The **Rough Guide**

Languedoc and Roussillon

written and researched by

Brian Catlos

ROUGH GUIDES

NEW YORK · LONDON · DELHI

www.roughguides.com

Contents

The Land of the Cathars colour section following p.216

Wines of Languedoc and Roussillon colour section following p.312

◀◀ Place de la Comédie, Montpellier ◀ Tree-lined road, Languedoc

Introduction to

Languedoc and Roussillon

The Languedoc and Roussillon region is one of France's best-kept secrets. While Provence and the Côte d'Azur just across the Rhône have been living it up, attracting movie stars and the masses, its less pretentious neighbour has remained in comfortable obscurity. And so much the better for those in the know. Dramatically varied landscapes, two distinct, proud cultures – Occitan and Catalan – a tradition of heresy and steadfast rebellion and age-old customs all combine to make this a great region unmatched in its romantic associations, at once epitomizing and defying everything that is France. Now shaking off centuries of sleepy neglect, Languedoc and Roussillon are emerging as one of the most enticing parts of the country, with remote villages and little-travelled byways affording a window onto a vanishing European rural culture, as well as beaches and cities offering a thrilling diversity of activity.

The boundaries of Languedoc have never been easy to fix. In its broadest – and original – sense, Languedoc includes the lands where the Occitan language (the *langue d'Oc*) was spoken in the Middle Ages, an area stretching along the north towards Savoy, through the Massif Central

▲ Cordes

Fact file

• The area covered by this guide includes most of the modern *région* of Languedoc-Roussillon and some of the most populated parts of the Midi-Pyrénées. The population of this area is approximately 3,400,000, concentrated in a handful of **urban centres**, including Toulouse, Montpellier, Nîmes and Perpignan. Mid-sized towns include Albi, Béziers, Narbonne, Sète and Carcassonne. Away from the coast, the broad plains of the Lauragais are lightly populated, and many areas of the hilly uplands are all but deserted.

• Languedoc's **terrain** is highly varied. The windswept coast, although rocky in the shadow of the Pyrenees, is generally a flat and sandy expanse, punctuated by salty inlets. Scrubby *garrigues*, rocky hills, rise out of the sun-baked littoral plain, providing shelter for vineyards. Further from the sea, the highlands of Haut Languedoc and the cordillera of the Pyrenees are covered by cooler and damper forests, and mark the transition from the Mediterranean to the Atlantic climate zone. On their far side, broad expanses of grain-lands are cut across by the occasional river-valley or ridge.

• Gone are the glory days of woad and silk; today, aside from the industry of Toulouse – and on a smaller scale, that of Carcassonne, Perpignan, Sète and Montpellier – the region's economy depends for the most part on wine and, increasingly, **tourism**. On the coast, mollusc farming supplements the still functioning but declining fishing industry.

and west along the Atlantic coast, taking in even Bordeaux. Nowadays, for administrative purposes, it has been lumped in together with its neighbour as the modern *région* of Languedoc-Roussillon, and trimmed down to the strip of coast running from Montpellier west to the border of Spain including the inland region jutting north of Nîmes. But this latter, narrow definition of Languedoc is as inappropriate as the traditional one is vague. In defining Languedoc in this guide we've avoided artificial boundaries in favour of cultural and historical cohesion and the logistics of travel, so that the region butts up to neighbouring Provence at the Rhône, and

5

■

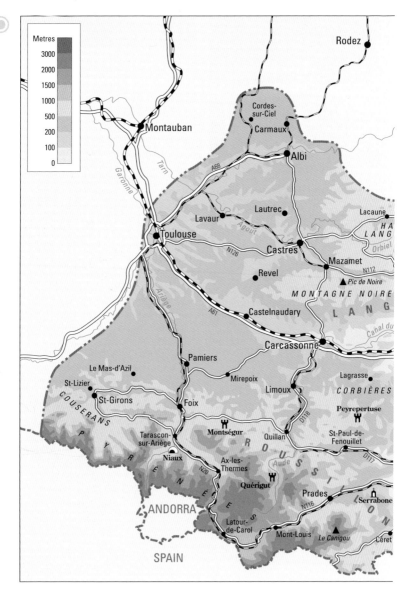

stretches west and inland to include the medieval capital of Toulouse, as well as the lands of Foix and Albi. Roussillon, Languedoc's accidental partner, squashed in between the eastern Pyrenees and the Corbières hills, is also characterized by a particular linguistic heritage, derived in

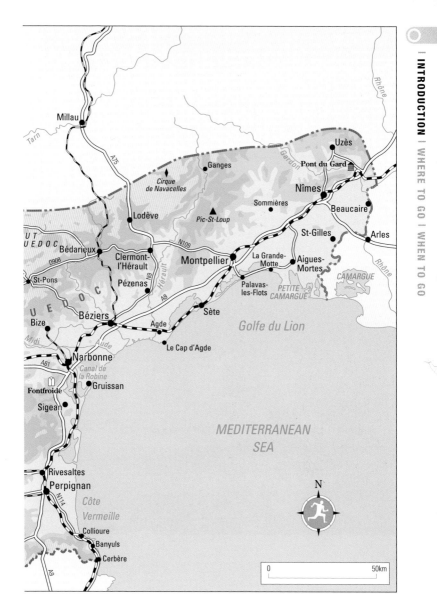

this case from a long history as part of the Catalan confederacy centred in Barcelona. Both regimes have distinct cultures but, in addition to their border, share a common history of occupation and of resistance and eventual submission to the modern France of Paris and the North.

Cathars

It's hard to imagine a more romantic episode of the Middle Ages. A peaceful people, living in a land of troubadours and poets, following the religion of their choosing, are declared heretics by a grasping and imperious papacy. This unleashes a series of brutal and drawn-out military campaigns, sanctified as Crusades, but in fact wars of aggressive colonialism waged by northern French nobles and churchmen on the unsuspecting locals. It's a story of knights and lords, martyrdoms, Inquisition, lost treasures, a proud but beleaguered nation and castles perched on rocky spurs, ending in the destruction of the Cathar faith, the suppression of Occitan culture and the subjugation of the people of Languedoc. The truth was far more complex than this popular and exaggerated Sir Walter Scott-ish version of the events, but the story of the Cathars is a fascinating and exciting introduction to the region's history, long buried by the modern French state. For the full story, see *The Land of the Cathars* colour section and Contexts p.394.

▼ Towers and fortifications of the Château de Foix

Where to go

With the tremendous range of sights and activities on offer in Languedoc and Roussillon, where you go will be determined by your interests and inclinations. **Toulouse** is the region's largest city and its most important cultural hub. Here you'll find a thriving nightlife and a collection of world-class museums and monuments, including the Les Abattoirs contemporary art museum and the basilica of St-Sernin. North of the city, the famous vineyards of Gaillac stretch up towards **Albi**, home to the Toulouse-Lautrec museum and an obligatory stop for anyone interested in modern painting. Nearby, the hills and forests of the **Parc du Haut Languedoc**, once the refuge of Protestant Huguenots, are now presided over by the herds of Brébais goats which give Roquefort cheese its famous flavour. To the south, the Ariège river, excellent for rafting in the summer, can be followed up into the Pyrenees. Here, south of medieval **Foix**, you'll find some of Europe's oldest and most enigmatic prehistoric caves. The mountains themselves have trails and pistes which make for spectacular hiking or skiing, depending on the season.

The **Canal du Midi**, a placid tree-lined waterway and the largest UNESCO World Heritage site on earth, leads east from Toulouse towards the Mediterranean, passing beneath the walls of **Carcassonne**, the greatest of the heretic fortresses and France's most recognizable medieval monument. Southeast of here, **Montségur** lies deep in Cathar country, at the upper end of the Aude and its stunning array of castle ruins, romantically perched on isolated cliff-tops.

Nothing could contrast with this more than the **Camargue**, the swampy delta of the Rhône, which forms Languedoc's northern frontier – home to the bull ranches which fuel the region's passion for the *corrida*. The beauty of the sun-baked *garrigues* just inland was well known to the Romans, whose monuments in and around **Nîmes**, including the famous **Pont du Gard** aqueduct, bear witness to the area's ancient glory. From here, you can either follow the path of the Roman super-highway, the **Via Domitia**, or the medieval Santiago pilgrim route past a series of atmospheric fortress-towns,

▼ Bize-Minervois

▼ The Feria in Nîmes

like **Aigues–Mortes** and **Sommières**, or you can dip down to the coast, a long swathe of sandy beach broken only by the salty inlets which are home to shellfish and windsurfers. Just south, **Montpellier** is a thriving multicultural city, close to the sea and with a lively street-life sustained by the student population of its famous university, which has been turning out graduates for eight hundred years. From here, the Hérault valley provides access to a rocky hinterland where you can visit the ancient monastery of **St-Guilhem-le-Désert** or hike through the spectacular **Cirque de Navacelles**.

▼ Main square, St-Guilhem

Food and drink

Languedoc and Roussillon present a culinary terrain as varied as their landscape. The coastal towns brim with freshly-caught fish and the cultivated shellfish of the saltwater *étangs*. In the east, the marshy Camargue is home to some of continental Europe's best beef. The rough hills which rise above the plain provide a range of fresh herbs and, in a brief season of glory, truffles. In the broad plains of the Lauragais, duck, the Frenchman's steak, is ubiquitous, along with its fellow fowl, goose, usually in the shape of rich foie gras. This is also the home of Languedoc's "national" dish, cassoulet – a baked-bean stew. In the desolate uplands, pork dominates in the form of chops, feet and a range of regional sausages, while sheep and goats provide the milk for cheeses, both pungent and sweet, and a series of micro-climate valleys produce a bounty of fruit. Aside

▲ Cassoulet

from Catalan, Spanish and North African food, there is little "ethnic" element in culinary Languedoc, although you will find other French cuisines well represented. The best respite from what can be delicious but eventually monotonous *terroir* fare, is *gastronomique* – adventurous cuisine blending regional elements with diverse ingredients and creative culinary techniques. Wherever you are, wash your meal down with the local wine. Languedoc has a wide selection of underrated vintages, while along the Tarn, at Gaillac, the interface between Atlantic and Mediterranean climate zones provides conditions for one of the most venerable of appellations.

At **Pézenas**, a town whose cobbled streets are girded by seventeenth-century palaces, the sun-baked Languedocian plain opens out. Medieval **Béziers** and Roman **Narbonne** preside over an expanse of archetypal Midi landscape. Blue skies are set off against the red soil and the iridescent green of seemingly endless vineyards. Only the ports, **Agde** and **Sète**, justly famed for their seafood and maritime traditions, manage to shake off the pleasant torpor of the plains.

Further south, Roussillon (French Catalonia), snuggles in the foothills of the Pyrenees, a region whose vivid contrasts have inspired artists including the Fauvists and Picasso. The capital, **Perpignan**, makes an ideal jumping-off point for visiting the rocky coves of the Côte Vermeille, or ascending the river valleys into the heart of the *département*. On the coast, **Collioure** and **Banyuls** are beautifully set beach towns, immune from the crass commercialism which characterizes the worst of the coastal resorts. Inland, the narrow-gauge Train Jaune winds upwards past **Le Canigou**, the mountain-symbol of the Catalan people, and the evocative old garrison towns of **Villefranche** and **Mont-Louis**, while the festivals at **Prades** and Céret make a great introduction to the lively Catalan folk traditions.

Canal du Midi

In the 1660s, a local tax-collector, Paul Riquet, dreamed of bringing prosperity back to Languedoc by building a canal to link it to the Mediterranean and the Atlantic. This mammoth civic engineering project was the most complex and greatest such undertaking since the time of the Romans. Although it bankrupted the visionary Riquet, who did not live to see its inauguration, by 1856 the canal was carrying one million passengers and more than 100,000 tonnes of freight per year. Struck down into sudden obsolescence by the invention of the steam engine, the canal system languished in over a century of disrepair, before being resurrected in the last few decades as a tourist attraction. The quintessential Languedoc experience is to boat, walk or cycle along Riquet's canal, travelling at an easy pace, the tree-lined hedges providing shelter from the same sun which coaxes up the region's famous grapes.

◄ Horse in the Petite Camargue

When to go

Whenever you visit, Languedoc and Roussillon offer a rich range of sights and activities to enjoy. The **summer season**, the time when most people come, offers a range of advantages but also some short-comings. In July and August you can count on long **museum and monument hours**, as well as the widest selection of hotels and restaurants, many of which are seasonal. The weather is generally **warm** and **sunny** enough that you can swim throughout the region, be it in the Mediterranean or in the nearest lake or river. Many of the region's village festivals take place in the summer, along with an array of special concert series. On the other hand, queues lengthen along with the opening hours. In summer months competition for accommodation is often fierce; you'll be forced to book ahead for hotels, particularly on the coast, and this can detract from the spontaneous aspect of your travels. Traffic is also increasingly problematic in summer; the coastal highways and byways are chock-a-block with frenzied drivers rushing to get either to the beach or back home. If you're thinking of a cycling holiday, you'll probably want to confine yourself to the quieter (and hillier) upland roads.

On the other hand, the long **off-season**, from November through to Easter, sees many services shut down and museum and monument hours reduced. Many of the villages, along with a lot of hotels and restaurants, all but shut down, with the exception of the Pyrenean **ski resorts** which, of course, are at their busiest. The weather is unreliable; it is frequently cold and grey, and a light layer of snow makes the Cathar ruins more **romantic** but less comfortable to explore. This is, however, arguably the best time to visit urban centres like Toulouse and Montpellier; with their student populations in residence, these cities spring to life.

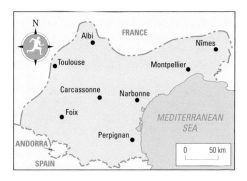

Not only do theatre and opera seasons get under way, but the **bars and clubs** pack out with throngs of young folk. Christmas and Lent breathe additional life into the countryside in the form of an array of colourful and unique festivities.

The best time to go is probably the **shoulder seasons**, May and June, and September, which offer a good balance between tranquillity and action. In early June you can visit a town like Cordes and find it quiet and not yet overrun. The cities will be winding down their university seasons and the cultural programmes are preparing their finales. With a bit of luck, you'll get good weather, although you may find swimming only suits the brave. The **grape harvest** and **bull-fighting** festivals are in full swing, and even the coastal roads are still relatively safe for two-wheelers. You'll also more or less have your pick of the hotels and restaurants and will generally still be charged low-season prices.

Average temperatures and rainfall

	Jan	Apr	Jul	Oct
Toulouse				
precipitation mm/in	50/2	60/2.4	38/1.5	58/2.3
average high temp °C/F	7/45	17/63	27/81	17/63
average low temp °C/F	3/38	6/43	15/59	9/48
Montpellier				
precipitation mm/in	50/2	60/2.4	38/1.5	58/2.3
average high temp °C/F	10/50	17/63	28/82	19/66
average low temp °C/F	2/36	6/43	16/60	9/48
Foix				
precipitation mm/in	68/2.7	54/2.1	22/0.88	61/2.4
average high temp °C/F	10/50	17/63	27/81	19/66
average low temp °C/F	2/36	9/48	17/63	10/50
Perpignan				
precipitation mm/in	51/2	56/2.2	18/0.7	89/3.6
average high temp °C/F	12/54	17/63	28/82	20/68
average low temp °C/F	4/40	9/48	19/66	12/54

things not to miss

It's not possible to see everything that Languedoc and Roussillon have to offer in one trip – and we don't suggest you try. What follows, in no particular order, is a selective and subjective taste of the region's highlights: outstanding natural features, spectacular cities, history, culture and beautiful architecture. They're arranged in five colour-coded categories to help you find the very best things to see, do and experience. All entries have a page reference to take you straight into the Guide, where you can find out more.

01 **Train Jaune** Page **366** • Twisting up into the high valleys of the Pyrenees, this revived narrow-gauge line is a worthy excursion in itself and perfect for hikers.

02 **Nîmes amphitheatre** Page **223** • The gladiators have been replaced by bullfighters but, 2000 years on, this 20,000-seat stadium still packs in the crowds.

04 **Rabastens** Page **186** • Get a rare glimpse of a medieval church in all of its painted glory.

03 **Water-jousting** Page **276** • Originating centuries ago in Sète, this sport is now a passionate fixture of Languedoc traditional culture.

05 **Oppidum D'Ensérune** Page **323** • A pre-Roman settlement perched on a ridge above the vineyards of Béziers.

06 **Beaches** Page **247** • From naked hedonism to romantic solitude, Languedoc's Mediterranean beaches, such as Le Grau-du-Roi, offer it all.

07 **Collioure** Page **382** ● Roussillon at its most Catalan: a picturesque beach town presided over by a medieval castle.

08 **Cordes-sur-Ciel** Page **181** ● Cruise the boutiques or enjoy the evocative atmosphere in this hill-top Cathar town.

09 Seafood Page **46** • Whether cultivated in the Bassin de Thau or fished from the sea, the area's seafood is a must.

10 **La Petite Camargue** Page 249 • Ride on horseback or cruise the canals and salt pans of Durrell's "Little Argentina."

11 **Christmas traditions** Page 349 • *Pessebres*, *caganers* and *cagatiós* set Roussillon's Christmas festivities apart from the rest of France.

13 Toulouse-Lautrec Page
174 • This Languedoc native revolutionionized nineteenth-century art; enjoy the largest collection of his work and visit his childhood estate.

12 Cirque de Navacelles
Page **292** • A dramatic oxbow canyon, which cuts through the causse of the upper Hérault.

14 Le Canigou Page **363** • Bonfires and a torch-light pilgrimage illuminate Catalonia's sacred mountain in mid-summer.

15 **Outdoor activities** Page **50** • The regions' rivers and hills offer a full range of hiking, trekking and water-sports.

16 **Montségur** Page **141** • The romantic and mysterious last redoubt of the Cathars.

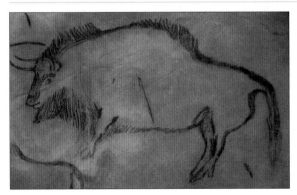

17 La Grotte de Niaux Page **158** • The finest of the Pyrenean caves, the remote Grotto de Viaüx is known for its enigmatic prehistoric paintings.

18 **The Orb valley** Page **334** • Follow this mountain river valley through near-forgotten hamlets, such as Lunas.

19 **Carcassonne** Page **117** • France's most famous and evocative medieval citadel.

20 **Tauromachie** Page **224** • Get swept up in the excitement and drama of the "art of the bull".

21 **Swimming at the Pont Du Gard** Page **234** • Take a dip under the lofty arches of this extraordinary Roman Aqueduct.

22 **Pézenas** Page **283** • Languedoc's former capital and the stomping ground of Molière still evokes the glory of the Age of Absolutism.

23 **The monastery of St-Roman** Page **240** • Medieval monks hewed out this underground monastic complex on the banks of the Rhône.

24 **Aigues-Mortes** Page **245** • Visit this perfectly preserved medieval walled town, romantically set among swamps and dunes.

Basics

Basics

Getting there

The quickest and most cost-effective way of reaching Languedoc and Roussillon from most parts of Britain is by air, though from the southeast of England it's worth considering the Eurostar, which links with fast and efficient TGV services south from Lille and Paris.

Getting to Languedoc and Roussillon **from North America** is straightforward; there are direct flights from over thirty major cities to Paris, from where you can either take an internal flight to the region or transfer to France's excellent train network. Many people heading for France **from Australia and New Zealand** travel via London, although there are scheduled flights to Paris from Sydney, Melbourne, Brisbane, Cairns, Perth and Auckland.

Airfares always depend on the **season**, with the highest being around mid-June to mid-September, when the weather is best; fares drop during the "shoulder" seasons – Easter to mid-June and mid-September through October – and you'll get the best prices during the low season, November to Easter (excluding Christmas and New Year). Note also that flying on weekends ordinarily adds to the round-trip fare; price ranges quoted below assume **midweek travel**.

Flights from the UK and Ireland

Flying is the quickest way of getting to Languedoc and Roussillon, with journey times from London to Toulouse of less than two hours. You can also get direct budget flights there from a variety of British regional airports.

Several **low-cost airlines** – Ryanair, BMIBaby, Flybe and EasyJet – offer scheduled flights into the region, or to hubs within easy striking distance of it. **Ryanair** flies from Dublin, East Midlands, Shannon, and Liverpool to Carcassonne; from East Midlands, Liverpool and Dublin to Nîmes; and from Stansted to Perpignan and Montpellier. **EasyJet** flies daily from Bristol and Gatwick to Toulouse, while **BMIBaby** flies from Manchester to Perpignan. **Flybe** flies from Birmingham and Southampton to Perpignan,

and from Birmingham and Bristol to Toulouse. Both EasyJet and Ryanair also have regular services from many British regional airports to **Girona** airport in Catalonia, just 60km from the border of Roussillon. Return fares on all the budget airlines start at around £20, but generally range from £60–150 for Carcassonne, and £45–125 for other destinations.

Air France and British Airways also offer scheduled flights from London to Toulouse from £120 return and to Montpellier for around £140. **Air France** flies from Heathrow at least once daily direct to Toulouse, and from Gatwick to Toulouse and Montpellier. **British Airways** flies several times daily from Gatwick to Marseilles, and once daily to Montpellier. Both airlines also have frequent daily flights from London and many British regional airports to Paris, from where travellers can continue overland (see p.31).

By far the most convenient way to fly from the **Irish Republic** to Languedoc and Roussillon is by flying direct from Dublin to Toulouse with Aer Lingus. Ryanair also has several routes to the region, including Dublin to Carcassonne and Nîmes, and Shannon to Carcassonne. There are no direct flights from **Northern Ireland** to Languedoc and Roussillon, but all the main budget airlines can get you there from Belfast via an English hub. Ryanair, for example, flies from Derry Airport to London Stansted for around £75, from where you can pick up an onward flight to their various Languedoc destinations. Alternatively, you could get a British Airways flight directly from Belfast City Airport to Paris CDG, and continue overland from there.

Flights from the US and Canada

To get to Languedoc and Roussillon from North America, you can either fly to London

Travelling with pets from the UK

If you wish to take your dog (or cat) to France, the **Pet Travel Scheme (PETS)** enables you to avoid putting it in quarantine when re-entering the UK as long as certain conditions are met. Current regulations are available on the Department for Environment, Food and Rural Affairs (DEFRA) website ⓦ www.defra.gov.uk/animalh /quarantine/index.htm or through the PETS Helpline (☎0870/241 1710).

and hook up with a **budget airline** (see p.27), or, better, fly to Paris and continue overland, by renting a car or using France's excellent **rail** system (see p.34).

Transatlantic fares to Paris **from the US** are very reasonable, thanks to intense competition. A typical return fare for a midweek flight costs around $850 from Houston, $750 from Los Angeles and $650 from New York. **From Canada**, prices to Paris are in the region of CAN$850 from Montréal and Toronto, and CAN$1100 from Vancouver. For contact details of airlines that fly from the US and Canada to Paris and London, see below.

Flights from Australia, New Zealand and South Africa

From Australia, New Zealand and South Africa, the best way to reach Languedoc and Rousillon is to fly to Paris then continue overland by train (see p.31). However, you can find a wider range of options by flying to another European capital – usually London – and picking up a budget flight there (see p.27). **Fares** are priced according to the French tourist seasons: the brief low season runs from early January to the end of February and through October and November; high season lasts from mid-May to the end of August and from December to early January. For contact details of **airlines** that fly to Paris and London, see below.

The best deals **from Australia or New Zealand** to Europe are routed via Asia, often with a transfer or overnight stop in the airline's home city. Flights via the US are usually slightly more expensive. Airfares **from east-coast gateways** to Paris are common rated, with regular tourist class fares starting at around Aus$2000 in low season, or AUS$2500 in high season. **From Perth and Darwin** flights cost around Aus$100–300 less via Asia, and Aus$400 more via the US.

From New Zealand, fares from Auckland start at around NZ$2000 in low season, up to NZ$3000 in peak season.

From South Africa, Air France flies direct from Johannesburg to Paris from around 6140ZAR return. BA, flying via London, comes in slightly more expensive, at around 10,000ZAR from Cape Town and 8600ZAR from Johannesburg. Flight times are around ten hours from Johannesburg to Paris, and 14 hours from Cape Town including a stopover.

Agents, airlines and specialist operators

Many airlines and discount travel websites offer you the opportunity to book your tickets **online**, cutting out the costs of agents and middlemen. Good deals can often be found through discount or auction sites, as well as through the **airlines'** own websites. There are also many tour operators offering **specialist tours** of Languedoc and Roussillon, such as walking, biking and boating.

Online booking agents and travel sites

ⓦ **www.expedia.co.uk** (in UK)
ⓦ **www.expedia.com** (in US)
ⓦ **www.expedia.ca** (in Canada)
ⓦ **www.lastminute.com** (in UK)
ⓦ **www.opodo.co.uk** (in UK)
ⓦ **www.orbitz.com** (in US)
ⓦ **www.travelocity.co.uk** (in UK)
ⓦ **www.travelocity.com** (in US)
ⓦ **www.travelocity.ca** (in Canada)
ⓦ **www.zuji.com.au** (in Australia)
ⓦ **www.zuji.co.nz** (in New Zealand)

Airlines

Aer Lingus UK ☎0870/876 5000, Republic of Ireland ☎0818/365 000, ⓦ www.aerlingus.com.
Air France UK ☎0870/142-4343, US ☎1-800/237-2747, Canada ☎1-800/667-2747, Australia ☎02/9244 2100, New Zealand ☎09/308

Fly less – stay longer! Travel and climate change

Climate change is a serious threat to the ecosystems that humans rely upon, and air travel is among the fastest-growing contributors to the problem. Rough Guides regard travel, overall, as a global benefit, and feel strongly that the advantages to developing economies are important, as is the opportunity of greater contact and awareness among peoples. But we all have a responsibility to limit our personal impact on global warming, and that means giving thought to how often we fly, and what we can do to redress the harm that our trips create.

Flying and climate change

Pretty much every form of motorized travel generates CO_2 – the main cause of human-induced climate change – but planes also generate climate-warming contrails and cirrus clouds and emit oxides of nitrogen, which create ozone (another greenhouse gas) at flight levels. Furthermore, flying simply allows us to travel much further than we otherwise would do. The figures are frightening: one person taking a return flight between Europe and California produces the equivalent impact of 2.5 tonnes of CO_2 – similar to the yearly output of the average UK car.

Fuel-cell and other less harmful types of plane may emerge eventually. But until then, there are really just two options for concerned travellers: to reduce the amount we travel by air (take fewer trips – stay for longer!), and to make the trips we do take "climate neutral" via a carbon offset scheme.

Carbon offset schemes

Offset schemes run by ⓦwww.climatecare.org, ⓦwww.carbonneutral.com and others allow you to make up for some or all of the greenhouse gases that you are responsible for releasing. To do this, they provide "carbon calculators" for working out the global-warming contribution of a specific flight (or even your entire existence), and then let you contribute an appropriate amount of money to fund offsetting measures. These include rainforest reforestation and initiatives to reduce future energy demand – often run in conjunction with sustainable development schemes.

Rough Guides, together with Lonely Planet and other concerned partners in the travel industry, are supporting a **carbon offset scheme** run by climatecare.org. Please take the time to view our website and see how you can help to make your trip climate neutral.

ⓦ**www.roughguides.com/climatechange**

3352, South Africa ☏0861/340-340,ⓦwww
.airfrance.com.

Air Canada US & Canada ☏1-888/247-2262, ⓦwww.aircanada.com.

Air New Zealand Australia ☏13 24 76, New Zealand ☏0800/737 000, ⓦwww.airnz.com.

American Airlines US ☏1-800/433-7300, Australia ☏1300/650 7347, New Zealand, ☏0800/887 997, ⓦwww.aa.com.

bmibaby UK ☏0870/264 2229, Republic of Ireland ☏1890/340 122,ⓦwww.bmibaby.com.

British Airways UK ☏0870/850 9850, Republic of Ireland ☏1890/626 747, US & Canada ☏1-800/ AIRWAYS, Australia ☏1300/767 177, New Zealand ☏09/966 9777, South Africa ☏011/441 8600, ⓦwww.ba.com.

Cathay Pacific Australia ☏13 17 47, New Zealand ☏09/379 0861, ⓦwww.cathaypacific.com.

Continental Airlines US & Canada ☏1-800/231-0856, ⓦwww.continental.com.

Delta Air Lines US & Canada ☏1-800/221-1212,ⓦwww.delta.com.

easyJet UK ☏0870/600 0000, ⓦwww.easyjet.com.

flybe UK ☏ 0870/889 0908, Republic of Ireland ☏1890/925 532, ⓦwww.flybe.com.

Northwest/KLM Airlines US ☏1-800/225-2525, Australia ☏1300 303 747, New Zealand ☏09/309 1782, South Africa ☏082/2345 747, ⓦwww.nwa.com, ⓦwww.klm.com.

Ryanair UK ☏0871/246 0000, Republic of Ireland ☏0818/303 030, ⓦwww.ryanair.com.

Qantas Australia ☏13 13 13, New Zealand ☏0800/808 767, ⓦwww.qantas.com.

South African Airways SA ☏011978-1111, ⓦwww.flysaa.com.

United Airlines US ☎1-800/241-6522, Australia ☎13 17 77, New Zealand ☎09/379 3800 or 0800/508 648, ⓦwww.united.com.
US Airways US & Canada ☎1-800/428-4322, ⓦwww.usair.com.
Virgin Atlantic Airways US ☎1-800/862-8621, Australia ☎02/9244 2747, New Zealand ☎09/308 3377, ⓦwww.virgin-atlantic.com.

Agents and operators

ebookers UK ☎0800/082 3000, Republic of Ireland ☎01/488 3507, ⓦwww.ebookers.com. Low fares on an extensive selection of scheduled flights and package deals.
North South Travel UK ☎01245/608 291, ⓦwww.northsouthtravel.co.uk. Friendly, competitive travel agency, offering discounted fares worldwide. Profits are used to support projects in the developing world, especially the promotion of sustainable tourism.
Trailfinders UK ☎0845/058 5858, Republic of Ireland ☎01/677 7888, Australia ☎1300/780 212, ⓦwww.trailfinders.com. One of the best-informed and most efficient agents for independent travellers.
STA Travel US ☎1-800-781-4040, Canada ☎1-888-427-5639, UK ☎0870/1630 026, Australia ☎1300/733 035, New Zealand ☎0508/782 872, SA ☎0861/781 781, ⓦwww.statravel.com. Worldwide specialists in independent travel; also student IDs, travel insurance, car rental, rail passes, and more. Good discounts for students and under-26s.

Specialist tour operators

Abercrombie & Kent UK ☎020/7730 9600, ⓦwww.abercrombiekent.co.uk; US & Canada ☎1-800/323-7308 or 630/954-2944, ⓦwww.abercrombiekent.com; Australia ☎03/9536 1800 or 1300/851 800, New Zealand ☎0800/441 638, ⓦwww.abercrombiekent.com.au. Upmarket biking and walking tours.
ACE Study Tours UK ☎01223/835055, ⓦwww.study-tours.org. Sophisticated educational tours including Romanesque art itineraries.
Adventure Center US & Canada ☎1-800/228-8747 or 510/654-1879, ⓦwww.adventurecenter.com. Hiking and "soft adventure" specialists.
Baronnie de Bourgade France ☎04.67.39.02.34, ⓦwww.baronnie-de-bourgade.com. This Béziers outfit offers week-long tours that combine regional highlights with wine tasting.
BKTours France ☎06.80.45.35.70 ⓦwww.bkwine.com. Swedish-based company which runs Languedoc wine tours around Nîmes.
Caprice Tours US & Canada ☎1-866-2FRANCE, ⓦwww.caprice-tours.com. Cultural and linguistic tours.

Château de Quarante France ☎04.67.89.40.41, ⓦchateaudequarante.com. Upmarket, gourmet living in a private castle by night, chauffeur-driven custom tours by day.
Discover France US & Canada ☎1-800/960-2221 or 480/905-1325, ⓦwww.discoverfrance.com. Bike and hiking tours in Languedoc.
Europe Through the Back Door US & Canada ☎425/771-8303 ext. 298, ⓦwww.ricksteves.com. Small-group and tailor-made tours.
Explore Holidays Australia ☎02/9423 8080, ⓦwww.exploreholidays.com.au. Accommodation, boat rental and package tours.
France OK France ⓦwww.franceok.com. Based in Argelès-sur-Mer; arranges canal, walking and gourmet tours in Roussillon.
France Unlimited Australia ☎03/9531 8787. All French travel arrangements, including châteaux stays, Alpine hiking and cycling tours.
French Cycling Holidays ⓦwww.frenchcyclingholidays.com. Cycling specialists who run both Leisure and Sport Cycling tours in Languedoc and Roussillon.
French Travel Connection Australia ☎02/9966 1177, ⓦwww.frenchtravel.com.au. Everything to do with travel to and around France.
Globus US & Canada ☎1-866/755-8581, ⓦwww.globusjourneys.com. Planned vacation packages.
Languedoc Nature France ☎04.67.45.00.67, ⓦwww.languedoc-nature.com. Organizes a range of tours based on outdoor activities, history, and gastronomy.
Passport Travel Australia ☎03/9867 3888, ⓦwww.travelcentre.com.au. Small-group walking and cycling holidays.
Peregrine Adventures UK ☎01635/872 300, Australia ☎1300/854 444, ⓦwww.peregrineadventures.com. Agent for a multitude of adventure companies, taking small groups on guided and independent walking and cycling holidays.
Rosé Exposé Events France ☎04.68.43.99.70 ⓦwww.drink-pink.com. Wine get-away weekends in the Aude.
Sherpa Expeditions UK ☎020/8577 2717, ⓦwww.sherpa-walking-holidays.co.uk. Self-guided inn-to-inn walks and cycle trips, or escorted group treks, including the Côte Vermeille.
Susie Madron's Cycling for Softies UK ☎0161/248 8282, ⓦwww.cycling-for-softies.co.uk. An easy-going cycle holiday operator. Although luggage transfer is not included in the deals, it can be arranged for an additional fee.
Tastes of Languedoc UK ☎020/8339 6050, ⓦwww.tastesoflanguedoc.com. Organizes custom wine tours in Languedoc and Roussillon.
Travel Notions Australia ☎02/9552 3355, ⓦwww.unitednotions.com.au/travelnotions. France

specialists and agents for leisurely "Cycling for Softies" tours.

Trek Holidays Canada ☏ 1800/661 7265, ⓦ www.trekholidays.com. Agent for a vast array of adventure companies, with hiking and cycling options in France.

Walkabout Gourmet Adventures Australia ☏ 03/5159 6556, ⓦ www.walkaboutgourmet.com. Classy food, wine and walking tours, including a Pyrenees itinerary.

By rail from the UK and Ireland

The quickest way to get to Languedoc and Rousillon by train is on **Eurostar** from London or Ashford in Kent through the Channel Tunnel to Paris or Lilles and then changing onto a fast TGV train to Toulouse (9–10hr), Perpignan (9hr), Montpellier (7–8hr) or Nîmes (7hr). The cheapest return ticket to Paris is currently £59, but Eurostar can also book the TGV leg: return fares from London to all four destinations above start at around £110, though these are non-flexible. Note that Inter-Rail passes (see below) give discounts on the Eurostar service.

Travelling by **regular train and ferry** or hovercraft via Calais, Boulogne or Dieppe, then making onward connections to Languedoc and Roussillon by train can work out slightly cheaper than using the Channel Tunnel, but it takes considerably longer, and is generally less convenient.

Rail passes

There's a huge array of **rail passes** available, which may be worth considering if you're visiting Languedoc and Roussillon as part of a longer pan-European journey. For details of local SNCF rail passes valid for journeys within France, see "Getting Around" p.34.

Inter-Rail pass

Inter-Rail passes are only available to European residents, and you will be asked to provide proof of residency before being allowed to purchase one. They come in over-26 and (cheaper) under-26 versions, and cover 28 European countries (including Turkey and Morocco) grouped together in zones. The Zone E Pass includes France, Belgium, the Netherlands and Luxembourg. The passes are available for 16 days (one zone only), 22 days, or one month and you can purchase up to three zones or a global pass covering all zones. Inter-Rail passes do not include travel between Britain and the continent, although pass holders are eligible for discounts on rail travel in Britain and Northern Ireland, including Eurostar, and cross-Channel ferries, plus discounts on other shipping services around the Mediterranean, Scandinavia and the Balearics.

Euro Domino pass

The **Euro Domino** pass is only available to European residents. Individual country passes provide unlimited travel in 28 European and North African countries. The passes are available for between three and eight days' travel within a one-month period; prices vary depending on the country, but include most high-speed train supplements. You can buy as many separate country passes as you want. There is a discounted youth price for those under 26, and a half-price child (age 4–11) fare.

Eurailpasses

The **Eurailpass**, which must be purchased before arrival in Europe (and cannot be purchased by European residents), allows unlimited free first-class train travel in France and seventeen other countries, and is available in increments of fifteen days, 21 days, one month, two months and three months. If you're under 26, you can save money with a **Eurailpass Youth**, which is valid for second-class travel or, if you're travelling with one to five other companions, a joint **Eurailpass Saver**, both of which are available in the same increments as the Eurailpass. You stand a better chance of getting your money's worth out of a **Eurailpass Flexi**, which is good for ten or fifteen days' first-class travel within a two-month period. This, too, comes in under-26/second-class (**Eurailpass Youth Flexi**) and group (**Eurailpass Saver Flexi**) versions.

In addition, a scaled-down version of the Eurailpass Flexi, the **Eurail Selectpass**, is available which allows travel in your choice of three, four or five of the seventeen countries Eurail covers (they must be adjoining, by either rail or ship) for any five days, six days, eight days, ten days or fifteen days (five-country option only) within a two-month period. In this plan, Belgium, the Netherlands and Luxembourg are taken as one "country". Like the Eurailpass, the Selectpass is also available in first-class, second-class youth, or first-class saver options.

Details of prices for all these passes can be found on the Eurail website (Ⓦwww .eurail.com).

Rail contacts

Europrail International Canada ☎1-888/667-9734, Ⓦwww.europrail.net. Sells Eurail, Europass and individual country passes.
Eurostar UK ☎0870/160 6600, Ⓦwww.eurostar .com.
International Rail UK ☎0870/751 5000, Ⓦwww .international-rail.com. Sells all major European rail passes.
Northern Ireland Railways UK ☎028/9089 9411, Ⓦwww.nirailways.co.uk. Reservations and rail passes, including student deals.
Rail Europe (SNCF French Railways) UK ☎0870/837 1371, US ☎1-877-257-2887, Canada ☎1-800-361-RAIL, Ⓦwww.raileurope.com. Sells discounted rail fares for under-26s and Eurostar tickets; also official agents for InterRail and Eurail passes, and sells rail passes for France.
Rail Plus Australia ☎1300/555 003 or 03/9642 8644, Ⓦwww.railplus.com.au. Sells Eurail passes and train tickets.

Trainseurope UK ☎0900/195 0101, Ⓦwww .trainseurope.co.uk. Sells a variety of rail passes as well as booking accommodation and other services.

By car and ferry from the UK and Ireland

It's a good nine hours' drive south from Calais on the north coast of France to Toulouse, but if you do want **to drive**, the quickest way across the Channel is via the Channel Tunnel (35 minutes), on **Eurotunnel's** (☎0870/535 3535, Ⓦwww.eurotunnel .com) daily shuttles. Due to the frequency of the service, you don't have to buy a ticket in advance (though it is advisable in mid-summer and during other school holidays), but you must arrive at least thirty minutes before departure; the target loading time is just ten minutes.

Fares are calculated per car, regardless of the number of passengers, and rates depend on the time of year, time of day and length of stay (the cheapest ticket is for a day-trip, followed by a five-day return); it's cheaper to travel between 10pm and 6am, while the highest fares are reserved for weekend departures and returns in July and August. A five-day, off-peak, low-season trip, for example, starts at £49 return (passengers included), increasing to £155 in the peak period.

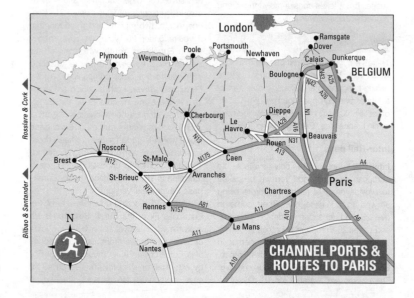

CHANNEL PORTS & ROUTES TO PARIS

Alternatively, you can get to France by **ferry** from various ports along England's south coast to the north coast of France. If you're coming from the north of England or Scotland, consider an overnight ferry to Zeebrugge (Belgium), either from Hull or from Rosyth. From Ireland you can take a ferry direct from Rosslaire (near Wexford) to either Cherbourg or Roscoff.

Ferry **prices** are seasonal and, for motorists, depend on the size of your vehicle. The popular Dover–Calais route costs from £120 one-way for a car and two adults. Note that return prices are substantially cheaper than one-way fares, but generally need to be booked in advance – details of routes and companies are listed below. You can either contact the companies direct to reserve space in advance – essential in peak season if you're intending to drive – or any travel agent in the UK or France will do it for you. All ferry companies also offer foot passenger fares from £20 one-way; accompanying bicycles can usually be carried free, at least in the low season, and for a charge of around £5 one-way in mid- and high seasons. The ferry companies also often offer **special deals** on three-, five- and ten-day returns, or discounts for regular users who own a property abroad, while the tour operator Eurodrive (℡020/8324 4009, 🖳 www .eurodrive.co.uk) can also arrange discounts on car-ferry crossings.

The cheapest way of getting to France **from Ireland** – though far from the quickest – is by ferry from Cork or Rosslare outside Wexford to Cherbourg or Roscoff, in Brittany, and then continuing overland.

If you don't want to drive far when you've reached France, you can take advantage of SNCF's **motorail**, which you can book through Rail Europe (see p.32), putting your car on the train in either Calais or Paris for Narbonne or Toulouse. This is a relatively expensive option though: for four people travelling from Calais to Toulouse, for example, the regular one-way price ranges from £289, dependent on the time of year.

Ferry contacts

Brittany Ferries UK ℡ 08703/665 333, 🖳 www.brittanyferries.co.uk, Republic of Ireland ℡021/4277 801, 🖳 www.brittanyferries.ie. Poole to Cherbourg; Portsmouth to Caen, Cherbourg and St Malo; Plymouth to Roscoff and Santander; Cork to Roscoff (March–Oct only).

Condor Ferries UK ℡0870/243 5140, 🖳 www .condorferries.co.uk. Portsmouth to Cherbourg (May–Sept); Poole to St-Malo (May–Sept); and Weymouth to St-Malo via the Channel Islands.

Irish Ferries UK ℡ 08705/171 717, Northern Ireland ℡ 00 353 818/ 300 400, Republic of Ireland ℡0818/300 400, 🖳 www.irishferries.com. Rosslare to Cherbourg and Roscoff (March–Sept).

Norfolkline UK ℡0870/870 1020, 🖳 www .norfolkline.com. Dover to Dunkerque.

P&O Ferries UK ℡ 08705/980 333, 🖳 www .poferries.com. Dover to Calais; Portsmouth to Bilbao; and Hull to Zeebrugge.

Sea France UK ℡0870/443 1653, 🖳 www .seafrance.com. Dover to Calais.

SpeedFerries UK ℡0870/220 0570, 🖳 www .speedferries.com. Dover to Boulogne.

Superfast Ferries UK ℡0870/234 0870, 🖳 www .superfast.com. Rosyth near Edinburgh to Zeebrugge (Belgium).

Transmanche Ferries UK ℡0800/917 1201, 🖳 www.transmancheferries.com. Newhaven to Dieppe.

By bus

Eurolines run regular bus-ferry services from London Victoria to over sixty French cities. Prices are much lower than for the same journey by train, with adult return fares of around £50 to Toulouse (£30 if booked 30 days in advance); the journey time is roughly nineteen hours. Regional return fares from the rest of England and from Wales are available, as are student and youth discounts. **Tickets** can be bought directly from the company, from National Express agents and from most high-street travel agents.

Bus contacts

Busabout UK ℡020/7950 1661, 🖳 www .busabout.com.

Eurolines UK ℡0870/5-808080, Republic of Ireland ℡01/836 6111, 🖳 www.nationalexpress .com/eurolines.

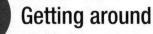

Getting around

France has the most extensive train network in western Europe, and rail is the best way of travelling between almost all the major towns within Languedoc and Roussillon. The nationally-owned French train company, the SNCF (Société Nationale des Chemins de Fer), runs fast, modern trains. In rural areas where branch lines have been closed, routes (such as Castres–Montpellier) are covered by buses operated solely by SNCF or in partnership with independent companies. It's an integrated service, with buses timetabled to meet trains and the same ticket covering both.

The private **bus** services that supplement the SNCF services are confusing and unco-ordinated. Some areas, such as the coast or around larger centres like Toulouse, Albi and Castres, are quite well served, while the service in less populated regions, like the Corbières and parts of the Pyrenees and Haut Languedoc, is barely existent – often designed to carry the inhabitants of hamlets to and from weekly markets, and thus not very useful for tourists. Weekends and holidays frequently have no service.

By rail

The SNCF has pioneered one of the most efficient, comfortable and user-friendly **railway systems** in the world. Its staff are, with few exceptions, courteous and helpful, and its trains – for the most part, fast, clean and frequent – continue, in spite of the closure of some rural lines, to cover much of Languedoc and Roussillon; a main rail corridor runs from Toulouse to Narbonne, where it joins the coastal line, linking Cerbère on the Spanish border and Beaucaire (Tarascon) at the Rhône, while spur lines run up major river valleys – including the Tarn, Ariège and Conflent. For national train **information**, phone ☎08.36.35.35.35 (€0.34 per minute) or check ⓦwww.voyages-sncf.com.

Pride and joy of the system are the high-speed **TGVs** (*trains à grande vitesse*), capable of 300kph, and their offspring Eurostar. There are several stations connected to the TGV in Languedoc and Roussillon, among them Nîmes (journey time from Paris 4hr), Montpellier (4hr 30min), Narbonne (5hr), Béziers (4hr 45min), Perpignan (6hr) and Toulouse (4hr 30min). The only difference between TGV and other train fares is that you pay a compulsory reservation charge (from €3), plus a supplement on certain peak-hour trains. Check the SNCF **website**, however, for a whole range of last-minute **special deals** and **upgrades**.

In person, it is easiest to use the counter service for **buying tickets**, though the touch-screen computerized system available in most stations can be read in English and is a good way to check fares and times – if need be, you can always press the red *annulment* button to cancel the transaction before committing yourself. All tickets – but not passes (see p.35) – must be **validated** in the orange machines at station platform entrances, and it is an offence not to follow the instruction *Compostez votre billet* ("Validate your ticket"). Train journeys may be broken any time, anywhere, for as long as the ticket is valid (usually two months), but after a break of 24 hours you must validate your ticket again when you resume your journey.

After a spate of terrorist bombings in the late 1990s, most train stations closed their **luggage lockers** (*consignes automatiques*); these days a few have reopened, and larger stations have a staffed luggage check-in, usually with limited hours (*consignes* are noted in the Guide).

Regional rail **maps** and complete **timetables** are sold in tobacconist shops (*tabacs*). Leaflet timetables for particular lines are available free at stations. *Autocar* or a bullet symbol at the top of a column means it's an SNCF bus service, on which rail tickets and passes are valid.

Aside from the regular lines there are a number of tourist-oriented railways, including the spectacular **Train Jaune** (see p.366) which winds its way up through the Pyrenees, and the **ATM train** (see p.322), which heads up into the hinterland of Narbonne.

French rail discounts and passes

SNCF offers a whole range of **discounted fares** within France on standard rail prices on *période bleue* (blue period) and *période blanche* (white period) days. A leaflet showing the blue, white (smaller discount) and red (peak) periods is given out at stations. In addition, any two people travelling together (*à deux*), or a small group of up to five people, are entitled to a 25 percent discount on return tickets on TGVs, subject to availability, or on other trains if they start their journey on a blue period day; the same reduction applies to a group of up to four people travelling with a child under 12, to under 26-year-olds, over-60s, and for anyone who books a return journey of at least 200km in distance, including a Saturday night away (this latter is called the *séjour*).

Finally, a range of train passes that give discounts (valid for a year) can be purchased from main stations and most travel agents in France. Over-60s can buy the **Carte Senior** for €53, which offers up to 50 percent off tickets on TGVs, or other journeys starting in blue periods, a 25 percent reduction on white period journeys, as well as a 30 percent reduction on international journeys involving most countries in western and central Europe. The same reductions are available for under-26s with a **Carte 12–25** pass, which costs €49. Under-12s can obtain the same advantages for themselves and up to four travelling companions of any age by purchasing the **Enfant Plus Carte** (€65). Those aged between 26 and 59 years can purchase a **Carte Escapades** (€85), but this only entitles the holder to a 40 percent reduction on normal, white-period fares. For details of pan-European rail passes, see Getting There, p.31.

By bus

The most convenient **bus services** are those run as an extension of rail links by SNCF, which always run to and from the SNCF station and access areas formerly served by rail. In addition to SNCF buses, private, municipal and *départemental* buses can be useful for mid- to long-distance journeys. The most frustrating thing about them is the multiplicity of services and the difficulty in obtaining departure information other than at bus stops and stations. In Toulouse, city buses can be used to access outlying villages, and in Montpellier the network goes as far out as the coast. Some *départements*, like the Hérault and the Tarn, have rural bus networks; their roadside stops usually have a copy of the schedule attached to the sign or shelter. Private operators cover much of rural Languedoc and Roussillon too – unfortunately, their routes miss some of the more interesting and less inhabited areas, and the **timetable** is constructed to suit working, market and school hours – all often dauntingly early. All buses are, generally speaking, cheaper and slower than trains.

Larger towns usually have a **gare routière** (bus station), often next to the gare SNCF. However, the private bus companies don't always work together and you'll frequently find them leaving from an array of different points (the local tourist office will usually help locate them).

By car

Driving in Languedoc and Roussillon can be a real pleasure, and gives you the freedom to explore parts of the region that would otherwise remain inaccessible, in particular the sparsely populated upland of Haut Languedoc, the Hérault and the Pyrenees. **Autoroutes** in the region run through the same corridors as the main rail lines, connecting Toulouse and Narbonne, and from here, running north and south along the Mediterranean coast. If you are in a hurry, it is well worth paying the toll (see p.36) for their use, as the free national routes, which also follow this corridor, tend to be heavily travelled by both local drivers and long-distance truckers. By *autoroute*, in good traffic conditions, you can reach Nîmes from Toulouse in 2–3 hours. Away from the main arteries, the older main roads or **routes nationales** (marked N9 or RN230, for example, on signs and maps) are generally uncongested and, passing through the centres of the towns along the way, make for a more scenic, if slower, drive than the *autoroutes*. Smaller **routes départementales** (marked D) should not be shunned. Although they are occasionally in relatively poor condition, you can often travel for kilometres across country, seeing few other cars, on broad and well-maintained roads.

The most challenging part of driving in Languedoc and Roussillon is likely to be entering large cities for the first time: as a general rule of thumb you can usually reach the centre by following signs for the tourist office. That said, **parking** is likely to be problematic, so you may instead want to follow signs for the gare SNCF, which will have some pay parking and most likely be within walking distance of the centre. Most cities also have sufficient underground parking **garages** (typical clearance 1.70–2m), where you may pay up to €30 over night. Outside of the city cores, street parking is usually free, although it may mean spending a considerable time hunting around. Many hotels have garages for which they typically charge €5 and up per night.

Of course, there are times when it is wiser not to drive: **congestion** is a major problem on the *Autoroute Méditerranéenne* in summer, particularly on the first and last few days of July and August, and the same goes for roads of all categories along the coast on summer weekends, when the going is frustratingly slow. The high cost of **petrol** (*essence*) can also be a discouraging factor: prices at the time of writing were around €1.28 a litre for four-star unleaded (*super sans plomb*) and around €1.10 a litre for diesel (*gasoil*). There are 3.8 litres to the US gallon. The cheapest petrol or diesel fuel can usually be found at out-of-town superstores or *hypermarchés*, though note that many of these are automated and do not recognize most non-French credit cards.

In addition, you have to pay a **toll** (*péage*) on most *autoroutes*. Rates vary, but to give you an idea, travelling only by motorway the 1039km from Calais to Montpellier would cost you around €59.60 for a car without trailer, plus €62.34 in fuel (based on a mid-sized car), and take approximately 10 hours.

All the major car manufacturers have **garages** and **service stations** in Languedoc and Roussillon, which can help if you run into mechanical difficulties. You can find them in the Yellow Pages (@www.pages jaunes.fr) under "*Garages d'automobiles*". For breakdowns, look under "*Dépannages*". If you have an accident or break-in, you should report it to the local police (and keep a copy) in order to make an insurance claim. Many car insurance policies cover your car in Europe, but you're advised to take out extra cover for motor assistance in case your car breaks down, costing around £50 for seven days. Check with your local automobile association before leaving home.

Traffic information and route planning

For up-to-the-minute **traffic information** regarding traffic jams and road works on *autoroutes* throughout France, ring ☎08.92.68.10.77 (€0.34/min; French only) or consult the bilingual website @www.auto routes.fr. Traffic information for other roads can be obtained from the *Bison Futé* recorded information service (☎08.26.02.20.22; €0.15/min; French only) or its website @www.bison -fute.equipement.gouv.fr.

For **route planning**, @www.viamichelin .com can provide you with point-to-point driving directions for itineraries throughout France.

Rules of the road

British, Irish, Australian, Canadian, New Zealand and US **driving licences** are valid in France, though an International Driver's Licence makes life easier if you get a police officer unwilling to peruse a document in English. If the vehicle is rented, its registration document (*carte grise*) and the insurance papers must be carried. GB stickers must, by law, be displayed, and a Green Card, though not a legal requirement, might save some hassle. If your car is right-hand drive, you must have your headlight dip adjusted to the right before you go – it's a legal requirement – and as a courtesy change or paint them to yellow or stick on black glare deflectors. Remember also that you have to be 18 years of age to drive in France, regardless of whether you hold a licence in your own country.

The law of *priorité à droite* – **giving way** to traffic coming from your right, even when it is coming from a minor road – is being phased out as it is a major cause of accidents. It still applies in built-up areas, so you have to be vigilant in towns, keeping a lookout along the roadside for the yellow diamond on a white background that gives you right of way – until you see the same sign with an oblique black slash, which indicates vehicles emerging from the right have right of way. At roundabouts the *priorité à droite* law no longer applies. *Stop* signs mean stop completely; *Cédez le passage* means "Give way". Other signs warning of potential dangers are *déviation* (diversion), *gravillons* (loose chippings), *nids de poules* (potholes) and *chaussée déformée* (uneven surface).

Speed limits in France are: 130kph (80mph) on *autoroutes*; 110kph (68mph) on dual carriageways; 90kph (56mph) on other roads; and 50kph (31mph) in towns. The town limit is constant, but in wet weather, and for drivers with less than two years' experience, the three road limits are 110kph (68mph), 100kph (62mph) and 80kph (50mph) respectively. The standard **fine** for exceeding the speed limit by 20kph (12mph), for example, is €90; above 40kph (25mph) you will not only be fined but will also have to go to court. The legal blood **alcohol limit** while driving is 0.05 percent alcohol (lower than in the UK and North America), and random breath tests are common: if you are caught over the limit, your driving privileges may be immediately suspended.

Car rental

Car rental in France costs upwards of €250 a week (from around €70 a day), but can be cheaper if arranged before you leave home. You'll find the big firms – Hertz, Avis, Europcar and Budget – at airports and in most big cities, with addresses detailed throughout the Guide. Rental from airports normally includes a surcharge. Local firms can be cheaper but you need to check the small print and be sure of where the car can be returned to. It's normal to pay an indemnity of €150–300 against any damage to the car – they will take your credit card number rather than cash. You should return the car with a full tank of fuel. The cost of car rental includes the basic legally necessary car insurance.

North Americans and Australians in particular should be forewarned that it is very difficult to arrange the hire of a car with **automatic** transmission; if you can't drive a manual you should try to book an automatic well in advance, possibly before you leave home, and be prepared to pay a much higher price for it.

Most rental companies will only deal with people over 25 unless an extra insurance premium, typically around €20–25 per day, is paid (but you still must be over 21 and have driven for at least one year). OTU Voyage (℡01.55.82.32.32, ⊛www.otu.fr), the student travel agency, can arrange car rental for young drivers.

Car rental agencies

Avis UK ℡0870/606 0100, Republic of Ireland ℡021/428 1111, US ℡1-800/230-4898, Canada ℡1-800/272-5871, Australia ℡13 63 33 or 02/9353 9000, New Zealand ℡09/526 2847 or 0800/655 111, ⊛www.avis.com.
Budget UK ℡08701/565656, Republic of Ireland ℡09/0662 7711, US ℡1-800/527-0700, Canada ℡1-800/268-8900, Australia ℡1300/362 848, New Zealand ℡0800/283-438, ⊛www.budget.com.
Europcar UK ℡0870/607 5000, Republic of Ireland ℡01/614 2888,US & Canada ℡1-877/940 6900, Australia ℡1300/131 390, ⊛www.europcar .com.
Hertz UK ℡020/7026-0077, Republic of Ireland ℡01/870-5777, US ℡1-800/654-3131, Canada ℡1-800/263-0600, Australia ℡08/9921-4052, New Zealand ℡0800/654 321, ⊛www.hertz.com.
Holiday Autos UK ℡0871/222-3200, Republic of Ireland ℡01/872 9366, Australia ℡1300/554 432, New Zealand ℡0800/144 040, ⊛www .holidayautos.co.uk.

Moped and motorbike rental

Mopeds and scooters are relatively easy to find; outside the mountainous areas everyone from young kids to grandmas seems to ride them, and although they're not built for any kind of long-distance travel, they're ideal for shooting around town and nearby. Places that rent out bicycles will often also rent out mopeds; you can expect to pay €40 a day for a 50cc Suzuki. No licence is needed for 50cc and under bikes, but for anything larger you'll need a valid **motorbike** licence. Rental prices are around €55 a day for a 125cc motorbike; also expect to leave a hefty deposit by cash or credit card – €1000 is not unusual – which you may lose in the event of damage or theft. Crash helmets are now compulsory on all mopeds and motorbikes.

Hitching

If you're intent on **hitching**, you'll have to rely almost exclusively on car drivers, as lorries very rarely give lifts. Even so, it won't be easy. Looking as clean and respectable as possible makes a big difference, and hitching the less frequented D roads is much quicker. In mountain areas a rucksack and hiking gear will help procure a lift from fellow hikers.

Autoroutes are a special case. Hitching on the *autoroute* itself is strictly illegal, but you can make excellent time going from one service station to another and, if you get stuck, at least there's food, drink, shelter and washing facilities at most service stations. It helps to have the *Guide des Autoroutes*, published by Michelin, which shows all the rest stops, service stations, tollbooths (*péages*), exits and so on. Remember to get out at the service station before your driver leaves the *autoroute*. The tollbooths are a second best (and legal) option; ordinary approach roads tend to be difficult and can easily lead to a fine.

For long-distance rides, or for greater security, you might consider using the national **hitching organization**, Allostop (☎01.53.20.42.42, ⓦwww.allostop.net); reservations are normally made through the Paris number, but there is also a local branch in Montpellier (see p.273). Similar net-based services include Covoiture (ⓦwww.covoiturage.com) and Gnafou (ⓦwww.gnafou.net). Generally the cost of using these services amounts to 20–40 percent of the price of normal public transport.

By bike

Bicycles (*vélos*) have high status in France, and the French respect cyclists – both as traffic and, when you stop off at a restaurant or hotel, as customers. In addition, municipali-ties like Toulouse and Montpellier, and their respective *départements* – Haute Garonne and Hérault – are actively promoting cycling, not only with city paths, but with comprehensive networks linking rural areas (frequently utilizing disused roadways and rail rights of way). These days more and more cyclists are using **mountain bikes**, which the French call VTTs (*vélos tout terrain*), even for touring holidays, although it's much less effort, and much quicker, to cycle long distances and carry luggage on a traditionally styled touring or racing bike. Your primary concern using bicycle transport in this region will likely be the traffic, which on the narrow two-lane *routes nationales* is frequently heavy and extremely fast. Dedicated and experienced cyclists may want to tackle all or part of the ten-day *Raid Pyrénéen*, a mountainous 879km route from Cerbère on the Med to Hendaye on the Atlantic. For more information or to get official recognition for having completed the *Raid*, contact Cyclo Club Béarnais (59 av L-Sallenave, 64000 Pau; ☎05.59.84.32.64 Fri only 6–7.30pm). The Fédération Française de Cyclotourisme (ⓦwww.ffct.org) is a further useful source of information on all things to do with cycling in France.

Restaurants and hotels along the way are nearly always obliging about looking after your bike, even to the point of allowing it into your room. Most large towns have well-stocked retail and **repair shops**, where parts are normally cheaper than in Britain or the US. However, if you're using a foreign-made bike which doesn't have standard metric wheels, it's a good idea to carry spare tyres. Inner tubes are not a problem, as they adapt to either size, though make sure you get the right valves.

The **train** network runs various schemes for cyclists, all of them covered by the free leaf-let *Guide du Train et du Vélo*, available from most stations. Trains marked with a bicycle in the timetable allow you to take a bike as free accompanied luggage. Otherwise, you have to send your bike parcelled up as registered luggage for a fee of €25. Although it may well arrive in less time, the SNCF won't guarantee delivery in under five days, and you do hear stories of bicycles disappearing altogether.

Ferries either take bikes free or charge a maximum of £5 one-way. British Airways and Air France both take bikes free – you may have to box them though, and you should contact the airlines first. **Eurostar** allow you to take your bicycle as part of your baggage allowance provided it is dismantled and stored in a special bike bag, and the dimensions don't exceed 120cm by 90cm. Otherwise it needs to be sent on unaccompanied, with a guaranteed arrival of 24 hours – (you can register it up to ten days in advance; book through Esprit Europe (☎08705/850 850, ⍟www.espriteurope.co.uk); the fee is £20 one-way.

Bikes – usually mountain bikes – are often available to **rent** from campsites, hostels and *gîtes d'étapes*, as well as from specialist cycle shops and some tourist offices for around €15–20 per day. The bikes are often not insured, however, and you will be presented with the bill for their replacement if they're stolen or damaged. Check whether your travel insurance policy covers you for this if you intend to rent a bike.

As for **maps**, a minimum requirement is the IGN 1:100,000 series (see p.60) – the smallest scale that carries contours. The UK's national cyclists' association, the CTC (☎0870/873 0060, ⍟www.ctc.org.uk), can suggest routes and supply advice for members, as well as running a particularly good insurance scheme. Companies offering specialist **bike touring holidays** are listed on p.30. Useful **vocabulary** for cyclists is given on p.426.

Walking

Long-distance **walkers** are well served in Languedoc and Roussillon by an extensive network of marked footpaths, including long-distance routes, known as *sentiers de grande randonnée* or, more commonly, **GRs** (see also p.51). They're fully signposted and equipped with campsites and rest huts along the way. Some of the main routes in the region are the GR10, which runs the length of the Pyrenees, the GRs 7 and 36, which wind their way down from Haut Languedoc through the Corbières, and GR653 which follows the medieval Arles–Jaca pilgrimage route (*le chemin de St-Jacques*) to Santiago in Spain. Other routes are composites, like the "Sentier Cathar", which utilizes various GRs and ARs (local paths) to link Cathar sites between Perpignan and Foix.

Each path is described in a *Topoguide* (available in Britain from Stanfords

which gives a detailed account of the route (in French), including maps, campsites, refuge huts and sources of provisions *Topoguides* are produced by the principal French walkers' organization, the Fédération Française de la Randonnée Pédestre, (☎01.44.89.93.93, ⍟www.ffrp.asso.fr). In addition, many tourist offices can provide **guides** to their local footpaths, especially in popular hiking areas, where they often share premises with professional mountain guides and hike leaders. The latter organize climbing and walking expeditions for all levels of experience.

The main **climbing** organization is the Club Alpin Français (☎01.53.72.87.00, ⍟www .ffcam.fr); most major towns in the region have a branch office, the most useful being the CAF de TOULOUSE, 3 rue de l'Orient, 31000 Toulouse (Mon 2–5pm, Tues–Fri 9am–noon & 2–7pm; ☎05.61.63.74.42, ⍟perso.wanadoo .fr/clubalpintoulouse). In the Pyrenees, CIMES (☎05.62.90.09.92, ⍟www.cimes-pyrenees .net) offers similar services and has its own network of refuges.

Inland waterways

Languedoc is home to one of France's most famous inland waterways, the **Canal du Midi**, which leads from Toulouse (where it hooks up with the River Garonne) to Agde and Sète, passing Carcassonne and Béziers en route. A spur, the **Canal de la Robine** passes Narbonne before reaching the sea at Gruissan and Port-Nouvelle. From Sète, you can enter the **Canal du Rhône à Sète**, which heads east, passing St-Gilles and Beaucaire, until it reaches the Rhône. Subsidiary canals branch out through the flatlands of the Petite Camargue, and penetrate the extensive Rhône delta. For information on maximum dimensions, documentation, regulations and so forth, ask at a French Government Tourist Office for their booklet *Boating on the Waterways*, or contact Voies Navigables de France, 175 rue Ludovic Boutleux, 62408 Bethune (☎03.21.63.24.24, ⍟www.vnf.fr), which has information on boating in Languedoc and Roussillon, and lists of French firms that rent out boats.

Accommodation

At most times of the year, you can turn up in any town in Languedoc and Roussillon and find a room, or a place in a campsite. Booking a couple of nights in advance can be reassuring, however, as it saves you the effort of trudging round. The "Language" section at the back of the Guide (see p.422) should help you make a reservation, though many hoteliers and campsite managers – and almost all hostel managers – speak some English. In most towns you'll be able to get a double room for around €35–50, or a single for €32–45; as a general rule the areas around train stations have the highest density of cheap hotels. Note that many municipalities charge a hotel tax, calculated on top of the posted rate, ranging from €0.20–€3 per night.

Problems with availability arise mainly between mid-July and the end of August, when the French take their own vacations en masse. The first weekend of August is the busiest time of all. During this period, hotel and hostel accommodation can be hard to come by, particularly in the coastal resorts, and you may find yourself falling back on local tourist offices for help and ideas. Some tourist offices offer a **booking service** but they cannot guarantee rooms at a particular price. All tourist offices can provide lists of hotels, hostels or organizations such as CROUS (see p.43) as well as details of campsites and bed-and-breakfasts. With **campsites**, you can be more relaxed about finding an empty space, unless you're touring with a caravan or camper van or looking for a place on the Mediterranean coast or upper Ariège valley.

Most French **hotels** are **graded** from zero to five stars. The price more or less corresponds to the number of stars, though the system is a little haphazard, having more to do with ratios of bathrooms-per-guest than genuine quality, and non-classified and single-star hotels are often very good. What you get for your money varies enormously between establishments. For under €30, the bed is likely to be old and floppy, there won't be soundproofing, and showers will be communal. Rooms usually have a sink (*lavabo*) in one corner, sometimes with a toilet (*WC*) behind a screen as well; bathrooms and showers (*douches*) are almost invariably found on the landing – referred to as *douche et WC dans le palier*. The shared showers are not usually free – they cost between €3 and €5 per shower (*douche*). If you plan to shower every day and there is more than one of you, it's worth adding up what the ultimate cost will be – you might be better off moving to a more expensive room with its own shower. Over €40 will get you a room with its own bath or shower though not necessarily a toilet (*WC*), and, though the decor may not be anything to write home about, comfortable furniture. If wandering dark halls late at night in search of a toilet is not your idea of fun, ask for a bathroom (*salle de bain*) which will get you both a toilet and a shower in a separate room; these occasionally have bath tubs (*bain*) too. This type of room can be had for around €50, and may also come with a TV. At more than €65, you should expect a

Accommodation price codes

All the hotels and guesthouses listed in this book have been price-coded according to the following scale. The prices quoted are for the cheapest available double room in high season.

❶ Under €30	❹ €55–70	❼ €100–125
❷ €30–40	❺ €70–85	❽ €125–150
❸ €40–55	❻ €85–100	❾ Over €150

higher standard of fittings and something approaching luxury. Hotels with one star or above have a telephone in the rooms, though some phones can only receive calls.

Big cities have a good variety of cheap establishments; in small towns or villages where the choice is limited, you may not be so lucky. The modern and cheesy resorts which have sprung up along the Languedoc coast have inordinately high July and August prices. If you are staying more than three days in a hotel it's often possible to negotiate a lower price, particularly out of season.

Breakfast is not normally included and can add €5–8 per person to a bill – though there is no obligation to take it and you will nearly always do better at a café. The cost of eating **dinner** in a hotel's restaurant can be a more important factor to bear in mind when picking a place to stay. Officially, it is illegal for hotels to insist on your taking meals, but they often do in places heavily dependent on seasonal tourism. However, this is not always such a bad thing, and you can sometimes get a real bargain. **Single rooms** are only marginally cheaper than doubles, so sharing always slashes costs. Most hotels willingly provide rooms with **extra beds**, for three or more people, at good discounts.

Note that many family-run hotels are closed every year for two or three weeks sometime between May and September – where possible we've detailed this in the text. In addition, some hotels in smaller towns and villages close for one or two nights a week, usually Sunday or Monday – if in doubt, ring first to check.

A very useful option, especially if it's late at night, are the **motel chains**. In contrast to the downtown hotels which often offer doubtful value (worn-out mattresses, dust, noise, etc) you can count on a decent and reliable standard in the chains even if they are without much charm. Among the cheapest is the one-star **Formule 1** chain (℡08.92.68.56.85, €0.34 per min; ⊛www.hotelformule1.com), well signposted on the outskirts of most big towns. They are characterless, but provide rooms for up to three people from €27. With a Visa, Mastercard, Eurocard or American Express credit card, you can let yourself into a room at any hour of the day or night. Other budget chains include **B&B** (℡08.92.78.29.29, €0.34 per min; ⊛www.hotel-bb.com) and the slightly more comfortable **Première Classe** (℡08.25.00.30.03, ⊛www.premiere classe.fr) and **Etap Hôtel** (℡08.92.68.89.00, €0.34 per min; ⊛www.etaphotel.com). More upmarket but still affordable chains include **Ibis** (℡08.92.68.66.86, €0.34 per min; ⊛www.ibishotel.com) and **Campanile** (℡01.64.62.46.00, ⊛www.campanile.fr), where en-suite rooms with satellite TV and direct-dial phones cost from around €40–50. If you are staying put in a town for three days or more, you might also look into local **Résidences de Tourisme**, which are slightly more economical than hotels and sometimes offer self-catering. Aside from the chains, there a number of **hotel federations** in France. The biggest of these is **Logis de France** (℡01.45.84.83.84, ⊛www.logis-de-france .fr), an association of over three thousand hotels nationwide. Other good resources include ⊛www.resinfrance.fr, an official central reservation service, or ⊛www.francehotel reservation.com.

Several cities in Languedoc and Roussillon participate in the **"Bon Weekend en Ville"** programme, whereby you book through the local tourist office and get two nights for the price of one (Oct–May only) at participating hotels, as well as an array of discount coupons and special deals. Participating towns include Albi, Carcassonne, Nîmes and Toulouse, but the list is growing, so it's worth enquiring about when you are making arrangements to stay in larger towns. If you are planning your trip in advance, contact local tourist offices before arrival; there are very often special accommodation deals on offer, especially outside high season.

Bed-and-breakfast accommodation

In country areas, you'll come across *chambres d'hôtes* and *fermes auberges*, **bed-and-breakfast accommodation** in someone's house or farm. These vary in standard and are rarely a cheap option, usually costing the equivalent of a two-star hotel. However, if you're lucky, they may be good sources of traditional home cooking and French company. The brown leaflets available in tourist offices list most of them.

If you are planning to stay a week or more in any one place it might be worth considering **renting a house**. You can do this by checking adverts from the private owners in, for example, British Sunday newspapers (*Observer* and *Sunday Times*, mainly), or trying one of the numerous holiday firms that market accommodation/travel packages (see p.30 for a brief selection of these). Otherwise, economical longer-term, self-catering options include the **gîtes rurauk** (rural homes renting for €300 and up per week, administered by Gîtes de France) and the Clévacances programme, which has mainly town properties for rent. Contact the Fédération Nationale des Locations de France Clévacances (☎05.61.13.55.66, ⊛www.clevacances.fr). Alternatively check local tourist office listings for **appartements** or **meublés**.

Gîtes de France (☎01.49.70.75.75, ⊛www.gites-de-france.fr), a government-funded agency which promotes and manages a range of bed-and-breakfast and self-catering accommodation in France, the latter usually consisting of a self-contained country cottage, known as a **gîte rural** or **gîte de séjour**. Further details can be found in their two national guides – *Chambres et Tables d'Hôtes* and *Chambres d'Hôtes de Prestige et Gîtes de Charme* – which are also sometimes on sale in bookshops and tourist offices. The national guides, however, are not exhaustive; complete listings (with photos) are available in the guides distributed by departmental Gîtes de France offices – you can either contact the main office for a complete list, or pick up copies from local and departmental tourist offices. If you're planning from home, the simplest way to make reservations is through their website. Rural bed-and-breakfast and dining accommodation can also be arranged through Bienvenue à la Ferme (☎01.53.57.11.44, ⊛www.bienvenue-a-la -ferme.com) which also publishes regional and departmental guides.

Gîtes d'étapes and refuges

In the countryside, **gîtes d'étape** provide basic hostel-style accommodation, often run by the local village or municipality (whose mayor will probably be in charge of the key). They provide bunk beds and primitive kitchen

and washing facilities from around €8, and they are marked on the large-scale IGN walkers' maps and listed in the individual GR *Topoguides*. In addition, mountain areas are well supplied with **refuge huts**, mostly run by the Club Alpin Français (CAF), but also by CIMES (in the Pyrenees). Many are open in summer only. They are the only available shelter once you are above the villages. Costs are from around €10 for the night, less if you're a member of a climbing organization affiliated to the CAF. Meals – invariably four courses – cost around €14, which is not unreasonable when you consider that all supplies have to be brought up by mule or helicopter.

More information can be found in the guides *Gîtes d'Étape et Séjours* published by Gîtes de France (see opposite), and *Gîtes d'Étape et Refuges*, published by Guides La Cadole (which also has the handy webpage ⊛www.gites-refuges.com), available in French bookshops for €18.30.

Departmental offices of Gîtes de France

Ariège 31bis av Général-de-Gaulle, BP 143, 09004 Foix ☎05.61.02.30.89, ℻05.61.65.17.34, ✉gites -de-france.ariege@wanadoo.fr
Aude 78 rue Barbacane, 11000 Carcassonne ☎04.68.11.40.70, ℻04.68.11.40.72
Gard CDT 3 pl des Arènes, BP 59, 30007 Nîmes ☎04.66.27.94.94, ℻04.66.27.94.95
Haute-Garonne 14 rue Bayard, BP 845, 31015 Toulouse ☎05.61.99.70.60, ℻05.61.99.41.22
Hérault Maison de Tourisme, 1977 av des Moulins, BP 3070, 34034 Montpellier ☎04.67.67.62.62, ℻04.67.67.71.69, ⊛www.gites-de-france-herault .asso.fr
Pyrénées-Orientales 30 rue Pierre-Breton- neau, 66017 Perpignan ☎04.68.55.60.95, ℻04.68.50.68.44
Tarn Maison des Agriculteurs, La Milliasolle, BP 89, 81003 Albi ☎05.63.48.83.01, ℻05.63.48.83.12

Hostels

At between €12 and €20 per night for a dormitory bed, and generally breakfast thrown in, **hostels** – *auberges de jeunesse* – are invaluable for single travellers on a budget. For hostels, **per-person prices** of dorm beds are given throughout the Guide. Many modern hostels now also offer rooms for couples, with en-suite showers, but they don't necessarily work out cheaper than hotels – particularly if you've had to pay a bus fare out to the edge of town to reach them. However, many hostels are beautifully sited, and they allow you to cut costs by preparing your own food in their kitchens, or eating in their cheap canteens.

There are three rival French **hostelling associations**: the main two ones are the Fédération Unie des Auberges de Jeunesse (FUAG; ☎01.44.89.87.27, ⓦwww.fuaj.org), which has its hostels detailed in the *International Handbook*, and the Ligue Française pour les Auberges de Jeunesse (LFAJ; ☎01.45.48.69.84, ⓦwww.auberges-de -jeunesse.com). Normally, to stay at FUAJ or LFAJ hostels, you must be a member of Hostelling International (HI) or the International Youth Hostel Federation (IYHF). If you don't join up before you leave home, you can purchase a **membership card** on arrival in the French hostel for €15.25 (€10.70 for under-26s). The third hostelling organization is the Union des Centres de Rencontres Internationales de France (☎01.40.26.57.64, ⓔinfo@ucrif.asso.fr), with 60 hostels in France; membership is not required.

A few large towns provide a more luxurious standard of hostel accommodation in Foyers des Jeunes Travailleurs/Travailleuses, **residential hostels** for young workers and students, where you can usually get a private room for around €14. They normally have a good cafeteria or canteen.

At the height of summer (usually July and Aug only), there's also the possibility of staying in **student accommodation** in university towns and cities. The main organization to contact for this is CROUS, (☎01.40.51.55.55, ⓦwww.crous-paris.fr). Prices are similar to the official hostels, from around €14 per person, and you don't need membership.

Camping

Practically every village and town in France has at least one **campsite** to cater for the thousands of people who spend their holiday under canvas – camping is a very big deal in France. The cheapest – at around €5–8 per person per night – is usually the *camping municipal*, run by the local municipality. In season or whenever they're officially open, they are always clean and have plenty of hot water; often they are situated in prime local positions. Out of season, those that stay open often don't bother to collect the overnight charge.

If you're planning to do a lot of camping, an **international camping carnet** is a good investment. The carnet serves as useful identification, covers you for third party insurance when camping and gives ten-percent reductions at campsites listed in the CCI information booklet that comes with your carnet. It is available in the UK from the AA, the RAC or the Carefree Travel Service (☎0247/642 2024), who also book inspected camping sites in Europe and arrange ferry crossings; in the US or Canada, contact Family Campers and RVers(☎1-800/245 9755, ⓦwww.fcrv.org).

On the coast around the beach towns, there are **superior categories** of campsite where you'll pay prices similar to those of a hotel for the facilities – bars, restaurants and sometimes swimming pools. These have rather more permanent status than the *campings municipaux*, with people often spending a whole holiday in the one base. If you plan to do the same, and particularly if you have a caravan, camper or a big tent, it's wise to book ahead – reckon on paying at least €8 a head with a tent or a camper van. Inland, *camping à la ferme* – on somebody's farm – is another possibility (generally without facilities). Lists of sites are detailed in the Tourist Board's *Accueil à la Campagne* booklet.

A number of companies in the UK also specialize in **camping holidays** with well-equipped tents provided: try Canvas Holidays (☎0870/192 1154, ⓦwww.canvas.co .uk) or Eurocamp (☎0870/9019 410, ⓦwww .eurocamp.co.uk). Twelve nights' camping at Argelès, near Perpignan, with Canvas, for example, costs about £900 in high season for two adults and up to four children, including Channel ferry.

Lastly, a word of caution: never **camp rough** (*camping sauvage*, as the French call it) on anyone's land without first asking permission, as you may well have to deal with an irate farmer and his dogs. On the other hand, a politely phrased request for permission will as often as not get positive results. Camping on public land is not officially permitted, but is widely practised by the French, and if you are discreet you will likely not meet with problems. On beaches, it's best to camp out only where other people are doing so.

Eating and drinking

Languedoc-Roussillon – a traditionally poor and marginalized region – isn't known for the elaborate haute cuisine which typifies French cookery in the popular imagination. The food of this overwhelmingly rural region tends to be simple, with little family restaurants serving classic peasant (terroir) dishes based on local produce for under €20 a head. As you cross the region, however, you'll find that the huge diversity of the landscape has contributed to a correspondingly wide range in local specialities – immediately obvious when you visit town and village produce markets – and in all but the most out-of-the-way hamlet you'll be able to find a more adventurous (and expensive) gastronomique restaurant. Due to its relative isolation Languedoc-Roussillon has also fared better than many regions in escaping the processed, boil-in-the-bag and ready-to-microwave productions – known in France as mal-bouffe ("bad grub") – of the global food industry.

In the rarefied world of **haute cuisine**, where the top chefs are national celebrities, a battle is currently raging between traditionalists, determined to preserve the purity of French cuisine, and those who experiment with different flavours from around the world to create novel combinations. At this level, French food is still brilliant – in both camps – and the good news is that prices are continuing to come down. Many gourmet palaces offer weekday lunch-time menus where you can sample culinary genius for around €50.

Languedoc and Roussillon are also great places for **foreign cuisine**, in particular North African, Caribbean (known as *Antillais*) and Asiatic. Moroccan, Thai or Vietnamese restaurants are not necessarily cheap options but they are usually good value for money. Chinese restaurants tend, on the other hand, to be inexpensive but disappointing.

On the whole, **vegetarians** can expect a somewhat lean time in Languedoc and Roussillon; *cuisine rurale* is relentlessly meat-based, and in some traditional farming villages even understanding the concept of vegetarianism can be a stretch. A few cities have specifically vegetarian restaurants (detailed in the text), but elsewhere you'll have to rely on crêperies and pizzerias, or hope you find a sympathetic restaurant willing to replace a meat dish on the *menu fixe* with an omelette. Remember the phrase "*Je suis végétarien(ne); il y a quelques plats sans viande?*" (I'm a vegetarian; are there any non-meat dishes?). **Vegans**, however, should probably forget all about eating in French restaurants and stick to self-catering.

For a **food glossary**, see pp.427–434.

Breakfast and snacks

A croissant, *pain au chocolat,* or a sandwich in a bar or café, with hot chocolate or coffee, is generally the best **breakfast** you'll get – at a fraction of the cost charged by most hotels. (The days when hotels gave you mounds of croissants or brioches for breakfast seem to be long gone; now it's virtually always bread, jam and a jug of coffee or tea for about €5.) Croissants and sometimes hard-boiled eggs are displayed on bar counters until around 9.30am or 10am. If you stand – cheaper than sitting down – you just help yourself to these with your coffee; the waiter keeps an eye on how many you've eaten and bills you accordingly.

At **lunch time**, and sometimes in the evening, you may find cafés offering a *plat du jour* (chef's daily special) at between €9 and €14, or *formules*, a limited or no-choice menu. *Croques-monsieur* or *croques-madame* (variations on the toasted-cheese sandwich) are sold at cafés, brasseries and many street stands, along with *frites* (potato fries), crêpes, *galettes* (wholewheat pancakes), *gauffres* (waffles), *glaces* (ice creams) and all kinds of fresh-filled baguettes (these very filling sandwiches usually cost €3–5 to take away). For variety, there are

Tunisian snacks like *brik à l'œuf* (a fried pastry with an egg inside), *merguez* (spicy North African sausage), Greek *souvlaki* (kebabs) and Middle Eastern falafel (deep-fried chickpea balls in flat bread with salad). Wine bars are good for regional sausages and cheese, usually served with brown bread (*pain de campagne*).

Crêpes, or pancakes with fillings, served up at ubiquitous crêperies, are popular lunch-time food. The savoury buckwheat variety (often called *galettes*) provide the main course; the sweet white-flour ones are dessert. They taste nice enough, but are usually poor value in comparison with a restaurant meal; you need at least three, normally at over €5 each, to feel full. **Pizzerias**, usually *au feu de bois* (wood-fire-baked), are also very common. They are somewhat better value than crêperies, but quality and quantity vary greatly – look before you leap into the nearest empty seats.

Gallic culture is incredibly **picnic**-tolerant, and there's no problem in pulling off the road and spreading your blanket wherever you are. It's a very economical and pleasant way of dining, with the local outdoor market or supermarket able to provide everything you need from tomatoes and avocados to cheese and pâté. Cooked meat, prepared snacks, ready-made dishes and assorted salads can be bought at *charcuteries* (delicatessens), which you'll find everywhere – even in small villages, though the same things are cheaper at supermarket counters. You purchase by weight, or you can ask for *une tranche* (a slice), *une barquette* (a carton) or *une part* (a portion).

Salons de thé, which open from mid-morning to late evening, serve brunches, salads, quiches and so on, as well as gateaux, ice cream and a wide selection of teas. They tend to be a good deal pricier than cafés or brasseries – you're paying for the posh surroundings. As bars are to men in France, *salons de thé* are to women, and they generally have a more female ambience and clientele. For cakes and pastries to take away, you'll find impressive arrays at every *boulangerie-pâtisserie*.

Meals

There's no difference between **restaurants** (or *auberges* or *relais* as they sometimes call themselves) and **brasseries** in terms of quality or price range. The distinction is that brasseries, which resemble cafés, serve quicker meals at most hours of the day, while restaurants tend to stick to the traditional meal times of noon to 2pm, and 7pm to 9.30pm or 10.30pm. After 9pm or so, restaurants often serve only à la carte meals (single dishes chosen from the menu) – invariably more expensive than eating the set *menu fixe*. In touristy areas in high season, and for all the more upmarket places, it's wise to make reservations – easily done on the same day. In small towns it may be impossible to get anything other than a bar sandwich after 10pm or even earlier; in major cities, town centre brasseries will serve until 11pm or midnight and one or two may stay open all night.

When hunting for places to eat, avoid those that are half empty at peak time, use your nose and regard long menus with suspicion. Don't forget that **hotel restaurants** are open to non-residents, and are often very good value. In many small towns and villages, you'll find the only restaurants are in hotels. Since restaurants change hands frequently and have their ups and downs, it's also worth asking locals for recommendations. This is the conversational equivalent of commenting on the weather in Britain and will usually elicit strong views and sound advice.

Prices, and what you get for them, are posted outside. Normally there's a choice between one or more *menus fixes*, where the number of courses has already been determined and the choice is limited, and choosing individually from the *carte* (menu). **Menus fixes** are normally the cheapest option. At the bottom end of the price range, they revolve around standard dishes such as steak and chips (*steak frites*), chicken and chips (*poulet frites*) and various concoctions involving innards. But further up the scale they can be much the best-value way of sampling regional specialities, sometimes running to five or more courses. If you're simply not that hungry, just go for the *plat du jour*.

Going **à la carte** offers greater choice and, in the better restaurants, unlimited access to the chef's specialities – though you'll pay for the privilege. A simple and perfectly legitimate tactic is to have just one course instead of the expected three or four. You can share dishes or go for several starters – a useful strategy for vegetarians. There's no minimum charge.

In the French **sequence of courses**, any salad (sometimes vegetables, too) comes separate from the main dish, and cheese precedes a dessert. You will be offered coffee, which is always extra, to finish off the meal.

Service compris or s.c. means the **service charge** is included. *Service non compris*, s.n.c. or *servis en sus* means that it isn't and you need to calculate an additional 15 percent. **Wine** (*vin*) or a **drink** (*boisson*) is occasionally included (*compris*) in the cost of a menu fixe. When ordering house wine, the cheapest option, ask for *un quart* (0.25 litre), *un demi-litre* (0.5 litre) or *une carafe* (1 litre). If you're worried about the cost ask for *vin ordinaire* or the *vin de table*. In the Guide the lowest price menu or the range of menus is given; where average à la carte prices are given it assumes you'll have three courses and half a bottle of wine.

The French are much better disposed towards **children** in restaurants than other nationalities, not simply by offering reduced-price children's menus but in creating an atmosphere – even in otherwise fairly snooty establishments – that positively welcomes kids; some even have in-house games and toys for them to occupy themselves with. It is regarded as self-evident that large family groups should be able to eat out together.

A rather murkier area is that of **dogs** in the dining room; it can be quite a shock in a provincial hotel to realize that the majority of your fellow diners are attempting to keep dogs concealed beneath their tables.

Regional specialities

Languedoc and Roussillon are extremely varied and exciting areas for cuisine. In the east, around Nîmes and in the **Gard**, the influence of Provençal cuisine is strongly felt – especially in the use of the herbs that spring up throughout the *garrigues* – while the *manades* (ranches) of the **Camargue** ensure that beef plays a notable role, especially in sausage and in the wine-marinated *brandade de la Gardienne*. Other prominent ingredients include truffles, gathered in the scrubby

woodland of the northern fringe around **Uzès**, olives, cultivated in low hills rising up from the coastal plains and yielding reasonable oil, and rice, which is grown locally in the Camargue. The fair sunny climate also favours vegetables and fruit, including asparagus, but more notably peaches and apricots (especially around St-Gilles).

Unsurprisingly, fish and seafood abound in the **coastal cuisine** of Languedoc, whether in brothy *coquillages*, the garlicky *bourride* of Sète, or baked or barbecued. Tuna, anchovy and sardine dominate, but the range of fish used is very broad. The shallow *étangs* are home to large-scale mussel and oyster farming, of which Mèze and Leucate are the main centres. In the uplands of the **Hérault**, the transition to cooler higher terrain is marked by an increase in sheep-based dishes (using both meat and cheese), although fruits such as figs also mark local cookery. Tripe (*tripoux*) is another staple along the whole inland strip of Languedoc.

The highland and forest ingredients are all the more accentuated in **Haut Languedoc**, where seasonal delicacies such as the ubiquitous mushrooms of late summer add variety. Some of the finest mutton comes from the Cabardès district, on the southern slopes of the Montagne Noire. Further northeast, the cereal lands of **Tarn** are notable for high-quality foie gras and land snails (*escargots*), while Lautrec is an undisputed garlic capital, famed for its pink version. Duck (*canard*), popular throughout France, is also a staple in the zone stretching from Toulouse to Albi, and you are likely to encounter it in the form of a *confit* (a jellied conserve). Tarn also falls heavily under the culinary influence of **Aude**, whose staple, cassoulet, a bean stew originating in Castelnaudary, has colonized the whole of Languedoc. Carcassonne marks something of a midpoint, between the wheat and bean fields which spread west to Toulouse, and the east, which is known for its olives. The city, and the lands along the Aude, are home to some of the region's most interesting sweets, ranging from the rosemary-tinged honey of the Corbières hills, to the nougat of Limoux and candied chestnuts, a traditional late-autumn treat. The cuisine of Aude, and its neighbour, **Ariège**, are transformed as the landscape rises towards the Pyrenees. While the foothills produce excellent beef, sheep and goats come to play an increasing role as the terrain climbs, appearing in well-reputed cheeses and supplementing or replacing pork in the ubiquitous sausage (*saucisson*).

Roussillon represents something of a shift, with its marked Catalan base and Spanish influence – immediately noticeable in the strong influence of olive oil. The region's dry and grilled pork sausages (in Catalan *embutits* and *botifares*) are particularly worth trying, and a countryside staple is the hearty pork-based *ollada* soup. Special occasions are celebrated with a *cargolada* – an elaborate dish of grilled land snails. Moving towards the milder climes of the coast, fruit makes a dramatic reappearance, in the cherries of Céret, as well as almonds, peaches and pears. The coastal hills are swathed in olive trees, while seaside villages like Collioure and Port-Vendres have long survived from fishing. Spanish influence in the twentieth century has also helped to popularize southern Spanish dishes such as paella and tapas.

Cheeses of Languedoc and Roussillon

You can find the great **cheeses** from all over France in Languedoc and Roussillon, but it is still worth hunting out local specialities. Many cheese-makers have successfully protected their products by AOC (*appellation d'origine controlée*) laws similar to those for wines, which means that the subtle differences between French local cheeses have not been overwhelmed by the industrialized uniformity that has plagued other countries. Although just about everything is available in supermarkets, farm-produced cheese will have to be hunted down in speciality shops (a *fromagerie*, or a regional produce outlet) and country markets.

Throughout the sheep-producing areas of the region, local cheeses can be picked up at country markets, or at times directly from the farms themselves. The milk which produces the famous Roquefort cheese comes exclusively from Haut Languedoc's sheep (specifically, an ancient breed of Lacaune), while a few noteworthy cheese varieties in Languedoc and Roussillon itself include **Pélardon des Cévennes**, a flavourful goats' (*chèvre*) milk cheese recently developed at St Hippolyte-du-Fort; the creamy but acidic **Pélardon des Corbières**, an older variant of the Cévennes version, round in shape and coated in natural mould, best served after about a week; and **Le Pérail**, a white *fromage de brebis* (sheep) from Gard, whose taste transforms as it ages – from a subtle freshness when first produced to a sharp tanginess when aged a fortnight.

Drink

Wherever you can eat you can invariably drink, and vice versa. **Drinking** is done at a leisurely pace whether it's a prelude to food (*apéritif*), a sequel (*digestif*), or the accompaniment, and cafés are the standard places to do it. Every bar or café has to display its full price list, usually without the fifteen-percent service charge added, with the cheapest drinks at the bar (*au comptoir*), and progressively increasing prices for sitting at a table inside (*la salle*), or outside (*la terrasse*). If you are sitting outside, particularly in a touristy area, unpleasantness can be avoided by checking the price with the waiter when you put in your order. You pay when you leave, and it's perfectly acceptable to sit for hours over just one cup of coffee.

Wine (*vin*) is drunk at just about every meal or social occasion. Red is *rouge*, white *blanc*, and rosé *rosé*. *Vin de table* or *vin ordinaire* – table wine – is generally drinkable and always cheap, although it may be disguised and priced up as the house wine, or *cuvée*. The price of AOC (*appellation d'origine contrôlée*) wines can vary from €1.80 to around €15 a bottle, and that's the vineyard price. You can buy a very decent bottle of wine for €3 to €5, and €10 and over will buy you something really nice. By the time restaurants have added their considerable mark-up, however, wine can constitute an alarming proportion of the bill.

The basic **wine terms** are: *brut*, very dry; *sec*, dry; *demi-sec*, sweet; *doux*, very sweet; *mousseux*, sparkling; *méthode champenoise*, mature and sparkling. A glass of wine is simply *un rouge*, *un rosé* or *un blanc*. You may have the choice of *un ballon* (round glass) or a smaller glass (*un verre*). *Un pichet* (a pitcher) is normally a quarter-litre. A glass of wine in a bar will cost around €3.

The best way to **buy bottles** of wine is directly from the producers (*vignerons*), either at vineyards, at Maisons or Syndicats du Vin (representing a group of wine-producers), or at Coopératifs Vinicoles (wine-producer co-ops). At all these places you can sample the wines first. It's best to make clear at the start how much you want to buy (if it's only one or two bottles) and you will not be popular if you drink several glasses and then leave without making a purchase. The most economical option is to buy *en vrac*, which you can also do at some wine shops (*caves*), taking an easily obtainable plastic five- or ten-litre container (usually sold on the premises) and getting it filled straight from the barrel. In cities, supermarkets are the best places to buy your wine, and their prices often beat those of the *vignerons*.

In Languedoc and Roussillon, some good **regional wines** can be found in the *vins de pays* category (also known as *vins d'Oc* in these parts). Quality wines are denoted by the *appellation d'origine contrôlée* (AOC), which strictly controls quality and the amount of wine that a particular area may produce. Within each *appellation* there is enormous diversity generated by the different types of soil, the lie of the land, the type of grape grown – there are over forty varieties grown in Languedoc and Roussillon – the ability of the wine to age and the individual skills of the wine-grower. For more details on local wines, see *Wines of Languedoc and Roussillon* Colour Section.

Familiar light Belgian and German brands, plus French brands from Alsace, account for most of the **beer** you'll find. Draught beer (*à la pression*) – usually Kronenbourg – is the cheapest drink you can have next to coffee and wine; ask for *une pression* or *un demi* (0.33 litre). A *demi* costs around €2.80. For a wider choice of draught and bottled beer you need to go to the special beer-drinking establishments or English-style pubs found in most city centres and resorts. A small bottle at one of these places will cost at least twice as much as a *demi* in a café. In supermarkets, however, bottled or canned beer is exceptionally cheap.

Strong alcohol is consumed from as early as 5am as a pre-work fortifier, and then at any time through the day according to circumstance, though the national reputation for drunkenness has lost much of its truth. Brandies and the dozens of *eaux de vie* (spirits) and liqueurs are always available. *Pastis* – the generic name of aniseed drinks such as Pernod or Ricard and a favourite throughout Languedoc – is served diluted with water and ice (*glaçons*). It's very refreshing and not expensive. Mixed with *crème de menthe* it's known as a *perroquet*. Among less familiar names, try Poire William (pear brandy), or Marc (a spirit distilled from grape pulp). Measures are generous, but they don't come cheap: the same applies for imported spirits like whisky (*Scotch*). Two drinks designed to stimulate the appetite – *un apéritif* – are Pineau (cognac and grape juice) and Kir (white wine with a dash of Cassis – blackcurrant liquor – or with champagne instead of wine for a Kir Royal). **Cocktails** are served at most late-night bars, discos and music places, as well as at upmarket hotel bars and at every seaside promenade café; they usually cost at least €7.

On the **soft drink** front, you can buy cartons of unsweetened fruit juice in supermarkets, although in the cafés the bottled (sweetened) nectars such as apricot (*jus d'abricot*) and blackcurrant (*cassis*) still hold sway. You can also get fresh orange or lemon juice (*orange/citron pressé*), at a price. A *citron pressé* is a refreshing choice for the extremely thirsty on a hot day – the lemon juice is served in the bottom of a long ice-filled glass, with a jug of water and a sugar bowl to sweeten it to your taste. Other drinks to try are syrups (*sirops*) of mint, grenadine or other flavours mixed with water. The standard fizzy drinks of lemonade (*limonade*), Coke (*coca*) and so forth are all available. Bottles of **mineral water** (*eau minérale*) and spring water (*eau de source*) – either sparkling (*gazeuse*) or still (*eau plate*) – abound, from the big brand names to more obscure spa product. But there's not much wrong with the tap water (*l'eau du robinet* or *une carafe d'eau*), which will always be brought free to your table if you ask for it.

Coffee is invariably espresso – small, black and very strong. *Un café* or *un express* is the regular; *un crème* is with milk; *un grand café* or *un grand crème* are large cups. In the morning you could also ask for *un café au lait* – espresso in a large cup or bowl filled up with hot milk. *Un déca* is decaffeinated, now widely available. Ordinary **tea** (*thé*) is Lipton's nine times out of ten and is normally served black, and you can usually have a slice of lemon (*citron*) with it if you want; to have milk with it, ask for *un peu de lait frais* (some fresh milk). *Chocolat chaud* – **hot chocolate** – unlike tea, lives up to the high standards of French food and drink and can be had in any café. After eating, **herb teas** (*infusions* or *tisanes*), served in every *salon de thé*, can be soothing. The more common ones are *verveine* (verbena), *tilleul* (lime blossom), *menthe* (mint) and *camomille* (camomile).

The media

English-language newspapers, such as The Times, the Washington Post, New York Times and the International Herald Tribune, are on sale the day of publication in some of the region's larger cities, including Toulouse, Montpellier and Nîmes, and the day after publication at many resorts. Of the French daily papers, Le Monde is the most intellectual; it is widely respected, but somewhat austere, while Libération, founded by Jean-Paul Sartre in the 1960s, is moderately left-wing, independent and more colloquial, with good, if choosy, coverage. Rigorous left-wing criticism of the French government comes from L'Humanité, the Communist Party paper. The other nationals are all firmly right-wing, with Le Figaro being the most respected. The top-selling national is L'Équipe, which is dedicated to sports, while Paris-Turf focuses on horse-racing. Languedoc-Roussillon's regional daily paper is the Midi-Libre: for visitors, it's mainly of interest for its listings, although it does have good local travel features.

Weeklies, along the lines of *Newsweek/Time*, include the wide-ranging and socialist-leaning *Le Nouvel Observateur*, its right-wing counterpoint *L'Express,* the boringly centrist *L'Événement du Jeudi* and the newcomer with a bite, *Marianne*. The best investigative journalism is to be found in the weekly satirical paper *Le Canard Enchaîné* while *Charlie Hebdo* is a sort of *Private Eye* equivalent. There is also *Paris-Match* for gossip about stars and royal families. **Monthlies** include the young, trendy and cheap *Nova*, which has excellent listings of cultural events, and *Actuel*, which is good for current events. There are, of course, the French versions of *Vogue*, *Elle* (weekly) and *Marie-Claire*, and the relentlessly urban *Biba*, for women's fashion and lifestyle.

Moral **censorship** of the press is rare. On the news-stands you'll find pornography of every shade, as well as covers featuring drugs, sex, blasphemy and bizarre forms of grossness alongside knitting patterns and DIY. You'll also find French **comics** (*bandes dessinées*), which often indulge such adult interests: wildly and wonderfully illustrated, they are considered to be quite an artform and whole museums are devoted to them.

Some of the huge numbers of homeless people in France (*les sans-abri*) make a bit of money by selling magazines on the streets which combine culture, humour and self-help with social and political issues. Costing €1.50, the best known of these is *L'Itinerant*.

French TV has six channels: three public (France 2, France 3 and Arte/France 5); one subscription (Canal Plus – with some unencrypted programmes); and two commercial open broadcasts (TF1 and M6). Of these, **TF1** and **France 2** are the most popular channels, showing a broad mix of programmes. **Arte/France 5** (also known as La Cinquième) is a joint Franco-German cultural venture that transmits simultaneously in French and German: offerings include highbrow programmes, daily documentaries, art criticism, serious French and German movies and complete operas. During the day (7am–7pm), France 5 uses the frequency to broadcast educational programmes. **Canal Plus** is the main movie channel, with repeats of foreign films usually shown at least once in the original language. **France 3** is strong on regional news and more heavyweight movies, including a fair number undubbed foreign films, while **M6** shows a lot of US imports and programmes aimed at a younger market. The main French **news broadcasts** are at 8pm on France 2 and TF1.

In addition there are any number of **cable** and satellite channels, including CNN, BBC World and BBC Prime, Eurosport, MTV, Planète, which specializes in documentaries, Ciné Première, and Canal Jimmy (*Friends* and the like in French). The main French-run **music channel** is MCM.

If you've got a **radio**, you can tune in to English-language news on the BBC World Service (⊛www.bbc.co.uk/worldservice) on 648kHz AM or 198kHz long wave from midnight to 5am (and Radio 4 during the day). The Voice of America (⊛www.voa.gov) transmits on 90.5, 98.8 and 102.4 FM. For radio **news in French**, there's the state-run France Inter (87.8 FM), Europe 1 (104.7 FM) and round-the-clock news on France Infos (105.5 FM).

Sports and outdoor pursuits

Languedoc and Roussillon offer a wide range of sports, both to watch and take part in. As well as seeing local teams play big league sports such as football, regionally popular games like rugby are also worthwhile seeking out. In addition, there's a variety of outdoor activities, including hiking, cycling and skiing, and water-borne diversions such as rafting and sailing.

As well as rugby, the outdoor spectacle of **bullfighting**, or more properly, *tauromachie*, is incredibly popular across the region, both in Spanish and indigenous styles. **Water-jousting** (see box, p.276), a coastal tradition which pits boat-borne jousting teams against each other in an effort to unseat their opponents, has its home at Sète, but is practised along the length of the coast. **Pétanque**, or *boules*, is a game you'll see played in towns and villages throughout the region, and which you can play yourself if you purchase a set (available at sports shops and large department stores).

Football and rugby

Languedoc and Roussillon are not the best places in France for **football**, and the only city in the region with a team in the First

Division (*Ligue 1*) is Toulouse, whose club tends to hover around the lower regions of the league. Montpellier are currently languishing in the second division, a far cry from their finest moment when they won the French Cup in 1990.

Rugby is the field game of choice in the region, and virtually every town of any size boasts a team. Top teams in the region include Toulouse, Narbonne, Perpignan, Nîmes and Castres, who have traditionally provided the core of the French national side. Rugby originated in 1832, in England, and although it arrived in France not long after, it only really caught on in the Occitan south – perhaps as an unconscious means of marking a difference from the northern French. Post-game camaraderie is a big part of the whole experience, and you'll find yourself caught up in the cheerful spirit of things whether you see a major team like Stade Toulousain in action, or a small-town match with teams of the level of Albi or Pamiers.

Tauromachie

Bulls have been raised in eastern Languedoc since time immemorial, and in the last centuries **tauromachie** – "the art of the bull" (see box, p.224) – has come to play an important role in the culture of the whole region. While the people of the Petite Camargue ranchlands see it as a measure of virility, Occitan patriots are attracted to it as a custom which has no equivalent in the north of France.

Two distinct types of *tauromachie* are practised in Languedoc and Roussillon, the better known of which is the Iberian-style **corrida**. This event, which can be seen at the *ferias* of Nîmes, St-Gilles and Béziers as well as smaller towns across Languedoc, and in Céret in Roussillon is a highly ritualized ceremony. In a typical afternoon, three matadors dispose of six bulls, each of which will face a number of torments, including being poked by horseback *picadores*, and pricked with spears by running *banderilleros*, before a series of choreographed passes is executed by the matador and the bull is killed. Crowds are extremely vocal; poor matadors are subjected to catcalls and shouts, while a successful performance is awarded with loud ovations.

The French **course**, which has its origin in the medieval *jeu taurin* ("bull-baiting") is quite distinct from the *corrida*. Less expensive and elaborate, it is more common in village *fêtes*, such as at Uzès or Aigues-Morte, and usually involves the bulls (or cows) being led into a ring and fitted with a rosette of ribbon and colourful tassels suspended between their horns. For fifteen minutes *raseteurs* provoke the bull into charging and attempt to snatch the rosette or tassels without getting trampled or gored. When all is complete, the bulls are herded out nervous, but otherwise unharmed, back to their pen. Unlike the ceremonial Spanish version, the *course* is more of a sport, with a stronger element of competition among the human participants.

Today *tauromachie* is more popular than ever; the **ferias** of Nîmes draw thousands of enthusiasts from all over Europe and are universally acknowledged as southern France's liveliest and most colourful festivities. *Tauromachie* has also taken firm root in the smallest of villages far from the *manades* of the plains: even if they can afford no more than an *encierro*, villagers pool their money in order to pay for some sort of taurine display, without which no *fête* is complete. In urban areas, however, there have been protests against the bull-fights, with *tauromachie* disappearing in Toulouse, and letter-bomb attacks on organizers in Nîmes.

Pétanque

Once the preserve of sweatered old men in berets, recently **pétanque**, or *boules*, has seen a surge in popularity and a broadening of appeal to include more young people and women. The game is similar to English bowls. Two equally numbered teams (from one to three persons) find a space of hard, compact ground and throw a *cochonnet* (jack) a few metres (technically 6 to 10). A small circle is then marked on the ground to show the limit of the area in which the throwers must stand (hence *pétanque* from the Provençal "pieds tanqués" or "feet together"). They then proceed in turns to launch a total of three balls (two in a 6-person match), each with the object of having their metal *boules* closest to the *cochonnet* at the end of the exchange. A point is gained for each ball that is closer than the nearest ball of the opposing team. The jack is then thrown again and play continues until one side scores 13. *Pétanque* matches invariably draw a crowd of onlookers, and you will not be considered rude if you stop to observe. The best times to watch are during village *fêtes*, which invariably include a tournament, drawing out the best players in the village.

Hiking, biking and riding

Walking is undoubtedly the way to get the most out of a visit to the region. Well-marked and maintained GR paths, signposted with their distinctive yellow and red bars, span the region, punctuated by *gîtes*, refuges and campsites along the way. The highest concentration of paths (and the best hiking scenery) is found in the Pyrenees and its foothills, where you will find an extensive network of yellow- and- red-marked GRP (*grandes randonnées du pays*) paths as well as HRP (*haute route des Pyrénées*) routes. In addition local AR footpaths abound, and in virtually every village you'll find an information board with a map outlining local itineraries of varying length and difficulty. Even if you're spending only a few hours in a village, it's worth enquiring at the tourist office which will almost certainly have a pamphlet outlining local walks.

Recently a series of excellent *Topoguides* has been published for each *région* and *département*, by the Fédération Française de la Randonnée Pédestre (☏01.44.89.93.90, ⓦwww.ffrp.asso.fr). Regional guides detail eighty walks and VTT routes (€13.95) and departmental guides have forty (€11.95); the series is widely available in bookshops. Most tourist offices also give away free or cheap (under €5) guides to local walks and bike trails. If you're travelling with children or are looking for less challenging routes, try the FFRP's *Les Sentiers d'Emilie*, which details thirty easy walks in the Pyrénées-Orientales. All these guides are in French, but even non-French speakers will be able to use them with the help of a pocket dictionary. For mountain refuges, the Club Alpin Français (ⓦwww.ffcam.fr) has online information and publishes an annual guide.

Biking is the next best option, and the cities of the south have been remarkably quick to adapt to two-wheeled transport, particularly Toulouse and Montpellier. Around Montpellier, Agde and Narbonne, extensive networks of bike paths, often using decommissioned roads, link the coastal villages and the cities. In the countryside disused rail lines, such as the Gijou Valley Trail (see p.198), have been set up as bicycle (VTT) routes, and canal towpaths make it possible to cross the region with ease. Traffic off the main roads is surprisingly light, and with the exception of the coastal plain you will find the biggest challenge to be the hilliness of the terrain.

While **horse-riding** is not practical as a means of transport, it is an excellent way of enjoying the countryside. Practically every town and many farms have equestrian centres where you can ride unaccompanied or with a guide on local trails. In the Pyrenees **mules** provide a more practical alternative.

Local tourist offices can give you information on riding centres or you can contact the regional equestrian tourism organization ATECREL, 14 rue des Logis, 34140 Loupian (☏04.67.43.82.50), or the Fédération Française d'Équitation (DNTE), 30 av d'Iéna, 75116 Paris (☏01.53.67.44.44, ⓦwww .ffe.com).For mule-trekking, contact the Fédération Nationale Ânes et Randonnées, Broissieux, 73340 Bellecombe-en-Bauges, (☏04.79.63.84.01, ⓦwane-et-rando.com).

Skiing, rafting and watersports

There are a number of **ski stations** in the eastern Pyrenees, and although they cannot offer anything to compare with the great resorts of the French Alps, you will be able to find some decent downhill skiing between November and April. Cross-country skiing, or *ski de fond*, is also a possibility, and the broad massifs of the Cerdagne and Ariège are particularly well suited to it. The relatively low altitude of some resorts is partially offset by the extensive use of snow-making machines. The most important and better-known resorts, among them Font-Romeu, Formiguères and Porté-Puymorens, are detailed in the Guide, and the Ariège and Pyrénées-Orientales tourist offices (see p.64) also have information, with the CDT Ariège website (ⓦwww.ariegepyrenees.com) often offering accommodation and lift-ticket deals. Alternatively, for wintersports (including snowshoeing) contact the Pyrénées Club de France, 8 rue de la Colombette 3100 Toulouse (☏05.62.73.56.35, ⓦwww .pyrenees-club.asso.fr).

While you are exploring the hilly uplands of the Languedoc and Roussillon, you ought to sample also the thrill of **rafting** down one of the region's many dramatic rivers. This sport has exploded in recent years, and you will scarcely pass a gorge which is not capped by a rafting outfit at its upper end. The biggest concentration is in the upper Hérault south of Ganges, but good opportunities can be found on the Orbiel, west of Lamalou, and on the Ariège around Tarascon. More placid paddling can by done by **canoe**, notably on the calmer stretches of water of the Aude and Gardon, and at the Pont du Gard. **Pot-holing** and **climbing** are also popular throughout Languedoc and Roussillon – tourist offices can hook you up with local guides and operators.

Most of the region's seaside towns are fully-developed resorts, and have facilities for the whole gamut of **watersports**: in summer months you'll find everything from jet-skis and sail-boards to houseboats and yachts for rent. If you are specifically looking for beachside activities, Le-Grau-du-Roi has the best range of facilities, with La Grande-Motte a close second. There are a number of scuba-diving clubs in the beach towns of Roussillon, such as Cap d'Agde, Banyuls, Argelès-Plage, Sète and Port-Camargue, which arrange outings and run certified basic diving courses.

Living and working in France

Unemployment in France is very high, and particularly so in traditionally depressed Languedoc and Roussillon, where it hovers around 23 percent. In the cities, bar work, club work, freelance translating, teaching English, software fixing, data processing and typing, or working as an au pair are some of the most likely employment options, while in the countryside, it comes down to seasonal fruit- or grape-picking (vendange), teaching English, busking or DIY odd-jobbing. Obviously, the better your French, the better your chances are of finding work.

Anyone staying in France for over three months must have a *carte de séjour* (see p.57), or residency permit – citizens of the EU are entitled to one automatically. France has a **minimum wage** (the SMIC – Salaire Minimum Interprofessionel de Croissance), indexed to the cost of living; it's currently around €6.85 an hour (for a maximum 169-hour month). By law, all EU nationals are entitled to exactly the same pay, conditions and trade union rights as French nationals, though in practice employers are more likely to pay lower wages to temporary foreign workers.

Some people find jobs **selling magazines** on the street and **leafleting** by asking other vendors for the agency address, while the American/Irish/British **bars** and **restaurants** in the main cities and resorts also sometimes have vacancies. You'll need to speak French, look smart and be prepared to work very long hours.

Temporary jobs in the **travel industry** revolve around courier work – supervising and working on bus tours or summer campsites.

You'll need good French (and maybe even another language) and should write to as many tour operators as you can, preferably in early spring. Getting work as a courier on a campsite is slightly easier. It usually involves putting up tents at the beginning of the season, taking them down again at the end, and general maintenance and troubleshooting work in the months between: Canvas Holidays (☏01383/644 018) are worth approaching. The British company PGL (☏01989/764 211, ⊛www.pgl.co.uk) runs several children's activity centres in France, employing people proficient in watersports or with youth-work experience, and offers general catering, domestic and driving work, between May and September every year; you should apply before April.

Teaching English as a Foreign Language (TEFL) is a good way to finance your stay in France. You can get a CELTA (Certificate in English Language Teaching to Adults) qualification before you leave home or even while you're abroad: International House has several branches in France (though none in Languedoc-Roussillon) which offer the course. The British Council's website, ⓦ www.britishcouncil.org, has a list of English-teaching vacancies.

An offbeat possibility if you want to discover rural life is being a **working guest** on an organic farm, for anything from a week to a couple of months. The work may involve cheese-making, market gardening, bee-keeping, wine-producing and building. For details of the scheme and a list of French addresses contact Willing Workers on Organic Farms (WWOOF) at ⓦ www .wwoof.org.

Useful publications and websites

A few **books** worth consulting are *Work Your Way Around the World* by Susan Griffiths and *Living and Working in France* by Victoria Pybus (both published by Vacation Work; ☎ 01865/241 978, ⓦ www.vacation work.co.uk), and *A Year Between* and *Working Holidays* (both Central Bureau). *Overseas Jobs Express* (☎ 01273/699 611, ⓦ www.overseasjobs.com) publishes a range of job vacancies fortnightly, but is only available by subscription, while Travel **magazines** like *Wanderlust* (every two months; £5) often advertise job opportunities with tour companies.

In France, check out the *"Offres d'Emploi"* (Job Offers) in newspapers such as *Le Monde*, *Le Figaro* and the *International Herald Tribune*. Young people may be able to get help and advice in a CIDJ, or *Centre d'Information et de Documentation Jeunesse* (ⓦ www.cidj.com): the main regional offices are at 17 rue de Metz, Toulouse (☎ 05.61 21.20.20, ⓦ www.crij.org), and 3 avenue Charles Flahault, Montpellier (☎ 04.67.04 36.66, ⓦ www.crij-montpellier.com). The national employment agency, the Agence Nationale pour l'Emploi (ANPE; ⓦ www .anpe.fr), advertises vacancies but doesn't go out of its way to help non-French citizens, especially non-French-speakers.

Buying property and relocation

After languishing in obscurity for centuries, the regions of Languedoc and Roussillon have been rediscovered by foreigners, notably the British. A combination of an inflated British housing market, and the rise in telecommuting has prompted many Brits to **relocate** or buy **second properties** in the region. With Provence overpriced and the Dordogne saturated, Languedoc, in particular, has become an obvious choice for its splendid climate and laid-back Mediterranean atmosphere – and whilst house prices are rising rapidly on the coast, inland areas still offer tempting bargains.

if you are contemplating such a move it is essential to thoroughly research the legal fine-points of any purchase. Using an **agency or intermediary** can facilitate the process but beware of unscrupulous operators. Be sure to get to know the area you are buying into, and do a **title search** and have a **survey** done of the property before signing a contract.

The region has a thriving ex-pat community, with plenty of businesses, services and cultural activities which cater to English speakers: two useful **resources** are the *Languedoc Sun* (ⓦ www.languedocsun. com), a free bi-monthly newsletter, and the website ⓦ www.frenchentree.com.

Study and work programmes

AFS Intercultural Programs UK ☎ 0113/242 6136, US ☎ 1-800/AFS-INFO, Canada ☎ 1-800/361-7248, Australia ☎ 1300/131736, NZ ☎ 0800/600 300, South Africa ☎ 27/11-339-2741, ⓦ www.afs.org. Global UN-recognized organization running cultural exchange programmes.
British Council UK ☎ 0161/957 7755, ⓦ www .britishcouncil.org. Recruits and trains TEFL teachers.
Erasmus UK ☎ 01227/762 712, ⓦ www.erasmus .ac.uk. EU-run student exchange programme.
ⓦ **www.studyabroad.com** Provides listings and links to study and work programmes.

Travel Essentials

Costs

Because of the relatively low cost of accommodation and eating out, Languedoc and Roussillon are not expensive by northern European standards. For a reasonably comfortable existence, including a hotel room for two, a light restaurant lunch and a proper restaurant dinner plus moving around, café stops and museum visits, allow around €100 a day per person. But by counting the pennies, staying at cheap hostels (around €18 for bed and breakfast) or camping (from €9), and being strong-willed about extra cups of coffee and doses of culture, you could manage on €45 a day, including a cheap restaurant meal.

For two or more people, **hotel accommodation** is nearly always cheaper and better value than hostels, though hotel rates rise throughout the region in July and August, most dramatically in coastal resorts, and major tourist towns, like Carcassonne. Many **restaurants** offer reasonable three- or four-course menus for between €12 and €25, though the lunch-time or *midi* menu is nearly always cheaper. **Wine** and **beer** are both very cheap in supermarkets, while buying wine from the barrel at village co-op cellars is even better value for money. The mark-up on wine in restaurants is high, though house wine in cheaper establishments is still very good value. **Drinks** in cafés and bars are what really make a hole in your pocket – remember that it's cheaper to drink at the bar than at a table. Also, given that a small bottled water typically costs €2.50–4, you can save considerably by ordering tap water – *une carafe d'eau* – which is always free.

French **trains** are good value, with many discounts available (see p.34 for details), though **buses** remain marginally cheaper. Admission to **museums and monuments** can be pricey, though reduced admission is often available for those over 60 and under 18 (for which you'll need your passport as proof of age) and for students under 26. Many museums and monuments

are free for children (the age bar for which may range from 12 to 18), and nearly always for kids under 4. Several towns operate a discount pass for their museums and monuments, which can be good value if you plan to visit a few.

Youth and student ID cards can soon pay for themselves in savings: full-time students are eligible for the International Student ID Card (ISIC, ⓦ www.isiccard.com, or ⓦ www.isic.org in the US and Canada), which entitles the bearer to reduced air, rail and bus fares and discounts at museums, theatres and other attractions. The card costs $22 in the US; Can$16 in Canada; AUS$16.50 in Australia; NZ$21 in New Zealand; £7 in the UK; and €12.70 in the Republic of Ireland. Those under 26 can buy the **International Youth Travel** Card, which costs US$22/£7 and carries the same benefits. Under-26s can also get a **youth card**, or *Carte Jeune*, available in France from main tourist offices for under €20 (valid for a year), which entitles you to reductions on museums, sights and other services in France. A university photo ID might also open some doors, though it's not as easily recognizable as an ISIC card.

Beaches

Beaches are public property within 5m of the high-tide mark, so you can kick sand past private villas, though camping on beaches is illegal.

Cameras and film

Film in France costs around the same as in the UK, but is considerably more expensive than in North America so stock up before travelling. If you're bringing a video camcorder, make sure any tapes you purchase in France are compatible.

Contraceptives

Condoms (*préservatifs* or *capotes*) are available at all pharmacies, as well as from many clubs and street dispensers (€2 for 4 condoms) in larger cities. You can also get spermicidal cream and jelly (*dose contraceptive*), plus suppositories (*ovules, suppositoires*) and (with a prescription) the Pill (*la pillule*), a diaphragm (*le diaphragme*) or IUD (*le stérilet*).

Crime

Petty theft is endemic in all the major cities and along the coast. Drivers, particularly with foreign number plates or in rental cars with Parisian registration, face a high risk of break-ins. Vehicles are rarely stolen, but car radios and luggage make tempting targets.

If you need to **report a theft**, go to the *commissariat de police* (addresses are given in the Guide for the major cities), where they will fill out a *constat de vol*: you'll need to show your passport, and vehicle documents if relevant. If you have an **accident** while driving, you have to fill in and sign a *constat à l'amiable* (jointly agreed statement); car insurers are supposed to give you this with the policy, though in practice few seem to have heard of it. For **non-criminal driving offences** such as speeding, the police can impose an on-the-spot fine.

The two main types of **police** that you are likely to come into contact with are the *Police Nationale*, who patrol cities and larger towns, and the *Gendarmerie Nationale*, who patrol the highways and rural areas. Some large cities also have a municipal force, which often has jurisdiction only over traffic. In the Pyrenees, you may also come across specialized mountaineering sections of the police, who provide rescue services and guidance, and are unfailingly helpful, friendly and approachable. In case of trouble or loss head for the nearest police station and they will direct you to the proper authorities.

Travellers of non-European origin, particularly those of African or Middle Eastern extraction, may encounter **racism**, such as hotels claiming to be booked up, police demanding to see papers and abuse. If you suffer a racial assault, you're likely to get a much more sympathetic hearing from your consulate than from the police. There are many anti-racism organizations which will offer support (though they may not have English-speakers): Mouvement contre le Racisme et pour l'Amitié entre les Peuples

(MRAP; ⊛www.mrap.asso.fr) and SOS Racism have offices in most big cities.

All these numbers are free
Fire brigade (pompiers) ☏18
Medical emergencies ☏15
Police ☏17
Rape crisis (SOS Viol) ☏08.00.05.95.95

Disabled travellers

For people in wheelchairs, the haphazard parking habits of the French and stepped village streets can be serious obstacles, while public toilets with **disabled access** are rare. In the major cities and coastal resorts, however, ramps or other forms of access are gradually being added to hotels, museums and some theatres and concert halls: look out for the Label National Tourisme Handicap (an APF initiative) affixed to disabled-friendly services and businesses.

Public transport is certainly not wheelchair-friendly, and although many train stations now have ramps for wheelchair-users to board and descend from carriages, at others it is still up to the guards to carry the chair. The high-speed TGVs (including Eurostar) have places for wheelchairs in the first-class carriage, which you must book in advance, though no higher fee is charged; on other trains, a wheelchair symbol on the timetable denotes whether that service offers special features, and you and your companion will again be upgraded to first class with no extra charge. The *Guide du Voyageur à Mobilité Réduite*, available free at main train stations, details all facilities. **Taxis** are obliged by law to carry you and to help you into the vehicle, also to carry guide dogs. Specialist taxi services are available in some towns: these are detailed in the *Guide des Transports à l'Usage des Personnes à Mobilité Réduite*, available at airports, main train stations and some tourist offices.

APF (Association des Paralysés de France), Head office, 17 bd Auguste-Blanqui, 75013 Paris ☏01.40.78.69.00; 116bis, rue des Amidonniers, Toulouse ☏05.62.30.64.00; 1620, rue St Priest, Parc Euromédecine, 34097 Montpellier ☏04.67.10.03.25; ⊛www.apf.asso.fr. National organization providing reliable information and lists of accessible accommodation. Their guide *Où Ferons-Nous Étape* is available at the office or by post to a French address.

CNRH (Comité National Français de Liaison pour la Réadaptation des Handicapés), 236bis rue de Tolbiac, 75013 Paris ☎01.53.80.66.66; 91 rue de Fenouillet, 31200 Toulouse ☎05.61.13.48.00. Information service that publishes various useful guides, including Touristes Quand Même!, which lists facilities throughout France though it's not updated regularly.

Fédération Française Handisport ☎01.40.31.45.00, ⊛www.handisport.org. Provides information on sports and leisure facilities for people with disabilities.

Electricity

This is almost always 220V, using plugs with two round pins. If you haven't bought the appropriate transformer with you, you can buy one for around €10 from the electrical section of a department store. Before you plug in, check that the transformer is of sufficient voltage and amperage for the appliance that you plan on plugging in.

Entry requirements

Citizens of EU (European Union) countries can enter and travel freely within France with just a passport. Citizens of Australia, Canada, the United States and New Zealand, among other countries, can enter France and stay for up to ninety days without needing a visa. However, the situation can change and it is advisable to check with the French embassy or consulate in your own country before departure.

EU citizens (or other non-visa citizens) who stay longer than three months are officially supposed to apply for a *carte de séjour*, for which you'll have to show proof of income at least equal to the minimum wage (around €1050 a month). However, EU passports are rarely stamped, so there is no evidence of how long you've been in the country. If your passport does get stamped, you can cross the border – to Spain, for example – and re-enter for another ninety days legitimately.

French embassies and consulates overseas

Australia Canberra ☎02/6216 0100; Sydney ☎02/9261 5779, ⊛www.ambafrance-au.org.

Britain London ☎020/7073 1200, ⊛www .ambafrance-uk.org; Edinburgh ☎0131/220 6324, ⊛www.consulfrance-edimbourg.org.

Canada Montreal ☎514/878 4385, ⊛www .consulfrance-montreal.org; Québec ☎418/694 2294, ⊛www.consulfrance-quebec.org; Toronto ☎416/925 8041, ⊛www.consulfrance-toronto .org; Vancouver ☎604/681 4345, ⊛www .consulfrance-vancouver.org.

Ireland Dublin ☎01/260 1666, ⊛www .ambafrance-ie.org.

New Zealand Wellington ☎04/384 2555, ⊛www.ambafrance-nz.org.

South Africa Johannesburg ☎11/778 5600, ⊛www.consulfrance-jhb.org; Le Cap ☎21/423 1575, ⊛www.consulfrance-lecap.org.

USA Atlanta ☎404/495 1660, ⊛www .consulfrance-atlanta.org; Boston ☎617/542 7735, ⊛www.consulfrance-boston.org; Chicago ☎312/787 5359, ⊛www.consulfrance-chicago .org; Houston ☎713/572 2799, ⊛www .consulfrance-houston.org; Los Angeles ☎310/235 3200, ⊛www.consulfrance-losangeles.org; Miami ☎305/372 9798, ⊛www.consulfrance-miami.org; New Orleans ☎504/523 5772, ⊛www .consulfrance-nouvelleorleans.org; New York ☎212/606 3600, ⊛www.consulfrance-newyork .org; San Francisco ☎415/616 4910, ⊛www .consulfrance-sanfrancisco.org; Washington ☎202/944 6200, ⊛www.ambafrance-us.org.

Festivals

It's hard to beat the experience of arriving in a small French village, expecting no more than a bed for the night, to discover the streets decked out with flags and streamers, a band playing in the square and the entire population out celebrating the feast of their patron saint. Apart from Bastille Day (July 14) and the Assumption of the Virgin Mary (August 15), there are many traditional **folk festivals** thriving in Languedoc and Roussillon. Moreover, local and municipal governments have invested heavily in summer *fêtes* and free concert series, designed to bring visitors into the region's villages.

Celebrations of local patron saints are concentrated in summer months and are the occasion for fireworks, dancing and *pétanque* competitions. These are particularly colourful in the fishing ports of the Languedoc coast, where saints' effigies are paraded down to the sea and events include **water-borne jousting** competitions. In wine country, there are inevitably festivals coinciding with the grape harvest, and in other regions with that of the dominant local product.Throughout the Languedocian plain – notably east from Béziers and in certain towns of the Pyrenees – *tauromachie* (see p.51), which involves Spanish-style *corridas* (bullfights) or indigenous *courses camarguaises*, occurs regularly throughout the summer, and at other big holidays, such as Pentecost and the pre-Lenten carnival. The most important and interesting regional festivals are outlined at the beginning of each chapter of the Guide.

Fishing

You get **fishing rights** by becoming a member of an authorized fishing club – tourist offices have details.

Gay and lesbian travellers

France is more liberal on **homosexuality** than most other European countries, with the legal **age of consent** being 16. In Languedoc, gay communities thrive in larger centres, such as Toulouse and Montpellier, and some beach towns, like Palavas, though lesbian life is rather less upfront.

In general, the French consider sexuality to be a private matter and homophobic assaults are very rare. On the whole, gays tend to be discreet outside specific gay venues, parades and certain coastal resorts. **Toulouse** has the reputation for being a city with a vibrant gay and lesbian culture, although there is no notable gay "ghetto" as such. **Montpellier**, traditionally politically left-wing and socially liberal, officially embraces gay culture, supporting many events in the city.

Contacts for gay and lesbian travellers

ARCL ☏ 01.46.28.54.94, ✉ archives.lesbiennes @wanadoo.fr. ARCL publishes a biannual directory of lesbian, gay and feminist contacts in France, L'Annuaire, and organizes frequent events.
Centre Gai et Lesbienne Toulouse, 4 rue de Belfort ☏ 05.61.62.30.62. Open Mon–Fri 5–8pm, Sat 3–8pm for information and advice, and also hosts a Sunday afternoon (3 –7pm) social event, Café Positif, which is great for meeting people.
Dykeplanet ⊕ www.dykeplanet.com. Sells Le dykeGuide, a guidebook listing lesbian-friendly places across France. Published annually, in French

only: also available from FNAC and other book stores.
Fréquence Gaie (FG) **98.2 FM**. 24-hour gay and lesbian radio station with music, news, chats, information on groups and events, etc.
Minitel 36.15 GAY is the Minitel number to dial for information on groups, contacts, messages, etc.
Guide Gai Pied The most comprehensive gay guide to France, published annually. Its website ⊕ www .gaipied.fr has a good selection of lesbian and gay contacts.
Lesbia The most widely available lesbian publication, available from most newsagents. Each monthly issue features a wide range of articles, listings, reviews, lonely hearts and contacts.
Têtu ⊕ www.tetu.com. Highly-rated French gay/lesbian magazine with events listings and contact addresses; you can buy it in bookshops or through their website, which is also an excellent source of information.

Health

With its gentle climate, easy pace of life and world-beating **healthcare system**, France is one of the world's healthiest destinations. All **tap-water** is safe to drink (except from taps labelled "*eau non potable*") and there are no nasty local maladies. No visitor requires any vaccinations. Languedoc and Roussillon will present you with few specific health risks, other than mosquito bites (especially on the coast and in the Camargue) or sun burn.

For minor ailments, your immediate recourse should be to a **pharmacy**, marked by a flashing neon green cross. *Pharmacies* tend to be expensive, but well stocked and extremely efficient, and the pharmacist is well qualified to dispense advice as well as remedies. Opening hours are normally the same as shops (roughly 8/9am–noon & 2/3–6pm). Cities maintain a *pharmacie de garde* that stays open 24 hours according to a rota; addresses and hours are displayed in all pharmacy windows.

For more **serious complaints**, pharmacists, tourist offices or police stations can direct you to a **doctor**, or you can always find one yourself by looking under "*Médecins généralistes*" in the *Yellow Pages* (*Pages Jaunes*). Many speak reasonably good English. Consultation fees, which you have to pay upfront, are €20 for a government-registered doctor (*un médecin conventionné*) – though fees are sometimes waived on an informal basis, partly to avoid paperwork. Non-registered doctors (*médecins non-conventionnés*), however, particularly specialists, may charge considerably more.

In serious **emergencies** you should take yourself off to the nearest *Centre Hospitalier* (hospital), or call an **ambulance** (SAMU) on ☎15. In an accident or injury situation, the **fire service** (*les pompiers*) is usually fastest, and firemen and women are trained in first aid: call ☎18. Hospital phone numbers are given in "Listings" at the end of the main city accounts in the Guide.

Healthcare charges and refunds

EU citizens are entitled to a refund (usually around seventy percent) of the standard fees of registered doctors and dentists. To apply for this refund, British citizens technically need a **European Health Insurance Card** (EHIC), available from post offices, which has replaced the old form E111. In practice, the card exists mainly to smooth the refund process rather than to guarantee it. If you don't have a card and need one, you can always apply for a "provisional replacement certificate". **Non-EU visitors**, including North Americans, should be sure to have their own adequate medical insurance cover.

French doctors are enthusiastic issuers of prescriptions (*ordonnances*), which can add to the final cost of treatment. You will be given a **Statement of Treatment** (*feuille de soins*) with little stickers (*vignettes*) for each medicine prescribed, and you can use this to claim against insurance. EU citizens, alternatively, can use it to claim back between 35 and 65 percent of the cost of prescription drugs and remedies. You have to take your *feuille de soins* to a local **Caisse Primaire d'Assurance-Maladie** (CPAM), or "Sickness Insurance Office" – ask the pharmacist for details – then wait around two months for the refund to be sent to you.

Similarly, if you're **treated at a hospital**, you'll have to pay upfront for out-patient treatment and then claim a refund at a CPAM branch. If you are hospitalized, inpatients who are EU citizens can proffer their European Health Insurance Card to get 75 percent refunds on bills. The other 25 percent, and a daily hospital charge (*forfait journalier*), however, are non-refundable.

Insurance

Even though EU health care privileges apply in France, you'd do well to take out an **insurance policy** before travelling to cover against theft, loss and illness or injury. Most insurance companies charge an extra premium to include so-called **dangerous sports**, so if you plan to do any skiing, whitewater-rafting, rock-climbing or potholing, make you sure you are covered.

If you need to make a claim on your insurance policy, you should keep **receipts** for medicines and medical treatment, and in the event you have anything stolen, you must obtain an **official statement from the police** (called a *constat de vol*).

Rough Guides has teamed up with Columbus Direct to offer you travel insurance that can be tailored to suit your needs. Products include a low-cost **backpacker** option for long stays; a **short break** option for city getaways; a typical **holiday package** option; and others. There are also annual **multi-trip** policies for those who travel regularly. Different sports and activities (trekking, skiing, etc) can usually be covered if required. See our website (☻www.roughguidesinsurance.com) for eligibility and purchasing options. Alternatively, UK residents should call ☎0870/033 9988; Australians should call ☎1300/669 999 and New Zealanders should call ☎0800/55 9911. All other nationalities should call ☎+44 870/890 2843.

Internet

Practically every reasonable-sized town in Languedoc and Roussillon has a **cyber-café** or Internet connection point of some sort, costing from €3 to €8 per hour. In less populated areas, many post offices now have public Internet terminals, which are operated with a prepaid card, though they are rather expensive at €7 for the first hour. In addition, France Telecom has street-side Internet kiosks in major cities. **Email** is the cheapest and easiest way of staying in touch with home while in France, and it's easy to open a free email account with Hotmail (☻www.hotmail.com) or Yahoo (☻www.yahoo.com).

Laundry

Laundries are common in French towns: some are listed in the Listings section of the

Guide, otherwise look in the phone book under "*Laveries Automatiques*". They are often unattended, so come pre-armed with small change. Machines are normally graded into 5kg, 8kg or 10kg wash sizes, and the smallest costs around €2.50 for a load, though some laundries only have bigger machines and charge around €4. If you're doing your own washing in hotels, keep quantities small as most forbid doing any laundry in your room.

Mail

French **post offices** (*bureaux de poste* or *PTTs*) – look for bright yellow *La Poste* signs – are generally open Monday to Friday 9am–7pm and Saturday 9am–noon. In smaller towns and villages, however, offices may close earlier and for lunch. Standard **letters** (20g or less) and postcards within France and to EU countries cost €0.52, to North America, Australia and New Zealand €0.90. **Stamps** (*timbres*) can also be bought from *tabacs,* often with less queuing. To post your letter on the street, look for the bright yellow postboxes.

Inside many post offices you will find a row of yellow *guichets automatiques* – automatic ticket machines – with instructions in English, where you can weigh packages and buy the appropriate stamps; sticky labels and tape are also dispensed. If you're sending parcels abroad, you can check prices on the *guichet* or in various leaflets: small post offices don't often send foreign mail and may need reminding, for example, of the reductions for printed papers and books. See Ⓦwww.laposte.fr for details on rates and services.

You can receive mail at the central post offices of most towns. It should be addressed (preferably with the surname first and in capitals) **"Poste Restante**, Poste Centrale", followed by the name of the town and its postcode. To collect your mail you need a passport or other ID and there may be a charge of a couple of euros. You should ask for all your names to be checked, as filing systems are not brilliant.

You can also use Minitel (see opposite) at post offices, as well as change money, make photocopies, send faxes and make phone calls.

Maps

The best up-to-date **road maps** are the 1:100,000 maps of France produced by Michelin (Ⓦwww.viamichelin.fr) or the Institut Géographique National (IGN; Ⓦwww.ign.fr). Both companies also issue good **regional maps** either as individual sheets or in one large spiral-bound "*atlas routier*"; Michelin's version is available in English as the *France Tourist & Motoring Atlas* (£13.99). Rough Guides also produces maps to France, and the Pyrenees.

If **walking or cycling**, it's worth investing in the more detailed IGN maps (see above). Their *Carte de Randonnée* series (1:25,000) is specifically designed for walkers, while the *Carte de Promenade* (1:100,000) is good for cyclists. For further details of walking guides, also see "biking and riding" on p.51.

Minitel

Many French phone subscribers still have the now-primitive **Minitel** telnet system which France pioneered. A sort of early email/Internet system, which allows access through the phone lines to directories, databases, chat lines and so on, it is still available in post offices, though it's gradually being displaced by the Internet. Most organizations, from sports federations to government institutions to gay groups, have a Minitel code consisting of numbers and letters, which you can call up for information, to leave messages and make reservations. You dial the number on the phone, wait for a fax-type tone, then type the letters on the keyboard, and finally press *Connexion Fin* (the same key ends the connection). If you're at all computer-literate and can understand basic keyboard terms in French (*retour* – return, *envoi* – enter, etc), you shouldn't find them hard to use. Be warned that most services cost more than phone rates. Directory enquiries (☎12) are free.

Money

The French **currency** is the euro (*eh-oo-ro;* €), with bank notes in denominations of 5, 10, 20, 50, 100, 200 and 500 euros, as well as coins of 1, 2, 5, 10, 20 and 50 cents and 1 and 2 euros. Current **exchange rates** are: €1.45 to the pound sterling (€1=0.70),

€0.84 to the US dollar (€1=$1.20), €0.64 to the Canadian dollar (€1=$1.55), €0.58 to the Australian dollar (€1=$1.70), and €0.51 to the New Zealand dollar (€1=1.94).

By far the easiest way to access money in France is to use your credit or debit card to withdraw cash from an **ATM** (known as a *distributeur* or *point argent*); most machines give instructions in a variety of European languages. Note that there is often a transaction fee, so it's more efficient to take out a sizeable sum each time rather than making lots of small withdrawals.

Credit and debit cards are also widely accepted in shops, hotels and restaurants, although some smaller establishments don't accept them or levy a minimum purchase. Visa – called Carte Bleue in France – is almost universally recognized, followed by MasterCard (also known as EuroCard). American Express is less widely accepted. Note that most French transactions require a PIN number: if your card is not a chip and PIN, explain that yours is a *carte à piste* and not a *carte à puce*.

If you prefer to take **travellers' cheques**, the most widely recognized brands are Visa, Thomas Cook and American Express, which most banks will change. American Express travellers' cheques can also be cashed at post offices. **Euro travellers' cheques** can be used as cash in some shops, hotels and restaurants, and you should get the face value of the cheques when you change them, so commission is only paid on purchase. Banks being banks, however, this is not always the case.

Rates and commission vary from bank to bank, so it's worth shopping around; the usual rate is a 1–2 percent commission on travellers' cheques and a flat rate charge on cash. Be wary of banks claiming to charge no commission – they merely adjust the exchange rate to their own advantage to compensate.

Standard **banking hours** are Monday to Friday 9am to 4pm or 5pm. Some close at midday (noon/12.30pm–2/2.30pm); some are open on Saturday 9am to noon. All are closed on Sunday and public holidays. They will have a notice on the door if they do currency exchange. **Money exchange counters** (*bureaux de change*) open longer hours than the banks: you'll find them at all the airports in the region and at the train stations in Toulouse and Montpellier, with usually one or two in town centres as well. You'll also find **automatic exchange machines** at airports and train stations and outside many money exchange bureaux. They accept £10 and £20 notes as well as dollars and other European currency notes, but offer a very poor rate of exchange.

Opening hours and public holidays

Basic **hours of business** are 8am or 9am to noon or 1pm, and 2pm or 3pm to 6pm or 7pm. In big city centres, shops and other businesses stay open throughout the day, and in July and August most tourist offices and museums are open without interruption. Otherwise almost everything closes for a couple of hours at midday, or even longer in the summer. Small food shops often don't reopen till halfway through the afternoon, closing around 7.30pm or 8pm just before the evening meal. Supermarkets tend to stay open 9am to 9pm Monday to Saturday.

The standard **closing days** are Sunday and/or Monday, with shops taking turns to close with their neighbours; many food shops such as *boulangeries* (bakeries) that open on Sunday will do so in the morning only. In small towns you'll find everything except the odd *boulangerie* shut on both Sunday and Monday, while, even in cities, **restaurants and cafés** also often close on a Sunday or Monday.

Museums tend to open between 9am and 10am, close for lunch at noon until 2pm or 3pm, and then run through to 5pm or 6pm, although in the big cities they will stay open all day: **closing days** are usually Tuesday or Monday, sometimes both. Many state-owned museums have one day a week (often Sun) when they're free or half-price. **Cathedrals** are almost always open all day every day, with charges only for the crypt, treasuries or cloister and little fuss about how you're dressed. **Church** opening hours are often more restricted; on Sunday mornings (or at other times which you'll see posted up on the door) you may have to attend Mass to take a look. In small towns and villages,

Public holidays

There are thirteen **national holidays** (*jours fériés*), when most shops and businesses (though not necessarily restaurants), and some museums, are closed. May in particular is a big month for holidays: as well as May Day and Victory Day, Ascension Day normally falls then, as sometimes does Pentecost.

January 1 New Year's Day
Easter Sunday
Easter Monday
Ascension Day (forty days after Easter)
Pentecost or Whitsun (seventh Sunday after Easter, plus the Monday)
May 1 May Day/Labour Day
May 8 Victory in Europe Day
July 14 Bastille Day
August 15 Assumption of the Virgin Mary
November 1 All Saints' Day
November 11 1918 Armistice Day
December 25 Christmas Day

however, getting the key is not difficult – ask anyone nearby or seek out the priest, whose house is known as the *presbytère*.

Pedestrians

French drivers pay little heed to **pedestrian/ zebra crossings** marked with horizontal white stripes on roads. It is very dangerous to step out onto one and assume drivers will stop as in Britain and Australia. Take just as great care as you would crossing at any other point. Also be careful at **traffic lights**: check cars are not still speeding towards you even when the green man is showing.

Phones

The easiest option – though by no means the cheapest – is to use a **mobile phone**. France operates on the **European GSM standard**, and mobiles bought in the UK, Australia and New Zealand should work here, though US cellphones won't unless they're tri-band. If you plan to make a lot of calls you might consider buying a French mobile (*portable*) using pre-paid charge-up cards (*mobicartes*); inexpensive deals are always on offer from one of the big companies. Mobile phone **reception** is generally good throughout Languedoc and Roussillon although in isolated mountain valleys coverage may be poor and in summer months relays can become saturated.

It's cheaper to make both domestic and international phone calls from a **telephone**

box (*cabine*), most of which use **phone cards** (called *télécartes*), available in €5 and €10 increments from *tabacs*, newsagents, post offices, tourist offices and some train station ticket offices. You can also use credit cards in many call boxes. **Coin-only boxes** still exist in cafés, bars, hotel foyers and rural areas; they take 10, 20 and 50 centimes and €1 pieces; put the money in after lifting up the receiver and before dialling.

Local calls cost €0.30 for four minutes; long-distance calls within France cost up to €1.20 for three minutes depending on the distance. **Off-peak charges** apply on weekdays between 7pm and 8am and after noon on Saturday until 8am Monday.

For **calls within France** – local or long-distance – simply dial all ten digits of the number. Numbers beginning with ☎08.00 are free numbers; those beginning with ☎08.36 are premium rate (from €0.34 per minute), and those beginning with ☎06 are mobile and therefore also expensive to call.

For **international calls**, it's cheaper to buy one of the private companies' pre-paid phone cards (*carte à codes*) from *tabacs*, newsagents and post offices, which can be used with any public or private telephone: Tiscali's "L'Astuce Internationale" (@www .prepaye.tiscali.fr), for example, gives you roughly three and a half hours to the UK, USA or Canada for €15.

To make a **reverse charge** or collect call – known in French as *téléphoner en PCV*

B

Useful numbers within Languedoc and Roussillon

Weather ☎08.36.68.02 + the number of the department: Ariège, 09; Aude, 11; Haute-Garonne, 31; Hérault, 34; Pyrénées-Orientales, 66; Tarn, 81.
Traffic and road conditions ☎08.36.68.20.00.
Telegrams by phone Internal ☎36.55; external ☎08.00.33.44.11 – all languages.
Time ☎36.99.
International operator For Canada and the US ☎00 33 11; for all other countries ☎00 33 followed by the country code.
International directory assistance For Canada and the US ☎00 33 12 11; for all other countries ☎00 33 12 followed by the country code.
French operator ☎13 to signal a fault.
French directory assistance ☎12.

Calling France from overseas
International access code + 33 + ten-digit number (minus the initial 0).

Calling overseas from France
Note that the initial zero is omitted from the area code when dialling the UK, Ireland, Australia and New Zealand from abroad.
US and Canada 00 + 1 + area code.
Australia 00 + 61 + area code.
New Zealand 00 + 64 + area code.
UK 00 + 44 + area code.
Republic of Ireland 00 + 353 + area code.

("pay-say-vey") – contact the international operator (see box above). For an English-speaking operator call ☎08.00.89.00.33 (in the UK) or ☎00.00.11 (in North America).

Swimming pools

Swimming pools (*piscines*) are well sign-posted in most French towns and reasonably priced, usually around €2.50–4 for a swim. Tourist offices have their addresses. You may be required to wear a bathing cap, whether you are male or female, so come prepared.

Time

France is **one hour ahead** of the UK, six hours ahead of Eastern Standard Time, and nine hours ahead of Pacific Standard Time. This also applies during daylight savings seasons, which are observed in France (as in most of Europe) from the end of March through to the end of October.

Toilets

Ask for *les toilettes* or look for signs for the WC (pronounced "vay say"); when reading the details of facilities outside hotels, don't confuse *lavabo*, which means wash-basin, with lavatory. Usually found downstairs along with the phone, French **toilets** in bars are still often of the hole-in-the-ground squatting variety, and tend to lack toilet paper. Standards of cleanliness are often not high, and men shouldn't expect much privacy in the urinal, which often won't have a door. Both bar and restaurant toilets are usually free, as are toilets in museums, though toilets in railway stations and department stores are commonly staffed by attendants who will expect a bit of spare change. Some have coin-operated locks, so always keep change handy for these and for the frequent Tardis-like public toilets found on the streets. These beige-coloured boxes have automatic doors which open when you insert coins and are cleaned automatically once you exit. Children under 10 aren't allowed in on their own.

Tourist information

Practically every town and many villages in Languedoc and Roussillon have a tourist office – usually an **Office du Tourisme** (OT) but sometimes a **Syndicat d'Initiative** (SI). For the practical purposes of visitors, there is little difference between them: SIs have wider responsibilities for encouraging business, while Offices du Tourisme deal exclusively with tourism; sometimes they share premises and call themselves an OTSI. In small villages where there is no OT or SI, the *mairie* (mayoral office), frequently located in the Hôtel de Ville (town hall), will offer a similar service.

From all these offices you can get specific local information, including listings of hotels and restaurants, leisure activities, car and bike rental, bus timetables, laundries and countless other things; many can also book accommodation for you. Most offices can provide a free town plan (though some places charge a nominal €0.75–1.50), and will have maps and local walking guides on sale. In mountain regions they display daily meteorological information and often share premises with the local hiking and climbing organizations. In the larger cities you can usually also pick up free *What's On* guides.

Regional and departmental tourist offices

Comité Départemental du Tourisme Ariège-Pyrénées: 31bis av de Général-de-Gaulle, BP 143, 09004 Foix ☎04.61.02.30.70, ⓦwww .ariegepyrenees.com
Comité Départemental du Tourisme Aude: Conseil Général, 11855 Carcassonne ☎04.68.11. 66.00, ⓦwww.audetourisme.com
Comité Départemental du Tourisme Gard: 3 pl des Arènes, 30010 Nîmes ☎04.66.36.96.30, ⓦwww.cdtgard.com
Comité Départemental du Tourisme Haute-Garonne: 14 rue Bayard BP 845 31015 Toulouse ☎05.61.99.44.00, ⓦwww.cdt-haute-garonne.com
Départemental du Tourisme Hérault en Languedoc: Maison du Tourisme, av des Moulins, BP 3067, 34043 Montpellier ☎04.67.67.71.71, ⓦwww.herault-en-languedoc.com
Comité Régional du Tourisme Languedoc-Roussillon: 20 rue de la République, 34000 Montpellier ☎04.67.22.81.00, ⓦwww.cr -languedocroussillon.fr
Comité Régional du Tourisme du Midi-Pyrénées: 54 bd de l'Embouchure, BP 2166, 31022 Toulouse ☎05.61.13.55.55, ⓦwww .tourisme-midi-pyrenees.com
Comité Départemental du Tourisme Pyrénées-Orientales: 16, av des Palmiers, 66005

Perpignan ☎04.68.51.52.53, ⓦwww.cdt-66.com
Comité Départemental du Tourisme Tarn: BP 225, 81006 Albi ☎05.63.77.32.10, ⓦwww .tourisme-tarn.com

Websites

Tourism and recreation

ⓦ**www.europe-today.com/france** English-language master-site for outdoor activities in Languedoc and Roussillon. Features contact details for a variety of sports and pursuits, from canyoning to parachuting.
ⓦ**www.franceguide.com** The official site of the French Government Tourist Office, with news, information on local festivals and useful links.
ⓦ**www.cr-languedocroussillon.fr** Languedoc-Roussillon's official website, with links to activities, accommodation, gastronomy and culture. One of the best starting points, but limited to the boundaries of the modern administrative *région*.
ⓦ**www.little-france.com** Roussillonaise weekly webzine with information on culture, tourism, art, politics and economy.
ⓦ**www.monuments-france.fr** Information on over 200 national monuments and museums – many in Languedoc and Roussillon – including news on special events.
ⓦ**www.pagesjaunes.fr** The complete French Yellow Pages, unbeatable for hunting down goods and services.
ⓦ**www.pyrenees-online.fr** The homepage of Pyrénées-Online, with information on accommodation, sights, recreational activities and regional specialities.
ⓦ**www.tourist-office.org** Useful database of France's municipal and local tourist offices arranged by *région* and *département*. Town listings have practical and cultural information and links to local websites.
ⓦ**www.viamichelin.com** The Euro-version of MapQuest allows you to map out detailed point-to-point driving itineraries around France and Europe, and gives you complete trip information and driving directions, free.

News and information

ⓦ**www.france2.fr** France TV 2's daily Web page has the latest on news, weather and road conditions, as well as listings and reviews of cultural events. Also has a youth section.
ⓦ**www.francedaily.com** English-language Web newspaper covering French, European and world news.
ⓦ**www.gksoft.com/govt** Gateway to English-language listings of all French government websites, including embassies, departmental and regional

tourist boards, political parties, municipalities and media.

ⓦ**www.lemonde.fr** The French-language version of one of France's most reputable daily newspapers. Includes national and international news, culture and sports.

ⓦ**www.midilibre.fr** French-language newspaper for Languedoc and Roussillon; good travel features, including ski information.

ⓦ**www.radio-france.fr** Radio France's official page has national and international news coverage, current affairs, as well as music, culture and the latest in French sports. French language only.

Arts and culture

ⓦ**www.bpi.fr** Home page of the Bibliothèque Pompidou, with good links to media and a very comprehensive list of arts and humanities pages for France.

ⓦ**www.cathares.org** Everything you ever wanted to know about the Cathars. A French-only site featuring information on culture, history and historical sites, as well as regular updates on related events and exhibitions.

ⓦ**web.culture.fr** French Ministry of Culture's page, with information on everything from monuments to exhibitions and also comprehensive links to organizations related to the whole gamut of artistic media.

ⓦ**www.ladanse.com** Multilingual site with comprehensive information on French and international dance including news, links and a database of artists and companies.

ⓦ**www.multimania.com/simorre/oc/presoc .htm** English-language website ideal if you want to learn more about the Occitan language. Links to history and literature (including works in translation), as well as information on grammar and a short tutorial.

ⓦ**www.occitanet.free.fr** A French-only site dedicated to the cuisine of Languedoc, and featuring weekly recipes, information regarding food-oriented events and festivals, and links to other culinary sites.

ⓦ**www.revue-spectacle.com** Arts page, set up by a group of newspapers and radio stations in cooperation with the Ministry of Culture. Covers theatre, dance and mime events and is updated monthly. No English version presently, but a link to the Babelfish translation page.

ⓦ**perso.wanadoo.fr/joseph.riera/menu.htm** French-language page dedicated to the history and culture of "French Catalonia" – Roussillon – with detailed explanations of history, customs and language.

Travelling with children

Children are generally welcome everywhere in France, including in most **bars and restaurants**. Especially in seaside towns, many restaurants have children's menus (*menu enfant*), while some will provide smaller portions of adult dishes on request. Most **hotels** charge by the room, with a small supplement for an additional bed or cot, while family-run places will usually babysit or offer a listening service while you eat or go out.

Under-4s travel free on SNCF **trains and buses**, while 4–11s pay half-fare (see p.35 for other reductions). In most **museums**, children under 4 are free, with discounts of 50 percent or more for under-18s, while entry to many monuments is free for under-12s.

If you're travelling with a baby, be aware that most French **baby foods** have added sugar and salt, and the milk powders may be richer than your baby is accustomed to – soy-based milk is only available at pharmacies, and is very expensive. Disposable **nappies/diapers** (*couches à jeter*) are available everywhere.

Most local tourist offices have details of specific **activities** for children – in particular, many resorts supervise "clubs" for children on the beach. Most **parks** have a children's play area; unfortunately the majority of parks are gravelled rather than grassed and when there are lawns they are often out of bounds (*pelouse interdite*). Something to beware of – not that you can do much about it – is the difficulty of negotiating a child's **buggy** over the large cobbles that cover many of the older streets in town centres.

Guide

Guide

Toulouse and around

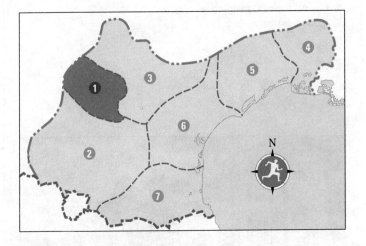

CHAPTER 1 # Highlights

✷ **Place du Capitole** The square at the heart of Toulouse, a bustling weekend market-place. **See p.80**

✷ **St-Sernin Basilica** Roman-esque Toulouse's finest monument, a crypt full of saints. **See p.81**

✷ **Hôtels Particuliers** The ancient mansions of the city's woad lords. **See p.83**

✷ **Les Abattoirs** Cutting-edge modern art gallery in a converted slaughterhouse. **See p.88**

✷ **La Montagne Noire** The northern slopes provide a scenic introduction to Languedoc's least populated area. **See p.102**

✷ **Cassoulet** Languedoc's emblematic dish; try it at Castelnaudary, where it was invented. **See p.105**

△ Place du Capitole, Toulouse

Toulouse and around

M idway between the cool shores of the Atlantic and the sun-baked Mediterranean coast, **Toulouse** and its surrounding area form the gateway to Languedoc. The city itself is a dynamo, undoubtedly the liveliest and most interesting on the west side of the Rhône; in addition to several notable museums, including the Musée des Augustins and Les Abattoirs, it has a vibrant cultural life and café and art scene and its medieval streets make for some of the most satisfying strolling in the South of France. The neighbouring countryside, though not especially dramatic, is a land of distinctive culture and cuisine.

Among the gently undulating wheat fields – the **Lauragais**, heartland of Toulouse's traditional agricultural prosperity – are little-known but colourful medieval towns like **Lavaur** and **Revel**. Scattered between these is an array of villages and castles whose ancient stones have witnessed both the success of the region's famous dye trade, and the violence and terror of Crusades and Wars of Religion. South of Revel is **Castelnaudary**, birthplace of the famous Languedocian staple, cassoulet, and the largest town in Toulouse's environs; it not only contains a number of unique historical buildings, but is also the main inland port of the **Canal du Midi**, an engineering marvel which stretches from Toulouse to the sea and is one of the emblems of the Southwest.

Toulouse is a major rail centre, with regular **trains** in all directions; these are complemented by SNCF and local buses, the former following several east–west routes across the Lauragais and the latter fanning out from Toulouse. Moving north to south across the area is more difficult, although the quiet roads make for good, if hilly, **biking**.

Toulouse

Although it falls into the modern administrative *région* of Midi-Pyrénées, **TOULOUSE** has a long tradition as the capital of Languedoc, while a solid industrial base, notably as the centre for French aeronautics, helps maintain it as the sixth largest city in the nation. It's a lively, cheerful place, with a vibrant arts community and a distinct Mediterranean look – as the sun edges towards the horizon, the hallmark pink brick buildings soak up the soft light and glow with a muted luminescence (hence its traditional nickname, *La Ville Rose*). For the traveller, the city has a lot to offer: aside from fine medieval churches and mansions, and first-rate galleries, there's an almost constant succession of **festivals** (see box, pp.74–75); in addition, it's the most cosmopolitan city in the

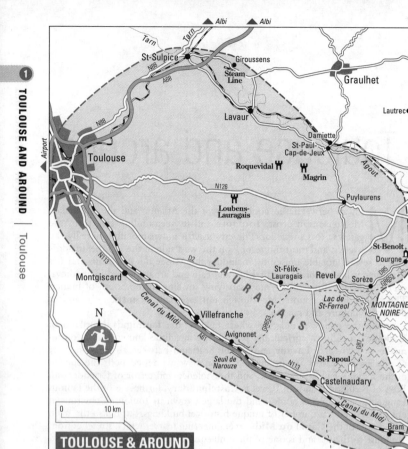

Southwest, with a vigorous nightlife fuelled by the massive student population of its famous university, and a range of immigrant cultures reflected in a variety of restaurants.

It's hard not to enjoy Toulouse, whether you are sitting in one of its multitude of outdoor cafés, strolling through its ancient streets or taking in some of the best museums west of the Rhône. A stay here is the easiest way to introduce yourself to southwest France, and you could easily spend a week exploring, but if you're short of time, the two sights which should not be missed are the Romanesque **Basilique de St-Sernin** and the modern art gallery, **Les Abattoirs**.

Some history

Originally located a bit further upstream on the Garonne from the present city centre, Toulouse (then called Tolosa) was moved to the plain which it currently occupies when the Romans took it over in 120 BC. With the disintegration of the empire the city briefly became the capital of the Visigoths in 414 AD, but when their centre of power shifted to Spain, the Franks moved in and gained control in 628. Under their feudal agrarian regime the town stagnated until the eleventh century, when the local **counts** (who were almost without exception named Raymond) began to encourage the nascent carpentry and leather industries. A century later a city council, or **Capitolo**, was set up to handle administration and justice and the wealthiest townsfolk – merchants and landholders – served as its members (the *capitouls*); the resulting convergence between their economic interests and political power allowed the city to flourish. Meanwhile, the counts – for all intents and purposes independent sovereigns – began to extend their influence over the other major families of the south, including the Trencavels (see p.117). By the late twelfth century they effectively controlled all of Languedoc, and adopted the surname of "St-Gilles", in honour of one of their favourite fiefs.

Both the counts and the city prospered until the reign of Raymond VI, by which time Cathar beliefs, considered heretical by the Church, had taken firm root in the region (see *The Land of the Cathars* colour section). Raymond may or may not have been a Cathar himself, but was content to let his subjects choose their religious beliefs, thus provoking the ire of the papacy and providing the northern French aristocracy with a justification for war against him. When their knights stormed into Languedoc on a campaign of religious and political conquest – the **Albigensian Crusade** – Toulouse fell to forces led by the cruel Simon de Montfort. Raymond, with the help of Catalan allies, recovered it in 1217, but it fell definitively under the power of the French Crown in 1271. One of the consequences of the Catholic takeover was the foundation, early in the thirteenth century, of Toulouse's **university**, which the strong presence of the Dominican Order helped make into the second most important theological centre in France after Paris.

Despite suffering grievously from a series of plagues, the city's prosperity soared with the booming woad **dye** industry in the 1400s (see box, p.97), and in the sixteenth century it became the official capital of Languedoc, although it later suffered – along with the whole of the South – as a result of the Wars of Religion, and as a consequence of the failed **revolt** against Cardinal Richelieu led by Henri de Montmorency (1595–1632), Governor of Languedoc. The Revolution of 1789, which the city fervently supported, heralded a new age of affluence as industry recovered and the Canal du Midi provided better market access for the agricultural hinterland. The good times were interrupted only by the Napoleonic Wars, during which the English general, Wellington, pursued the retreating Soult to the city in 1814; the French field marshal broke through the near encirclement, dealing the English a minor defeat before escaping towards the Montagne Noire.

Occupied by the Germans during World War II when it was an important centre of the Resistance, Toulouse passed through the war more or less unscathed, and today the city is best known for its thriving aerospace industry, along with electronics and related hi-tech manufacturing. Home to Airbus Industries, the principal manufacturer of commercial airliners in Europe, this is where the successful A340 and A440 crafts, the first "fly-by-wire" (entirely electronically controlled) planes are assembled, and where the A380 was launched, a daringly designed two-level super-liner, bigger even than Boeing's largest Jumbo. On 21 September 2001, Toulouse made the world news when a massive explosion ripped through a petrochemical plant in the south of the city, devastating the surrounding industrial suburbs, leaving 40 hectares of city razed, 29 dead and almost 2500 wounded. Despite early speculation that the tragedy was terrorist-related, investigations revealed it was the result of industrial malpractice. Nor was Toulouse immune from the riots which spread across France in late 2005 in which young French of North African origin reacted against the

Toulouse and the surrounding area aren't the best places to look for folk or traditional festivals – for these you're better off heading for the uplands of Languedoc or the Pyrenees to the south. Toulouse's strength is the arts – its splendid galleries and museums are complemented by a series of **music**, **dance** and **art festivals** which bring in top-notch names from around the world. Where we haven't given contact details, enquire at the tourist office (see p.76).

Mid-Jan to mid-Feb Toulouse: *C'est la Danse Contemporaine* ☏05.61.59.98.78, ⓦwww.cdctoulouse.com. A month-long programme of innovative contemporary dance featuring choreographers and ensembles from around Europe.

Feb 17 Dourgne: *Fête Médiévale du Romarin*. A one-day medieval pageant ostensibly to celebrate the herb rosemary, the symbol of the village, but in reality a typical but entertaining *terroir* fête, including music, dancing, sports competitions and, of course, a market of crafts and local produce.

First or Second Saturday in February Toulouse: *Fête de la Violette* (International Violet Meeting). The city's massive violet market features exhibitions relating to flower production, as well as a market and events.

Mid-March Toulouse: *Festival Irlandais*. A festival of Irish music, theatre and dance leading up to the St Patrick's Day festivities and featuring-highly rated Irish performers. For information contact TILT, 27 rue Ste-Blanche, 31200 Toulouse (☏05.61.13.20.08).

Mid-March Toulouse: *Rencontres Cinémas d'Amérique Latine* ☏05.62.32.98.83, ⓦwww.cinelatino.com.fr. Long-running eight-day film festival, held in various venues around town. Both feature-length and short productions are shown, ranging from documentary and drama to the experimental. Also colloquia and exhibitions.

Late March Toulouse: *Printemps du Rire* ☏05.62.21.23.24, ⓦwww.printemps-du -rire.com. A festival featuring France's most renowned comedians as well as local talent. Performed at various venues.

Late March Toulouse: *Festival Flamenco* ☏05.62.25.81.21. A new addition to the city's cultural calendar, featuring live performances, exhibitions, and film.

Late March to early-April Toulouse: *¡mira!* ☏05.34.45.05.05, ⓦwww.mira-toulouse .com. An exciting program of Spanish and Portuguese music, dance and other cultural events held at the TNT and other venues.

Late June Toulouse: *¡Rio loco!* ☏05.61.32.77.28, ⓦwww.rio-loco.org. An annual international festival featuring dance, music, film and a variety of events. Each year focuses on a different country, such as Senegal and Spain.

Throughout June and July Toulouse and St-Félix: *Festival Déodat-de-Séverac* ☏05.61.83.01.83, ⓔjjcubaynes@netscape.net. Wednesday- and Thursday-night series of concerts at the church of St-Pierre-des-Cuisines and various venues in St-Félix, featuring works of or inspired by the celebrated nineteenth-century St-Félix-born composer.

marginalization from which their communities suffer. On a brighter note, since 1985 the city's violet cultivation industry – once a major concern, but dormant for nearly a century – was revived thanks to "test tube" technology. The annual flower fair (see box above) is once again a major event.

Arrival, information and city transport

Toulouse's **airport** (☏05.34.61.80.00, ⓦwww.toulouse.aeroport.fr) is located 6km northwest of the centre in the suburb of Blagnac. It has better services than many regional airports, with banking and exchange facilities including an

Late June & Early July Toulouse: *Les Siestes Électroniques* ☎05.61.23.80.57, ⓦwww
.les-siestes-electroniques.com. A celebration of electronic and ambient music, featuring
performers from around the world. Free afternoon concerts (Sat & Sun 4pm) are held in
the Jardin Raymond VI, behind Les Abattoirs on the left bank of the Garonne.

Throughout July Toulouse: *Toulouse d'Été* ☎05.62.27.60.91, ⓦwww.toulouse.fr.
Eclectic programme of concerts held in the Couvent des Jacobins, Notre-Dame-de-
la-Daurade and Zénith on Tuesday and Thursday nights, featuring a diversity of styles
– from classical, to gospel and Flamenco.

Throughout September Toulouse: *Piano aux Jacobins* ☎05.61.22.40.05, ⓦwww
.pianojacobins.com. Nightly recitals in the cloister of the Jacobins by pianists from
around the world. For programme details, contact the Piano aux Jacobins, 61 rue de
la Pomme, 31000 Toulouse.

One weekend in September Toulouse: *Estrambord Garones* ☎05.61.29.80.01.
Traditional Occitan water-jousting (see p.276) matches are held on the Garonne,
amidst a lively street-festival.

Late September to Early October Toulouse: *Festival Occitania* ☎05.61.11.24.87,
ⓦwww.ieotolosa.com. A week-long festival of Occitan and Mediterranean culture,
featuring music, food, arts and crafts.

Late September to mid-October *Toulouse: les Orgues* ☎05.61.53.81.16, ⓦwww
.toulouse-les-orgues.org. Using some of the city's finest antique organs, this music
and choral series features Saturday and Sunday night concerts in the city's famous
churches.

Late September to mid-October Toulouse: *Le Printemps de Septembre*
☎01.43.38.00.11, ⓦwww.printempsdeseptembre.org. A three-week-long visual arts
festival, in which artists invited from around Europe use the city as their canvas.

Mid-October Toulouse: *CineSpaña* ☎05.61.12.12.20, ⓦwww.cinespagnol.com.
This well-established event brings in Spanish directors and actors for twelve days of
screenings and awards.

End October Toulouse: *Jazz sur Son 31* ☎05.24.45.05.92, ⓦwww.jazz31.com. The
world-class jazz, blues and salsa festival of the Haute-Garonne attracts the biggest
and best names in jazz, blues and salsa. Past performers include Miles Davis,
Campay Segundo and Carlos Santana. Programme available early September.

Second week in November Toulouse: *Salon des Antiquaires* ☎05.61.21.93.25, ⓦwww
.salon-antiquaires-toulouse.com. Internationally renowned antiques fair, featuring 300
pre-selected antiques dealers from around Europe. Held at the Parc des Expositions.

Late November Toulouse: *Séquence Court-Métrage* ☎05.61.62.92.46, ⓦhttp
://sequence.free.fr. Ten-day programme and competition of short films. Screenings
at various venues.

December Toulouse: *Marché de Noël*. A large Christmas market, featuring gifts and
arts and crafts, both traditional and new. Held in Place du Capitole.

---

automatic exchange dispenser, car rental offices (all the major companies) and
a small selection of shops and travel agencies, although it lacks a left-luggage
facility. A **shuttle bus** runs to the centre (from 5am–8.20pm every 20min,
returning 7.35–12.15am; €4; tickets can be bought from driver), making various stops in town, including the Compan-Caffarelli, place Jeanne d'Arc (near
St-Sernin), place Jean-Jaurès (near place Wilson) and the *gare routière*. A **taxi**
(☎05.61.30.02.54) to the centre will cost around €25.

Trains arrive at the grand old **Gare Matabiau** on boulevard Pierre-Sémard
along the banks of the Canal du Midi – a twenty-minute walk northeast of the

old town. The large station has a good café, but the left-luggage facility is still closed for security reasons. Any of the city buses which stop here will take you down to the boulevard de Strasbourg (the ring road around the old town), while bus #2 carries on through old Toulouse, passing rue de Metz and the Grand Rond; the place du Capitole is just two stops away from Matabiau on the *metro*. **Buses** pull in at the modern **gare routière** right beside the gare SNCF, which has an excellent information desk (Mon–Sat 7am–8pm). **Driving** into town, follow directions for the "Centre" and you will wind up on the A61 ring road – from this take any one of exits 14–17 or 21–30. There are plenty of car parks, as well as metered street parking and free parking in place St-Sernin in the centre, place St-Auban east of the centre and les allées Jules-Guesde south of the centre. For contact details regarding departures from Toulouse see "Listings", p.95.

The main **tourist office** (June–Sept Mon–Sat 9am–7pm, Sun 10am–1pm & 2–6.15pm; Oct–May Mon–Fri 9am–6pm, Sat 9am–12.30pm & 2–6pm, Sun 10am–12.30pm & 2–5pm; ℡05.61.11.02.22, ⓦwww.toulouse-tourisme.com) is housed in a restored tower in place Charles-de-Gaulle, directly behind the Capitol building (*metro* Capitole). This large and efficient office can help make hotel reservations, sells tickets to many festivals and events and organizes walking tours of the city (in English, mid-July to mid-Sept Sat 2pm; €9). If you don't feel like going with a group, you can buy a booklet of self-guided tours for €1.50. If you're staying for more than a day or two, consider the "Toulouse en liberté" **discount** card (€10), which gives ten percent discounts in many shops and fifty percent off museum tickets, as well as other savings: for an extra €3 you can add an accommodation option (*option héberegement*) which gives a 30–60 discount on hotels.

The narrow streets of the old town necessarily make **walking** the best way to see Toulouse; the account below has been written with this in mind. **Cycling** is also an excellent option, particularly given the economical rates of the municipal bike rental co-op, Movimento (see listings, p.95). The tourist office distributes a map of bike paths, as well as a brochure detailing three routes which take in the major sights. Additionally, there's a comprehensive bus and metro network, which covers Toulouse and its outlying villages. Although more are planned, for the time being there is just one **metro** line, running from the northeast (via Gare Matabiau) to the new university campus in the southwest; for visitors it comes in handy for getting from the *gares* to the main hotel districts (metro Jean-Jaurès or Capitole), or over the river to see the Les Abattoirs (metro Cyprien-République). With the exception of getting to outlying sights, like the Cité de l'Espace or the campsite, Toulouse's **bus** network is of little use – it's also quite elaborate, so you'd do well to pick up a transport map, available at the Tisseo-Connex **information office**, 7 place Esquirol (℡05.61.41.70.70, ⓦwww.tisseo-connex.com; metro Esquirol), or at the tourist office and metro stations. **Tickets** serving both bus and metro are available from bus drivers, as well as at metro stations and tobacconists: a single costs €1.30, a return €2.40, a day-pass €4, and a ten-trip ticket €10.70. If you're going far afield or clubbing in the suburbs, bear in mind that the buses stop at 10pm and the nightbus network, whose hub is the *gare*, winds up at 1am, with the metro keeping more or less the same hours (first/last departures Sun–Thurs 5.15am & midnight, Sat & Sun 5.15am & 12.42am). If time is short and you want to see the highlights, **taxis** offer a special "taxi touristique" tariff: €35 for a one-hour circuit and €60 for a two-hour circuit of the town, for up to three people (see "Listings", p.95).

Accommodation

Unless you are planning on staying in Toulouse for a lengthy period you will be more or less confined to **hotels** – and there's no shortage of them, in every

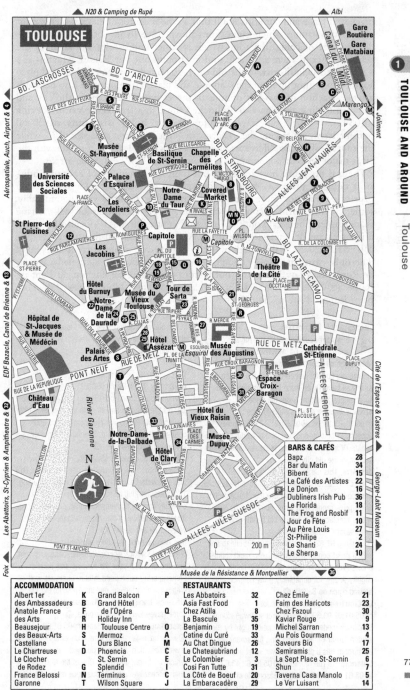

TOULOUSE

N20 & Camping de Rupé ▲   ▲ *Albi*

Aérospatiale, Auch, Airport & 4
EDF Bazacle, Canal de Brienne & 13
Les Abattoirs, St-Cyprien & Amphitheatre & 32
Foix

Joliment
Cité de l'Espace & Castres
George-Labit Museum

Musée de la Résistance & Montpellier ▼   ▼ 36

Map labels:
Gare Routière
Gare Matabiau
Marengo
Canal du Midi
Musée St-Raymond
Basilique de St-Sernin
Chapelle des Carmélites
Université des Sciences Sociales
Palace d'Esquiral
Les Cordeliers
Notre-Dame du Taur
Covered Market
St Pierre-des Cuisines
Les Jacobins
Capitole
Théâtre de la Cité
Hôtel du Burnuy
Notre-Dame de la Daurade
Musée du Vieux Toulouse
Tour de Sarta
Hôpital de St-Jacques & Musée de Médecin
Palais des Artes
Hôtel d'Assézat
Musée des Augustins
Cathédrale St-Etienne
Espace Croix-Baragon
Château d'Eau
Hôtel du Vieux Raisin
Notre-Dame-de-la-Dalbade
Hôtel de Clary
Musée Dupuy
J.-Jaurès
Capitole
Esquirol

Place Jeanne-d'Arc
Place Victor-Hugo
Place Wilson
Place St-Georges
Place Occitane
Place St-Pierre
Place St Jacques
River Garonne
Pont Neuf
Pont St-Michel

0   200 m

BARS & CAFÉS	
Bapz	28
Bar du Matin	34
Bibent	15
Le Café des Artistes	22
Le Donjon	16
Dubliners Irish Pub	36
Le Florida	18
The Frog and Rosbif	11
Jour de Fête	10
Au Père Louis	27
St-Philipe	2
Le Shanti	24
Le Sherpa	10

ACCOMMODATION			
Albert 1er	K	Grand Balcon	P
des Ambassadeurs	B	Grand Hôtel	
Anatole France	F	de l'Opéra	Q
des Arts	R	Holiday Inn	
Beausejour	H	Toulouse Centre	H
des Beaux-Arts	S	Mermoz	A
Castellane	L	Ours Blanc	M
Le Chartreuse	D	Phoencia	C
Le Clocher		St. Sernin	E
de Rodez	G	Splendid	I
France Belossi	N	Terminus	I
Garonne	T	Wilson Square	J

RESTAURANTS			
Les Abbatoirs	32	Chez Émile	21
Asia Fast Food	1	Faim des Haricots	23
Chez Atilla	8	Chez Fazoul	30
La Bascule	35	Kaviar Rouge	9
Benjamin	19	Michel Sarran	13
Catine du Curé	33	Au Pois Gourmand	4
Au Chat Dingue	26	Saveurs Bio	17
Le Chateaubriand	12	Semiramis	25
Le Colombier	3	La Sept Place St-Sernin	6
Cosi Fan Tutte	31	Shun	7
La Côte de Boeuf	20	Taverna Casa Manolo	5
La Embaracadère	29	Le Ver Luisant	14

bracket of price and comfort. You'll find a whole cluster of establishments right around the station, which range from inexpensive to moderate, but have the disadvantage of being in a zone which is rather nondescript and far from the centre. Closer in, there are cheap options around place de Belfort, which is also a sort of red-light district. In the old town, the hotels concentrated around place Victor Hugo (just up from the Capitole and place Wilson) are an easy bet, with a wide selection of two-star options in the ❸ bracket. Rooms in the city and the surrounding area can also be booked through a **free reservation service** (℡0892-700-297, Ⓦwww.reserv-hotels.fr). For **hotel discounts** of 30–60 percent, it's worth buying the "*Toulouse en liberté*" discount card (see p.76), while the tourist office also offers various 2–3 day package deals, to coincide with the city's major festivals; ask about its "*Forfaits courts-séjours*" before you arrive.

There is no youth hostel as such, but there are a number of **accommodation centres**, primarily designed for students but also useful for visitors who plan on staying for more than a few days. Their facilities vary considerably: some provide dorm accommodation, others private rooms or self-catering shared suites. The local youth information centre, the CRIJ (Centre Régional d'Information de Jeunesse), 17 rue de Metz (Mon–Sat 10am–1pm & 2–7pm; ℡05.61.21.20.20, Ⓦwww.crik.org) can inform you about current availability. The only **campsite** close enough to be of use is the well-equipped *Camping de Rupé*, just a few kilometres north from the centre on chemin du Pont du Rupé (℡05.61.70.07.35, Ⓔchristian.lagarde31@wanadoo.fr; bus #59 from place Jeanne-d'Arc to "Rupé").

Budget hotels

des Ambassadeurs, 68 rue Bayard ℡05.61.62.65.84, Ⓦwww.hotel-des-ambassadeurs.com. Very friendly little hotel run by a young couple, just down from the station. Its rooms all have TV, en-suite bath and phone – a surprisingly good deal given the price. ❷

Anatole France 46 pl Anatole-France ℡05.61.23.19.96, Ⓕ05.61.21.47.66) Another acceptable bottom-end option, the *Anatole-France* boasts TV in each room, and is located in a quieter section of the old city. ❶

des Arts, 1bis rue Cantegril ℡05.61.23.36.21, Ⓕ05.61.12.22.37. On a corner diagonally opposite the Augustins museum, this is a top choice in the lower price range, with large, quirky rooms (some with a fireplace) in a superb old building. ❷

Beauséjour, 4 rue Caffarelli ℡ & Ⓕ05.61.62.77.59. Basic, but dirt cheap and with a great copper-balconied facade and sound-proofed rooms. This is the best of the hotels in this slightly dodgy but engagingly gritty neighbourhood around place de Belfort. ❶

Le Chartreuse, 4bis bd Bonrepos ℡05.61.62.93.39, Ⓔla.chartreuse@wanadoo.fr. Efficiently modern if soulless choice, right by the station. Great value, considering the amenities: each room has a private shower, toilet and TV. ❷

Splendid, 13 rue Caffarelli ℡05.61.62.43.02, Ⓕ05.61.62.43.02. Another reasonable cheapie

in the place de Belfort area. Very basic (no television), clean, and very cheap. Reception closed Sun afternoons. ❶

Moderate hotels

Albert 1er, 8 rue Rivals ℡05.61.21.17.91, Ⓦwww.hotel-albert1.com. Set in a quiet side street just off the Capitole and close to the central market in place Victor-Hugo. A small, comfortable and good-value establishment. Special weekend deals are sometimes available. ❺

Athénée, 13bis rue de Matabiau ℡05.61.63.10.63, Ⓦwww.athenee-hotel.com. This well-renovated hotel offers all mod cons, including TV, garage parking and a cocktail bar, amidst a carefully chosen contemporary décor. Quiet, despite its location between the station and the old town. Wheelchair accessible. ❹

des Beaux-Arts, 1 pl du pont-Neuf ℡05.34.45.42.42, Ⓦwww.hoteldesbeauxarts.com. Located in a 150-year-old building, this hotel's contemporary but refined interior contrasts well with its ageing facade, making for solid, old-world elegance. Each room is individually decorated and some have views of the Garonne. ❻

Castellane, 17 rue Castellane (℡05.61.62.18.82, Ⓦwww.castellanehotel.com). A cheerful hotel with a wide selection of room types and sizes, most of which are bright and quiet. One of the few wheelchair-accessible hotels in this price range. ❹

Le Clocher de Rodez, 14 pl de Jeanne-d'Arc ☎05.61.62.42.92, ⓦwww .leclocherderodez.com. Comfortable and central, with secure parking and all mod-cons. Despite its size, it exudes a very personal hospitality. Wheelchair accessible. ❺

France Belossi, 5 rue d'Austerlitz ☎05.61.21.88.24, ⓦwww.hotel-france-toulouse .com. One of the better options in the rue d'Austerlitz/ place Wilson area. Clean rooms with cable television and AC. ❸

Grand Balcon, 8 rue Romiguières ☎05.61.21.48.08, ⒻF05.61.21.59.98. Just off place du Capitole, this ageing classic was frequented by the aviation pioneers, such as St-Exupéry (whose former room you can view), who first established Toulouse as a capital of manned flight. It's currently being renovated but should re-open some time in 2007.

Ours Blanc Victor Hugo, 25 pl de Victor-Hugo ☎05.61.21.62.40, ⓦwww .hotel-ours-blanc.fr. Right by the covered market and steps from the Capitole, this welcoming hotel is one of the city's better bargains, although room quality varies. The entire building has been renovated and each room has TV, air conditioning, telephone, and a private bath: there's also free Wifi access. The owners run two other similar-standard hotels nearby, the *Ours Blanc Centre*, 2 rue Porte Sardane, and the *Ours Blanc Wilson*, 2 rue Victor Hugo. ❸

Phoenicia, 7 bd Bonrepos ☎05.61.63.81.63, ⓦwww.hotel-phoenicia-toulouse.com. Weird retro décor but good service and facilities in this three-star place near the stations. The staff are friendly, and it has a small cocktail bar on the main floor. ❹

St-Sernin, 2 rue St-Bernard ☎05.61.21.73.08, ⒻF05.61.22.49.61. Well-renovated old hotel in one of the best districts of the old town, around the basilica – close to all the action, but far enough away to provide peace in the evening. ❸

Terminus, 13 bd Bonrepos ☎05.61.62.44.78, ⓦwww.terminus31.com. This old three-star station-side hotel has large, renovated rooms that make it worth the price, and there are special room prices for off-season weekends and a buffet breakfast (€8) available, the only drawback being that the hotel is rather far from the sights. ❹

Wilson Square, 12 rue d'Austerlitz ☎05.61.21.67.57, ⓦwww.hotel-wilson.com. Clean and well-kept place at the top of rue d'Austerlitz, with TV, AC and a lift. Also has a great pâtisserie on street level. ❹

Expensive hotels

Hôtel Garonne, 22, descente de la Halle-aux-Poissons ☎05.34.31.94.80, ⓦwww.hotelsdecharmetoulouse.com. A chic little hotel tucked away down an alley near the Pont Neuf, with fourteen rooms of understated luxury looking out over the river and the old town. The most romantic of the city's hotels. ❾

Grand Hôtel de l'Opéra, 1 pl du Capitole ☎05.61.21.82.66, ⓦwww.grand-hotel -opera.com. The grand dame of the city's hotels presides over the place du Capitole in the guise of a seventeenth-century convent. The rich décor, peppered with antiques and artwork, underlines its sophisticated atmosphere. Also has a fitness centre for working off that second helping of *foie gras*. ❾

Holiday Inn Toulouse Centre, 13 pl Wilson ☎05.61.10.70.70, ⓦwww.hotel-capoul.com. The best of the hotels on place Wilson, combining elegance with warmth and contemporary design; it has all the conveniences and amenities you'd expect and the staff are attendant, professional and friendly. ❽

Mermoz, 50 rue de Matabiau ☎05.61.63.04.04, ⓦwww.hotel-mermoz.com. Immaculate, comfortable rooms in a 1930s Art Deco-style hotel close to the station. Also has wheelchair access and a parking garage. ❼

The City

Toulouse's **old town**, straddling a curve in the River Garonne and hedged by a busy, roughly hexagon-shaped ring road (which marks the course of its former defensive walls), is where you'll find most of the city's points of interest. Its heart is the majestically broad **place du Capitole**, the town hall square near the northeastern edge, from which crooked streets radiate out, web-like, to a series of *places*. East from the place du Capitole is primarily a business district, where you'll find a great deal of the city's offices, hotels and restaurants. To the north, the area around the wonderful **Basilique de St-Sernin**, with the nearby archeological museum, forms the university quarter, while west of the Capitole towards the river lies the bulk of medieval Toulouse – major sights here include the Dominicans' **Les Jacobins** complex, plus a number

Toulouse museums

The normal entrance fee for Toulouse's historical museums is €3, except for the first Sunday of each month, when they are free. You can also buy museum **passeports** for three or six visits (€6 and €9 respectively) to the following museums: the Augustins, the Musée St-Raymond, the Musée Paul-Dupuy, the Musée Georges-Labit and the Jacobins.

of noteworthy churches: St-Pierre-des-Cuisines, Notre-Dame-de-la-Dalbade and Notre-Dame-de-la-Daurade. It is also home to most of the city's majestic Renaissance-era **hôtels particuliers** (private mansions), some of which, like the magnificent **Hôtel d'Assézat**, are now open as museums; most though are simply worth seeing for their striking and varied facades. The city's shopping district, focused on rue d'Alsace-Lorraine and rue St-Rome, stretches south to intersect with rue de Metz, south of which again, after the **cathedral**, a further series of *places* leads down to the formal gardens, the **Grand Rond** and **Jardin des Plantes** at the southeast corner of the old town. Beyond this, you'll find the town's canal port and a couple of small museums. Across the Garonne to the west, the neighbourhood of **St-Cyprien** is of interest for its stunningly reno-vated cutting-edge modern art gallery, **Les Abattoirs**, while the only reason to visit the **suburbs** is to see two modern exhibitions revolving around the city's aeronautical tradition.

Place du Capitole and place Wilson

Place du Capitole, the sweeping plaza containing Toulouse's historical seat of government, the **Capitole**, forms the administrative and civic hub of the city. Apart from when it fills up with market stalls on Wednesday and Sunday mornings, the *place* is a magnet for rollerbladers and host to a constant surge of pedestrian traffic – great for people-watching. Prettiest at sunset, when perme-ated by a pink glow reflected off the huge Capitole's brickwork, the square is best appreciated from one of the bank of cafés which line its western side – the perfect spot from which to contemplate the Neoclassical symmetry and elegance of the building's 130-metre-long facade. Deriving its name from the twelfth-century administration of the city (see p.73), the palace dates back to the sixteenth century, although the frontage you see today was raised in the mid-eighteenth. In addition to its function as the centre of municipal govern-ment, it serves as home to the city's most prestigious opera and ballet venue (see p.95). There's not much to see in the cavernous seventeenth-century **foyer** (Mon–Fri 9am–7pm, Sat & Sun 9am–5pm; free), aside from a gallery of paintings extolling the glories of France and celebrating the execution of revolt-leader Montmorency, which took place in the square, but you can stroll through to place Charles-de-Gaulle on the other side of the palace. Sadly, this small patch of green, presided over by Viollet-le-Duc's (see box, p.124) restored 1529 pseudo-medieval *donjon* – the only remnant of the original Capitole and now the tourist office – has become a haven for local junkies.

East of here along rue la-Fayette is the oblong **place Wilson**, which, edged by modern, expensive hotels, retains a certain grandeur despite the traffic. Directly north of place Wilson is the lively triangle of streets centred on the town's main **indoor market** (Tues–Sun 6am–noon) in place Victor-Hugo. The market sells local agricultural produce, meat and fish, and the surrounding area is home to an array of cheapie hotels and restaurants, as well as some great places to pick up regional culinary goodies – look out for the Ducs de Gascogne delicatessen at 1 rue du Remparts Villeneuve, and the Chocolatier de Bayonne, next door. **Rue d'Alsace Lorraine**, the western boundary of the triangle, is Toulouse's principal shopping street, its towering nineteenth-century apartments for the most part converted into shops and office space. Nevertheless, the magnificent facades, with their monumental doorways, elaborately carved cornices and wrought-iron balconies, still exude *fin-de-siècle* elegance. Heading west from the market on rue Salé you'll come to the **Chapelle des Carmélites** (Tues–Sun: May–Sept 9.30am–12.30pm & 2–6pm, Oct–Apr 10am–1pm & 2–5pm; free) at 1 rue du Périgord. Once part of a sprawling Carmelite convent, this seventeenth-century chapel, richly decorated with period murals by Antione Rivalz (the architect and official artist of the Capitole) is all that remains.

North to the Basilique de St-Sernin and beyond

Leading north out of place du Capitole, rue de Taur is a street full of lively studenty cafés and shops, a reminder that Toulouse has long been a university city. Just along from the *place* is the church of **Notre-Dame du Taur**, the original resting place of St-Sernin, boasting a turreted facade; further up the street, you'll pass the sprawling sixteenth-century Palace d'Esquiral, now home to the city's main cinema and a meeting place for student literary groups.

This is just steps from the **Basilique de St-Sernin** (July–Sept Mon–Sat 8.30am–6.15pm, Sun 8.30am–7.30pm; Oct–June Mon–Sat 8.30–11.45am & 2–5.45pm, Sun 8.30am–12.30pm & 2–7.30–pm; free), which, with its wedding-cake bell tower – an emblem of Toulouse – is arguably southern France's greatest Romanesque church and the largest of its style in Western Europe. Begun in 1080 to hold the remains of the city's first bishop, who was killed by the Romans in 250 AD – dragged to death by a bull (hence the name of the street). Later, the church was an important stop on the pilgrimage to Santiago de Compostela. Despite the fact that the present building was not completed until the fourteenth century, it has almost no Gothic elements: it's this stylistic purity, combined with the sheer size of the construction, that makes it such a singular monument. The most striking feature of its exterior is the early twelfth-century **Miégeville door**, whose restrained but expressive biblical sculptures mark it as a product of the pivotal era in the evolution of medieval art. Inside, the uniform simplicity of the cavernous nave is impressive; the plain marble altar, which is still used today, was consecrated by Urban II in 1096. But the real attraction is the church's incredible collection of **reliquaries** (daily 10am–6pm; €2), which it amassed over the years under the patronage of kings and with the financial help of donations from Santiago-bound pilgrims. Body parts of all of the major saints can be found here reposing in carved and gilded boxes set into the walls and chapels of the ambulatory and stored in the crypt below the altar, including a spectacular bust of James the Greater, whose thirteenth-century painted effigy is decked out in pilgrim's garb. The crypt also contains some very good examples of fourteenth-century polychrome saints' **statues**.

On the other side of place St-Sernin, which is unfortunately used as a car park, is the small **Musée St-Raymond** (daily: Oct–May 10am–5pm; June–Sept 10am–6pm; €3), which holds the city's archeological finds. The best part of this collection is the prehistoric and Bronze Age section on the first floor, which includes not only the usual arrowheads and brooches, but a decent range of pre-Roman jewellery, weapons and even chariot wheels. The Roman religious sculpture and third-century portraiture is also worth seeking out. In the basement you'll find the remains of part of the city wall as well as the excavations of Roman and medieval cemeteries.

North from the *place*, up rue Gatien-Arnoult, there's a small but lively **African quarter**, populated by immigrants from the Maghreb, in particular and the shops and restaurants of rue Trois Pilliers exude wafts of mint and parsley. Narrow rue Gramat, just before Trois Pilliers, is also worth a look – after a long campaign to convince the city, local artists were permitted in July 2000 to decorate the walls, cheering up the previously decrepit street with a series of colourful murals. From here, the concrete blight of place Bernard marks the end of the old town and a dull zone of low-rent apartments and university buildings. It's better to turn back and follow a series of quiet neighbourhood squares – des Tiercerettes, St-Julien and Peyrou – each of which has a couple of small café-restaurants. From place du Peyrou, rue des Lois will take you back to the Capitole.

Les Jacobins and west

The most colourful part of Toulouse's old town is found in the labyrinth of streets radiating west and south from the place du Capitole, and dominated by the former Dominican headquarters, known as **Les Jacobins** (daily 10am–7pm; €3), tucked away off rue Lakanal. Built in 1230, this was the first-ever permanent convent of St Dominic's Order of Preachers (the Dominicans), founded in the city in 1215 to combat the Cathar heresy. From its humble beginnings the Order quickly grew in power, soon taking charge of the Church's Holy Inquisition and exercising, for a time, a near monopoly over the bishoprics and universities of the medieval Latin West. This building is, in fact, Toulouse's original university, home of the theology Faculty which the Dominicans established in order to strengthen Catholic orthodoxy. The cavernous fourteenth-century **interior** (free entry), through which you enter the complex, contains a single file of seven enormous supporting columns, from which a web of delicate interlacing ribs fan out across the vaulted ceiling. These ribs, still bearing their original painted pattern of red and black bands, contrast beautifully with the cream-coloured brick they support. In a modest gilt box under the grey marble altar in the centre of the nave rest the remains of **St Thomas Aquinas** (1225–74), the great Dominican philosopher who strove to introduce the thought of Aristotle into Catholic theology – there's still a pilgrimage here on his feast day (Jan 28). Leaving the church, you enter a low Gothic **cloister**, which, with its stubby and unadorned columns, is as sober in style as the Order that built it. In fact, the cloister isn't original, but the structures along its north side are, including the large **chapterhouse**, which also preserves its wall decoration, and the fourteenth-century **chapel of St-Antonin**, whose walls are graced by richly detailed period paintings. The old **refectory**, also accessed from the cloister, now houses high-quality temporary art exhibitions of a decidedly secular character.

From the north end of rue Lakanal, rue Pargaminières leads to the placid little **place St-Pierre** on the banks of the Garonne. There are a couple of small pubs here and, on its northern side, **St-Pierre-des-Cuisines** (June Mon 10am–1pm, July daily 2–7pm; €2), an ancient church reputed to be the oldest ecclesiastical building in Southwest France, constructed over a substantial Gallo-Roman necropolis, accessed via the church's **crypt** (guided tour June Mon at 11am, July daily at 4pm; €2.50). Built on the site of a late-Roman church, the present edifice dates from the twelfth century, and now houses a four-hundred-seat concert hall.

Just west of the *place*, the languid **Canal de Brienne** angles away from the river through a nineteenth-century industrial area, where newly erected student apartment buildings abut old warehouses and cigarette factories. The

River Garonne has been exploited for industrial purposes since grain mills were first set up here in the twelfth century. They became a symbol of the city's prosperity, which was at that time based on local wheat production, and achieved such renown that the sixteenth-century satirist Rabelais cited them as the most powerful in the world. In 1890 the **EDF Bazacle** (Tues–Fri 2–7pm, Sat & Sun hours vary, art exhibits only; closed Aug; free), a generating plant that powers up Toulouse to this day, was built on the banks at the former site of the mills, about a ten-minute walk from St-Pierre. Here you can see both the modern and original turbines churning away, have a look at the cascading fish ladder, and take in the local and international art exhibits, displayed in the main foyer.

Back at place St-Pierre, an old ironwork bridge still decked out with gaslight fixtures leads south over the Garonne. This is the most direct route to the Les Abattoirs art gallery in St-Cyprien (see p.88) – you can see the mammoth cupola of the St-Joseph hospital ahead. If you prefer to stay on this side of the river, your best bet is to climb down to the riverside promenade Henri-Martin, whose grassy verge will take you down towards the place de la Daurade.

Toulouse's hôtels particuliers

One of the hallmarks of Toulouse is its multitude of luxurious private mansions, or **hôtels particuliers**, scattered throughout the old town. Built for the most part in the fifteenth and sixteenth centuries, they are testament to the tremendous prosperity which the town enjoyed at that time as a result of the *pastel* dye industry, which turned the local merchants and bankers into veritable princes (see box, p.97). The earliest mansions have some sections of timber and daub, but the majority are constructed from local brick, which – ageing badly – detracts somewhat from their majesty. There is often, however, wonderful **masonry**; the mansions' splendour tends to reside in their stone doorways and window frames, which were embellished with carved figures, statues, coats of arms and floral designs. Stone was relatively expensive here, so more masonry was a sign of greater wealth; the most opulent buildings have facades constructed entirely from stone. In later examples, you'll find Renaissance flourishes, imported from Italy to lighten the solid, but rather plain and chunky, medieval building style, and which can be distinguished by a movement towards greater symmetry and complexity of carving. Some of these "mature" *hôtels* have graceful **turrets**, built to reflect the status of the owner; only the chartered elite – those who were wealthy enough to serve as *capitouls* – could add a tower. The heady times of mansion-building, however, were not to last, and in the late sixteenth century declining *pastel* production precipitated the end of the woad lords, leaving their magnificent homes to fall into gradual decay. Today they serve a variety of functions, including apartments, offices, schools and museums.

△ Hôtel particulier, Toulouse

Place de la Daurade and around

A rare green space in the old town, **place de la Daurade** makes a great spot to take a break and loll by the riverside, or, should you wish to get on the river, is also the point from where boats depart on cruises (see "Listings", p.95). Across the Garonne you can see Toulouse's medieval hospital, the Hôtel-Dieu St-Jacques, with the stub of the old bridge still poking out from its walls, while on the flood banks above the square you'll find the city's oddest church, **Notre-Dame-de-la-Daurade** (opening times vary), a curious compound of disparate architectural styles. The church started out as a pagan temple and was then converted to Christian worship in the fifth century, but today's building, with its weighty Neoclassical facade, dates from the eighteenth. Entering the church through the modern parish hall tacked incongruously on the north side, you'll be met by a hive of painted Baroque busyness, with fields of trompe l'oeil held back by armies of cherubs, all presided over by a massive array of organ pipes. At the centre of it all sits the *Vierge noire*, a black Madonna reputedly empowered to cure ailments and bring good fortune to the unborn child. It's still the object of popular pilgrimage even today, with many devotional plaques fixed around the entrance. Next door, on quai de la Daurade, you'll find the **Palais des Arts**, now sadly abandoned except when used for temporary exhibitions (free), but possessing a typically nineteenth-century facade, which attempts in vain to immortalize a series of forgotten French artists.

Back in place de la Daurade, the *Café des Artistes* (see p.93) makes a handy refreshment stop. If you head up back to the Capitole keep an eye out for the sixteenth-century **Hôtel de Burnuy**, one of Toulouse's famed *hôtels particuliers* (see box, p.83), at the beginning of rue Gambetta. Although it is now part of a school, you can still poke your head inside to have a look at the two luxurious courtyards. This was the home of Jean de Burnuy, the town's wealthiest woad merchant, who was rich enough to literally afford a king's ransom. In fact, he stood his fortune as security to pay for François I's release from captivity at the hands of the Hapsburgs, against whom the king had fought in vain for the title of Holy Roman Emperor. Even when the palace is closed, its 1504 **facade** will draw your attention – the square windows are complemented by delicate Gothic details, while its cherub-topped main entrance completes the strange stylistic mix. Stepping back from the building, you'll see its slender tower rising high above the street.

Rue St-Rome and the Hôtel d'Assézat

A number of less grand but still intriguing sights can be found along the pedestrian promenade which heads straight south from the place du Capitole. This route starts with **rue St-Rome**, a busy shopping street lined with clothing stores and sandwich stands. The second street on the right after the *place* leads to the sixteenth-century **Hôtel du May**, built by a regent dean of the university's medical faculty, and now home to the **Musée du Vieux Toulouse** (Tues–Sun 10am–12.30pm & 1.30–6pm; €2.20). One of the town's least ornate *hôtels* – with only a simple door decoration to boast – it is proof that even then academics were underpaid. Nor is the museum itself particularly stimulating, as its collection consists of items of purely local interest: ceramics, paintings of local grandees and nineteenth-century knick-knacks.

Back on rue St-Rome, opposite rue de Muy, is an old Neoclassical bank building, dating from 1734, and behind it, at no. 4 rue Jules-Chalande, another courtyard, whose small tower marks it as the home of a former *capitoul*. Rue Chalande itself leads into an eminently explorable warren of narrow streets punctuated by tiny, and wonderfully serene, *places* – most of which have some sort of bar and a number of shops. Back on St-Rome, you can look down rue Tripière, where an old timber-and-brick **mansion** is studded with stone decorations in the form of rabbits (guided tours every 30min Wed 2.30–6pm; free). A little further south, rue St-Rome turns into rue des Changes, dominated by the three-storey **Tour de Sarta**, another former palace. The length of this old street is lined by overhanging sixteenth-century homes, until it opens up abruptly at the nineteenth-century place Esquirol.

To the west of rue des Changes is a little commercial area of wholesalers and workshops, centred around the place dela Bourse. The main reason for venturing into this neighbourhood is to find the **Hôtel d'Assézat**, which you enter from rue de l'Écharpe. This is Toulouse's most famous and possibly most luxurious *hôtel particulier*, home to a hugely successful woad merchant, Pierre d'Assézat, and which for a time hosted the *jocs florals* (see p.418). The former owner's wealth is evident in the predominance of stone over brick in its construction, endowing it with a sense of majesty which many of the town's best buildings lack. Assézat commissioned Nicholas Bachelier, a renowned local architect, to build the mansion in 1555 in cutting-edge style – its weighty, columned stone facade anticipates the Neoclassicism which would soon dominate European architecture. Inside, the patio is no less splendid, with a magnificent covered porch and columns. Despite his riches, d'Assézat suffered a tragic fate: having taken up Protestantism, he was deprived of his fortune, and Catholic repression forced him into exile.

Today the building is home to an impressive art gallery, the **Foundation Bemberg** (Tues–Sun 10am–6pm, Thurs until 9pm; €4.60, plus €3 for temporary exhibits, Ⓦ www.fondation-bemberg.fr). On the first floor up you'll pass through a collection of Renaissance furniture, including painted leather chairs and cabinets, before reaching a gallery displaying fifteenth- and sixteenth-century Flemish art, dominated by portraiture. Works by Lucas Cranach the Elder, in particular *Venus and Cupid*, and his portrait of a young woman, stand out. Further along there's a collection of sixteenth-century decorative statuary, whose kinetic realism bears an odd but striking resemblance to early twentieth-century Art Nouveau. Upstairs you'll find a worthy collection of more recent art, with the Impressionists and their successors well represented, among them Monet, Gauguin, Matisse and Bonnard, who has a whole roomful of works here, including *Still Life with Lemons*. On the museum's covered porch you can enjoy a coffee or light snack from the in-house café and soak up the atmosphere of the courtyard.

Place Esquirol to place du Salin

South of **place Esquirol** the street opens almost immediately into **place de la Trinité** – one of the many squares which punctuate the old town south of rue de Metz. Like the others, Trinité is dominated by a pleasant fountain, and there are several lively bars and brasseries where you can stop for a drink or a meal. While on the square, look out for the high-relief allegorical statues on the facade of the Maison Lamothe, one of the city's finest nineteenth-century buildings. From here, rue des Filatiers, the continuation of the shopping area, heads south to the place de Carmes. This is the site of the city's other big **covered market** (Mon–Sat 6am–noon); unfortunately, the several storeys of car park rising above it blight the square. Heading west on either of the streets leading off the *place* you come to the church of **Notre-Dame-de-la-Dalbade**. This sixteenth-century brick monster, scrubbed white inside in the best spirit of the Catholic Reformation, is itself hardly worth a stop, but the street of the same name, leading south, takes you through the heart of the old district that used to house the faculty of theology, an evocative neighbourhood with several fine *hôtels*. On the right you'll pass the magnificent **Hôtel de Clary**, whose stone Neoclassical facade of 1613 is very flamboyant, with high-relief *faux* columns separating the window casings, which in turn are capped by ornate lintels. The simpler, and grimy, courtyard is also worth a look.

At the end of the street, **place du Salin** opens up in front of the massive brick Palais de Justice, built on the site of Toulouse's medieval castle, and its predecessor, the Roman fort. On the adjacent place du Parlement, at no. 7, you'll find the house where St Dominic and his early disciples stayed when they arrived in Toulouse in 1215 to preach against Catharism. The building is abutted by a scrap of the city's ancient Gallo-Roman wall. From the place du Parlement, rue du Renfort will take you over to the bank of the Garonne, where a pleasant path leads back up to La Daurade. Alternatively, head northeast out of place du Salin on Grande Rue Nazareth towards the cathedral and another cluster of fine squares and mansions.

The cathedral and around

Although it holds ecclesiastical priority, Toulouse's **Cathedral St-Étienne** (Mon–Sat 8am–7pm, Sun 9am–7pm; free) has always played second fiddle to its rival St-Sernin. The discord between its average-sized brick entrance, which dates from the beginning of the thirteenth century, and the incongruously massive choir plonked on the back some seventy years later is obvious, and continues when, on entering, you discover that the huge ambulatory isn't even lined up squarely with the older church. The reason for this lack of harmony is that the cathedral was slated to be rebuilt on a much grander scale – the original nave demolished and a new one of the same proportions as the entrance added on – but money ran out, and the church was left as it is today. The **interior** of the cathedral holds few surprises, but is worth a quick look, if only for the Renaissance tapestries which line the walls of the nave, the sixteenth-century carved walnut choir, and the details of some the chapels behind the main altar: there are several good **stained-glass windows**, going back as early as the fifteenth century, and some carved ceiling medallions date from the 1200s.

Place St-Étienne itself is surprisingly quiet, boasting little more than the city's oldest fountain – the Griffoul – dating from 1546. Head west from here, and a short walk down rue Croix-Baragnon will take you past the city's oldest house (at no. 15) and **Espace Croix-Baragnon** (Tues–Sat noon–7pm) at no. 24: here, two small exhibition rooms house local paintings, sculpture and audio-visual art. Next you'll come to the lively place Rouaix, bounded to the northeast by the town's impressive eighteenth-century Chamber of Commerce building. On the far side of this, you'll be back in place Esquirol, right at the Musée des Augustins.

South from the cathedral you'll find a quiet neighbourhood of old houses and narrow streets. There are fewer shops and restaurants here, although each of the small **places** – and there seems to be one at every intersection – has somewhere to sit and have a drink or bite to eat. Rue Perchepinte, the continuation of rue Nazareth, leads to the pretty place Ste-Scarbes, the centre of Toulouse's antique furniture trade.

Further along, towards the place du Salin, was the wealthiest neighbourhood in the city during the age of *pastel*. You'll find a series of grand mansions on the streets near the *place*, notably rue Languedoc and rue Ozenne. One of the best, the compact fifteenth-century **Hôtel du Vieux Raisin** at the junction of rue Ozenne and rue du Languedoc, now houses law offices, but you can still take a peek at the courtyard, which is normally open during the day. On tree-lined rue Ozenne, the old Hôtel Pierre-Bresson houses the **Musée Paul-Dupuy** (daily: June–Sept 10am–6pm; Oct–May 10am–5pm; €3), one of the least inspiring museums in the city. Its holdings represent the collected knick-knacks of Dupuy, which include various medieval artefacts, a transplanted sixteenth-century pharmacy shop and a vast and dull collection of architectural drawings. If you do want to visit, aim to go on the first Wednesday of the month at 3pm, when the ornate nineteenth-century Orientalist-themed automaton, "The Singing Lesson", is put in motion.

The Musée des Augustins

The former home of the city's powerful canons of the Augustinian Order now houses what was, until the opening of Les Abattoirs, Toulouse's largest and most important museum, the **Musée des Augustins** (Thurs–Tues 10am–6pm, Wed 10am–9pm; Ⓦwww.augustins.org; €3). The collection is dominated by medieval sculpture, and unless you are an aficionado, you may be surprised by the reputation the museum enjoys. Nevertheless, it deserves a visit – the quality of work here is undeniable and the building itself is well worth a look. An externally featureless fourteenth-century brick precinct, covering an area almost as big as the place du Capitole and dominated by a strikingly huge bell tower, the monastery was founded in 1309 on the authority of Pope Clement V and is a fine example of southern French Gothic style, with an extensive cloister and large chapterhouse surviving from the original construction. Its smaller Neoclassical cloister dates from the seventeenth century, and it also has an apparently medieval refectory, though this is, in fact, one of Viollet-le-Duc's dubious nineteenth-century reconstructions.

The museum's **collection** consists of two disparate sections: superb medieval sculpture and less remarkable eighteenth- and nineteenth-century paintings. The former is made up of stone carvings – found in the course of excavations for the museum itself and from the ruins of local churches and cloisters – of exceptional quality, thanks to the wealth of the city's twelfth-century counts. The complex was only restored to its original size in the last thirty years, and in the course of these works, more medieval treasures were discovered and added to the displays. The main floor consists of a series of rooms and chapels opening out onto the cloister; these contain a substantial part of the sculpture collection, with pieces not just from France, but from as far afield as northern England. The star attraction here is the forest of Romanesque **columns** on the bottom floor of the refectory, found just off the cloister on the west side. Rescued from the ruins of the town's various churches, these were crafted by a school of Toulouse sculptors that thrived under the patronage of the counts in the first half of the twelfth century, their consummate skill evident in the impressively carved capitals. Moving through the refectory, you can follow the development of the Toulouse school, as the elaborate vegetal forms of the 1120s to 1140s give way to busy narrative scenes in increasingly high relief as the century progresses and draws to a close. The last examples, many taken from the cathedral's destroyed cloister, are the most spectacular – wonderfully carved scenes centred around episodes such as the death of John the Baptist. From the refectory, a monumental staircase leads to the upper floor, which, along with the stifling third storey, contains a collection of largely unimpressive **paintings**, amassed by city councillors of the post-Revolution period. On your way out, back on the ground floor, you'll walk past a series of grounded gargoyles set upright on the floor and apparently yawning, unimpressed by their surroundings.

North of the museum, up rue des Arts is place St-Georges, now packed with restaurants. From here the elegant rue St-Antoine, a narrower version of rue d'Alsace-Lorraine, continues up to place Wilson, and rue de la Pomme heads northwest to arrive at the Capitole.

St-Cyprien and Les Abattoirs

Although the old neighbourhood of **St-Cyprien** was also enclosed within the medieval city's defensive walls, its location on the west bank of the Garonne meant that it became marginalized. Home to tanners and butchers, professionals banned from the main town for sanitary reasons, from the Middle Ages it was also the home of Toulouse's hospitals, where the sick were kept in semi-quarantine. Thus, on this side of the river, you won't find the grand mansions of *capitouls* and merchants, but nondescript streets containing fairly ordinary houses. That said, you should not leave Toulouse without setting foot in St-Cyprien, if only to visit the splendid modern art gallery, Les Abattoirs, and once you cross over there's a clutch of smaller museums which are also worth a look. Coming from the station or the old town, you can get to St-Cyprien by bus (#1 or #14) and *metro* ("St-Cyprien République" stop), but the best way to get there is to walk, which at the most leisurely pace shouldn't take more than fifteen minutes.

Crossing the Pont Neuf at the western end of rue de Metz brings you over to the broad grassy bank of the Prairies des Filtres. On the left side of the bridge you'll see the **Château d'Eau** (Tues–Sun 1–7pm; free), a former pumphouse, now a small photographic museum holding good-quality monthly exhibitions. On the north side of the bridge is the old **hospital of St-Jacques**. Modern hospitals grew out of the hospices which cared for pilgrims en route to the Holy Land or Santiago, and which eventually took over the care of sick people in general. Toulouse, being on the pilgrim route and the site of a major university, was a pioneer in medieval medicine. In the plague-ridden centuries preceding the Revolution, the most contagious patients arrived at the hospital directly by boat, so as not to infect the town. Today, these buildings house the administrative offices for Toulouse's centralized medical services, as well as a small **Musée dela Médecine** (Mon–Sat 2–6pm; free) with collections of surgical instruments and pharmaceutical equipment. Further along the riverbank you'll see the huge dome of the sixteenth-century **hospital of St-Joseph de la Grave**, which is still a working hospital. Hard-core philatelists will want to head over to the Centre Municipal de l'Affiche, a small **stamp museum** and resource centre (Mon–Fri 9am–noon & 2–6pm; free), nearby at 58 allée Charles-de-Fitte.

The main reason for visiting St-Cyprien – indeed a good reason for visiting Toulouse itself – is to see the contemporary art gallery, **Les Abattoirs** (Tues–Sun 11am–7pm; €8, free first Sun of month; Ⓦ www.lesabattoirs.org) at 76 allées Charles-de-Fitte, the avenue which marks the precinct of the city's former western wall, just behind the great cupola dominating the river's left bank. This splendid venue, opened in 2000, is not only one of France's best contemporary art museums, but also an inspired piece of urban regeneration. The massive brick complex was constructed in 1828, and functioned as an abattoir until 1989, when environmental concerns forced it to close. The space itself is massive, with huge chambers perfectly suited to display even the largest canvases. Comprising over 2000 works by 130 artists, the collection covers everything from painting to multimedia exhibits. Most European and American schools are well represented, with the major post-war French movements, including Support-Surface, Art Brut and Figuration Libre, plus Italian and Spanish works a particular strength. The most striking piece is undoubtedly **Picasso**'s massive 14m-by-20m theatre backdrop, *The Stripping of the Minotaur in the Harlequin Suit*, painted in 1936 for Romain Rolland's *Le 14 Juillet* and towering over the lower gallery. Other avant-garde works which stand out are the untitled canvases of **Tàpies** and **Barceló**, **Bettencourt**'s provocative mosaic *The Conversion of St Paul* and a large collection of **Dubuffet**'s paintings. More unusual exhibits include a sculpture made up of transparent pipes into which you drop coins, but the collection is so large and varied that, whatever your tastes, you're unlikely to come away disappointed. The complex also includes libraries and a resource centre, interactive terminals on which you can manipulate digital images and a fantastic children's play area; light meals and refreshments are available in the museum's **café** (Tues–Sun 11am–9pm). Behind the museum, the grassy Jardin Raymond IV stretches out towards the river, along an impressive section of the city's fourteenth-century **walls**.

South and east of the old town

If you have the time and energy, the areas south and east of the old town are also worth exploring. The southern district is marked off from old Toulouse by the wide allées Jules-Guesde, the southernmost stretch of the former walls and site of an **antiques market** from Thursday to Sunday. On its northern side is the grassy Jardin Royal, while at its eastern end, a roundabout encircles the surprisingly tranquil **Grand Rond**, with its pretty flower-rimmed fountain (a favourite for wedding photographs). The town's main park, the formally styled **Jardin des Plantes** (daily 7.45am–dusk), can be entered through a large arch off Jules-Guesde. The park itself is a lively place, complete with kids' rides, ice-cream stands and an ersatz mountain and waterfall. Near the entrance stands the city's natural history museum, scheduled to re-open in 2007. At the southern end you'll find the **Monument à la Résistance** (Mon–Fri 10am–noon & 2–5pm; free), where you can enter a solemn stone commemorative chapel.

If this theme interests you, continue down allée des Demoiselles opposite the park; among the fading glory of the Art Deco mansions you'll come across plaques marking the spots where Resistance fighters were shot dead by the Germans in the street-fighting of 1944. Finally, at no. 52, you'll arrive at the **Musée de la Résistance et de la Déportation** (Mon–Fri 9.30am–noon & 2–6pm, Sat 2–5pm; free). Founded to mark the fiftieth anniversary of the liberation of Toulouse on June 19, 1944, this resource centre and museum commemorates through photos, artefacts and dioramas the life of the maquis, the plight of those living under occupation and the crimes of the occupiers, including the massacre of the Forest of Bouconne.

A ten-minute walk up rue du Japon, just outside the museum's doors, brings you to the tiny mansion belonging to the traveller and collector, Georges Labit. This nineteenth-century pavilion is pure Orientalist fantasy, a Gilbert and Sullivanesque vision of the East, while the **museum** (daily: June–Sept 10am–6pm; Oct–May 10am–5pm; €3) holds a small but incredibly varied collection of Asiatica, including Chinese artefacts dating from the tenth century, temple carvings from Northern India and two complete samurai suits of armour. Just a stone's throw away, a canalside path leads up to the remains of old Canal du Midi port, **Port St-Saveur**, now being refitted as a modern pleasure port. From here it's a short walk north along boulevard Monplaisir back to the Grand Rond; incidentally, the towpath running parallel forms the first leg of the canal-side bike and walking route from Toulouse to the **Seuil de Naurouze** (see box p.111). Heading back north along the west side of the canal, beyond the Halle aux Grains, you'll enter the St-Aubin *quartier* (which extends up to allées Jean-Jaurès). Although it has no sights, this inner-city neighbourhood makes for an interesting evening or afternoon excursion, with its marked North African flavour and increasingly diverse selection of bars, restaurants and nightclubs.

The suburbs

A number of specific sights may tempt you to leave old Toulouse and its immediate environs and head for the suburbs. Most popular of these is the **Cité de**

l'Espace (Feb–Aug daily 9am–5/7pm; Sept–Dec Tues–Sun 9am–5/6pm; ⓦwww
.cite-espace.com; €18.50, children under 5 €12), east of the city centre by exit
17 of the *périphérique est* ring road. This is a massive high-tech science centre, with
scores of exhibits on the theme of space and its exploration, including satellite
communications, space probes, a real Ariane rocket and, best of all, the opportunity
to walk inside a mock-up of the MIR space station – a fascinating, but absolutely
chilling and inhuman environment. Many of the exhibits are interactive and,
though it's on the pricey side, you could easily spend half a day here, especially
if you've got children in tow. Unfortunately, getting here by public transport is
tricky: the closest bus lines (#16 and #19, from place Esquirol and Gare Matabiau
respectively) leave you a good twenty-minute walk north of the park.

Only slightly more down to earth is the tour of **Aérospatiale**'s huge assembly
plant in Colomiers, near the airport. In 1970 Toulouse became home to the
French branch of the European conglomerate Airbus Industries, which manu-
factures passenger jets. The planes are assembled, painted and tested in a vast

Toulouse: the history and future of air travel

Toulouse has long been a centre of innovation in aviation. An early hero was **Antoine de Saint-Exupéry** (born 1900 in Lyon), a pilot who joined a local company and
pioneered airmail routes over Africa and the South Atlantic, but is better known today
as an author and journalist. Joining up in 1939 to fight the Germans, and despite
physical disabilities, he flew reconnaissance missions for the Free French forces from
1940 onwards. A man of courage and conviction, he soon fell out with the authoritar-
ian de Gaulle and, despite his exemplary record, became the subject of accusations
of disloyalty. Meanwhile he authored a string of acclaimed books, the most famous
of which, the children's fable *The Little Prince* (1943), has become a world-wide classic. A year after the book's publication Saint-Exupéry mysteriously vanished during
a flight over the Mediterranean, and his ultimate fate remained a mystery until 2004,
when a Corsican fisherman turned up the pilot's identity bracelet.

Today it is corporate rather than personal heroics which characterize aviation in
Toulouse. Airbus, which has been giving stiff competition to major American airline
manufacturers like Boeing, has upped the ante with its development of a new **super-
liner**, the A-380. With a passenger capacity of 656, this two-storey colossus almost
doubles the size of Boeing's 747, and promises to usher in a new era of air travel. But
the cost of development has not been cheap. The massive components manufactured in Germany, Britain and elsewhere in France can be shipped to Bordeaux, but
then must be taken by road to Toulouse. And there's the rub – their size makes transport on existing highways impossible, and thus 250km of highway have been altered
or built anew to accommodate trucks bearing loads up to 13m in height and 300m
long (travelling at the break-neck speed of 20km/h). Needless to say, there are grave
concerns over the environmental impact of such a project, and several *départements*, notably the socialist-run Les Landes, Gers and Lot-et-Garonne, have resisted
the development. Whilst a long list of orders has already been taken for A-380s, the
plane is far from off the ground; in June 2006 a scandal provoked the firing of the
project's entire upper management, while rising fuel prices and wiring problems have
cast further doubts on the plane's viability, and delayed delivery.

Meanwhile, with Toulouse's airport also feeling the pinch, plans are afoot to construct a new larger air hub for southwest France near the city and the authorities are
casting around for possible locations. The flat lands of the *pays de Cocagne* on the
Tarn's left bank seem to be an ideal site: level, open and with good transport links to
the city. This has the villagers of Rabastens and Lisle-sur-Tarn nervous, as they rightly
feel that such a monstrosity would spell the end of the bucolic life of their villages,
which has continued, unhurried, for almost a thousand years.

hangar, L'Usine Clément Ader, before taking their maiden flights from next-door Blagnac airport. You can choose between a ninety-minute **guided tour** (Mon–Sat) of the assembly bays, where crews of one hundred people churn out five Airbuses a week, assisted by scores of computerized robots (€14), or a visit to the now defunct Concorde (€4.50): tours must be booked well in advance (July & Aug contact the tourist office; Sept–June ring ☏05.61.18.06.01, ⓌWww.taxiway.fr). The closest bus route to the factory is #64 (from *metro* Arènes), and the bus driver will direct you to the site.

In the northern suburbs, you'll find the scant remains of Roman Toulouse's **amphitheatre**, constructed in the first century and used through to the end of the fourth. There are also the vestiges of Roman baths and you can visit a small archeological centre (Sat & Sun: June, Sept & Oct 2–6pm; July & Aug 2–7pm; €3). The site is about halfway to the airport, 5km downstream from the centre on the Garonne, on avenue des Arènes-Romaines and can be reached by buses #66 (from *metro* St-Cyprien to "Cautarets") or #70 (from place Jeanne-d'Arc to "Purpan").

Eating and drinking

There's no shortage of good **eating** options in Toulouse, although on Sundays you will find your choice drastically reduced. The city's ethnic mix has engendered a culinary cosmopolitanism, and for French cooking you'll find a multitude of choices in every category of style and price. Toulouse is also a city which loves its **cafés** and **bars** – not surprisingly, given that the population swells by almost a quarter with the annual inundation of university students. The establishments listed below are only a fraction of what's out there – whichever part of town you find yourself in, you're never far from a drink or a meal.

Restaurants

There are several good areas for **restaurants**. Rue de la Colombette in the St-Aubin district, just across boulevard Carnot, has some attractive and fashionable choices. The area surrounding St-Sernin is particularly good: just north, place Arnaud-Bernard and the tiny adjacent place des Tiercerettes have attractive options; between the basilica and place Bernard there's a compact knot of **Arabic** and **Maghrebi** restaurants; and rue du Taur has a number of **Vietnamese** places and sandwich bars. Should you feel stuck for a choice, you can always head south of place Wilson to place St-Georges, where you'll find a gaggle of typical terraced eateries, or to the bottom end of rue des Filatiers where there's a cluster of late-night restaurants and tapas bars. Several of the *bistrots* on place Wilson are distinguished not so much by their fare, but by the fact that you can eat as late as 1am.

If you're on a tight budget you can pick up **picnic** supplies in the Monoprix department store at 39 rue d'Alsace-Lorraine, or head from place du Capitole down rue St-Rome, where there's a string of inexpensive and good kebab and sandwich stands. The best lunch-time bargain is in the covered **market** on place Victor-Hugo (closed Mon), whose upper floor has a group of very cheap food counters. As a last resort, you'll find a late-night grocery store at 67 rue des Pargaminières.

Budget

Les Abattoirs 97 allée Charles-de-Fitte ☏05.61.42.04.95. A family-run restaurant for two generations, the last of the traditional slaughterhouse-side meat emporia, with a reputation for top-of-the-line intestinal delicacies such as calves, brains and pigs' feet. *Menus* from €18. Closed Sun, Mon & Aug.

Asia Fast Food 4 rue Bayard. If you want a quick bite on the way to the station, drop into this cheerful self-service cafeteria at the southern end of rue Bayard. Chinese, Vietnamese and Thai dishes at budget prices. Open daily till midnight.

Benjamin 7 rue des Gestes ☎05.61.22.92.66. A long-standing institution for economical *terroir* food; service is pleasant and professional, although the atmosphere is somewhat anonymous. A wide selection of duck-based lunch and dinner *menus* €11–19. Open daily.

Le Chateaubriand 42 rue Pargaminières. Named after the politician rather than the steak, this casual little restaurant serves an excellent cassoulet, made with flavourful *haricots Tarbais*, and scrumptious home-made desserts. Lunch *menus* from €11, or €19–29 for dinner. Closed Aug, Sat lunch & Sun.

Chez Atilla In the market at pl Victor-Hugo. The best of the market restaurants, this no-nonsense lunch-time establishment is also one of Toulouse's best options for seafood – their Spanish *zarzuela* stew is a fish-lover's dream. *Menus* from €12. Closed Mon & part Aug.

Chez Fazoul 2 rue Tolosane ☎05.61.53.72.09. Welcoming restaurant serving local dishes in a pleasant, brick-walled dining room. *Menus*, featuring steak, cassoulet, *confits* and *cèpes*, for €12–27. Closed Sun.

L' Colombier 14 rue Bayard ☎05.61.62.40.05. Cassoulet's the thing in this elegant restaurant, but there are other regional delights, such as *gésiers* ("gizzards") and *foie gras*, as well as seafood and game. *Menus* from €18. Closed Sat lunch & Sun.

La Embarcadère 11 rue de la Bourse. Good selection of generous-sized salads, dessert crêpes and other light fare for under €8. Closed Mon.

Faim des Haricots 3 rue du Puits Vert ☎05.61.22.49.25. A good vegetarian option, with generous all-you-can-eat salad and dessert buffets (both €9), "bottomless" bowls of soup and a *plat du jour*. Open Mon–Sat lunch & Thurs–Sat dinner; closed first half Aug.

Saveurs Bio 22 rue Maurice-Fonvieille ☎05.61.12.15.15. Toulouse's best vegetarian place, offering everything from spinach quiche to alfalfa salads, and with various set meals for under €15 and a *grande assiette* at €8. Closed Sat eve & Sun.

Taverna Casa Manolo 24 rue des 3 Piliers ☎05.61.23.85.06. Lively Spanish taverna hidden away amongst the couscous places north of St-Sernin. Generous tapas from €5 and a massive two-person paella at €30. Open Tues–Sun 7pm to late.

Le Ver Luisant 41 rue de la Colombette ☎05.61.63.06.73. A bar and simple restaurant frequented by the arty set. The good food – mostly regional but with some cosmopolitan touches – is copious and the atmosphere fun. *Plat du jour* €10

at lunch time, or €18–30 for an evening meal. Closed Sat lunch & Mon.

Moderate

La Bascule 14 av Maurice-Hauriou ☎05.61.52.09.51. A Toulouse institution. Its chromy interior is pure Art Deco and the food well preprared and presented. The *menu* includes regional dishes like cassoulet, *foie de canard* and oysters from the Bay of Arcachon. *Menus* from €20. Closed Sun.

Cantine du Curé 2 rue H-de-Grosse. Cosy little *terroir* restaurant, housed in a small but atmospheric old building, complete with wooden beams, by the entrance to the Dalbade church. One of the two tiny dining areas has a fireplace. Evening *menu* from €28. Closed Sun eve & Mon.

Au Chat Dingue, 40bis rue Peyrolières. Small, hip bistro with cool blue decor across from the *Petit Voisin* bar. The selection is not overly imaginative, with a solid southern French base and occasional Italian incursions (usually in the form of pasta). *Menus* cost €18–22, but considerably more à la carte. Closed Sun.

Cosi Fan Tutte 8 rue Mage ☎05.61.53.07.24. Highly-reputed and stylish Italian place with rich garish red decor. Ordering à la carte or dining in the evening is considerably more expensive (€44–85) than the €18 daily specials. Closed Sun & Mon.

La Côte de Boeuf 12 rue des Gestes ☎05.61.21.19.61. This simple and compact street-side restaurant is not the cheapest in the neighbourhood, but the quality of its wood-fire home-cooking (superb duck and *foie gras*) and the genuine friendliness of the family who run it put it a step above neighbouring *Benjamin*. Extras (such as coffee and liquor) are pricey. Expect to spend €18–47. Closed Sun, Mon & Aug.

Kaviar Rouge 21 place Nicholas Bachelier ☎05.61.62.31.19. Toulouse's Russian restaurant is located in the St. Aubin district. Sample a wide selection of Caucasian delicacies, including caviar (€25–160 per 50g) and the cities best selection of Polish and Russian flavoured vodkas (from €5) in the cosy atmosphere of a *faux* Siberian log cabin. Generous dinner *menu* at €25.

Semiramis 23 rue des Peyrolières ☎05.6123.66.11. Extremely popular Lebanese and Syrian cuisine, with typical *mezze*, including home-made *kibbeh*, spinach pie and other Middle-Eastern favourites. Dine inside or on the street for around €22. Open daily.

Le Sept Place St-Sernin 7 pl St-Sernin ☎05.62.30.05.30. A small house behind the basilica conceals a lively and cheerful restaurant which serves inventive and original cuisine with a constantly changing *carte*, followed by dazzling desserts. *Menus* from €18–45. Closed Sat lunch & Sun.

Shun 35 rue Bachelier ☎05.61.99.39.20. Surprisingly well-priced Japanese restaurant at the north end of the St-Aubin district. Basic *menus* at €9–15 at lunch but plan on spending more in the evening. Closed Sun & Mon.

Expensive

Chez Émile 13 pl St-Georges ☎05.61.21.05.56. One of Toulouse's best restaurants, and well situated on this busy oblong square. Regional cuisine downstairs and seafood upstairs, at €18–48 on the *menu*. Closed Sun & Mon.

Les Jardins de l'Opéra 1 pl du Capitole ☎05.61.21.05.56. The *Grand Hôtel*'s restaurant is Toulouse's best and most luxurious. If you fancy a splurge this is the place to do it – the food is

outstanding – but you will pay for it: a basic *menu* starts at €40. Closed Sun & Mon lunch & part Aug.

🏃 **Michel Sarran** 21 bd Armand-Duportal ☎05.61.12.32.32. Justifiably renowned *gastronomique* restaurant, a 15min walk from the place du Capitole (follow rue des Lois and rue des Salenques to the end, and turn left). Imaginative dishes with a strong Mediterranean streak are served with style and warmth. *Menus* from €45 at lunch and €95 at dinner. Closed Sat, Sun, Wed lunch & part Aug.

🏃 **Au Pois Gourmand** 3 rue Émile Heybrard ☎05.61.31.95.95. Great location in a nineteenth-century riverside house with a beautiful patio. The quality French cuisine does not come cheap here (*menus* from €22–64), but is of a predictably high standard, and the *carte* presents a pleasant departure from purely regional dishes. Bus #66 or #14 from *metro* St-Cyprien-République. Closed Sat & Mon lunch, Sun & Aug.

Cafés and bars

Many establishments cater to a mellow coffee and beer clientele during the day and put on the music after 10pm. Regular daytime **café**-lounging can be pursued around the popular student/arty hangout of place Arnaud-Bernard, while place du Capitole is the early evening meeting place. Place St-Georges has been somewhat inundated by restaurant terraces but remains another option, while the more elegant terraces of place Wilson are good if you don't mind the traffic.

Bapz 13 rue de la Bourse. English-style bakery and tearoom – definitely not your typical "caff", with good breakfasts and snacks. Smart service (and prices). Closed Sun.

Bar du Matin 16 pl des Carmes. Great old street-corner bar in the finest beer, peanuts and *pastis* tradition. A friendly and deservedly popular place. Closed Sun.

Bibent 5 pl du Capitole. On the south side of the square, this is Toulouse's most distinguished café, with exuberant plasterwork, marble tables and cascading chandeliers. Open daily.

Le Café des Artistes pl de la Daurade. Lively, young café overlooking the Garonne. A perfect spot to watch the sun set on warm summer evenings, as floodlights pick out the brick buildings along the quays. Open daily.

Le Donjon Bar 2 rue du Poids de l'Huile. Tiny bar on the south side of the Capitole building. Impossibly crowded but great fun for watching rugby or having a drink. Open until 2am. Closed Sun.

Dubliners Irish Pub 15 av Crampel. Toulouse's biggest Irish pub. Few surprises. Open until 2am. Closed Sun.

Le Florida 12 pl du Capitole. Relaxed café with a nicely retro air. One of the most pleasant places to hang out on the central square. Open daily.

The Frog and Rosbif 14 rue de l'Industrie. Stop by this friendly British pub, just off bd Lazare-Carnot, for a pint of Darktagnan stout, or one of their other excellent home brews. Quiz nights, football and fish and chips draw an international crowd. Open until 2am, Sat until 4am. Closed part Aug.

Jour de Fête 43 rue de Taur. Funky tearoom and brasserie with a small street-side patio. Friendly service and a young studenty crowd. Open until 2am Fri & Sat.

Au Père Louis 45 rue des Tourneurs ☎05.61.21.33.45. A lively, old-fashioned bar with *chansons* and music some nights. Open till 10pm. Closed Sun.

St-Philipe 19 rue Arnaud-Bernard Escoussières. Just off place Bernard to the north of the St-Sernin, on the edge of the Maghrebi neighbourhood, this bar attracts a mixed crowd of locals, students and business people. There's a pool table, table-football and video games to keep you busy over your beer. Open daily.

Le Shanti 21 rue Peyrolières. A funky "Indian" tea house featuring a wide range of non-alcoholic refreshments as well as the opportunity to relax with a *narghila* (Arab water-pipe; €6). Open daily 2pm–2am.

Le Sherpa 44 rue de Taur. Another of the city's many tea rooms. Popular with the university crowd and conveniently located by the Cinemathèque. Closed Sun.

Nightlife

The annual influx of university students ensures that the city's **nightlife** is active, sustaining a whole range of **music-bars** and **clubs**; if the French are not famous for exuberant partying, Toulouse helps belie the stereotype. Things slow down from July to September, when the academic year breaks, but even in the summer you'll have no trouble drinking and dancing as late as you like. Unfortunately some of the city's best venues lie in the suburbs, which means paying for a taxi, though there's no shortage of options closer to the old town. Entrance fees to discos and clubs may be charged depending on the night and event, but generally you're expected to buy a rather expensive drink (€8–10), while at venues which are essentially bars you can enter free of charge.

Music-bars and clubs

L'Ambassade 22 bd de la Gare. Downbeat club where funk and soul rule. Live jazz on Sunday nights. Open until Tues, Fri & Sun until 2am, Sat till 5am.

Bar de la Lune 24 rue Palaprat. This evening drinking spot in St-Aubin draws an arty crowd with its occasional exhibitions and concerts. Daily from 7pm.

Le Bikini 55 chemin des Étroits, rte de Lacroix-Falgarde (@www.lebikini.com). On the city's southern outskirts, this is *the* hangout of Toulouse rockers, and a prime venue for live gigs. Open Thurs–Sun.

Bodega-Bodega 1 rue Gabriel-Péri. The old *Telegraph* newspaper building makes a superb venue for this bar-restaurant, with its hugely popular disco after 10pm. Daily until 2am, Sat 4am.

Café Classico 37 rue des Filatiers. Trendy, designer-ish establishment that's a café by day and music-bar by night. House, hip-hop and jungle. Daily until 1am, Sat 4am.

Le Cri de la Mouette pl Héraclès (@www .lecridelamouette.com). Popular disco featuring reggae, rock, funk and soul. Cover from €5. Daily 11pm–5am.

Erich Coffie 9 rue Joseph-Vié. Just west of the river in the *quartier* St-Cyprien, this is one of the city's liveliest and most enjoyable music-bars, with an eclectic music policy. There's food available and live bands most evenings. Open Tues–Sat from 10pm.

Le Griot 3 rue Amélie. Massive super-bar and concert hall, with dance floors, videos, pool room and restaurant. Happy hours 7–8pm & 10–11pm. Daily until 2am.

La Luna Loca 15 rue Pierre Rubens. Cultural centre and club for lesbians. Men admitted on Wed & Fri only. Nightly 8pm–late.

Le Petit Voisin 37 rue Peyrolières. A neighbourhood place, just like the name, "the little neighbour", says. Laid-back during the day when workers and businessmen stop for a drink, and livelier at night, when it fills with a student crowd. Open until 2am, Sat 4am. Closed Sun & mid-Aug.

Puerto Habana 12 port St-Etienne. Toulouse's hottest salsa venue, in a superb setting beside the Canal du Midi. Also has an excellent restaurant and a house band Thurs–Sat. Mon–Fri until 2am, Sat till 5am.

Le Purple 2 rue Castellane (@www.purepurple .fr). Southwest France's temple of cool and Mecca of House, with food, drinks and dancing. Tues–Sat 11pm to dawn.

Le Rex 15 av Honoré-Serres. Located in an converted cinema, just north of the old town, this bar/concert hall usually features ska and punk acts. Opening hours vary so check with the local entertainment magazines for concerts and events.

Le Shanghai 12 rue de la Pomme. One of the city's most established gay and lesbian clubs, which attracts a mixed crowd including transvestites and transsexuals. Wed–Sun 11pm–late (on Sat right through to Sun 1pm).

L'Ubu 16 rue St-Rome. Long-standing pillar of the city's dance scene, that remains as popular as ever. Mon–Sat 11pm till dawn.

Entertainment and festivals

Drinking and dancing aside, there's plenty to do in Toulouse. Several **cinemas** regularly show v.o. films, including ABC, 13 rue St-Bernard (℡05.61.29.81.00), Cinémathèque, 68 rue de Taur (℡05.62.30.30.10, Ⓦwww.lacinematheque detoulouse.com), and Utopia, 24 rue Montardy (℡05.61.23.66.20, Ⓦwww .cinemas-utopia.org). The city also has an extremely vibrant **theatre** culture. The official Théâtre de la Cité, 1 rue Pierre-Baudis (℡05.34.45.05.05, Ⓦwww .tnt-cite.com) is home to the Théâtre National de Toulouse Midi-Pyrénées, which has a narrative theatre programme livened up by occasional dance performances, while the workshop Nouveau Théâtre Jules-Julien, 6 av des Écoles-Jules-Juliens (℡05.61.25.79.92) has a reputation for staging provocative drama, with a particular emphasis on Absurdist productions. The large venue Odyssud, 4 av du Parc Blagnac (℡05.61.71.75.15; bus #66) features both theatre and **opera**, but the place to head for the latter, as well as **ballet** and **contemporary dance** performances, is the Théâtre du Capitole, housed in the Capitole building (℡05.61.63.13.13, Ⓦwww.theatre-du-capitole.org), a highly acclaimed venue where you can also hear recitals and chamber music. **Classical music** fans also have the Orchestre National du Capitole, with its base in the Halle aux Grains in place Dupuy (℡05.61.99.78.00, Ⓦwww.onct.mairie -toulouse.fr). The city's biggest **rock music** venue, with nine-thousand seats, is Zénith, at 11 avenue Raymond Badiou (℡05.62.74.49.49; *metro* Arènes), which features both French and foreign groups, including visiting jazz and blues performers, while for something a little less energetic, Cave-Poésie, 71 rue de Taur (℡05.61.23.62.00, Ⓦwww.cave-poesie.fr.st) is home to various **literary workshops** and gatherings of a decidedly bohemian spirit.

Toulouse's **festivals** calendar is packed out, with a back-to-back programme of artistic, musical or literary events throughout the year. For a full rundown of these, see the box, pp.74–75. To get up-to-date **information** on the latest cultural events check the weekly magazines *Toulouse Hebdo* (€1) or *Flash* (€3), which have detailed concert and event listings and are available at news-stands. The monthly *Ramdam* (€2.20) has listings for the whole region of Midi-Pyrénées, while the *mairie* distributes a free magazine, *Cultures Toulouse*, and has comprehensive event listings at Ⓦwww.mairie-toulouse.fr.

Listings

Airlines Air France ℡08.20.82.08.20, Ⓦwww.airfrance.com; American Airlines ℡08.10.08.72.08.72, Ⓦwww.aa.com; BMI Baby ℡00.44.87.02.64.22.29, Ⓦwww.bmibaby.com; British European ℡00.44.13.92.26.85.00, Ⓦwww .flybe.com; Delta ℡05.62.27.26.05, Ⓦwww.delta .com; easyJet ℡08.26.10.26.11, Ⓦwww.easyjet .com.

Airport Aéroport Toulouse-Blagnac ℡05.61.42.44.00 & 05.24.61.80.00, Ⓦwww .toulouse.aeroport.fr; for shuttle bus information ℡05.34.60.64.00.

Banks and exchange Most major French banks have offices and ATMs around the place du Capitole. The Banque de France is at 4 rue Deville (Mon–Fri 9am–12.20pm & 1.20–3.30pm). For bureaux de change Banque Populaire has an office at the airport (Mon–Fri 8am–7pm, Sat 8am–12.30pm) and C2E Capitole Exchange is in the centre at 30 rue du Taur (Mon–Fri 9am–12.30pm & 2–6pm & Sat 10am–noon & 2–6pm).

Bike rental The municipal bike co-op Movimento (Mon–Fri 8am–7pm, Sat & Sun 10am–7pm; Ⓦwww.movimento.coop), has branches at sq Charles-de-Gaulle (opposite the tourist office) and 5 Port Saint-Saveur. Rates are €1 for a half-day, €2 for a full day and €3 overnight, and you must leave a credit card deposit of €260. Holiday Bikes, 9 bd. des Minimes (℡05.34.25.79.62, ℮toulouse @holiday-bikes.com) also rents out scooters and motorcycles. Serious cyclists planning a longer trip may want to contact the Association Vélo, 2 rue de la Daurade, 31000 Toulouse (℡05.61.11.87.09, Ⓦmembres.lycos.fr/velotlse).

Boat trips and rental Various outfits offer tours on the Garonne and the canals du Midi and de Brienne. Le Capitole has several daily and night-time departures from pl de la Daurade for a ninety-minute journey on the Garonne (€5; reserve at the tourist office; @www.toulouse-croisieres.com). Baladine (@www.bateaux-toulousains.com) has a variety of full day programmes, as well as a 75-minute cruise of historic Toulouse departing from the Quai de la Daurade (daily in summer at 2.30, 4 & 5.30pm, otherwise Wed, Sat & Sun; €7). For houseboat rental, contact Navicanal, 139 rue Bonnat (☎05.61.55.10.91, @www.navicanal.com).

Books The best general bookshops are Castéla, on place du Capitole, and FNAC, at 16 allées F-Roosevelt. Toulouse Presse, 60 rue Bayard, stocks a good range of IGN maps and guides while Ombres-Blanches at 50 rue Gambetta is another good choice for travel literature. For English-language books, Books and Mermaides, 3 rue Mirepoix, specializes in second-hand tomes and will exchange, while The Bookshop, 17 rue Lakanal, stocks new titles. There are book markets on Thursday mornings in place Arnaud-Bernard, and all day Saturday in place St-Étienne.

Bus departures *Gare routière* (information booth Mon–Fri 8.30am–4pm; ☎05.61.61.67.67) beside the gare SNCF.

Car rental A2L, 81 bd Déodat-de-Séverac ☎05.61.59.33.99; Avis, gare SNCF ☎05.61.63.71.71; Budget, 49 rue Bayard ☎05.61.63.18.18; Europcar, 15 bd Bonre-pos ☎05.61.62.52.89; Hertz, gare SNCF ☎05.61.62.94.12.

Consulates Canada, 10 rue Jules de Resseguier (☎05.61.52.19.06, ©consulat.canada .toulouse@wanadoo.fr); USA, 25 allées Jean-Jaures (☎05.34.41.36.50, @www.amb-usa.fr); the closest British Consulate is in Bordeaux at 353 bd Wilson (☎05.57.22.21.10).

Gay and lesbian For information contact the gay and lesbian students' group Jules et Julies, Comité des Étudiants, Université du Mirail, 5 allée Mach-ado, 310589, or Gais et Lesbiennes en Marche (☎06.11.87.38.81, ©gelem@altern.org).

Hospitals There are two major hospitals, both outside the A61 ring road: CHR Ranguiel, chemin du Vallon (☎05.61.32.25.33) to the south, and CHR Purpan, pl du Dr Baylac (☎05.61.77.22.33) to the west. Emergency ☎15 or 05.61.12.77.77.

Internet access Cyber Media-Net, 19 rue de Lois (Mon–Fri 9am–11.30pm, Sat 10am–midnight), or @fterbug, 12 pl St-Sernin (Mon–Fri noon–2am,

Sat noon–5am, Sun 2.30–10.30pm). Aside from these, the CRIJ office at 17 rue de Metz has a free terminal, and you can also get online at the main post office, and at Telecom France kiosks at 11 rue Alsace-Lorraine and 18 place Wilson.

Language courses Alliance Française, 9 pl du Capitole (☎05.34.45.26.10, @www.alliance -toulouse.org), and Maison de l'Europe, 35 rue Croix-Baragnon (☎05.61.54.53.86.43, @www .maisondeleurope.org) both run French-language courses.

Laundry Lavomat, 20 rue Arnaud-Bernard (daily 7am–10pm), and Lavaria Auto, 7 rue Mirepoix (daily 7am–9pm).

Markets Antiques in place St-Sernin and allées Jules-Guesde (Thurs–Sun 8am–4pm). Produce and clothes in place du Capitole (Wed & Sun 8am–1pm). There is also a mammoth food and clothing market on Sun and Mon along boulevard de Strasbourg, and more produce markets at places des Carmes, St-Cyprien and Victor-Hugo (all Tues–Sun). For a complete rundown of the city's many markets, ask at the tourist office.

Pharmacy There are pharmacies in the place du Capitole and dotted throughout the city. The Pharmacie de Nuit, 70–76 allées Jean-Jaurès (entry on rue Arnaud Vidal) is open Mon–Sat 8pm–8am & Sun 8pm–9am.

Police 23 bd de l'Embouchure ☎05.61.12.77.77; emergency ☎17.

Rugby Toulouse is a centre of excellence for French rugby – many players in the national team hail from these parts. You can see their first-rate Stade Toulousain team in action at their stadium at 114 rue de Troènes (☎05.61.57.05.05, @www .stadetoulousain.fr; bus #16 to "Stade").

Swimming There are several public pools in town. Alfred Nakache is open year-round, allées Paul-Bienes (☎05.61.22.31.35).

Taxis Capitole (☎05.34.25.02.50); Taxi Radio Toulousain (☎05.61.42.38.38). For taxis to the airport call ☎05.61.30.02.54.

Train departures Tickets can be bought at the gare SNCF, or at the Tisseo-Connex building, 7 pl Esquirol (Mon–Fri 2–6pm). Information on ☎08.92.35.35.35, @www.voyages-sncf.com.

Travel agencies USIT Voyages (@www .usitconnect.fr) has branches at 16 rue Pierre-Paul Riquet (☎05.61.99.38.47) and 5 rue de Lois (☎05.61.11.52.42); Nouvelles Frontières (@www.nouvelles-frontieres.fr) is in 2 pl St-Sernin (☎08.03.33.33.33).

Around Toulouse

Predominantly flat, and ribbed by a multitude of small streams, the hinterland fanning out to the north and east of Toulouse has long been the source of the city's wealth. The woad boom of the fifteenth and sixteenth centuries may have powered its prosperous golden age, but the **cereal farming** carried out in this immensely fertile region has been Toulouse's traditional financial mainstay. Field after field of wheat dominates the rolling landscape, cut across by narrow bands of wood, and dotted by the church steeples of modest, introverted hamlets – havens of determined rural existence where elderly farmers speak French with a rounded Occitan accent. The region is hedged to the north by the River Agout and to the west by the rising peaks of the Montagne Noire (see pp.194–195), but is most notable for its southern boundary, the Canal du Midi. With its generally low relief and comparatively little traffic, it makes **cycling** enjoyable and reasonably safe here.

The northern stretch of the region, known as the *pays de Cocagne* (see box below) is dominated by **Lavaur**, once a stalwart Cathar centre, with its beautifully preserved old town. On either side of this, a series of quiet hamlets, **St-Sulpice**, **Giroussens**, **St-Paul** and **Damiette**, line the Agout, crossing it with narrow old trestle bridges. The easternmost town in the area, sitting on the edge of the Parc du Haut Languedoc, is the old *bastide* of **Revel**, with an impressive medieval covered market-place. Just south of here, at **St-Ferreol**, you'll find part of the incredible catchment system of the Canal du Midi, while just to the northeast, **Sorèze** and **Dourgne** embody the past and present of the monastic traditions of the Benedictines and their heirs. The flat Lauragais district stretches southwest of Revel: **St-Félix** is its prettiest town, but

---

The woad to riches

From the mid-fifteenth to the mid-sixteenth century Toulouse and Albi experienced an unprecedented wave of prosperity, based on the humble **woad** plant (*Isatis tinctoria* or in French, *pastel*). When craftsmen in Albi discovered that the innocuous weed, which was used for medicinal purposes across the Mediterranean, yielded a rich blue dye, they knew they were onto a good thing; blue was one of the colours for clothing most in demand by the growing middle class, and up to that point it could only be produced from rare and expensive raw materials.

With capital from Toulouse, intensive woad cultivation operations were set up across the Lauragais, which had ideal soil and climate conditions for the plant. Once the woad had been harvested, the process of dye production lasted approximately four months, during which time the leaves were picked, crushed and rolled into balls (*coques*) and left to ferment for two weeks, whereafter the sticky dye could be pressed out and rolled into balls (*cocagnes*). Demand from textile manufacturers across Europe brought staggering wealth to the region, which became known in common parlance as the **pays de Cocagne** (a play on words, also meaning "the land of plenty"). Some 30–40,000 tonnes were shipped annually. The woad merchants, many of whom became *capitouls* of Toulouse, erected fine mansions, the *hôtels particuliers*, which even today bear witness to their former wealth. By the late sixteenth century, however, *pastel* began to be superseded by cheaper indigo-based dyes brought over to Europe from the Indies, and production went into decline. The violent upheavals of the Wars of Religion, ravaging fields and interrupting transport, provided the final blow, and the dye, along with the incredible affluence it generated, became a thing of the past. Today, you can purchase traditionally dyed items at La Fleurée de Pastel at 20 rue de la Bourse in Toulouse, near the Hôtel d'Assézat.

Castelnaudary – the area's capital – contains a surprising number of monuments and mansions. More significantly, it is also the main town on this stretch of the **Canal du Midi**, the engineering marvel constructed in the seventeenth century to link the Mediterranean and the Atlantic, and now a favourite with boating enthusiasts and cyclists.

Lavaur and around

Thirty-seven kilometres east of Toulouse, **LAVAUR** is the biggest town on the Agout west of Castres, and the traditional capital of the surrounding *pays de Cocagne*. It's also a key town in the history of Catharism, the twelfth-century heretical movement (see *The Land of Cathars* colour section). Seat of a Cathar bishop, the "citadel of Satan," as it was known to Catholic forces, was besieged twice by the crusading northern French aristocracy. It resisted in 1181, but when the violent leader of the papal military forces, Simon de Montfort, arrived in March 1211, he meant business. After nearly two months of encirclement the walls were breached, and the town taken – with bloody consequences: Guiraude de Laurac, widow of the town's lord and leader of the defence, was thrown down a well and pelted with stones; her brother, along with nearly a hundred knights, was put to the sword; and some four hundred Cathars were burnt at the stake. Despite such brutality the heresy persisted, prompting the papacy and crown to establish a series of religious foundations here, starting with a Dominican house to run the local Inquisition and finally, in the fourteenth century, a cathedral. In the sixteenth century the town was a Huguenot hotbed, pitting itself once more against the Catholic establishment and the seigniorial powers of the North. Nevertheless it prospered, profiting first from the lucrative woad industry and, later, silk manufacture. Today Lavaur is an attractive if quiet rural centre, surrounded by the wheat fields of the Agout valley.

The town's main landmark, the brick-built former **cathedral** of St-Alain, stands on a wide plaza above the river. The present structure was built in 1254, replacing that destroyed by the Crusaders, and although the interior has been given a hideous nineteenth-century remodelling, the exterior still holds a few surprises. These include a wooden door on the south side, which survives from the original pre-Crusade building, an eleventh-century marble altar, a highly stylized fifteenth-century doorway and an incredible mechanical clock, perched high above the ground in one of its two towers. This *jacquemart* – a clock which strikes using a mechanical figure in the form of a soldier wielding a hammer – dates back to 1523 and still marks every half-hour. Looking across the river from the plaza, you'll be treated to a vista of old mansions set in the fields along its banks, while heading southwest from the cathedral entrance a series of signs leads you on a pleasant stroll past the highlights of the town. Chief among these is the fourteenth-century **church of St-François**, dedicated to St Francis of Assisi, founder of the Franciscans, the first group established to preach against heretics and the Dominicans' great rivals, who also came here to rehabilitate the Cathar population. Set in the town's old main street, the Grande Rue, this church has weathered the centuries, losing its cloister and other appendages to Huguenots and revolutionaries. Nevertheless the graceful simplicity of its single nave and surviving columns make it worth a look. In the adjoining **garden** keep an eye out for the old dovecote, one of the first along the route des Colombiers (see p.100). Nearby, the **church of the Cordeliers**, built in the years immediately following the Crusade, also merits a visit for its elegant Gothic interior. As you walk around the town you'll see a number of timber-and-brick houses, many dating from the fourteenth to sixteenth centuries;

there may be no major sights in Lavaur, but the narrow old streets make for a pleasantly atmospheric whole. Finishing up, the circuit through the old town leads back towards the cathedral, passing the eighteenth-century Neoclassical *mairie*, which houses the local historical and archeological museum, the Musée du Pays Vaurais, currently under indefinite renovation.

Practicalities

Trains and buses stop at Lavaur's **gare SNCF**, located northeast of the old quarter on the place de Stalingrad. From here it's a fifteen-minute walk to the **tourist office** (June–Sept Tues–Sat 9.30am–noon & 2.30–6.30pm; Oct–May 9.30am–12.30pm & 4–6pm; ℡05.63.58.02.00, ⓦwww.ville-lavaur.fr), which is housed in a small turret on the riverside quai Tour de Rondes. Decent **hotels** include the comfortable if unremarkable *le Terminus* (℡05.63.58.00.18, ℱ05.63.58.15.11; ❸) by the station, and the basic *Pasteliers*, 7 rue d'Alsace-Lorraine (℡05.63.58.04.16, ℱ05.63.58.58.75; ❸), but the best place to stay is the **chambres d'hôtes** ⚿ *Les Chambres du Pastel*, 5 rue du Père Colin (℡05.63.58.38.95, ⓔpierrick.broustet@free.fr; ❸), an ancient house located just a short walk from the old cathedral with four small but cosy rooms. It also has a great bar, worth a visit whether you're staying there or not. For eating, the best choice is the **restaurant** at *Le Jacquemart* (℡05.63.58.04.17; closed Sun eve & Mon) which does good local food from €18.50 and also has rooms (❸). A second choice is the dining-room *Terminus* (closed Sat), a friendly place serving up inventive *terroir*-based food (around €20). You'll also find a clutch of places in the elongated square stretching up from the tourist office, the most interesting of which is *Pitcholina* (closed Sun), a Basque restaurant where you can get a half-chicken lunch with wine for only €9. Lavaur's **country market** is on Saturday morning throughout the old town, and there's a **horse-fair** held on the third Saturday of each month near the *gare*.

Giroussens and St-Sulpice

Some fifteen kilometres northwest of Lavaur, the ancient village of **GIROUS-SENS** huddles on the slope of a high ridge. For thousands of years and right up to the present day, this town has been a centre of pottery production, as the shops which line the road through town reveal. Pottery fans can also visit the **Maison de la Céramique**, a museum/shop featuring local wares (Tues–Sun: May–Aug noon–6pm, Sept–April 10am–noon & 2–6pm, closed part Jan & Feb; €3). Aside from this and an attractive thirteenth-century **church**, there's little to draw you here, but if you are walking, cycling or driving by, it makes a good place to spend the night. Just across the river on the south bank of the Agout, you'll find the hamlet of **St-Lieux-lès-Lavaur**, site of a much-touted **steam train** (mid-April to mid-July, Sept & Oct Sun 2.30–5.30pm; late July Sat–Tues 2.30–4.30/5.30pm; Aug daily 2.30–4.30/5.30pm; Nov to mid-April Sun & school holidays only 2.30–4.30/5.30pm; subject to cancellation if less than ten tickets sold; €5), which runs a one-hour return trip eastwards along the river valley. Its highpoint is crossing over a twenty-metre-high viaduct: note that sometimes the steam train is substituted with a regular diesel engine. Also in St-Lieux is the **Jardin des Martels** (late March Sun 1–6pm; April, Sept & Oct Mon–Fri 1–6pm, Sat & Sun 11am–6pm; May–Aug daily 11am–6pm; Nov Sat & Sun 1–6pm; €6), a botanical garden with thousands of varieties of flowers and plants, as well as a petting zoo. The train and garden make a good combination if you are travelling with children. The best place to **stay** or **eat** in Giroussens is *L'Échaguette* (℡05.63.41.63.65, ℱ05.63.41.63.13; ❷), in the lower part of the village. This beautiful thirteenth-century building has several well-furnished rooms and a small, intimate dining room, with delicious *terroir*-based *menus* (from €24 at dinner). Alternatively, you can stay at the Reynaud's B&B, *Le Pepil* (closed late-Aug to early-Sept; ① & ⑤05.63.41.62.84; English spoken; ②), set in an attractive old farm building.

You're only likely to make a stop in tiny **ST-SULPICE**, 8km further west, if changing buses or trains en route to Toulouse or Albi from Lavaur or the Montagne Noire. The village is quite plain, apart from an attractive old suspension **bridge** over the Agout, which flows into the Tarn just west of town. There's also a mildly interesting fourteenth-century **church** just south of the old bridge, whose crenellated facade shows it originally served as part of the town's defences. On one of the doors you can see a depiction of Moses descending from Mount Sinai bearing the Ten Commandments and sprouting ram's horns. The origin of this curious motif, recurrent in Catholic art, is an error on the part of St Jerome, who translated the Bible into its popular Latin version, the Vulgate, in the fourth century. Led astray by the Hebrew text (in which vowels are not written) he confused two adjectives; the original read that Moses returned from his interview with God "radiant", but Jerome read it as "horned". Medieval artists, faithfully following scripture, dutifully depicted the patriarch sprouting horns. Just east of the church, below the ruins of the twelfth-century **château du Castela**, you can visit the castle's underground passages, 142 metres in length. Dress warmly for the 40-minute tour (July–Sept daily 3–7.30pm; Oct–June on demand at tourist office; €3).

The **tourist office** is at Parc Georges-Spenale (Tues–Sat 3–7pm; ①05.63.41.89.50, ⑩www.ville-saint-sulpice-81.fr). For **accommodation**, you can choose between the *Hôtel Le Relais Fleuri* (①05.63.41.80.20, ⑩www.federal-hotel.com; ②), and several **chambres d'hôtes**, including *Le Cambou* (①05.63.41.82.66; ③). There's also a **campsite** in town, *Borio-Blanco* (①05.63.41.89.55), which is open all year. If you are looking for a **meal**, head out on the RN88 to ✗ *L'Auberge de la Pointe* (closed Tues, Wed & Thurs eve & part Nov; ①05.63.41.80.14), one of the best *gastronomique* restaurants on this stretch of the Tarn, where you can enjoy subtle and elaborate *menus* overlooking the river for €18–38. If you have transport, the nineteenth-century manor house at St-Lieux has reasonable rooms in impressive surroundings (①05.63.41.60.87; ③; English spoken). Market day is Wednesday (morning only).

The route des Colombiers, St-Paul-Cap-de-Joux and Damiette

If you are cycling or driving from Lavaur, you should take time to explore the **route des Colombiers**, a loose circuit of approximately 20km which you can start on the southern bank of the Agout heading east out of the town. *Colombiers*, elaborate and varied **dovecotes**, have been constructed here among the farm fields since the Middle Ages to house the pigeons which formed a valuable part of the rural economy, providing food and fertilizer. The tourist office in Lavaur has a map with directions to all of the dovecotes (many are private and hardly visible from the road) as well as some explanatory text. If you don't want to do the whole circuit, which leads about 10km east before looping back, you'll pass a good number of dovecotes by taking the small riverside road from Lavaur towards St-Paul (follow signs for "Flamarens"). There are also plenty to see right along the main D112 highway which runs between Lavaur and Castres, in addition to half a dozen in Lavaur itself.

Ten kilometres after the river road and the main road meet you'll come to a bridge over the Agout, abutted on the south side by **ST-PAUL-CAP-DE-JOUX** and on the north by **DAMIETTE**. These two sleepy little towns

△ *Colombier* near Lavaur

don't hold any attractions themselves but are the closest places to the castles of Magrin and Roquevidal to the southwest, and make a possible meal stop if you are cutting south by car through the *pays de Cocagne* towards Revel and the Canal du Midi. St-Paul has a small **tourist office** in avenue de Strasbourg (mid-June to mid-Sept Mon–Sat 10am–noon & 2–6pm; mid-Sept to mid-June Tues 10am–12.30pm & 4.30–6.30pm; ☎05.63.70.52.10), which can give you information for the whole of the valley downstream of Castres. Unfortunately, the old *Hotel Central*, on rue Jeanne d'Arc opposite the church, no longer rents rooms, but you can still get a light meal here (*menu* €12), and there is a well-equipped **gîte** (☎05.63.70.66.03; ❸) at En Nassalit, 4km from town. Damiette has a **gare SNCF** on the Toulouse–Revel line and a **campsite** (mid-June to mid-Sept; ☎05.63.70.66.07, ✉bernard.belin@wanadoo.fr).

If you have your own transport, head ten kilometres down the twisting D40 road from St-Paul and you'll come to the **Château-Musée de Magrin** (mid-July to Aug daily 10.30am–noon & guided tours in French 3–6pm; late-Sept to June Sun guided tours 3–6pm; €6.50). Largely ruined, this castle dates to before the Albigensian Crusade, although most of what survives is from the Renaissance. Included in the visit is a museum of woad, set in the castle's old dye works, featuring displays, reconstructions and models illustrating the techniques of *pastel* manufacture. A few more kilometres to the west you'll find the **Château de Roquevidal** (Aug Sun 3–7pm; €4), a square thirteenth-century keep remodelled as a manor house in the late fourteenth century. Its collection of antique furniture and knick-knacks, complemented by old typewriters and printing presses, is anything but exceptional, but makes for a pleasant stop if you happen to be driving through.

South from St-Paul towards Revel there's little to detain you. The old town of **Puylaurens**, once a centre of local Huguenot learning, is not worth stopping in – continue, instead, on the N126 towards Toulouse, that passes near **Loubens-Lauragais**, dominated by its old seigniorial **castle** (2.30–6.30pm: May, June & Sept to mid-Nov Sun & hols; July first & last Sun; Aug Thurs–Sun; €5). Most of the present structure dates from the sixteenth century, and the setting is idyllic, with stately white geese lolling in the pond by its gate. Inside, you'll find a collection of antique furniture (including some good Aubusson tapestries) amassed by the family that has lived here for 22 generations.

Revel and around

Situated at the westernmost point of the long **Montagne Noire** massif, **REVEL** is a tiny but busy district capital, which serves as a regional bus hub – this is where you catch the bus to Sorèze and Dourgne – and a good base for exploring the surrounding area. It was founded as a *bastide* in 1342 by Philip IV, and the deliberate plan of the town is reflected in its octagonal layout and regular streets; indeed, Revel's original charter prescribed a uniformity which even regulated the size of the houses which could be built. Today, it is still dominated by the immense market which covers the entirety of the town's central square. The market was built soon after the town was founded, its rows of stout pillars supporting a single-gabled roof, converging at a stone-constructed tower. Revel was the principal market town for the farmland of the region before becoming a centre for furniture manufacture in the nineteenth century, taking advantage of the wooded slopes of the Montagne Noire to its east. There's nothing much to see or do here, but if you are changing buses or hiking out of the hills it is a good place to spend a comfortable night and get your laundry done. At any rate, you should take a walk around the compact old town and look at the many medieval houses which remain. Local workshops still turn out exceptionally crafted wooden furniture, and if you are interested in how it used to be done check out **Sylvéa**, the "Woodworkers Conservatory", at 13 rue Jean Moulin (Nov–April Tues–Sat 2–6pm; May–Oct Mon–Fri 10am–noon & 2–6pm, Sat & Sun 2–6pm; €4.50) on the northeast corner of the main square. Here you can see a collection of old tools, watch furniture being made according to traditional techniques and, naturally, make a purchase.

Practicalities

Buses passing through **Revel** stop on the place de la République, on the main road just north of the town's covered market, where there is a small SNCF bus ticket office (Tues–Fri 9am–noon & 1.30–6.30pm, Sat 9am–noon; ☎05.61.83.53.73). The **tourist office** (July–Aug Mon–Fri 9am–6.30pm, Sat 9am–7pm, Sun 10am–12.30pm & 3–6pm; Sept–June Mon–Sat 9.30am–12.30/1pm & 2.30/3–6.30pm & Sun 10am–12.30pm & 3–6pm; closed Sun in Jan; ☎05.34.66.67.68, ⓦwww.revel-lauragais.com), located in the tower in the market's centre, can give you information about neighbouring towns too (including Sorèze and Dourgne).

The best of the **hotels** here is the *Auberge du Midi*, set in a refined old nineteenth-century mansion at 34 boulevard Gambetta, just north of the market (closed late-Nov to early Dec; ☎05.61.83.50.50, ⓦwww.logis-de-france .fr; ❷). Close by, at 7 rue de Taur, the *Commanderie Hôtel* (☎05.34.66.11.24; closed part Feb, part June, part Sept; ❸) is a good second choice, with an old timber-framed facade and a remodelled interior. The municipal **campsite** is walking distance from the main square (mid-June to Aug; ☎05.61.83.32.47). For **eating**, the *Auberge* also has the town's best restaurant choice (*menus* from €19–45; closed Sun eve and Mon noon) and there are a number of places on the market square to get a drink or a light meal, including *Le Progrès*, with a daily €11 *menu*, and the *Café des Arcades*, for sandwiches and drinks. Across the square, the old *Hôtel du Centre* no longer offers accommodation, but still has an atmospheric **bar**. For a chance to see the old covered *halles* in use, try to catch the Saturday morning **market**.

Lac de St-Ferrol

Three kilometres southwest of Revel is **Lac de St-Ferreol**, an artificial reservoir created in 1672 with the completion of a massive 780-metre-long dam. This was part of the incredible Canal du Midi project (see p.108), and took some seven-thousand workers five years of hard labour to construct. It was here that run-off from the Montagne Noire was collected to feed the canal, flowing down the Rigole de Canal du Midi to Naurouze, some 25km to the southwest. Nowadays it is a popular weekend spot: the woods make for easy walking, and you can **swim** or **sail** on the lake. A variant of the **hiking** trail GR7 swings by the reservoir, linking up with the G653 west at the Rigole, and passing close to Castelnaudary to the south.

Lac de St-Ferréol has a profusion of **hotels** and **campsites**, most of them clustered along the northwest corner, where the road from Revel meets the lake. Two of the better places to stay are the *Hôtellerie du Lac* – turn right coming from Revel – (☎05.62.18.70.80, ⓦwww.hotellerie-du-lac.com; ❹; closed late-Dec to early Jan), which also has suites with kitchenettes, and *La Renaissance* (closed mid-Dec to mid-March; ☎05.61.83.51.50, ⓦwww.hotellarenaissance .fr; English spoken; ❸), right at the main intersection. The *Hôtellerie* also has a decent **restaurant** (*menus* from €12). The campsites around the lake tend towards the deluxe multi-facility type, with the closest to the water being *En Salvan* (April–Oct; ☎05.61.83.55.95). You can rent **bikes** and **sailboats** through Le Bivouac (☎05.61.27.53.94), in rue des 4 Vents, behind the *Hôtellerie*.

St-Félix-Lauragais

Seven kilometres west of Revel, on the road back to Toulouse, the tiny picturesque hill-top hamlet of **St-Félix-Lauragais** – birthplace of the composer Déodat-de-Séverac (1872–1921) – dominates the flatlands stretching west towards the capital of Midi-Pyrénées. Nothing remains of the time when the town was a meeting place for Cathar clergy, but it does retain a fine wooden **market** with a small stone tower, a curious Gothic-style **church** tucked away amongst the buildings of the main street and a profusion of timber-frame houses.

The excellent **hotel-restaurant** ⚜ *Auberge du Poids Public* (closed Jan & part Nov; ☎05.62.18.85.00, ⓦwww.auberge-du-poidspublic.com; ❹) is reason enough to stay in St-Félix. Located in a large old house beside the town's public weighbridge, the hotel has been restored and decorated in warm luxury, while the restaurant is widely praised for its regional gastronomic creations – try the rabbit and pigeon dishes (*menus* €24–58) – served up with fine Gaillac vintages; you'll need to book ahead if you plan to stay or eat.

Sorèze and Dourgne

Taking the D85, the scenic route from Revel to Castres, you'll pass through two small villages, which, with few attractions themselves, are worthy of a visit only if you happen to be driving, walking or biking through, or if you wish to use them as bases for exploring the western reaches of the Montagne Noire. This is cattle-grazing land, an idyllic expanse of rolling green pasture with the wooded ridge of the mountains rising up sharply along the south side of the road. Narrow forest roads (the D45 from Sorèze and the D12 from Dourgne) twist and turn up into the hills, converging in the shadow of Mount Alric (813m) before arriving at Arfons (see p.206).

SORÈZE, just 6km east of Revel, is an ancient town which grew around a monastery founded in 754 by Pepin the Short, forerunner of Charlemagne. The only remaining vestige of the once huge religious complex is the curious octagonal **bell tower**, dating from the fifteenth century and located near to where the mountain road winds out of town. The other sight worth a stop is the old Dominican **convent-school**, which was converted into a military academy in the eighteenth century. The nineteenth-century Latin American hero Simón Bolívar is its most famous *alumnus*. An unremarkable hour-long guided tour takes visitors through the building (daily 10am–noon & 2–5.30/6pm; €5). The convent is also home to a luxurious **hotel-restaurant**, the ⚜ *Abbaye-École* (☎05.63.74.44.80, ⓦwww.hotelfp-soreze.com; ❸) with great old timber-beamed rooms: the restaurant has *menus* from €34. Less luxurious accommodation can be found at the B&B, *Le Moulin du Chapître* (☎05.63.74.18.18, Ⓔmoulin.chapitre@libertysurf.fr; ❸; English spoken) on the outskirts of town, or at the **campsite**, *St-Martin* (mid-June to mid-Sept; ☎ & Ⓕ05.63.73.28.99). The town's **tourist office** (daily 10am–noon & 2–5.30/6pm; ☎05.63.74.16.28, ⓦwww.ville-soreze.com) is off the main square, in rue Saint-Martin, though more up-to-date information on the Parc Naturel de Haut Languedoc, which begins in the hills above the town, can be found at the former Maison du Parc, on the main road at the west end of town, which now houses the **municipal museum** (July & Aug Wed–Mon 2–6.30pm; Sept–June Sat, Sun & hols 2–6pm; €2). You can **eat** or get a **drink** at the *Pub St-Martin*, in a restored rustic stable building in the old town centre, at 4 rue St-Martin (☎05.63.74.18.71). There is a lively country market on Friday mornings.

Just a few kilometres beyond Sorèze lies the even smaller village of **DOURGNE**, still marked on the east side by the crumbling walls of an ancient abbey. Today the town's monastic tradition is as alive as ever, revived in the nineteenth century with the founding of two Benedictine communities just up the road at **En Calcat**. The larger of the two is the **Monastère de St-Benoît**, which you can visit to sit in on any of the five daily services and hear a chanted Mass; the smaller convent of **Ste-Scholastique** is the home of nuns who pass the time in devotion and weaving. Although the town is quite pretty, with its old streets and arcaded houses, the only other sight is a rather unexceptional sixteenth-century church. The **tourist office** (Tues–Sat 8.30am–12.30pm & 1.30–6.30pm; ℡05.63.74.27.19, ⓦwww.paysdedourgne-tourisme.com) is in the centre of the village, on place Jean-Bugies. If you are hungry, stop in at the **hotel-restaurant** *Hôtellerie de la Montagne Noire*, 15 place des Promenades (closed part Feb, part Sept & part Nov; ℡05.63.50.31.12, ⓦwww.logis-de -france.fr; ❸), which serves up hearty *terroir*-inspired food (*menus* €12.50–31; closed Sun eve & Mon). Alternatively, there are two fine **chambres d'hôtes**: Rose Pauthe (℡05.63.50.31.30; ❷), and the bucolic *Domaine de Béthanie* (℡05.63.50.15.92, ⓔbethanie@tiscali.fr; ❷), as well as a tiny one-star municipal **campsite** (mid-June to mid-Sept; ℡05.63.50.31.20).

Castelnaudary

The biggest stop on the Canal du Midi between Carcassonne and Toulouse, **CASTELNAUDARY** holds the joint honours of being the legendary birth-place of that most Occitan of dishes, cassoulet, and the capital of the Lauragais region, the flat grain-producing hinterland of Toulouse. With its wide **Grand Bassin**, or reservoir, the town is the major pleasure port on the Canal, and a great place to start a waterborne trip towards the Mediterranean. Like the surrounding region, Castelnaudary's past is intimately linked with Cathar history – the town endured no fewer than three sieges during the Albigensian campaigns, and was also the birthplace of Pierre de Castelnau, the papal legate whose murder prompted Pope Innocent III to proclaim the Crusade. When the Inquisition arrived here in 1235, the grey-robed Dominicans' efforts to root out heretics were thwarted by the solidarity of the townsfolk, who refused to implicate their fellows. It was also just outside the town that the last dream of Languedocian independence died, with the capture in 1632 of the rebellious Henri de Montmorency, who was borne away to Toulouse and executed on orders of Cardinal Richelieu.

Arrival, information and accommodation

Trains arrive at Castelnaudary's **gare SNCF** (℡04.68.94.41.55), located on the south side of the Canal du Midi. At the end of the avenue de la Gare, the

---

Cassoulet

One of the great pillars of Southern French *terroir* ("country" or "local") cuisine is the humble **cassoulet**. A simple but tasty baked dish, made up of white beans and garlic cooked with bits of pork and sausage, cassoulet is a staple you'll find just about everywhere between the peaks of the Pyrenees and the banks of the Rhône. Legend has it that the dish originated in Castelnaudary in the mid-fourteenth century, when the Black Prince, Edward, besieged the town during the course of the Hundred Years' War. The defenders, gathering their last provisions, which amounted to some beans and scraps of meat, not only managed to concoct a culinary triumph under extreme duress but, thus fortified, put the English troops (whose own inferior syrupy brown baked-bean diet could not compete) to flight. Today the "original" recipe is safeguarded by the amusingly solemn Confraternity of the Grand Cassoulet, a collective of local chefs who occasionally dress up in distinctive medieval-style robes for culinary events and fairs. You'll have plenty of chances to eat cassoulet in Languedoc and Roussillon, but be warned, local wisdom (and common sense) says that it is a dish best avoided in the summer.

road running directly from the station, turn right onto avenue Arnaut-Vidal, which will lead you over the river and straight to the place de la République, in the centre of town. The **gare routière**, on the other hand, is on the north side of town, on avenue Frédéric-Mistral. Following this street as it veers right (now called rue du 11 Novembre) also takes you to the central *place*, and the town's **tourist office** (April–June & Sept Mon–Sat 9am–12.30pm & 2–6pm; July & Aug Mon–Sat 9am–1pm & 2–7pm; & Sun 10am–12.30pm & 3–6pm; ☎04.68.23.05.73, ✉ot@ville-castelnaudary.fr). The office can arrange guided tours (in English) of the town and excursions to St-Papoul (€4.50–14). **Bicycles** can be rented at Trigano Cycles (☎04.68.23.09.77), in St-Martin-Lalande, 4km east on the RN113. For **Internet** access, head to the main **post office**, 18 cours de la République.

There are several **hotels** to choose from in town, the best of which is the friendly, canalside *Hôtel du Canal* (☎04.68.94.05.05, ⓦwww.hotelducanal.com; ❸), at 2 avenue Arnaut-Vidal – a comfortable place with all mod cons (including satellite television) and a garage. Second choice is the *Hôtel du Centre et du Lauragais* (closed Jan to mid-Feb; ☎04.68.23.25.95, ⓕ04.68.94.01.66; ❹), a converted nineteenth-century house, centrally located at 31 cours de la République. Other decent options include the three-star *Hôtel de France et Notre-Dame*, at 2 avenue Frédéric-Mistral (☎04.68.23.10.18, ✉hdf@cassoulet.com; ❸), and the simple but welcoming *Grand Hôtel Fourcade* (☎04.68.23.02.08, ✉hotelfourcade@ataraxie.fr; closed Jan; ❷), at 14 rue des Carmes, near the covered market. The municipal **campsite**, *La Giraille* (July to mid-Sept; ☎04.68.23.11.28) can be found west of town, a twenty-minute walk along avenue Georges-Pompidou from the bridge at the foot of cours de la République.

The Town

Although Castelnaudary's main attraction is its canal port (see opposite), there are a number of sights worth seeing in the town itself. The first you are likely to encounter is the **halle aux grains**, the former cereal market. It's a handsome building with a plain but dignified arcaded front on the west side of place de la République, and now houses the tourist office, as well as hosting occasional theatre and dance productions. Heading uphill from the *halles* along allée du Cassieu you can follow the main road west to the thirteenth-century **church of St-François**, inside which you'll find a well-crafted statue of the Virgin and Child, dating from the same period. Another 800m further on (turn up towards the cemetery on the impasse Claude-Chappe), is the curious **Tour Chappe**. This tower was once part of the immense semaphore network which covered much of France. Napoleon used the system extensively, and on a clear day messages could be passed from Strasbourg to Paris in just over three hours, using over 180 of these signal stations. The network was a huge success, until the introduction of the electric telegraph in 1859 rendered it obsolete.

Alternatively, continue straight uphill from the *halles* to rue du Château; this will take you to the old **Moulin de Cugarel** (mid-July to Aug Mon–Sat 10am–12.30pm & 2.30–6pm, Sun 2.30–6pm; rest of year by reservation at the tourist office; €1), the last of the town's wind-powered grain mills. With the building of the Canal du Midi, farmers suddenly had access to markets as far afield as Toulouse and the Mediterranean, and so 32 mills were built to process the wheat which they brought to be sold. The *moulin* is an attractive stone structure; its superb grinding mechanism was fully restored in 1962. Below the mill the heart of the old town makes a rough trapezoid, marked off by place de Verdun and rue Goufferand on the east and west sides, and Grande Rue and rue de Dunkerque on the north and south. **Place de Verdun** was the medieval town's main square. Ringed by handsome mansion facades, including that of the Hôtel Dupuy on its north side, the *place* is home to the town's main covered *halles*, as well as the site of the colourful Monday market originally instituted on June 1268 by order of Alphonse de Poitiers, Count of Toulouse, who wanted to spark the town's economy. Following Grande Rue from the market-place will lead you past two more attractive seventeenth-century **mansions**, the Hôtel de Laudun-Courtiade at no. 26, and the Hôtel Latapie, on the corner of rue de la Terrasse. Turning the corner you'll soon reach the southern-Gothic-style collegiate **church of St-Michel**, built in the fourteenth century. Its exterior is notable for its beautiful steeple, towering 55m above the neighbouring place de St-Just, as well as two fine doorways on the north side, but the interior, clinically white, has little to recommend it. Rue du College, which continues from St-Michel, leads into place Auriol, at the far end of which you can ascend to the **Présidial**. This sombre stone building was raised on the site of the town's castle in 1585, when Henri III made the town capital of the Lauragais. First serving as a courthouse and later a prison, it now holds a rather dull **museum of pottery** (July & Aug Mon–Sat 10am–12.30pm & 2.30–6pm, Sun 2.30–6pm; Sept–June by reservation at the tourist office; €2.50).

Finally, there are two more points of interest in the old town, both along rue de l'Hôpital, north of place Auriol. The first of these is the chapel of **Notre-Dame-de-Pitié**, founded in the eleventh century and a popular stop on the medieval pilgrimage route to Santiago de Compostela. The dazzling interior of the chapel, which was reworked in the sixteenth century (and which you can peek at through the grills), contains a feast of gilt wooden low-relief panels depicting angels and biblical scenes in the most outrageously flamboyant Baroque style. Castelnaudary's best restaurant, *Le Tirou* (see below) is just a short walk beyond.

The Grand Bassin

Castelnaudary's biggest draw is the section of the **Canal du Midi** which runs through the town and is punctuated by the broad **Grand Bassin**. This roughly oblong pool, some seven hectares in area, is the largest reservoir along the length of the navigable canal. Constructed as a port, where barges could turn around, get repaired and load up with the grain harvested in the Lauragais, it now serves as a **pleasure port** and point of embarkation for tours and trips along the inland waterways of the Midi and Languedoc. To the west, the Grand Bassin empties into the Petit Bassin, marked by the two road bridges over the canal, before narrowing to wind its way towards Toulouse. On the east side, a remarkable series of six locks, the **Écluse de St-Roch** lowers barges and boats bound for the Mediterranean. If you want to rent a boat for a few hours or a few weeks, take a tour or simply take in the variety of modern and historical craft which you can find on the canal, this is the place to do it (see Canal du Midi "Practicalities" on p.109).

Eating and drinking

There is no shortage of **restaurants** where you can sample cassoulet and other *terroir* treats. The best, and most expensive, is undoubtedly ✠ *Le Tirou* at 90 av Monseigneur de Langle (℗04.68.94.15.95; closed Wed, Thus & Sun eve, late Dec to late Jan & part June), in an old stone house with a pleasant garden and an excellent *terroir carte* (€16–32). Of the hotel restaurants, the best is the *Centre et Lauragais*, with a traditional Midi dining room (closed Mon–Fri eve; *menus* from €16–30), while *La Belle Époque* (closed Tue eve & Wed; ℗04.68.23.39.72), at 55 rue Général-Dejean, serves a great cassoulet (basic *menu* €10). If you're tired of beans and *foie gras*, there's good quality Chinese and Vietnamese cooking at *Le Dragon*, 22 rue Soumet (closed Wed; ☎04.68.23.33.61), by the market; Italian pizza and seafood at *Le Gondolier*, 10 rue Maréchal-Foch (closed Tues, part April & part Aug; *menus* from €11); and the local kebab joint, *Agadir*, at 9 Grand Rue.

You can also pick up take-away cassoulet and other regional delicacies from the town's well-reputed *traiteurs* and *conservateurs*, artisanal butchers and confectioners. There are a number of them in the old town, including Le Regal, at 30 rue Dunkerque, Escudier, at no. 9, and Au Gourmet Chaurien at 38 cours de la République. The local market is held on Mondays.

Around Castelnaudary

If you happen to be in Castelnaudary on April 30 or at Christmas you can get a glimpse of the closed world of France's notorious **Foreign Legion**, whose base, 2km southeast of town on the D33, opens its doors to the public on these two occasions (the tourist office has details). Another short excursion, 8km east on the D113, is to the **abbey of St-Papoul** (April–June & Sept–Oct daily 10–11.30am & 2–5.30pm; July & Aug daily 10am–6.30pm; Nov–March Sat, Sun & hols 10–11.30am & 2–6.30pm; €3.50, reduction with "Carte Intersite" pass – see p.129), set on the edge of the Lauragais plain. Founded in the eighth century by Pepin the Short, it went on to huge success after 1317 when its abbot was elevated to the status of bishop. The church itself is impressive, with some sections dating back to the twelfth century. The most important feature, however, is the **carved capitals** on the upper rim of the exterior of the apse, which can be viewed without entering, executed by the "Master of Cabestany" (see box below) and depicting Daniel in the lions' den.

Along the Canal du Midi from Toulouse to Carcassonne

The **Canal du Midi** runs a roughly straight path through the wheat-producing lands of the Lauragais, clearing the compact suburbs of Toulouse and steering

---

The Master of Cabestany

The actual name of the **Master of Cabestany** has long been forgotten, but the work of this genius of masonry comprises one of Languedoc's most important medieval legacies. The twelfth-century itinerant sculptor, whose speciality was human figures in high relief, worked as far afield as Tuscany and Catalonia, but the greatest concentration of his works can be found in a wide band of territory stretching from Castelnaudary to the sea. Doorways, cloisters, tombs and tympanums – over 120 works found so far – all bear the distinctive mark of his vivid style. His large-handed, bulbous-eyed portraits are set apart not so much by their realism, but by the obvious brilliance with which they were executed, which seems to endow the mute stone figures with a life and soul of their own. The most dramatic example of his work can be found at St-Hilaire (see p.129), while others survive at Cabestany (p.354), Lagrasse (see p.317), Rieux-Minervois (see p.320), Passa (p.373), St-Papoul (see above) and Le Boulou (see p.373). Several works have been identified just over the border in Catalonia, including at the magnificent monastery of San Pere de Rodes (only 25min by car from Le Boulou) and one piece now resides in the Cloisters collection of the Metropolitan Museum of Art in New York. A museum and resource centre dedicated to this rediscovered master and to the history of Romanesque sculpture has been opened in Cabestany, outside Perpignan (see p.355).

its tree-lined course east, parallel to the Hers River, towards its highest point, at the Seuil (or "threshold") de Naurouze. From here it descends to the basin at Castelnaudary, as the Montagne Noire, the source of the canal's water, comes into view to the north. From the Grand Bassin, the waterway cuts eastwards across the plain, bridging the 32km to **Carcassonne**, where it begins to adapt to the contours of the Aude valley, and start in earnest its descent towards the sea (see Chapter 6). The towns along the route are not especially notable, but afford you a glimpse of rural France at its most antiquated and peaceful.

The first town of any size which you'll pass is the old *bastide* of **Montgiscard**, some 10km from the port of Toulouse. There's not much to see here, but if you are tempted to stop, take a look at the medieval church, part of which was remodelled by the same architect who designed Toulouse's Hôtel d'Assézat. Next along you'll come to **Ayguesvives** and **Montesquieu-Lauragais**, both of which have impressive nineteenth-century *châteaux*. Eighteen kilometres from Toulouse you'll reach the **écluse de Négra**, which is where you leave the canal to reach **Villefranche**, and was once the first post-stop on the way to Agde – several of the old canal-side buildings survive. Just to the east, **Avignonet-Lauragais** was once a wealthy woad town, and is notable for being the place where, in 1242, the Cathars, holed up in Montségur, launched an attack on and massacred a contingent of the Dominican Inquisition; the resulting counterattack brought about the destruction of Montségur castle and the mass execution of its garrison and population (see p.141). Today the town has a fourteenth-century church with a fine retable dating from 1632. The last stop before you reach Naurouze is the modern **Port-Lauragais**, built specifically for pleasure boating. There's a **restaurant** here, as well as an **information centre** (daily 10am–6pm; ℡05.61.27.14.63) which houses permanent and temporary exhibitions on the building of the canal. **Naurouze**, the highest point on the canal's path, is where the Rigole, or feeder canal, arrives bearing the water gathered on the slopes of the Montagne Noire; it has long been a point of transit, as the vestiges of Roman road here testify. The area around the canal junction has been set up as a **picnic area** and **park** (unfortunately with no toilets), and nearby you'll find a rather sombre monument to the Canal's founder, Pierre-Paul Riquet. Incidentally, this is also the site where Soult signed his surrender to Wellington in 1814. From Naurouze it's another 12km to Castelnaudary (see p.105).

The only place of any interest between Castelnaudary and Carcassonne is **BRAM**, an ancient village where the houses are arranged in tight circles around the church; it dates back to the thirteenth century. Bram's villagers resisted the Albigensian Crusaders in 1210, and when the town eventually fell to the Catholic forces, the inhabitants came to a grisly end. Simon de Montfort ordered a hundred prisoners to be blinded and mutilated; the refugees, carrying their amputated body parts, were then sent to the as yet unvanquished fortress of Cabaret, led by the only villager with an eye remaining ungouged.

Practicalities

The head office of Voies Navigables de France is at 2 Port St-Étienne in Toulouse (℡05.61.36.24.24, ⓦwww.vnf.fr), with English-speaking port offices at Carcassonne (℡06.84.81.96.20), Castelnaudary (℡06.84.81.96.23) and Port St-Saveur (℡06.84.81.96.21). There's also a small **tourist office** at Villefranche, in place Général-de-Gaulle (℡04.61.27.20.94). For port information and administration in Toulouse contact La Capitannerie, 7 Port Saint-Saveur (℡05.61.14.17.25, ⓔinfos@toulouse-croisieres.com) and for general information as well as accommodation, sights and activities see ⓦwww.canaldumidi.com.

The Canal du Midi

The **Canal du Midi** runs for some 240km from the River Garonne at Toulouse, via Castelnaudary, Carcassonne and Béziers, to the Mediterranean at Agde or Sète, and via its subsidiary, the **Canal de la Robine**, to Narbonne, entering the sea at Gruissan. The waterway was the brainchild of Pierre-Paul Riquet, a minor noble and the holder of the lucrative salt-tax concession for Languedoc (the *gabelle* – a tax levied on the sale of salt – was one of the royal treasury's most lucrative sources of income). Riquet succeeded in firing the imagination of Louis XIV (and more importantly, his first minister, Colbert) with the idea of linking the Atlantic and the Mediterranean via the Garonne (in reality the connection wasn't actually to happen until long after the principal stretch had been finished).

The main canal, begun in 1667, took fourteen years to complete using tens of thousands of workers. At the start, an engineering problem automatically presented itself: how to feed the canal with water when the Mediterranean was obviously at sea level, the Garonne at 132m above sea level, and, in the middle, the Col (or Seuil) de Naurouze at 201m. Riquet's solution was to build a system of dams and reservoirs at St-Ferréol, Lampy and on the Alzeau in the Montagne Noire, channelling run-off water from the heights down to Naurouze. He spent the whole of his fortune on the canal (sacrificing even his daughters' dowries) and, sadly, died just six months before its inauguration in 1681. But the waterway, built to accommodate barges of up to 30m in length, was a success and sparked a wave of prosperity along its course, thanks to the access it provided local farmers, manufacturers and raw material industries to foreign markets (via the Mediterranean). Traffic increased steadily until 1856, when it carried 111,000 metric tonnes of material as well as one million passengers, and the official link-up to the Garonne and the Atlantic opened. The next year the Sète–Bordeaux railway opened, and rail transport being faster and more cost-effective, traffic on the canal dropped to all but nothing almost immediately.

In the last ten years or so, however, the canal has been revived as a course for pleasure craft, and it's not difficult to see why. It remains a marvel of engineering and beauty, incorporating no fewer than 99 locks (*écluses*) and 130 bridges. The various topographical challenges were met with imagination, including the construction of canal **tunnels** and **bridges**, the latter allowing water to cross valleys and gullies, suspended in the air. No less beautiful are the stone foot and road bridges, most of which date back to the first era of construction. The graceful oval **lock-basins**, built in that shape for more strength, are guarded by uniform *maisons d'éclusier*, where the controls of the mechanism are housed; and, as along any major route, inns and restaurants punctuate the canal's course. Even the double file of plane trees which lines most of the waterway's length, giving it a distinctive "Midi" look, serves a technical as well as an aesthetic purpose: to shade the water and impede its loss through evaporation.

Unsurprisingly, the canal was designated a UNESCO World Heritage Site in 1996, ensuring its conservation. You can follow it by road, and most sections have foot or bicycle paths, but the best way to travel it (and an ideal way to spend a family

For **boat rental** in Toulouse contact Navicanal, 139 rue Bonnat (℡05.61.55.10.91, ⊛www.navicanal.com). In Castelnaudary the biggest boat rental company is Crown Blue Line, Le Grand Bassin, Castelnaudary (℡04.68.94.52.72, ⊛www.crownblueline.com), whose fleet consists mostly of modern craft, so if you are hoping for a more authentic-looking barge, you may have to shop around and book well ahead; another option is Connoisseur (℡04.68.94.09.75, ℮info@connoisseur.fr). At Carcassonne you can rent from Nautic (℡04.68.71.88.95, ⊛www.nautique.fr), while Locaboat (℡03.86.91.72.72, ⊛www.locaboat.com) rents out *pénichettes* (traditional canal or group holiday) is, of course, **by boat**. It's a gentle, restful chug down a tunnel of greenery enhanced in spring by the bloom of yellow iris and wild gladioli, with occasional glimpses of a world beyond: a distant smudge of hills or the pinnacles of Carcassonne. There are outfits in all of the major ports which **rent houseboats and barges** – most of which will also rent **bikes** as an extra, perfect for exploring the sights along the waterway. Or, if you prefer to be driven rather than drive, there are many cruises too. The canal is navigable from March to November, but the high season of July and August is best avoided – boat availability declines, prices rise and the canal gets quite crowded. Finally, if you don't want to commit the time and money to rent a houseboat, most ports also rent smaller **electric boats**, suitable for one to six people by the hour (usually €20) or half-day (around €50). Navigation itself is straightforward (quite literally) and an orientation session by the boat rental company is all you need to get you on your way – no licence is required. Generally, **locks** are open from 8am to 12.30pm and 1.30pm to 7.30pm: they open daily from mid-March to early-November, and Monday to Friday from mid-December to mid-March, but close on major holidays. There's no charge for passage, and you can count on about a quarter of an hour for a basin to fill or empty. With a maximum permitted speed of 6km per hour, you should count on being able to travel no more than 250km in a week of cruising. Canal **information** can be found at the port offices of Voies Navigables de France, the government organization in charge of inland waterways – we've given the details of these in the relevant parts of the Guide.

Biking and hiking

The easiest part of the canal's route along which to **bike** or **hike** is the initial – paved – stretch from **Toulouse to the Seuil de Naurouze**, following a path from Port St-Saveur (see p.89). The surrounding farmland, which gradually ascends the further you go, doesn't make for the most spectacular of backdrops, but the canal – its tree-lined placidity interrupted only by the "putt-putt" of passing boats – is beautiful in its own right. The total distance along the paved path is 50km, which can be biked in about five hours and walked in under twenty. If you decide on the latter course of action you need not commit yourself to going the whole way – you can stop at Villefranche-Lauragais at the 30-kilometre-mark to catch a bus back or onwards, or spend the night at *En Jouty* (closed Nov–Feb; ☎05.61.81.57.35; ③), a **chambres d'hôtes** near the centre of Avignonet. From Port-Lauragais, a further 12km from Villefranche, you have the option of continuing the rest of the journey to Naurouze on a boat cruise (see "Practicalities" p.109). The paved path ends at Écluse Océan, shortly after the port, and a gravel towpath (fine for mountain bikes) continues to Carcassonne; should you wish to continue beyond Castelnaudary and on to Bram, there's a *chambres d'hôtes* at *Domaine de Pigne* (☎04.68.11.40.70, @bernard.linepiquet@wanadoo.fr; ③) on the outskirts of the village, and the **hotel** *Clos Saint Loup* at 69 av des Razes, just south of the old *circulade* (closed Dec 24–28; ☎04.68.76.11.91, @www.logis-de-france.fr; ③). You'll find filling local *menus* in the *Clos*'s dining room, ranging from €12–30.

boats), and also has a branch in Montequieu-Lauregais (☎05.61.81.36.40) between Toulouse and Castelnaudary. Castel Nautique (☎04.68.76.73.34, @www.castelnautique.com) in Bram rents out both traditional and electric boats, as well as bicycles. At any of these firms expect to pay between €700 and €1600 per week for a three- to five-person boat.

If you don't feel like navigating yourself, Le St Roch, in Castelnaudary's Grand Bassin (☎04.68.23.49.40, @www.saintroch11.com), organizes canal tours lasting from thirty minutes to two hours (€4–10 per person), while Croisières Cathy (☎06.09.33.15.96, @http://croisières-cathy.chez-alice.fr), also in Castelnaudary, runs half- and full-day programmes with optional on-board meals. Trips must be booked in advance: full-day cruises, which depart at 9am, cost €30 including a meal; non-dining afternoon cruises depart at 2.15pm for €9.50. Additionally, just west of Naurouze at Port-Laugarais, the *Lucie* runs a thirty-minute circuit to the Seuil and back (April–Sept daily; €5), as well as other longer itineraries whenever ten or more passengers assemble.

Travel details

Trains

Toulouse is the rail hub for this region, on the Narbonne-Bordeaux/Paris trunk line with smaller lines going to Albi and Carmaux, and La-Tour-de-Carole, as well as services to Revel and Castres. SNCF buses may run in lieu of trains on some of these lines; services are reduced on Sundays and holidays.

Toulouse to: Albi (8–19 daily; 1hr); Avignonet (1–7 daily; 42min); Ax-les-Thermes (20–24 daily; 1hr 55min); Béziers (12 daily; 45min–1hr 30min); Bram (6–10 daily; 1hr 4min); Carcassonne (6–15 daily; 45min–1hr); Carmaux (10 daily; 1hr 45min); Castelnaudary (6–13 daily; 30min–1hr); Castres (6–8 daily; 1hr 6min); Cordes/Vindrac (4–11 daily; 50min–1hr 12min); Damiette (7–8 daily; 50min); Foix (24–36 daily; 47min to 1hr 12min); Gaillac (10–30 daily; 48min); L'Hospitalet (11–12 daily; 2hr 30min); Latour-de-Carol (7–11 daily; 2hr 30min); Lavaur (6–8 daily; 50min); Lavelanet (Fri & Sun 1 daily; 1hr 55min); Lisle (10–22 daily; 38min); Mazamet (6–8 daily; 1hr 28min–1hr 55min); Montpellier (15–18 daily; 2hr 15min–2hr 55min); Narbonne (7–8 daily; 1hr 18min–1hr 50min); Nîmes (15–18 daily; 2hr 45min–3hr); Pamiers (24–36 daily; 36min–1hr 10min); Paris (30–42; 5hr 25min–7hr 10min); Rabastens (10–22 daily; 29min); St-Gaudens (12 daily; 50min–1hr 15min); St-Sulpice (12–27 daily; 22–30min); Tarascon (20–24 daily; 1hr 20min); and Villefranche (6–13 daily; 18–33min).
Castelnaudary to: Bram (6–13 daily; 10min); Carcassonne (6–19 daily; 20–27min); Narbonne (5–8 daily; 50min); Revel (Mon & Fri 1 daily; 20min); Sorèze (Fri 1 daily; 54min).
Damiette/ St-Paul to: Castres (7–8 daily; 25min).
Lavaur to: Castres (6–8 daily; 32min); St-Sulpice (7–8 daily; 12min).
St-Sulpice to: Albi (7–15 daily; 50min); Castres (6–8 daily; 45min); Gaillac (12–27 daily; 12–26min); Lavaur (6–8 daily; 8min).

Buses

In the Haute-Garonne most lines have no Sunday service; holidays and school holiday periods often have little or no service (see partial schedule of regional lines at ⊛www.cg31.fr/bus.asp).
Toulouse to: Albi (12–16 weekly; 2hr 40min); Avignonet (1–12 daily; 1hr 25min); Ax (1–2 daily; 2hr 11min); Carcassonne (1 daily; 2hr 20min); Castelnaudary (1–12 daily; 1hr 25min); Castres (8–12 weekly; 1hr 40min–2hr); Foix (2–4 daily; 1hr 30min); Gaillac (4 daily; 1hr 25min); Grauhle (8–12 weekly; 1hr 35min); Lavaur (6–8 weekly; 1hr 10min); Lavelanet (1–2 daily; 2hr 30min); Mas d'Azil (2 daily; 1hr 50min); (Mazamet 6–8 weekly; 2hr); Mirepoix (1–2 daily; 2hr); Pamiers (3–5 daily; 1hr– 1hr 30min); Revel (2–6 daily; 1hr 10min); St-Félix-de-Lauragais (1–2 daily; 1hr); St-Girons (3 daily; 2hr 30min); St-Sulpice (2–6 daily; 30min); Sorèze (3 daily; 1hr 20min); Villefranche (1–12 daily; 44min).
Castelnaudary to: Alet-les-Bains (daily; 1hr 5min); Axat (daily; 1hr 50min); Bram (4–6 weekly; 30min); Carcassonne (5 daily; 45min); Fanjeux (0–1 daily; 40min); Limoux (1–2 daily; 1hr); Quillan (2–4 weekly; 1hr 30min); Sorèze (Mon 1 daily; 30min); Villefranche (1–12 daily; 20min).
Lavaur to: Castres (4–6 daily; 45min–1hr); Gaillac (4 daily; 35min); St-Paul (4 daily; 15min); Toulouse (4 daily; 50min).
Revel to: Castres (4 daily; 1hr); St-Félix (3 daily; 20min).
St-Sulpice to: Albi (6–8 weekly; 1hr 5min); Gaillac (6–8 weekly; 50min); Toulouse (2–6 daily; 20min).

Carcassonne,
Upper Aude
and Ariège

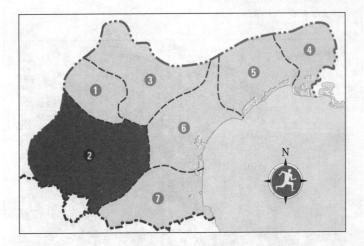

CHAPTER 2 # Highlights

✳ **Carcassonne** Southern France's most visited monument, this reconstructed medieval citadel is a must-see. **See p.117**

✳ **Carnaval** Limoux's famous Lenten festival draws crowds from around the Southwest to see its elaborately costumed dancers. **See p.128**

✳ **Rennes-le-Château** A mecca for occultists and conspiracy theorists following the trail of a nineteenth-century priest. **See p.131**

✳ **Rafting** The Upper Aude and Ariège provide excellent opportunities for a range of skill levels. **See p.135**

✳ **Montségur** The legendary site of the heretic Cathars' last stand. **See p.141**

✳ **Mirepoix** The region's best preserved medieval town features a stunningly carved fourteenth-century town hall now converted into a hotel. **See p.143**

✳ **La Grotte de Niaux** Caves painted by our most remote European ancestors. **See p.158**

△ Limoux Carnaval

Carcassonne, Upper Aude and Ariège

The citadel of **Carcassonne** is quintessential Languedoc: a medieval fortress with the foothills of the Pyrenees rising off to the south, the peaks of the Montagne Noire looming to the north, and the languid waters of the Canal du Midi gliding past towards the Mediterranean. Although it fell to Catholic forces early in the Crusade, Carcassonne was held to be the epicentre of the Cathar heresy in Languedoc: the castles which form a far-flung ring in the Corbières and the Pyrenean slopes to the south were referred to as the heretic capital's "sons". The land fanning southwest of the city rises in a series of ridges and plains, cut through by two rivers. The first, the **Aude**, runs north to Carcassonne, skirting the highlands of the **pays de Sault** on its way down from the mountains; journeying up this valley and into the *pays*, a region littered with narrow gorges and high passes, is like flipping through the pages of Cathar history – from the site of their greatest fortified city to the ruins of their last redoubt, **Montségur**. The second river, flowing down from Andorra to Toulouse, gives its name to the *département* – **Ariège** – constituting the remainder of this chapter. **Foix**, once the thriving capital of a proudly independent county, sits at the centre of the *département*, standing sentinel over the course of the rapid river, after it has twisted through the northern slopes of the Pyrenees past the skiing and hiking country around the spa of **Ax-les-Thermes** and **Tarascon-sur-Ariège**, with its incredible array of **prehistoric caves** – justification alone for a trip to the region. The plain northeast of Foix was the haunt of troubadours and men of religion, be they Cathar *parfaits* (see *The Land of Cathars* Colour Section) or the Inquisitors sent to hunt them. Reduced to a ruin in the Wars of Religion, today its ancient, near-abandoned villages with their arcaded squares and crumbling walls offer the only faded record of the district's rich past. At the southwestern limits of the *département*, the **Couserans**, snowcapped peaks ranged in breathtaking cirques, form a virtually impenetrable barrier to Spain beyond.

Today, the Aude valley – with the exception of ever-popular Carcassonne – and the Ariège *département* are two of the least developed regions in the

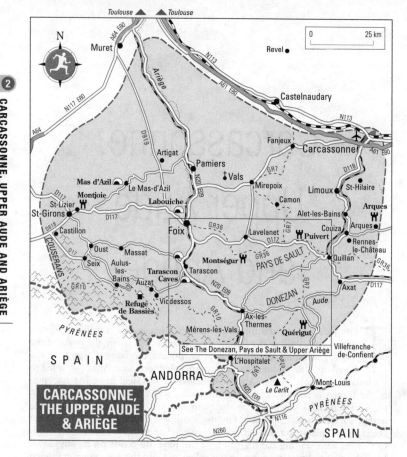

Toulouse ▲ ▲ Toulouse

N

0   25 km

Muret   Revel ●

Castelnaudary

Fanjeux   Carcassonne

Artigat
Pamiers   Vals
Mirepoix   Limoux   St-Hilaire
Mas d'Azil   Le Mas-d'Azil   Camon   Arques
Montjoie   Labouiche   Alet-les-Bains
St-Lizier   Arques ●
St-Girons   Lavelanet   Puivert
Castillon   Foix   Couiza   Rennes-
Oust   Massat   Montségur   PAYS DE SAULT   le-Château
Seix   Aulus-   Tarascon   Quillan
les-   Tarascon
Bains   Caves
Auzat   DONEZAN   Aude   Axat
Refuge   Vicdessos
de Bassiès   Aude
Mérens-lès-Vals   Ax-les-
Thermes   Quérigut
PYRÉNÉES   Villefranche-
See The Donezan, Pays de Sault & Upper Ariège   de-Confient
SPAIN   L'Hospitalet
ANDORRA   Le Carlit   Mont-Louis
                                  PYRÉNÉES
CARCASSONNE,
THE UPPER AUDE   SPAIN
& ARIÈGE

French Southwest. Isolated by difficult terrain, and afflicted for generations by the emigration of youth to the better prospects of the northern cities, there is little economic base here apart from farming and herding. In recent years, tourism has rescued the area from its relentless decline, and to a certain extent, the construction of **ski resorts**, spas and local museums has served to improve the region's prospects. But these recent initiatives, if they have stimulated the local economy, have not detracted from the essential flavour of the area – a refuge of mountain tradition.

As you'd expect, the region is not the best for **public transport**. There's a good rail service running up the Ariège valley, from Toulouse to beyond the Col de Puylaurens (and hooking up with the Tech service of Roussillon), while the other line, from Carcassonne to Quillan, has considerably fewer services. Bus services, even between larger towns, are infrequent: consult the "Travel Details" on p.163, and obtain current local information before planning a route.

Carcassonne

Your first view of **CARCASSONNE**, its fairy-tale citadel perched high above the grassy verges of the River Aude, is likely to be a memorable one. The famous **cité**, declared a UNESCO World Heritage site in 1997, enjoys must-see status on any trip through southwest France, and if it has suffered through the ages – beaten, burnt and dismantled – you'd never guess from looking at it. Aside from the walled town, with its castle and basilica, there's the medieval lower town, or **ville basse**, set on the far side of the Aude. Together, the two complement each other: the first is outstandingly beautiful, while the latter is lively, with a sprinkling of good services. Good transport links by bus, rail, canal and air also make Carcassonne an ideal base for exploring the surrounding areas: the uplands of the Ariège and the Aude covered later in this chapter, and to the north, the ominous Montagne Noire (see p.203).

Carcassonne was settled as far back as the sixth century BC, passing through the hands of Romans and Visigoths before its golden age under the great Languedocian family, the **Trencavels**. This family, which had various holdings in Languedoc, became vassals of the counts of Toulouse (the "St-Gilles" family) in 1163, and used Carcassonne as their principal residence, ensuring the town a prosperous economic base. As a consequence of the Crusade against the Cathar heretics, the town was besieged and taken in 1209, eventually passing to the notorious Simon de Montfort, who made it "**capital**" of the extensive territories he was taking over from local nobility. After the feared warrior died outside the walls of Toulouse in 1218, the Trencavel Raymond-Roger VII briefly recovered the town, only to see it pass to royal control in 1229. Some twenty years later, King Louis IX laid out the *ville basse*, a *bastide* which would serve as a regional market and increase the town's wealth, on the far banks of the river. Carcassonne thus prospered until the **Black Prince** invaded during the course of the Hundred Years' War and, frustrated by his inability to seize the strong citadel, burnt the *ville basse* to the ground in 1355. Despite this setback, the town's citizens rallied and rebuilt the lower town, and for the rest of the Middle Ages Carcassonne enjoyed a healthy economy, profiting handsomely from its location – perfect for a market – on the frontier of the old French kingdom. With the annexation of Roussillon in 1659 all of this changed, the border shifted south, and Carcassonne entered a period of stagnation, during which time the citadel was abandoned and eventually quarried for its stones. This is how it remained until it was rediscovered in the nineteenth century by **Viollet-le-Duc**, whose visionary fifty-year restoration project rescued it from obscurity.

Today Carcassonne continues to flourish largely because of that vision, which brings in thousands of visitors every year. Despite the fact that the citadel is the only sight as such, and there is essentially very little to do here, it is nevertheless a great place to spend a relaxing few days. Additionally, the *cité* has become something of a symbol of medieval France; its yearly **pageants** and spectacular Bastille Day celebrations (see box, p.118), featuring the second largest fireworks display in France, keep the streets full of both French and foreign tourists.

Arrival and information

Carcassonne's **airport** is just west of town; there's a bank with exchange services, several shops and car rental offices in the arrivals hall. A shuttle bus (*navette*; hourly; 15min; €5) leaves from outside the terminal and stops in town at the gare SNCF, place Gambetta and the *cité*; a **taxi** to the centre

July and August are the best months for **festivals** in Ariège. The lively *fêtes locales* invariably feature live music and dancing, and are a good opportunity to pick up country produce; several have colourful (if not always accurate) medieval re-enactments. The biggest festival is Carcassonne's Bastille Day, but bear in mind that the town gets packed out for the event, with parked cars lining the route nationale for several kilometres from the *cité*. Limoux's Carnaval is also a unique event, worth planning for if you're in the area.

Mid-Jan to Easter Limoux: *Carnaval*. An extended Lenten celebration featuring vividly costumed dancers in the old town squares. Three sets of performances (11am, 4pm & 10pm) on Saturdays and Sundays.

May–June St-Lizier & the villages of the Couserans: *Festival d'Art Sacré* ☏05.61.96.77.77. A two-week celebration of religious artistic expression coinciding with the Ascension, with a heavy emphasis on the medieval. Concerts ranging from Gregorian chant to choral music are performed in the cathedral and in the village parishes, alongside art exhibitions and performances of dramatic works.

June Couserans: *Transhumances en Couserans* ⓦwww.transhcouserans.free.fr. In a revival of the ancient tradition, 4000 sheep are driven up the valleys of the Couserans into the high pasture lands. Each village they pass through celebrates with markets, displays of folk traditions and general festivities.

19–23 June Saint-Girons: *Sent Joan Beth e Gran* ☏05.61.04.65.53, ⓦwww.ville-st -girons.fr. Celebration of Saint John's day culminating in the traditional bonfire: four days of folk concerts and dances feature groups of the Couserans as well as foreign troupes.

Throughout July Carcassonne: *Festival de Carcassonne de la Cité & Festival de la Bastide* ☏04.68.25.33.16. Month-long festival of dance, music and theatre with nightly performances in the castle's amphitheatre and free performances in the squares of the cité. The highpoint is the Bastille Day (July 14) celebration, which culminates in a giant fireworks display.

First two weeks of July Tarascon: *Résistances* ⓦwww.capmedia.fr/resistances. Festival of new, cutting-edge film, with a predominantly French programme.

Second weekend of July Seix: *Fête de la Transhumance* ⓦwww.ville-st-girons.fr. Three-day celebration timed for the traditional passing of the sheep flocks. Market with traditional products and crafts and various events.

Mid-July Pamiers: *Fiesta* ☏05.61.67.52.52, ⓦwww.pamierstourisme.com/fiesta. Five days of Spanish and Latin American dance and music with a strong accent on flamenco.

Mid-July Foix: *Résistances* ☏05.61.05.13.30, ⓔrésistances@wanadoo.fr. Annual film festival of national stature. Each year a different theme and over a hundred screenings in ten days.

Third weekend of July Mirepoix: *Les Médiévales de Mirepoix* ☏05.61.68.83.76. Medieval horsemanship, pageantry, market and fair in the arcaded squares around the cathedral.

Late July Limoux: *Festival du Folklore*. Five-day international festival featuring traditional storytelling, theatre, dance and music.

Late July Quillan: *Festival du Folklore International*. Held over six days, this international festival features storytelling and theatre with an impressive repertoire of groups from as far afield as East Asia and South America.

Late July Ax-les-Thermes: *Spectacles de Grands Chemins* ☏05.61.64.38.00, ⓦwww.ax-animation.com. A three-day festival of street theatre celebrating local *montagnard* culture and featuring over twenty French companies.

Late July Foix: *Jazz à Foix* ☎ 05.61.01.18.30, ⊛ www.jazzfoix.com. Five nights of jazz, swing and blues featuring a predominantly French and American programme.

Late July Tarascon: *Tarascon-Latino* ☎ 05.34.09.88.87, ⊛ www.tarascon-latino.com. Eight days of music, dance and food from Central and South America.

Late July to mid-Aug St-Lizier: *Festival de Saint-Lizier* ☎ 05.61.66.67.89, ⊛ www.austriar.chez.tiscali.fr. Long-running three-week music festival with an impressively varied programme, ranging from the Baroque to Prokofiev and Stravinsky.

Late July to late Aug Foix: *Si L'Ariège M'Était Contée... Il était une Foix... L'Ariège* ☎ 05.61.65.03.03, ⊛ www.foixterredhistoire.fr. Massive outdoor exhibition glorifying Foix's medieval past, culminating in a fireworks display. Nightly at 10pm, ticket required.

Early Aug Mirepoix: *Festival de la Marionette* ☎ 05.61.68.20.72, ⊛ www.filentrope.free.fr. Three-day festival of puppetry along with a large craft and produce market.

First week of Aug St-Girons: *Rite* ☎ 06.07.32.77.58, ⊛ www.bethmalais.org. Ten-day festival of traditional culture, including music, song and dance, and featuring over two hundred performers drawn from countries as diverse as Mongolia and Angola.

First weekend of Aug St-Girons: *Autrefois le Couserans* ⊛ www.ville-stgirons.fr. Two days celebrating the region's rural traditions, including performances, a market and horse and donkey races.

Mid-Aug St-Girons: *Festival de Théâtre* ☎ 05.61.96.85.66. French-language theatre festival featuring a programme ranging from the classical (such as Molière) to puppetry.

Mid-Aug Carcassonne: *Spectacle Médiéval* ☎ 04.68.71.35.35, ⊛ www.terredhistoire.com. Medieval costumes and pageantry and a theatrical re-enactment with a different theme each year.

First two weeks of Aug St-Lizier: *Festival de Musique* ☎ 05.61.96.67.89. Nightly classical concerts, ranging from Mozart to Paganini to classical guitar works, performed in the cathedral by international artists. The *fête locale*, including markets, music and a weekend-long Gallo-Roman festival, is also held at this time.

First two weeks of Aug Limoux: *Vigne et Terroir* ☎ 05.61.96.67.89. A celebration of local culinary traditions, with concerts, street performances and good food and drink in abundance.

Last weekend of Aug Carcassonne: *Fiesta y Toros*. A weekend of taurine events including bullfights and *abrivados*, equestrian displays, and a Spanish-style street party (bullfights €30; ☎ 04.68.71.01.00).

First two weeks of Sept Foix: *Fêtes de Foix*. An annual festival, with produce markets, music and a medieval theme, centred on the illustrious figure of Gaston Fébus.

Mid-Sept Mirepoix: *Grande Fête de St-Maurice*. Held over four days, a lively festival with market and some costumed events.

Sept 21 Vicdessos: *St-Matthieu*. Transhumant livestock fair, formalized by the Count de Foix in 1313. Nowadays, the tradition continues with a lively market and celebration.

Early Oct Couserans: *Transhumances en Couserans* ⊛ www.transhcouserans.free.fr. Fattened on the rich mountain grasses in summer, massive flocks of sheep are driven back down to the shelter of the valleys, an occasion for celebration in the villages through which they pass (see June, above).

Late Oct/Early Nov Lavelanet: *Jazz'velanet* ☎ 05.61.01.22.20, ⊛ www.jazz-velanet.com. Eclectic four-day programme of jazz featuring acts from around the world.

Dec 17 to Sunday before Christmas Carcassonne: *Marché au Gras*. Lively Christmas market featuring produce and regional crafts.

costs €8–15. The **gare SNCF** (T08.36.35.35.35) is on the north side of the *ville basse*, just over the Canal du Midi from boulevard Omer Sarraut. From the station you can catch the *navette*, or simply follow the ring road around to place Gambetta and the main **tourist office** at 15 boulevard Camille Pelletan (July & Aug daily 9am–7pm; Sept–June Mon–Sat 9am–6pm & Sun 9am–noon; T04.68.10.24.30, F04.68.10.24.38, Wwww.carcassonne-tourisme .com); there's a second tourist office (daily: June & Sept 9am–6pm; July & Aug 9am–7pm; Oct–May 9am–5pm; T04.68.10.24.36) in the *cité*, just inside the main entrance. Both branches sell the handy *Rando-Guide* (€1), outlining six walks and hikes in the Carcassonne area. Finally, there is a canal-side information office (daily: April–June, Sept & Oct noon–6pm; July & Aug 9am–6pm) at the town's port. The town has no *gare routière* as such; **buses** arrive along the broad boulevard de Varsovie on the west side of the *ville basse*, a ten-minute walk from the tourist office. If you're arriving **by car**, there's a car park up by the *cité* (€3.50–4.50), but there are cheaper options ringing the *ville basse*, as well as free and metered street parking.

Place Gambetta is the **local transport** hub; all city buses and *navettes* (€1.10) leave from here – a *navette* to the *cité* (€1.50 return) and campsite departs from near the Caisse d'Épargne bank (mid-July to mid-Sept 7am–10.30pm; every 15min). Local transport information, including maps, can be picked up at the tourist offices, or you can contact Carcassonne's urban transport company (T04.68.47.82.22). For **bikes** and **motorbikes**, see p.127.

Accommodation

Although your first impulse may be to get a room in the *cité*, beware that if you are hoping to pass the evenings in a medieval idyll you will most likely be disappointed. There is little **accommodation** here and it is expensive; furthermore, the citadel is very busy – verging on lunacy in high season. You may be more satisfied with a room along the slopes down towards the riverbank, or in the *ville basse* (from where you get the view of the *cité*). Be warned, also, that Bastille Day (July 14) is very big here; hotels book up a year in advance and traffic jams clog

The Legend of Dame Carcas

The origin of Carcassonne's strange-sounding name has given rise to a number of interesting stories, the most enduring and popular of which is that of Dame Carcas. Legend asserts that when the town was under Muslim control in the early Middle Ages, the Emperor Charlemagne arrived to lay siege, knowing that if his army attacked for long enough, eventually the town would run short of food. However, just when defeat looked inevitable, Carcas, the Muslim ruler's wife, ordered a pig to be force-fed with the last of the town's precious grain and tossed over the battlements. When the pig hit the ground it immediately split open, and Charlemagne's troops, seeing the contents, despaired, believing that the town must have abundant supplies. They lifted the siege and retreated, and as the town's church bells pealed in celebration, the townsfolk cried "Carcas, sonne!" ("Ring, Carcas!"). It's a great story, but pure fantasy of course. A Muslim ruler, for whom pork would have been considered unclean, would never have kept pigs within the confines of his fortress, and in the early ninth century the locals spoke something more akin to Latin than modern French. Nevertheless it is decidedly more poetic than the truth, which is that the town's name derives from two Occitan roots: carac, for "rock" (after the spur on which it is built), and sonne, for "wood" (for the forests which surrounded it).

approaches to the town for kilometres in every direction. From November to March the tourist office operates a "Bon Week-end" programme, which gives you two nights for one at participating hotels.

Cité hotels

All the hotels below are marked on the *Cité* map on p.122.

🏃 de la Cité place de l'Église ☎04.68.71.98.71, 🌐www.hoteldelacite .com. If you can afford it, this luxurious hotel with its beautiful enclosed courtyard will separate you from the maddening crowds of the *cité*. The price matches the opulence. Closed mid-Jan to mid-Feb. **❾**

Le Donjon 2 rue du Comte Roger ☎04.68.11.23.00, 🌐www.hotel-donjon.fr. The other *cité* hotel is surprisingly affordable for what you get: a thoroughly renovated hotel with well-equipped rooms. Just a stone's throw from the donjon. **❻**

Éspace Cité 132 rue Trivalle ☎04.68.25.24.24, 📧hotel-espace-cité@wanadoo.fr. What this hotel lacks in charm it tries hard to make up for with amenities such as AC, TV and garage parking. Just downhill from the main gate to the *cité*; wheelchair accessible. **❸**

Montmorency 2 rue Camille St-Saëns ☎04.68.11.96.70, 🌐www.lemontmorency.com. Provides a good range of services and is well located for visiting the citadel, as it is just one street north of the *cité*. Wheelchair access and a swimming pool. **❹**

du Pont Vieux 32 rue Trivalle ☎04.68.25.24.99, 🌐www.hoteldupontvieux.com. Perhaps the best all-round choice in town this "olde worlde" hotel is on a lively, atmospheric little street which winds up from the medieval bridge towards the *cité*. TV and parking; pets are welcome. **❸**

Ville Basse hotels

All the hotels below are marked on the *Ville Basse* map on p.125.

La Bastide 81 rue de la Liberté ☎04.68.71.96.89, 📠04.68.71.36.28. A good deal in the *ville basse*, down a quiet side-street not far from the station. You get TV, a lift and car park at one-star prices. **❷**

🏃 du Soleil Terminus 2 av de Maréchal Joffre ☎04.68.25.25.00, 📠04.68.75.53.09. Fading steam-age luxury in this station-side hotel,

which has a splendid *fin-de-siècle* facade. Also has a good bar, lifts and TV in the rooms. Closed Dec–Feb.

Ibis Centre 5 pl Gambetta ☎04.68.72.37.37, 🌐www.ibishotel.com. With a range of amenities, this well-kept establishment is convenient for the old town. Wheelchair accessible and a parking garage. **❸**

Montségur 27 allée d'Iéna ☎04.68.25.31.41, 📧info@hotelmontsegur.com. Comfortable rooms in an impressive-looking nineteenth-century townhouse. Located a 15min walk west of the cathedral, off boulevard Barbès, it is not the closest hotel to the *cité*, but it's competitively priced. Closed late Dec to Jan. English spoken. **❹**

Au Royal 22bd Jean-Jaurès ☎04.68.25.19.12, 📧godartcl@wanadoo.fr. This hotel has a good location, and all rooms have TV. Closed late Dec to late Jan. **❷**

Hostels and campsite

All the listings below are marked on the *Cité* map on p.122.

Camping de la Cité Rte St-Hilaire ☎04.68.25.11.17, 🌐www.campeoles.fr. Exceptional ground with good shady sites, some bungalows and a shop. Tucked away in parkland to the south of town, it can be reached by local bus #8 or by a 20min walk from the *cité*. If you point your tent in the right direction you get a view of the citadel poking up over the trees. Open mid-Mar to mid-Oct.

HI hostel rue Trencavel ☎04.68.25.23.16, 📠04.68.71.14.84, 📧carcassonne@fuaj.org. Excellent, modern hostel in the heart of the citadel. Its dorms (€16) and the 4–6 person rooms are clean and bright, there's a large patio for respite from the crowds outside, plus a bar. Membership (available on site) required in summer. Open Feb to mid-Dec.

Notre Dame de l'Abbaye 103 rue Trivalle ☎04.68.25.16.65, 📠04.68.72.71.74. A second choice for hostel-style accommodation. Great location in a beautiful street, comfortable dorms (€13) and sheet rental available (€3).

The Town

Carcassonne's layout can be initially confusing. The town is divided into three main parts, the oldest of which is the **cité** – the compact, walled citadel perched on a hill on the east bank of the Aude. Descending from here you pass through the medieval suburb of La Barbacane and cross the river to arrive at the **ville basse**, formally known as La Bastide de St-Louis – a typical grid of thirteenth-century streets, ringed by a one-way system where there was once a wall. Splayed out around this is the **new town**, a nondescript series of suburbs which holds nothing of interest for the visitor.

The Cité

From whichever direction you approach, Carcassonne's magnificent citadel, its stout ramparts and pennant-capped towers piercing the sky, presents one of the South of France's most striking images – straight out of a medieval fantasy. However, much of Carcassonne is, in fact, fabrication – a piece of imaginative reconstruction by the nineteenth-century restorer Viollet-le-Duc, whose enthusiasm for "the medieval" inspired him to invent inaccurate features like the conical towers and arrow-slits, which the original medieval fortress lacked.

Nevertheless, as you cross over the moat, passing the wide grassy verges between the thick double walls, you do feel as though you're entering another world. Although you can enter through the **Porte d'Aude**, on the citadel's

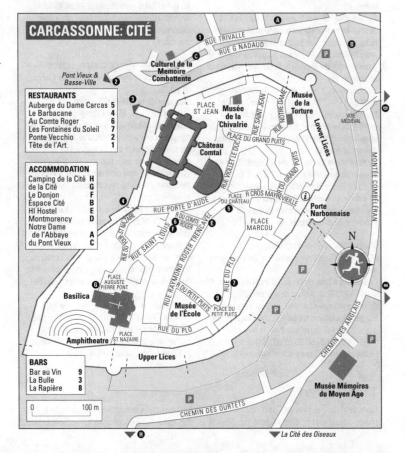

CARCASSONNE: CITÉ

RESTAURANTS
Auberge du Dame Carcas 5
Le Barbacane   4
Au Comte Roger   6
Les Fontaines du Soleil 7
Ponte Vecchio   2
Tête de l'Art   1

ACCOMMODATION
Camping de la Cité   H
de la Cité   G
Le Donjon   F
Espace Cité   B
HI Hostel   E
Montmorency   D
Notre Dame
 de l'Abbaye   A
du Pont Vieux   C

BARS
Bar au Vin   9
La Bulle   3
La Rapière   8

0   100 m

La Cité des Oiseaux

western side (and closer to the *ville basse*), a more visually impressive and evocative option is to head to the main **Porte Narbonnaise**, where the local *navettes* and main car park are found – on the far side of the *cité*. From here, rue Cros Mayrevieille, with its phalanxes of souvenir shops and ice-cream stands, leads to the entrance of the twelfth-century **Château Comtal** (daily: April–Sept 9.30am–6pm; Oct–March 9.30am–5pm; by guided tour only; €6.50), the castle where Count Raymond-Roger Trencavel made his last stand against the northern knights, and surrendered, in 1209. Although you can wander around the *cité* for free, the ticket office for the Château Comtal is just inside the Porte Narbonnaise, on the left-hand side. The mandatory **guided tours** of the *château* (35–40min, occasionally in English in summer only) begin in the main castle courtyard (at the end of the street), from where the guides lead you through the scanty remains of the now open-roofed keep. The tour continues southwards along a section of the citadel's three kilometres of walls and through three of its 31 towers (some of whose Roman foundations can be discerned) before arriving at the modern **amphitheatre**, built on the side of the fortress's former abbey-church and used since 1908 for theatre, dance and musical performances. Take care along the walls, as stairways can be slippery and the inadequate railings are no match for curious children. The ruins themselves are anything but spectacular – Carcassonne is best when looked at from outside – but the views from the walls are good, and the guides' frank account of the history of the town is lively and informative. Appropriately, the castle also hosts an exhibit on the life and work of Viollet-le-Duc (see box, p.124).

The tour ends at place St-Nazaire, behind the **basilica** of the same name (Mon–Fri 8.45am–12.45pm & 1.45–5/6pm, Sat & Sun 8.45–10.30am & 2–5/6pm; free), a late eleventh-century church that was originally Romanesque, but underwent major Gothic and neo-Gothic remodellings, first in the thirteenth century and then again in the nineteenth, by Viollet-le-Duc. As you follow the building round to the entrance in place Pierre Pont look up to see a stunning series of **gargoyles** along the eaves, as well as amusingly carved heads above the door. Inside, the church's plain nave betrays its pre-Gothic origins – the choir and rosette window are thirteenth-century additions – and at the southern end you'll find the tomb where Simon de Montfort lay until his body was transferred to his family's main fief at Montfort l'Amaury near Paris.

There's not a great deal else to see or do in the *cité* apart from wander the narrow, crooked streets, and absorb the convincingly medieval ambience. From behind the basilica, follow the walls east along rue du Plô. At no. 3 there's the small **Musée de l'École** (daily: July & Aug 10am–7pm; Sept–June 10am–6pm; €4), a reconstruction of a *fin-de-siècle* classroom, and slightly further along you'll pass a little park at place du Petit Puits, with its old well – a good place to pause and soak up the atmosphere – before eventually reaching the restaurant-clogged **place Marcou**. On the nearby place St-Jean, you'll find the small **Musée de la Chivalrie** (Easter–Oct 10am–noon & 3–6pm; €5), further capitalizing on themes medieval, with a collection of arms and armour. The small section of town on the far north of rue Cros Mayrevieille is somewhat less developed and provides a bit of respite from the teeming masses of visitors. Here you can visit the **Musée de la Torture**, in rue du Grand Puits (daily: July & Aug 10am–8pm; Sept–June 10am–6pm; €6.50), with mock-ups, models and some genuine instruments of pain dating from the Middle Ages to the French Revolution.

Before finishing up your visit of the *cité*, you should also take the time to walk around the grassy **lices**, a narrow space some 1100m in length, created with the building of the second set of walls in 1200s, and divided into two sections. The **lower lices** run from the Porte Narbonnaise to the Porte de l'Aude around the northern perimeter of the citadel; starting out from the former, you'll notice a section of brick-and-stone-constructed wall dating back to the end of the period of Roman occupation. Walking along the slightly longer

Viollet-le-Duc

It can be something of a disappointment to discover that so many of the buildings of medieval France are in fact, reconstructions, reassembled or repaired in the nineteenth century. Up until then, the Middle Ages was considered to be a period of "Gothic" barbarism best forgotten, but in the early 1800s European intellectuals began to look back at the medieval era as the time when their own nations were born, and all over western Europe projects were undertaken to recover its neglected art and architecture. The major figure in this movement in France was Eugène Emmanuel **Viollet-le-Duc**, the prolific restorer-extraordinaire who left his – often fantastical – mark all over the country, but particularly in Languedoc and Roussillon.

Born in Paris in 1814, Viollet-le-Duc studied art history at the Sorbonne before embarking on an extended tour of France and Italy in his early twenties. On his return to Paris, he assisted in the renovation of the glorious stained glass and stone-carved interior of the **Ste Chapelle**; it was here that he found his calling and made his reputation, and in the years that followed he was inundated with contracts to restore buildings such as Narbonne's Hôtel de Ville (see p.306) and the basilica of St-Nazaire in Carcassonne – accomplished works which served to further his renown. By 1853, when Louis-Napoleon, prince-president of the Second Republic, had given him overall supervision of the restoration of all of France's medieval buildings, Viollet-le-Duc had already begun the massive reconstruction of Carcassonne's walled **cité** – a project which would take fifty years to complete and which he would not live to see finished. After drawing up the restoration plans, he returned to his old university to butt heads with critics and colleagues and dabble as a professor of art history but, finally disillusioned with the criticisms his theories provoked, he left, returning to his work and writing, eventually dying in his adopted home of Switzerland in 1879.

Viollet-le-Duc's idiosyncratic **theory** of restoration dictated that buildings should not necessarily be returned to their exact previous state, but rather modified according to their essential underlying architectural principles (as he saw them, naturally). As a result, the elaborate restorations – in which he sometimes started from nothing more than a pile of stones – are reflections of Viollet-le-Duc's imagination, and bear little or no relation in design or form to their originals. Works such as the Ste Chapelle, which were taken on early in his career and not under his direct supervision, tend to be more faithful, but with later renovations he was more or less given free rein. In Carcassonne's *cité* for example he not only made "improvements", such as adding arrow-slits and crenellation to the walls, but adopted features which are aesthetically pleasing but, quite simply, inaccurate: the pointed roofs on the towers are German-style as opposed to the flat Languedocian version. In this way he created France's medieval heritage almost single-handedly – a heritage which reflects historical reality as much as Sir Walter Scott's *Ivanhoe* or Cecil B. de Mille's movies, but which now forms a focus for French national and Occitan regional identity, as well as the foundation for the booming tourist industry of the twenty-first century. Whatever you think about Viollet-le-Duc's easy attitude to verisimilitude, as you travel around Languedoc and Roussillon, bear in mind that – for better or worse – almost all the great medieval monuments here have "benefited" to some degree from his endeavours. There is a permanent exhibit dedicated to the restorationist, including many original sketches and plans, in Carcassonne's castle.

southern circuit of the **upper lices** gives you good views of the elaborate towers added to the citadel's defences under Philip III in the late thirteenth century. Once a space for medieval archery practice and other military exercises, the *lices* now provide a favourite route for horsedrawn *calèches* and a great place to have a picnic.

Outside the Porte Narbonnaise, on the chemin des Anglais, the **Musée Mémoires du Moyen Âge** (Museum of Memories of the Middle Ages; 10am–7pm; €4) houses a collection of dioramas depicting battalions of medieval soldiers hacking and slashing at each other – strictly for kids. A fifteen-minute walk south at Colline de Pech Mary you'll find **La Cité des Oiseaux**, an animal park which runs exciting 40- to 60-minute-long live **falconry** and wolf shows (daily: late April to June & Sept–Nov 2–6pm; July & Aug 10am–12.30pm & 2–7pm; €8.50).

The Ville Basse

When you leave the *cité*, instead of backtracking through the main gates and past the car park, a better option is to take the gate at the end of rue Notre Dame, off place du Grand Puits, and cut down to rue Trivalle, a world away from the touristy scrum in the fortress above. Here, the **Centre Culturel de la Mémoire Combatteante** (Mon–Fri 9am–noon & 2.30–3.30pm; free) is a small museum showcasing a rather random selection of military bric-a-brac. The street continues to the picturesque fourteenth-century **pont vieux**, adorned on its far side by the small and simple Gothic structure of the twelfth-century Notre Dame de la Santé **chapel**. The riverbanks on the *cité* side have been kept free of building and make a nice grassy spot to relax or have a picnic.

Just up from the bridge you reach the southeastern edge of the **ville basse** at place Gambetta, which, despite the traffic, has an airy feel, as well as some attractive nineteenth-century facades. Keep an eye out for the impressive Art Deco facade of the Groupe Scolaire Jean-Jaurès on the northwest corner. Rue Verdun (formerly Grande Rue) runs from here straight into the grid of the thirteenth-century *bastide*: at no. 1, an eighteenth-century *hôtel* is home to the **Musée des Beaux-Arts** (mid-June to mid-Sept Wed–Sun 10am–6pm; mid-Sept to mid-June Tues–Sat 10am–noon & 2–6pm; free), which, aside from its large but unremarkable collection of eighteenth-century landscapes, sometimes hosts interesting temporary exhibitions. Further along you'll arrive at place Carnot, the heart of the old *ville basse* – a wide square with shops, cafés and bars as well as a good **market** (Tues, Thurs & Sat mornings). At the far end of rue Verdun, the **Maison des Mémoires** at no. 53 (Tues–Sat 9am–noon & 2–6pm; free) pays homage to local-born surrealist poet Joë Bousquet (1857–1950). Left paraplegic by battle wounds received at Vailly in 1918, Bousquet lived out the rest of his life bedridden in this house in Carcassonne, comforted by opium and producing dark and mystical poetical reflections which attracted the attention of the interwar intelligentsia. Near the fourteenth-century cathedral of St-Michel you'll find the most substantial remains of the town's once stout defences; the **Porte des Jacobins**, a medieval gate which was widened and remodelled in Neoclassical style in 1778, is in good shape, while beside it lie the remains of the old ramparts. Otherwise, keep an eye out for some of the impressive old private *hôtels* which can be found in the *ville basse*, both along rue Verdun and rue Aimé-Ramond, where you'll find the plain, medieval-styled facade of the fourteenth-century Maison du Sénéchal, at no. 70, and a more flamboyant Renaissance *hôtel* at no. 50.

If you're heading back to the *cité*, the unpleasant walk along the modern road bridge east of place Gambetta will give you a great view of the citadel and the *pont vieux*. On the other side, cut across to the old bridge and follow rue de la Barbacane up past the church of St-Gimer. From here you can get to the Porte de l'Aude, walking between the double walls to re-enter the *cité*.

Eating, drinking and nightlife

You'll never have a problem getting something **to eat** in Carcassonne, whether in the *cité*, where every other facade seems to belong to a bistro, or in the *ville basse*, which has a good selection of simple and smarter establishments. Place Marcou in the *cité*, in particular, is home to a mass of indistinguishable patios all of which have *menus* in the €12 range. For something lighter, rue Cros Mayrevieille at the entrance to the *cité* is crammed with *crêpe* and sandwich stands, while there are traditional café-bars in and around the *bastide*'s place Carnot.

Cité restaurants

All the restaurants below are marked on the *Cité* map on p.122.

Auberge de Dame Carcas 3 pl du Château ☎04.68.71.23.23. Large restaurant with several dining rooms, serving up excellent-quality traditional and regional cuisine, including roast meats cooked over an open fire. With *menus* from €13.50, this is one of the best-value places in town, so book ahead. Closed Sun eve, Mon lunch & Feb.

Le Barbacane Pl de l'Église ☎04.68.71.98.71. The most elegant (and expensive) of the three restaurants operated by the *Hôtel de la Cité*. Adventurous gastronomique cuisine with four-star service. You'll pay upwards of €60. Open evenings only.

Au Comte Roger 14 rue St-Louis ☎04.68.11.93.41. One of Carcassonne's better choices for *terroir*. Renowned chef Pierre Mesa imaginatively combines local Lauragais basics with subtle gastronomique touches. *Menus* €27–33. Closed Sun & late Jan to late Feb.

Les Fontaines du Soleil 32 rue de Plô. One of the best deals in the *cité*: small, friendly and cheap with good local, home-style cooking. You can eat well here for about €15 in a quiet little interior patio. Closed Jan.

Ponte Vecchio 22 rue Trivalle ☎04.68.71.33.17. Fine Italian dining and hospitable atmosphere in the shadow of the *cité*. *Menus* €14.50–17.50. Closed Mon & mid-Nov to mid-Dec.

Tête de l'Art 37bis rue Trivalle ☎04.68.71.23.11. Located on the atmospheric thoroughfare which connects the old bridge and the *cité*, with an unassuming exterior girded by a tiny sidewalk patio, and an interior festooned with the contemporary painting and sculpture. Excellent *terroir* fare from €11.50–35 with a filling vegetarian option at €13.

Ville Basse restaurants

All the restaurants below are marked on the *Ville Basse* map on p.125.

La Divine Comédie 29 bd Jean-Jaurès ☎04.68.72.30.36. An Italian restaurant, serving decent pasta, as well as local standbys like cassoulet and *confit de canard*. *Menus* from €12. Closed Sun & late Dec to early Jan.

L'Écurie 43 bd Barbès ☎04.68.72.04.04. Elegant dining in a converted eighteenth-century stable, with *menus* from €15–28. Serves local cuisine as well as dishes with adventurous touches, such as mackerel brochettes in thyme sauce: popular with gays and lesbians. Closed Sun eve & Wed.

Le Jardin de la Tour 11 rue Porte d'Aude ☎04.68.25.71.24. Just outside the citadel's Porte d'Aude, this is a good option for local and Mediterranean cuisine, with a small garden dining area. *Menus* from €20; closed Sun eve, Mon eve & Nov.

Le Petit Couvert 18 rue de l'Aigle d'Or. Snappy and cheerily decorated little restaurant with good cheap *menus* based around combinations of salads and simple meat dishes (from €11) and a small street-side terrace. Also light options for vegetarians. Closed Sun, Mon & March.

Le Quai Bellevue 2 rue des 3 Couronnes ☎04.68.25.05.60. Good regional cuisine served on a riverside terrace, with excellent views of the medieval bridge and the walls of the *cité*. Expect to spend about €15. Closed Oct–April.

Bars and nightlife

For a small city, Carcassonne does quite well for **nightlife**, with a good selection of late-night **bars** (normally open until 2am, sometimes 4am or 5am at weekends) in the *ville basse*. *Le Café de Nuit*, 32 boulevard Omer Sarraut, livens up later with a mixed gay/straight crowd, while *La Fiesta Bodega*, at 49 avenue Henri Goût, is a rather pricey Spanish-Mexican restaurant by day, but stays open late as a lively tapas bar. Tiny rue de l'Aigle d'Or, just off place Carnot, is the centre for local hipsters, with bars like *Le Conti*, at no. 16, which has two dance floors (daily till 5am), and the rockish *Le Not*, at no. 18 (Tues–Sat till 2am), while the cosy British *Pub Sheridan* can be found nearby, at 13 rue Victor-Hugo. In the *cité* itself, *Bar au Vin*, in rue Plô, is the best place for a drink – a post-show favourite for visiting actors and musicians. For **dancing**, try *La Bulle* (closed Mon & Tues), just below the *cité* at 115 rue Barbacane, or *La Rapière*, a house-sound disco popular with under-25s, just outside the main gates.

Listings

Airlines Ryanair ☎04.68.71.96.65, ⊕www.ryanair.com.

Airport information ☎04.68.71.96.46 & 04.68.71.96.65, ⊕www.carcassonne.cci.fr.

Banks Most major French banks, plus ATMs, are represented. Try, for example, Caisse d'Épargne, 5 bd Camille Pelletan, which also has a 24hr automatic change machine, or Crédit Agricole, 8 pl Carnot; after 5pm use the post office (Mon–Sat till 7pm).

Bicycle rental Évasion 2 Roues, 85 allée d'Iéna, ☎04.68.25.28.18; Espace 11, 3 route de Minervoise (☎04.68.25.28.18, ℮espace11@wanadoo.fr)

also has motorbikes and scooters. Both are closed Sun & Mon.

Boat rental Nautic (☎04.68.71.88.95, ⊕www.nautique.fr); Locaboat (☎03.86.91.72.72, ⊕www.locaboat.com). Voies Navigables de France has an office (☎04.68.71.74.55) at the port.

Bus departures Various bus lines operate from Carcassonne, departing from along bd de Varsovie; tickets and information for destinations within the Aude *département* (no buses Sun) can be found at the main tourist office. Tickets for long-distance buses and Eurolines can be bought from Verdier Voyages, 1 av Maréchal-Joffre (℡04.68.25.09.06).

Car rental Avis, 52 rue Antoine Marty ℡04.68.25.05.84, ⓦwww.avis.com; Budget, 5 bd Omer Sarraut ℡04.68.72.31.31, ⓦwww.budget .com; Europcar, 7 bd Omer Sarraut ℡04.68.25.05.09, ⓦwww.europcar.com; Garage la Bouriette, 58 bd Denis Papin ℡04.68.47.80.00; Location Occitan de Véhicules, 36 av Franklin Roosevelt ℡04.68.11.74.10. All of these companies, except for Garage la Bouriette, also have offices at the airport.

Hospital Centre Hospitalier Général, rte de St-Hilaire (℡04.68.24.24.24), on the south side of town.

Internet access Alert Rouge, 73 rue de Verdun (Mon–Fri 10am–1am, Sat 2pm–3am).

Laundry 5 sq Gambetta & 31 rue Aimé-Ramond.

Lost property 13 rue Jean Bringer ℡04.68.10.27.00.

Pharmacy There several in rue Verdun: try Pharmacie Serin at no. 56; after 8pm enquire at the police station.

Police 4 bd Barbès ℡04.68.11.26.00.

Swimming pool Grazailles, rue du Moulin de la Seigne (℡04.68.47.81.83) is the one municipal pool open year-round (bus #2 or #3). Locals also head for the Lac de Cavayère, signposted from the Narbonne road, just east of the *cité* (#7 bus).

Taxi Radio Taxi ℡04.68.71.50.50.

The upper Aude valley

The River Aude, whose course can be followed due south from Carcassonne, is like a highway of Catharism – the majority of the most famous sights and ruins associated with the heretical sect lie along its path as it ascends into the Pyrenees. The river's lower regions hold fewer attractions but are consequently less visited, making quiet towns like **Limoux** and **Alet-les-Bains** good places to get away from the summer crowds, but as the valley winds its way up to the modern service centre of **Quillan** more and more relics of the area's history reveal themselves. On the way you'll pass the mysterious site of **Rennes-le-Château**, a favourite of occultists' and treasure-hunter's. Just south, the so-called "Cathar castles" (many of which, in reality, postdate the heretics), form a rough chain stretching from Foix in the west, passing Quillan, and on to the Fenouil-lèdes to the east. South of Quillan, the valley narrows into a series of gorges as you begin the climb into the mountains, eventually reaching the isolated **Donezan** region. This upper portion of the river, skirting the southeastern edge of the highlands of the pays de Sault, has a good network of trails and *gîtes*, stretching out over varied terrain – a great area for **hiking**. From Quillan, you can connect to Foix and access the caves along the River Ariège, while a network of hiking trails leads over the Donezan, southwest towards Tarascon and southeast to the Têt valley of Roussillon.

Limoux and around

Famous for its sparkling white *blanquette* ("little white") wine, first vinted in 1531, **LIMOUX** is the first major town you will arrive at as you follow the course of the Aude upstream from Carcassonne. It is pleasant enough, but there's little to write home about, apart from the Lenten Carnaval **festival**, held from January through to March in the town's main place de la République and featuring displays of masked dancers and live music.

Limoux has dominated this neck of the woods since the Middle Ages and the same **bridge** which spans the Aude today brought prosperity in the form of merchants and traders as far back as the fourteenth century, when the town was rebounding from the repression it suffered as a consequence of its Cathar tendencies. At this time the town, like many of the "new towns" of the era, was governed by a board of consuls rather than by a noble lord, and was wealthy enough to construct a formidable set of **defensive walls**, part of which can still be seen along the riverside. But these did not prove strong enough to keep out either the Black Death or the Black Prince in the 1300s, and a century and a half later Calvinism arrived, bringing religious strife, quickly followed by a poverty from which it never quite recovered.

Today, Limoux is quiet and has something of an air of neglected decay, but at least it provides an opportunity to stretch your legs on the way towards the Pyrenees. The heart of the town is the **place de la République**, a wide square with some fine old stone arcading, a number of timber-frame houses and the requisite café and restaurant patios. Just down rue St-Martin, the town's main **church** has some top-notch stained-glass windows and remarkably restrained sixteenth- and seventeenth-century decor in the side chapels. Behind it the canalized Aude separates the old town from the newer districts. Heading away from the river from place de la République, the quiet streets lead past a hideous nineteenth-century market and on to promenade de Tivoli, the Carcassonne–Quillan highway. Here, you'll find the small **Musée Petiet** (July & Aug daily 9am–7pm; Sept–June Mon–Fri 9am–noon & 2–6pm, Sat & Sun 10am–noon & 2–5pm; €3) in the same building as the tourist office. Its collection of paintings, dominated by local nineteenth-century pointillism and allegory, contains some works of surprising quality. The town's newest attraction is a **piano museum** (July & Aug Wed–Mon 2–6pm; €2), touted as the only one if its kind in France. And, just in case you'd forgotten you were in Cathar country, **Catha-rama** (daily: April–June, Sept & Oct 10am–5pm, July & Aug 10am–6pm; €5), across the street from the museum, will remind you; it has a cheesy thirty-minute audiovisual show in four languages, emotionally recounting the repression of the religious movement, now a pillar of a manufactured regional identity. Alternatively, if you're more interested in the local *blanquette* (a dry, sparkling white), head to the *domaine* Caves Sieur d'Arques (Mon–Sat 10–11am & 3–5pm; free) on avenue de Mauzac, 1km west on avenue Charles de Gaulle from the main roundabout. Here you can learn about the history of the vintage, as well as sample and buy some to take home.

If you have a car or bike, you may want to follow the winding D104 from Carcassonne to Limoux rather than the main D118, stopping at **ST-HILAIRE**, where you can visit the **abbey-church** (April–June & Sept daily 10am–noon & 2–6pm; July & Aug daily 10am–7pm; Oct–March Sat, Sun & hols 10am–noon & 2–5/6pm; €4) of the same name. This sixth-century foundation, once the choice burial place of the counts of Carcassonne, is best known for a splendid sarcophagus, carved in vivid relief by the Master of Cabestany (see box, p.108), and depicting the martyrdom of Toulouse's first bishop St Sernin. On the right-hand side of the main panel, there is a representation of Toulouse's medieval Capitole building. Aside from the sarcophagus you can visit the compact cloister, and a small wine-cellar. It was the monks of St-Hilaire who invented the Blanquette of Limoux, which, pre-dating the sparkling wines of Champagne

---

The Carte Intersite pass

If you are planning on visiting a few of the Cathar sites in the region, consider buying a "**Carte Intersite**" pass (€4) from participating sites or local tourist offices. Valid for a year, it gives you reductions on the entrance fee to selected castles and monuments of the Aude *département*, including the castles of Aguilar, Arques, Carcassonne, Caunes-Minervois, Fontfroide, Lastours, Minerve, Montségur, Peyrepertuse, Puilaurens, the Puivert museum, Quéribus, St-Hilaire, St-Papoul, Saissac, Termes, Usson, Villelongue and Villerouge, plus the abbey of Lagrasse. Total savings, if you visit all of these sites, is €17.20.

by a century, is claimed to be the original "Brut." Following the twisting D104 west for the 12km to Limoux will take you past **Notre-Dame de Marceille** (9am–7pm), a Romanesque church with a fine polychrome interior and an eleventh-century Virgin and Child reputed to perform miracles. It is still a place of pilgrimage for local Catholics.

Practicalities

Trains arrive at Limoux's **gare SNCF**, on the east bank of the river, a good twenty-minute walk from the old town, while **buses** (℡04.68.31.09.64) stop outside the cinema on allées des Marronniers, in the old town. The **tourist office** (July & Aug daily 9am–7pm, Sept–June Mon–Fri 9am–noon & 2–6pm, Sat & Sun 10am–noon & 2–5pm; ℡04.68.31.11.82, ✆www.limoux.fr) is on promenade de Tivoli, just south of the main roundabout.

There is little reason to spend the night in Limoux, but should you want to, the best **accommodation** options are the splendid and stately ⚜ *Modern & Pigeon* (closed Wed; ℡04.68.31.00.25, ✆www.grandhotelmodernepigeon .fr; ❻) in place Général Leclerc, and the humbler *Des Arcades* (closed mid-Dec to mid-Jan & Wed; ℡04.68.31.02.57, ✆www.logis-de-france.fr; ❷), south of the church at 96 rue St-Martin: both are comfortable and have amenities such as television and parking. At St-Hilaire, the *chambres d'hôtes* at 3 avenue de Limoux (℡04.68.11.40.70; ❸) is a better option than the grimey *l'Abbaye* (℡04.68.69.67.23), which offers basic rooms (❶), generous meals (€12) and perhaps the slowest service in France. Limoux's municipal **campsite** (June–Sept; ℡04.68.31.13.63) is on the east bank of the river, south of the old bridge.

Restaurants range from the excellent but expensive dining room of the *Modern & Pigeon* (closed Sat lunch & Mon), with elaborate *menus* (€29–55), to the *Grand Café*, 25 place de la République, one of several on the square where you can enjoy a *menu* inside or on the sunny terrace for only €12. Otherwise, *Maison de la Blanquette*, at 46 bis promenade de Tivoli, is a good place to wash down regional cuisine with some bubbly white (from €16), or try *l'Hibiscus* (closed Mon), a *gastronomique* restaurant at the edge of town en route to St-Polycarpe (€13–45; closed Mon). Limoux's **market** is held on Fridays. **Bike rental** is available from Cycles Taillefer (℡04.68.31.02.01).

Alet-les-Bains

Sixteen kilometres further upstream, **ALET-LES-BAINS** is a better place than Limoux to make a stop. This ancient little village still owes its modest prosperity to the **hot springs** which bubble out of the ground on the north side of town, and which were first harnessed for curative purposes by the Romans. From the ninth century the town flourished as the site of a Benedictine abbey, and from the fourteenth as a bishopric, before declining into obscurity with the Wars of Religion. Today it is largely overlooked, which helps to preserve an atmosphere of antiquity in the village, whose quiet streets conceal some surprising relics. A seventeenth-century **bridge** still connects Alet with the Limoux–Quillan highway, and just across it loom the ruins of the **abbey of Notre-Dame** (daily: July & Aug 10am–noon & 2.30–7pm; Sept to mid-Dec 10am–noon & 2.30–6pm; mid-Dec to June 10am–12.30pm & 3–6pm; €5), destroyed in 1577 during the Religious Wars and subsequently plundered to strengthen the town's walls. From here, the narrow rue du Séminaire leads back to the town's **square**, boxed in by timbered houses and the stone **Maison des Consuls**, the medieval home of the town council. Following the narrow and evocative rue de la Cadène north from the square will take you through a gate and on to a few **Roman**

relics, including a scrap of ancient road. South from the square, sleepy rue de la Rose leads to another gate and a long section of twelfth-century walls. Just inside the gates, to the west, you'll find several tiny **medieval houses**, which, 800 years ago, housed merchants' families.

Practicalities

Buses between Limoux and Quillan drop you on the main road by the old bridge, from where it's a short walk to the town's **tourist office** (daily: July & Aug 10am–12.30pm & 2.30–7pm; Sept–June 10am–12.30pm & 2.30–6pm; ☎04.68.69.93.56,ⓦwww.info.aletlesbains.free.fr) in rue Nicolas Pavillon, beside the ruined abbey. **Staying** in Alet-les-Bains is made all the more worthwhile by its excellent hotel, the ☀ *Hostellerie de l'Évêché* (closed Nov–March; ☎04.68.69.90.25, ⓦwww.hotel-eveche.com; ❸), in a wooded garden just over the old bridge. If this is full, head for the *chambres d'hôtes* at the friendly, English-run *Maison Val d'Aleth* (☎04.68.69.90.40,ⓦwww.valdaleth.com; ❸) on the same street, who also run the town's well-equipped, riverside **campsite** (book far ahead in summer), further along rue Nicolas Pavillon. The only **restaurant** in town is *L'Évêché*'s dining room (closed Sun; *menus* €22–40), which serves high-quality regional cuisine.

Rennes-le-Château and Arques

There is little to detain you along the road from Alet-les-Bains to Quillan, but if you have time, it's worth detouring away from the Aude at **Couiza** to the ancient abbey-town of Rennes, and the castle at **Arques**, east of the main highway.

RENNES-LE-CHÂTEAU (not to be confused with the nearby spa town of Rennes-les-Bains) sits at the end of a four-kilometre mountain road winding up from Couiza, with impressive views over the Aude valley. It was here that the enigmatic Bérenguer Saunière, Rennes' parish priest, died in 1917 after having lived in luxury for nearly thirty years, building himself a private villa, conservatory and library, and renovating the church in garish style. Together these sites form the mysterious **Espace Bérenguer Saunière** (March, April, mid-Sept to mid-Nov & mid-Dec to mid-Jan daily 11.30am–4/4.30pm; May to mid-Sept daily 10.30am–6pm; mid-Nov to mid-Dec Sat & Sun 11.30am–4pm; €4.25), a magnet for treasure-seekers, occultists and crop-circle aficionados, and inspiration for *The Da Vinci Code*. Entry to the **church**, a small medieval chapel built on an ancient foundation, is free, as is the pavilion beside it, which served as Saunière's office. Behind this you'll find the cemetery where he lies next to his "housekeeper", Marie Denardaud. The compact church is entered through the side door, above which a Latin inscription welcomes the visitor to this "terrible place" – perhaps a reference to the decor. Inside, you are greeted by a rather sinister wooden carving of a grimacing demon surmounted by four angels. The interior itself is painted in medieval style and filled with a healthy contingent of carved Baroque saints. Although to the uninitiated these may seem rather ordinary church furnishings, enthusiasts have uncovered a complex code in their details and arrangement, one which corresponds either to Kabbalistic theory, UFO-influence or the secret "Priory of Zion" society (depending on whom you ask).

Next door to the church is the humble farmhouse in which Saunière lived, now converted into a **museum** and containing important relics, such as the hollow late Visigothic base which once supported the church's altar and which some believe contained ancient parchments which led the priest to a buried treasure. From there you enter Saunière's spacious garden, girded by a fanciful

△ Carving, Rennes-le-Château

fortified wall capped by two turrets, one of which once served as his library, while adjacent to the farmhouse sits "Béthania", a more luxurious house where he entertained guests and installed his own chapel once he had been banned from conducting the Catholic Mass. The house may seem humble now, but when you reflect on how isolated and poor the hamlet must have been in the late 1800s, it would have seemed like a palace. For more, see the box opposite.

Bérenguer Saunière arrived to serve as the priest in the tiny and backward hamlet of Rennes in 1885, at 33, a cranky, royalist reactionary whose political views had already earned him the ire of the Church authorities. But his exile was to take an unexpected turn. Within a few years the humble priest was renovating the tiny and ancient **parish church**, decking it with a collection of eccentric fineries bought on order in Paris. By 1891, he began buying up considerable tracts of land, the title to which he put in the name of **Marie Denardaud**. Marie, born in 1868, was the daughter of his first housekeeper in Rennes, and became his life-long companion. In 1899, Saunière began construction work on the house and gardens of **Béthania**, as he called the smartly appointed villa which he raised next to the church. Luxurious by local standards, it was finished in 1904. Meanwhile, the *abbé* and his consort lorded it over the hamlet, on the one hand dispensing generous donations and throwing magnificent *fêtes*, and on the other maintaining an iron grip on his affairs. Such was the awe Saunière inspired that when villagers begged Marie for access to the priest's cistern to put out a fire, she refused them, rather than rouse him to get his permission.

By 1907 Saunière's activities and outspoken politics had attracted the attention of the Church authorities. He was investigated by the bishop of Carcassonne and deposed on a string of charges, ranging from abuse of power and finances to traffic of Church offices. His initial appeal failed in 1911 and, **defrocked**, he filed a second appeal to the Holy See in Rome. Meanwhile, the construction of the villa continued; banned by canon law from officiating over Mass in the church, he performed the sacraments in the stained-glass annexe built onto Béthania. On January 22, 1917, after giving his last confession, Saunière died of a heart attack and was buried in the cemetery behind the church. Marie Denardaud, much to Saunière's family's disappointment, was his only heir, and she remained faithful to her *"chéer disparu"* till her end, refusing to divulge his secrets. Since her death in 1953, they have lain in adjacent graves.

The question, of course, was where Saunière's money came from. It is generally believed he stumbled upon a cache of medieval coins, perhaps after finding ancient parchments either in the hollow stone **Visigothic** altar-support, in a secret compartment in a wooden column or under a carved flagstone which sat before the altar. After his death, Marie made cryptic references to the "gold" over which the "villagers were walking", which would be enough to "support the village for a hundred years". These tales attracted the attention of a steady string of **treasure-hunters** who became so troublesome and disruptive that even today signs forbid any digging in the vicinity of the town.

The story of the treasure and the bizarre symbolism of the church's decor have spawned scores of occult theories over their origin and significance, including possible links to a secret society called the Priory of Zion, the Templars, **Solomon's treasure**, Cathars, the **Holy Grail** and a Christ who escaped crucifixion. In the last decades this has turned into a small industry and there are dozens of books written on the subject. Most are full of the kind of incoherent and self-contradictory pseudo-scientific ramblings which typify this genre. The ground-breaker was Lincoln, Baigent and Leigh's *Holy Blood, Holy Grail*; other titles include Hudson Newman's *Pathways of the Gods* and Gabriel's *The Holy Valley and the Holy Mountain*. It was these tales that inspired American author Dan Brown to write the popular novel, *The Da Vinci Code*, drawing the various strands together (see p.131). Inevitably, this interest in the town has sparked a series of reports of other parapsychological and extra-terrestrial events in the vicinity, including a miraculous image of the Virgin and Child, discernible in a 1967 aerial photograph, UFO visitations and crop circles. With all of this, an open mind and sense of humour makes Rennes-le-Château a unique site.

Arques

The **donjon d'Arques** is around 10km east of Couiza along the D613, which winds slowly uphill following the course of the Orbieu. Coming into view, the perfectly preserved square **keep** (daily: March & Oct to mid-Nov 10.30am–12.30pm & 1.30–5pm, April–June & Sept 10.30am–6.30pm; July & Aug 9.30am–8pm; €5) is unmistakable as it rises 25m above the surrounding fields. Both the remains of the walled perimeter and the tower of this so-called Cathar castle date from after the famous Crusade, but it is without doubt the most beautiful of the region's *château*. The central *donjon*, which dates back to the thirteenth century, is extremely well preserved, with graceful Gothic vaulting sustaining two of its great chambers and a number of ogival (pointed-arch) windows dating from the period of its original construction. The third-floor hall is dominated by an impressively huge fireplace, while the walls, which were constructed in the following century, are breached by a simple gate and buttressed by a square guard tower on the southwest corner. Outside, there's a group of beehives clustered just to the side of the entrance, where you can buy fresh honey.

About 1500m east of the castle, the village of **ARQUES** is a nondescript little hamlet, with a fourteenth-century church, some contemporary buildings and a small, dull exhibit on Catharism housed in the **Maison de Déodat Roché** (same hours and ticket as castle), the home of the Freemason and pioneering nineteenth-century historian of the heretical movement. From Arques the road continues (no public transport) through ever more untamed and isolated terrain towards the castles at Termes and Villerouge-Termenès (see p.315), and the abbey-town of Lagrasse (see p.317), a route very much worthwhile exploring either by car or bicycle.

Practicalities

If you have no transport, you can reach Rennes and Arques by **taxi** from Couiza (T04.68.74.25.36), although, if you are up to it, the demanding uphill walk can be enjoyable. Cycling is another option – *Au Fil de l'Aude* (T04.68.74.16.69) in Couiza rents **bikes**. There's a **tourist office** in Rennes (daily: mid-June to mid-Sept 10am–7pm; mid-Sept to mid-June 10am–5.30pm; T04.68.74.72.68, Wwww.rennes-le-chateau.org), who can arrange English-language guided tours of the Saunière complex, which must be booked at least a month in advance.

There are no hotels in Rennes, but there is the attractive, English-run *Maison du Chapelier* **chambres d'hôtes** (T04.68.74.22.49, Wwww.esperazabedand breakfast.com; ④) with free Wi-Fi, in the village, or the luxurious *Château des Ducs de Joyeuse* (T04.68.74.04.20, Wwww.chateau-des-ducs.com; ⑤) in Couiza. In Arques, there's a **B&B** (T04.68.69.82.74; English spoken; ②) in the town's old smithy at 19 route des Corbières, and you'll find **campsites** in both Arques (T04.68.69.88.30, Wwww.relaisoleil.com; Feb–Oct) and Rennes (T04.68.74.09.32, Ecamping.rennes-les-baines@wanadoo.fr; May–Oct).

Good *terroir* **restaurants** are scattered throughout the area, the best being the *Château des Ducs* in Couiza, which sometimes has a dinner-theatre show (closed Sun & Mon eve, mid-Nov to March; *menu* from €30). Also worth trying are *Jardins de l'Abbé* in Rennes, with live music on Friday evenings (closed Sun & Mon lunch & Nov–April; T04.68.74.31.16; from €20), and *Auberge du Moulin d'Arques* in Arques (T04.68.69.80.61; closed Sun & Mon, Jan–March; from €15).

Quillan

Clustered on the west bank of the Aude about halfway along its course, **QUILLAN** is a half-heartedly industrialized place with a number of services, its main attraction being its proximity to the Pays de Sault (see p.137), plus the river itself, a sturdy torrent running right past the town providing ample canoeing and rafting possibilities (see below). The only monument of interest is the ruined **castle**, on the east bank of the Aude just across the *pont vieux*. Built on the site of a Visigothic fortress, it was burned by the Huguenots in 1575 during the course of the Religious Wars and partly dismantled in the eighteenth century, but the remnants are still worth a scramble.

The **gare SNCF** and **gare routière** are both central, on boulevard Charles-de-Gaulle. The **tourist office** occupies a prominent kiosk beside the train station (Jan to mid-May Mon–Fri 9am–noon & 2–6pm, Sat 9am–noon; mid-May to mid-Sept Mon–Sat 9am–noon & 2–7pm, Sun 9am–1pm; mid-Sept to Dec Mon–Fri 9am–noon Sat 9am–1pm; ℡04.68.20.07.78, Ⓦwww.aude-en-pyrenees.fr), and can help with Grotte de l'Aguzou reservations (see p.136), among other things. Opposite, you'll find Quillan's least expensive **hotel**, *Le Terminus*, at no. 45 boulevard Charles-de-Gaulle (℡ & Ⓕ04.68.20.94.67; 1). The rest of the town's accommodation is also on the same, noisy street, which doubles as the D117: for more comfort, there's the *Cartier*, at no. 31 (℡04.68.20.05.14, Ⓦwww.hotelcartier.com; ❸) and the *Canal* at no. 36 (℡04.68.20.08.62, Ⓦwww.hotel-canal.com; ❷). All the hotels have attached **restaurants** (*menus* €12–35), though the *Canal's* shuts on Sunday evening and Monday. The Centre International de Séjour Sports et Nature, at the southern edge of town en route to Axat, has a **gîte d'étape** (℡04.68.20.33.69; dorm beds €14), and organizes **canoeing** and **rafting**, as well as climbing and canyoning trips. *La Sapinette* (℡04.68.20.13.52; April–Oct) at 21 rue René-Delpech, off boulevard Jean Bourrel, is the closer and better equipped of two **campsites**. The town's produce **market** is held on Wednesdays (8am–4pm). You can rent **bikes** from Cycles Bénassis (℡04.68.20.18.91).

South from Quillan

The road **south from Quillan** provides a fabulous approach to the eastern peaks of the Pyrenees. Coursing down from the Capcir plateau, the Aude has cut successively through granite, gneiss and schist, and finally soft limestone, carving spectacular **caves** (*grottes*) and ever deeper **gorges** along the way. Public transport here is limited to a summer **bus** service to Quérigut, 44km south of Quillan. There's a map of the region on pp.138–139.

Défilé de Pierre-Lys and Axat

Gorge country begins almost immediately after you leave Quillan heading south, with rock overhangs blasted as necessary to allow passage. The narrowest section is the cliff-lined **Défilé de Pierre-Lys**, 8km to the south, where climbers can usually be seen swinging above the road. Four kilometres beyond the *défilé*, there's a **campsite**, *Le Moulin du Pont d'Aliès* (April–Nov), and simple restaurant, at the crossroads of the same name, where the D117 highway peels off east towards the Fenouillèdes.

Continuing south 1km beyond the crossroads on the D618 brings you to **AXAT**, where an old bridge, under which rafters often put in, links the through-road district with the east-bank quarter. There's one **hotel** here, the very basic *Auberge La Petite Ourse*, 16 route Nationale, the main street (closed part Sept; ℡04.68.20.59.20; ❹ half-board), and a municipal **campsite** (mid-March to mid-Nov; ℡04.68.20.53.27, Ⓦwww.alies.fr). A few kilometres south of Axat, the D17 forks left off the main highway leading over the desolate and beautiful Colline de Jau towards **Molitg-les-Bains** and **Prades** (see p.359).

Grotte de l'Aguzou

A visit to the **Grotte de l'Aguzou**, 15km southwest of Axat towards the upstream end of the Gorges de l'Aude, provides a unique opportunity to get an in-depth look at one of the region's famous caves. The guided tour of this magnificent complex is as close as a non-speleologist can get to the real thing and is very popular, so book well in advance (contact Philippe Moreno; €50 full day, €30 half-day; ☎04.68.20.45.38, ⊛www.grotte-aguzou.com). Equipped with overalls, helmet and lamp, groups of four to ten people are taken into the unlit cave system at 9am, to be conducted through the *grandes salles* of stalactites, stalagmites, columns and draperies, some of which are 20m high. Lunch (you bring your own) is taken 600m underground, and then it's on to the so-called "gardens of crystals" – a fantastic array of forms and shapes, some growing from the rock in long, thin needles, or like pine cones dusted by hoar frost, and others clear and convoluted like a Venetian glass-blower's accident. The best place to **stay** for an early start is the designated *camping sauvage* area by the river, 300m from the cave entrance.

The Donezan

In the twelfth century the **Donezan** region, and its then capital Usson – in the southern neck of the Gorges de l'Aude – became a sort of forerunner to Andorra: separated from the rest of Ariège by the **Col de Pailhères** (2001m), it was granted special financial privileges on account of its inaccessibility. Today **USSON**, like the rest of this remote region of seven villages, houses barely enough people to function as a *canton*; the spa of Usson-les-Bains 1km downstream is boarded up and for sale, while the dry-stone walls around the fields are as dilapidated as the **château** (Feb–April hols 2–6pm; May & June Sat, Sun & hols 1–6pm; July & Aug daily 10am–1pm & 3–7pm; early Sept daily 2–6pm; mid-Sept to mid-Oct Sat & Sun 2–6pm; €3.50), which was the first place of safety for the four Cathars who escaped the massacre at Montségur (see *The Land of Cathars* colour section). Dating back to at least the eleventh century, the castle, between the thirteenth and sixteenth centuries, marked the eastern boundary of the possessions of the counts of Foix, once champions of the Cathars and resolutely hostile to the French Crown.

Just above Usson, 3km along the D25 to Ax-les-Thermes, **MIJANÈS** is an immensely attractive stone-built village, with the only year-round **hotel-restaurant** between Quillan and Quérigut, the simple but perfectly adequate *Relais de Pailhères* (☎04.68.20.46.97; ④), with well-sized, wooden-floored rooms: reservations advisable at weekends. When there's good snow the small, laid-back **ski station** of Mijanès-Latrabe (☎05.61.20.41.37, ⊛www.donezan .com/sation_mijanes) opens, but this is not so frequent, given that the lifts only reach an altitude of 2060m. There are also cross-country trails here.

These days, **QUÉRIGUT**, 7km south of Usson, is the capital of the region. It stands at the head of a slope of neglected terraces, notable only for the stump of the **Château de Donezan**, the last stronghold of the Cathar leadership, who held out here for eleven years after the fall of Montségur. Although the area's **tourist office** (July & Aug daily 8.30am–12.30pm & 1.30–5.30pm; Sept–June closed Sat & Sun; ☎04.68.20.41.37, ⊛www.donezan.com) is actually in **Le Pla**, a hamlet 5km north of Quérigut on the D16 (half-way to Mijanès), Quérigut makes a good walking base for jaunts southwest through the forest; the only **accommodation** and **restaurant** is at the ageing *Hôtel le Donezan* (☎04.68.20.42.40, ⑤04.68.20.47.06; ②), uphill from the church opposite the fountain, though there is also a **campsite**, *Le Bousquet*, down by the stream below the village.

The Pays de Sault

The magnificent **PAYS DE SAULT** – the upland area more or less bounded by the rivers Aude and Ariège and, to the north, the main road from Quillan to Foix – is pure Cathar territory, as evinced by its most famous sight, the cliff-top stronghold of **Montségur**. For visitors it also offers some of Languedoc's most outstanding scenery; the vast highlands are composed primarily of limestone, and thus riddled with caves and ravines like the spectacular **Gorges de la Frau**. Above ground, the region's agricultural methods seem to have changed little since Cathar times – pesticides have yet to infiltrate the region's ecosystem, so the silhouettes of birds of prey can often be seen.

There are various ways to explore the *pays*. The only public transport consists of two regular **bus** services, both of which take you just part of the way to Montségur: the first runs along the region's northern perimeter, linking the train station in Quillan with that in Foix, via **Puivert** and **Lavelanet**; the other runs along the central plateau southwest from Quillan via Belcaire and Camurac to **Comus**, from where you can walk to Montségur via the Gorges de la Frau. Because departures are slightly more frequent from the east, the two routes to the castle described below approach from Quillan.

This is an excellent **hiking** region, which can be crossed in a few days, making occasional use of the sporadic public transport. A network of walking itineraries – the "Tour du Pays de Sault", the "Tour du Massif de Tabe", the "Piémont" and the GR107, plus forestry tracks – provide various routes, but the most popular is the "**Sentier Cathare**". This is best picked up at Foix and arrives at Montségur in two stages via Roquefixade (see p.142), then continues on to the Mediterranean, taking advantage of the descent towards the sea, via Puivert; it's easy walking much of the year (avoid mid-winter and mid-summer), with strategically placed accommodation in *gîtes d'étape*.

Much of the Pays de Sault is a spacious agricultural plateau, but it contains more vertiginous terrain, too. At the southeastern edge, the dramatic D107 road from Axat to Ax-les-Thermes runs through the **Rebenty** and **Joucou** gorges and over the **Col du Pradel** (1673m), a tough but wonderful **cycling** route. Another possible activity in the uplands is **skiing**, although neither of the region's downhill ski stations is worth much effort: the Monts d'Olmes resort, southwest of Montségur, is crowned with a seedy apartment development, while the one at Camurac comprises a "village" of decaying chalets – and both have impossibly low top-lifts of only 1940m. There is, however, good **cross-country skiing** on the plateau, with a small rental and tuition operation at Comus and especially good terrain at the **Col de Marmare**.

Puivert

Although it's just a twenty-minute drive from Quillan, the countryside around **PUIVERT** feels quite different, a vast upland planted with corn and sunflowers, buzzed by amateur pilots using the small local airport. Standing alone like a child's cardboard cut-out atop a gently rounded hill 1km or so east of the village, the **château** (daily: April–Sept 8am–8pm; Oct–March 10am–sundown; €4), fell to the Albigensian Crusade in 1210. More a place of culture than of arms, it was closely associated with the troubadour poets, whose preoccupation with romance might seem incompatible with the asceticism of the Cathars. What united them was the Occitan language, then spoken all across southern France. For the troubadours the *langue d'Oc* ("tongue of Oc") was simply the natural language of poetry and love; for the Cathars it expressed their defiance

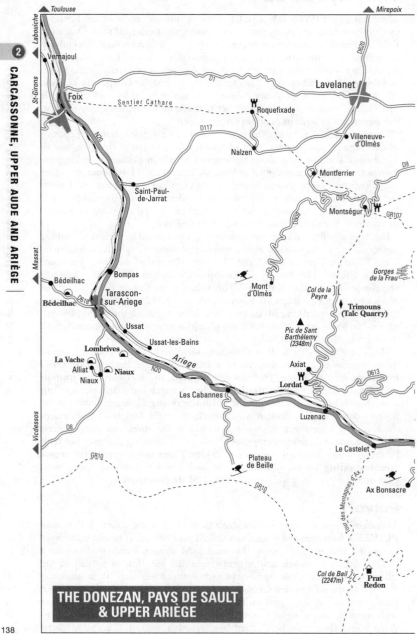

THE DONEZAN, PAYS DE SAULT
& UPPER ARIÈGE

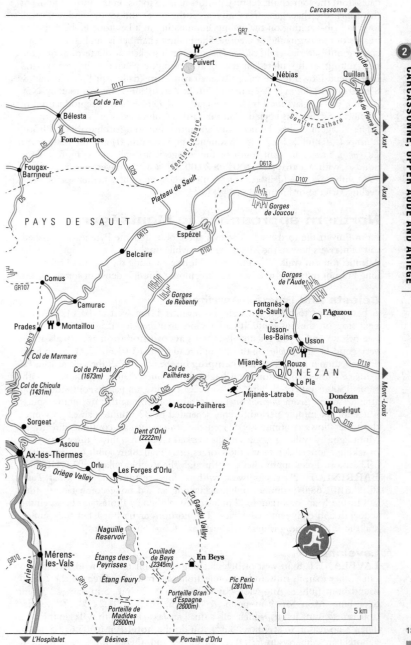

of the North. Little remains of the pre-1210 structure; most of what's visible dates from the fourteenth century. Visitors tend to focus on the various floors of the *donjon*; the chapel features vigil seats at the north and south windows, a wall font and rib-vaulting on the ceiling, culminating in a keystone embossed with images of the Virgin and St George. The highest chamber is dubbed the "musicians' room" after its eight *culs-de-lamps* or torch sockets at the termini of more rib-vaulting, each sculpted in the form of a figure playing a different period instrument. Down in the village, a small **museum** (daily: April to mid-July & Sept 10am–12.30pm & 2–6pm, mid-July to Aug 10am–7pm; Oct to early-Nov 2–5pm; €4) displays local traditional crafts and a collection of reproductions of medieval instruments copied from the castle's sculptures.

The village itself has the necessary amenities, including a **chambres d'hôte**, *L'Irenée* (☎04.68.20.95.79, ⓦwww.irenee-puivert.com; ❸) and the **restaurant** *Le Pamir*. Less than 1km south of the village is a small lake – more a large pond – with a **campsite** (☎04.68.20.00.58, ⓦwww.puivert.net; May–Sept) and swimming area (daily except Mon), a welcome sight whether you've been cycling, driving or hiking.

Northern approaches to Montségur

From Puivert the road heads west over the Col de Teil, the Pyrenean watershed: east of it, rivers flow to the Mediterranean, while on the west they empty into the Atlantic. You can **walk** from Puivert to Montségur along the "Sentier Cathare", a long but not difficult day of some 25km, mostly through dense fir forests.

Bélesta and Fougax-Barrineuf

A better place to begin the walk, however, is 11km west at **BÉLESTA**, the next stop on the bus route. It's a far more manageable village than Lavelanet (see below), and if you get stranded there's **accommodation** and **meals** at the very good *Le Troubadour*, on the through road (☎05.61.01.60.57; ❸; lunch from €10.50, dinner from €15), and **camping** on the east side of the village at *Le Val d'Amour* (June–Sept). Attractions begin almost immediately on the way south: some 1500m out of Bélesta, the route to Montségur passes Fontestorbes, an artesian spring (*source intermittente*) under a rock overhang that in summer spurts water for six-minute periods evenly separated by 32-minute pauses (in winter the water flows continuously). From the *source* you can continue directly to Montségur by walking along various marked GRs – roughly a three-hour trip, or taking a longer detour via the Gorges de la Frau, 8km south (see opposite).

The most direct approaches pass through the double village of **FOUGAX-BARRINEUF**, 2km southwest, with a fine **restaurant**, *Les Cinq Fours* (☎05.61.01.68.04; summer only), occupying an old bone-comb factory (this was formerly an important local industry, established by Protestants between the sixteenth and eighteenth centuries). The portions aren't huge, but they suffice, and the €16.50 *menu* is quite adequate as a four-course lunch.

Lavelanet

LAVELANET, 8km west of Bélesta along the Quillan–Foix road, has little to offer other than its onward bus connections and **tourist office** on the central roundabout (July & Aug Mon–Sat 9am–noon & 2–7pm, Sun 9am–12.30pm; Sept–June Mon–Sat 9am–noon & 2–6pm; ☎05.61.01.22.20, ⓔlavelanet.tourisme@wanadoo.fr), which sells a small *rando guide* (€2) to walks in the area. There's no reason to stay here, but if you do the **hotel** *Parc* (☎05.61.03.04.05, ⓔhotel.parc@libertysurf.fr; ❷) is adequate, and there's the clean, modern

campsite *Camping de Lavelanet* (April–Sept; ☎05.61.01.55.54), southwest of the centre. The town's main **market** is held on Friday, but there is also a smaller one on Wednesdays. Further information on the region, including detailed itineraries for numerous walking, cycling and riding trails can be found at Ⓦwww.paysdolmes.org.

The southern approach to Montségur via Comus

From Monday to Friday there are two late-afternoon buses daily along the main D613 from Quillan to Comus, about 40km southwest. They pass through **BELCAIRE**, where you'll find the homey hotel *Bayle* (☎04.68.20.31.05, Ⓔhotel-bayle@ataraxie.fr; ❶), perhaps due for redecoration but with comfortable rooms and a decent restaurant. Three kilometres before Comus, buses also stop at **Camurac** – with a **gîte**, *Auberge du Pays de Sault* (☎04.68.20.32.09; ❷) and **campiste**, *les Sapins* – from where you can walk to Montségur via **MONTAILLOU** village, a detour which takes about two hours. Montaillou subscribed to the Cathar heresy long after the fall of Montségur, until the Inquisition, directed by the bishop of Pamiers, set to work here during the 1320s. The records compiled by the inquisitors were so precise that historian Emmanuel Le Roy Ladurie was able to recreate every aspect of the villagers' lives from them, from the minutiae of domestic economics to the details of their sexual habits, in his book, *Montaillou*. Fewer than twenty people live here permanently now, all of them descendants of the Cathars, as you can see by comparing their surnames with those on the headstones in the ancient graveyard.

COMUS isn't a lot bigger than Montaillou, but does have an excellent **gîte d'étape** (☎04.68.20.33.69, Ⓦwww.gites-de-france-aude.com; ❷) attached to the *Centre École Pleine Nature*, which specializes in **caving**, the limestone hereabouts being peppered with two hundred known caves. Montségur is 13km away, through the **Gorges de la Frau**. From Comus take the GR107 (formerly the GR7B) which drops down as a mule track between fields to a wide gorge that suddenly becomes a *défilé*, where thousand-metre-high cliffs admit the sun only during the early afternoon. When the gorge widens again, you meet the dead end of the D5 coming south from Bélesta and Fougax-Barrineuf. There are two ways of continuing to Montségur: either along the Sentier Cathare westwards, wrapped in tree shade alongside a stream (turn off at the first farm, 45min along the D5), or via a bridle trail beginning about an hour along the tarmac, offering higher, more open ground. Either way, walking time from Comus is four hours.

Montségur

The ruined castle of **MONTSÉGUR** lives up to the promise of its distant view, its plain stone walls poised emphatically above the straggling, namesake village on a 1207-metre-high *pog* (a local variant on the Occitan *puèg*, or "hill"). The original fortifications were built by Guillaume "Short-Nose", duke of Aquitaine, but between 1204 and 1232 it was reconstructed as a bastion of the Cathars under the direction of Guilhabert de Castres, leader of the sect. Drastically eroded into naked vertical faces and gullies, the *pog* would have been a formidable defence. Only on the western side is it possible to walk up to the summit (about 30min), through what is now called the *prat dels cremats*, where the surviving Cathars were burned to death after the castle fell (a stone memorial pays tribute to them).

The beauty of **the site** (daily: Feb 10.30am–4pm; March 10am–5pm; April & Sept–Oct 9.30am–6pm; May–Aug 9am–7.30pm; Nov 10am–5.30pm; Dec 10.30am–4.30pm, €4) is what hits you first; the original walls were reduced by half after the siege, and all internal structures are gone except the simple keep, now open to the sky. Then you begin to wonder how that last Cathar community of five hundred people could have held out so long in such a small space. Even given that some lived in now-vanished houses at the foot of the walls on the north and west faces, there was still a sizeable garrison to be accommodated, together with the *faydits* – local aristocrats dispossessed by the crusade against Catharism. What's left of the castle takes no more than a few minutes to explore – rather disappointingly, you're no longer allowed to climb up on the walls, merely to traverse the keep to visit the west *donjon* – but it isn't so much what you see at Montségur that makes the trip unforgettable, as what your imagination can recreate from its remnants.

Down in the village, 1km below, a one-room **archeological museum** (April–Nov daily 10am–1pm & 2–7pm; €0.25, or free with castle ticket) displays artefacts excavated since the 1950s from the original village beside the walls, from both pre- and post-Cathar periods – mostly food bones, personal effects, tools and surviving fragments of houses.

Practicalities

Despite its small size, tourist numbers at Montségur village have prompted a **tourist office** (Feb–June & Oct–Dec Wed–Sun irregular hours; July–Sept daily 10am–noon & 2–6pm; ☎05.61.03.03.03, ⊛www.citaenet.com/montsegur), of most use for information on the precise route of the GR107. If you'd like to stay the night – and the beautiful scenery certainly appeals – there are a couple of **hotels**: the old-fashioned *Couquet* (☎05.61.01.10.28, ⊛www .montsegur-village.org; ❷), a rambling country *pension* of wood-furnished rooms with washbasins, and the adjacent two-star *Costes* (☎05.61.01.10.24, ⊛www.chez-costes.com; ❸), just uphill. There are also several **gîtes** and a **chambres d'hôte** *L'Oustal* (☎05.61.02.80.70, ⊛serge.germa@wanadoo.fr; closed Jan; ❷), The closest **campsite** (tents only) is the *Point Accueil Jeunes* (mid-March to mid-Oct; ☎05.61.01.10.27), at the lower end of the village on the Bélesta side. The *Costes* has a reasonably-priced **restaurant** attached, featuring game and *Ariègeois terroir*, while *L'Occidadelle*, near the centre, specializes in organic fire-cooked *foie*, sausages and local trout (from €11; closed Fri).

Roquefixade

Approximately 8km west of Lavelanet, the village of Nalzen is the best point along the D117 for access to **ROQUEFIXADE**, westernmost of the Cathar castles and last stop on the "Sentier Cathare" before Foix. A two-kilometre side road leads up to the eponymous village, refounded after the Albigensian Crusade as a *bastide*. From the high end of the village it's a twenty-minute climb to the unenclosed castle (free), which takes its name (originally *roca fissada* from the vast natural fissures augmenting its defences. Perched at the western end of a long ridge, it's bigger than it appears from below but utterly ruined; your main reward is the view over the valley below with its clustered villages, and south – weather permitting – to the high Pyrenean ridge. There are two **hotels** here, both with **restaurants**, the small *Relais des Pogs* (☎05.61.01.14.50, ⊛www.perso.wanadoo.fr/gite-relais-des-pogs; doubles ❷, dorm beds €13), and the three-star *Trois Châteaux* (closed late-Nov & mid-Jan to mid-Feb; ☎05.61.01.33.99, ⊛www.troischateaux.com; ❸).

Mirepoix and the lower Ariège valley

The lower part of the Ariège valley winds a leisurely course through a broad, rolling upland, whose rich dairy and wheat farms set it apart from the dry, vine-dominated scrub of most of Languedoc and Roussillon. The plain adjacent to this part of the river, centred on **Mirepoix**, was, like its southern counterpart the pays de Sault, a land of Cathars and castles; today it is home to a series of surprising and unique medieval **monuments**. Along the river proper you'll pass through unprepossessing **Pamiers** to **Foix**. Head of Ariège, France's smallest *département*, Foix was once the capital of a proudly independent principality, whose ambitions of independence were as strong and as fruitless as those of Toulouse county. Today the only testament to this is the town's strikingly positioned castle.

Mirepoix and around

The village of **MIREPOIX**, tucked away amongst the undulating hills of the Hers valley is served by just four daily buses running each way between Pamiers to the west and Lavelanet to the south. Without a car it would take a day's cycling to cover the 48km from Carcassonne, or a lengthy 30-kilometre trek along the GR7 from Villepinte (near Castelnaudary), via Fanjeux. Nevertheless the village receives a steady stream of visitors, who have yet to eradicate its considerable charm.

Mirepoix was a Cathar stronghold which paid dearly for its heresy, suffering a massacre at the hands of the Catholic Crusaders; but this in fact was only the beginning of its misfortunes, as a generation later it was all but destroyed by a flood. The present town dates back to 1290, when the noble Jean de Lévis laid out a new *bastide* in a safer location. At the centre of the village sits the broad place Général-Leclerc (or place de Couverts), arguably the most beautiful town **square** west of the Rhône. Almost the entire perimeter is rimmed by broad arcades supported by stout old beams, above which rise two storeys of pastel timber-frame houses. Although the *place* as a whole is beautiful, its star attraction is the fourteenth-century **Maison des Consuls** (now a hotel, see p.144) in the centre of the north side, at no. 6. This old council-house, courthouse and prison dates from the fourteenth century and is decorated by nearly 150 **wooden heads**, carved in high relief at the ends of the beams supporting the second storey. Each carving is individual, the portraits ranging across the gamut of medieval social classes and professions and including exotic and foreign peoples (including some very early portrayals of black Africans), as well as demons, monsters, animals and assorted grotesques. They make a singular masterwork.

By passing through an attractive nineteenth-century wrought-iron **market hall** on the south side of the square, you arrive at another arcaded *place*, Philip de Lévis – not as stunning as its larger counterpart, but also impressive. In the middle stands the fourteenth-century **cathedral of St-Maurice** (Mon–Sat 9am–noon & 2–6pm), whose broad single nave is the widest of any Gothic-style church in France. Local lore attributes the absence of supporting columns to the clergy's desire to monitor parishioners, checking that they were not carrying out forbidden Cathar practices, but this is doubtful given that the cathedral was not consecrated until 1509. The interior itself has suffered a rather excessive Baroque renovation, but the massive pipe organ and large carved gallery are impressive. There's also an unremarkable **museum** (daily 2–6pm) of rural life attached to the church.

Aside from a small thirteenth-century **gate** and a section of the old town wall a few metres west of place Leclerc, all of the town's sights are grouped around

△ Mirepoix

the two squares. There is little else to do, but the beauty of the town makes it the perfect spot to relax on a terrace, have a drink and soak up the atmosphere. On Monday mornings both of the *places* fill with the **market** stalls of local farmers – an excellent opportunity to prepare a picnic lunch.

Practicalities

Buses passing through Mirepoix stop within sight of the cathedral, and it's a short walk from there to the **tourist office** (Mon–Sat 9am–noon & 2–6pm; ℡05.61.68.83.76, ⓦwww.ot-mirepoix.fr), located in the only modern building on place Leclerc. There are two upmarket **hotels** to choose from: the *Relais Royal* (℡05.61.60.19.19, ⓦwww.relaisroyal.com; ⓪) in an eighteenth-century mansion in rue Maréchal Clauzel, and the gorgeous, and slightly more affordable, ⚿*Maison des Consuls* (℡05.61.68.81.81, ⓦwww.maisondesconsuls.com; ⓺). Those on a budget should head for the pleasant and well-maintained *Commerce*, in cours du Docteur Chabaud (closed Jan & part Nov, plus Sat from Sept–June; ℡05.61.68.10.29, ⓦwww.chez.com/lecommerce; ⓷). There is also a **campsite** (mid-June to mid-Sept; ℡05.61.68.28.63) on the road to Fanjeux.

Mirepoix boasts a number of **restaurants**, most ritzy of which is *Le Ciel d'Or* (in *Relais Royal*), although the *menus* (€29–70) are frankly overpriced. Better value, and more satisfying, is the simpler fare at *Le Comptoir Gourmand*, on cours Maréchal de Mirepoix (closed Mon; ℡05.61.68.19.19), and *La Flambée*, 17 rue Porte d'Amont (closed Sun eve & Mon; ℡05.61.68.16.59), both of which are in the €15-and-up range and specialize in cassoulet and dishes based on locally raised beef. Another good choice is *Les Remparts*, 6 cours Louis Pons (℡05.61.68.12.15), which has a medieval dining room and features *terroir* specialities from €15. On the main square, *Le Cantegril* at no. 25 (closed Wed out of season) serves cassoulet and *foie gras* (from €12), while *Café-Crème*, at no. 32 (closed Tues) is a good economy choice (*menus* from €10). The square is also home to a couple of surprisingly hip-looking **cafés**, the stylish *Castignolles*, and *Atmospher*, which is popular with a younger crowd.

Fanjeux

Halfway between Mirepoix and Carcassonne, tiny **FANJEUX** is a town which has fallen from medieval glory into virtual obscurity. Once the capital of Occitan troubadours, it was here that the *jocs florals* ("floral games"), a competition of Occitan poetry and song in which the winners were awarded gilded flowers for their efforts, were first held in 1323 (see p.418). In 1206, St Dominic de Gúzman passed through town and, contemplating the horizon from the town's belvedere, saw a series of miraculous fireballs. Inspired by this divine meteorological phenomenon he founded a convent at nearby Prouille, the precursor of his communities of preaching friars, the **Dominicans**. Nowadays, not even the buses stop in Fanjeux; the streets are quiet, and the various vestiges of its medieval splendour, the old Dominican headquarters and the town's church, moulder away unvisited except by groups of nuns on field trips. The one day it does come to life is August 16, when a medieval-style procession is held. If you are intent on exploring the town, there is an **information office** (Mon–Fri 10.30am–12.30pm & 3–7pm; ⓔfanjeux-bram-montreal@fnotsi.net) in the *mairie* which may be able to get you access to the monuments. And if you're passing through on the GR7, you might want to stay the night in any of a number of sporadically open **chambres d'hôtes**, or grab a meal in the town's **restaurant**, *La Table Cathare* (closed Sun & Mon), on the road out of town to Mirepoix. The local **campsite**, *Les Bruges* (☏04.68.24.70.26) is open June to September.

South to Camon

The hamlet of **CAMON**, 13km southeast of Mirepoix along the GR7, makes for a more rewarding stop than Fanjeux, and one which can be visited on a one-day walking trek from Mirepoix. Taking up the trail by the small bridge across the River Hers just east of Mirepoix's main roundabout, you'll walk along the well-marked trail over gentle, hilly farmland for 8km, until you reach **Lagarde**. There is a dramatic-looking ruin here, an ancient **château** (private and closed to visitors) whose empty window-frames set in broken walls romantically frame the blue sky behind. Continuing along for 3km the trail merges into a paved country lane, arriving at Camon shortly thereafter.

This tiny settlement, founded by Charlemagne himself, is still dominated by its **abbey-castle** and surrounded by parts of its two sets of walls (fourteenth- and sixteenth-century). The castle is private and operates as a luxurious bed-and-breakfast, but its richly appointed sixteenth-century interior can also be taken in as part of a guided tour (€5), arranged by the small **tourist office** on Grand Rue (Mon–Sat 9am–noon & 2–5pm; ☏05.61.68.88.26, ⓦwww.camon99.org), who can also get you into the town's unexceptional fourteenth-century church. If you can afford to splash out, ⚹ *L'Abbaye-Château* (☏04.61.68.31.23, ⓦwww .chateaudecamon.com; ❾) is the best place to **stay** the night; if you can't, you should at least enjoy a drink in its *salon de thé*, *La Tartine*. A cheaper option is the **chambres d'hôtes** *La Besse* (☏05.61.68.13.11; ❷), which also operates a **campsite** (☏05.61.68.64.63, ⓦwww.camping-labesse.com) and has a pool. If you continue south from Camon on the GR7, keep an eye out for the *cabanes*, sturdy little stone shepherds huts, hidden amongst the growth.

Vals

Perhaps the most interesting sight in the vicinity of Mirepoix is the church at **Vals**, 12km west of town on the north bank of the Hers. Vals itself is little more than a cluster of a half-dozen farmhouses – a dusty hamlet, with no services – where you are as likely to encounter a cow as a person walking down the street. About 20m from the main road a small and incredibly ancient **subterranean church** (daily 9am–6pm; free), once a stopping-point on the pilgrims route to Compostela, is built on a rocky spur. Entering through a hobbit-sized doorway you climb a staircase carved in the rock, passing through a pseudo-crypt of pre-Roman origin before reaching the church itself. When you enter, grope for the light switch to the left of the door to illuminate the curious three-chambered vertical structure; in the arches of some of its windows you'll find well-preserved late eleventh- and early twelfth-century frescoes of saints and angels, which recall the styles of painted churches of the Pyrenees. Lacking bicycle or car, you can reach Vals by getting off the Pamiers–Mirepoix bus at the turn-off from the D40 (just east of Les Pujols) and walking the remaining 4km.

Pamiers and the Grotte du Mas d'Azil

The town of **PAMIERS** is loaded with history, but suffered so gravely in the Wars of Religion that there is virtually nothing left to see here. Founded by returning Crusaders – who named it after the ancient city of Apamea in Syria, which they had captured – Pamiers later played the role of headquarters for the anti-Cathar Crusaders. In 1321, the Inquisition burned the last Cathar *parfait* Guillaume Bélibaste here. Now, of the town's vanished medieval glory only a scattering of old bell towers survive, poking above the rooftops in the tight knot of streets on the east bank of the Ariège, which make up Pamiers' bland old town. If you're here at the weekend, cross the bridge over the Ariège to see the small twelfth-century **Abbaye de Cailloup** (Sat & Sun 3–7pm; free), used as a farm building until 1980 but now restored to its former condition.

Trains and buses stop at Pamiers' **gare SNCF**, just east of the old town, and a short walk from the **tourist office** (July & Aug daily 9am–noon 2–6pm; Sept–June Mon–Sat 9am–noon & 2–6pm, Jan–March closed Sat pm; ☎05.61.67.52.52, ⓦwww.pamierstourisme.com) on boulevard Delcassé, at the southeastern corner of the ring road. If you want to stay, best value is the *Hôtel de France* on 5 cours du Rambaud (closed late Dec; ☎05.61.60.20.88, Ⓔcontact@hotelfrancepamiers.com; ❸), a welcoming, old-style hotel with good facilities. Alternatively, there's the *Hôtel de la Paix*, in place Albert Tournier (☎05.61.67.12.71, ⓦhoteldelapaix-pamiers.com; ❸), or the adequate two-star *Le Roi Gourmand* (☎05.61.60.12.12, ⓦhotel-roigourmand09.com; ❷), opposite the train station. All the hotels have **restaurants** (the *de France* being the cheapest with a €15 *menu*), and there are other places scattered about the town, but nothing outstanding. The town's three-star **campsite**, *Village d'Apamée* (mid-May to Oct; ☎05.61.60.06.89), also rents **bikes**, as does Cycles Passion (☎05.61.60.14.05).

The cave and village of Mas d'Azil

The swathe of land which sweeps northwest of Pamiers towards the banks of the Garonne and Toulouse holds virtually nothing of interest, its flat landscape peppered by farming hamlets and populated largely by cattle. There is, however, a good route for **biking** (if you're in good shape) or driving (if you're not) across the western spur of the low Plantaurel mountains to the **Grotte du Mas d'Azil**, and on to St-Girons. Pick this up by crossing the Ariège west of Pamiers' old town on the D110 (direction St-Victor); 7km later you'll hook up with the main D119. Thereafter, the road climbs steeply before dipping into the valleys of the Lèze and Arize.

At Sabaret a gruelling series of hairpin curves ascends to the village of **MAS D'AZIL**, whose massive cavern is not only noteworthy for being the most northerly and largest of the great Pyrenean prehistoric *grottes* (see p.159), but also as Europe's only **drive-through cave**. The gaping maw (some 50m in height) opens up just to the south of the town, swallowing the D119 road whole, before disgorging it several hundred metres later. Once a lair of the giant cave-bears which populated the south of France in the days of the great mammals and, roughly 30,000 years ago, a home for our own humble ancestors, historically the cave has provided refuge for a whole series of endangered species, including early Christians, Cathars and Huguenots. Indeed, it was here and in the village that a group of Protestants made a valiant and desperate stand in 1625, fending off a Catholic army which outnumbered them fifteen to one. If you're interested in seeing more than simply what passes by your window, other sections of the cave are **accessible by foot** (March, Oct & Nov Sun 2–6pm; April & May Mon–Fri 2–6pm, Sun 10am–noon & 2–6pm; June & Sept daily 10am–noon & 2–6pm; July & Aug daily 10am–6pm; Dec–Feb school hols 3–4.15pm; €6.10), and you can stroll through galleries littered and decorated with the vestiges of its former inhabitants. Nearby, a new museum, **La Forêt aux Dinosaures** (Wed–Mon: May, June & Sept 10am–noon & 2–6pm; July & Aug 10am–7pm; Oct–April 2–5/6pm; €6.10) is an outdoor exhibition of fossils and dinosaur replicas that will delight children.

The village itself, which lost its fortifications to a spiteful Richelieu, has a small **museum** (March, Oct & Nov Sun 2–6pm; April–June & Sept Tues–Sun 2–6pm, July & Aug daily 11am–1pm & 2–7pm; free with cave or €4.60) by the church, with prehistoric knick-knacks collected from the cavern and a section on the local glass-making tradition. The same building houses the local **tourist office** (April–Sept daily 10am–1pm & 2–6pm; ☎05.61.69.97.22 ⓔtourisme .arize.leze@wanadoo.fr). The only **hotel** in the hamlet is the family-run *Hôtel Gardel* (closed mid-Nov to mid-March; ☎05.61.69.90.05, ⓕ04.61.69.70.27; ❷), and there is a municipal **campsite** (June to mid-Sept) a twenty-minute walk away. The best place to eat is the homely **restaurant** with **rooms**, *Le Jardin de Cadettou* (closed Sat lunch time, Sun eve & Mon; ☎05.61.69.95.23; ❸),

The Return of Martin Guerre

In 1548 Martin Guerre, a surly young farmer who had been accused of theft, suddenly vanished from Artigat, abandoning his wife Berthrande and their infant son. Eight years later Martin returned, to the joy of his wife and family. By 1559, however domestic bliss had given way to family tensions; when Martin sued his uncle for part of his father's inheritance, Pierre Guerre countered with the incredible charge that Martin was, in fact, an imposter. After a series of suits and counter-suits the case was brought before the *capitouls* of Toulouse in 1560. Martin was in closing arguments with legal victory in his grasp, when suddenly a man claiming to be the true Martin Guerre appeared in court. And so it was that the defendant was found guilty and sentenced to be hung at the very doors of the house he had fraudulently inhabited. This tale, all the more incredible for its historical accuracy, was brought to international attention in 1983 by historian Natalie Zemon Davis's *The Return of Martin Guerre* (see Books, p.408) and became the subject of a 1982 film of the same name starring Gérard Depardieu and Nathalie Baye. The film, is excellent: a vivid evocation of rural life in the sixteenth-century Pyrénées and a must-see for travellers to the region. Sadly, little remains of the Artigat of Martin Guerre; the town was captured and all but destroyed by Protestants on 7 March 1621.

serving excellent *menus* of regional cuisine from €15. Alternatively, there's the *Gardel*, whose family-run dining room also has *menus* from €15.

Emerging from the cave, the road meanders through attractively forested uplands before meeting the main highway at Lescure, just 8km east of St-Girons (see p.152). Fans of the film and book *The Return of Martin Guerre* (see box, p.147) will want to visit **Artigat**, a bucolic little village west of Pamiers, over 20km of winding lanes, which is best reached via the D919. There's nowhere to stay here, but it's a pleasant place to wander through and makes a good stop on the way between Foix and Toulouse.

Foix and around

Eighteen kilometres upstream from Pamiers, **FOIX** has few specific sights itself but is the most agreeable base in the valley, with connections by train and bus into the mountains. It has a good range of services, and is surprisingly lively for a relatively small town. What's more, people tend to hurry past, so that although Foix is located in the midst of the greatest concentration of prehistoric caves in France, it is never overwhelmed by visitors and retains an appealing intimacy and freshness.

Arrival, information and accommodation

The **gare SNCF** sits on the right bank of the Ariège, a ten-minute walk north of the centre; most **buses** stop on the central cours Gabriel-Fauré, near the Resistance monument, although some will drop you off behind the post office. The **tourist office** at 45 cours Gabriel-Fauré (mid-June to mid-Sept 9/9.30am–noon/12.30pm & 2–6pm; mid-Sept to mid-June Mon–Sat 9am–noon & 2–6pm; ☏05.61.65.12.12, ⓦwww.ot-foix.fr) can be reached from the train station by walking south along the east bank of the Ariège and then crossing the Pont-Neuf. If you plan on doing any hiking, pick up a free *randonnées* booklet here, published by the *département* of Ariège.

Most **accommodation** is found in the old town, on the west bank of the Ariège, though little of it is inspiring. The quietest and most comfortable option is the three-star *Hôtel Lons*, 6 place Duthil, near the Pont Vieux (closed late Dec to early Jan; ☏05.61.65.52.44, ⓦwww.hotel-lons-foix.com; ❸). The *Eychenne*, 11 rue Noël-Peyrevidal (☏05.61.65.00.04, ⒻD05.61.65.56.63; ❸) is second choice if only for its location in the heart of the old town; the rooms are decent enough, though the bar on the ground floor can get noisy. Across the street at no. 16 is the friendly **youth hostel** *Auberge Léo Lagrange* (☏05.61.65.09.04, ⓦwww.leolagrange-foix.com; ❷), with one- to four-person rooms. Rather better and more bucolic accommodation can be found at the riverside *Hôtel du Lac* (☏05.61.65.17.17, ⒻD05 61 02 94 24; ❸), 3km north of the town centre off rue Leclerc; the municipal **campsite**, *Lac de Labarre* (May–Oct; ☏05.61.65.11.58), is just further on.

The Town

Foix has a well-preserved **old town** of narrow alleys, wedged in the triangle between the Ariège and the Arget rivers. A few of the overhanging houses here date from the fourteenth to sixteenth centuries, and especially attractive are **place Pyrène** and **place St-Vincent** with their fountains, though many junctions in the old quarter sport some sort of water feature. All lanes seem to lead eventually to the conspicuously large **church of St-Volusien** in the east of the old town, originally Romanesque but almost completely reconstructed after being razed during the Wars of Religion. Its eponymous square, along

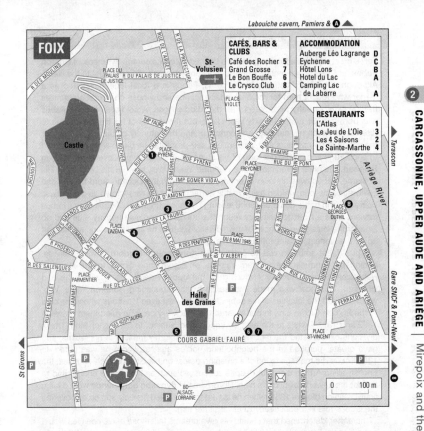

with the Halles des Grains just off cours Gabriel-Fauré, hosts lively Wednesday and Friday **markets** – farm produce and plants at the *place*, and meat, cheese, savouries and pastries at the metal-roofed *halles*, which on other days is a prime drinking venue.

Presiding over the old town is Foix's grey hill-top **castle**, not so much a single fortification as three magnificent, dissimilar towers from different eras: a slender twelfth-century turret, a bulky square fourteenth-century keep and a broad and rounded fifteenth-century tower – dramatic when viewed from any angle. From 1012 the castle on this site was the seat of the counts of Foix, whose association with the Cathar faith led to its being besieged four times by Simon de Montfort, who failed to break the fort's resistance. One of these counts, Roger-Bernard II "Le Grand", was a determined opponent of the Albigensian Crusade, but perhaps made his most lasting contribution to history by marrying Ermensende of Castellbó early in the thirteenth century, thereby linking the fortunes of Foix and Andorra. Although the dynasty ended illustriously with Huguenot king Henri III of Foix-Béarn and Navarre, who annexed what had become a Pyrenean mini-state to the Crown on becoming Henri IV of France in 1589, the biggest name in Foix is that of the fair-haired knight whose features can be seen on postcards all over town – Gaston III, known as Gaston Fébus (see box, p.150).

Looming over the town, the **castle** (daily: May, June & Sept 9.45am–noon & 2–6pm; July & Aug 9.30am–6.30pm; Oct–April Wed–Sun 10.30am–noon

Gaston Fébus

Foix's greatest hero, a towering figure in the history of the central Pyrenees, is **Gaston Fébus** (or Phébus, in French), Count of Foix and Viscount of Béarn (just to the west). Although ultimately frustrated in his plans, Fébus is a local legend, revered as a leader who fought hard for regional independence and whose character epitomizes the ideals of chivalry associated with the Middle Ages. A soldier and poet, Fébus was born in 1331 and died sixty years later, but the details of his life are difficult to disentangle. With his dashing, aristocratic image he naturally became a subject for the songs of troubadours and, a relentless self-promoter, he did everything he could to encourage and embroider tales of his own valour and prowess, even inviting Jean Froissart, the great chronicler of the Hundred Years' War, to write his biography. His surname, Fébus, was his own invention, derived from the Occitan word for sun and celebrating his long, golden hair. What is certain is that he was known as a dauntless soldier, and in battle could be found leading his men with the cry *Fébus avan* ("Fébus forward"). As a ruler he was very much the image of medieval nobility – he had no time for the legislative councils of town dwellers, which he abolished, and set himself up as the highest judicial authority in his realms.

Fébus' great ambition was to create an **autonomous kingdom** in the Pyrenees, adding by conquest the western regions of Bigorre and Soule to the lands of Nébouzan, Béarn and Foix (including all the upper Ariège valley), which he had inherited. This goal was made impossible by the continuing Hundred Years' War, which divided the loyalties of his subjects: in the west lived Gascons who were loyal to the English Crown, and in particular to the Black Prince, who ruled them between 1362 and 1371 – while to the east lay Languedoc, subject to the French king. These divisions exacerbated the feuding of the leading knightly families in his realms, and gave greater purpose to the neighbouring nobles against whom he was pitted. In 1362 Fébus did manage to inflict a crushing defeat on his Gascon arch-enemies, the English-allied Armagnacs, but despite successes such as this, in the end he had to accept the unworkability of his plan. His dreams of **dynastic dominance** were dealt a final, crushing blow in 1380, when he is said to have killed his only son on discovering the latter's role in a conspiracy to assassinate him.

Thereafter, determined that should his own dreams fail, those of his enemies would not succeed, Fébus dedicated himself to campaigning for a strong, **united France**, pledging his lands to the Crown by inheritance. But this too was initially thwarted, with the d'Albret family, one of his rivals, gaining the throne of Béarn and keeping it out of French control until 1589. Nevertheless, Gaston Fébus' ideals and endeavours have come to represent all that is romantic about the medieval era, and, in Foix especially, he is celebrated with festivals in July and August and remembered fondly for **l'hypocras**, a spiced wine drink which he invented and which is enjoyed in the region to this day.

& 2–5.30pm; €4.20) is reached by ascending a steep flight of stairs. Inside, two of the three towers hold exhibits relating to the history of the building and the County of Foix; others are home to rather uninspiring interactive displays of local crafts and products. On a clear day the views from the crenellated turrets reward those who puff up the narrow key-stone staircases. On weekend evenings (July & Aug) the castle forms the venue for an elaborate *son et lumière* and theatre performance with a massive cast (10pm; €22). If the castle seems rather too cramped to have served as a noble residence, bear in mind that the counts' regular residence was the roomier castle of Orthez in Béarn – they just stopped in here on occasion to reassert their power over the town.

Eating, drinking and nightlife

The best area for **eating** is rue Lafaurie, the old blacksmiths' bazaar at the centre of the old town, where the best of several establishments is *Les 4 Saisons* at no. 11 (closed Sat & Sun in season, plus Sun–Thurs eve off-season), whose gimmick is to bring to your table a hotplate – a *pierrade* – on which you cook fish and meat yourself; they also do a wide range of crêpes (€14–20). *Le Jeu de L'Oie* (closed Sun & Mon in winter) nearby at no. 17 is also worth trying for more traditional fare (lunch from €10). A pricier, but worthwhile option is *Le Sainte-Marthe* (℡05.61.02.87.87; closed Wed off-season), at 21 rue Peyrevidal, which has a range of specialties (*menus* €36–44) including cassoulet, with a dog-free dining-room and street-side terrace. *L'Atlas* (closed Mon lunch) on place Pyrène offers up delicious Moroccan cuisine (€14.50–22) in the shadow of the town's church.

There is a row of café-restaurants which occasionally double as night-time **music-bars** on the west side of the cours Gabriel-Fauré, on either side of the old market hall. *Café des Rocher*, *Grand Grosse* and *La Bonne Bouffe* all have decent if unspectacular dinner *menus* for €10–15, and stay open for drinking. Later on, you can head to the **disco** *Le Crysco Club* (Wed–Sat 10pm–3am) at 3 cours Irénée Cros, on the far side of the *pont vieux* over the Ariège.

Listings

Car rental ADA, 59 av du Général-Leclerc, ℡05.61.68.38.38, Ⓦwww.ada.fr, Europcar, Route d'Espagne, ℡05.61.02.32.74, Ⓦwww.europcar .fr; and Hertz RN20 Peysales, ℡05.61.65.15.99, Ⓦwww.hertz.fr, have offices in or near town.

Internet access To get online head to the friendly Bureau de' Information Jeunesse (Mon 1–5pm, Tues–Fri 10am–5pm; closed Aug) on rue Roger, off rue du College behind the tourist office, or to the pay-terminal at the post office, also on rue Roger.

Laundry There's a coin-operated launderette (daily 7am–9pm) on place Lazéma.

Swimming pools Indoor and outdoor swimming pools are located at place du Champs de Mars, behind the main post office (€2.50 admission).

Watersports The narrow Lac Labarre reservoir, just north of town, has the usual gamut of waterside facilities; ASPTT (℡05.61.02.62.99) rents kayaks and canoes, and organizes rafting trips.

West of Foix

Heading west from Foix, the main road, the D117, climbs rapidly to the **col de Bouich** (599m) before descending through the Aujole and Baup valleys to arrive at St-Girons and St-Lizier, near the western limit of the *département*. On this particular road, there's little to detain you, although you might stop at **La Bastide de Serou**, just under half way, to have a drink in the square outside its old market building. Just past the village, a treacherous forest road provides cuts up towards Mas d'Azil (see p.147).

If however you take the Vernajoul road from the town centre, which eventually links up with the D117, you'll come to the subterranean **river-cavern of Labouiche**, some 3km northwest of Foix (daily: Easter–June & Sept to mid-Nov 10–11.15am & 2–5.15pm; July & Aug 9.30am–5.15pm; €8): it claims to be the longest such navigable cave in western Europe, although the water levels in winter are so high as to block access completely. The same amusement-park atmosphere prevails here as at Lombrives (see p.160): twelve-person boats travel for 75 minutes in opposite directions along the 1500m of galleries open to the public. Entry is either via the natural entrance, or an artificial one bored at the upstream end, on either side of the ticket office – you're told which to assemble at. Highlights of the cavern are the **waterfall** at the upstream end of the river and a small chamber full of formations below the artificial entry; these and other oddities along the way are described by the guides, who do their best to keep up a witty patter while hauling the craft via ceiling-mounted cables.

There are also two unusual English-run **chambres d'hôtes** off the road between Foix and St-Girons. At Rimont, 34km from Foix, there is – a rarity in France – excellent and reasonably priced vegan (not even eggs) accommodation, at ⚐ *Le Guerrat*, Suzanne Morris and Trevor Warman's working organic farm (mid-May to mid-Oct; ☎05.61.96.37.03, ⓦwww.leguerrat.org; ❸), while at Lescure, 4km further on, Nicholas Goldsworthy's *La Baquette* (May–Oct; ☎&ⓕ05.61.96.37.67; ❷) can arrange guided walks and tours of the local wildlife and flora. Heading south from La Bastide de Serou towards Massat, you'll come upon one of the better hotels in this area, ⚐ *Auberge les Myrtilles* (☎05.61.65.16.46, ⓦwww.perso.wanadoo.fr/auberge.les.myrtilles; ❷; closed Nov–Feb) in Col des Marrous, a beautiful rustic hotel with an indoor pool and jacuzzi, as well as a fine *terroir* restaurant (from €17).

The Couserans

Southwest of Foix, the peaks and the northern slopes of the Pyrenees shelter a series of high river valleys known collectively as the **Couserans**. As the Garbet, Salat, Arac and Alet rivers drain off the high glaciers they flow down through a country traditionally as poor and isolated as it is majestically beautiful. Cattle-farming, herding and forest industries were the original means of subsistence for the meagre population of this area, while later, mineral exploitation and spa development brought tenuous fits of humble prosperity and sustain the area today. The two towns which dominate this region, **St-Girons** and **St-Lizier**, are worth a visit if only to appreciate a subtle cultural shift offered by the mid-Pyrenees – the westernmost zone of Occitan influence coloured by contacts with Navarre, the Basque country and the flatlands of Gascony. The lowlands around the two towns were prosperous in the Middle Ages, as the cluster of romanesque churches in the country-side around them testifies to. If you have the time, energy and perseverance, exploring the highlands to the south will lead you through some of the most remote and splendid scenery, and distinctive culture, the Pyrenees have to offer.

Given the area's isolation, it should come as no surprise that there is little by way of public transport in the region. There are bus links from Toulouse and Foix to St-Girons, and a regular service up into the Couserans, but unless you have a **car**, to do any real exploring you'll have to resort to **hiking** – cycling in these hills is strictly for the dedicated.

St-Girons and St-Lizier

The two complementary towns of St-Girons and St-Lizier, 45km west of Foix along the D117, and separated from each other by only 1500m of riverbank, to all intents and purposes form a single unit. The former is the administrative and commercial centre, which, with good transport links to Toulouse and a range of services, is most useful as a base for exploring the mountains. The latter, which was the capital of the Couserans until the role was ceded to St-Girons, is where you'll find the sights.

Apart from its long association with making cigarette papers, the most striking thing about **ST-GIRONS** is its pavements, made of a local dark-grey marble veined with white, and with finely chiselled gullies to carry away the rainwater. And although there are no other memorable sights, it's a far from unpleasant place, with a couple of decent **festivals**: folklore in mid-July and theatre in early August. The simplest centre for orientation is the **Pont-Vieux**. Straight ahead on the right bank of the River Salat, the bridge points you into the old commercial centre of the town, with some marvellously old-fashioned shops, their fronts and fittings unchanged for generations. To the right is the typically provincial **place des Poilus**, its cachet largely due to the faded elegance of the *Grand Hôtel de France* and the equally old-fashioned *Hôtel de l'Union*, opposite, where you can still stay (see p.154). The *Grand Café de l'Union* on the square is a splendidly balconied period café that faces the *mairie*. Beside it, along the riverbank, a wide gravelled *allée* of plane trees, the **Champ de Mars**, provides the site for a big general market on the second and fourth Mondays of every month, and for a regular produce market every Saturday morning.

St-Girons' older and prettier sibling, **ST-LIZIER**, occupies a little hillock, still partially enclosed by walls and towers built under the Romans in the third and fourth centuries. Strolling along its narrow streets, keep an eye out for the carved facades of its numerous fifteenth-century palaces, particularly around the places de l'Église and des Entends, and on the rues des Nobles and d'Horloge. Of special note is the late seventeenth-century **bishop's palace**, from the terrace of which you get a great view over the Couserans rising to the south, with the snowcapped peaks of the Pyrenees as a backdrop. Inside, the **museum** (April, May & Oct to early-Nov Tues–Sun 2–6pm; June & Sept Tues–Sun 10am–noon & 2–6pm; July & Aug daily 10am–7pm; €4) contains an uninspiring collection of local handicrafts, bric-a-brac, and household items.

The main attraction here is the **cathedral of St-Lizier** (Mon–Sat 9am–noon & 2–6/6.30pm, Sun 2–6/6.30pm; free), an eleventh-century structure built on Roman foundations, with a magnificent array of Romanesque frescoes on the walls and ceiling of its twelfth-century apse; the figure of Christ, as *Pantocrator* ("Lord of all") presides over angels, apostles and various other figures who descend in hierarchy towards the floor. The adjacent **cloister** is particularly noteworthy for the carvings of its capitals – in addition to the usual floral motifs and monsters are extraordinary narrative scenes illustrating the highlights of the Old and New Testament. Over the five centuries after its founding the church was completed piecemeal, with sections added on in a strange higgledy-piggledy manner, and though there hardly seems to be a right angle in the floor plan, somehow it all holds together. Apart from the building itself, the church's **treasury** is host to a stunning sixteenth-century reliquary bust of St Lizier, as well as other pieces dating back to the eleventh century.

Four kilometres north-east of St-Lizier, just off the highway to Foix, the tiny, beautifully-preserved *bastide* hamlet of **Montjoie** evokes a sense of history which the larger villages and towns of the region have all but lost. Hunkered down within fourteenth-century walls, it boasts a striking fortified church. There's also a notable romanesque church in **Eycheil** (contact the tourist office in St-Girons; €1.50), 3km southeast of St-Girons on the Massat/Aulus route.

Practicalities

Buses from Toulouse and the Couserans arrive in St-Girons on the left bank of the river at place des Capots. There's a **tourist office** here, in the central place Alphonse-Seintein (July & Aug Mon–Sat 9am–6.30pm, Sun 10am–1pm; Sept–June Mon–Sat 9am–noon & 2–6pm; ☎05.61.96.26.60, ⓦwww.ville-st -girons.fr), and seasonal one up in St-Lizier (June–Sept Mon–Sat 10am–noon & 2–6/7pm, Sun 2–6/7pm; ☎05.61.96.77.77, ⓔot.saintlizier@wanadoo .fr). The best **accommodation** in town for both atmosphere and comfort is

St-Lizier's *Hôtel de la Tour* (☎05.61.66.38.02, ✉hoteldelatour06@wanadoo.fr; ❸) in a remodelled old building down by the riverbank. In St-Girons, there's the elegant *Hotel Eychennes*, on av Paul-Laffont (☎05.61.04.04.50; ✉eychen @club-internet.fr; ❹), or the cheaper *Hôtel del Union*, on allée Champs de Mars (☎05.61.66.09.12, ℻05.61.04.81.73; ❶). Alternatively, on St-Girons' southern edge, the ⚘ *Château Beauregard* (☎05.61.66.66.66, ⓦwww.perso.orange.fr /domainedebeauregard; ❹) is a nineteenth-century estate with its own park, swimming pool, two hotels and a fine restaurant. If you look like a hiker, the St-Lizier tourist office will arrange a berth in the pilgrim **hostel** for a single night (dorm beds €15), while the nearby **campsite** *Parc des Palettes* (March–Sept; ☎05.61.66.06.79) also rents out bungalows. The *département* website (ⓦwww .ariege.com) also has comprehensive listings of *gîtes*, B&Bs and hotels in the isolated hinterlands.

The **restaurants** at the hotels *Eychennes* and *Château Beauregard* (both closed Sun eve) serve fairly adventurous and expensive fare, while the *de la Tour* (also closed Sun eve) is more economical, with a strong *terroir* streak. There are also a number of standard-fare **brasseries** in St-Girons. **Bikes** can be rented at Horizon Vertical in St-Girons (☎05.61.96.08.22), who also do caving trips, and at Cycles Solana in St-Lizier (☎05.61.96.26.60).

Over the Couserans to Tarascon

Looping back to Tarascon (see p.157) in the Ariège valley provides an opportunity to take in the stunning terrain of the **COUSERANS**, which buttress some of the highest peaks in the Pyrenees and, culturally, remains a unique and independent zone, quite different from Languedocian Foix. Gascon is still spoken here, and if you have the good fortune to visit during local festivities, you'll be treated to the area's singular costume and music: men wearing white embroidered jackets (reminiscent of traditional Greek styles) and red *baretos* (hats) sport curious wooden shoes with high (up to 30cm) pointed toes, while women wear long dresses draped with colourful scarves; the clarinet-like *haut-bois*, accompanied by drums, supplies the sounds for traditional dances. The villages in the region are likewise distinctive, built low in stone and timber to resist the high mountain clime. The Couserans has traditionally been a difficult area to access and even more so to govern, the proud mountain people resentful of any infringement of their liberties or threat to their way of life. As late as the nineteenth century, the villagers waged a guerrilla war against the French government – the so-called Guerre des Demoiselles ("war of the girls"), when they dressed up as women in a surprise attack on local property owners, government foresters and police.

The magnificent landscape is accessible by road and trail, with a number of rewarding circuits. Most of the villages of the Couserans have tourist offices, but hours can be irregular and confirmation is best made at the office in St-Girons, which has information and **walking** itineraries for the whole region. You may also want to contact the Ariège tourist board for **information** (CDT Ariège Pyrénées, 31bis avenue du Général de Gaulle, BP 143, 09004 Foix; ☎05.61.02.30.70, ℻05.61.65.17.34, ⓦwww.ariegepyrenees .com). There are three main **routes** which traverse the Couserans from west to east, only one of which is partially accessible by public transport from St-Girons (a single bus route climbing from St-Girons to Aulus-les-Bains), and all of which are fairly demanding drives. Hikers will find comprehensive information on **cabins** and **refuges** at ⓦwww.pyrenees-refuges.com and ⓦwww.ariege.com.

Via Massat

Striking out from the Salat, south of St-Girons, through the dramatic **Gorges de Riabouto** will bring you to the confluence of the Arac and Riabouto. Here, you can take the more direct of the two routes to Tarascon by heading due east to the village of **MASSAT**. As you approach, the fifteenth-century bell tower of its church rises 60m above the village in a marvellous Pyrenean tableau. There is a **tourist office** here (Tues–Fri 10am–noon & 2–6pm, Sat 10am–1pm & 4.30–6pm; ☎05.61.96.92.76, Ⓔotmassat&wanadoo.fr) and good shops and services, including the *Hôtel Le Globe* (☎05.61.96.96.66, Ⓔleglobe2 @wanadoo.fr; ❷) and the *Hostellerie des Trois Seigneurs* (Easter–Oct; ☎05.61.96.95.89, Ⓕ05.61.04.94.18; ❸), both of which provide food as well as lodging. A **market** is held on the second and fourth Thursday of every month, and Sundays in summer. Continuing east, the road climbs in a seemingly endless succession of hair-raising bends until you reach the 1250m-high Col de Port. On the left rise the wooded slopes of the **Montagnes de l'Arize**, while on the right the barren **Pic des Trois Seigneurs** (2199m) scratches the clouds. A steep eighteen-kilometre descent then brings you to Tarascon, passing the Parc de la Préhistoire (see p.158) at the entrance to the town.

Via Seix and Aulus-les-Bains

From the mouth of the Riabouto gorge, the road heads further up the Salat to **OUST** (Ⓦwww.ariege.com/oust). The squat twelfth-century **church** in neighbouring Vic (contact the tourist office in St-Girons; €1.50) is the only real attraction, there are some good **accommodation** options, including the two-star *de la Poste* (☎ & Ⓕ05.61.66.86.33, Ⓔhotel-de-la-poste3@wanadoo.fr; ❷) and the year-round **campsite** *Quatre Saisons* (☎05.61.96.55.55, Ⓔcamping @cegetel.net), which also has bungalows.

From Oust, a relatively straight road leads up the Garbet Valley to Aulus-les-Bains, though if you are travelling by bus you'll continue on to **SEIX**, a few kilometres beyond, where the peaks of the **cirque** at the valley's head come into view. This market town, lorded over by a fifteenth-century castle and with a distinctive church tower, makes a good base if you plan to do some hiking in the region: the traditional and homey *Auberge du Haut Salat* (☎05.61.66.88.03, Ⓔaubergeduhautsalat@wanadoo.fr; ❷) is good place to **stay**. The **tourist office** (☎05.61.96.52.90, Ⓦwww.haut-couserans.com) in the town centre provides up-to-date hiking information, and can tell you about the **mountain biking** circuit just south of town. La Marmotte (☎05.61.66.91.60) rents **bikes**, and the local Crédit Agricole bank handles currency **exchange**. In summer a **market** is held on the second and fourth Wednesday of the month, and local products are also sold at the annual **horse fair** on October 18.

From Seix, the bus continues up the Alet river to its terminus at **AULUS-LES-BAINS**, a spa village and adjunct to the mediocre ski station of **Guzet-Neige** (☎05.61.96.00.11, Ⓦwww.guzet.com), separated from Spain's Vall de Cardós by a ten-kilometre-wide mountain wall, and lying among lush and fragrant meadows ringed by dramatic peaks. In summer the station becomes a centre for a variety of sports including para-gliding, rafting and hiking. The most remote point of the traditionally poor Couserans, Aulus was once famous for its bear trainers, who toured the wealthier lowlands. The classic walk here involves heading south along the GR10 to the **Cascade d'Ars** waterfall, a round trip of about five hours. Aulus' **tourist office** on allée des Thermes (daily: 9am–noon/12.30pm & 2/3–6/7pm; ☎05.61.96.01.79, Ⓦwww.haut -couserans.com) can provide detailed information on hikes, as well as accommodation options. Thanks to the spa industry which keeps the town busy from May to November, and the skiing which brings people in winter there are a number of places to stay and eat. The best **accommodation** deal is the *L'Oustalet* (closed Nov; ☎05.61.96.00.90, ℻05.61.96.03.29; ❷) with comfortable rooms and an excellent and affordable **restaurant** (from €14). A more attractive choice is the *Hôtel les Ousaillès* (☎05.61.96.03.68, ✉jcharrue@free .fr; ❸), while the cheapest beds are at the **gîte**, *Presbytère* (☎05.61.96.02.21; ❶). For light meals, the tearoom and bar *La Cascade* (weekends only in winter) can fix you up with snacks from about €5. The nearest **campsite** to Aulus is *Le Couledous* (year-round; ☎05.61.96.02.26) in a holiday complex neighbouring the town. Sunday is **market**-day (morning).

From Aulus, a narrow mountain road and the GR10 wind separate paths along the northern fringe of the **Pic Rouge de Bassiès** (2676m), weaving in and out of the tree line. Looking back, you'll see the high-walled crenellated cirque formed by the peak and its nearest neighbour, the Pic des Trois Comtes; the drama of the cirque's heights is underscored by wedges of snow lying beneath the sheerest faces, while below, the steep slopes are luxuriant with beech. The road rises to the east, then the north, skirting the small Étang de Lers and passing herds of grey cows grazing the alpine meadow, to arrive at the pass, the **Port de Lers** (1517m). Eventually passing the waterfall, the **cascade d'Arbu**, some 3km beyond, you begin a sharp descent towards Vicdessos. The GR10, on the other hand, continues due east to the Port de Saleix (1794m) where it meets two other paths. The main trail takes a right, arriving 2km later at the CIMES **refuge**, *de Bassiès* (☎05.61.64.89.98, ⊛bassies.free.fr; meals available June–Oct; open weekends only May & Sept–Oct; dorm beds €11), and then, passing a series of reservoirs, it branches east, crossing the **Pic du Far** and descending to Auzat and Vicdessos – in total some 16km of often demanding trail. In the final leg of the hike, keep an eye out for the squat stone shepherds' shelters, or *orris*, hidden among the underbrush – some are as much as 700 years old.

There is little to detain you in **VICDESSOS**, the capital of a remote and poor *canton*, and nearby **AUZAT** is remarkable chiefly for the large and ugly aluminium factory which dominates it. It is however at these villages that the footpath and road route converge again, and where the main road descends the river valley, passing the Grotte de Niaux (see p.158), shortly before entering **Tarascon**. You may want to take a **room** or **meal** at the homely *Hôtel Henri Hivert* (☎05.61.65.88.17; ❶) in Vicdessos. Alternatively the local **campsite** (☎05.61.64.82.22, ⊛www.labexanelle.com) also rents bungalows off-season. For those on a budget, *La Bonne Auberge* (☎ & ℻05.61.03.80.99; ❶) in Auzat has cheap rooms and well-priced *menus* (from €12). The town is also the headquarters of the departmental association of *accompagnateurs*, 1 rte de la Prade (☎05.61.64.83.96), which can set you up with a reliable **guide** for hikes up into the Couserans. Vicdessos' **market** is held on Thursdays, and there is an annual fair on 21 September. For further information on the area, check ⊛www.pays-du-montcalm.com.

Via Castillon-en-Couserans

The longest but most rewarding route over the Couserans to Tarascon begins by heading southwest from St-Girons along the broad Bouigane Valley to **CASTILLON-EN-COUSERANS**. This is the most populated and prosperous part of the region, testified to by the ancient **churches** clustered around the town. The best can be found at Arrout and Andressein, en route to Castillon, and Ourjout, just beyond: all can be visited (€1.50) by prior arrangement with the St-Girons tourist office.

Whilst hardly a bustling metropolis, Castillon's central position means it has long been an important market town. It is set at the crossroads ("*Cruz de Camisses*" in Gascon) of the four "B" valleys – Biros, Bethmale, Balaguères and Bellongue – and, as such, is the Couserans heartland. Its **tourist office** (hours vary; ☎05.61.96.72.64, ⓔotcastil@club-internet.fr) provides detailed information on the whole area, including local B&Bs. The main reason to stay here is to use the town as a base for hiking, with the best **accommodation** being at the magnificent townhouse, *Le Clos Enchanté* at 58 rue Peyrevidal (☎05.61.04.64.47, ⓔmyriam.peat@wanadoo.fr; ❸).

From Castillon, it's a tense 35km drive of hair-raising switchbacks up the **Vallée de Bethemale** to Seix. However, you'll be rewarded by spectacular views, both in the tree-lined valley, and once the road breaks into open ground at the Col de la Côte, just past the halfway mark.

The upper Ariège valley

South of Foix, the **upper Ariège** narrows rapidly, and forest slopes rise sharply on either side as the riverbed twists and cuts down through gneiss and schist of the Pyrenean foothills towards **Tarascon**. It is along this part of the river that you'll find in thick concentration many of France's best and most famous prehistorically inhabited **caves**, decorated by hand-prints, etchings and animal figures left by our ancestors up to a quarter of a million years ago. This, along with the beauty of the countryside, has made the upper Ariège an extremely popular destination, especially for French tourists. High season, particularly August, is mayhem, and if you're hoping to see the renowned cave art you should plan (and reserve) as far ahead as possible. Further up in the hills towards the Spanish and Andorran frontiers, the high peaks of the Pyrenees loom ever closer. Here, around **Ax-les-Thermes**, there is breathtaking mountain scenery and great possibilities for **walking**. There's a map of the region on pp.138–139.

Tarascon-sur-Ariège and the caves

A small, utilitarian mining and metallurgy centre with traffic roaring past on the bypass highway, **TARASCON-SUR-ARIÈGE** has nothing about it to suggest that this is the heart of one of the most fascinating areas in Europe. Yet any account of the emergence of the human species must include the **caves** around the town, which taken as a group constitute an unequalled display of prehistoric painting and artefacts. The *grottes* served as shelters – and, arguably, as places of worship – for early humans, later coming in handy as hideouts for religious dissidents during the Christian era. Their high concentration in the Ariège is due to the limestone which constitutes the hillsides here – permeable rock ideally suited to the work of cavern-creation. There are four main sites, all accessible in a single day if you have your own transport.

Tarascon itself is rather dull and hardly worth a stop, although riverside cafés provide pleasant vantage points over the Ariège, with a narrow pedestrian lane leading past a string of craft shops into the old quarter. Here the church of St-Michel presides over a partly arcaded square, and various surviving bits of the medieval walls, razed in 1632, crop up here and there: the **Tour St-Michel**, and the **Porte d'Espagne** with a fountain inside. From the gate, the short hike past walled orchards up to the **Tour du Castella**, now a clock tower, is worthwhile for the views over the five valleys which converge here. Tarascon is the site of two lively livestock **fairs**, on May 8 and September 30, timed for the passing of the transhumant herds. A regular **market** is held on Wednesday morning in the place de l'Horte, and Saturday morning in the place de l'Ayroule as well as during the annual fairs on May 8 and September 30.

If you haven't managed to make reservations at the caverns, you can still experience the Neolithic era, albeit vicariously, at the **Parc de la Préhistoire** (April–June & Sept to early-Nov Mon–Fri 10am–6pm; Sat & Sun 10am–7pm; July & Aug daily 10am–8pm; €9.40), 5km outside Tarascon – take the N20 north, and you'll see it signposted at the junction for St-Girons. This rambling park contains nature trails, and prehistory-related exhibits including replica bison and reproductions of some of the more important and inaccessible cave art – a good alternative to the real thing if you have children.

Practicalities

Buses and trains call frequently from nearby Ax-les-Thermes and Foix, on the line from Toulouse to Latour-de-Carol; the **gare SNCF**, which also serves as the bus stop, is on the left bank of the Ariège, in the northern half of town. The **tourist office** (July & Aug daily 9am–7pm; Sept–June Mon–Sat 9am–6pm; ☎05.61.05.94.94, ✉pays.de.tarascon@wanadoo.fr) is inside the multipurpose hall known as the Espace François Mitterand, on avenue des Pyrénées in the centre.

Quietest and most attractive of the **hotels** is the *Confort* on the riverside quai Armand-Sylvestre (☎05.61.05.61.90, ✉hotel.comfort@wanadoo.fr; ❷), with some rooms facing a courtyard. For quieter rooms facing the river, the comfortable *Hostellerie de la Poste*, is 200m north on the main through road (☎05.61.05.60.41, ⓦwww.hostellerieposte.com; ❸), with a cosy fireside lounge. The best option, however, is the eighteenth-century manor house, *Domaine Fournie* (☎05.61.05.54.52, ✉contact@domaine-fournie.com; ❸), 1km from the town centre on rte Saurat, and set within impressive grounds. There are two **campsites**: *La Bernière* (☎05.61.05.78.01), near the junction of the road to Bédeilhac, and the municipal *Pré Lombard* (☎05.61.05.61.94, ⓦwww .flowercampingsariege.com), upstream from town on the right bank. All the hotels have attached **restaurants**, with the best food and service at *Hostellerie de la Poste,* which offers a reasonably priced Gascon *menu* featuring *auzinat*, a rich hotpot of cabbage, potato, sausage, game and other goodies: the *Domaine Fournie* has a €18 *menu*. **Markets** are held Tuesday and Saturday morning, as well as during the annual fairs on May 8 and September 30.

Grotte de Niaux

Unquestionably the finest of the Pyrenean caves is the **Grotte de Niaux**, 2km southwest of Tarascon. Rivals like Lascaux in the Dordogne and Altamira in Spain are now closed or very nearly so, but the only restriction on access to Niaux is the mandatory **reservation** for places on the twenty-person 45-minute **guided tour** (daily: Jan to mid-April & Oct to late Dec 10.15am–4.15pm, closed some Mondays; mid-April to June & Sept 9.45am–5pm, English tour at 1pm; July & Aug 9.15am–5.30pm, English tours at 9.30am & 1pm; €9.40).

The current entrance to Niaux is a tunnel created in 1968 near the low and narrow natural opening under an enormous rock overhang. Using torches for illumination, you penetrate 900m (from a total 4km of galleries) to see just some of the famous black outlines of **horse** and **bison**, minimally shaded yet capturing every nuance. Analysis has established that these drawings, and those of the ibex and stag in the recess further back, were produced around 10,800 BC with a "crayon" made of bison fat and manganese oxide. A line of **footprints** left by the artists can be seen in a part of the cave that was opened up

Pyrenean cave art

The **painted caves** of the Pyrenees are known to have been created by nomadic and semi-nomadic communities of Cro-Magnon *Homo sapiens* during the Late Paleolithic period, between 10,000 and 35,000 years ago. Almost everything else about them is conjecture.

According to the pioneering French paleo-anthropologist **Father Breuil** (1877–1961), known as the "Pope of Prehistory", cave art served a **magical function**, to ensure an abundance of game. The frequency with which animals appear on the walls seems to back up this theory, but there are objections to it, the most obvious being that the animal remains found in the caves show that the species depicted were not the main food supply. Breuil's disciple **André Leroi-Gourhan** (1911–86) and his colleague **Annette Laming-Emperaire** focused on the **layout** of cave designs. As a result of extensive surveys, they observed, for example, that hands were depicted only at the entrance to caves or in the centre, and that mammoths and bison were confined to the centre. They suggested that the arrangement reflected a sexual polarity, with bison symbolizing the female element, and horses the male. However, poor lighting would probably not have allowed the artists to see the cave decorations as a unity. Moreover, successive paintings were superimposed to the extent that they became indecipherable, even though suitable areas of blank rock were available nearby. Nevertheless, most experts agree that there is some sort of pattern: bison and horses, for example, are thirty times more likely to occur in the central area than are deer, a statistic difficult to dismiss as coincidence.

The most cogent refutation of the above theories was published in 1996 by **Jean Clottes**, a French prehistorian, and **David Lewis-Williams**, a South African expert on the Kalahari Bushmen, one of the last surviving hunter-gatherer societies, with strong parallels to European Paleolithic culture. Their *Les Chamanes de la Préhistoire* (Éditions Seuil) proposes that the images may have been executed by **shamans** in an altered state, and that "the paintings and engravings do not represent real animals… rather they are visions drawn from the subterranean world of spirits." More prosaically, **Dale Guthrie**, at the University of Alaska, has shown that most of the art was done by teenage males, and – with its strong sexual content – may, in fact, be the prehistoric equivalent of modern graffiti.

Undoubtedly the caves will continue to stimulate speculation. The apparent stylistic development of the paintings, for example, along with similarities between decorative work in caves hundreds of kilometres apart suggests that there was some sort of coherent "school" of artistic development, as well as communication between widely dispersed groups. A great many decorated caves of the Pyrenees are closed to the general public, an essential precaution if they are to be preserved; application through a caving organization might gain access to some of these. The most spectacular examples, though, are open to all. After the Tarascon group, the major Pyrenean cave is **Gargas**, with its vast array of hand-prints in red and black, many with apparently mutilated fingers. Whatever the uncertainties about its significance and the ways in which it was made, seeing the Pyrenean cave art is an extraordinary experience – one which allows us to connect in an intuitive and immediate way with our most remote human ancestors.

in 1970, while their primitive form of **writing** is represented by the dots and bunches of lines on the wall of the main cavity.

NIAUX village itself, between the cave and Tarascon, has a small, private **Musée Pyrénéen** (daily: July & Aug 9am–8pm; Sept–June 10am–noon & 2–6pm; €8) which displays a splendid collection of tools, furnishings and archival photos illustrating the vanished traditions of the Ariège. Exhibits also explain local Pyrenean architecture, with its use of *lauzes* (stone slabs), *ardoise* (slate) and occasionally *chaume* (thatch) for roofing. About halfway between Niaux and Tarascon, keep your eye peeled also for the picturesque remains of a medieval smelting works by the riverside.

Grotte de la Vache

The **Grotte de la Vache** (daily: Easter–June, Sept & off-season school holidays 2.30–4pm; July & Aug 10am–5.30pm; other times groups only; ℡05.61.05.95.06, ✉contactgrotte@club-internet.fr; €8) at Alliat is well worth the 2km journey across the valley from Niaux, south on the road to Vicdessos: walkers can slightly shortcut the road, by taking the path beginning some 150m before the Niaux museum. Excavations here over two decades sifted through the detritus of ten thousand years of habitation, beginning between 15,000 and 12,500 BC and ending in the Bronze Age. Around 30,000 fragments of flint tools were unearthed and over 6000 complete tools, mainly for engraving in rock; some pieces are displayed in the cave.

Grotte de Bédeilhac

To reach the **Grotte de Bédeilhac** (Easter–June & Sept Mon–Sat 2.20–5pm; July & Aug daily 10am–5.30pm; Oct–Easter Sun 3pm; ℡05.61.05.95.06, ✉contactgrottee@club-internet.fr; €9) above the eponymous village, you have to return to Tarascon and cover 5km along the D618 towards Saurat. This cave, a hollow in the ridge of Soudour, contains examples of every known technique of Paleolithic art, including polychrome painting (now faded to monochrome). The imposing entrance yawns 35m wide by 20m high, making it easy to understand how the Germans managed to adapt the cavern as an aircraft hangar during World War II. Although the art within is not as immediately powerful as that at Niaux, its diversity compensates, with low reliefs in mud, paintings of bison, deer and ibex, and stalagmites used to model figures.

Grottes de Lombrives

The **Grotte de Lombrives** (daily: June & Sept tours at 10am, 2pm, 3.30pm & 5pm; July & Aug 10am–7pm; other holiday periods tours at 2 & 3.30pm, or by appointment, ℡05.61.05.98.40, ✉grotte.lombrives@laposte.net), 3km south of Tarascon along the N20, near Ussat-les-Bains, could only disappoint if you've already seen Niaux, Vache and Bédeilhac. The access by underground train gives it something of an amusement-park feel – as do the nocturnal *spectacles* regularly staged here in July and August – but the stalagmite formations are superb, and the sheer size of the complex is impressive. It is, in fact, the largest cavern in Europe, and would take five days' walking to see it in its entirety. Lombrives was inhabited around 4000 BC, but all the material found here now rests in museums such as that at Foix. Its later history is embellished by legends of the last Cathars walled up inside in 1328, and of 250 soldiers subsequently disappearing without trace, the victims of cave-dwelling bandits.

There are three **routes for visitors**: a 90min walk to the first cavern (€7.50), a 2hr tour of the great cavern (€10), and a three-hour underground hike (€18). Groups of eight or more can arrange for three- or five-hour walk-throughs by ringing the number above, while serious cave buffs can book on one of the "*Visites longue durée caractère spéléologique*", which are run from June to September.

Ax-les-Thermes and around

AX-LES-THERMES, 26km southeast of Tarascon on the main N20 road, is an unobjectionable spa resort with little specifically to see – owing to numerous disastrous fires in centuries past – other than a lively Monday market along the river promenade. However, it makes a good base for skiing or walking in the Ariège region, with **hikes** routed in circuits from the town, and several **ski resorts**, both downhill and Nordic, within a convenient distance.

Ax dates back to at least Roman times, while the commercial exploitation of its hot springs dates from the thirteenth century; the smell of sulphur that early twentieth-century travellers commented on can still be whiffed from the spring water coursing through the gutters, and the ambience of a spa remains. Four *thermes* still exist, all of them part of the central *Hôtel Royal Thermal*, and in total there are more than forty *sources*, producing a volume of water in excess of 600,000 litres per day, some at temperatures hotter than 70°C. The town itself is small and pleasant enough, but there's little to see once you've wandered a couple of streets in the quarter to the right of the N20, which forms the main street. Rue de l'École and rue de la Boucarie retain a few medieval buildings, and above place du Breilh, the **church of St-Vincent** is of architectural interest for its Romanesque tower. Just across the road you can join the locals and dangle your feet for free in the **Bassin des Ladres**, a pool of hot sulphurous water (77°C) dating to 1250, which was once incorporated into the now-vanished hospital founded in 1260 by St Louis for leprous soldiers returning from the Crusades.

Practicalities

The **gare SNCF** is on the northwest side of town, just off the main avenue Delcassé; **buses** stop in the town centre. On the northside of the main road, halfway through town, the helpful **tourist office** (daily 9am–noon & 2–6/7pm; ℡05.61.64.60.60, ⓦwww.vallees-ax.com) provides information on hiking and contact guides, and sells a range of *Topoguides* and maps. Thanks to the baths and the local skiing, there is a wide selection of **hotels** in and around town: *L'Auzeraie* in avenue Théophile Delcassé (℡05.61.64.20.70, Ⓔauzeriae@free .fr; ❷) is a good cheap option, with *Le Breilh*, on place Breilh (℡05.61.64.24.29, ⓦwww.ariegehotellebreilh.com; ❷), a close second. The three-star *L'Orry Saquet* on the main highway (℡05.61.64.31.30, ⓦwww.auberge-lorry.com; ❹)

Skiing around Ax-les-Thermes

The nearest **ski station** to Ax **is Station d'Ax** (ⓦwww.ax-ski.com), 8km south up the D820 – an agglomeration of three resorts, Bonascre, Saquet and Campels. The station itself is a hideous knot of high-rises, but once you get into the *télécabine* (€6.50 to Bonascre; €10 to Saquet) and up to the **Plateau du Saquet**, with the beautiful Andorran frontier peaks as a backdrop, it's a different matter. The snow record here is good, there are 75km of pistes (some over 3km long), and the top lift is at 2305m. There's an alternative station 13km east of Ax at **Ascou-Pailhères** (ⓦwww .vallees-ax.com/html/hiver/ascou_fr.htm), with 15 downhill runs and a top station of 2020m. It's a pretty drive up to the station, and though it only has one black piste, it's quite a challenging one.

Three valleys west of Bonascre, the **Plateau de Beille** (ⓦwww.lespyrenees.com /plateau-de-beille) has been developed for **cross-country skiing**. The 55km of pistes range in length from one to twenty kilometres, at an altitude of just under 2000m – which should ensure adequate snow. The station can be reached by *navette* (weekends in the ski season and daily during school hols) from the village of Les Cabannes, 15km north of Ax along the main N20 road. There's also good cross-country skiing to the north of Ax around the **Col de Chioula** (1431m).

is also a good deal. The vast municipal **campsite**, *Malazéou* (year-round; ☎05.61.64.22.21, ⓦwww.campingmalazeou.com), is beside the Ariège, 500m from the train station.

All the hotels above have **restaurants** with *menus* from €15. Alternatively, try the hip *La Petitè Fringale*, on rue Piétonne, for its *montagnard* cuisine and shady terrace (from €16). Otherwise the *Terminus Bar* near the station and *Grand Café*, on the same square as the Bassin des Ladres, serve passable light fare. For **snacks** on the hoof, there are numerous cheap *boulangeries* and over-the-counter pizza places in rue de l'Horloge, leading off the place du Marché. The most atmospheric venues for a **drink** are the *Grand Café*, and *Brasserie Le Club* on place Roussel. The **market** is held on Tuesday and Sunday mornings (also Thurs in summer), and **bikes** can be rented at L'Eskimo Sport, in nearby Savignac (☎05.61.64.02.85).

The Oriège valley

Extending east from Ax, the damp, leafy **Oriège valley** allows access to both the Carlit peaks for hikers (see opposite) and the **Réserve Nationale d'Orlu**, created south of the road in 1975 to benefit a growing herd of isards (Pyrenean chamois, a goat-like animal) as well as roe deer, golden eagles and lammergeiers (Europe's biggest birds of prey). Under the shadow of the distinctive Dent d'Orlu, beloved of technical climbers, the D22 road heads up the valley to **ORLU**, where there's camping at the *Municipal* (☎05.61.64.30.09) and a popular *gîte d'étape* aimed at walkers, the *Relais Montagnard* (☎05.61.64.61.88, ⓕ05.61.64.30.12; ❻, including obligatory half-board). A path from **Les Forges d'Orlu** further up the valley permits a link-up with the "Tour des Montagnes d'Ax" (see below), via a climb from near the power station to the dam at Naguille.

At a popular picnic area some 8km beyond Orlu, the asphalt ends and a jeep track, prohibited for all private cars, climbs south into the *réserve* through the En Gaudu valley, before meeting the GR7 below the Étang d'en Beys, with its refuge. If you're approaching the Carlit via the Oriège, it's well worth splashing out for a taxi to the picnic grounds: the walk in is tedious and steep, with little chance of a lift in either direction.

Walks near Ax-les-Thermes

Next door to the tourist office in Ax, the **Bureau des Guides et Accompagnateurs Montagne des Vallées d'Ax** (☎05.61.64.31.51) maintains a list of seventeen brief **walks** around the town, ranging in length from twenty minutes to seven hours, though most of these prove rather short and over-generously timed; it also keeps information on all the mountain huts and refuges, climbing courses and weather forecasts. To fill a day properly, take the suggested itinerary to the attractive village of **SORGEAT** and link this hike with other sections.

Among the long-distance hikes in the area, the five-day, four-night **Tour des Montagnes d'Ax** is most recommended, since it covers a variety of terrain, including parts of the Carlit. You can begin at **Le Castelet**, on the main road 5km northwest of Ax, climbing south for a day to hook up with the GR10 at the **Col de Beil** (2247m); the closest crude shelter is at **Prat Redon**. The route then heads eastwards to cross the Ariège valley at Mérens-les-Vals, your second overnight stop. From here, stick with the GR10, and later the GR7, and it's a very long day's walk to the *Refuge d'en Beys* (☎05.61.64.24.24, ⓦrefuge.enbeys .free.fr; late May to Sept & weekends in May & Oct by arrangement; dorm beds €15), where you'll spend your third night, unless you stay at the refuge *Les Bésines* (☎05.61.05.22.44, ⓦbesines.free.fr; meals available June–Sept, otherwise open weekends only by reservation; dorm beds €15) at the junction of the two trails. From *Les Bésines,* you've a shorter day up to the gentle **Couillade de Beys** (2345m), then past the easterly Étang des Peyrisses and the Naguille dam before the descent to the floor of the Oriège valley.

Mérens and L'Hospitalet

The reputation of **MÉRENS-LES-VALS,** 8km south of Ax along the N20, rests on the stocky frame of the **Mérenguais horse,** a breed which – partly on the strength of the Niaux cave paintings (see p.158) – is considered the closest thing in western Europe to the wild horse of prehistory. Nowadays there are more specimens outside the mountains of Mérens than in them, but the village remains a place of pilgrimage for horse lovers. Mérens itself, though, is unexceptional, one part clustered on the main road, the other spread out on the slopes to the east around a Romanesque church. The village straddles the GR10, which accounts for the attractively restored **gîte d'étape,** *La Soula,* in the upper village (April–Oct; ℡05.61.64.32.50, ℻05.61.64.02.75; ❶), a congenial place to base yourself for a few days' walking, serving excellent food. The **campsite** (℡05.61.64.33.77, ℮camping.merens@wanadoo.fr) is just off the main road, near the river, and doubles as a **tourist office.**

Mérens makes a good base for **walks,** short or long. A popular one-day circuit involves following the GR10, and then a local path, southwest up the Mourgouillou valley, where Mérenguais horses still graze, to the **Étang de Couart,** and then dropping back down to the train station at L'Hospitalet by using the **HRP** (the Haute Route des Pyrénées, a trail which traverses the whole range). Alternatively, heading southeast, the GR10 offers a more appealing, if more strenuous introduction to the **Carlit range** than the HRP from L'Hospitalet (see below), but be warned that both French and translated *Topoguides* sketch the route on the wrong bank of the River Nabre.

L'Hospitalet

Ten kilometres south of Mérens is **L'HOSPITALET-PRÈS-L'ANDORRE,** whose sole interest – in the absence of any monumental or natural attraction – is as a route convergence: the HRP goes through here, as do buses to and from adjacent Andorra, and trains south into the Cerdagne and north to Toulouse. There is a basic and unremarkable one-star **hotel,** the *Puymorens* (℡05.61.05.20.03; ❷), plus a **gîte** (℡05.61.05.23.14, ℮gitedetape.lhospitalet @libertysurf.fr; closed Nov; doubles ❸, dorm beds €19), and a **campsite.** Heading into the Carlit massif, the **HRP** gets you quickly to grips with the mountains, offering the shortest approach from the west as it climbs unusually gently to the dam and pair of refuges at Bésines (see opposite), where you link up with the GR10. Heading south of L'Hospitalet, a 7km-long road tunnel pierces the Col de Puymorens (1915m), reducing the road distance to Latour-de-Carol on the Spanish border to only 20km.

Travel details

Trains

The main rail corridors in this region are Toulouse/ Narbonne, and Toulouse/Latour-de-Carol which hooks up with the *Train Jaune* (p.366) to Perpignan.

A spur line runs from Carcassonne to Quillan and the Fenouillèdes line (p.356) from Rivesaltes terminates at Axat. SNCF buses may run in lieu of trains on these lines; services are reduced on Sundays and holidays.

Carcassonne to: Alet-les-Bains (3 daily; 35min); Bram (6–13 daily; 10min); Castelnaudary (6–19 daily; 20–27min); Lézignan (8–12 daily; 20min); Limoux (4–9 daily; 25min); Montpellier (15–18 daily; 1hr 30min–4hr); Narbonne (13–17 daily; 35min); Nîmes (15–18 daily; 2hr 5min–3hr 10min); Perpignan (18–24 daily; 1hr 15min–2hr); Quillan (4–5 daily; 1hr 15min); Toulouse (6–15 daily; 45min–1hr).

Foix to: Ax-les-Thermes (20–24 daily; 50min); L'Hospitalet (14–16 daily; 1hr 10min–1hr 30min); Latour-de-Carol (11–13 daily; 2hr); Pamiers (24–36 daily; 15–25min); Tarascon-sur-Ariège (24–28 daily; 15–25min); Toulouse (24–36 daily; 45min–1hr 15min).

Latour-de-Carol to: Ax-les-Thermes (11–13 daily; 55min); Bourg-Madame (5 daily; 15min); Foix (11–13 daily; 2hr); L'Hospitalet (11–13 daily; 25min); Mont-Louis (4 daily; 1hr 20min); Tarascon-sur-Ariège (11–13 daily; 1hr 25min–1hr 45min); Toulouse (7–11 daily; 2hr 30min); Villefranche-de-Conflent (6–7 daily; 2hr).

Limoux to: Quillan (4–7 daily; 30–45min).

Pamiers to: Foix (24–36 daily; 15–25min); Latour-de-Carol (7–11 daily; 1hr 55min–2hr 10min); Lavelanet (Fri & Sun; 35min); Toulouse (24–36 daily; 50min–1hr 10min).

St-Girons/St-Lizier to: Toulouse via Boussens (5–8 daily; 1hr 45min–2hr).

Buses

In the Aude and Ariège, weekend services are much reduced, with most lines having no buses on Sundays, and holidays and school holidays often having little or no service; for full schedules and map, see Ⓦwww.cg09.fr.

Ax-les-Thermes to: Toulouse (1–3 daily; 2hr 10min).

Axat to: Castelnaudary (1 daily; 1hr 50min); Limoux (1 daily; 50min).

Carcassonne to: Albi (1 daily; 2hr); Axat (1 daily; 1hr 45min); Castelnaudary (5 daily; 45min); Castres (8 daily; 1hr 50min); Homps (2 daily; 55min); Lézignan (6 daily; 45min); Marseillette (2 daily; 22min); Narbonne (2 daily; 1hr 25min); Quillan (2 daily; 1hr 20min); St-Hilaire (2 daily; 45min); Toulouse (1 daily; 2hr 20min); Trèbes (8 daily; 15min).

Comus to: Quillan (1–2 daily; 1hr 5min).

Foix to: Auzat (1–2 daily; 1hr 50min); Ax-les-Thermes (1–5 daily; 1hr 20min); La Bastide (2–4 daily; 25min); Lavelanet (1–2 daily; 35min); Lescure (2–4 daily; 40min); Niaux (1–3 daily; 1hr); Pamiers (1–2 daily; 30min); St-Girons (2–4 daily; 50min); Quillan (1 daily; 2hr); Tarascon (1–10 daily; 35–55min); Toulouse (1–2 daily; 1hr 30min); Ussat (1–5 daily; 55min); Vicdessous (1–3 daily; 1hr 20min); Villeneuve d'Olmes (4 weekly; 30min).

Latour-de-Carol to: Font-Romeu (4 daily; 50min); Perpignan (4 daily; 3hr 5min).

Lavelanet to: Belesta (4 weekly; 20min); Foix (1–2 daily; 35min); Mirepoix (1–6 daily; 20min); Pamiers (1–6 daily; 1hr); Quillan (2 daily; 1hr); Toulouse (1–2 daily; 2hr 5min).

Limoux to: Castelnaudary (3 daily; 35min).

Mas d'Azil to: Toulouse (2 daily; 1hr 50min).

Pamiers to: Niaux (1–3 daily; 1hr); Tarascon (1–3 daily; 55min); Vicdessous/Auzat (1–6 daily; 1hr 20min).

Quillan to: Axat (1–2 daily; 15min); Carcassonne (2 daily; 1hr 20min); Comus (1–2 daily; 1hr 5min); St-Paul-le-Fenouillet (1 daily; 30min); Quérigut (3 weekly in summer; 1hr 30min).

St-Girons to: Aulus-les-Bains (2 daily; 45min); Castilon (2–6 daily; 13–25min) Foix (2–4 daily; 50min); Lescours (2–4 daily; 25min); Mas d'Azil (1–2 daily; 35min); Massat (2–3 daily; 35min); Oust (2 daily; 30min); Seix (2 daily; 25min); Toulouse (3 daily; 2hr 30min).

Tarascon-sur-Ariège to: Niaux (1–3 daily; 1hr); Vicdessos/Auzat (1–3 daily; 1hr 25min).

Albi and Haut
Languedoc

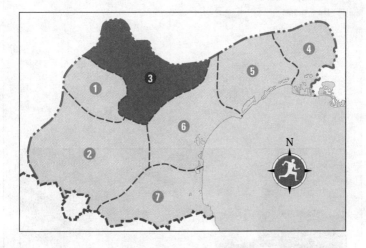

CHAPTER 3 # Highlights

✳ **Albi Cathedral** Distinctive brickwork construction gives this medieval cathedral a surreal look. See p.174

✳ **Toulouse-Lautrec** See the world's largest collection of the diminutive Impressionist's distinctive work. See p.174

✳ **Cordes-sur-Ciel** Once a refuge for heretics, now a town of artisans, perched "on the sky" west of Albi. See p.181

✳ **Gaillac wines** Sample one of the country's oldest and most venerable AOCs. See p.184

✳ **Rabastens** A brilliantly restored painted church set by the tranquil banks of the Tarn. See p.186

✳ **Parc du Haut Languedoc** A wild and under-populated area, perfect for hiking and cycling. See p.194

△ Albi

Albi and Haut Languedoc

T**arn**, the *département* to the east of Toulouse, consists of two contrasting zones. The northwest is wine country: the rolling landscape on the banks of the river after which the administrative area is named is punctuated by towns which grew up on the modest prosperity of the grape and other products of the soil, including garlic and woad. The southeast, on the other hand, is a rugged upland where herding and wool have sustained a precarious living for the villagers of the high valleys as far back as can be recalled. Today Tarn is not the most of dynamic of regions – it has fallen victim to the rural depopulation which typifies much of southern France, with the result that there is almost no industry. Nevertheless, there's much to see here and though, like Toulouse, it falls outside the modern administrative *région* of Languedoc-Roussillon, it is culturally and historically inseparable from the Occitan coastal lands.

In the northwest, **Albi**, Tarn's principal town, was ruled for centuries by the counts of Toulouse, and its name is synonymous with the Cathar sect with which modern *languedociens* still proudly identify. The undulating lowlands which surround the town are defined by the flow of the Tarn: to the east, descending from the Grandes Causses, it follows a rapid, rocky course, cutting down through forested hills and meandering dramatically around **Ambialet**; north of the capital, gritty **Carmaux** sits atop a coal-rich landscape, the Ségala, scarred by the centuries-long search for the black stuff; to the west, the stunningly preserved medieval citadel of **Cordes** marks the transition to the Aveyron valley; and finally, passing Albi, the Tarn flows west toward **Gaillac** and one of the most praised wine regions of the South of France, veering south, past the ancient *bastides* of **Lisle** and **Rabastens**, before being met by the tributary Agout. The region's interior, south of Albi, has a scattering of sleepy old towns set amidst fields of corn and wheat, slumbering since the leather industry which sustained them in the Middle Ages declined. Moving away from the river past Graulhet and Réalmont, the land becomes more hilly, and here you'll find **Lautrec**, the most beautiful town of the Albigeois.

To the southeast, **Haut Languedoc** ("Upper Languedoc"), a wild hinterland of rocky hills that provides an unexpected contrast with the bustle of the nearby coast, has a history of religious and political nonconformity – it was once a remote hotbed of Protestant Huguenots. At its base lies **Castres**, Albi's poorer cousin, a lively little provincial town, birthplace of the socialist hero

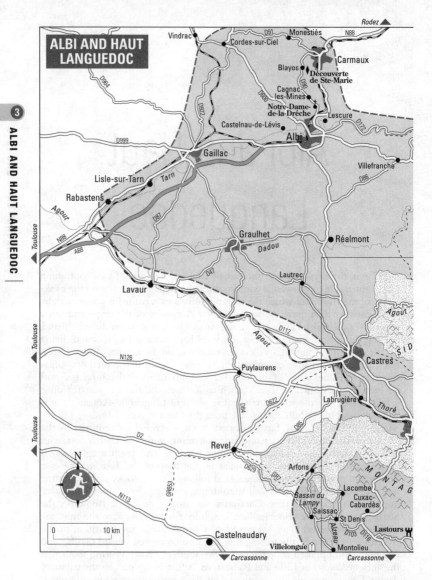

ALBI AND HAUT LANGUEDOC

Rodez ▲

Vindrac • Monestiés

Cordes-sur-Ciel • • N88

Carmaux

Blayes ◆ Découverte
de Ste-Marie

Cagnac •
les-Mines

Notre-Dame-
de-la-Drèche

Castelnau-de-Lévis • Lescure

Albi

Gaillac

Villefranche •

Lisle-sur-Tarn • Tarn

Rabastens •

Agout

N88

A68

Graulhet • **Réalmont**

Dadou

Lautrec •

Lavaur •

Agout

N126 D112

Puylaurens • Castres

Labruguière •

Thoré

Revel •

Arfons •

Lacombe
Cuxac-
Cabardès

Bassin du
Lampy St Denis

Saissac Lastours

N113 Castelnaudary • Villelongue

Montolieu

▼ Carcassonne Carcassonne ▼

N

0   10 km

Jean Jaurès and home to an important collection of Spanish art. In the uplands, most of which have been incorporated into the **Parc Naturel Régional de Haut Languedoc**, dark woods and high pasture are interspersed with a series of largely forgotten villages, including Lacaune, La Salvetat and St-Pons. This is easy walking terrain, crisscrossed by *grandes randonnées* and local trails like the Gijou Valley Railway Path. Further south the **Montagne Noire**, rising south of **Mazamet**, presents an even more isolated and untamed landscape, guarded on its southern side by the ruined fortress of **Saissac** and the Cathar castles of **Lastours**. Chilling out in Castres is a good option, especially given its

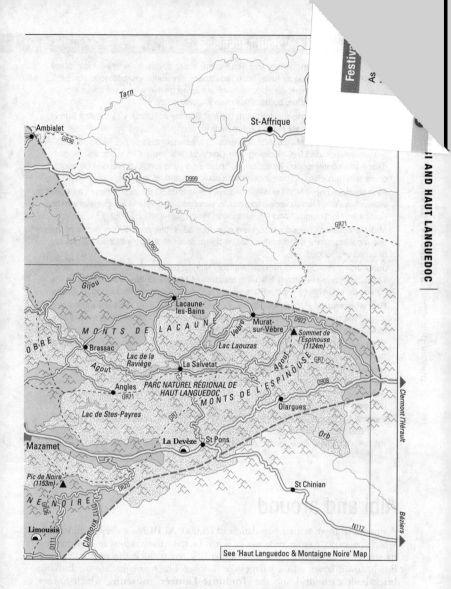

See 'Haut Languedoc & Montaigne Noire' Map

museums and amenities, while the rest of the region features rugged country-side, ideal for rambling or back-road motoring and cycling.

Despite its general isolation, the area of Albi and Haut Languedoc is well served by public transport. The main Toulouse–Rodez rail line follows the course of the Tarn up to Albi and Carmaux, with branch-offs to Cordes and Castres. Cordes acts as a bus hub for the western part of the Parc Naturel Mazamet, while other routes are now served by regular SNCF buses or local lines, but getting to smaller villages is more difficult; penetrating the heart of the park is best done from St-Pons.

elsewhere in Languedoc and Roussillon, most towns have their local **fêtes** between June and August here, featuring dances, fireworks and *pétanque* competitions. Some of the more exceptional ones are listed below; where we haven't given a number for information, contact the town's tourist office.

Feb–March Albi: *Carnaval.* Held from the last Sunday in February to the first Sun in March, Albi's traditional French Lenten festival.

Late Feb to early March Albi, Castres & Mazamet: *reBonds* ☎05.63.38.55.56, ⊛www.athanor.asso.fr. Coinciding with *Carnaval*, this festival of sculpture, modern dance and contemporary music brings together a wide range of French choreographers and musicians, in conjunction with sculpture and art exhibits.

First weekend April Albi: *Un Week-end avec Elles* ☎05.63.60.55.90, ⊛www.arpeges ettremolos.com. Female vocals and music, emphasizing *chanson française* as well as European, North African and US acts (Joan Baez head-lined in 2006).

Mid-May Gaillac: Wine contest. Held over four days, this competition is one of the two most important dates on the Gaillac calendar, when the new year's vintages are debuted and judged.

June–July Albi: Open-air theatre festival. Nightly performances of mostly French works, covering everything from the classics of Molière to the avant-garde, at the Palace de la Berbie (9.45pm). Runs from the last week of June through to mid-July.

First weekend July Monastiès: *Pause Guitare* ☎05.63.60.55.90, ⊛arpegesettremolos .com. Free concerts dominated by *chanson française*, but also featuring solid world-music acts (such as Greame Allwright in 2006).

Early July Albi: Jazz festival. A week-long festival drawing French and international musicians alike, playing in a range of indoor and outdoor venues.

Mid-July Cordes: *Fêtes du Grand Fauconnier* ⊛www.cordes-sur-ciel.org. This four-day medieval festival converts the town into a costumed extravaganza, complete with concerts, exhibitions on medieval crafts and falconry. Daily admission to the old town is €7.

Early July Castres: *Les Extravadanses* ☎05.63.71.56.58, ⊛www.ville-castres.fr. An eight-day festival featuring music, dance and cinema in free open-air venues and at the town's theatre. An eclectic program with an international flavour.

Albi and around

A provincial town with a population of 65,000, **ALBI** has a sleepy atmosphere which belies its role as *préfecture* of Tarn. Despite the visitors, in the evening its streets are deserted, even in summer. By ten o'clock the restaurants shut down, and it lapses into a village-like slumber. The highlights are the hulking brick-built **cathedral** and the **Toulouse-Lautrec museum**, which houses the world's largest collection of paintings by the native artist. In addition, the town offers a well-preserved **medieval quarter** of winding cobblestone alleys and centuries-old mansions. Set picturesquely on a high bank of the Tarn, it makes a comfortable base for exploring the nearby sights: the medieval vestiges of **Lescure** and **Castelnau**, and the coal country to the north. Albi is easily explored on foot, and you can take in the main sights in a single day.

After the decline of Roman power, the former Celtic settlement here passed through the Visigothic and Frankish hands before coming under the power of the counts of Toulouse in the eleventh century. It was under them that the

Mid-July Cordes: *Musique sur Ciel* ℡05.63.56.00.75, ✉acadoc.festival@libertysurf .fr. Each year this ten-day festival focuses on the work of a different contemporary composer, and features the most promising of young French soloists playing programmes of classical music.

Last two weeks of July Castres: Goya festival. Nightly performances of classical music, theatre and opera, all performed on an outdoor stage in the place du 1er Mai. Brings in symphonies and companies from around France and western Europe.

Late July Blayes-les-Mines (Cagnac): Summer festival ℡05.63.38.55.57, ✉info @rocktime.org. Long-running outdoor summer rock festival (camping available) held over a weekend, featuring international acts as well as notable local acts, such as Zebda.

Late July Réalmont: *Ré'alcroche* ℡05.63.55.52.89, ⊛www.realcroche.com. Massive outdoor weekend festival of bluegrass, rock, blues, Celtic and Cajun music, bringing in world-class acts and attracting over 30,000 spectators.

First three weeks Aug Castres: *Couleurs du Monde* ℡05.63.71.59.84. Free world-music performances held nightly in the place du 1er Mai, and featuring performers from Africa, the Caribbean, Latin America and across Europe.

First weekend Aug Gaillac: *Fête du vin*. Gaillac's second wine festival is timed to coincide with the beginning of the grape-harvest season, with wine contests and tastings, as well as concerts and cultural events.

Mid-Aug Rabastens: *Grande Cavalcade*. Typical village *fête* held for two days and featuring dancing, fireworks, and a parade through the town centre.

Mid-Nov Albi: *Les Œillades* ℡05.63.38.25.17, ⊛www.oeillades.free.fr. A one-week festival of new French feature films (with some entries from Belgium and Québec) with an emphasis on young film-makers. Plenty of seminars, and prizes are awarded for the films, actors and directors. Held at Ciné-forum, 104 av Colonel-Teyssier.

Nov 23 Albi: Ste Cécile Day. Feast of the patron saint of the cathedral, with a special Mass held, and a market in the adjacent square.

pont vieux was built over the Tarn, stimulating the town's growth as a centre for trade and attracting immigrants from as far away as the Rhine. The anti-Cathar Crusade let the town's burghers and bishops play the counts and kings against each other, increasing their own autonomy, and under the rule of the bishops from the 1300s onwards, Albi rode a wave of prosperity, based on the same woad trade that powered Toulouse (see box, p.97). But when demand for the dye declined, the town's fortunes diminished, and by the 1700s the adventurous were turning to the sea, some becoming renowned navigators. Industrialization came with the development of coalfields to the north; glass-working and textiles becoming the mainstay. These industries persist in Albi on a modest scale, and today the town is something of a backwater, living on under the shadows of its cathedral and the legacy of its most famous son, the artist Henri Toulouse-Lautrec (see box, p.175).

Arrival, information and accommodation

Albi's **gare SNCF**, midway along the Toulouse–Rodez line, is southwest of the old town on place de Stalingrad, which can be reached in fifteen minutes

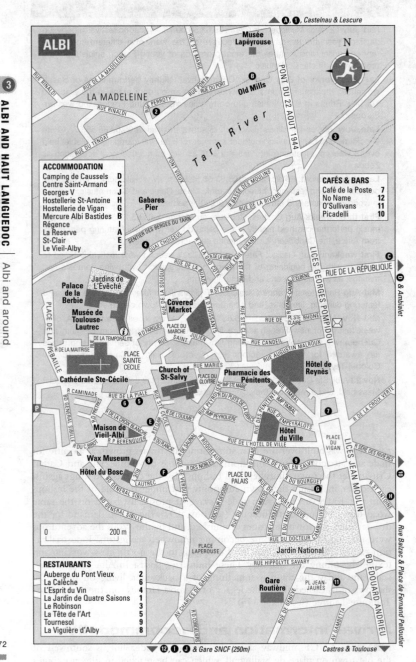

ALBI

ACCOMMODATION

Camping de Caussels	D
Centre Saint-Armand	C
Georges V	J
Hostellerie St-Antoine	H
Hostellerie de Vigan	G
Mercure Albi Bastides	B
Régence	I
La Reserve	A
St-Clair	E
Le Vieil-Alby	F

CAFÉS & BARS

Café de la Poste	7
No Name	12
O'Sullivans	11
Picadelli	10

RESTAURANTS

Auberge du Pont Vieux	2
La Calèche	6
L'Esprit du Vin	4
La Jardin de Quatre Saisons	1
Le Robinson	3
La Tête de l'Art	5
Tournesol	9
La Viguière d'Alby	8

0   200 m

by foot, or by local bus (#1; every 30min; €0.80) to place du Vigan, on the eastern side of the old town. The *gare* has a car rental office and small café, but no left-luggage service. The **gare routière** is on place Jean-Jaurès, southeast of the old town, a little over ten minutes by foot from the cathedral and the **tourist office** (July & Aug Mon–Sat 9am–7pm, Sun 10am–12.30pm & 2.30–5pm; Sept–June Mon–Sat 9am–12.30pm & 2–6pm, Sun 10am–12.30pm & 2.30–5pm; ☎05.63.49.48.80, ⓦwww.albi-tourisme.fr), which is housed in the Palace de la Berbie, next door, and can change money when banks are closed. The tourist office also sells the *Albi Pass* **discount card** (€5), which gives free entry into the Toulouse-Lautrec museum and the cathedral choir and provides reductions for other sights, as well as discounts on restaurants, boat tours, shopping and other activities.

Given its size, Albi offers a surprisingly wide selection of **hotels**, though rock-bottom budget places are scarce. One of the few is the **hostel** run by the local diocese, the *Centre Saint-Armand* (☎05.63.48.18.29, ⓔdiocesalbi -saintamarand@wanadoo.fr), at 16 rue de la République, which offers dorm accommodation for €15. The two-star **campsite**, *Camping de Caussels*, is a thirty-minute walk east of the centre in Parc de Caussels (Easter–Oct; ☎05.63.60.37.06; Albibus #5 to "Camping" from place Jean-Jaurès). Ask at the tourist office for the "*Bon Séjour à Albi*" a set-price hotel package, offering a double room for €54 for the first night, €44 for subsequent nights, and including an *Albi Pass*.

Georges V 29 av Maréchal-Joffre ☎05.63.54.24.16, ⓦwww.hotelgeorgev .com. Located by the train station, a small 80-year-old hotel in a converted house. Each room is individually decorated in modern pastel tones, and there's a garden to breakfast in. You'll need to book ahead. ❷

Hostellerie St-Antoine 17 rue St-Antoine ☎05.63.54.04.04, ⓦwww.saint-antoine -albi.com. Classy establishment founded in 1734 and run by the same family for five generations. The sumptuous rooms are appointed with antique furnishings, but the hotel also has modern facilities such as parking and AC. ❺

Hostellerie de Vigan 16 pl du Vigan ☎05.63.43.31.31, ⓔhotelduvigan@wanadoo .fr. Near the *gare routière*, this modern building is more functional than charming, with big but bland rooms. Comfortable, clean and quiet, it has all the amenities. ❷

Mercure Albi Bastides 41 rue Porta ☎05.63.47.66.66, ⓔmercure.albi @wanadoo.fr. A luxury establishment in a restored eighteenth-century mill, with modern facilities and decor, and a highly rated and well-priced restaurant. Ask for one of the riverside rooms,

which have spectacular views over the river to the cathedral. ❺

Régence 27 av Maréchal-Joffre ☎05.63.54.01.42, ⓦwww.hotellaregence.com. Next door to, and a virtual replica of the *George V*, and a fine second choice when that hotel is full. ❶

La Réserve, rte de Cordes ☎05.63.60.80.80, ⓦwww.relaischateaux.com/reservealbi. Opulent luxury for those willing to pay. Set on a rambling green estate at the northwest end of town, this beautiful hotel has four-star amenities and five-star service. Open May–Oct. ❾

St-Clair 8 rue St-Claire ☎05.63.54.25.66, ⓔmichelandrieu@hotmail.com. In a converted old brick-and-timber house in the heart of the old town only 50m from the cathedral, this friendly establishment is clean and well maintained. Also has parking. Closed part Jan. ❷

Le Vieil-Alby 25 rue Toulouse-Lautrec ☎05.63.54.15.69, ⓦperso.wanadoo.fr/le -vieil-alby. Comfortable, quiet and set in a renovated medieval house in the centre, this hotel is possibly the best deal in town. It also has a great restaurant (closed Sun eve & Mon) with *menus* at €12–35 and very friendly management. Closed part Jan & early July. ❸

The Town

All Albi's sights are within or adjacent to the compact limits of the once-walled **old town**, whose northern boundary is formed by the steep banks of the Tarn, and which is now completely surrounded by the sprawl of the new town. Across the river, the eighteenth-century suburb of **La Madeleine** is also worth a look, primarily for the spectacular views of the Tarn which it affords, with medieval Albi perched above.

The Cathédrale Ste-Cécile

The rounded arches and towers and red-brick construction of the **Cathédrale Ste-Cécile** (daily: June–Sept 9am–6.30pm; Oct–May 9am–noon & 2.30–6.30pm; free) dominate Albi, evoking a mix of the Middle Ages and Art Deco that makes it without doubt the most curious medieval cathedral you are likely to see. Financed by the proceeds of the Inquisition, the first bricks were laid in 1282, some fifty years after the Cathar defeat, but the 30-metre-wide nave and 78-metre-tall tower were not completed for more than a century after. The cathedral's clean lines, narrow windows and hulking mass reflect its role as a bastion of militant Catholicism in a region plagued by heresy, but two alterations spoil its unity: a gaudy and incongruous sixteenth-century stone porch, and a Baroque frenzy of *trompe l'oeil* festooned about the interior. In better harmony with the structure are the fifteenth-century **statues** of saints and biblical figures which decorate the rood screen to the right of the entrance, while the west wall is dominated by a giant contemporary **mural** of the Last Judgement – sadly marred by the later construction of a chapel – replete with nasty devils carrying off teeth-gnashing souls to the inferno. To the immediate right of the entrance, a doorway leads to the **choir** (€1), consisting of wooden stalls backed by elaborately carved stonework and more statuary, similar to that of the nave. The **treasury** (€3), reached by a spiral staircase on the north wall, is disappointingly small. If you can, catch the **organ recitals** held in the cathedral in July and August (Wed 5pm & Sun 4pm; free), or the tourist office's night-time **tours** (June–Sept daily 9.30pm; French only; €5). Weekend nights in summer (10.15pm), the cathedral is the venue for an elaborate French-language *son et lumière* (€10).

The Palace de la Berbie and the Musée de Toulouse-Lautrec

Next to the cathedral, the matching brick-built **Palace de la Berbie** ("bìshop", in local parlance), the fortified redoubt of Albi's lord-bishops, squats over the slow-passing Tarn. This complex began as a simple keep in the thirteenth century, but was elaborated in succeeding centuries by its wealthy owners, who strengthened its fortifications, linked it to the cathedral and laid out a classical garden. Today the palace houses the **Musée de Toulouse-Lautrec** (April–June & Sept daily 9am–noon & 2–6pm; July & Aug daily 9am–6pm; Oct–March Wed–Mon 10am–noon & 2–5/6pm; €5), the most important public collection of the painter's work, and the only part of the palace interior which is open to the public. Conceived and endowed by the artist's mother and opened in 1922, the museum is comprehensive (boasting both his first and last works) – a must for any fan of the diminutive Albigeois. His famous depictions of the entertainers and prostitutes of *fin-de-siècle* Paris, such as the provocatively matter-of-fact *In the Salon in Moulin Street*, or the erotic *Woman Disrobing*, are complemented by many **posters** and lesser-known works inspired by his family life in the local countryside. Off in a corner up a spiral stairway, you'll find a sumptuous thirteenth-century **chapel**, with a beautiful ceiling of gold-painted stars on a blue background – once the audience chamber of the bishops. The top floor of the museum's three storeys houses works by other modern French artists, including Brayer (see also Cordes, p.181), Gauguin and Matisse.

The palace also has a partly covered gallery (free) with a shady outdoor **café** providing views of the old bridge and the far riverbank, as well as access to the

Henri de Toulouse-Lautrec

Perhaps the most famous of Languedoc's artists is the painter and illustrator **Henri de Toulouse-Lautrec**. Born into the venerable family of the viscounts of Toulouse-Lautrec in 1864, Henri was deprived of a traditional aristocratic upbringing due to a congenital bone condition; his frailty kept him out of school, and after two falls at his home in Albi resulted in broken legs, any hope of pursuing a "normal" life ended. He thus turned to painting, and his earliest works, scenes from his family's milieu such as *Artilleryman Saddling a Horse*, and portraits – particularly of his mother – showed great promise. With the support of his family and the encouragement of their friend, the painter René Princeteau, Henri moved to Paris to study under Bonnat and Cormon, two successful conservative artists. Settled in bohemian Montmartre and accompanied by his friend and fellow student **Vincent Van Gogh**, he came under the spell both of the Impressionists and of the seedy underside of the city, and it was here that his own vivid style began to flourish. Seduced by the subversive Parisian **nightclubs**, he began to convey their dynamism in charcoal sketches like *Gin-Cocktail* and *Chocolate Dancing*, which were published in popular newspapers and magazines. By the early 1890s he was renowned as an illustrator, doing colourful line-drawn adverts, posters for the famous **Moulin Rouge** cabaret and covers for magazines like *La Revue Blanche*. By 1894, when he began his series of sketches and paintings of Paris **brothels**, including *In the Sitting Room at Moulins Street* and *The Two Girlfriends*, he was already successful.

Henri's disabilities did not prevent him from living life to the full: he travelled widely, drank copiously and, of course, patronized with gusto the brothels he depicted (he was known to Parisian prostitutes as the "teapot", owing to his short rotund figure and excessive endowment). In the end his vices aggravated his already fragile state, and by 1899 he was seeking treatment for **alcoholism**. In September 1901, at the age of 37, he died in a family castle near Bordeaux. What compelled Lautrec's dissolute lifestyle is uncertain (it wasn't his family relations, as he remained close to his parents throughout his life) but his contribution to the artistic world is unquestionable; with a unique illustrative style – a peculiar outgrowth of Impressionism – he not only influenced successive movements such as the Fauvists, but set the precedent for innovative poster design; to this day his Moulin Rouge adverts remain some of the most reproduced pictures in the world. His other great legacy is the **chocolate mousse**, a dessert invented by the painter, for whom culinary experimentation was also a passion.

garden (July & Aug 9am–6pm; Sept–May 8am–noon & 2–6pm); you enter it from the place de l'Archevêché, on the east side of the complex.

The old town and La Madeleine

Albi's **old town** is a chaotic jumble of narrow streets spreading east and south of the cathedral-palace complex. From the square by the tourist office, you'll see the red-brick spire of the much mistreated **church of St-Salvy**, which marks the old town's centre. Between 474 and 584, it served as the town's first cathedral, while after the revolution it was used as a storage shed for fodder. While the interior of the building is nothing special, its simple Romanesque **cloister** is a great place to read or just take a break: it can be entered from the streets to either side (daily: 7am–8pm; free). Just east, in rue Timbal, sits the sixteenth-century brick-and-timber **Pharmacie des Pénitents**, once a wealthy merchant's mansion and now a pharmacy, with playfully carved faces on its wooden beams, while across the street lies the rather more austere Renaissance and Gothic **Hôtel de Reynès** (courtyard open Mon–Fri 8am–noon &

1.30–5.30pm; free). To the south a hulking Renaissance mansion, now housing the **Hôtel de Ville**, holds a huge, timbered council chamber within its regal interior (Mon–Fri 8am–noon & 1.30–5.30pm; free). West from the town hall, the narrow cobbled streets overhung with balconies of medieval houses evoke the age when the bishops and woad merchants held sway. Here, on rue de la Croix Blanche, you'll find the medieval **Maison du Vieil Alby** (Mon 3–7pm, Tues–Sat 10.30am–12.30pm & 3–7pm; €2), a museum displaying items of local interest, including memorabilia of the young Toulouse-Lautrec, and – more interestingly – a period town-house interior. Close by, on rue Lautrec, are the artist's childhood home, the **Hôtel du Bosc** (no entry), and a laughably shabby **wax museum** (Mar–May & Oct–Dec Tues–Sat 2.30–5pm; June–Sept Tues–Sat 10am–noon &2.30–6pm; €3.20).

Across the river from the main body of the old town lies the eighteenth-century suburb of **La Madeleine**, best reached by the oft-repaired eleventh century *pont vieux* to the east of the bishop's palace. Before you cross over, however, you might want to explore the banks of the Tarn, where under the shadow of the palace walls, *gabares* (traditional river boats) depart downriver for **excursions** around town (30min; May–Sept 10.45am–6.30pm; €5) or to Aiguelèze (2hr; July & Aug Mon & Wed 5.45pm & Sun 9am; €15) about halfway to Gaillac. La Madeleine itself is a compact knot of residential houses, with a number of disused eighteenth-century mill buildings clustered along the riverbank on its eastern side. Part of the mill complex, back from the river, holds the **Musée Lapeyrouse** (July & Aug Mon–Fri 9am–noon & 2–6pm, Sat & Sun 10am–noon & 2–7pm; Sept–June Tues–Sun 9/10am–noon & 2–5/6pm; €2.50), named in honour of the adventurous navigator (1741–88) who fought the British in New France before embarking on a scientific voyage to South America, Japan, Siberia and the East Indies, where he perished in a shipwreck. The museum reviews the admiral's career in a lively display of personal and period artefacts, maps and dioramas.

Eating, drinking and nightlife

Culinary variety is not a high priority in Albi and most of the **restaurants** specialize in local *terroir* ("country cooking"), with the usual dishes – cassoulet, foie gras and duck, accompanied by fine Gaillac wine. You can also get *lou tastou*, tapas-sized portions which permit you to sample a variety of dishes without breaking the bank. Pizzas and *briques*, quick and cheap, can be found on the place du Vigan. Numerous **cafés** and **bars** lining place de l'Archevêché and place du Vigan have terraces for a daytime drink, including *Café de la Poste* on the north side of place du Vigan, with a good selection of Belgian beers. For night-time **music** (predominantly Latin), there's *Picadelli* (nightly till 2am) at 44 rue Séré des Rivières, and *No Name* (weekends till 2am) in Edmond-Canet. *O'Sullivans*, 44 pl Jean Jaurès is the Irish-style option.

Restaurants

Auberge du Pont Vieux 98 rue Porta
℡05.63.77.61.73. On the north bank of the Tarn, this popular establishment serves traditional Albigeois cuisine and offers both a vaulted dining room and a riverside terrace. *Terroir menus* go from €16. Closed Wed lunch & Thurs off-season & Oct–May.
La Calèche 8 rue de la Piale ℡05.63.54.15.52. Comfy dining room built under the supporting

vaults of the cathedral, with a wide range of lunch and dinner *menus*, including cassoulets, *escargots*, excellent salads and Moroccan dishes (starting from €13.50). The service is fast and professional, yet friendly. Wheelchair accessible.
L'Esprit du Vin 11 quai Choiseul
℡05.63.54.60.44. Under the shadow of la Berbie, this place scores on both decor and quality with imaginative *gastronomique* cuisine, balancing sweet and savoury with duck, lamb and fish dishes

as well as excellent home-made desserts. Dinner *menus* €42. Closed mid-Feb to May.

Le Jardin des Quatre Saisons 19 bd de Strasbourg ℡05.63.60.77.76. Hearty *terroir* fare prepared with market-fresh ingredients. Dine in AC comfort inside, or on a shaded terrace. *Menus* from €20. Closed Sun eve & Mon.

Mercure Albi Bastides 41 rue Porta ℡05.63.47.66.66. A luxurious, but affordable restaurant, with fine views of the old town across the river. Match this with quality food and good service and you have a winner. Lunch *menus* from €15. Closed Sat & Sun lunch & late Dec.

Le Robinson 142 rue Edouard-Branly ℡05.6346.15.69. Reached by a footpath from the new bridge and set in a riverside park, this converted house definitely gets an 'A' for atmosphere. Come in the afternoon for a cocktail and enjoy a selection of grilled meats and other *terroir* treats. *Menus* from €17. Closed Mon, Tues & Nov–March.

La Tête de l'Art 7 rue de la Piale ℡05.63.38.44.75. Decidedly unrestrained atmosphere and wacky decor makes a pleasant change from its more formal rivals. *Menus* consisting of plentiful portions start at €14. Closed Tues & Wed off-season & Aug.

Tournesol Rue de l'Ort-en-Salvy, off pl du Vigan ℡05.63.38.44.38.14. Albi's herbivorous option; expect to pay €15 for a variety of salads, quiches and other organic options. Open lunch only, Tues–Sat.

La Viguière d'Alby 7 rue Toulouse-Lautrec ℡05.63.54.76.44. Long an Albigeois *terroir* institution, the cuisine here has now taken a *gastronomique* twist. *Menus* from €17 at lunch to €60 in the evening. Closed Jan, part June & July, Sun eves & Mon.

Listings

Banks Most of the major French banks have branches in the old town offering currency exchange and ATMs. After bank hours, change money at the tourist office.

Bike rental Basile Sarl, 28 av Maréchal-Foch ℡05.63.38.43.09

Bus information ℡05.63.53.31.28.

Car rental Auto Gita, 6 rte de Millau (℡05.63.47.79.30, ⓦwww.rentacar.fr); Avis, 70 av François Verdier (℡05.63.54.76.54); Budget, rte de Castres (℡05.63.47.97.00); Cars Coulom, 4 av Gambetta (℡05.63.54.18.39, ⓔcarscoulom @wanadoo.fr); Europcar, 24 av François-Verdier (℡05.63.48.88.33); and JLC Tourisme, 2 rue Denis-Papin (℡05.63.45.03.03, ⓔjlctourisme@wanadoo.fr).

Hospital Centre Hospitalier, bd Général Sibille (℡05.63.47.47.47), southwest of the old town.

Internet access Les Royaumes Virtuels, 44 rue Croix Verte (daily 2pm–midnight); Ludi.com, 62 rue Séré de Rivière (daily 11am–midnight).

Laundry Lavatop, 10 rue Émile Grand (daily 8.30am–8pm).

Police Police Municipale, Hôtel de Police, 11 licés Georges-Pompidou.

Shopping and markets Flea market in the Halle de Castelviel (Sat 8am–noon), just west of the cathedral, and produce markets in pl Ste-Cécile and pl du Marché (Tues–Sun 8am–noon). Organic foods are sold in pl. F-Pelloutier (Tues 5–7pm) and at Aliments Naturels, 1 rue Puech Bérenguier (℡05.63.54.44.86).

Swimming Espace Caussels is a waterpark just north of town on the Cordes road with an Olympic-sized pool and activities for children. Daily June–Aug 10am–8pm, €3.30 (€2.20 children).

Taxi Albi Taxi ℡05.63.54.85.03.

Train information ℡08.92.35.35.35, ⓦwww .voyages-sncf.com.

Around Albi

Albi makes a good base for a number of easy excursions, most of which are well served by public transport (either Tarnbus or private firms). On the north bank of the Tarn, 6km west of Albi, tiny **Castelnau-de-Lévis** boasts the ruins of a hill-top **castle** (free entry) founded after the Albigensian Crusade by a rehabilitated Raymond VII of Toulouse. Little remains apart from a single slender tower, but climbing its 198 steps provides breathtaking views of Albi and the plains of the *pays de Cocagne*. There's an excellent **B&B** here, *Jussens* (℡05.63.45.59.75, ⓔmichele.roose@wanadoo.fr; ❹), in an old farm house.

Another vantage point from which to take in the panorama of Albi is the nineteenth-century octagonal sanctuary of **Notre-Dame-de-la-Drèche**, set

The Albi–Castres rail line trail

The most pleasant, if not the fastest way to get from Albi to Castres is to follow the former rail line, now converted Into a **hiking**, **cycling** and **riding** trail, which connects Albi and Castres. There are no major sites on the way, but this is an excellent way to enjoy a typical slice of Midi landscape – gently rolling hills with alternating pastures, wheat fields and sunflowers. The walk is suitable for all ages and fitness levels. The total distance is 45km, which can be walked in approximately sixteen hours, making an overnight stop at Lautrec (see p.187), 26km along. The trail can be picked up 1km south of the Albi ring road, on rue Bourgelat, near the old cemetery, just off the southbound N112. After 800m you'll meet the D71, which should be followed south for 900m to regain the trail. A further 7km will lead you past the ruined church of Montsalvy and along the N112 until you reach a parking lot. Following the yellow trail markings you'll take a small lane on your right, and continue straight, over the quiet N120, as the trail once again becomes dirt. After 400m, branch off to the right (south-east) to regain the rail line. Turning right it continues for 3.5km, passing below the hamlet of Lombers, and continuing 12km to Lautrec, the turn-off for which is marked by a disued crossing-house. Leaving Lautrec the trail can be regained at the same point, or by taking the D83 (direction Castres) south for 1.5km, where you'll pass a grain silo on the left. From here the trail continues the remaining 16km to Castres, emerging near the town's *gare*.

on a rise 6km north of town. Founded by returning missionaries, it houses a small museum (Mon–Sat 9.30am–12.15pm & 4–6pm; free) recalling their efforts overseas; the grassy grounds outside the church are a popular picnic spot, and make an ideal rest stop for those returning by foot or bike from Cagnac (see p.180). A visit to the sanctuary can also be combined with a trip to **Lescure**, on the northeast edge of Albi, whose draw is the must-see eleventh-century **chapel of St-Michel** (hours vary). Founded by the monks from Gaillac and presently used for photography and art exhibitions, the ancient church boasts a striking twelfth-century Romanesque doorway and is festooned inside and out with carvings of gargoyles, animals and biblical scenes. Die-hard Toulouse-Lautrec fans will want to trek 45km north to **Château du Bosc** (45-min guided tours in French; daily 9am–7pm; €5), the family's principal estate, easily accessible from Albi by car or train to Naucelle-Gare, and then 3km southeast (follow signs for "Bosc"). The rambling estate is presided over by a magnificently appointed manor house still owned by the painter's family. In addition to family furnishings and *objets*, there are galleries featuring temporary exhibitions.

Ambialet

Following the twisting and rocky bed of the Tarn 21km east from Albi you reach **AMBIALET** (on the GR36), a mandatory stop on the way to Millau and worthy of exploration in its own right. Here the river doubles back in a dramatic oxbow, leaving a spit of land only 25m across at its narrowest point – a truly striking location. First mentioned in 924 AD, Ambialet belonged to Toulouse until it was seized by Simon de Montfort during the Albigensian Crusade. Over the following centuries it suffered in the Hundred Years' War and Wars of Religion; by the nineteenth it lay abandoned and even today it exudes a certain sleepy desolation. The main sight here is the austere Roman-esque **church** (daily 7.15am–10pm; free), still used by the resident monks whose chanted masses are open to the public. Perched on the top of the hill it provides an impressive panorama of the town below. You reach the church by climbing up a path from the "old town", which sits at the narrowest part of the river's meander (the "new town" is above the road tunnel), and return either the same way, or by following the road behind the monastery for 2km. The countryside south of Ambialet is agricultural land – high plains deeply etched by winding rivers. Apart from pleasant scenery, there is little of interest until you reach the Monts de Lacaune of the Parc du Haut Languedoc (see p.196), some 35km south.

Buses stop in the car park on the south bank, near which you'll find Ambialet's summer **tourist office** (July & Aug Tues–Sun 10am–noon & 3.30–7pm; ⓦwww.si-ambialet.fr). On the north bank, the village's only **hotel**, the well-appointed *Du Pont* (closed Jan–Feb; ☎05.63.55.32.07, ⓦwww .hotel-du-pont.com; ❸), has been run by the same family for almost two centuries. Its **restaurant** (open daily) offers *menus* from €21–50. Ambialet also has three **campsites** (May to mid-Sept), all clustered along the river-bank near the bridge: the municipal site (☎05.63.55.32.93); the *Mise à l'Eau* (☎05.63.79.58.29); and the *Pont d'Ambialet* (☎05.63.56.43.53), which also has two *gîtes*. **Bikes** can be rented at the hotel, while **kayaks** and **canoes** can be rented near the bridge on the same side of the river, and at other locales along the length of the river on the way to Albi. Wednesday's "country" **market** (July & Aug) is strictly a tourist affair.

Carmaux and around

Lying 16km north of Albi, down-to-earth **CARMAUX** owes its minor wealth to the thirty-square-kilometre coalfield over which it sits, and its few visitors are drawn by the relics of the defunct mining industry around the town: the open pit of **Ste-Marie** and the museum of **Cagnac**. These sights can be taken in by car, bicycle or even by foot, and, combined with a visit to the church of Notre-Dame-de-la-Drèche (see p.177), make a good day's outing from Albi. The countryside hereabouts is flat, scarred by excavation, and not particularly welcoming, but it improves as you head west towards Cordes, passing through **Monestiés**, home to a well-preserved ensemble of late medieval statues. If you're reliant on public transport, you'll have to catch one of the frequent buses which follow the old highway to see the mining sites, but there's no public transport link between Carmaux and Monestiés.

Carmaux's **coal** vein has been used since the twelfth century, but mining on a grand scale didn't begin until the 1700s, when the local squire, Georges Solages, received a royal licence to exploit the deposit. Late in the nineteenth century, the massive coalface at nearby Cagnac was discovered and became the focus of a boom. By the end of that century though, brutal conditions prompted miners, supported by Jean Jaurès, to unionize; in the half-century that followed the mines enjoyed their greatest period of production. In the 1970s things began to wind down, and the last mine, the great open pit, closed in 1997.

Carmaux itself offers little to visitors aside from a refreshing roughness – a relief after the pretensions of one too many polished-up *bastide*. In fact, the only "attraction" is the deceptively named **Musée du Château**, the former Solages estate 1km west of the centre, now housing a **museum** of mining and glass-working (French-only 1hr guided visits: June–Aug Mon–Sat 9am–noon & 2–6pm, Sun 3–6pm; Sept–May Mon–Fri 9am–noon & 2–6pm, Sat & Sun

3–6pm; €5). The mansion itself is unremarkable and run-down, and is unfortunately not redeemed by the insubstantial and dull subterranean exhibition, which is dominated by examples of local glass products and over-technical displays on coal mining.

Practicalities

Carmaux's **gare SNCF**, on the Albi–Rodez line, sits on the west side of the town centre. Turning left out of the station, boulevard Malroux leads north 100m to avenue Jean-Jaurès, the main street; at the junction turn right and you'll arrive three minutes later at the *place* of the same name, the town's centre. Two streets beyond lies place Gambetta, where the same kiosk serves as the **gare routière** and **tourist office** (Mon–Sat 10am–noon & 2–6pm; T05.63.76.76.67, Wwww.carmaux.fr). Of the town's **hotels**, the non-descript *Terminus* (closed Sat, mid-Aug & late Dec; T & F05.63.76.50.28, Wwww .logis-de-france.fr; ❶), across from the train station on avenue Jean-Jaurès, is the best option: failing that, there's the more basic *Gambetta* (T05.63.76.51.21; ❶), on place Jean-Jaurès. The **campsite** (May–Oct) is beside the museum. The town's best **restaurant**, *La Mouette* (closed Sun & Mon eves & mid-Feb; T05.63.36.79.90), is on place Jean-Jaurès, and offers original and varied *menus* featuring grilled meats and *confits* starting at €12 for lunch, up to the deluxe dinner-time "*menu* surprise" at €44. **Bikes** can be rented from Patrick Gelac (T05.63.56.05.64) on boulevard Augustin-Malroux, near the station.

Blayes, Cagnac and the Cap Découverte

With the land sloping down towards Albi, it makes the most sense to start a trip through the once coal-filled landscape to **Cagnac** from Carmaux. Just 2km south of town, the mining hamlet of **Blayes-les-Mines** is now a centre for industrial-history tourism, and a remarkable example of creative economic rehabilitation of what had become a post-industrial wasteland. The town makes an interesting stop, particularly if you are travelling with children. The first thing you'll come upon is the abandoned *découverte*, or **open pit**, of Ste-Marie, now transformed into the amusement park **Cap Découverte** (mid-April to mid-July daily 11am–7pm; mid-July to mid-Sept daily 11am–8pm; mid-Sept to mid-April Sat & Sun 11am–7pm; Wwww.capdecouverte.com), with a wide range of activities including go-karting, water-skiing and a beach: the activities are payable individually, or with a day-pass (adults €24, children €18). The site also plays host to various concerts and cultural events. The day-pass includes entrance to the adjacent **Jardins du Carbonifère** (same hours) featuring nature trails among the local fauna, while the silent hulks of rusting machinery parked along the rim of the pit can be explored in the **Parc des Titans** (free).

Further along the D90 you'll pass the **Cité du Homps**, a little industrial suburb of single-storey wooden huts, built for the Polish miners who immigrated in the 1950s, until you reach the **Musée Mine de Cagnac** (May–June & Sept–Oct daily 10am–noon & 2–6pm; July & Aug daily 10am–7pm, Nov–April Tues–Sat 10am–noon & 2–5pm & Sun 10am–noon & 2–6pm; €7), a vivid recreation of the world of the coal mine, and undoubtedly the region's most original museum. It consists of a stimulating, if claustrophobic, ninety-minute guided tour through 350m of galleries, excavated by out-of-work miners, and over a century of mining history, as you're shown different types of tunnels and machinery, a broad coal face and the miners' day quarters.

In **Blayes**, **accommodation** is available at *L'Auberge* near the Cap (T05.63.80.21.35, F05.63.80.21.36; ❷), while *La Grande Couverte* serves

The Cérou Valley

From Monestiés to Cordes-sur-Ciel the **Cérou** river meanders down from the scrubby highlands of the Ségala towards the rocky hills of the Tarnais *causses*, before emptying into the Lot. The pleasant and unchallenging sixteen-kilometre trip along the wooded riverbank can be made by car or **bicycle**, but can also be **hiked**, following a gentle path, in four to five hours. Leaving from the sports ground on the north side of Monestiés, follow the disused rail-bed which runs parallel to the D91 highway for 6km to the hamlet of Salles. Crossing the river, follow the directions through town for Virac, but turn right when you come to Salles' medieval church. At the end of that street follow the sealed road which ascends towards the Vignasse farm. After 200m or so, take the first trail branching off to the right. After 800m or so, following the yellow trail markings, you should reach the top of a T-junction. Cross this and proceed 30m, before the trail turns off left through the trees. Regaining a country lane 60m later, turn right, passing a bridge on your right, and a turn on your left, before coming to a T-junction. Here, take the left branch, which descends, becoming a dirt trail for 250m before reaching the D7 road. Cordes should now be in view. Descending along the D7 for just over 1km you'll pass a sign saying *"virages sur 2000m"*; here you can pick up the trail which leads to the town itself (1km further).

up traditional fare (from about €11). In **Cagnac** village, 1km further along, you'll find a couple of simple **café-bars** and the welcoming **B&B** *les Mailhoc* (℡05.63.53.90.10, ✉somaury@wandoo.fr; ❸), which also serves meals. From Cagnac, the D90 begins a rapid descent, reaching Notre-Dame-de-la-Drèche (see p.177) after 3km, before continuing to Albi.

Monestiés

Some 8km west of Carmaux is the rather run-of-the-mill village of **MONESTIÉS**, remarkable only for a much-touted set of fifteenth-century religious **statues** housed in its **Chapelle St-Jacques** (Mon 2–5/6.30pm, Tues–Sun 10am–noon & 2–5/6.30pm; €3.50). The stone carvings on display are a set of four works representing a group of figures in Christ's tomb, the Crucifixion and a *pietà*; they are well executed and preserved, but most likely only fans of late medieval art will feel that the admission price is justified. The town is also home to the small **Bajén-Vega Museum** (Tues–Sun 10am–noon & 2–5/6.30pm; €3, or €5 with chapel), displaying works by the two unexceptional local twentieth-century artists after whom it is named. It is housed in the same building as the **tourist office** (same hours; ℡05.63.76.19.17, ⒲www.monesties .com). The only **hotel** is the *Hostellerie de Saint-Jacques* (℡05.63.76.11.72, ⒲www.logis-de-france.fr; ❷), opposite the *chapelle*, or you can stay at the B&B *Les Voisins* (℡05.63.76.48.78, ⒲www.lesvoisins.nl; English spoken; ❷). There is a basic riverside municipal **campsite** off the road to Cordes. *Auberge Occitane* (closed late Aug to Sept & Wed), on the main street, is friendly and serves two-course **meals** from €15; the grocery store rents **bikes** (℡05.63.76.11.51).

Cordes-sur-Ciel

CORDES-SUR-CIEL, 27km northwest of Albi and just west of Monestiés, is the most spectacularly preserved of the Albigeois fortified planned towns, or *bastides*. Dramatically situated on a steep hill, the origin of the town's surname *sur-ciel* ("in the sky") can be appreciated on mornings when fog cloaks the foot of the hill and the medieval *cité* pokes through, apparently suspended in the clouds. No single sight brings people to Cordes; rather, the town as a whole, girded by several concentric medieval walls and endowed with a score of old houses, is something of an open-air museum and artisanal centre. It can be seen in an afternoon, but if you can afford the relatively expensive hotels, it makes for an atmospheric place to spend a night or two.

Founded in 1222 by Count Raymond VII of Toulouse at the height of the war against his Cathar subjects, Cordes provided a durable and defiant

△ Cordes-sur-Ciel

stronghold against Simon de Montfort's attacks. Its forename comes from the **leatherworking** industry (a craft associated with Córdoba, in Spain) which supported and enriched the town, bringing rapid growth; in the 1200s alone the walls had to be enlarged no less than seven times. Things took a downturn, however, with the arrival of the plague in the 1400s. Although Cordes later recovered, and had a notable lace industry in the nineteenth century, its real renaissance didn't come until the 1970s, when hippies, including the **craftsmen** and **artisans** whose wood, metalwork and other studios now cram the upper town, arrived to put Cordes back on the map, attracted by the place's beauty and air of antiquity.

The Town

The traveller, who from the terrace of Cordes regards the summer's night, knows that he has no need to go further, and that if he allows it, day after day, the beauty here will raise him out of any solitude.

Albert Camus

Camus' words give some idea of the town's allure, and hard though it may be to achieve such a placid state when the streets are packed during summer days, in the evening or out of season the romance of Cordes returns. To watch the sun rise from the ramparts is worth getting up for, and with every other building a medieval mansion, walking the town before the crowds arrive is a delight. Its layout is simple: the old citadel – the "**upper town**" – runs along and down the sides of the long and narrow ridge which juts up from the plain, while the modern "**lower town**" consists of a clump of streets at the foot of the old town's eastern tip. The best route to the upper town is the knee-cracking Grande Rue Basse ascending from the lower tourist office (see p.184), although at busy times, it is more pleasant to take one of the picturesque but less crowded side-streets. Alternatively, a *petit train* (July & Aug; €2.50) makes frequent trips from outside the tourist office. Along the way a series of medieval **gates** leads to the compact upper town.

Entering the last of the fortified entrances, you'll reach the **Musée Charles-Portal** (Easter–June, Sept & Oct Sun & hols 3–6pm; July & Aug daily 11am–1pm & 3–7pm; €2.30), housing a display on the medieval wells which riddle the town, and which were used in time of siege for water supply or to store grain. Further along, on Grande Rue, the elegant and symmetrical arcaded face of the fourteenth-century Maison du Grand Fauconnier houses the **Musée d'Art Moderne et Contemporain** (daily: Feb, March, Nov & Dec 2–5pm; April, May & Oct 11.30am–12.30pm & 2–6.30pm; June–Sept 11am–12.30pm & 2–7pm; €4). The museum features works by the figurative painter Yves Brayer, who lived in Cordes from 1940, a motley collection of modern art, including minor pieces by Picasso, Miró and Klee, and a French-only audio presentation explaining the town's lace-making tradition – hardly worth the stop. Across the street squats the ancient covered market, where you can peer down one of the town's famously deep wells. Continuing along Grande Rue, you'll pass the **Maison du Grand Veneur** ("House of the Great Hunter") – whose otherwise plain stone facade is festooned with amusingly sculpted and extremely well-preserved medieval caricatures of beasts and hunters. A few doors down is the similarly impressively carved frontage of Raymond of Toulouse's old palace, now home to the hotel *Grand Écuyer* (named after the finely sculpted horse figure) while, just beyond, the contemporary **Porte des Ormeaux** ("Gate of the Elm Saplings") takes you out of the old town.

There are more than forty **boutiques** in Cordes, including some which are thinly disguised as "museums". If price is not an issue, you could easily spend an afternoon or two here shopping for leatherwork, metal and handicraft items. Many of the stores double as workshops, so even window-shopping is quite interesting. One of the better deals is *Le Petit Bois*, in the place de l'Église, which has ingenious toys and gifts.

Practicalities

Trains stop 5km to the west of Cordes at **Vindrac** (℡05.63.56.05.64), from where it's a pleasant hour-long walk, or take the *navette* (€4.50). **Buses** arrive in the lower town, near the summer-only **tourist office** (May to mid-June & early Sept Sat 2–6pm, Sun 10.30am–12.30pm & 2–6pm; mid-June to Aug Mon 2–6pm, Tues–Sun 10.30am–12.30pm & 2–6pm), while the main tourist office (Jan Sat & Sun 2–6pm; Feb & March daily 2–6pm; April–June, Sept & Oct daily 2–6pm, plus Tues–Fri 10.30am–12.30pm; July & Aug daily 10am–1pm & 2–7pm; ℡05.63.56.00.52, ⓦwww.cordes-sur-ciel.org) is in the heart of the *cité*. If you're driving, **parking** can be a challenge – in the summer months the area a few metres east of the lower tourist office soon fills up and cars line the roads leading into town. Don't be tempted to drive into the old town.

Famed Tarnaise pastry chef and chocolatier Yves Thuriès presides over several of Cordes' **hotels**, including the lavish four-star ⚜ *Grand Écuyer* (closed mid-Oct to Easter; ℡05.63.53.79.50, ⓦwww.thuries.fr; ⑥), housed in Raymond's former palace, the atmospheric three-star *Vieux Cordes* (closed Jan; ℡05.63.53.79.20, ⓦwww.thuries.fr; ❸), and the two-star, *Hôtel de la Cité*, (closed Nov–April; ℡05.63.56.03.53, ⓦwww.thuries.fr; ❹). There's also a decent **campsite**, *Le Garissou* (open mid-April to Oct; ℡05.63.56.27.14, Ⓔlegarissou@wanadoo.fr), in Les Cabannes to the west of town. The best **restaurants** are in the hotels, including that in the *Grand Écuyer*, a one-star Michelin restaurant known for its *foie gras* and other regional dishes (*menus* €40–80). There's plenty of choice for more economical fare around the central place de la Halle and adjacent place de la Bride, while *Les Ormeaux*, at 3 rue Saint-Michel (closed part Jan; *menus* from €25), offers an appetizing middle ground.

Gaillac and around

Twenty-three kilometres west of Albi along the Tarn, **GAILLAC**, located at the heart of the wine region bearing its name, is a town built on the grape. It has an ideal climate for viticulture, and its inhabitants started putting corks in bottles more than 2500 years ago. But the industry really took off in the eighth century with the founding of the Benedictine abbey of St Michel – as part of their rule, monks are given a healthy daily ration of wine which, along with that needed for Holy Communion, ensured a high demand for the local product. In the tenth century the entrepreneurial Order decided to guarantee the qualify of their vintage by laying down the rules as to which wines could quality as Gaillacoises – and thus one of France's most famous AOCs was born. Today, Gaillac continues to live off the deserved reputation of its wine, but the commercial success of such a class-conscious product has led the simple town to adopt certain pretensions unmerited by its provincial reality. The chief reason for staying here longer than a few hours is to use it as a base for exploring the old *bastide*-villages of **Lisle** and **Rabastens**, further downstream.

The Town

Gaillac, with its compact medieval core, sits on the north side of the river. The focal point of the old town is the ponderous **abbey-church of St-Michel**, constructed in the eleventh century, and impressively large for its era. The interior is unadorned, apart from a fourteenth-century painted Virgin and Child on the left-hand side of the nave. The uninspiring **Musée de l'Abbaye de la Vigne et du Vin** (daily 9.30am–1pm & 2–7pm; €2.50), adjacent to the church, is dedicated to wine-making, with a twenty-minute French-only audiovisual show and displays of old grape presses, barrels, tools and bottles, but its chief attraction is its location in the old monastery cellars. The real business in Gaillac goes on down in the **Maison des Vins de Gaillac** (daily 10am–noon & 2–6pm; free) in the same complex, where you can sample and buy local vintages.

The old town spreading out to the north and east of the abbey-church retains a number of brick-and-timber houses worth a look, while a few minutes' walk northwest from place Lapérouse across the old Pont Château-de-Homps sits the **natural history museum** (July & Aug 10am–noon & 2–6pm, Sept–June Fri–Sun 10am–noon & 2–6pm; €2.30), with a collection of specimen cases stacked with the usual stuffed birds, dead bugs and sea creatures. Behind the monastery, off place Eugénie de Guérin, lies the medieval *faubourg*, whose twisting lanes lack grand monuments but are loaded with atmosphere. On its eastern side, in shady **Parc Foucaud**, the surprisingly good **Musée des Beaux-Arts** (July & Aug daily 10am–noon & 2–6pm; Sept–June Fri–Sun 10am–noon & 2–6pm; €2.50), houses some contemporary art that rises well above the usual quality of a country museum: the nineteenth- and twentieth-century Impressionist works of local artists Raymond Tournon and Henri Loubat, in particular, deserve a look.

Practicalities

Gaillac's **gare SNCF** (☎05.63.57.00.23), which is also where **buses** stop, is to the north of the old town, a good twenty-minute walk from the wine centre and the **tourist office** (daily 10am–noon & 2–6pm; ☎05.63.57.14.65, ⓦwww.ville-gaillac.fr) at the heart of things. **Accommodation** is plentiful and relatively cheap: the best is at ⅄ *La Verrerie* (closed mid-Oct to mid-April; ☎05.63.57.32.77, ⓦwww.la-verrerie.com; ❸; English spoken), a converted glass factory set in its own grounds in rue de l'Égalité. Another good option is the well-equipped *Hôtel Occitan* (☎05.63.57.11.52, ⓦwww.hotel-occitan -gaillac.com; ❸) at 41 rue Georges-Clémenceau, while Lucile Pinon, 8 place St-Michel (☎05.63.57.61.48, ⓦlucile.pinon.hotes81.monsite.wanadoo.fr; ❸) has **chambres d'hôtes** in her comfortable seventeenth-century *faubourg* house. The municipal **campsite** (June to mid-Sept; ☎05.63.57.18.30) is nicely situated along the river, beneath the shadow of the abbey. The best **restaurant** in town is *Les Sarments* at 27 rue Cabrol (closed Sun eve & Mon; ☎05.63.57.62.61; *menus* from €23), a *gastronomique* place tucked away in a medieval cellar in the *faubourg*. Alternatively, the much cheaper *Aux Charmes Gaillacois*, on rue Denfert-Rochereau near the train station, offers inexpensive and abundant four-course *menus* including wine and home-made desserts from €12. The local **market** is held on Tuesday, Friday and Sunday mornings.

Lisle-sur-Tarn and Rabastens

Only a ten-minute ride (7km) south on one of the frequent buses or trains from Gaillac, **LISLE-SUR-TARN** is a tranquil twelfth-century *bastide* known for its *pountets*, the overhead covered passages which connect many of its brick-built medieval houses. There is little to detain you here apart from a stroll through the town and a relaxed drink in arcaded place Saissac, at its centre. The small local **museum** (April to mid-Oct Tues–Sun 10am–noon & 2–6pm; €2) is tucked away to the southeast of the square and contains works by the native designer Raymond Lafage (who studied under Michelangelo). To the east, a street descends to the riverside and a point which long ago was the town's pier – an evocative spot. By the modern bridge just downstream sits the town's strikingly bold fourteenth-century brick **church**.

Lisle's **tourist office** (May, June, Sept & Oct Tues–Sun 10am–noon & 2–6pm; July & Aug daily 10am–12.30pm & 2.30–7pm; Nov–April Tues–Fri 2–5pm & Sat & Sun 10am–noon & 2–5pm; ☎05.63.40.31.85, ⓦwww.ville-lisle-sur -tarn.fr) is on the east side of place Saissac. The town's only **hotel** is *Le Princinor*, on the road to Rabastens (☎05.63.33.35.44, ⓔle.princinor@wanadoo.fr; ❷) – don't be fooled by its box-like exterior, the rooms are comfortable and the *menu* has a distinctly northern French flavour (from €12 at lunch and €15 at dinner; closed Fri eve, Sat lunch & Sun eve). There's a tiny one-star **camp-site** (July–Sept; ☎05.63.33.35.18) near the *Princinor*. **Bikes** can be rented from the local mechanic, Fauroux (☎05.63.33.35.06).

RABASTENS, the next village downriver on the Tarn, can be reached easily by bicycle or on foot and is a better choice than Lisle for an overnight stop. On weekend evenings the streets fill with young people, giving it a vivacity surprising for its size and making it a welcome contrast to the sleepier villages of the Albigeois. Still guarded by vestiges of its brick ramparts, Rabastens was founded in the time of the fifth-century barbarian invasions, when it served as a refuge for the inhabitants of a huge Gallo-roman villa. In the Middle Ages, the tanning industry brought it considerable prosperity, reflected in its surprisingly rich architecture. The sight which makes Rabastens an obligatory stop is the twelfth-century **Notre-Dame du Bourg** (Mon–Sat 10am–noon & 2–6pm, Sun 2–6pm). In the 1860s its incredible painted interior was rediscovered and restored. The magnificent, vibrant **frescoes** cover virtually every surface, and provide a rare chance to see what medieval churches really looked like, before the "puritans" of the Catholic Reformation scrubbed them clean. Also of note is a chapel dedicated to St James, donated by the archbishop of Santiago, grateful for the wealth which the pilgrimage route was bringing his diocese. The **Musée du Rabastinois** (Feb–Nov Mon–Sat 10am–noon & 2–6pm, Sun 3–6pm; €2.50) is just down the street and contains pieces from the Gallo-Roman and medieval periods.

Buses from Lisle pass through the centre of Rabastens, though the **gare SNCF** is located just across the river in Couferoul – about a ten-minute walk from the centre. The **tourist office** (March to mid-June & Sept–Oct Tues–Sat 10am–noon & 2–6pm; mid-June to Sept daily 9.30am–2pm & 3–6.30pm; Nov–Feb Tues–Sat 10am–noon & 1.30–5.30pm; ☎05.63.40.65.65, ⓦwww .cc-paysrabastinois.fr), at 12 rue Pont del Pâ, is by the old bridge and the church. The best **hotel** in Rabastens is the *Hostellerie du Pré-Vert* (closed Sun, Mon & Jan; ☎05.63.33.70.51, ⓔinfo@leprevert.com; ❸), an eighteenth-century mansion on the promenade des Lices. The one-star **campsite**, *Les Auzerals* (May–Aug; ☎05.63.33.70.36), is situated 3km northwest of town, on a small lake. As far as food and drink goes, any of the bistros and **restaurants** on the main promenade can provide solid Tarnaise sustenance, but for something different head to the *Hôtel de la Poste*, on place St-Michel (just off the main road), which has authentic Andalucian ambience and *menus* from €15, including wine (closed Sun eve & Mon).

Graulhet, Réalmont and Lautrec

The undulating wheat lands stretching southeast from Gaillac towards Castres are dominated by three small *bastides*. Of these, **Graulhet** and **Réalmont** are better served by public transport (both being on the Albi–Toulouse bus route), but are less interesting. **Lautrec**, on the other hand, picturesquely set on a windmill-capped spur, is a nice place to spend an afternoon or evening, but can only be accessed from Albi either via Graulhet or Castres.

Graulhet

Sixteen kilometres southeast of Gaillac and 30km northwest of Castres, on the Dadou river, **GRAULHET** is a grim, unsmiling town, whose unremarkable old quarter has decayed into a shambles. The town's name is derived from *groule*, the Occitan word for leather, which has been the source of its meagre prosperity since the Middle Ages – as early as the twelfth century raw hides from the pasture lands of the Montagne Noire were brought here to be tanned and finished. About the only reason to stop here is to change buses on the route from Albi to Lautrec: **buses** stop in place du Jourdain, across the river from the main road, below the old quarter capping the low rise on the north side of the square. The **tourist office** on place Foch (Mon–Sat 9am–noon & 2–6pm; ☎ & ℱ05.63.34.75.09, Ⓦwww.ville-graulhet.fr) has maps of the town's paltry highlights. If you do need to **stay** here, *Le Grandgousier* in place du Jourdain (☎05.63.34.50.32, Ⓔpaul.fernandez@wanadoo.fr; ❷) has reasonable rooms and a **restaurant** (€14.50–21). Finer dining can be found at the acclaimed 🏵 *La Rigaudié*, 2km east of town on the St-Julien-du-Puy road (closed Mon, Sat & Sun eves, Aug & late Dec; ☎05.63.34.50.07), with an excellent fish *menu* from €24. The town is at its best on Tuesday, Thursday and Sunday when the local **market** is held.

Réalmont

Seventeen kilometres east of Graulhet, **RÉALMONT** is one of the "royal *bastides*" founded by the twelfth-century Capetian kings to weaken the power of the local nobility. Today, only a few vestiges of its medieval past – the arcades of the main square and the grid of streets typical of medieval "new towns" – survive. The town's **church**, dating from the sixteenth century, is unremarkable. Wednesday morning is the best time to stop in here; the country **market** has local produce at excellent prices – a great opportunity to stock up for a picnic. The **tourist office** (July & Aug Tues–Sat 10am–noon & 2–6.30pm, Sun 10am–12.30pm; Sept–June daily 10am–noon & 2–6pm; ☎05.63.79.05.45, Ⓔoffice-tourisme-realmont@wanadoo.fr) is in 8 pl de la République, behind the town's only **hotel**, the charming but slightly decayed *Hôtel Montréal* (closed Sun eve, Mon & Feb; ☎05.63.55.52.80, Ⓦwww.logis-de-france.fr; ❷), which also provides excellent meals (from €18; closed Sun eve & Mon). There's a basic **campsite** 2km away on the Graulhet road (May–Sept; ☎05.63.55.50.41). The best-value **restaurant** is *Les Routiers* on boulevard Armengaud (closed Sun & part Aug; ☎05.63.55.65.44), which serves up solid *menus* starting from as low as €7.50. A country **market** is held on Wednesday mornings (July & Aug).

Lautrec

The most picturesque of the towns between Albi and Castres, **LAUTREC** is located on a minor road 15km southeast of Graulhet. The vanes of the windmill still churn on top of the hill where the castle once stood, and the hamlet gathered around it is a warren of steep, twisting streets, interspersed by little arcaded squares. It was here that a marriage alliance in 1196 established the family of the counts of Toulouse-Lautrec (the artist Henri's forebears). Nowadays the town prides itself on its pungent pink **garlic**, first brought by Spanish merchants in the eighteenth century. Four thousand tonnes of the stuff are harvested here every year, but smaller quantities can be purchased at the town's Friday **market**, and it even has its own festival (Aug 6).

Entering the old town through rue du Mercadial, where the main road passes on the north side, the *mairie* is just on the left, in a building which also houses the tourist office and the two-room **archeological museum** (Thurs–Sun 3.30–6.30pm; €2). A fairly humble affair, the museum has a display on local medieval burial customs and information on the scores of wells which perforate the old town and served primarily for grain storage. Continuing from the museum to the first crossroads, you can either descend on the left towards Lautrec's remaining twelfth-century **gate** or continue to the fourteenth-century collegial **church**, now a Baroque monstrosity inside. To get to the functioning seventeenth-century **windmill** perched above the town (early May to mid-June Sat 2–6pm & Sun 2–7pm; mid-June to Aug Thurs–Mon 2–6pm; €2), climb the street to the right immediately before the church. As you enter the mill on a windy day, the sight and sound of the large, rapidly spinning wooden mechanisms are exhilarating. The hill top also offers a superb panoramic **view** towards the south.

There is no hotel here, but there are a number of **chambres d'hôtes** in or near the town: the most homely is Alain Rouquier's house in place du Monument (T05.63.75.30.02, W www.cadalen81.com; ❸), while the grander *La Terrasse* (T05.63.75.84.22, W www.laterrassedelautrec.com; ❹) is a seventeenth-century mansion with an impressive French garden. A full list of the *chambres d'hôtes* in the area is available from the **tourist office** in rue du Mercadial (mid-June to mid-Sept Mon–Sat 10am–12.30pm & 2.30–6.30pm, Sun 2–5.30pm; mid-Sept to mid-June daily 2–5/5.30pm, plus Tues–Sat 10am–noon; T05.63.75.31.40, W ot.lautrec.free.fr) has a complete list. The two best **restaurants** are *le Moulin Gourmand*, rue Edmond-Michelet, below the windmill, which serves home-made food using garden-grown ingredients (closed Mon & Tues eve, plus Wed & Thurs eve off-season; from €11–33), and *Le Garde Pile* (T05.63.75.34.58; Fri noon to Sun noon only), located in a converted granary, just outside town on the Castres road, which serves a selection of lively dishes, strong on the local pink garlic (*menus* from €18). Friday morning is **market** day.

Castres and around

Southeast of Lautrec, the rolling agricultural landscape comes to an abrupt end as the land begins to rise and you approach Haut Languedoc, a highland ridged by peaks rising up to 1100m. **CASTRES**, on the western edge of the uplands, 42km south of Albi, began some two thousand years ago as a Roman military base (as its name, from the word for "camp" or "fort" recalls). An important Benedictine monastery was built here in the seventh century but, like the Roman town, its traces have all but vanished. In the twelfth century Castres was swept up in the Cathar movement, and it was here that the first Albigensian **martyrs** were burned at the stake in 1209. The ever-rebellious population took up the Protestant banner four centuries later, and the town became an important centre of **Huguenot** administration. Today, still supported by the textile industry which boomed in the eighteenth century, Castres is a town with energy – worth visiting in its own right and an ideal point of access to the northern and western parts of the Parc Naturel Régional du Haut Languedoc (see p.194). Boasting a colourful medieval core and a pleasantly diverse populace, it is also enlivened by two summer **music festivals**. In addition, it has a couple of good museums: one dedicated to Castres' native son, the nineteenth-century socialist Jean Jaurès, and the other to Spanish art. The Sidobre, a granite massif to the east famed for its peculiar rock formations, makes an easy excursion. Castres is also the end-point of the Gijou Valley Trail, a hiking, riding and mountain-bike route, leading up into the isolated heights of Haut Languedoc (see p.198).

Arrival, information and accommodation

Castres' **gare SNCF** is at avenue Albert 1er, a 25-minute walk west of the old town (bus #7; €0.90). The **gare routière** on place Soult is on the far eastern edge of the centre – a short walk from the river. For those driving, **parking** on the street in old Castres is possible, but check the signs carefully: between the market days and street-cleaning schedule, you could easily get your car towed.

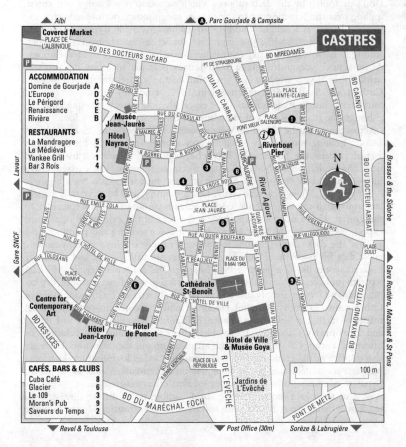

CASTRES

ACCOMMODATION
Domine de Gourjade A
L'Europe D
Le Périgord C
Renaissance E
Rivière B

RESTAURANTS
La Mandragore 5
Le Médiéval 7
Yankee Grill 1
Bar 3 Rois 4

CAFÉS, BARS & CLUBS
Cuba Café 8
Glacier 6
Le 109 3
Moran's Pub 9
Saveurs du Temps 2

The **tourist office** is at 3 rue Milhau-Ducommun, along the riverbank in the old town, by the *pont vieux* (July & Aug daily 9.30am–12.30pm & 1.30–6.30pm; Sept–June Mon–Sat 9.30am–12.30pm & 2–6pm; ☎05.63.62.63.62, ⓦwww .ville-castres.fr): in summer it sells the "**Passe culturel de l'été**" (€4), which gives admission to the town's three museums and is valid for one month.

Castres has two marvellous seventeenth-century mansions converted into luxurious but affordable **hotels**: the more deluxe is the ⚜ *Renaissance* at 17 rue Victor Hugo (☎05.63.59.30.42, ⓦwww.hotel-renaissance.fr; ❺), which also owns the *L'Europe*, just up the same street at no. 5 (☎05.63.59.00.33; ❹). Alternatively, the *Rivière*, 10 quai Tourcaudière (☎05.63.59.04.53, ⓔhotelriviere @wanadoo.fr; ❷), has pleasant views over the Agout and helpful staff, while the very friendly and clean *Le Périgord*, 22 rue Émile Zola (☎ & Ⓕ05.63.59.04.74; ❶) is a bargain, with a *bain complet* in every room, and great half- and full-pension plans. The three-star **campsite** in Parc Gourjade (April–Sept; ☎05.63.59.72.30, ⓦwww.campingdegourjade.com) also has bungalows, with walking trails and watersports facilities in the Parc itself: get there by buses #3, #6 or #7 (direction Borde-Basse) or by the *Miredames* river-boat (see "Listings" p.192).

The Town

Don't be fooled by the drab suburbs which surround it – Castres' **old town**, spilling over the River Agout to the east, its rough square outline reflecting the Roman layout, is a delight. The brightly painted riverside **dyers' houses** are the town's hallmark, while the impressive sixteenth-century mansions hidden among its narrow streets make the medieval quarter a pleasure to stroll through. At its centre, café-girded **place Jean-Jaurès** is home to a bustling produce market four days a week, while just south of the square, the unprepossessing **Cathédrale St-Benoît**, constructed in 1677, stands on the site of the old monastery church. It's a squat and not especially noteworthy Baroque building, although the marble statues of saints around the choir are worth a look.

Across the street, the **Hôtel de Ville** reposes within the former bishop's palace, a dour, hulking square edifice, whose grey sobriety contrasts with the bright formal gardens, the **Jardins de l'Évêché**, which stretch out on its southern side. The building also houses Castres' foremost museum, the **Musée Goya** (July & Aug daily 9am–noon & 2–6pm; Sept–June Tues–Sun 9am–noon & 2–5/6pm; €2.30), which was established a century ago by private donation, and now holds the biggest collection of Spanish paintings in France apart from the Louvre. Dominating its largest salon, the core of the exhibition is, as you'd expect, taken up by the artist after whom it is named, but the paintings here are not the dark, sinister visions for which **Francisco Goya** is most famous, but rather his portraiture, including his *Self-portrait with Glasses*, and politically inspired works like *The Junta of the Philippines Presided over by Ferdinand VII*. A separate room features several series of his satirical pen-and-ink cartoons, depicting vices and virtues and popular adages, as well as series on bullfighting and war. Other rooms contain numerous pieces by other seventeenth-century Iberian masters – including **Velázquez**'s *Portrait of Philip IV*, **Murillo**'s *Virgin with Rosary* and **Zurburán**'s *Carthusian Martyr*. Flemish-influenced medieval paintings by fifteenth-century Catalan and Spanish artists round out the collection. There are also displays of old coins, royal seals and assorted archeological knick-knacks, as well as a room dedicated to the local war-time Resistance. An adjacent gallery (separate admission) houses temporary exhibits of impressive quality.

West of the Goya museum along rue Chambre de l'Édit are three palatial residences dating from the sixteenth and seventeenth centuries. On rue Guy, the first street on the right, the seventeenth-century **Hôtel de Poncet** stands out, with its classically inspired Renaissance facade and caryatid columns supporting an elegant Ionic-columned loggia. Further along rue Chambre de l'Édit you'll find the earlier **Hôtel Jean-Leroy**, notable for its stately carved casement windows and topped by a defensive tower. Next door to that, **Hôtel de Viviès**, built along the now-vanished city walls, was once the seat of the town's Huguenot judicial court and now houses the small **Centre for Contemporary Art** (Tues–Fri 10am–noon & 2–5.30pm, Sat & Sun 3–6pm; €1), which hosts temporary exhibitions of local and international modern works. Castres' shopping district stretches north from here, on the far side of which, in rue Thomas, you'll find Castres' grandest *hôtel particulier*, the **Hôtel de Nayrac**, built in the brick-and-stone style of the Toulouse mansions, with three sober facades boxing in a broad symmetrical courtyard. Just beyond is the **Musée Jean-Jaurès** (same hours as Musée Goya; €1.50), which pays homage to the life of Castres' favourite son (see box below), recounting the martyred activist's career with newspaper reports, memorabilia and contemporary artefacts.

Jean Jaurès

Jean Jaurès, the nineteenth-century labour activist, politician and martyr, is a figure whose presence travellers can scarcely escape in Languedoc. Nearly every town has at least one street or square – usually a main one – and a building or two named after this **socialist hero**, whose tireless struggle for workers' rights and international peace eventually cost him his life.

Born in Castres in 1859, Jean Jaurès showed exceptional promise as a student and won a scholarship to complete his studies in Paris. When these were finished, rather than stay in the capital he returned to his home *département* of Tarn and took a post teaching philosophy in **Albi's** *lycée* (high school), and giving lectures at the University of Toulouse. But the miserable conditions under which his **working-class** neighbours toiled drew him out of the academy; their dangerous working environment, underpayment and near-total lack of rights and representation could have been lifted straight from the pages of **Émile Zola's** contemporary *Germinal*. Jaurès ran for political office and at the young age of 26 was elected a deputy (or legislative representative) of Tarn. One of his first projects was to help the glass-workers at Albi found the collectively run V.O.A. bottle factory, which still operates today. Continuing in politics and the cause of social justice, in 1893, as socialist deputy for **Carmaux**, he supported the miners' struggle for better working conditions (see p.404), and his renown as a social reformer began to spread.

However, Jaurès' desire for reform went beyond simply improving the lives of those around him. Five years later he joined other liberals, including Zola, in defence of the Jewish army captain, **Alfred Dreyfus**, convicted on unfounded charges of espionage. National feelings of resentment against Dreyfus were running high, but despite this Jaurès persisted in his defence of the underdog, and – eventually – got him pardoned. The patriotically charged issue temporarily cost Jaurès his popularity, but he was soon back on the stage, founding the Communist daily *L'Humanité* in 1904 (still one of France's major newspapers; ⓦwww.humanite.fr) and the following year helping found the socialist SFIO party. With the dawn of World War I, however, Jaurès' internationalist brand of socialism revealed itself again in an outspoken and unpopular **pacifist** stand – and led to his **assassination** in Paris by a nationalist extremist in July 1914. On his death he was hailed as a martyr, the perfect hero for the Tarn – a local politician who improved the quality of life in this underdeveloped and marginalized region, and who wasn't afraid to take on the political establishment of Paris in order to defend a higher justice.

Over on the far side of the river, the scruffier east bank of the Agout is home to a number of interesting little restaurants and cafés, and although it lacks historical buildings the neighbourhood's proletarian feel is refreshing. The sparsely adorned medieval **fountain** in place Fagerie, just north of the Pont Neuf, is also worth seeking out, if only for the "undiscovered" atmosphere of the square in which it sits.

Eating, drinking and nightlife

For its size, Castres has an impressive range of **restaurants**. The *l'Europe* hotel has an excellent all-you-can-eat buffet (€10) both at lunch and dinner-time (daily noon–2pm & 8.30–10.30pm), featuring a range of *terroir* fare and an impressive selection of desserts. *La Mandragore*, 1 rue Malpas (closed Sun & Mon lunch; ☏05.63.59.51.27), is praised both for its *gastronomique* cuisine and selection of wines *(menus* range from €15–30), while for a no-nonsense quality **brasserie**, try *Le Médiéval* at 44 rue Milhau-Ducommun (closed Sun & Mon; ☏05.63.51.13.78), whose eleventh-century dining room sits poised above the Agout, with a funky pseudo-medieval décor *(menus* from €18). Along rue Fuzies, which runs east from the Pont Vieux, you'll find a number of cheaper but no less interesting options: in addition to a selection of kebab stands and Chinese places, the *Yankee Grill* (closed Sun noon) offers Tex-Mex à la carte from €12. The jazzy *Bar 3 Rois*, in rue des Trois Rois, also has a small upstairs dining room.

A good **café** is *Saveurs du Temps*, 4 rue Fuzies, and you can get a pint at the very un-Irish *Moran's Pub* at no. 18 in rue d'Empare. Aside from this, any of the **bars** around place Jean-Jaurès will do for a coffee or drink, with *Glacier*, on the south side, being particularly popular with locals for its gigantic ice-cream sundaes (€6), and sometimes hosting live music. Late-night diversion is provided by the rock **club** *Le 109* (after 11pm), through the graffitied door (no sign) in passage Henri IV, and the cool cocktail and tapas bar *Cuba Café* at 8 rue d'Empare (Wed–Sun 6pm–2am).

Listings

Banks There are several banks with ATMs in the old town, including Crédit Agricole in pl Jean-Jaurès.
Bike rental You can rent bikes from Soual à Bouti Cycle (☏05.63.75.46.19),
Boat trips The Miredames river-boat does a 45min round-trip down the Agout, leaving from the pier outside the tourist office (May–Oct at noon, 2.20pm, 3.40pm & 5.10pm; €4).
Bus information ☏05.63.35.37.31.
Car rental Ada, 32 av Charles de Gaulle ☏05.63.51.10.26; Avis, rte de Toulouse ☏05.63.72.82.21; Budget, rue Albert 1er ☏05.63.71.31.28; Europcar, 67 rue Maillot

☏05.63.72.24.69; Hertz, av François Mitterand ☏05.63.59.01.14; and Lavail, rte d'Albi ☏05.63.71.93.34.
Hospital Centre Hospitalier, pl Alsace-Lorraine, just south of the Hôtel de Ville ☏05.63.71.15.15.
Internet access Multimedia Cultural Centre, 2 av de Sidorbe ☏05.63.62.41.60.
Laundry Lavanderie Express, 8–9 rue Fuzies (daily till 9pm).
Market Tue, Thurs, Fri & Sat in pl Jean-Jaurès and pl l'Albinique.
Police 2 av Charles de Gaulle ☏17 or ☏05.63.35.40.10.
Taxis ☏05.63.59.99.25.

Around Castres

Castres is not only a comfortable place to stay for a day or two, but an ideal base for exploring a number of day-trip destinations in the vicinity. Just to the east lies the hundred-square-kilometre granite plateau known as the **Sidobre**.

This heavily promoted area is known for the boulders which litter it, either eroded into evocative shapes or balancing precariously. Many are found within a three-kilometre radius of Lacrouzette, including the rock-strewn waterfall, **Saut de la Truite**, and while some of the formations are truly remarkable, others are really rather lame – the **Trois Fromages** ("Three Cheeses"), for example, merely comprises a group of three roundish boulders set on top of each other. South of these groups lies the **Peyro Clabado**, an 800-tonne boulder perched on a smaller stone, and the **Rochers de Sept-Faux**, "logan stones" – two giant rocks balanced in such a way that the upper one, 900 tonnes in mass, can be rocked simply by pushing on it. The wooded paths which lead to the sites are well maintained and make for pleasant walking, although on weekends they're crowded with families. Bring sufficient water or be prepared to pay over the odds at the cafés and drinks stands near the trails. To explore the region by foot or bicycle, pick up the free *Les Circuits du Tarn* brochure in Castres, which provides detailed descriptions of routes.

All the sights of the region are easily accessed by **bus** from Castres, but if you want to stay locally, **accommodation** can be found in nondescript **Lacrouzette**, at *L'Auberge du Crémaussel* (Easter–Nov; ℡05.63.50.61.33; ❸), which also has a restaurant serving generous *menus* from €16 (closed Sun eve, Wed all year, Jan & winter weekends), or *Au Relais du Sidobre* (℡05.63.50.60.06, Ⓦwww.hotel-restaurant-sidobre.com; ❸). Alternatively head to nearby **Burlats**, where there's great chambres d'hôtes accommodation in a luxurious fourteenth- to sixteenth-century castle (℡05.63.35.29.20, Ⓔle.castel.de-burlats@wanadoo.fr; ❹). *Le Clos du Roc* **restaurant** in nearby **St-Salvy** serves excellent cuisine at economical prices, in a converted barn, (closed Wed eve, Sun & Mon & part Feb; ℡05.63.50.57.23; *menus* €12–30; book ahead),

South of Castres: Labrugière

South of Castres on the way to Mazamet, you may pass through **LABRU-GIÈRE**, a quaint *circulade*, or "round village" (see box below), laid out in concentric circles around the village church. Dating back to 985 AD, the town owes its notoriety to the 1484 **witch trial** of Péronne Bachère. Accused of making a pact with the Devil, casting spells and killing a neighbour with magic powder, she confessed all when interrogated and was burnt at a nearby crossroads. The parchment which recorded her trial can be seen today in a display at the *mairie* on the town's main square.

The Parc du Haut Languedoc

The southeastern half of the *département* of Tarn is dominated by the mountain-ridged highlands of Upper Languedoc. In this region of isolated hamlets the scant population has traditionally subsisted on herding and agriculture, supplemented nowadays by a growing outdoor recreation industry. Long a backwood of proudly self-sufficient Calvinist Huguenots, these hills later proved a fertile recruiting ground for anti-German resistance after the occupation of Vichy France. The zone is dominated by the sprawling **PARC NATUREL RÉGIONAL DU HAUT LANGUEDOC**, an imprecisely bounded region which, in the thirty years or so since its establishment, has grown to encompass additional territory

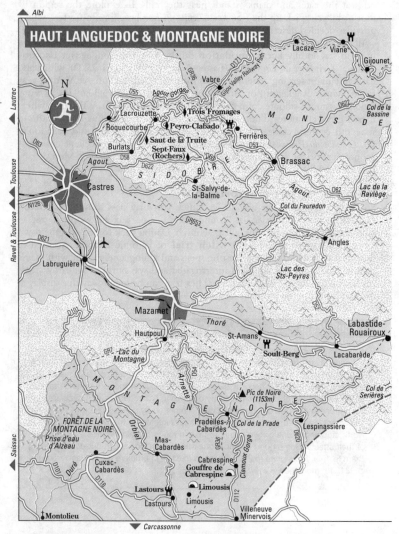

almost yearly. Its designation as a park is primarily administrative, which can lead to confusion – the boundaries aren't well marked, and there's no change in the landscape or villages which distinguishes the park from the surrounding area. That said, a good approximation is to define the park more or less by the mountains which cross it: the **Monts de Lacaune** in the north, the **Monts de l'Espinouse** to the east, and the north face of the Montagne Noire range (see p.203), tacked onto the park's southwest. The man-made **lakes** which punctuate the highland near **La Salvetat**, **Fraïsse** and **Anglès** are the focus of a thriving tourist industry: each is ringed by campsites and boat-rental outfits which do a brisk trade in the summer months. Although public transport across the park is poor, it serves **hikers** well, crisscrossed by a network of footpaths: *grandes* and

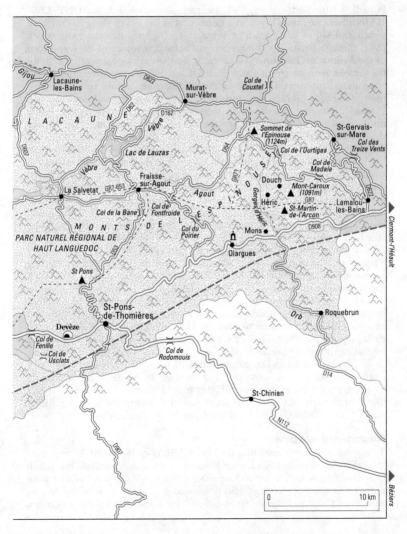

petites randonnées, and local routes, such as the **Gijou Valley Railway Trail** linking **Lacaune-les-Bains**, **Vabre** and **Brassac**. Native wildlife, which still includes some wild boar and deer, is less frequently encountered as the park becomes more popular – although you might see the ancient breed of mouflon sheep if you cross the Monts de l'Espinouse – and despite straddling the border of the Atlantic and Mediterranean climatic zones, the bulk of the park lies in the cooler, humid northern zone, where the flora is dominated by forests of sturdy oak and chestnut. Detailed park **information** can be obtained at the **Maison du Parc** offices in **St-Pons**, the "capital" of the park, and **Murat**; local tourist offices sell a guide to fifteen **bicycle** itineraries in the area.

Lacaune-les-Bains and around

Poised on the northern edge of the park, slate-roofed **LACAUNE-LES-BAINS** lies east from Castres, at a distance of either 67km along the tortuous Agout and Gijou valley road, or 46km along the mountainous route which passes through Brassac. At 885m, it sits just below the source of the Gijou river in the **Monts de Lacaune**, whose sheep are the exclusive source of milk for the famous blue cheese of Roquefort. The town was a curative spa (specializing in urinary tract ailments) in the Middle Ages, a role commemorated by a fourteenth-century iron **fountain** in the town centre known as "Les Pisseurs", featuring four tiny but impressively endowed male figures peeing into a pool below. Beside the fountain, in place du Friggoul, is the **Musée du Vieux Lacaune** (April–June & Sept–Nov Tues–Sun 2.30–6pm; July & Aug daily 10am–noon & 2–6pm; free), which offers an unexceptional look at local nineteenth-century rural life. In similar vein, the **Filature Ramond** is a wool workshop from the same era, where you can watch the various tools and machines being used (Mon, Wed & Fri 11am, 2 & 3pm; €2). Aside from taking in the surroundings there is little to do in Lacaune, apart from enjoying the Sunday-morning local **market** and a larger regional **fair** on the 21st of each month. The town has good bus connections, but the best way to explore the area is on foot or by bike along the Gijou Valley Trail, a disused narrow-gauge railway line heading west towards Castres (see p.188).

Buses trundle through Lavaur stopping at place de la République, where a small **tourist office** (mid-June to mid-Sept Mon–Fri 9am–noon & 2–6.30pm, Sat & Sun 10am–noon & 2–6.30pm; mid-Sept to mid-June Mon 2–5pm, Tues–Fri 9am–noon & 2–5pm, Sat 10am–noon & 2–5pm; ☎05.63.37.04.98, ⊛www.lacaune.com), provides detailed information on walks in the area, and rents out **bikes**. If you want to **stay** the night, the *Central Hôtel Fusies* on rue de la République (☎05.63.37.02.03, ⊛www.hotelfusies.fr; ❸) offers three-star amenities, though the small family-run hotel *Calas*, tucked away in the place de la Vierge (closed mid-Dec to mid-Jan; ☎05.63.37.03.28, ⊛www.pageloisirs .com/calas; ❷), is more attractive and cheaper. Its owner, Claude Calas, a fourth-generation chef, also runs a highly praised **bistro** (closed Fri & Sat eves Oct–Easter; *menus* €11–35). The local municipal **campsite** is on the Murat road (all year; ☎05.63.37.03.59, ⊛www.pageloisirs.com/le-clot).

Murat-sur-Vèbre

Twenty-six kilometres east of Lacaune lies **MURAT-SUR-VÈBRE**, an ancient but otherwise unremarkable hamlet bisected by a tributary of the Vèbre, which undoubtedly saw its heaviest traffic passing through when it was a way-stop on the pilgrim route to Santiago. Hikers who want to relive a bit of the Middle Ages can follow the "chemin de St-Jacques" (now the GR653) east to Castres.

△ Les Pisseurs, Lacaune-les-Bains

If you stop here it will most likely be to pick up information from the **Maison du Parc** (July & Aug Mon–Sat 10am–noon & 2–6pm; Sept–June 10am–noon & 2–5pm; ☎05.63.37.45.76), an annexe to the local **tourist office** (same hours; ☎05.63.37.47.47), which rents out **bikes**. Should you decide to stay, the only **hotel** is the rather basic *Durand* (☎05.63.37.41.91, ⊜hoteldurand@wanadoo.fr; ❸), with a reasonable but unexceptional **restaurant** (closed Fri eve & Sat out of season), and there's also a **campsite**, *Les Adrets* (June–Sept; ☎05.63.37.41.16).

Alternatively, Cristiane Roque's farm, *Félines*, just outside town (℡05.63.37.43.17, ℻05.63.37.19.85; ❷), has rooms and can provide meals.

The Gijou Valley Railway Trail

Half a century ago locomotives still threaded the tortuously meandering Agout and Gijou valleys, steaming up the cliff-hanging **narrow-gauge railway** connecting Castres with Vabre and Lacaune to the east, and branching off to Brassac to the south, 16km up the Agout valley. The trains have long disappeared, but the rail-bed has been brought back to life as a **hiking** and **mountain-biking** trail – a route best travelled from Lacaune westwards for the simple reason that it's downhill. This defunct railway winds along steep and forested banks, dramatically crossing the riverbed on ancient trestle bridges and only rarely passing tiny hamlets of slate-shingled houses and solitary farmsteads.

Leaving Lacaune, the trail arrives at **Gijounet** after a couple of hours walk, just after a small waterfall. Continuing along for 5km, it skirts the slightly larger **Viane**, with a ruined *château* perched above, and then at **Lacaze**, several hours beyond, a medieval bridge spans the river, beside a once-stately fifteenth-century **mansion**. From this point the river gains force and begins to wind erratically through the cliffs girding it; fifteen kilometres now remain to **Vabre**, a larger town with a twelfth-century bridge. The distance from Lacaune to Vabre is 40km, which will take around eleven hours on foot. A few kilometres after Vabre, the Gijou empties into the Agout, and it is here that the railway branches off southwards and uphill towards **Brassac** 16km away (see below), passing the still fiercely Huguenot village of **Ferrières**, which has a private **castle** (closed), and a paltry **Musée du Protestantisme** (April–June & Sept–Oct Sun & hols 2–6pm; July & Aug Mon & Wed–Sat 10am–noon & 3–7pm, Tues & Sun 2–6pm; €3) at the halfway mark. From the Vabre junction, the mainline trail continues to Roquecourbe, threading the gorges which mark the northern limit of the Sidobre; from here the D89 can be followed for 8km to Castres. Alternatively, 3km out of Roquecourbe, take the tarmac road towards Le Carla generating station to regain the river and follow it to Castres via Burlats (adding 12km to the route). The Topoguide *Le Tarn …à pied* details the trail, but starting from Castres in the opposite, uphill, direction.

There are few opportunities to pick up supplies en route – Lacaze, with a **store** and **café**, is the first good spot to refuel – but for those who plan on making the journey over a night or two, each of the villages along the line has a very basic and free **campsite**. Vabre has a number of services, including a **tourist office** in the *mairie* (June–Sept Mon–Fri 10am–12.30pm & 3–6.30pm; ℡05.63.50.48.75), and a Thursday morning **market**. In Ferrières, Davina Doughan's B&B *La Ramade* (℡ & ℻05.63.40.52.57, ✉ddoughan@aol.com; English spoken; ❸) also provides meals (€15), though the municipal **gîte**, which can be booked through the *mairie* (℡05.63.74.40.60, ℻05.63.74.40.64; doubles ❶, dorm beds €15), is a better deal.

Brassac

BRASSAC, lying some 20km southwest of Lacaune, is undoubtedly the most attractive town on the west side of the park. Here the Agout, girded by nineteenth-century textile plants and the towers of a small medieval **castle**, is crossed by a picture-postcard twelfth-century **bridge**. Brassac has some decent amenities, including shops and ATMs, making it a good base for exploring the western sector of the park. The former staging-post, the *Café de Paris* (closed Sun & Mon out of season; ℡05.63.74.00.31; ❸) has **accommodation** and

The Huguenots of Haut Languedoc

The rugged and isolated hills of Haut Languedoc remain a bastion of France's once much-mistreated but stubborn Protestant community, or **Huguenots**. During the sixteenth century, Protestantism, like Catharism before it, exercised a strong attraction on the inhabitants of Languedoc. In an age when political and religious obedience were perceived as parallel, the people of the south felt exploited, on the one hand by an absolutist monarchy in Paris and on the other by a Church which manifested itself most visibly as a tax-collector.

The new faith arrived in the Haut Languedoc close on the heels of Martin Luther's defiance of Church authority in 1519; the first Protestant was burned in Toulouse only eight years later. The Huguenot movement – named after an obscure Swiss political event – however, tended to follow the Frenchman **John Calvin**'s teachings, which had a more politically revolutionary message: his principle of "Inferior Magistrates" dictated that people were morally justified in disobeying and deposing an unfit ruler. The established order was clearly under threat from the dangerous new religion, and when the Crown and Church attempted to eradicate it, arresting reforming theologians and preachers and impounding French-language versions of the Bible, the people of the south, backed by the equally dissatisfied local nobility, retaliated, and the long and bloody **Wars of Religion** ensued. In a dynamic reminiscent of the Cathar era, the nobility, already divided into factions, used the theological conflict as justification for open warfare: the princely house of Guise and their allies championed Catholicism, while the rival Bourbons took up the Protestant flag. After a prolonged series of military campaigns and massacres the wars ended, or rather paused for a while, with a compromise when the formerly Protestant Henri IV passed the **Edict of Nantes** in 1598, recognizing limited Huguenot rights. Castres became a "protected zone" for Protestants, and eventually home to one of the four courts of the land empowered to mediate legal disputes between Catholics and Huguenots. Almost a century later however, this uneasy accommodation ended when the supreme autocrat Louis XIV outlawed Calvinism again in 1685, and set in motion a harsh period of **repression** in Haut Languedoc. Soldiers were billeted in suspected Protestant homes, and possession of the Bible in French (instead of the official Latin) became a criminal offence. Huguenots reacted by escaping into exile or going underground, like the community in Ferrières, which hid Bibles in secret wall-compartments or women's bonnets, and held clandestine services in the forest. Eventually many villages fled en masse to the even more isolated Cévennes to the east, out of reach of royal officials and the army. Many returned only in 1787, when the **Edict of Toleration** finally established Protestant liberties; with the foundation of the secular revolutionary government two years later, Catholicism ceased to be an official measure of "Frenchness". Although Protestantism declined as a result of centuries of persecution, today nearly every hamlet in the highlands and every sizeable town in Languedoc has a Huguenot church (or *temple*), and country folk of Haut Languedoc still recall the stalwart non-conformity of their ancestors with pride.

a **restaurant** serving *menus* from €14 (Sept–June closed Sun). Across the street, the *Centre* also offers rooms and meals (℡05.63.74.00.14; ❷), and has a little **bar**. You'll find a basic municipal **campsite** just north of the village (℡05.63.74.09.11).

The Plateau des Lacs

Sandwiched between the mountains of Lacaune and l'Espinouse, and stretching from Murat in the northeast almost as far as Mazamet to the southwest, the rambling upland of the park, the **Plateau des Lacs**, is punctuated by three large, artificial lakes along the Vèbre and Agout rivers, which converge here. **LA SALVETAT-SUR-AGOUT**, smack in the middle of the uplands, is the hub of the plateau, and the terminus of the Béziers to St-Pons bus route. The attractive little town has not been spoiled by the souvenir shops which dot its centre, and when the daily hubbub subsides, the tangled knot of streets which makes up the old town evokes the eleventh century, when La Salvetat was founded. There is nothing in particular to look at in the village, but two historical relics lie just outside of town: a twelfth-century Romanesque **chapel** (July & Aug daily 3–7pm), which contains a "black Virgin"– a Romanesque statue discoloured by time – and the stone bridge next to it, used by medieval pilgrims en route to Santiago. The town is a short walk from the ten-kilometre-long **Lac de la Ravièrge**, which has been extensively developed as a holiday spot – here you'll find **beaches**, and plenty of **canoe**, **sail** and **motorboat** rental outlets. Those wishing to explore the surrounding area on foot can purchase a booklet with twelve well-laid-out *petites randonnées* (€1) from La Salvetat's **tourist office** (Mon–Fri 9am–noon & 2–6pm, Sat & Sun 10am–noon & 2–5pm, Sept–June closed Sun; ☏ & 🖷04.67.97.64.44, 🖲www.lasalvetatot.com), which can also help find furnished flats and cottages to rent.

Alternatively, inexpensive **rooms** and generous portions of home-cooking (for guests only) can be found at the English-owned *La Pergola* (☏04.67.97.60.57, 🖷04.67.97.56.76; ❶), just off the main road by the *place* where the **buses** from St-Pons stop. There's also **chambres d'hôtes** accommodation at *Hameau de Meges* on the northern side of the town (☏04.67.97.56.65, 🖾pommier.pierre @wanadoo.fr; English spoken; ❸), and at *La Moutousse*, an old farm 4km out of town on the GR653 (Easter–Oct; ☏04.67.97.61.63, 🖲www.lamoutouse.com; ❸). **Bikes** can be rented at *Loca Surf* (☏04.67.97.65.13). There are four **camp-sites** within walking distance; the nearest is *La Blaquière* on allée St-Étienne de Cavall just north of the centre (June–Aug; ☏04.67.97.61.29, 🖲www.blaquiere .fr.st), while down by the lake there's the small *Calcia* (☏04.67.97.63.45). Of the several **restaurants** in town, the only notable one is *La Table Forestière* (☏04.67.97.56.01), on the route de Lacaune, which is open all year.

Fraïsse-sur-Agout and Lac de Lauzas

Although **FRAÏSSE-SUR-AGOUT**, 10km east of La Salvetat by road (D14) or trail (GR71), is only 2km south of **Lac de Lauzas** as the crow flies, the winding road which crosses the intervening hills clocks in at nearly 10km. This hamlet, set at a hilly crossroads, has become rather touristy in summer, but still retains its bucolic air thanks to its diminutive size and the isolated beauty of its surroundings. From the ancient bridge over the Agout, a short trail leads south-wards uphill for 2km to the **Prat d'Alaric** and a traditional working **farm museum** (Thurs 10am–noon; free).

Fraïsse has a **tourist office** (May, June & Sept Sat & Sun 10am–12.30pm & 2–5pm; July & Aug daily 10am–12.30pm & 2–5pm; ☏04.67.97.61.14), and you can **stay** at the homey *Auberge de l'Espinouse* (☏04.67.95.40.46; 🖲www .aubergespinouse.net; ❸) which also has a good *terroir* restaurant (May–Nov; *menu* €17). Nearby Lac de Lauzas is devoted to developed waterside **camping**, with a full gamut of activities: its main campsite is *Rieu Montagné* on the north side of the lake (mid-June to mid-Sept; ☏05.63.37.15.42), or there's *Le Pioch* (May–Sept; ☏04.67.97.61.72, 🖲www.lepioch.com) in Fraïsse itself.

Anglès

Some 16km south of Brassac on the St-Pons road, **ANGLÈS** consists of a collec-tion of houses which is home to no more than a handful of families. It's likely to be of most interest to hikers following the GR71 west from La Salvetat or the GR653 east from the Sidobre, though the hamlet can also be reached by regular buses from Mazamet. Although in Julius Caesar's time it served as a border post guarding the frontier against the Gallic barbarians, its oldest presently surviving monument is a small twelfth-century **gate**. The village is about 5km from **Lac des Sts-Peyres**, on the westernmost edge of the plateau, which remains undeveloped for tourism and is a good spot for a bit of peace and quiet. Anglès' seasonal **tourist office**, just south of town (daily: Easter–June 10.30am–12.30pm & 2–7pm; July & Aug 10.30am–12.30pm & 2–7pm; ☎05.63.74.59.13,) is adjoined by a two-star rural **hotel**, *Le Manoir de Boutaric* (Easter to mid-Oct; ☎05.63.70.96.06, ⓦwww.boutaric.com; ❸), with a **campsite** (April–Oct). The *Manoir's* **restaurant** is open in July and August only; the rest of the year you can get a hearty meal for about €15 at *Aux Épis*, in Anglès itself.

St-Pons-de-Thomières and around

Deep in the folds of the Jaur valley, 52km from Castres and 35km due east on the N112 from Mazamet, sits **ST-PONS-DE-THOMIÈRES**, the park's principal information centre, separated from the Plateau des Lacs to the north by a high ridge, the western spur of the Monts de l'Espinouse (see p.195). It is also a transport hub for the park, with two main **bus** routes (Béziers–La Salvetat and Castres–Montpellier) intersecting here. This ancient town's curious compound name originates with local count Raymond Pons, who founded a monastery (hence the "St" part of the name) across the river, north of the hamlet of Thomières in 936.

St-Pons' old quarter is worth a walk around – on the edge of it, on the north side of the modern road, is poised the twelfth-century **cathedral** (€3), with its incongruous, slapped-on seventeenth-century facade, around the back of which you can still see the statues on the medieval tympana, faces chipped off by iconoclastic Huguenots in the sixteenth century. The bulk of the old town, however, lies south of the main road on both sides of the Jaur, which is crossed by a medieval **bridge**. Amidst the ancient alleys the square fourteenth-century defensive tower, the **Tour de l' Évêché**, pokes above the rooftops. To the west of the old town, the **Musée de la Préhistoire** (mid-June to Oct 10am–noon & 2.30–6pm; Nov to mid-June Wed, Sat & Sun 10am–noon & 2–5pm; €3.50) has information on the area's menhirs as well as an exhibition of local Flintstonian relics, and also arranges speleological **safaris** in the neighbouring Ponderatz cave complex (☎05.67.97.22.61; check for availability of English-speaking guides). Cave fans will also want to check out the **Grotte de Devèze**, 5km west of St-Pons on the N112, and its **Musée Français de la Spéléologie** (daily: April & May 2–5pm; July & Aug 10am–6pm; June & Sept noon–2.30pm & 3.30–4.30pm; at other times call to book; ☎04.67.97.03.24, ⓔcourniou.les.grottes @wanadoo.fr; €6.50). Opened in 1932, the cave contains a variety of rock forms, including an impressive stone cascade and several calcite "draperies".

Buses pull up near the main crossroads of St-Pons, on the south side of which is the town's **tourist office** (July & Aug Mon–Sat 9.20am–1pm & 2–7pm, Sun 9.30am–1pm; Sept–June Tues–Sat 10am–noon & 2–6pm; ☎04.67.97.06.65, ⓦwww.saint-pons-tourisme.com), which also houses the central information office for the park, the **Maison du Parc** (ⓦwww.parc-haut-languedoc.fr). The best **hotel** in town is *Le Somail*, near the tourist office (☎04.67.97.00.12, ⓕ04.67.97.05.84; ❷), though more luxurious accommodation can be found 1km east of town at the *Bergeries de Ponderach* (☎04.67.97.02.57, ⓦwww .bergeries-ponderach.com; ❽), a seventeenth-century country estate with a fine restaurant. The municipal **campsite** (reserve through the tourist office) is open in summer only, while the year-round *Cerisiers du Jaur* (☎04.67.97.06.65) is just out of town on the road to Bédarieux. *La Route du Sel* in 25 Grand Rue has delicious *menus* from €13.50 (dinner reservations in advance on ☎04.67.97.05.14).

③ Olargues and around

From St-Pons, the Jaur river snakes northeast, skirting the **Monts de l'Espinouse** that loom over the north bank, to arrive at **OLARGUES**. Approached from the west, this hamlet presents an impressive vista: a high and gracefully arched medieval **bridge** backed by the steep hill where its castle once stood. From a covered staircase just west of the parking area along the main street, a ten-minute climb through the steep medieval alleys leads up to the lonely **clock tower**, the only remaining vestige of the eleventh-century fortress. Nearby, the Romanesque **priory** of St-Julien makes a good hike or a short drive, its shady wooded surroundings providing a great picnic spot and wonderful **views** of the Jaur Valley; take the Bédarieux road east for 2.5km and climb steeply on the left up the narrow signposted road a further 1500m.

The Monts de l'Espinouse

Olargues is a natural place to begin a circuit of the **Monts de l'Espinouse**, an area whose isolated beauty is preserved in part by its inaccessibility; there's no public transport here. From the village the D14 switchbacks steeply up past slate-covered hamlets clinging to near-perpendicular slopes until you reach the central pass of the **Col de Fontfroide** (971m). Here, **trails** (including the main GR7-71) crisscross the barren hillsides, and a sombre **monument** commemorates the German occupation. To the east on the lonely D53 the forest gets thicker (a picnicker's paradise) as you approach the 1124m **summit** (sommet de l'Espinouse). A few kilometres later, rounding the Col de l'Ourtigas, the country opens up dramatically into a series of broad gorges, the vibrant green landscape contrasted with dull grey rock. Continuing for 4km, you come to the turn-off for **Douch**, after which the road descends to **Lamalous-les-Bains**. Douch is a good place to pick up the GR7 trail to reach either **Mont Caroux** (1091m; 2hr round trip) or the **Gorges d'Héric**, which you access via the tiny stone hamlet of Héric, 2km west of Douch. The deep and narrow gully of sparkling red granite shaded by thickly covering oak descends rapidly to the River Orb, 6km below, and the beauty of the gorge accounts for its popularity with day-trippers. Easier access to the trails of the gorge is found at **Mons la Trivalle**, just off the main St-Pons–Bédarieux highway.

Practicalities

Olargues' **tourist office** (July & Aug daily 9am–1pm & 4–7pm; Sept–June Mon, Tues & Thurs–Sat 9am–noon & 2–5pm; ☎04.67.97.71.26, ⓦwww .olargues.org) is on the main road. There is a deluxe country **hotel**, the *Domaine de Rieumégé* (☎04.67.97.73.99, ⓦwww.domainederieumege.com; ❻) just outside town on the St-Pons road, but a better deal is Pauline Giles' homely ⌂ *Les Quatr' Farceurs* in rue de la Comporte (☎04.67.97.81.33, ⓦwww.olargues .co.uk; ❸), which serves huge meals with free-flowing wine for €20, or *Au Fil de l'Eau* (☎04.67.97.27.04, ⓦlefildeleau.online.fr; ❹), in an old house at the foot of the bridge, with a €20 *menu*. In nearby Mons, at the base of the Gorges d'Héric, there's a comfortable B&B, *Manoir le Trivalle* (☎04.67.97.85.56, ⓦwww.monslatrivalle.com; ❺). Olargues has a seasonal municipal **campsite** (mid-April to mid-Sept; ☎04.67.97.71.50) and **bikes** can be rented from Oxygène (☎04.67.97.87.00).

Mazamet and the Montagne Noire

The highlands of Haut Languedoc are bounded on their southwest side by the deep valley of the River Thoré, which empties into the Agout just west of Castres. A separate massif, the **MONTAGNE NOIRE**, stretches in a narrow 50km band along the south side of the river course and westwards to Revel (see p.102), its highest peak, the **Pic de Noire** (1153m), located more or less at the centre of the range.

The two sides of the Montagne Noire present a stark contrast: the north face, which has been incorporated into the Parc du Haut Languedoc, is thickly covered in a mixed forest of oak, beech and spruce, while the south presents a scrubby Mediterranean landscape of brush and vine. This whole district has traditionally been even poorer and more isolated than Haut Languedoc proper: near-subsistence farming and herding continue to be the only activities through most of the zone now that the mining of Salsigne and cloth industry of **Mazamet**, which boomed in the nineteenth century, have been reduced to shadows of their former selves. The Montagne Noire's chief attraction is its isolated wilderness, even more extreme than that to the north; you'll find that the outdoor facilities which have sprung up in the main body of the park are lacking here. South of Mazamet, which is the closest service town to the range, the ruin of medieval **Hautpoul** is a popular stop.

There are two direct **routes** over the mountains: the first starts at Hautpoul before continuing to the Pic de Noire and Carcassonne via the **Clamoux Gorges**; the second, ten kilometres west and roughly parallel to this route, follows the dark and evocatively lush Orbiel valley down to the Cathar castles of **Lastours**. Further west still, on the far side of the main Mazamet–Carcassonne road, you can skirt the massif to medieval **Saissac**, a good base from which either to ascend to the forests around Arfons, or descend via **Montolieu** – known for its bookshops – past the ruined abbey at **Villelongue** and on into the open country around Carcassonne. Public transport in this neck of the woods is more or less non-existent, the only regular service being the Mazamet–Carcassonne bus.

Mazamet and around

Lying 17km southeast of Castres, **MAZAMET** is a pale imitation of that town, owing its meagre prosperity to the cloth industry. The town's single sight is the **Musée Mémoire du Catharisme Occitan** (Feb–April & Oct–Dec Tues–Sun 2.30–5.30pm; May–Sept daily 3–6pm; €3) in the old Fuzier-family mansion – an unimpressive exhibition consisting mainly of a fifteen-minute French-language slide show lamenting the fate of the Cathars. More interesting is the short trip to **Hautpoul** – the precursor of Mazamet – a Cathar redoubt perched on a hillside, which was all but levelled by the unstoppable de Montfort in 1212. The trip up to the village follows the serpentine **Route des Usines**, climbing the bed of the Arnette, where windowless relics of hulking nineteenth-century factories lurk at every hairpin. Now consisting of nothing more than one winding street and the sparse vestiges of the **castle**, Hautpoul is lorded over by the **Maison du Bois** (July & Aug daily 2–7pm; Sept–June Wed, Sat & Sun 2–6pm), an artisanal operation churning out wooden toys. Despite having relatively little to offer, Hautpoul is a popular spot for excursions, in part because of the strong Cathar connection. But even if you aren't a Cathar fan, you'll still enjoy the hamlet's breathtaking setting, with views over the seemingly endless forested hills. If you have neither a car nor the desire to walk up to the hamlet, take one of the tourist office's **organized trips** (regular departures March–Oct; €5).

Practicalities

Mazamet's **gare SNCF** is located just off the Castres road, a fifteen-minute walk from the town centre; **buses** stop here or 300m further south on avenue Rouvière, by the post office. The **tourist office** (Mon–Sat 9/9.30am–noon/12.30pm & 2/3–6.30/7pm, Sun 2/3pm–5/6pm; Jan closed Sun; ☎05.63.61.27.07, ⓦwww.ville-mazamet.com) is further south on the cours René Reille, where you can park. Inexpensive **hotels** are plentiful in Mazamet: try the basic and ageing *Le Nord* at 4 place Olombel (closed part June & Sun; ☎05.63.61.00.53, ⓕ05.63.61.57.74; ❸), or the more comfortable *Le Boulevard*, 24 boulevard Soult (closed late Dec; ☎05.63.61.16.08, ⓔdegruel@aol.com; ❸). Better still is the rustic ⌖ *La Métairie Neuve*, 3km east in Bout de Pont l'Arn (closed mid-Dec to mid-Jan; ☎05.63.97.73.50, ⓦwww.metairieneuve.com; ❺). The three-star **campsite** *La Lauze* (May–Sept; ☎05.63.61.24.69) lies some 5km east of town. Once again, the hotel **restaurants** are the best bet for food here – *Le Boulevard* has a good-value *menu* with wine included (€12–23).

St-Amans-Soult and the Thoré valley

Climbing east from Mazamet, the **Thoré valley** still maintains its long-established role as a transport link between Castres and the Mediterranean coastlands, now the N112. Not far east of Mazamet you reach **ST-AMANS-SOULT**, a nondescript town which changed its name in honour of its native son, Field Marshal **Nicolas Soult** (1769–1851), Wellington's would-be nemesis of the Peninsular War. The warrior's sombre and monolithic tomb is hardly worth stopping to see, but not so his palatial estate, **Château de Soult-Berg** (June–Sept Wed & Sun guided tours at 3 & 4pm; €5), set amidst a wooded park. The richly furnished rooms here are immaculately preserved, and the mansion's rich library reflects the eighteenth-century ideal of the Renaissance man: aristocratic, learned and soldierly. From here the highway continues, passing through tiny **Labastides** and eventually reaching St-Pons.

St-Amans and Labastides will be of interest to hikers in need of supplies or yearning for a hotel. The former is crossed by the **GR36** on its way to the Pic de Noire, and the latter by the **GR7**, descending from the Monts de l'Espinouse. In St-Amans the only **hotel** is the *Hostellerie des Cèdres* (☎05.63.98.36.72, ⓦwww.promenades-gourmandes.com/cedres.htm; ❷), while 1.5km north of Labastides, *La Bouriotte* offers comfortable and cheap **farm accommodation** and plentiful home-cooked food (☎05.63.98.07.64; ❷). Both St-Amans (☎05.63.98.87.31) and Labastides (☎05.63.98.49.74) have **campsites**.

South via the Pic de Noire

If you are heading towards Carcassonne from Mazamet, and you have your own transport, there are a couple of interesting routes which you can take across the Montagne Noire. To cross via the **Pic de Noire**, continue up the Arnette, past the turn-off to Hautpoul, for 3km, until you reach a junction from which the massive transmission tower crowning the summit should be in easy view. An arm-wrenching series of switchbacks then takes you to the flat and barren mountain-top around the antenna's base, and a breathtaking combination of cool, thin air and sweeping panorama. From the peak, the tortuous road descends several kilometres to the hamlet of **Pradelles-Cabardès**, with its medieval **church**, before threading through the steep and forested cliffs of the **Clamoux gorges**, where, after 12km, you'll pass the turn-off for the **Gouffre de Cabrespine** (daily: March & Nov 2–5.30pm; April–June, Sept & Oct 10am– noon & 2–6pm; July & Aug 10am–6.30pm; €8), a huge vertical subterranean cavern with a main chamber 250m in height ("higher than the Eiffel Tower!"). The route continues to **Villeneuve-Minervois**, a quiet little town with some traces of medieval buildings, including the remains of its **castle**. Services along this route are minimal and you should plan to complete it before nightfall. In Pradelles there is a basic **campsite** on a nearby reservoir, and a **café** which also serves simple meals, while in Villeneuve the **restaurant** *La Clamoux* (*menu* from €17) also has **rooms** (℡04.68.26.15.69; ❷).

South via the Orbiel valley

An alternative route across the Montagne Noire, which you pick up by turn- ing east off the D118 just after Lac du Montagne, is via the **Orbiel valley**, and south to the castles at **Lastours**. As you descend the valley, the blanket of iridescent green forest threatens to swallow the steep and narrow stone- buttressed road, and the continuous series of hairpin curves makes the 11km to Mas-Cabardès seem at least twice as long as it should. Driving here is an effort, however, which the scenery makes worthwhile.

After the long descent you'll pass the romantically ruined church of St-Pierre- de-Vals, just outside **Mas-Cabardès**, a village which makes a good spot to stretch your legs before the tortuous second leg of the trip. While here check to see if the medieval **church**, crowned by a fifteenth-century bell tower, is open; if it is, step inside to see the fourteenth-century statuary within. Onwards from Mas-Cabardès, the road bends sharply as you approach Lastours, where the old textile mill which serves as the entrance to the grounds of the **Châteaux de Lastours** (Feb, March, Nov & Dec Sat, Sun & hols 10am–5pm; April–June & Sept daily 10am–6pm; July & Aug daily 9am–8pm; Oct daily 10am–5pm; €4) looms on the right. A cluster of four separate forts, perched dramatically on the points of the rocky hill dominating the river-bend, these are the northernmost of the Cathar castles, although in fact, only two of them, eleventh-century Cabaret and twelfth-century Surdespines, date from the era of the Crusade. When Simon de Montfort had conquered Minerve to the east and Termes to the south, the survivors took refuge in these forts, which were the redoubt of the Cathar-protecting lord, Pierre-Roger Cabaret. Efforts to besiege them proved vain and de Montfort only took the castles in 1211, when Pierre-Roger surrendered in exchange for a pardon. Two more castles were built in the fourteenth century. A path climbs the steep and scrubby hill, and leads from one small castle to the next – an exhilarating walk which takes about two hours. The *châteaux* are quite ruined, and really their location is more evocative than their remains, so if you don't want to climb, you can drive to the look-out point (same ticket), set on a ridge to the west, which affords the best perspectives. There's a basic **campsite** (June–Sept; ℡04.68.77.56.01) beside the belvedere in Lastours, which has a great location overlooking the castles, and simple **restau- rants** in Mas-Cabardès and Lastours.

Before continuing south, cut over 5km on the D111 to **Limousis**, whose **cave complex** (tours: March & Oct daily 2.30–5.30pm; April–June & Sept daily 10.30am–5.30pm; July & Aug daily 10am–6pm; Nov Sun 2.30–4.30pm; €8) boasts impressive calcite formations, including the largest known cluster of the crystalline mineral, aragonite. The lively English-speaking guides make the visit particularly enjoyable.

Saissac and around

By traversing the Montagne Noire and heading west along its lower slopes you'll arrive at **SAISSAC**, an ancient hamlet whose steeply sloping lanes lead downhill from the main road to a large ruined fortress looking out towards Carcassonne – the medieval walls and towers can be clearly made out in the distance. Although little remains of the fifteenth-century **castle** (Feb, March, Nov & Dec Sat, Sun & hols 10am–4.40pm; April–June & Sept daily 10am–5.40pm; July & Aug daily 9am–7.40pm; Oct daily 10am–4.40pm; €3.50), which can be reached from the road in about ten minutes, the hollow ruin is evocative – and a great place for viewing sunsets, but hardly worth the price of admission. Up on the road itself, a solitary tower surviving from the town's now-vanished walls holds a dull **museum** (April–June & Sept daily 10am–1pm & 2–6pm; July & August daily 9am–1pm & 2–6pm; Oct–March Mon–Fri 10am–1pm & 2–5pm, Sat & Sun during school hols; €2.50) containing an exhibition of tools used in local crafts and agriculture.

If you are leaving Saissac by car, you can easily reach the **Bassin du Lampy**, the smallest of the Park du Haut Languedoc's reservoirs, and a quiet place to have a swim, 5km up the D4 (picked up just west of Saissac). From the reservoir, the road continues north, through ever-thickening forest, to **Arfons**. Set among a series of grassy clearings, this little hamlet has an enchantingly forgotten air and is a great place to buy freshly picked mountain produce, including splendid wild mushrooms in late summer. The forest road continues north, eventually forking off to Dourgne and Sorèze. South of Arfons a turn-off to the east leads towards Lacombe, following a narrow path through the **Forêt de la Montagne Noire**, lush, dark and green woods which make for another prime picnicking zone. In the heart of the *forêt*, at the hamlet of La Galaube, a path leads south for twenty minutes to the **Prise d'eau d'Alzeau**, the uppermost reservoir of the Canal du Midi's catchment system. The easy-to-follow trail to the site, where a statue to the visionary engineer stands, is a good way to get a feel for the forest of this region.

Saissac's **tourist office** is in the same tower as the museum (July & Aug daily 10am–12.30pm & 2–6.30pm; ☎04.68.24.47.80, ✉saissac@fnotsi.net), while its only **hotel**, *Montagne Noire* (☎04.68.24.46.36, ℉04.68.24.46.20; ❷) is nothing special. You're better off heading out to the Bassin du Lampy, where the *Domaine du Lampy-Neuf* (☎04.68.24.46.07, ⓦwww.domainelampy-neuf.com) offers deluxe **chambres d'hôtes** (❸) and gîte dorms (€15), or to *La Galaube*, by the Prise d'eau d'Alzeau (closed mid-Sept to mid-Jan; ☎04.68.26.51.23; ❷), which has simpler rooms and an inexpensive year-round **restaurant**. In Saissac itself, the restaurant *Au Beau Site*, (closed Sat & Sun Sept–June; ☎04.68.24.40.37) in the town below the tower, has good views and *menus* from €30. There are basic **campsites** at the Bassin du Lampy and at Arfons (ask at the bakery), which also has a bar and restaurant.

Montolieu and Villelongue

A short drive south of Saissac, **MONTOLIEU** has striven to make a mark since 1990 as a "town of books", a contrived (and pale) imitation of England's famous Hay-on-Wye. One shop, the aptly titled English Bookshop in rue de la Mairie, specializes in English-language titles, while several of the rest concentrate on New Age and occult books. You can also look round a collection of old presses and book-binding tools in the **Musée Michel Braibant** (daily: July & Aug 10am–12.30pm & 2–6.30pm; Sept–June 9am–12.30pm & 2–6pm; €2.50) at the north end of the village. West of Montolieu, tucked away in a wooded vale down a seemingly endless country lane, lie the ruins of the twelfth-century Cistercian **Abbey of Villelongue** (May & Oct daily 10am–noon & 2–6.30pm, June–Sept Sun–Fri 10am–noon & 2–6.30pm, Sat 10am–noon & 2–4pm; €4) – worth driving to if only for the picturesque location on the banks of the Vernassonne. The remains of the abbey include a thirteenth-century vaulted cellar, a fourteenth-century Gothic cloister and the ruins of the abbey-church, now surrounded by a garden.

Montolieu's **tourist office** is in the *mairie* (Mon–Fri 10am–noon & 2–6pm; ☏04.68.24.80.80, ⓦwww.montolieu.net), and you can stay at the bright, new **B&B** *Les Anges au Plafond* (☏04.68.24.97.19, ⓦwww.lesangesauplafond.com; ❸), or in greater luxury at the *Château de Villeneuve* (☏04.68.24.84.08, ⓦwww .chateauvilleneuve.com; ❹), a wine *domaine* just north of town. The former monastery in Villelongue also offers **rooms** (☏04.68.76.92.58; ❹), but these are rather spartan and monkish given the price. There's a basic **campsite** in Montolieu (☏04.68.24.80.88), and *Le Grillon* in pl de l'Église (Thurs–Sat only off-season) is a good spot for a **meal** (€17).

Travel details

Trains

A regional train line runs along the Tarn from Toulouse to Albi and Carmaux, while Castres and Mazamet are also served from Toulouse. SNCF buses may run in lieu of trains on these lines; service is reduced on Sundays & holidays.

Albi to: Carmaux (7–13 daily; 30min); Gaillac (8–19 daily; 20–40min); Naucelle (6–9 daily; 1hr); St-Sulpice (7–15 daily; 22min); Toulouse (8–19 daily; 1hr).

Castres to: Damiette (7–8 daily; 20min); Labrugière (8–14 daily; 8min); Lavaur (6–8 daily; 40min); Mazamet (8–14 daily; 20min); St-Sulpice (6–8 daily; 1hr 5min); Toulouse (6–8 daily; 1hr 5min).

Gaillac to: Lisle-sur-Tarn (10–22 daily; 8min); Rabastens (10–22 daily; 15min); St-Sulpice (12–27 daily; 22min); Toulouse (10–30 daily; 50min); Vindrac (for Cordes; 4–11 daily; 20min).

Mazamet to: Castres (8–14 daily; 20min); Labrugière (8–14 daily; 10min); St-Amans (2–3 daily; 15min); St-Pons (2–3 daily; 40min); Toulouse (6–8 daily; 1hr 30min–1hr 55min).

Buses

Many lines in Tarn-et-Garonne have reduced or no service on Saturdays, Sundays and holidays, and in the summer months. For regional lines see ⓦwww.federteep.org; for buses to Béziers, see ⓦwww.herault.fr.

Albi to: Ambialet (3–5 daily; 30min); Blayes (4–10 daily; 15min); Cagnac (1–3 daily; 30min); Carcassonne (1 daily; 2hr); Carmaux (4–10 daily; 20min); Castres (6–15 daily; 40min–1hr 40min); Cordes (2–3 daily; 35min); Gaillac (6–12 daily; 35min); Graulhet (5–9 daily; 40min); Lacaune (1–3 daily; 1hr 35min); Lavaur (3 daily; 1hr 20min); Lisle (5–9 daily; 1hr); Rabastens (5–8 daily; 1hr 15min); Réalmont (1–2 daily; 25min); St-Sulpice (4–7 daily; 1hr); Toulouse (2–4 daily; 2hr 40min).

Carmaux to: Blayes (4–10 daily; 10min); Cagnac (2–3 daily; 20min).

Castres to: Béziers (2 daily; 2hr 50min); Brassac (3–6 daily; 50min); Carcassonne (8 daily; 1hr 50min); Dourgne (2–6 daily; 40min); Gaillac (2–4 daily; 1hr 15min); Gijounet (2–4 daily; 1hr 15min); Graulhet (4–7 daily; 40min); Labrugière (2 daily; 15min); Lacaune (daily; 1hr 15min); Lautrec (2 daily; 30min); Lavaur (4–11 daily; 45min–1hr); Mazamet (8–12 daily; 20–30min); Murat (1 daily; 2hr); Réalmont (2–4 daily; 25min); Revel (2–4 daily; 45hr); St-Paul (3–5 daily; 45min); St-Pons (2–4 daily; 1hr 15min); The Sidobre (frequent; 20min); Sorèze (3 daily; 45min); Toulouse (2–4 daily; 1hr 40min–2hr); Vabre (1–2 daily; 45min).

Gaillac to: Graulhet (4–7 daily; 30min); Lavaur (2–4 daily; 40min); Lisle (4–8 daily; 10min); Rabastens (4–8 daily; 20min); Toulouse (4 daily; 1hr 25min).

Graulhet to: Albi (2 daily; 40min); Lautrec (2–4 daily; 30min); Lavaur (4–8 daily; 25min); Toulouse (4–8 daily; 1hr 35min).

La Salvetat to: Béziers (3 weekly; 2h); St-Pons (3–5 daily; 40–55min).

Mazamet to: Anglès (2 daily; 20min); Labastides (2 daily; 35min); Labrugière (2 daily; 10min); Lacabarède (2 daily; 30min); La Salvetat (2 daily; 45min); Lavaur (2 daily; 1hr 10min); Réalmont (2–4 daily; 55min); Revel (1 daily; 45min); St-Amans (2 daily; 20min); St-Paul (2 daily; 55min);

St-Pons (4 daily; 45min); St-Sulpice (2 daily; 1hr 30min); Toulouse (2 daily; 2hr).

Réalmont to: Graulhet (daily; 20min).

Revel to: Dourgne (daily; 5min); Sorèze (daily; 10min).

St-Pons to: Bédarieux (4–6 daily; 1hr 20min); Béziers (4 daily; 1hr 20min); Lamalou-les-Bains (4–6 daily; 55min); La Salvetat (3–5 daily; 40–55min); Montpellier (1–3 daily; 2hr 25min); Sorèze (3 daily; 45min); Castlenaudary (Mon; 30min); Saint-Félix (3 daily; 20min); Toulouse (3 daily; 1hr 20min).

Nîmes and around

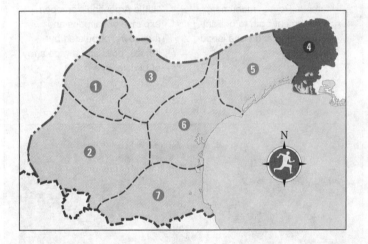

CHAPTER 4 # Highlights

✳ **Nîmes Amphitheatre** Once the scene of gladiatorial combats, this 20,000-seat stadium still functions after 2000 years. See p.223

✳ **Tauromachie** The "art of the bull" is practised in the Gard with a passion and intensity unparalleled north of the Pyrenees. See p.224

✳ **Pont du Gard** France's most famous Roman monument, a testament both to brilliant engineering and slave labour. See p.234

✳ **The Monastery of St-Roman** An underground monastery cut from the living rock, tucked away in the hills above the Rhône. See p.240

✳ **Aigues-Mortes** A picture-perfect medieval walled town, set among the swamps and dunes of the Mediterranean coast. See p.245

✳ **La Petite Camargue** Durrell's "Little Argentina", an open expanse of saltpans and meadows, populated by horses, bulls and a wide array of birdlife. See p.249

△ Flamingoes in La Petite Camargue

4

Nîmes and around

N îmes is Languedoc's most revitalized city, on the way up after an eighteen-hundred-year slump following its decline as an imperial settlement. Chock-full of the region's most impressive Roman monuments, and a showcase for its most exciting new architecture, it's a busy little place, embodying an intriguing combination of ancient glory and modern style. The lands around the city comprise the southern half of **Gard**, the easternmost *département* of Languedoc-Roussillon – hemmed in on the east by the mighty Rhône river and on the west by the humble River Vidourle. On the Mediterranean coast, the **Petite Camargue**, the western section of the Rhône delta, rises tentatively out of the sea. This is desolate and windswept country, dominated by bull and horse farms near the seaside, and vineyards closer inland. As you move away from the sea, the sand dunes gradually give way to the brushy hills known as the **garrigues**, around Nîmes itself and to the north. These in turn are cut through by the deep gorge of the Gardon river, on the far bank of which runs the band of flatland once dominated by the ducal castle of **Uzès**. Vineyards cover the river valley, but in the scrub-covered hills stunted holm oaks compete with hardy thistles, lavender and thyme.

Although the numerous and majestic **Roman ruins** of southern Gard, including Nîmes' **Les Arènes** and the magnificent **Pont du Gard**, attest to the area's prosperity in Roman times, this corner of the south has for centuries been something of a poorer cousin of neighbouring Provence, relegated to secondary status as the House of Toulouse collapsed in the wake of the Albigensian Crusade. This traditional economic marginalization is reflected in the faded glory of the former medieval port towns of **Beaucaire** and **St-Gilles**, although further south, recent revival has drawn developers to the **beaches** and **pleasure ports** of the Camarguaise coast. To the west, the gentle Vidourle is still spanned by **Roman bridges** and dotted by all but forgotten hamlets.

The weather in Gard tends to extremes: hot summers and mild winters, punctuated by violent rainstorms in autumn and the merciless buffeting of the cold mistral wind in spring. In recent years, the autumn storms have become even more volatile, turning city streets into rivers and causing large-scale destruction, particularly along the Gard river. The best season to visit is undoubtedly summer, but if you want to see Nîmes and Gard at their most traditional, try to visit during the local **festivals**, which invariably entail *tauromachie* – bullfighting and horsemanship, both Camarguaise and Spanish-style.

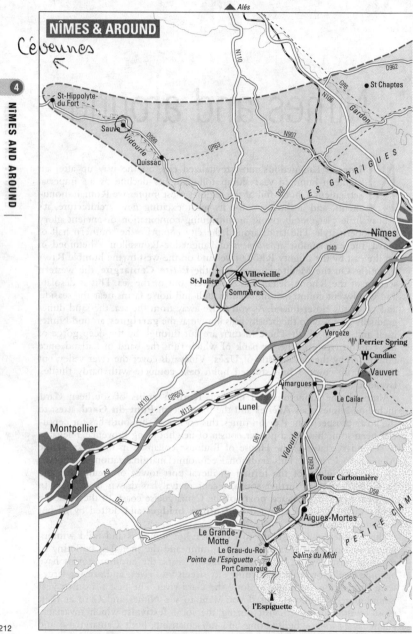

NÎMES & AROUND

Cévennes ←

▲ Alés

N110

GR6
D962
● St Chaptes

St-Hippolyte-
du Fort

Sauve
D999
Vidourle
Quissac
GR63
N907
N106
Gardon

LES GARRIGUES
D22

Nîmes

D40

St-Julien ✝ ■ Villevieille
Sommières

Vergèze
△△ Perrier Spring
♨ Candiac

Vauvert

Aimargues
Le Cailar

N110
GR653
N113
Lunel

Vidourle
D979

Montpellier

A9
D61

Tour Carbonnière
D58

D21
D62
D62
● Aigues-Mortes
PETITE CAM

Le Grande-
Motte
Le Grau-du-Roi
Pointe de l'Espiguette
Port Camargue
Salins du Midi

⚲ l'Espiguette

UZES

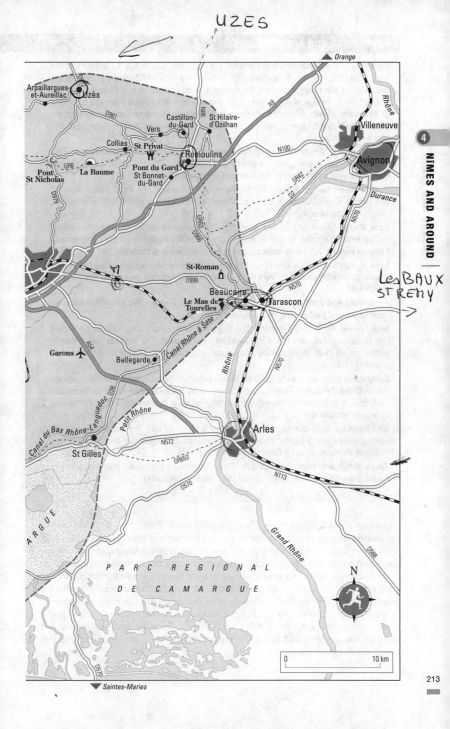

Arpaillargues-et-Aureillac · Uzès

D981

Castillon-du-Gard · St Hilaire-d'Ozilhan

Vers

Collias · St Privat

Pont St Nicholas · La Baume · St Bonnet-du-Gard · Pont du Gard

GR6

D579

N86

Remoulins

N100 · Villeneuve

A9

Avignon

Rhône

GR42

D2

Durance

N570

St-Roman

D999

Beaucaire

Le Mas de Tourelles · Tarascon

N570

Garons

Bellegarde · Canal Rhône à Sète

A54

D38

Canal du Bas Rhône-Languedoc

Petit Rhône

St Gilles

N572

GR653

D570

Rhône

Arles

N113

N570

D598

CAMARGUE

PARC REGIONAL DE CAMARGUE

Grand Rhône

N

Orange

Les BAUX St REMY

0   10 km

Saintes-Maries

Festivals in and around Nîmes

Festivals in the *département* of Gard have a decidedly bullish flavour to them. In the bigger places – Nîmes, Beaucaire and St-Gilles – full-blown Spanish-style *corridas* are held for the most important occasions, but otherwise, nearly every small town will somehow involve **bulls** in their celebrations. Aside from these there are a number of fairs and events which commemorate the area's medieval past or its regional products. Where no specific information number is given, contact the relevant tourist office for details.

Late January Nîmes: *Festival Nîmes Flamenco* ⓦ www.theatresdenimes.com. This annual five-day event gathers top Flamenco stars for performances of music and dance, as well as a series of conferences and exhibitions.

Fourth week before Easter Nîmes: *Feria de Primavera*. The local celebration for pre-Lenten Carnaval, and the first of Nîmes' famed *ferias*, a street festival including music and *tauromachie*.

Late March St-Gilles: *Carnaval*. Held for one week and similar to the Nîmes event, but on a much smaller scale and with emphasis on the traditions of the Camarguaise cowboy culture: horsemanship, *courses camarguaises* and *corridas*.

Late March to Sept Le Grau/Port Camargue: *Courses camarguaises* are held every weekend in order to decide the year's winners of the Trophée de As and the Trophée de l'Avenir.

First Weekend April Sommières: Medieval festival. A street festival with costumed merchants and performers, markets, music and cookery.

May Nîmes: *Feria de Pentecôte*. The city's most important festival and a frenzied rite of spring, held on the fifth weekend after Easter. The festival has a heavy emphasis on bullfighting, along with music, dancing and a large street market in the old town.

Early June Beaucaire: *Fête du Drac*. A three-day medieval festival, held in conjunction with neighbouring Tarascon, and celebrating the legend of the river beast, La Tarasque, a child-eating amphibious monster of local medieval folklore. Admission charge of €9 per day.

Mid-June Le Grau-du-Roi: Fisherman's festival. Along with the traditional *courses camarguaises*, water-jousting competitions are held in the harbour and canals in this four-day celebration of Le Grau's traditional industry.

Throughout July Nîmes: *Les Jeudis*. Every Thursday night, street markets with live music are held in nearly every square (and many restaurants).

Getting around in southern Gard presents some difficulties if you're reliant on **public transport**, and want to get off the main routes. Nîmes is the hub, with good train and bus services to most of the region's towns, services to the coast becoming more frequent in summer. Crossing between the various routes from Nîmes, or accessing out-of-the-way areas like the Petite Camargue or the *garrigues*, however, is more inconvenient. That said, the flattish terrain makes for relatively easy walking and, as elsewhere in the south, local drivers are generally helpful when it comes to hitching. Unfortunately for **cyclists**, heavy traffic makes the country roads of the coastal plain unpleasant and dangerous, but amongst the *garrigues* and along the Vidourle there are some excellent and not overly challenging routes.

Mid-July Sauve: African festival ☎04.66.77.59.96. Yearly three-day festival which brings in performers of traditional and modern music from across Africa. Concerts held in the town's Théâtre de Verdure. Admission €20.

Late July Uzès: *Autres Rivages*. A World-Music festival featuring primarily African groups. Performances are held in sites of architectural and archeological interest in the countryside around town.

Late July Beaucaire: *Les Rencontres Équestres Méditerranéennes*. France's largest gathering of Iberian horses, held in the Parc de l'Institut St Félix, just east of the town centre on the banks of the Rhône.

Throughout July & Aug Beaucaire: *Les Beaux Quais du Vendredi*. Friday-night open-air concerts, featuring live acts ranging from blues to World Music, plus a lively canalside street market.

Early Aug Quissac: *Les Vidourlades* ☎04.66.77.15.13, ⓦwww.vidourlades.com. A three-day World Music festival with a Spanish and North African bent. Nightly performances are held in the medieval ruins atop the town's hill.

Early Aug Aigues-Mortes: *Les Nuits de Sel. For three consecutive nights dance companies from France and abroad perform outside the south ramparts.*

Mid-Aug St-Gilles: *Feria de la pêche et de l'abricot*. A one-week harvest festival, celebrating two of the area's major agricultural products, peaches and apricots, with the emphasis on ranch culture and *tauromachie*.

Late Aug Aigues-Mortes: *Fête de St-Louis*. Held on the closest weekend to August 25, a medieval pageant and reconstruction of St Louis' departure for the Crusades, celebrating the day when the saint-king set out to fight the Muslims.

First week Sept Fourques (near Beaucaire): *Foires aux Chevaux*. A traditional two-day horse-market, which brings together *manade*-owners and *gardians* from across the Camargue, in addition to some 10,000 spectators, for a boisterous carnival.

Second week Sept Le Grau/Port-Camargue: *Fête locale*. A major event on the taurine calendar, the twin towns' festivities include bull-running, *courses camarguaises*, water-jousting and the usual markets, street parties and general exuberance.

Third week Sept Nîmes: *Feria des Vendanges*. The third great *feria* in Nîmes, celebrating the wine harvest. Another *tauromachie* extravaganza, with live open-air concerts, parades and a market.

Mid-Oct Aigues-Mortes: *Fête locale*. A three-day annual party featuring Gardois *tauromachie* performed alongside the medieval walls of the old town.

Nîmes

NÎMES is a city inextricably linked to its Roman past. Its location on the Via Domitia – the main chariot route from Spain to Rome – helped make it a favourite with a series of emperors of the first and second centuries AD, who endowed it with the outstanding collection of monuments which dominate the place today; the **Maison Carrée**, the **amphitheatre** (or "Arènes") and the **Temple of Diana** are all testament to the city's bright, if short-lived, splendour. Since then, over the last eighteen hundred years, Nîmes has had something of a tough time of it, having to vie with neighbouring rivals Arles, Avignon and Montpellier (see p.258), which each in their time stole the city's limelight. Through the 1980s and 1990s, however, a succession of two flamboyant mayors have promoted the city within and without, engaging in a series of audacious building projects (including a retractable cover for the Roman amphitheatre), sponsoring concerts and festivals and drawing in artists and musicians. Their efforts have succeeded, kindling a spark that not even the massive mudslide of 1988, which covered the city in two and a half metres of muck and claimed the lives of seven people, could extinguish. Nowadays, crowds come not only to see the shrines of the Caesars and the dusted-off **mansions** of the cloth-making bourgeoisie, but a collection of provocative contemporary urban architecture in a city which is redefining itself. Nîmes also has two surprisingly good **art galleries**, and hosts some of the South of France's most colourful **festivals** – February's *Carnaval*, and the *ferias* of Pentecost and September, when the arena fills with **bullfighting** aficionados and the bars and restaurants are packed late into the night with noisy revellers.

Some history

Nemausus had been a Roman colony since 40 BC, but didn't really take off until Augustus Caesar (then, Octavian, and not yet emperor) defeated Mark Antony and Cleopatra at Actium in 31 BC, bringing Egypt under his power. As a reward, he settled his veterans here, laying out a Roman grid-plan city and endowing it with powerful fortifications. In honour of their victory in Egypt, his soldiers adopted the ensign of a crocodile (the Nile) chained to a palm tree, which subsequently became the city's **symbol**. As the town grew, water-demand outstripped the resources of its sacred spring and, under Claudius, a 50km-long canal, of which the Pont du Gard (see p.234) is part, was constructed to supply water. A century later, the city was at its zenith, enjoying the special patronage of the emperor Antoninus Pius, whose mother's family hailed from these parts. It was a sprawling city enclosed by some 7km of thick walls (which survived as late as 1786), reinforced by thirty stout towers and pierced by seven monumental gates. From that glorious era, however, things went rapidly downhill. Within a decade of Antoninus' death, the Roman Empire spun into a temporary political crisis, and by the time the situation had restabilized, Christianity had replaced paganism in the empire, and Christian Arles had supplanted polytheistic Nîmes as the local capital.

With the Roman decline, Nîmes was to suffer conquest by Germanic "barbarians". For 250 years the town was held by the Visigoths, in turn displaced by Muslims who came up from Spain in about 724. Only seven years later the Muslims were forced out, and for the next four hundred years the town was incorporated into a series of rapidly dissolving principalities including West Francia, Aquitaine and Septimania. In 1185 it came under the control of the **counts of Toulouse**, under whom the town briefly flirted with Catharism; the mere sight of de Montfort's powerful army, however, was enough to make it "repent" and return to the Catholic fold. Nîmes was absorbed by the French Crown in 1226, but by this time little was left of the glorious Roman city – only two clusters of houses huddled around the cathedral and amphitheatre.

After three sleepy centuries as a poor market town, Nîmes began to discover a new vocation as a textile centre – until the **Wars of Religion** wracked the region. Calvinist preachers found eager ears in Nîmes' new prosperous class of cloth-makers, to the extent that local Huguenots destroyed the eleventh-century cathedral and, on St Michael's Day of 1567, massacred some two hundred clergy. Following their repression in the wake of the Wars, Protestants from Nîmes as well as exiles from Haut Languedoc rose up together in the Camisard rebellion, brutally suppressed by royal forces in 1704, following its leader's defection to the Catholic forces at Nîmes. Many Protestants fled, while others persevered,

The Land of the Cathars

From the rolling hills around Albi to the
coasts of the Mediterranean it's impossible
to travel through Languedoc without
crossing paths with the Cathars. Mixing
Christianity with Middle Eastern
philosophies, the Cathar cult was
bought to the region by returning
Crusaders in the twelfth century,
and gained popularity as a
reaction to the wealthy and
corrupt Catholic Church. Cathars
believed in the struggle between
the good spirit world and the evil
material world, and practised
asceticism (self-denial and
abstinence) as a path to salvation.
Monk-like perfecti (or parfaits)
presided over the believers,
who aspired to become perfecti
themselves just before death,
so that they could die pure and
escape the material universe.

The rise of Catharism

By the 1140s, the sect had become a formal church, which spread rapidly throughout northern France and the Low Countries, with Italy, Spain and, of course, **Languedoc** all becoming important centres. In Languedoc, the religion was welcomed by urban tradesmen, by the regional nobility (who resented the papacy's political expansion and feared a Church-backed takeover by the French Crown), and by peasants who were attracted by the dedication of the *perfecti* and the Cathar cosmology. Thus, Cathar beliefs fused with **Occitan identity**, and came to be associated strongly with the region. By 1200, the Catholic Church could no longer ignore the rival religion, and **Pope Innocent III** (1198–1216) undertook a series of initiatives against them, culminating in a military campaign.

The Albigensian Crusade

On July 22, 1209, the papacy sent an army of knights to surround **Béziers**, lead by Arnaud-Amaury, Abbot of Cîteaux, the most powerful monastery in northern France. As the noose around the town tightened, a band of Béziers citizens, both Catholic and Cathar, took refuge in the **Church of the Madeleine**, within which, according to Catholic law, no blood was to be shed. Arnaud-Amaury, however, gave the order to set fire to the church, exclaiming, "Burn them all, God will know his own!"

◀ The Albigensians

This was the start of the **Albigensian Crusade**, a ferocious campaign waged against the Counts of Toulouse, who were tolerant of their Cathar population, by the papacy and the northern French nobility. **Simon de Montfort** was one of the leaders of this brutal campaign of terror: his treatment of the populace was pitiless, with massacres and mutilation commonplace.

De Montfort came to an appropriate end in June 1218 at the **Siege of Toulouse**, when a missile from a catapult fired by a squad of women and children, bashed his brains out. His relentless attacks, however, left Languedoc unable to withstand the pressure of the French Crown, and led ultimately to the destruction of Catharism and the fall of independent Languedoc.

The Inquisition

In the aftermath of the Crusade, the Papacy undertook the task of converting the "hearts and minds" of the Cathars and their supporters. This was taken on by two

▲ The village of Minerve

Top 10 Cathar sites

▼ Villerouge, site of the last Cathar burning

new religious orders, the **Franciscans** (1209) and **Dominicans** (1215), backed up by the **Inquisition**, part secret police, part travelling court, which went from town to town investigating locals' religious leanings and sniffing out secret heretics. Guilt was frequently assumed, and torture frequent. Once condemned by the Church, the victim was handed over to local authorities for execution. Not surprisingly, the Inquisition did little to endear the people of Languedoc to the Catholic authorities, and it contributed to the region's residual distrust of "foreign" authority.

The Siege of Montségur

In 1242 a band of Cathar warriors struck out from **Montségur** castle and attacked and killed a party of Dominican Inquisitors at **Avignonet-Lauragais**, sparking a series of rebellions across the region. The royal response was swift: a massive force was raised and in May 1243 they lay **siege** to the castle. Inside, 150 knights, led by **Pierre-Roger of Mirepoix**, and several hundred Cathars endured eight months of siege and bombardment, before Pierre-Roger negotiated for clemency in exchange for surrender. But the Cathar faithful would not betray their cause and when the castle was opened to the French, some 225 were led out to a field below the fort and **burnt alive**. Nevertheless, it took the **Inquisition** over a century to finish the job: the last **burning** took place at **Villerouge-Termenès** in 1321, and in 1412 the last remaining community of Cathars was discovered in the village of **Montaillou** and prosecuted in an Inquisition led by the Bishop of Foix.

Montségur's Lost Treasure

Legend has it that a handful of perfecti slipped out of the encirclement of Montségur carrying the group's valuables. Within time the story of the **Lost Treasure of the Cathars** grew, and become tangled up with occultist notions as well as tales of the **Holy Grail** and the **Templars**. In the 1930s, Otto Rahn, a Grail and Cathar enthusiast, brought the legend's attention to the Nazi authorities in Germany, who believed the treasure offered a mystical link to the supposedly Aryan Visigoths who overran Rome and Languedoc in the fifth century. **Himmler** took a personal interest and supported the investigations. Since then, a small army of books has been published about Montségur's "lost treasure", which have fuelled the legend and become a lucrative marketing tool for local tourist boards.

▶ Montségur Castle

having to disguise their faith. After the Revolution, religious issues were laid aside, and Nîmes, still predominantly Protestant, got back down to making money, which it did by spinning silk and cotton. The town's product became so successful that the cotton cloth "de Nîmes" (thus "denim") went west, where in 1848 an American, Levi Strauss, hit upon the idea of attaching small red labels to trousers made out of the material. Recent city history has been dominated by the flamboyant mayor Jean Bousquet, who embarked on a daring policy of reconstruction, including drawing leading avant-garde architects to the city and opening its first university. His communist successor Alain Clary, followed by the current right-wing mayor Jean-Paul Fournier, seemed to have remained loyal to this vision, and Nîmes' new-found élan continues.

Arrival and information

Located 10km south of Nîmes along the D42, just outside St-Gilles, Garons **airport**, which also serves Arles, has few facilities other than an ATM and car rental desks. From here the trip to the city can be made by *navette* (2–4 daily; ☎04.66.29.27.29; "Gambetta" or "Imperator" stop; €5), or by taxi (at least €28, or €33 at night). Nîmes' **gare SNCF** and **gare routière** are both located at the end of avenue Feuchères, about a ten-minute walk south of the old town. Arriving **by car** on the A9, take either exit and follow signs for the centre (north of the *autoroute*); there are underground parking spaces on the ring road, and street parking is also legal, if often difficult. The **main tourist office** (Easter–Sept Mon–Fri 8am–7/8pm, Sat 9am–7pm, Sun 10am–6pm; Oct–Easter Mon–Fri 8.30am–7pm, Sat 9am–7pm, Sun 10am–5pm; ☎04.66.58.38.00, ⊛www .ot-nimes.fr) is about a twenty-minute walk from the *gares* at 6 rue Auguste, and can also be reached by bus #8 ("Antonin"). Up-to-date information on Nîmes and other places covered in this chapter can be found at ⊛www .tourismegard.com.

Unless you're staying at the campsite, hostel or one of the far-flung motels, you'll most likely have no use for Nîmes' city transport system. The **bus** network's hub is avenue Feuchères, through which all the main lines pass, the most useful of which, line #8, circles the city centre. Transport **maps** are available from tourist offices, and single **tickets** (€1) can be bought from the drivers. **Bikes** can be **rented** from Cycles Rebour, at 38 rue Hôtel Dieu (☎04.66.76.24.32), as well as from the youth hostel (see p.219) and campsite. To see the city in comfort, TRAN **taxis** (see "Listings", p.228) charge €27 for a fifty-minute tour of Nîmes for a maximum of six people (€6 extra for hotel pick-up and drop off).

Accommodation

Accommodation options in Nîmes are plentiful, although rock-bottom budget places aren't so easy to come by. You can reserve many hotels in the city through a **central reservation** office (☎04.66.36.96.30, ⊜groupes @ot-nimes.fr.com), and should book ahead as far as possible for visits during any of the city's celebrations. If you are here at the weekend, check the tourist office's **hotel package**, the "Pass Romain," which includes admission to the city's museums, the Pont du Gard, a "Roman" meal, and one night's accommodation (from €75 per person, depending on hotel rating).

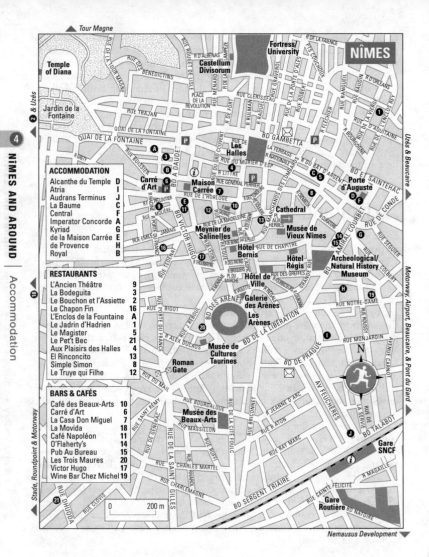

Most of Nîmes' cheaper **hotels** are located between the Arènes and the train station. At *feria* times, you may have to resort to the cluster of chain motels around the Nîmes-Ouest exit of the A9, which includes the *Holiday Inn* (☎04.66.29.86.87, Ⓔcontact@holidayinn-nimes.com; ⑥), *Mercure* (☎04.66.70.48.00, Ⓔho558@accor.com; ⑥), *Mas de Galoffre* (☎04.66.38.15.36, Ⓦwww.gallofre.com; ③) and *Formule 1* (☎04.66.38.14.05, Ⓕ04.66.29.77.85; ②). As well as the HI hostel (see opposite), there are several private **hostels** (*résidences*), some for under-25s, others with self-catering suites (contact the tourist office for details).

Hotels

Alcanthe du Temple 1 rue Charles Babout ☎04.66.67.54.61, ⓦ www.hotel-du-temple .com. This is one of the old town's best bargains. Friendly, well-kept and quiet, set in an eighteenth-century house. Rooms have fans, TV and en-suite showers. Closed Jan. ❸

Atria 5 bld de Prague ☎04.66.76.56.56, ⓦ www .novotel.com. Just south of the old town, this modern building is something of a monstrosity compared with Nîmes' other hotels, but it has all the mod cons – at a price. ❼

Audrans Terminus 23 av Feuchères ☎04.66.67.66.20, ⓦ www.hotel-terminus-nimes .com. Right by the train station, this is a well-decorated and lively hotel, with attentive staff. Amenities include cable TV. ❷

La Baume 21 rue Nationale ☎04.66.76.28.42, ⓦ www.new-hotel.com. Located in a tastefully-decorated former mansion, with friendly and professional service: slightly pricey, but worth it. ❼

Central 2 pl du Château ☎04.66.67.27.75, ⓦ www.hotel-central.org. Just behind the temple and the Porte d'Auguste, this is a small but cosy hotel which also has secure parking. ❷

Imperator Concorde Quai de la Fontaine ☎04.66.21.90.30, ⓦ www.hotel-imperator.com. Nîmes' best and most prestigious hotel, with top service and amenities in an atmosphere-loaded *fin-de-siècle* mansion with a stately garden. Prices quadruple during *ferias*. ❾

Kyriad 10 rue Rossy ☎04.66.76.16.20, ⓦ www .hotel-kyriad-nimes.com. One of Nîmes' newer hotels, the *Kyriad* is a solid two-star option with an impressive range of amenities. Its location just outside the old town makes street parking a convenient possibility. ❹

de la Maison Carrée 14 rue de la Maison Carrée ☎04.66.67.32.89, ⓔ aaaaa@abtel.fr. Right by the famous temple, this small hotel has cheery decor and a great rooftop breakfast terrace. Extras include AC and TV. Reception closes at 11pm, and the check-out is a rather early 10am. ❸

de Provence 5/7 square de la Couronne ☎04.66.76.04.92, ⓦ www.hoteldeprovence.net. Well located near the train and bus stations and the amphitheatre. Rooms have cable TV; parking is extra. ❸

Royal 3 bd Alphonse-Daudet ☎04.66.58.28.27, ⓔ rhotel@wanadoo.fr. The *Royal* has a cool Spanish-style decor which draws in passing *toreros*. The rooms are individually decorated with a distinctly Iberian flavour, and the place exudes a certain cool chic. It's also home to the *Bodeguita* tapas bar. ❹

Hostel and campsites

FUAJ/ HI hostel, Chemin de la Cigale, ☎04.66.6803.20, ⓦ www.hinimes.com. A comfortable hostel 2km northwest of the centre (take bus #2 dir: Alès or Villeverte to "Stade"), with dorm beds for €9: also has camping facilities. July & Aug membership required; Sept–June no curfew.

Municipal campsite ☎04.66.62.05.82, ⓦ www .camping-nimes.com. Open year-round, on the route de Générac, 5km south of the centre, beyond the A9 autoroute (bus #D: "La Bastide" stop).

The City

The heart of Nîmes can be found in the place de la Maison Carrée, where an august two-thousand-year-old temple, the **Maison Carrée**, faces off against its gleaming twentieth-century doppelganger, the **Carré d'Art**. Fanning out from here to the east, a compact warren of pedestrian streets makes up the city's **old town**, a triangle hemmed in by the boulevards Gambetta on the north, Amiral-Courbet on the southeast, and Victor-Hugo on the southwest, and home to the city's medieval and early modern sights. Nîmes' oldest

---

Discount passes

If you plan on visiting more than one of the Roman sights, consider buying a "*Billet Global*", a combined ticket allowing entry to Les Arènes, La Maison Carrée and the Tour Magne for €9.50: it can be bought at Les Arènes and the tourist office. Alternatively, a €9 ticket gives entry to all Nîmes' museums.

remains – its **Roman monuments** – lie for the most part on the edge of the old town, like the famous **Arènes** coliseum, and off to the north and east, clustered around the blunt Mont Cavalier. There are several worthwhile museums here, all to be found in the city centre, whereas Nîmes' famous modern architecture is concentrated in the far south, in the newer suburbs.

The Maison Carrée and Carré d'Art

The **Maison Carrée** ("square house"), a tiny but perfectly proportioned temple, once the centrepiece of the city's forum, was founded in 4 or 5 AD and dedicated to Augustus' adopted grandson. Size, of course, is not everything, and as Henry James remarked, it is precisely because of its compactness that "it does not overwhelm you, you can conceive it." This is perhaps the world's best preserved Roman temple (rivalled only by Lebanon's stupendous Temple of Apollo at Baalbek), and can still boast all of its columns, an intact roof and *cella* (inner sanctum). If, over the ages, its functions – including use as a stable – haven't always done it justice, its aesthetic perfection has long drawn notable admirers: Colbert, Louis XIV's prime minister, wanted to carry it off lock and stock to Versailles; Thomas Jefferson modelled the Virginia Capital building on it; and Napoleon took it as inspiration for the Magdalene church in Paris. Today it houses a **museum** (daily: March & Oct 9am–6pm; April, May & Sept 9am–7pm; June–Aug 9am–8pm; Nov–Feb 10am–5pm; €4.50), showing short 3D films on the history of Nîmes.

The Carré d'Art

On the far side of boulevard Victor-Hugo sits Norman Foster's 1993 **Carré d'Art** (Tues–Sun 10am–6pm; free), a twentieth-century descendant of the Roman temple. Four fine columns support the high portico with seeming effortlessness, paying homage to the chunkier Ionic columns of the smaller Maison Carrée, reflected in the inscrutable glass face of Foster's building. The building is home to a library and resource centre, and the top two floors house the city's **Musée d'Art Contemporain** (€4.90), which contains an impressive survey of French and Western European art of the last four decades. Emphasis

---

Nîmes' avant-garde architecture

Through the mid-1980s and 1990s Nîmes embarked on an audacious project of **urban renewal**, contracting high-flying architects from around the world to construct public housing developments, sport centres and civic spaces. These new buildings – Nîmes' modern pride – vary in originality and effect; you may judge them to be either wonders or monstrosities. Some of them you'll pass as you make the rounds in the centre, while the rest (which are really only of interest to hard-core modern architecture fans) are scattered around the southern edge of the city and are best visited either by bike or taxi.

The best work by far is Norman Foster's great **Carré d'Art** (1993; see above). Also in the old town are two remodelled urban *places*: Martiel Raysse's **la place d'Assas** (1989) and Philippe Starck's **Arbibus** (1987), both offering simple landscape architecture and decidedly underwhelming modern sculpture. The peripheral sites include the whale-like and rapidly ageing social housing development **Nemausus 1** (Jean Nouvel, 1987), its monstrous rejoinder, **Nemausus 2** (Alain Amedeo and Jacek Padlewski, 1989), and three sports complexes – **Stade des Costières** (Vittorio Gregotti and Marc Chausse, 1989), **Salle Omnisports** (Gregotti, 1993) and already-dated **Le Colisée** (Kisho Kurokawa, 1991) – which, with their lunging surfaces of concrete and glass, complete the discordant collection.

is on Gallic movements such as Nouveau Réalisme and Support-surfaces, but Mediterranean and northern European art is also strongly represented.

The Cathedral and around

With the core of the Roman city long buried and built over, and most of the medieval buildings destroyed in the course of the Wars of Religion, Nîmes' **old town** is for the most part a testament to the success of the local cloth-merchants of the seventeenth to nineteenth centuries – the builders of the grandiose *hôtels* which pepper the streets emanating south and west from the **Cathédrale de Notre-Dame et St-Castors**, a five-minute stroll east of the Maison Carrée. This church serves as a fitting transition point from Roman to early-modern Nîmes, set as it is on the foundations of the former temple of Apollo. Of the original cathedral, founded in 1069, only the bell tower and the badly chipped friezes of the facade survived the Huguenots' wrath – the rest was rebuilt in the 1700s. The new building is rather nondescript and the drably remodelled interior is hardly worth a visit. On the south side of the square sits the seventeenth-century **bishop's palace**, now home to the **Musée du Vieux Nîmes** (Tues–Sun 10am–6pm; free), whose lively collection focuses on the city's artisanal and industrial past, including, of course, the manufacture of denim, and will appeal to both adults and children. It is a well-organized exhibition, rounded out by a noteworthy furniture collection, which includes a nineteenth-century billiard table and sedan chairs.

Northeast of the cathedral, following the narrow lane which runs along its north wall, you'll eventually come upon the excavated **Porte d'Auguste**. This surprisingly well-preserved triumphal entryway into the city, sunk by the rising ground level, was only discovered in the eighteenth century with the destruction of the medieval palace which had been built around it. It is through this gate that the **Via Domitia** entered Nîmes from the east: the larger central passages were for chariots and the smaller side entrances for pedestrians. Just beyond, in place des Carmes, the Protestant Grand Temple and the Catholic church of St-Baudille contemplate each other uneasily.

The Hôtels of the denim lords

Heading south from the cathedral on rue des Marchands, you'll pass the plain facade of a medieval shop at no. 15 – a rare "commercial" survivor of the Middle Ages – before passing **Hôtel Régis**, a former merchants' house with a stately sixteenth-century courtyard in rue du Chapitre. The street ends at Grande Rue, where you'll be confronted by the clean Neoclassical lines of the former **Jesuits' Chapel** (Tues–Sun 10am–6pm; free). Inside, there's a spacious and luxuriously appointed Baroque interior, now used for exhibitions and concerts. In rue des Greffes, to the south, sits the late Renaissance **Hôtel de Ville**, built in 1700 – look for the stuffed crocodiles suspended above the staircase inside the entry hall, gifts to the city from contented (and rich) eighteenth-century burghers.

West from here, the saurian theme continues in place du Marché, where a twentieth-century homage to the city's emblem has been paid in a **fountain** designed by Martiel Raysse and Silvio and Vito Tongiani. Just to the north-west, innocuous among the colourful boutiques and restaurants, sits the **Hôtel Bernis**, one of the town's earliest surviving mansions, its fifteenth-century facade studded by casement windows and concealing an atmospheric old court-yard with a well in the centre. Nearby, at 8 rue l'Aspic, you can see three early Christian sarcophagi incorporated into the walls of the **Meynier de Salinelles**

△ Place de l'Horloge, Nîmes

mansion, as well as a splendid staircase leading up from its courtyard. Further along rue l'Aspic is the place de l'Horloge, whose solitary eighteenth-century **clock tower** is now crowded by the tables of café terraces; place aux Herbes is just to the east.

The Museum of Archeology and Natural History

Abutting the back of the Jesuits' Chapel is the **Museum of Archeology and Natural History** (Tues–Sun 10am–6pm; €4.90), housing two collections with little in common. The archeological section is disappointingly poor in Roman artefacts considering the city's ancient Latin glory; items are limited to a sizeable but visually monotonous collection of Latin epigraphy and an assortment of household goods, though it does have some fine Greek lacquerware and pre-Roman Etruscan statuary.

The quirky natural history exhibition comprises a jumbled collection of Polynesian masks and spears, and a hotchpotch of stuffed animals, including a Royal Bengal Tiger. In fact, the museum rather resembles a large curio cabinet – a journey into the nineteenth-century European mind, which saw the world beyond its borders as a hunting ground for collectables.

Les Arènes and around

The city's other famous Roman monument squats at the south end of boulevard Victor-Hugo, and although not the largest surviving Roman amphitheatre, **Les Arènes** (March & Oct 9.30am–5.30pm; April, May & Sept 9am–6pm; June–Aug 9am–7pm; Nov–Feb 9.30am–4.30pm; closed during special events; €7.70) is one of the best preserved. Dating from the first century, the 133-metre-long and 101-metre-wide oval surges 21 metres above the street, thanks to its uniquely intact upper galleries, and still holds the crowds of 20,000 spectators for which it was designed. An ingenious access system allows the public to enter and exit through the *vomitoria* – the great arched entryways which ring the building – quickly and with minimal jostling. Before the Christians banned gladiatorial matches in the fourth century, these entertainments, along with spectacles involving killing exotic animals, were the big draw. Since the decline of these games the building has managed to escape destruction thanks to its more or less continued use. With the town's occupation by the Visigoths it was used as a fortress throughout the twelfth century (in the east section, two contemporary windows remain). Thereafter it quickly filled up with houses, shops and churches, coming to constitute a veritable slum, which was only cleared out when restoration work began in 1809.

Since the nineteenth century the amphitheatre has been used again for public spectacles, including bullfights. Once you have appreciated the grandness of its structure, however, the inside of the arena holds little interest; the long series of impressively vast but near-identical passages, stairways and bench-rows is a tribute to Roman engineering, but hides few surprises. Unfortunately, the concerts and events held here often obscure the building with scaffolding and stage-works, and although the retractable cover which was added in the late 1980s makes winter-time shows possible, it frustrates efforts to imagine the building's ancient ambience. The best way to visit Les Arènes is to come for a **bullfight** (see box, 224) during one of Nîmes' *ferias*. Outside the main entrance of the arena you'll see a sombre reminder of the seriousness of the *corrida*, the statue of Christian Moncouquiol, a promising young *torero* known as "el Nimeño II," who was gored to death in 1991.

Whether or not you manage to see a matador in action, be sure to check out the two taurine museums near the Arènes: the small **Galerie des Arènes** on the north side of the boulevard des Arènes (Tues–Sun 11am–6pm; free) features local painters, while the nearby **Musée des Cultures Taurines,** at 6 Rue Alexandre Ducros (June to mid-Nov daily 10am–6pm; mid-Nov to May

Tues–Sun 10am–6pm; €4.90), is dedicated to *tauromachie*, with a permanent collection of posters and relics, and engagingly themed annual exhibits.

From the temple, it's a fifteen-minute jaunt southwest to rue de la Cité Foulc and the **Musée des Beaux-Arts** (Tues–Sun 10am–6pm; €4.90), whose highlight is a huge Roman mosaic depicting the mythical "marriage of Admetus". The rest of the collection – mostly Flemish, Italian and French paintings from the sixteenth to eighteenth centuries – is endowed with works of surprising quality, including Rubens' uncharacteristically static *Portrait of a Monk*, and a fine example of the transition from medieval to humanist style in Giambono's *Mystical Marriage of St Catherine*.

Along the way, in rue Porte de France, you'll pass through the **Roman gate** of the same name. It's worth pausing here to consider the immense size of the Roman city – the whole area between here and the Tour Magne was contained by its walls.

The Castellum Divisorum, La Tour Magne and Temple of Diana

Tucked away north of boulevard Gambetta, beside the cold and sinister facade of the town's eighteenth-century **fortress**, now the Centre Universitaire du

Bullfighting and tauromachie

Bulls have been raised in the Petite Camargue and the plains to its north for centuries, and for the people of the ranchlands around St-Gilles, **tauromachie** or *la bouvine* – the art of bull-handling – has come to represent a measure of virility, testament to their proud rural roots. Its significance however, is also region-wide: in addition to the exciting action and dangerous elements of bull-handling – which naturally began to attract audiences – the growing cultural awareness of the mid-nineteenth century prompted intellectual Occitan patriots to find in it a further mark of the uniqueness of their local culture, thus sealing *tauromachie*'s transformation into a popular spectacle throughout Languedoc and Roussillon.

The traditions of the **bullfight**, which seem now to be so essential to the spirit of Gard, are in fact almost exclusively recent innovations. A *jeu taurin*, wherein ranch hands and sometimes other animals were pitted against bulls as entertainment, had developed by the Middle Ages, but it wasn't until the Iberian customs arrived, thanks to a visiting Spanish nobleman, that French *tauromachie* came into its own. The first real **corrida** (Spanish bullfight) in France was held in 1853 at Bayonne. It was a great success and soon spread throughout the Midi and into Provence. Nîmes' first official *corrida* was held at Les Arènes in 1865, and by 1880 the spectacle could be seen across the south. Meanwhile, the local tradition, the **course** – in which men on foot would try to pull ornaments off the foreheads of charging bulls – had also been formalized, and achieved such popularity that when the government tried to ban it because of high fatality rates, the population defiantly opposed the plan.

The standard Spanish-style *corrida* which can be seen at the *ferias* of Nîmes, Beaucaire, St-Gilles and Sommières is a highly ritualized **ceremony** – a fatal dance in which the bull is an unwitting but respected partner. In a typical afternoon, three matadors will dispose of six bulls, each of which will face a series of torments: first, after a few initial passes with the large cape (*capote*), the bull is subjected to the long, barbed spear of the mounted *picadores*; next, the graceful *banderilleros* run at the bull and plant their colourful barbs in its shoulder; and finally, the matador executes a series of choreographed passes with his small red *mula* until, to the minor strains of a *paso doble*, the president of the *corrida* gives the order for the bullfighter to finish off

Vauban (free), sits one of Nîmes' most important but least known Roman artefacts – the **castellum divisorum** (daily: mid-March to mid-Oct 7.30am–10pm; mid-Oct to mid-March 7.30am–6.30pm; free), the rare remains of a first-century waterworks (the only similar ones are at Pompeii in Italy and Tiermes in Spain), which mark the start of the Roman circuit. It was from this innocuous-looking open basin that the water carried to the town via the Pont du Gard was distributed to the various parts of the Roman city by lead pipes, which are still partly visible – at the Pont du Gard museum (see p.235) multi-media installations show how the complex worked. Following the quiet residential streets west from here takes you to the **Jardin de la Fontaine**, a formal eighteenth-century garden with a complex series of fountains and pools, at the foot of the forested **Mont Cavalier**.

La Tour Magne and Temple of Diana

From the *place* at the foot of the Mont, follow the signs up the serpentine path which takes you to the ruins of the **Tour Magne**. This **watchtower** (daily: July & Aug 9am–7pm; Sept–June 10am–5pm; €2.70), based on an earlier Celtic structure, dates from about 15 BC, and as the Roman settlement grew, was eventually incorporated into the city walls. The tower has suffered its share of indignities, including the loss of the top fifteen of its original 45-metre

his partner. Crowds at the event are extremely vocal and demonstrative: a poor matador and bull will be pelted with seat cushions, while a very successful matador will be greeted with cheers, showered with roses, rewarded with a gift of the bull's ears and tail and borne out of the ring on the shoulders of the crowd. The happiest ending, however, is the rare *indulto*, when the bull is also rewarded for his performance, and retired, to be used for breeding and allowed to die of contented old age.

The French *course* is quite distinct, although it has been permeated by an undeniable Spanish flavour. Less expensive and elaborate, it is more common in village *fêtes*, such as at **Uzès** or **Aigues-Mortes**. The bulls (or cows) are first led to the ring in an *abrivado*, herded by a tumult of mounted *gardians* – if this takes place within a confined area, it is called an *encierro* (a "running" of the bulls). Once in the ring the animals are outfitted with a rosette and tassels suspended between their horns, and for fifteen minutes *raseteurs* (named after the hooked handgear they wear) provoke the animal into charging, and attempt to snatch the rosette or tassels without getting trampled or gored. When all is complete, the bulls are herded out with great fanfare and frenzy (the *bandido*) and back to the pen.

Aside from these entertainments, a rather more workaday manifestation of *la bouvine* has also become a staple of local spring-time festivals. This is the *ferrado*, in which year-old bulls are driven from their pens by mounted *gardians*, wrestled to the ground by their colleagues on foot and then branded with a hot iron, marking them with the arms or initials of the *manade* to which they belong.

La fé di bioù ("love of the bull") has proved contagious, and today *tauromachie* is more popular than ever. The *ferias* of Nîmes draw thousands of enthusiasts from all over Europe and are universally acknowledged as southern France's liveliest and most colourful festivities. And the practice has taken firm root even in the smallest of villages far from the *manades* of the plains; even if they can afford no more than an *encierro*, villagers pool their money in order to pay for some sort of taurine display, without which no *fête* would be seen as complete. In recent years, however, some events have been marked by small but vocal protests and in 2006 several organizers of the local *tauromachie* were injured by letter bombs.

height and the frantic diggings around the foundations by a treasure-hunting seventeenth-century gardener deluded by a prediction of Nostradamus, but it is impressive even in its ruined state. Broken off and eroded, the tower evokes the romantic etchings of the nineteenth-century travellers who marvelled at it, and it is still the best place from which to survey Nîmes and its surroundings.

As you return to the foot of the hill, to the right of the Jardin sit the shambolic ruins of the "**Temple of Diana**" (daily: mid-March to mid-Oct 7.30am–10pm; mid-Oct to mid-March 7.30am–6.30pm; free). Originally a *nymphaeum*, a sacred fountain dedicated to Nemausus (the god of the spring), the structure was taken over by Benedictine monks in the Middle Ages, in whose care it remained until destroyed by Huguenot mobs. Today the hulking half arches and ruined walls are the only remnants of the temple, but are enough to give you an impression of the scale of the building in Roman times.

Eating, drinking and entertainment

Three culinary traditions – Spanish, *gastronomique* and, of course, Gardois *terroir* dominate Nîmes' **restaurants**, with Indian and North African establishments adding a cosmopolitan flavour. The cuisine of Gard has a distinctly Mediterranean taste, with a strong current of olive and garlic, plus rosemary, basil, bay and mint, all of which sprout up in the *garrigues*. Look out for *boeuf à la Gardianne* (slow-cooked marinated beef), *soupe au pistou* (vegetable soup with pesto), and *brandade de morue* (cod and olive-oil purée); wash these down with the wines of the Costières, or with the famous Côtes-du-Rhône vintages.

Restaurants

Many of the cheapest **restaurants**, including self-service cafés and budget sandwich stands, can be found along the boulevard Amiral-Courbet, and the whole of the old town is thick with small restaurants and brasseries, with a veritable colony of street-side bistros in the narrow alleys around place du Marché (many in the €12–20 range). When weather permits, you'll be threading through the tables which spread into the streets and squares.

L'Ancien Théâtre 4 rue Racine ☎04.66.21.30.75. Just a 5min stroll west from the Maison Carrée, with zippy Mediterranean cuisine. *Menus* from €13. Closed Sat noon, Sun, Mon & early July.

La Bodeguita 1 Pl d'Assas ☎04.66.58.28.27. A solid choice for Spanish food and tapas, with a good view of the Maison Carrée. A meal costs about €25, tapas from €5.

Le Bouchon et l'Assiette 5bis rue de Sauve ☎04.66.62.02.93. Worth the walk out past the Temple of Diana – come here for elaborate *gastronomique* variations on traditional *tarnaise* themes. Very reasonably priced, with *menus* from €15–44. Closed Tues & Wed, part Jan & most of Aug.

Le Chapon Fin 3 rue Château Fadaise ☎04.66.67.34.73. Basic but hearty *terroir* cuisine in simple surroundings; a good value-for-money choice. Closed Sat lunch & Sun. *Menus* €11–30.

El Rinconcito 7 rue des Marchands ☎04.66.76.17.30. Nîmes' Chilean restaurant offers a range of South American favourites, including *ceviche*, *empanadas* and fish pie. Wash it down with Chilean vintages or *pisco*, inside or on the indoor patio. But get there early, the last dinner order is taken at 9.30pm. Lunch from €8.50. Closed Sun & Mon.

L'Enclos de la Fontaine Quai de la Fontaine ☎04.66.21.90.30. Set in the luxurious *Hotel Imperator*, with a shady garden, its carte treads a line between *terroir* and *gastronomique*. Splurge on the *Menu Impérator* for €60. Open daily.

Le Jardin d'Hadrien 111 rue Enclos-Rey ☎04.66.21.86.65. Inventive cuisine based on local southeastern Gard tradition. Reasonable prices, too, with *menus* at €17–26. Closed Mon & Wed lunch & Sun (July & Aug); Wed, Tues & Sun dinner (Sept–June) & late Aug to early Sept.

Le Magister 5 rue Nationale
☎04.66.76.11.00. Daring experimentation is the order of the day at this good *gastronomique* restaurant. Cod and salmon act as a springboard for the most adventurous combinations, which blend tangy herbs with the sweetness of fruit, while the lamb cutlets are also of exceptional tenderness. The €30 *menu* is a solid option, and includes wine; otherwise *à la carte* is pricey. Closed Sat lunch & Sun, part of Feb, July & Aug.

Le P'tit Bec 87bis rue de la République ☎04.66.38.05.83. The best mid-range place for typical Gardoise cuisine, including the ever-present *boeuf à la gardianne* and *brandade de morue*. *menu* options from €18, plus children's *menus*. Closed Sun eve & Mon & Wed eve.

Aux Plaisirs des Halles 4 rue Littré ☎04.66.36.01.02. Located between the tourist office and the new *halles*, serving up market-fresh food combining a traditional olive oil base with the enticing flavours of the herbs of the *garrigues*. *Menus* from €24–55 (€20 at lunch). Closed Sun & Mon.

Simple Simon 11 rue Xavier Sigalon ☎04.66.76.01.21. Any restaurant in France daring to advertise English cuisine deserves credit. If you're tired of duck and "under-cooked" meat with too much sauce, you can savour the culinary glory of Britain, including fish'n'chips and pasties, for €14–24. Closed Sun & Mon.

La Truye qui Filhe 9 rue Fresque. Basic self-service place, incongruously tucked away in a fourteenth-century building. Fill up with *croque-monsieur*, salads and the like from €9. Lunch only, closed Sun & Aug.

Bars and cafés

Bars in Nîmes are smoking – literally. Over the course of an evening many establishments fill with the thick blue haze of Gaulloises and Gitanes; appropriately enough, given that the person who introduced tobacco to France in the sixteenth century was Nîmes native Jean Nicot (also the drug's namesake). Nîmes' two dominant types of drinking establishments are sedate neighbourhood **café-bars**, and louder and larger **music-bars**, which usually feature a DJ (or more rarely, unexceptional live music) on weekend nights. Smaller bars can be found scattered among the narrow streets of the town core, while the large, traditional-style café-bars are found on the wider streets such as boulevards Amiral-Courbet or Victor-Hugo, on either side of the old town. Nimes' **clubs** tend to be located in far-flung suburbs or out of town altogether, making them all but impossible to get to without a car.

Café des Beaux-Arts Pl aux Herbes. A cheerful and airy place with a good patio that's well located for people-watching, or simply for soaking up the ambience of the old medieval heart of Nîmes. Closed Sun.

Café Carré d'Art Bd Daudet. Great views of the city from inside the glassed-in interior or outside on the patio atop the museum of the same name. Open the same hours as the museum.

La Casa Don Miguel 18 rue de l'Horloge. This popular and late-opening Spanish-style *bodega* is known for its cocktails and large variety of tapas. Occasional flamenco, salsa and jazz shows. Closed Sun.

La Movida 2 la Placette. A Spanish bar with decent tapas and a Romany/flamenco atmosphere that explodes during the *ferias*. Closed Sun & most of Aug.

O'Flaherty's 26 bd Amiral-Courbet. British beer – seven kinds on tap – plus food and regular Thursday concerts of Irish, country and bluegrass (except July & Aug). Open till 2–3am daily.

Café Napoléon Top end of bd Victor Hugo. Famous old neighbourhood café – complete with faded wood decor, cigar-chomping old men in cardigans and unbeatable Gallic ambience. Great place for a refreshing mid-afternoon *pastis* break and right on the edge of the old town. Closed Sun.

Pub Au Bureau 24 bd Amiral Courbet. Massive bar and pool hall which also features live music on most weekends from Oct to May. Open late.

Les Trois Maures 10 bd des Arènes. Fantastic old high-ceilinged bar beside the Arènes, festooned with bullfighting and rugby memorabilia and exceptionally busy during *ferias*. Open late. Closed Sun in July & Aug.

Victor Hugo 36 bd Victor-Hugo. The favourite hotspot of Nîmes' younger set, hosting local DJs and specializing in electronic, funk and house music. Daily till 1am.

Wine Bar Chez Michel 11 square de la Couronne. This is *the* place to begin your acquaintance with the wines of Languedoc (at €20–200 a bottle), served with traditional Gard cuisine. Closed Mon & Sat noon & Sun.

Entertainment and festivals

Generally, the city's high-brow cultural programme is disappointing, possibly because of its proximity to more prestigious centres like Avignon and Montpellier. That said, there's a steady stream of theatre groups and musicians, ranging from symphonies to rock and blues acts, coming to town – drawn primarily by the presence of an excellent venue in the Roman amphitheatre; groups who can't fill Les Arènes play on various smaller stages scattered about the town. The **cinema**, Sémaphore, 25 rue Porte de France (℡04.66.67.83.11, ⓦwww .lesemaphore.free.fr), shows films in *version originale*. For information and reservations for films, concerts and plays, contact the main tourist office and also check the annual *Guide Culturel* booklet for major shows.

The most important dates in the Nîmes calendar are those of the **ferias**, lively street festivals featuring parties, music and *tauromachie*. The city is the French capital of the *corrida*, the Spanish tradition of bullfighting which the Occitans have striven to make their own, and during the three great annual ferias – **Primavera** (February), **Pentecôte** (seven weeks after Easter) and **des Vendanges** (mid-September), the best local and Spanish *toreros* come to Les Arènes to practise the brutal pageantry of their art. During the *ferias*, particularly Pentecost, the centre of Nîmes becomes a massive round-the-clock party; the bars fill with boisterous revellers and the best hotels get booked a year in advance. If you plan to visit the city during one of the festivals, it is essential to make reservations for accommodation; for tickets to bullfights throughout the year, contact the Bureau de location des Arènes, at 1 rue Alexandre-Ducros (℡04.66.67.28.02).

Listings

Airlines Air France ℡08.02.80.28.02 ⓦwww .airfrance.com; Air Littoral ℡08.25.83.48.34, ⓦwww.airlittoral.fr; Ryan Air ℡08.92.55.56.66, ⓦwww.ryanair.com.

Airport The Aéroport International Garons ℡04.66.70.49.49.

Banks and exchange A number of banks have branches in the old town which offer currency exchange and ATMs.

Books Secondhand English books can be bought and sold at Bouquinerie, 21 av Amiral-Courbet (beside *O'Flaherty's* pub).

Bus departures Intercity service leaves from the *gare routière* on bd Natoire (℡04.66.29.52.00; ⓦwww.stdgard.com), connected by a footbridge to the gare SNCF. The main carriers are the SNCF and Cévennes Cars (℡04.66.29.27.29), although Sommières is served by Cariane Cars (℡04.66.38.13.98).

Car rental ADA, 2614 rte de Montpellier ℡04.66.04.79.99; Apex 2, 72 rue de la République ℡04.66.38.09.66; Avis, 1800 av du Maréchal Juin ℡04.66.29.05.33; Budget, 1800 av du Maréchal Juin ℡04.66.38.01.69; Europcar, 1bis rue de la République ℡04.66.21.31.35; National, 14 av Carnot ℡04.66.21.03.62; Hertz, 5 bd de Prague

℡04.66.76.25.91. All except Apex have airport offices as well and Avis has an office at the *gare*.

Children's activities A good place to take the kids is Parc Aquatropic (℡04.66.38.31.00), a waterslide theme park near the Nîmes-Ouest *autoroute* exit, accessible by bus #D from outside the Halles shopping centre on bd Gambetta. Adults pay €4.90, kids €1.30. Open summer only 9am–10pm.

Hospital Carremeau Hospital is at Nîmes University (℡04.66.68.68.68). Emergency (℡15).

Internet access Cyber Café Vauban, 34 rue Clérisseau (daily 10am–11pm).

Laundry There's a launderette on rue de Grand Couvent, at the corner of rue de Agau (daily 7am–9pm).

Market Farmers' market (Fri) and flea market (Mon morn) on bld Jean-Jaurès; also general open-air crafts market throughout the old town in July & Aug (Thurs 6–10pm).

Police *Mairie*, rue Hôtel de Ville (℡04.66.76.70.54); emergency (℡17).

Taxi TRAN (℡04.66.29.40.11) runs an excursion to the Pont du Gard with a thirty-minute wait for €40.

Train information ℡08.92.35.35.35, ⓦwww .voyages-sncf.com.

Around Nîmes

For such a small area, the southern portion of Gard contains a surprising number of attractions for visitors. Just across the river Gardon to the north of Nîmes lies **Uzès**, the "First Duchy" of France, its castle still in the hands of a family which traces its roots back to Charlemagne. A few kilometres east of the city lies the **Pont du Gard**, perhaps the most famous of all Roman aqueducts, now developed into a major attraction, while along the Rhône, medieval **Beaucaire**'s castle and the uniquely sculpted facade of the church of **St-Gilles** deserve a visit. The southern edge of the *département*, sweeping west of here, is dominated by the westernmost branch of the swampy Rhône delta, the **Petite Camargue** – an important way-station for migratory birds. On the west, the medieval walls of **Aigues-Mortes** are now besieged only by invading sunseekers who crowd the beaches south of the town, around **Le Grau-du-Roi** and **Port-Camargue**. Upstream from Le Grau, on the River Vidourle, **Sommières** and **Sauve** lie quietly languishing in forgotten obscurity, far from the bustle of the coast. Roman ruins pepper the entire area, including aqueducts, arches and stretches of road still marked by milestones, and towns throughout the region share Nîmes' enthusiasm for the *corrida*; if possible trips should be planned to coincide with village *ferias*. The best time to visit the southern Gard is during the summer, when pleasure ports and beaches are busy, although inland towns follow a rhythm not so dependent on the sun.

Public transport in the region is fairly good and, with the unfortunate exception of Uzès, the main towns are served by frequent bus and train routes. Distances, however, are not great, and the generally even landscape makes **hiking** a good option. Unfortunately, south of the *garrigues*, **cycling** is made hazardous by the intense and rapid traffic on the area's narrow highways.

Uzès

Long disdained by the French literati as the proverbial "middle of nowhere", **UZÈS**, nestled among the rocky *garrigues* twenty kilometres north of Nîmes, has now been discovered. Like so many towns of the Gard, Uzès traces its history back to the time of the toga, when it served as an agricultural and local market centre, and it became the seat of a bishop as early as the fifth century. Changing hands many times over the following centuries, it eventually came under the control of the counts of Toulouse. When they lost the town to the French Crown in 1229, their former underlings, lords of Uzès, battled it out with the bishops for local control. These barons served the French kings well and were rewarded when the town was given the rank of the "First Duchy of France" in 1632. The title had belonged to the dukes of Montmorency until then, but they lost it as a consequence of Henri de Montmorency's failed revolt (see p.400). Like Nîmes, Uzès violently embraced Calvinism – becoming the fifth most important Huguenot centre in France – but once the movement was suppressed and the majority of Protestants fled, those "Catholics" that remained turned it into a wealthy silk town, which it remained for the next three hundred years. The early twentieth century brought depression, and when the railway bypassed the town, the writing of Uzès' decline was on the wall. The history of the town's celebrities is also one of near misses: Guillaume de Grimoard, later to become Pope Urban V, was not from Uzès, but did live here for a while; the great seventeenth-century poet Jean Racine had an uncle from the town, and spent a year and a half here; and Charles Gide, father of Nobel-laureate author André, was a native – the junior Gide passed his childhood summers here.

But Uzès, historical marginalization belies its beauty. As André Gide remarked, "O little town of Uzès! Were you in Umbria, the tourists of Paris would rush to see you!" In fact, today the town fairly packs out with tourists in summer months; each medieval stone arcade now conceals a bistro, and when the weather is good the restaurant patios which dominate the squares are frequented by buskers of surprising quality. Saturday's traditional **market** is particularly lively, while gourmands will want to sample the **truffles** for which the town is renowned. If you're reliant on public transport and short on time the town is best visited on a day-trip that also takes in the **Pont du Gard**, 20km southwest.

Arrival, information and accommodation

Uzès' **gare routière** (⊤04.66.22.00.58) is located just west of the old town on Esplanade Maréchal de Lattre de Tassigny; from here it's a five-minute walk north along boulevard Gambetta to the **tourist office** (June–Sept Mon–Fri 9am–6/7pm, Sat & Sun 10am–noon & 1–5pm; Oct–May Mon–Fri 9am–12.30pm & 2–6pm, Sat 10am–1pm; ⊤04.66.22.68.88, ⓦ www.uzes-tourisme .com) in place Albert 1er, just north of the Duché. **Bikes** can be rented one block west of the tourist office, at Et Paysan, on avenue Général Vincent, which

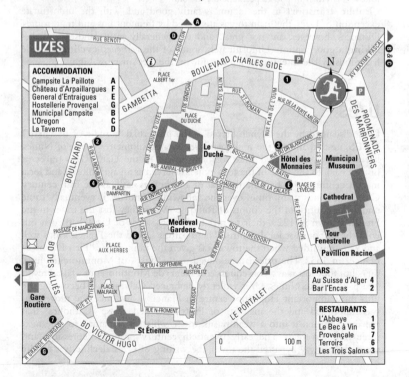

has a free brochure of bike routes, including one to the Pont du Gard. *Cyberland* **Internet** café is on place Austerlitz (noon–2am);

Most of the town's **hotels** reflect its noble past – which is to say, luxurious but pricey. The cheapest beds can be found at the attractive ☂ *La Taverne* (☎04.66.22.13.10, ✉lataverne.uzes@wanadoo.fr; ❹), behind the tourist office at 4 rue Xavier Sigalon, or try the friendly *Hostellerie Provençale* (☎04.66.22.11.06, ⓦwww.hostellerieprovencale.com; ❺) at 1 rue Grande Bourgade, near the church of St-Étienne. The deluxe ☂ *Général d'Entraigues*, 8 rue de la Calade (☎04.66.22.32.68, ⓦwww.hoteldentraigues.com; ❹), is in a converted fifteenth-century mansion opposite the cathedral: its owners also run the *Château d'Arpaillargues* (April–Oct; ☎04.66.22.14.48, ⓦwww.chateaudarpaillargues.com; ❼), a rural mansion converted into a hotel, 4km northwest of town. There are two seasonal **campsites**: the municipal site (mid-June to mid-Sept; ☎04.66.22.11.79), on the riverside 500m northeast of town on avenue Pascal; and *La Paillote* (mid-March to mid-Oct; ☎04.66.22.38.55), 500m along rue Xavier Sigalon. The local **gîte d'étape**, *L'Oregon* (☎04.66.22.16.25; April–Oct), is 1.5km north of Uzès, following avenue Pascal. It has one double room (❷), as well as a dorm (€12) and guests have use of a kitchen.

The Town

Uzès, the core of which can be walked in about an hour, is extremely easy to find your way around; the compact **old town** – shaped roughly like a kidney bean – is ringed by a broad one-way system. Within this perimeter the town is still dominated by the twelfth-century castle, **the Duché**, just south of the tourist office, while its other focal point, the place aux Herbes, lies a bit further southwest of the fortress. The **cathedral** overlooks the Alzon river on the eastern edge of the old town, as if pushed aside by the power of the town's dukes.

The Duché

The old ducal castle of the de Cressol family, the **Duché** (daily: mid-June to mid-Sept 10am–1pm & 2–6.30pm; mid-Sept to mid-June 10am–noon & 2–6pm), is the centrepiece of Uzès, and the sight of its towering *donjon* topped by the family's red and yellow-banded pennant makes a Hollywoodesque but authentic medieval tableau. The compact walled *enceinte* rises dramatically from amidst the old town's buildings, concealing a courtyard presided over by a majestically columned Renaissance facade, and a small garden, as well as the bulky and crude keep. Claiming roots which go back to Charlemagne and St Louis, the de Cressols are proud of their long lineage, and their motto *ferro non auro* – "by iron [i.e. the sword], not gold" – sets them apart from the later families who bought rather than fought their way into the aristocracy. Their stay in Uzès has not been continuous, however, as the Revolution precipitated a hiatus which lasted until 1954. Among the most colourful of its members was the Duchess Anne, grandmother of the present Duke; monarchist, suffragette and enthusiastic hunter (she killed over 2000 animals), she rode until the age of 87, and was France's first female driver – and the first to receive a speeding ticket. Despite the fact that it is still a part-time residence for the dukes, the castle can be visited on a lively hour-long **guided tour** (€12; an English-language handout is provided), although the budget-conscious may opt only to climb the tenth-century **Tour Bermonde** (€7), whose summit gives fine views from between the battlements. The main tour through the family's apartments is entertaining and offers an intimate look at a disappearing aristocratic world, with personal effects set amongst the rare furnishings and ancient books.

André Gide

André **Gide** was born in Paris in 1869, the son of a wealthy Huguenot family from Uzès. A sensitive, nervous soul, the young Gide's introspection and uncertainty was no doubt nourished by the tensions he felt regarding his sexual identity. His disquietudes came to be expressed through literature, and his exceptional promise was reflected in the fact that he published his first work at the age of 20. Five years later he married his cousin and childhood sweetheart, Madelaine. Their marriage was never consummated, although in 1923, he had a daughter by another woman. His *Si le grain ne meurt* ("If It Die"; 1924–26), recalls in part the summers of his youth, spent in Uzès. Like so many nonconformist contemporaries he was drawn to exotic and liberating French North Africa, where he confronted and eventually came to celebrate his bisexuality, as in the landmark *The Fruits of All Earth* (1897) – a work which decisively influenced the young Albert Camus and Jean-Paul Sartre. He became a close friend of Oscar Wilde, whom he met in Algiers. In the English-speaking world his best-known novels are *The Immoralist* (1902) and *The Counterfeiters* (1926). He died in 1951, recognized as a seminal moral and social iconoclast of the modern age, four years after having received the Nobel Prize for Literature. In 1952 his books were placed on the Catholic Church's Index of forbidden reading.

The visit ends in the castle's ancient cellars, where guests are invited to taste the Duke's own vintage (also on sale, of course) and buy over-priced Provençal statuettes.

The rest of the old town

The castle is far from Uzès' only attraction, and a wander through the dense and evocative alleys of the old town is a true pleasure. Leaving the Duché and following it around to the left, rue Dampmartin leads towards the arcaded **place aux Herbes**, the route punctuated by the carved stone doorframes and casement windows of several elegant sixteenth- to eighteenth-century mansions. Crossing the *place* towards the eighteenth-century St-Étienne **church**, with its thirteenth-century belfry, brings you past the old Gide house, with the streets behind the church pleasantly quiet, unlike the café- and boutique-crammed area around the *place* to the west. Rue Foussat leads back into the heart of the old town and rue Port Royal, where you'll find the entrance to the recreated **medieval garden** (April–June & Sept Mon–Fri 2–6pm, Sat & Sun 10.30am–12.30pm & 2–6pm; July & Aug daily 10.30am–12.30pm & 2–6pm; Oct daily 2–5pm; €3). Set in the courtyard of the former bishop's palace, it contains the herbs and plants which were collected or cultivated in the area during the Middle Ages and makes a great stop for children. Further up, at the dour entrance to the plain **Hôtel des Monnaies** (the former bishop's mint), you can either loop back to the Duché, or turn right to pass the sumptuous Hôtel du Baron de Castille to arrive at the cathedral.

Following the fate of other churches of the region, the medieval **cathedral** of Uzès fell victim to the violence of the Wars of Religion but, thankfully, the twelfth-century bell tower, the **Tour Fenestrelle** survived. Rising 42m above the plaza on which it sits, the six levels of arched windows on this round structure – unique in France – recall strongly the Leaning Tower of Pisa. The new cathedral, on the other hand, dates from the seventeenth to nineteenth centuries and is hardly of interest, apart from its flamboyantly styled seventeenth-century organ. The broad verge to the south of the cathedral, the **promenade de Racine**, provides pleasant views of the countryside and river, and sports a curious

△ Uzès Tour Fenestrelle

eighteenth-century **pavilion** resembling a Victorian bandstand, built on one of the town wall's old towers. On the north side of the cathedral the sombre and hulking episcopal palace is home to the **municipal museum** (Tues–Sun: March–Oct 3–6pm, plus July & Aug 10am–noon; Nov, Dec & Feb 2–5pm; €2), which holds Polynesian relics carried home by local missionaries, some decent eighteenth-century portraiture and a room dedicated to the Gide family, consisting of manuscripts, photographs, furniture and personal effects.

Eating and drinking

Uzès' recent tourist boom has been good news for diners, as the town has a surplus of **restaurants** – stiff competition meaning good prices. Among the terraces which clutter the old town and line the ring road, a number of establishments stand out. The finest and most expensive dining can be found at the *Général d'Entraigues*, where you can eat on a panoramic terrace *(menus €24–50)*. For cheaper *terroir* cuisine, try the traditional family-run bistro *L'Abbaye*, 24 boulevard Charles-Gide (closed winter; ℡04.66.22.91.21), with *menus* from €15. At 5 pl aux Herbes, *Terroirs* (closed Mon off-season) has amiable service and excellent local cuisine from €13, while *Provençale*, on rue Grande Bourgade (℡04.66.22.11.06) has lunch *menus* featuring dishes from neighbouring Provence from as low as €9. Other good options include *Les Trois Salons* at 18 rue Blanchard (Tues–Sun; ℡04.66.22.57.34) with excellent *gastronomique* meals from €21, and *Le Bec à Vin*, on rue Entre-les-Tours (℡04.66.22.41.20; closed Sun), for its innovative Mediterranean fare (from €15–30).

For a **drink**, try *Au Suisse d'Alger* on rue République, near place aux Herbes; it has a lively terrace, where you can drink very reasonably priced wine by the glass. Later in the evening *Bar l'Encas*, at the corner of Gambetta and République, is the place to head for – in addition to its pool table and good selection of beers, it has a terrace where off-duty buskers often sit down for an impromptu jam.

The Pont du Gard and around

No one with even a passing interest in history or architecture should go through the Gard without seeing what is arguably the world's most famous Roman aqueduct, the **PONT DU GARD**, 20km to the northeast of Nîmes. The area around the Pont was devastated by serious flooding in 2000, but since then the site has been developed as a major tourist attraction, with an activities centre and an impressive modern **museum** which, together with the pleasant but stony river-beach, excellent **picnic** and **hiking** possibilities and a wide range of accommodation and activities, make it a good base, particularly if you are travelling with children. Several of the hamlets nearby are worth checking out too, as is the **medieval bridge** of St-Nicholas, further up the Gardon river. The aqueduct can be visited as a day-trip from Nîmes and combined with a visit to Uzès, or you can stay by the Pont itself, in the service town of **Remoulins**, 2km away or, particularly if you have some transport, in one of the hamlets between Uzès and Remoulins.

The Pont du Gard

When the Romans needed to supply growing Nîmes with water, they found that the nearest suitable source was some 50km away on the Eure river, near Uzès. Despite the deep Gardon gorge which cut through the route, with Roman single-mindedness (and slave labour), they set about constructing a waterway. This remains nothing short of a technical marvel, descending only 17m in altitude along its course and bridging the Gardon with a monumental aqueduct, the **Pont du Gard** (free access). Most likely constructed in the mid-first century, the Pont's three tiers of arches span an incredible 275m in length, carrying water 49m above the riverbed below. Pillaged for stone through the ages, and first used as a bridge in 1295, the aqueduct has suffered various misfortunes, including an earthquake of 1448, but there was enough of the structure remaining to begin a comprehensive restoration in the eighteenth century. Such was its impact that when Rousseau passed by shortly after this work had been undertaken, the sight of the monument was enough to make him say he wished he'd been born a Roman. A visit here used to be a must for French journeyman masons on their traditional tour of the country, and many of them have left their names and home towns carved on the stonework. Among these, the markings made by the original builders to facilitate construction can also still be found. For the moment, the top tier is under renovation (reopening has been continually postponed), and you can only cross the broad lower level. The best way to enjoy this ancient engineering wonder, however, is to take it in from different perspectives, climbing up to the lookout areas at the top of either end, or viewing it upriver from the bed of the Gardon. Seen from here on a sunny day, the utilitarian but gracefully symmetrical beauty of the aqueduct's yellow-stone structure presents a striking contrast to the blue sky.

The new **Site du Pont du Gard** visitors' complex offers a whole range of activities and attractions. The **museum** (daily: May–Sept 9.30am–7pm; Oct–April 9.30am–5pm; €6) is an incredible multimedia installation, fully multi-lingual and incorporating archeological finds, working models, film, sound effects, and interactive terminals. Themes include the role of water in Roman society and culture, the building of the aqueduct, and its later decay and rediscovery. This is a must-see, not only for technology and engineering buffs and children, but for anyone remotely interested in the past. In the same building you'll find the Ludo, an interactive activity centre for **children** (closed Mon morn; €4.50), a resource centre, and a cinema. Out back, the Mémoires de Garrigue is a 15-hecatre garden with **nature trails** highlighting the local fauna (April to mid-Oct daily 9.30am–6pm; €4). Finally there are a number of activities and displays particularly suited to children including **workshops** for making Roman-style crafts and weapons (daily 10am–6pm), and **gladiator** demonstrations (daily noon & 5.30pm). The whole site is suitable for visitors with disabilities. A combined one-day **ticket** for all the permanent attractions costs €10 (or €20 per family), while the *Site Pont du Gard* **pass** (€15) gives unlimited access to all the attractions, including temporary exhibits and parking (see below).

Around the Pont du Gard

The Pont du Gard is a great place to cool down on a hot day (although the river slows to a trickle in August), and this part of the Gardon is an easy stretch for **canoeing** and **kayaking** (see p.236). Two kilometres south of the aqueduct lies the **château de St-Privat**, the site where Richelieu signed the Peace of Alès with the Huguenots in 1629 (the lords of the castle, the Faret family, were Protestants) and famous for its elaborate formal garden, which dates back to 1644. One of the garden's three sections, the "Avant-park", is home to the **War Sacrifice Chapel**, commissioned after World War I by then-owner Jacques Rouché; its walls are decorated with painted works of metaphysical allegory, mixing biblical figures with depictions of *poilus* (French common soldiers). Unfortunately the property can only be visited on a ninety-minute **guided tour** (contact the tourist office at Remoulins or Pont du Gard for details).

Moving on from the aqueduct, the best way to leave is to hike along the **Gardon gorge** to the Pont St-Nicholas. The GR6 on the north bank and the AR6 on the south (passing St-Privat) lead to **Collias** 4km away, formerly a hippie Mecca, from where the GR6 can be followed upriver. Aside from the rugged beauty of the riverbed's red cliffs, look out for the **Grotte de la Baume**, on the north bank after Collias, a cave with a medieval chapel set amongst what were once the rocky abodes of hermits. Finally, some 10km after Collias, you reach the ponderous and chunky thirteenth-century **Pont St-Nicholas**, now incorporated into the main Uzès–Nîmes highway. There are also some interesting hamlets along the Uzès–Remoulins road, the most intriguing of which (and also the one where the most buses stop) is **Vers**, 4km north of the Pont, where you'll find bits of ruined arches and chunks of Roman road lying around town, and an eleventh-century church. Other nearby villages include **St-Hilaire** and **Castillon-du-Gard**, ancient and picturesque farming settlements which don't have any particular sights, but are worth wandering around.

Practicalities

The Pont itself can be reached by **bus** direct from Nîmes (there is a stop on the south riverbank), or via **Remoulins** (a thirty-minute walk away), which is served by buses from Uzès and Nîmes. Those arriving by **car** can park in official spaces (€5 per day, or €8 for an annual pass) on either bank of the river, or for free in Remoulins, 3km from the site. **Tourist information** is provided at the ticket counter of the activity centre on the north bank (la rive gauche), where you'll find the closest parking. The centre also has a couple of fast-food outlets, though there's better dining on the far bank, at the pleasant **restaurant** *Cuisiners Vignerons* (*menu* from €15). For **canoe rental**, Kayak Vert on the south shore (℡04.66.22.80.76, ⓦwww.canoe-france.com), can arrange trips (including pick-up or drop-off) in either direction, the best being the downstream paddle from the Pont St-Nicholas, as well as renting out mountain **bikes**. If you're just going to splash around, keep your sandals on or buy some cheap plastic shoes to survive the pebbly bed of the Gardon; on the upriver side of the aqueduct there are places deep enough to dive in, but the river level varies considerably, so check carefully before taking the plunge. Conveniences such as **banks** and **supermarkets** can be found at Remoulins, where there's also a larger **tourist office** in place des Grands Jours (July & Aug Mon–Fri 9am–7pm, Sat & Sun 10am–1pm & 2–6pm; Sept–June Mon–Sat 9am–12.30pm & 2.30–6pm; ℡04.66.37.22.34, ⓦwww.ot-pontdugard.com).

Accommodation

The websites of the Uzès (ⓦwww.uzes-tourisme.com) and Remoulins (ⓦwww.ot-pontdugard.com) tourist offices are great for **accommodation**: the former has an excellent central reservation system which covers much of this area and the latter has many options for rural accommodation. The cheapest beds in the region around the Pont are at the Turions' three-room **gîte d'étape** (May–Sept; ℡06.86.90.44.84; ❶), near their farm in Vars, where they also have several well-appointed rooms (Easter–Oct; ℡04.66.37.16.25; ❸).

There are four **campsites** in the area, all with cabins or trailers for rent, though in high season, they get booked up very quickly. The *Gorges du Gardon* in Vers (mid-March to Oct; ℡04.66.22.81.81, ⓦwww.le-camping-international .com) is the cheapest campsite around, but *Le Barralet* in Collias (March to mid-Sept; ℡04.66.22.84.52, Ⓕ04.66.22.89.17) wins out on both location and value – located on the riverside, it is cheap and far from the maddening crowds. *La Sousta* on the south bank of the Gardon, right by the Pont (March–Oct; ℡04.66.37.12.80, Ⓔlasousta@aol.com) has the widest range of facilities, with the more expensive *La Soubeyranne* on the other side of Remoulins (late March to mid-Sept; ℡04.66.37.03.21, ⓦwww.soubeyranne.com).

L'Arceau 1 rue de l'Arceau, St-Hilaire
ⓣ04.66.37.34.45, ⓦwww.hotel-arceau.com. One
of the best value-for-money options, an eighteenth-
century home set in a picturesque hamlet 3km
from the aqueduct. Mid-Feb to late-Nov. ❹

🏃 **Bégude St-Pierre** CD 981, Vers
ⓣ04.66.63.63.63, ⓦwww.hotel
-saintpierre.fr. Excellent value, good location and
a swimming pool make this seventeenth-century
former post-house on the edge of Vers village a
first-rate option. ❻

Le Columbier avenue Pont du Gard, Remoulins
ⓣ04.66.37.05.28, ⓔhotelresto.columbier@free
.fr. The best of Remoulins' hotels: a mid-sized
establishment with good amenities and helpful
staff. ❸

Le Gardon Collias ⓣ04.66.22.80.54, ⓦwww
.hotel-le-gardon.fr. Another excellent mid-range
choice. An old farmhouse in a village just up-river
from Remoulins. Mid-March to mid-Oct. ❸

Hostellerie Le Castillas Grand' Rue, Collias
ⓣ04.66.22.88.88, ⓦwww.lecastellas.com. Three
luxuriously if idiosyncratically restored seventeenth-century houses are home to this small and
welcoming hotel. Closed Jan & Feb. ❼

Mas de Raffin, Chemin Mas de Raffin, Castillon
ⓣ04.66.37.13.28, ⓕ04.66.27.14.78. A good
mid-range option, this small but stately restored
five-roomed mansion sits on the outskirts of the
village and also boasts a swimming pool and has
English-speaking staff. ❺

🏃 **Le Moulin** av Pont-du-Gard, Castillon
ⓣ04.66.22.44.28, ⓦwww.lemoulinduroy
.net. Small but homey hotel set in an medieval mill
on the riverside. One of the best bargains close to
the aquaduct. ❸

🏃 **Le Vieux Castillon** Rue Turion Sabatier,
Castillon ⓣ04.66.37.61.61, ⓦwww
.vieuxcastillon.com. This gloriously restored rambling
country estate with a swimming pool provides pricey
top-end accommodation. Closed Jan–March. ❾

Eating

The most pleasant option for **eating** is to have a **picnic** on the banks of the
river. All the hotels listed above have restaurants, most with *terroir menus* in the
€15–30 price range – the most sophisticated are those at *Le Vieux Castillon*,
which features an eclectic *carte* (and *menus* from €29) and *Bégude St-Pierre* in
Vers (*menus* from €29), which features variations on local *terroir* themes (notable
for the predominance of beef) as well as the surrounding country's best selection of wines. Alternatively, *Le Clos de Vignes* in Castillon (closed Mon & Tues
lunch & mid-Jan to mid-Feb; ⓣ04.66.37.02.26) serves up good, inexpensive
local food on two pleasantly situated terraces (€16–25).

Beaucaire and around

BEAUCAIRE doesn't necessarily merit making a special effort to visit, but can
be a rewarding stop for those passing through. This is particularly worth considering if you have your own transport, as the interesting **Roman** and **medieval**
vestiges around the town are better reached by car, although **hiking** and **biking**
are possible as well. The best time to visit Beaucaire is during June's *Fête du Drac*,
a traditional festival in honour of the town's dragon mascot, marking the arrival
of summer and featuring parades and *tauromachie*, or July's *Estivales*, a medieval
pageant celebrating the town's once-famous fair. Located on the banks of the
Rhône and crossed by the Roman Via Domitia, Beaucaire is a town whose
success was grounded in its position as a crossroads, and as one of the region's
main gateways – Provençal Tarascon lies just across the river.

From the second century BC Beaucaire was a Roman wine entrepôt known
as Ugernum, but this disappeared along with the empire. Centuries later, the
town thrived under the patronage of the counts of Toulouse. During the Albigensian Crusade, de Montfort's forces seized the castle, and when Raymond VII
of Toulouse re-took the walled town in 1216, Simon's men would not let him
into the castle. So, aided by the townsfolk, Raymond laid siege to the castle from

within the town, while Simon, who had arrived in the meantime, encircled the town from without. Raymond prevailed in this strange double siege – a rare defeat for the fierce de Montfort – and the jubilant count granted the town the right to hold a yearly **trade fair** as a reward. Bringing merchants from all over Europe, the Middle East and North Africa, the market survived the town's transition to the French Crown in 1229 and continued to be held through the nineteenth century. Trade routes shifted, however, and by the time Richelieu ordered the castle torn down in 1632, Beaucaire was already a backwater.

Nowadays, the town presents a strange dichotomy. Although in summer, the tree-lined canal is alive with waterfront restaurants and the busy leisure of the boaters who ply the canals to Sète and Montpellier, the old town is a singularly decrepit area – a marginalized industrial neighbourhood which shows the stresses of high unemployment and unintegrated immigration. At night it takes on a fairly unpleasant aspect: dark and narrow streets and small deserted squares where care should be taken when walking; you should also avoid parking here.

The Town

The limits of Beaucaire are roughly defined by the Sète canal on the south, the Rhône river on the east, and the castle-topped hill which rises sharply on the north side. Walking from the canal, there are only one or two sights as you make your way across the old town towards the castle. Just north of the tourist office sits the town's most noteworthy building, the Neoclassical **Hôtel de Ville**. This fine seventeenth-century edifice has a colonnaded facade and window casements lavishly carved in floral motifs; inside, the courtyard (Mon–Fri 10am–noon & 2–5pm) is girded by slender columns and dominated by a monumental staircase. Unfortunately the *hôtel*'s beauty is diminished by its surroundings; the scruffy and inhospitable place Georges-Clémenceau. On the south side squats the small nineteenth-century metal-and-glass **market**, whose picturesque quality is offset by the decaying shop fronts and miserable-looking bars neighbouring it. Beaucaire's main **church**, Notre-Dame des Pommiers, lying two streets beyond, has a plain facade which hides a gaudy and unexceptional late Baroque marble interior. The church's real treasure is found on the building's exterior, which you will pass if you follow rue Charlier towards the castle – here, high up on the east wall, is the only remaining part of the original Romanesque structure: a remarkable low-relief frieze recounting scenes from the eve of the Crucifixion. Aside from these specific sights, you should also keep an eye out in Beaucaire for the seventeenth-century merchant's **mansions** which pop up en route to the castle, notably along rue de la République at the foot of the hill. The palace at no. 23, for example, has a strikingly elaborate facade, including caryatid columns on either side of the entrance. From the west end of rue de la République a stiff climb leads up the rise, dramatically crowned by the remains of the former keep.

Poised on a rocky promontory rising 35m above the Rhône, Beaucaire's **castle** provides dramatic views of the surrounding countryside and Tarascon's own castle. Fortunately, Richelieu did not manage to destroy the fortress completely, and the fourteenth-century **curtain wall** survives, as do several towers, including the striking **Tour Polygonale**, shooting dramatically skyward out of the living rock of the hill. The only way of visiting the castle ruins is to take in the entertaining medieval **falconry** display, "*Les Aigles*", with hourly live demonstrations (daily: late-March & Sept–Nov 2.30–4.30pm; April–June 2–4.30pm; July & Aug 3–6pm; closed Wed off-season; €9). The eighteenth-century listed **gardens** which fill the outer courtyard, however, can be visited free of charge (daily: April–Oct daily 10am–noon & 2.15–6.45pm; Nov–March 10.15am–noon &

2–5.15pm). Within the gardens, the municipal **Musée Auguste-Jacquet** (same hours; €3) houses several small collections of medieval bits and bobs, local rocks and paraphernalia relating to Beaucaire's annual fair. On Friday nights in summer the castle is the backdrop for the *son et lumière* "Raymond VII and the Siege of Beaucaire" (July & Aug daily at 10pm), which floods the castle buildings in garish colour while recounting the town's moment of medieval glory.

Practicalities

To get to Beaucaire by **train** you will arrive at Tarascon's **gare SNCF** (℡08.36.35.35.35) on boulevard Gustave-Desplaces, just across the Rhône. From here, you cross over the bridge, a ten-minute walk which brings you to the Rhône–Sète canal, or take a Nîmes-bound bus from the *Café de Fleurs* stop across from the station. Arriving by **bus** (information on ℡04.66.29.27.29), get off at *Passarelle* (the footbridge), which is the third stop coming from Nîmes, and the first from Tarascon. Those who come by **car** should avoid the more isolated public parking spaces; it's safest to park outside the tourist office or on the far side of the canal. Beaucaire's friendly **tourist office**, 24 cours de Gambetta (Mon–Fri 8.45am–12.15pm & 2–6pm, Sat 9.30am–12.30pm; Easter–Nov also Sat 3–6pm; July & Aug also Sun 9am–12.30pm; ℡04.66.59.26.57, ⓦwww.ot-beaucaire.fr) is on the north side of the canal, opposite the footbridge, and can provide information package excursions to the Camargue. At Beaucaire's pleasure port, you can **rent boats** ranging everything from pedal-boats to yachts: try Arolles Marine (℡04.66.01.75.15) or Connoisseurs Cruisers (℡04.66.59.46.08). You can also take **organized cruises** down the Rhône into the bird-rich delta of the Camargue: one of the best itineraries is to the bird sanctuary at Pont de Gau, off the Petit Rhône. Beaucaire has two **car rental** outlets: Avis, in the Total petrol station at 6 rue Général-de-Gaulle (℡04.66.59.29.89), and ADA, in the Le Mistral petrol station on route de Nîmes (℡04.66.59.37.77).

Accommodation

Beaucaire does not have a huge selection of **hotels**: the three-star *Doctrinaires*, (closed mid-Dec to mid-Jan; ℡04.66.59.23.70, ⓦwww.hoteldoctrinaires.com; ❸) in a seventeenth-century building on Quai Général de Gaulle overlooking the port, is the best for comfort, atmosphere and location. Alternatively, *Les Vignes Blanches*, at 67 av Farciennes on the western edge of town, about 1500m from the castle (℡04.66.59.13.12, ⓦwww.bestwestern.com; ❺), has excellent amenities and a pleasantly bucolic ambience. At the lower end of the scale, the basic *Napoléon*, at 4 place Frédéric Mistral (℡04.66.59.05.17; €50 per person, including compulsory half-board), reposes in the shadow of the *digue*, the massive flood dyke which protects the town from the Rhône. The 65-bed **HI hostel** is in Tarascon at 39 boulevard Gambetta (closed mid-Nov to Feb; ℡04.90.91.04.08, ⓦww.fuaj.org/aj/tarascon; dorm beds €8.40), a ten-minute walk north of the Tarascon train station. It has dining facilities, a washing machine, and an 11pm curfew. Those with transport should head 6km south of Beaucaire to the luxurious and relaxing *⚘Domaine des Clos* (℡04.66.01.14.61, ⓦwww.domaine-des-clos.com; ❹; English spoken), an eighteenth-century Provençal farm on the route de Bellegard.

Eating

Beaucaire's best-value **restaurant** is the *Auberge de l'Amadin* on Chemin de la Croix de Marbre (℡04.66.59.55.07; mid-April to Oct Tues–Sun lunch

Although not as famous as its sister to the west, the **Rhône–Sète canal** is an inland waterway which also offers great sightseeing and leisure possibilities, either on its own or combined with a trip along the Canal du Midi. Not only is the Rhône–Sète waterway less crowded than its more popular counterpart, the general evenness of the landscape means that there are no locks (on the main line) and fewer queues to contend with, even in high season. The various **subsidiary canals** also offer the opportunity to explore the backwaters of the Camargue in relative isolation.

The canal begins from the River Rhône at **Beaucaire**, heading southwest 11km through the flat Camarguaise wine-country past Bellegard. From here, a further 11km brings it to **St-Gilles**, where you can turn off on a secondary canal to **Vauvert**, a handy stop for supplies, particularly when its market is in full swing, on Wednesday and Friday mornings. Otherwise, if you keep on the main canal, after 30km of salty marshland, rich in birdlife, you'll pass the medieval **Tour Carbonnière**, which marks your arrival at **Aigues-Mortes**. From here, St Louis' thirteenth-century canal can be followed to **Le-Grau-du-Roi** and **Port-Camargue**.

Alternatively, from Aigues-Mortes follow the main canal west as it weaves its way past the Étang de Maugaio, before arriving at Carnon and **Palavas-les-Flots**, which provides a handy base for exploring **Montpellier**, and whose branch-canals lead inland to **Villeneuve-lès-Maguelone** and Lattes. Heading west, the canal threads a series of *étangs*, gliding past the ancient **cathedral** of Maguelone, before the Montaigne de la Guardiole rises to the north, and **Frontignan**, an ancient *circulade* with a **medieval church**, is reached. Finally the canal arrives at its terminus, Sète; from here you can continue into the broad expanse of the Bassin de Thau, skirting the oyster-beds, to visit its colourful fishing towns: Balaruc, **Mèze** and Marseillan. At the far end of this salt-water lagoon, an access canal leads 5km to **Agde**, from where the **Canal du Midi** can be accessed.

Boats can be rented at most of the ports of call along the canal (see the entry for each town in this guide), which also have sanitary facilities and fresh-water supplies. The local Capitainneries can also direct you to the nearest **bicycle** rental, handy for exploring the canalside towns.

only), with an €18 *menu*. For something more simple and central, several canalside bistros along quai de Gaulle have €8–14 *formules*, while the more formal *Doctrinaires* (closed Sat lunch) is as fancy as it gets here; service and atmosphere are good and there is a solid range of meat and fish options for up to €40.

Around Beaucaire

Four kilometres northwest of Beaucaire, off the Remoulins road just before the dam on the Rhône, lies the turn-off for the **underground monastery of St-Roman** (April–Sept daily 10am–6/6.30pm; Oct–March Sat & Sun 2–5pm; €5.50); to get there, follow the narrow road (no RVs) 3km to the monastery car park, then walk 500m to the site itself. This incredible complex, founded in the fifth century, is one of the oldest monasteries in France. Later covered over by a castle which was subsequently destroyed, the huge abbey was not redis-covered until 1966. The subterranean main chapel – built to house the sacred remains of St Roman – still contains the impressive carved seat from which the abbots presided over their community until the sixteenth century. Inside you'll also find small tombs carved in the floor, and set with recesses in which oil-lamps were placed in honour of the dead. This church, the monks' cells and other chambers were cut into the living rock of the hill in what must have been gruelling labour. The terrace of the monastery offers a sweeping panorama of the Rhône, with the hills of Provence easily visible in the distance.

Eight kilometres west of Beaucaire on the D38 (no public transport) is the recreated Roman winery of **Le Mas de Tourelles** (Easter–June & Sept daily 2–6pm; July & Aug Mon–Sat 10am–noon & 2–7pm, Sun 10am–noon; Oct–Easter Sat 2–6pm; €4.80). It's an entertaining stop, where you can watch toga-clad types making wine using first-century AD technology; you can taste the final result before drawing your own conclusions as to its Roman authenticity. From the vineyard it's a thirty-minute signposted walk north to a well-preserved eight-kilometre stretch of the **Via Domitia** that leads west from Beaucaire, and still boasts three Roman **milestones**; when you reach the road, turn right and you will arrive shortly at the milestones.

Finally, while visiting Beaucaire it would be a shame not to walk or drive across the bridge which spans the Rhône to visit the **castle** at **Tarascon** (April–Aug daily 9am–7pm; Sept–May Tues–Sun 10am–6pm; €6.50). This immaculately preserved fortress, rising majestically from the banks of the Rhône, provides a stunning contrast to the ruins of Beaucaire's fortress. The rectangular *enceinte* was constructed in the 1200s by the count of Provence to guard his western border; the present towers were raised in the following two centuries. It was here that the anonymous medieval poem (possibly a musical play), *Nicolette and Aucassin*, was written, recounting the tale of the star-crossed love affair between Aucassin, a fictional heir of Beaucaire, and Nicolette, a beautiful Muslim slave girl who had been bought by the viscount of Tarascon and raised as a Christian. Close by, the **church** of St Martha features a masterful Romanesque portal on the south side, and in the crypt you'll find a carved third- to fourth-century sarcophagus.

St-Gilles and around

Twenty-six kilometres southwest of Beaucaire and 20km south of Nîmes lies the former pilgrims' stop of **St-Gilles**, another town whose candle blew out in the late Middle Ages, and whose only present attraction is the magnificent and fortunately preserved facade of its former **abbey-church** (a UNESCO World Heritage monument). St-Gilles is also one of the gateways to the vast and swampy Petite Camargue (see p.249) which surrounds it on the eastern and southern sides; moving away from town, the stony ground becomes increasingly sandy and marshy, and vineyards give way to flower farms, rice paddies and bull and horse **ranches** (*manades*), as the Rhône spills out to sea. The band of flat grape-growing land which stretches west from the town to the River Vidourle is punctuated by nondescript hamlets; it is here, near the town of **Vauvert**, that the famous **Perrier spring** and bottling plant sits – a site of modern Gallic pilgrimage.

St-Gilles

Perched on the edge of the Camargue, quiet **ST-GILLES** – with its tiny, entirely residential old centre – is, like Beaucaire, a town rescued from complete oblivion only by its medieval monuments and the Rhône–Sète canal, each of which ensures a steady stream of passers-by in summer months.

The town takes its name from a legendary sixth-century hermit who converted the Visigothic king Wamba to Christianity. The ever-astute Cluniac monks promoted the cult of the saint in order to make the town (already on the Arles to Santiago de Compostela route) a lucrative stopping point early in the twelfth century. By this time it was a favourite of the counts of Toulouse, and the Crusader Raymond IV even preferred to be called "de St-Gilles". A good port and liberal market privileges further boosted prosperity and drew traders from around the Mediterranean, but within a few hundred years the unstoppable silt of the Rhône and the tide of the Reformation conspired to kill both the port and the pilgrim route. The **Wars of Religion** were especially bitter in St-Gilles – at one point a Protestant mob is said to have thrown the church's choristers down a well – and by the time the great abbey-church was virtually destroyed by Huguenot mobs in 1622, the town had already passed into history. Today the town's two principal roles have been revived: it has both a busy canalside **pleasure port** and the pilgrim route to Compostela, which lives on as the GR653, coming into town from Arles and heading on west through the flat vineyards to Vauvert (see p.244) and on to Montpellier. The biggest festivities in St-Gilles take place in mid-August, with the *Feria de la Pêche et de l'Abricot* ("The Peach and Apricot Festival") featuring *abrivados*, *encierros* and full-blown *corridas*.

The Town

The only part of St-Gilles which is likely to interest you is the **old town**, which lies on the eastern side of rue Gambetta, the main Arles–Montpellier road. Rue Gambetta ends at the tourist office, opposite which an arched passageway leads into the rue Porte des Marchaux, which takes you into the old centre and up to the **abbey-church**; as you round the last bend in the street and enter the compact place de la République, you'll be greeted by the stunning sight of its broad facade.

Although the Religious Wars destroyed almost all the church, fate spared the most interesting work of medieval art of the region: the great twelfth-century Romanesque **frieze** of the church's west entrance. Spreading between and over the three great doorways (reminiscent of a Roman triumphal arch), a series of bas-reliefs convey the story of Jesus' return to Jerusalem and subsequent Crucifixion, representations of the Apostles, the three Marys and St Paul, and scenes based on the Old Testament and medieval iconography. These carvings are of superlative workmanship, a unique blend of Byzantine, Classical and medieval stylings setting them apart from the mass of contemporary work: they're best viewed (and photographed) in the afternoon, when the sunlight plays across the carvings. Aside from this entrance, two other interesting remains of the medieval church can be seen: the **choir** and the **crypt** (April–Oct Mon–Sat 9am–12.30pm & 2/3–6/7pm; Nov–March Mon–Fri 8.30am–noon & 1.30–5.30pm, Sat 9/10am–noon/1pm; guided visit €4). Located behind the modern building, the ruins of the former choir hint at the grandeur of the medieval church. On the north side lies the *vis* ("screw"), a twelfth-century stone **spiral staircase** which once climbed to the church's upper gallery: an architectural marvel – a massive self-supporting key-stone stairway – it was, like the Pont du Gard, a mandatory stop on the traditional masons' tour of the country. From a gate on the south side of the church entrance, you can enter the massive vaulted eleventh-century crypt, which contains the **tombs** of St-Gilles and Pierre de Castelnau, and which is where services for the crowds of passing pilgrims were also held.

Opposite the church sits the **Maison Romane**, a restored medieval house in which it is claimed Gui Folques, who became Pope Clement IV in 1265, was born; it now houses a municipal **museum** of slight interest (Mon–Sat: July & Aug 9am–noon & 3–7pm; June & Sept 9am–noon & 2–6pm; Oct–Dec & Feb–May 9am–noon & 2–5pm; free), mostly full of chunks of carved stone salvaged from the wrecked abbey-church as well as a dusty exhibition of stuffed

The Chemin de St-Jacques

The pilgrimage route to Santiago de Compostela (known in Spain as the "Camino de Santiago") was Languedoc's and Europe's first grand tourism venture (and inspired the first European guidebooks). It all started in the ninth century when a priest at Iria Flavia in northwestern Spain miraculously discovered the burial site of **St James the Greater**, the Apostle, in a local cemetery. The remains were shifted to a nearby hamlet, which was subsequently renamed as **Santiago** (St James) de Compostela (traditionally attributed to the "field of stars" which signalled the saint's resting place, but actually derived from the Latin for "little burial ground"). The tomb became a rallying point for the Christians of northern Spain, who lived under the shadow of the Muslim Caliphate of Cordoba. But it was in the late eleventh century that things really got going. By this time the Catholic Church had introduced pilgrimage as a way of doing penance for sins, and although Rome, the home of the papacy, was the most prestigious site, it was soon exceeded in popularity by Santiago. Pilgrimage became popular with common folk and nobles alike, who saw it as a way to travel, see the world and escape the mundanities of daily existence, as well as a way to score points for salvation of the soul. The volume of travellers brought wealth and prosperity not only to Santiago, but to the churches and monasteries along the route which, like **St-Sernin** in Toulouse (p.81), **St-Guilhem** in Hérault (p.295) and **St-Gilles** in Gard, made showcases of their own relics to attract the faithful on the way. Other notable stops on the pilgrim route include **Vals** in the Aude (p.145), **St-Lizier** in Ariège (p.153), **Rabastens** in the Tarn (p.186), **Joncels** (p.334), **Murat** (p.196) and **La-Salvetat** (p.200) in Haut Languedoc, and **Clermont l'Hérault** (p.288) and **Santa María Vilar** in Roussillon (p.381). Today, hikers continue to follow the pilgrimage route, designated a UNESCO World Heritage site in 1998, and a fascinating window into a world long past.

birds. Before leaving St-Gilles, it is well worth wandering around the narrow lanes and arch-covered streets of the old town – many of the tiny houses here retain their medieval details and it won't take long for you to discover small doors set in slowly sagging walls, and half-open windows revealing pastel-toned plaster walls and ceiling beams within.

Practicalities

St-Gilles' **gare routière** (℡04.66.87.31.32), 100m south of the tourist office and just north of the canal, is a fifteen-minute walk northeast of the centre. Arriving by **car**, park in the free municipal car park on the west side of the old town, just off rue Gambetta. You'll find the **tourist office** at place Frédéric Mistral (daily 8.30am–noon & 2–5.30pm; ℡04.66.87.33.75 @www.ot-saint-gilles.fr), at the northern end of rue Gambetta. The town's **hotels** all lie within a few minutes' walk of the *gare routière* and the canal. The best budget option is the *Ste-Gillois* at 1 rue Neuve (℡04.66.87.33.69, ℻04.66.28.99.57; ❷), which also offers good-value half-board. For better amenities, try *Le Cours*, 10 allée Griffeuille (closed mid-Dec to Feb; ℡04.66.87.31.93, @www.hotel-le-cours.com; ❸), or the three-star *Heraclée*, 30 Quai du Canal (℡04.66.87.44.10, @www.hotel-heraclee.com; ❸). The **campsite**, *Chicanettes* (mid-April to Sept; ℡04.66.87.28.32, @camping .la.chicanette@libertysurf.fr) is in town, just behind the public car park.

St-Gilles offers a number of unremarkable but adequate *terroir* **restaurants** and pizzerias around the canal port, while *Le Cours* serves up well-executed and imaginative cuisine in its recently renovated dining room for around €10–28 the local speciality is *taureau* (beef) *à la gardianne*. The local **market** is held on Thursday and Sunday mornings in avenue Emil-Cazelles.

Around St-Gilles

Although Aigues-Mortes is better situated for exploring the **Petite Camargue**, St-Gilles can also serve as a jumping-off point to the region by either boat or on horseback. The portion of the delta near St-Gilles is far from the coast, and comparatively dry and uniform: an expanse of salt marshes, with a bull or horse farm set wherever the land rises far enough above the water table. Several of the horse farms near St-Gilles offer half- and full-day **horseback** and **carriage tours** around their land, the cheapest of which is Manade Lebret (℡04.66.87.22.04), some 10km from St-Gilles (east on the N572 to the D37, and then south). Whether you approve of the *corrida* or not, a visit to a bull farm (or *manade*) is an interesting experience – a chance to see the traditional lifestyle of the ranches of the delta, and witness the impressive equestrian skills of the *gardians* ("cowboys") who manage the herds. The tourist office in St-Gilles has a list of the twenty or so ranches in the area and can indicate which have English-speaking guides and which charge admission to visitors. Crown Blue Line (℡04.66.87.22.66, ⓦwww.crownblueline.com) in St-Gilles **rents boats**, while L'Isle de Stel (℡06.80.83.82.01) runs organized **cruises** on various itineraries along the network of canals and the Petit Rhône.

The flat band of plain between St-Gilles and the Vidourle river 20km to the west comprises a sort of transition zone between the salty swamps to the south and the rocky hills around Nîmes. A shadeless countryside of vineyards and indistinguishable hamlets, it is, however, home to one of France's proudest commercial institutions, the **Perrier spring and bottling plant**, located a few minutes' drive north of **Vauvert**, just before you reach the village of Vergèze. The source of France's second most famous bubbly stuff, the much-advertised **spring** (Feb–June & Sept–Dec Mon–Fri 9.30–10.30am & 1–4pm, Sat & Sun 1.30–5pm; July & Aug Mon–Fri 9.30–10.30am & 1–6pm, Sat & Sun 10–10.30am & 1–6.30pm; €8) is a site venerated by the Gallic hordes who arrive daily, blissfully shelling out for the two-hour **tour**, sharing vicariously in the glory of the water which has come to signify France abroad. The spring was known in Roman times, but subsequently languished in obscurity until 1894, when a certain Dr Perrier of Nîmes bought the property and set up the Perrier Spring Company in partnership with a young, disabled English aristocrat, who came up with the distinctive shape for the bottle inspired by the dumbbells he used for his physiotherapy. The **guided tour** includes a walk through the vast and modern bottling complex, a visit to the spring itself and ends at the former owner's mansion, this last now the Perrier "museum" – a thinly disguised shop where you can pay ridiculously high prices for various bits of merchandising. Judging by the guest-book, the tour is a big domestic hit, but non-French – unless they are avid spring-water enthusiasts – are likely to regard the experience as time and money misspent.

About halfway to the Perrier plant from Vauvert, you'll see the turrets of **Château du Candiac**, on the riverbank off the right-hand side of the D56. This is the birthplace of the Marquis of Montcalm (1712–59), who unsuccessfully defended Québec against the English general James Wolfe. Montcalm could not save the French colony from the invaders, and both he and his adversary died in the battle fought on the Plains of Abraham outside the city.

The Camarguaise coast

Lying 35km south of Nîmes, set amidst the flat swampy land of the westernmost reaches of the Rhône delta, sits **Aigues-Mortes**, its perfectly intact rectangular walls rising out of the plain like a storybook image of a medieval town. An ancient canal leads southwest to **Le Grau-du-Roi**, once a humble fishing town, now a teeming **summer resort**, exploiting the great unbroken band of dunes which stretches along the coast from the town's eastern limits all the way to the mouth of the Petit Rhône. **Port-Camargue**, a modern adjunct to Le Grau, is a purpose-built yachting complex – the biggest pleasure port on the whole of the Mediterranean. Heading east from Aigues-Mortes, you penetrate the heart of the **Petite Camargue**, the western portion of the Rhône delta, a ten-thousand hectare band of inhospitable terrain which forms a temporary home to a wide variety of migrating birds and, along the coast, crowds of summer-time sunbathers. Driving, cycling or horse-riding is the best way to explore the hinterland of the Carmargue.

Aigues-Mortes

Originally intended to be France's principal Mediterranean port, **AIGUES-MORTES** was swallowed up in short order by the silt of the Rhône, which pushed the sea south and consigned the town to stagnation among the "dead waters" surrounding it. Founded by Louis IX in 1246, it was from here that the saint-king embarked on two of his expeditions: to Cyprus on the Seventh Crusade of 1248, and to Tunis in 1270, where he met his death. His son, Philip, gave the medieval town its present form – commissioning Genoan engineers to build walls in emulation of those of Damietta in Egypt, the site of Louis' early (but Pyrrhic) triumph. Local salt beds and trade privileges brought initial success, but by the end of the fourteenth century it had become a backwater, stranded by the waves of silt brought downriver by the Rhône. Aigues-Mortes' misfortune, however, has preserved the town's striking profile, which may have otherwise been built over and around. Today it is a mandatory photo-stop, and a tour of the **fortifications** and the grid of thirteenth-century streets is a pleasant

△ Aigues-Mortes

way to pass an hour or so, combining well with a trip to the **beaches** to the south. If you have the fortune to visit during a festival, try to catch a bit of the *course Camarguaise*; watching the crowds and the bulls beneath the medieval ramparts is a truly evocative sight.

Arrival and accommodation

The **gare SNCF** (℡04.66.53.74.74), on the spur line which runs down from Nîmes to Le Grau-du-Roi, is on the route de Nîmes, about 100m north of the old town, while **buses** stop on avenue de la Liberté, across the canal from the *gare*. From either of these head south towards the massive Tour de Constance (see below) on the northwest corner of the old town. Drivers are directed by a signal system to free spaces in the **car park** along the east wall of the town. The **tourist office** (June & early-Sept Mon–Fri 9am–6/7pm, Sat & Sun 10am–noon & 2–6/7pm; July & Aug Mon–Fri 9am–8pm, Sat & Sun 10am–8pm; mid-Sept to May Mon–Fri 9am–noon & 1–6pm, Sat & Sun 10am–noon & 2–6pm; ℡ & ℻04.66.53.73.00, ⓦwww.ot-aiguesmortes.fr) is just inside the Porte de la Gardette, one of the old town's five monumental gates, east of the Tour de Constance on the north wall. **Bikes** can be rented from Découvrir Aigues-Mortes, at 14 rue Théaulon (℡06.15.37.88.45), and there's **Internet** access at Sarah Phone, 5bis, avenue de la Liberté.

There are a number of **hotels** in and around Aigues-Mortes, though they get booked up early in high season, and room prices are relatively high and don't offer great value for money – hotels in Le Grau, only 8km away, tend to be more reasonable. *L'Escale*, right by the Tour de Constance, (℡04.66.53.71.14, ⓦwww.hotel.escale.free.fr; ❷), is the best deal, with a traditional homely atmosphere, as well as a good restaurant. Just outside the old-town walls, the *Tour de Constance*, at 1 boulevard Diderot (closed Nov–March; ℡04.66.53.83.50, ℻04.66.77.36.02; ❷), lacks ambience, but is economical and has larger rooms for families and groups. More expensive but with more amenities (TV and air conditioning), *Le Victoria* (℡04.66.51.14.20, Ⓔlevictoria@wanadoo.fr; ❸) is on the same square as the tourist office. Moving upscale, *Les Arcades*, 23 boulevard Gambetta (℡04.66.53.81.13, ⓦwww.les-arcades.fr; ❺), is a small, tastefully-appointed hotel in a beautiful old building; the rooms are not huge, but the service is attentive. The **campsite**, *Fleur de Camargue* (late April to late Sept; ℡04.66.88.15.42, ⓦwww.fleur-de-camargue.com) is a four-star super-site, a massive complex with a café-bar, laundry facilities and a gamut of other services, located 3km west of town.

The Town

Aigues-Mortes' **old town**, where the sights, hotels and restaurants are concentrated, is laid out on a rectangular grid, girded by stout walls. It is well maintained, but its success as a day-trip and weekend destination has cluttered the streets with photo-developing shops and souvenir boutiques, the regular street pattern adding to an air of artificiality and tweeness. Henry James's observation of a hundred years ago is equally valid today: Aigues-Mortes, he wrote, "can hardly be said to be alive; but it has been very neatly embalmed".

On the far side of the open *place* where the tourist office sits, looms the massive **Tour de Constance** (daily: May–Aug 10am–7pm; Sept–April 10am–5pm; €6.50), the main fortress of the town – once a lighthouse and for many years a prison for uncooperative nobles and stalwart Huguenots. Protestant women were confined in the cells on the top floor, including the stoic Marie Durand, who spent almost forty years here in the eighteenth century, and whose graffiti remain etched in the stone to this day. It is also through the tower that you access the walk along the **town walls**, which provides sweeping views over the flat terrain of the delta and allows a close-up look at the city's defences: arrow-slitted battlements, and stone ducts for pouring boiling oil on would-be attackers. Those on a budget, however, should skip this steeply priced visit; a pleasant (and free) option is to walk across town from the Porte de la Gardette and take in the walls from the fields to the south. Looking back at the town from here, the tower which you see on the far left is "**the tower of the salted Burgundians**", the curious nickname dating back to a grisly episode of the Hundred Years' War. When the town was seized in a raid by English-allied Burgundian forces in 1418, royalist Armagnacs came to try to retake the town. They were foiled by the strong fortifications, but one night a local citizen opened one of the smaller gates to let their forces in. Sneaking up on the sleeping Burgundian garrison, the Armagnacs slaughtered them before they knew what was happening, but rather than bury the bodies (no easy task in the fetid marshes surrounding the town), the victorious forces stuffed them into this tower, and layered them with salt so they would not putrefy – leaving them, literally, in a pickle. Other sites in town include the melodramatic **Musée de la Torture** at 3 rue République (July & Aug daily 10am–7pm; Sept–June Fri–Sun 10am–7pm; €7), and the fossil collection of **Musée Paleo Passion** at 33 rue Jamais (mid-June to mid-Sept daily 2–6pm; free). Otherwise, the country **market**, held on Wednesday and Sunday mornings on the broad esplanade of avenue Frédéric-Mistral (75m north of the town walls), sells excellent produce and prepared dishes, and you could do much worse than buy a **picnic** and enjoy it with a bottle of the local *vin de sable*, "sand wine", on the grassy verge by the ramparts.

Eating and drinking

On the **restaurant** front the old town fares quite respectably, with the culinary champion being the highly-praised *Café de Bouzigues* at 7 rue Pasteur (☎04.66.53.93.95), where you can enjoy plentiful, elaborate *menus* on the cosy interior patio or in the comfortable dining room (about €14 at lunch). Many establishments specialize in seafood, mostly in the €14–25 range, including *La Citadelle*, 10 place St-Louis (☎04.66.53.86.68), while *Le Galion*, 24 rue Pasteur (☎04.66.53.86.41), with its unique stone-cooked dishes, is a solid, reasonably-priced option. Though rather touristy, *La Camargue* at 19 rue République (☎04.66.53.86.88), is good fun, with a performance by local "gypsies" each evening, and decent *terroir* food (€32).

Le Grau-du-Roi and Port Camargue

LE GRAU-DU-ROI and its sister **PORT CAMARGUE** comprise, between them, a bustling contrast to Aigues-Mortes. Like its fortress neighbour, Port Camargue is also a purpose-built port complex, but one dedicated to pacific hedonism rather than violent idealism. Le Grau (Occitan for "sand bar") has been a fishing village since the time of Henri IV in the sixteenth century, but it was only with the building of Port Camargue in 1969 that prosperity finally arrived. Now summer months fill the town with boaters from around the world, and sun-worshippers from France and abroad who seek out the duned expanses stretching off towards the mouth of the Rhône in the east. If on one hand the town resembles a package-tour nightmare, on the other, there's no shortage of bars, cheap food and beachside fun. Off season, of course, it's another story entirely; things wind down quickly and, as happens in so many seaside towns, a certain air of cold desolation sets in.

Basically, the only reason to stay in Le Grau or Port Camargue is the beach. West of the mouth of the canal which passes through Le Grau's centre, a narrow band of sand, hemmed in closely by road, leads 5km west to La Grande-Motte (see p.273), whose curious triangle-shaped buildings can easily be made out on a clear day. This is the most accessible swimming area, but the best **beaches** are east of town, once you pass the busy little bay between Le Grau and Port Camargue. Just beyond Pointe de l'Espiguette, the spur of land jutting westwards on the south edge of Port Camargue, is where the real beach starts – an uninter-rupted swathe of dunes stretching 5km east to the lighthouse and from there towards the horizon. Naturally the busiest area is around the **lighthouse** itself, which can be accessed by road from Le Grau, and where you will be charged a €4.50 fee to park. The further east you go, the more the crowds thin out, and the more laid-back beach etiquette becomes. **Nudists** have staked their claim on one stretch of beach to the east of the lighthouse, and if you are prepared to go far enough away you can find seclusion even at the busiest time of year. The main attraction here aside from the seaside is the **Seaquarium** (daily: May, June & Sept 10am–8pm; July & Aug 10am–midnight; Oct–April 10am–7pm; €9.80), one of the biggest indoor aquariums in Europe, located in the Palais de la Mer between the two towns. The fairly steep admission price also gives access to the **Musée de la Mer** ("The Sea Museum") in the same building, which features exhibits on local marine life and nautical history.

Le Grau and Port Camargue have facilities for a wide range of **water sports**, including outfits which rent sail-boards, sailing boats, kayaks and jet-skis, many offering instruction (see below), as well as waterborne jousting competitions during the *fêtes* of mid-June and September. For children, there are no fewer than three **water parks** around the towns. Le Grau/Port Camargue is also a big centre for **bull**-related activities, including a series of *courses* (held every week-end from the end of March to September), the climax of which is the *Trophée de As* competition in mid-August, and *corridas* held throughout July and August.

Practicalities

Both **buses** and **trains** approach the town along the narrow sand spit lead-ing from Aigues-Mortes and deposit passengers more or less smack in the middle of Le Grau, at the small **gare SNCF** (℡04.66.51.40.93), just off the canal on the east side. The large and efficient **tourist office**, 30 rue Rédarès (daily: May & Sept 9am–7pm; June–Aug 9am–9pm; Oct–April 9am–12.15pm & 2–6pm; ℡04.66.51.67.79, ⓦwww.ville-legrauduroi.fr), is on the east side of Le Grau, five streets south of the train station. Vélo Évasion, 1291 rue de Camargue (℡04.66.51.48.65), and Loca Loisirs, avenue Jean Lasserre (℡04.66.53.45.12), both rent **bicycles,** while for **watersports** head to Surf Loisirs on boulevard Front de Mer (℡04.66.52.40.01) or Société Nautique on quai d'Escale (℡04.66.53.29.47). **Diving** can be organized by Espace Mer (℡04.66.51.75.25) in the Nouveau Port de pêche. The tourist office has a full list of places that rent out **canal boats**, or contact A2M, at 1 rue Esprit Fabre (℡04.66.51.42.54, ⓔa2mglad@wanadoo.fr).

Accommodation

The dozen or so **hotels** in Le Grau and Port Camargue range from smaller and more attractive establishments in the old town to larger beachside places. Surpris-ingly, prices tend to be fairly reasonable. In the **old town**, the least expensive choices are the *Splendid* on boulevard Front de Mer (℡04.66.51.41.29, ⓦwww .splendidcamargue.com; ❸), and the basic *L'Étoiles*, 119 avenue de Camargue (℡ & ⓕ04.66.51.41.31; ❸). The best of the smaller, old town hotels is the

Bellevue et d'Angleterre, Quai Colbert (closed Jan; T04.66.51.40.75, Wwww
.hotelbellevueetdangleterre.com; ❸) a pleasant, airy and clean place with good
views. In **Port Camargue** hotels tend to be more expensive, but with more
facilities. *Le Spinaker*, pointe de la Presqu'île (March–Oct; T04.66.53.24.91,
Wwww.spinaker.com; ❼) is cosy and discreetly set in a green patch in the
midst of the port, while *Oustau Camarguen*, 3 route des Marines (March–Nov;
T04.66.51.51.65, Wwww.oustaucamarguen.com; ❻) is larger but has a more
authentically maritime feel. **Campsites** abound, with three set conveniently
on route de l'Espiguette between Le Grau and Port Camargue, all with
excellent facilities: *L'Espiguette* (mid-March to early Nov; T04.66.51.44.00,
Wwww.campingespiguette.fr) and *du Soleil* (March–Oct; T04.66.51.50.07,
Wwww.campingdusoleil.fr) are both two-star, while *L'Eden*, (April–Oct;
T04.66.51.49.81, Wwww.campingleden.fr) is a four-star, 400-pitch monster-
site, which also rents out chalets.

Eating

Eating in Le Grau and Port Camargue means **seafood**, and on every corner
there is a restaurant serving up bouillabaisse, *moules frites*, *coquillages* and fish.
Competition means prices are good, even if the product is often indistinguishable – most establishments have *menus* in the €12–24 range. The bargain places
are *Le Pistou* on rue de la Rotonde and *Le Provençal*, 45 rue des Combattants,
both serving lunch from €9.50. At the other end of the scale, *Le Spinaker*'s
restaurant is the best eatery in the area, with *menus* priced accordingly (€59–
81). Of the towns' many **bars**, the only one which stands out from the crowd is
Leon, at 2 avenue de la Gare, the home turf of the local bullfighting aficionados
association. **Markets** are held every morning (except Sunday) either at place de
la République or Boucanet on the far bank of the grau.

The Petite Camargue

The **PETITE CAMARGUE**, which Lawrence Durrell called "Little Argentina", stretches east from Le Grau and Aigues-Mortes, an inhospitable expanse
of marshes, crisscrossed by canals, and dominated by great saltwater *étangs*
("lagoons"). This is a lightly populated and unwelcoming area, with no villages
to speak of, only isolated ranches, rice farms and salt works. It is temporary
home, however, to an incredible variety of **waterfowl** – some four-hundred
different species – including a steady stream of migrating birds crossing the
Mediterranean between Europe and Africa; look out especially for pink flamin-
gos, herons, grand cormorants and egrets. The delta is also where Gard's strong
traditions of horsemanship and *tauromachie* originate, on the great ranches
where wild bulls are left to graze the salty scrub freely. The *gardians*, whose
simple huts dot the plain, have been the proud masters of the delta since at least
1512, when they established a formal confraternity. Riding their distinctively
small "Camargue" ponies they pursue and corral the black bulls, rounding them
up for branding in the springtime *ferrade*. The Camargue proper, which lies in
Provence, has been incorporated since 1970 into a national park, but there is no
visible characteristic which distinguishes the official parkland from the section
of the delta near Aigues-Mortes and Le Grau.

Heading east from Aigues-Mortes into the Petite Camargue you pass the
curious **Tour Carbonnière** on the left. Once the guard-post on the only land
access to the medieval port-town, this twenty-metre-high tower, perched on a
rare mound of *terra firma* and pierced by a gate through which the road once
led, is now a popular place for a picnic. Penetrating the heart of the area, the

road rolls by a flat, unchanging landscape until you reach the bridge over the Petit Rhône. Heading in the other direction from Aigues-Mortes down to Le Grau you'll see the salt pans of the **Salins du Midi** to the south, which can be visited by *petit train* (1hr 15min; €7.10) or bus (2hr 15min; €10.30), with a guide explaining their history and the techniques of salt harvesting. The train is booked at the tourist office in Aigues-Mortes (see p.246), but check in advance if you need an English-speaking guide. Just beyond the salt works are the **Caves de Listel**, a wine *domaine* where locally produced "sand wine" can by sampled and purchased. On the far side of Le Grau, on the way to the lighthouse, you'll pass the **bird observatory**, a discreet cabin overlooking one of the shallow, salty *étangs*; early morning and evening in summer are the best times to look.

If you are exploring the Petite Camargue with your own vehicle, don't be tempted onto the unpaved roads and lanes leading out through the fields – quite often they are deceptively soft and you may find yourself walking back to civilization. The best ways to visit the more remote areas are on an organized one-day safari or boat tour: Le Gitan in Le Grau (☏04.66.52.04.99, ✉legitansafari@libertysurf.fr) runs **four-wheel drive** expeditions; Isle de Stel in Aigues-Mortes (April–Oct; ☏04.66.47.52.69) offers a half-day **boat** tour of the nearby *étangs* and canals; while Cabane de Boucanet in Port Camargue (☏04.66.53.25.64), organizes **horseback** rides of the area.

The Vidourle valley

West of Nîmes, the border of Gard is marked by the **Vidourle valley**, which begins as a trickle on the southern edge of the Cévennes mountains at the northwest of the *département*. This is a quiet corner of Gard, relatively unexplored, and on the whole the villages here, some of which are impressively ancient, lack both the sights and amenities to draw travellers. Notable exceptions though are **Sommières**, where the breadth of the river is still spanned by a Roman bridge and watched over by the richly preserved castle of Villevieille; **Sauve**, an ancient hamlet which makes a convenient stopping-point en route from Nîmes to Ganges; and, further on, at the edge of the *département*, just 15km from Ganges to the west, **St-Hippolyte-du-Fort**.

Sommières

SOMMIÈRES, the largest town along the Vidourle, lying halfway between Nîmes and Montpellier, is one point on the way west from Nîmes which definitely merits a stop. Its easy, unspoilt charm seduced the English author Laurence Durrell into spending the last 33 years of his life here, and prompted him to remark, in *Spirit of Place*, that he had seen "nothing prettier". Walking through the old town or along the riverbank it's hard not to sympathize with Durrell's judgement – Sommières remains a peaceful, idyllic village. Strongly Protestant, it was all but destroyed during the Wars of Religion as it repeatedly changed hands before being conquered personally by Louis XIII in 1622. Today Sommières makes a pleasant stop for a bite to eat and a wander around, and those looking for a few days of quiet relaxation could fare a lot worse than to spend some time here, away from the crowded beaches of Le Grau and the busy streets of Nîmes. April through to September is the season for *courses camarguaises*, held on Sunday afternoons.

The **Roman bridge** which spans the river remains an integral feature of Sommières, uniting the newer town on the west bank with the old town on the east. Something of a curiosity, it was built in the first century and originally consisted of seventeen arches, but half a dozen have been gradually covered over by the encroaching town. A testament to Roman engineering, it continued to carry all of the car and truck traffic passing through the town up until the recent opening of a new bypass. At the bridge's western end the walled old town is entered by passing through the **tour de l'horloge**, home to a ponderous seventeenth-century clock. From here you can descend to the left to the **bas marché** (lower market), now the place des Docteurs M. et G. Dax, or proceed along the course of the old Roman road to the **haut marché** (upper market), the place Jean-Jaurès – both arcaded squares still serve as market places for local farmers. From the upper market, an alley leads to the steep stairs at the foot of the town's **castle**. Not much remains of this fortress, built in the tenth century and all but destroyed by Catholic forces in 1573, but you can climb to the top of the square **tower** (July & Aug daily 4–7pm; €2) for a dramatic panorama of the Vidourle plain. Aside from the confines of the old *enceinte*, the quai Griolet, between the town walls and the riverbank, makes for a particularly evocative stroll downriver, with the geese which mill about the small dam honking emphatically at each other and passers-by.

Practicalities

Buses arriving in Sommières drop passengers off at the place de la République, along the northern wall of the old town. The **tourist office** (Mon–Sat 9am–12.30pm & 2–6/7pm; July & Aug also Sun 9.30am–12.30pm & 2–5pm; ℡46.68.80.99.30, ⓦww.ot-sommieres.fr), on rue du Général-Bruyère, just west of the Place de la République, distributes a pamphlet detailing local walking routes. The best **hotel** in Sommières is the ⚜ *L'Estelou* (℡04.66.77.71.08, ⓦhoteldelestelou.free.fr; ❸), an arty hotel set in the town's old *gare*, with a swimming pool, and good service. Other good choices are the **chambres d'hôtes**, *l'Orangerie* (℡04.66.77.79.94; ❹), a seventeenth-century mansion tucked away in rue de Baumes in the shadow of the castle; Colette Labbe's *La Mas Fontclaire*, 8 avenue Émile Jamais (℡&ⓕ04.66.77.78.69; ❹), with a pool set in a verdant garden (meals from €16); and Billy Gérard's cosy **gîte**, *Le Parvis* at 8 rue Docteur Chrestien (℡04.66.80.35.66; ❸). The **campsite** (Easter–Sept; ℡04.66.80.33.49) is on rue Eugène Rouché, on the west bank of the Vidourle, heading north out of town.

L'Olivette, 11 rue Abbé Fabre (closed Tues eve & Wed; ℡04.66.80.97.71), is the best **restaurant** in the area serving exciting regional cuisine, with *menus* from €25. For good quality, simple *terroir* fare, try *Le Bodegón* at 9 place du Marché (Sept–June closed Mon–Fri eve; ℡04.66.80.09.55), where you can eat for around €15. On Saturday morning a **market** is held in place du Marché.

Around Sommières: the Château de Villevieille

Perched on the rise which dominates the old town of Sommières, the **Château de Villevieille** (May & June daily 2–7pm; July–Sept daily 2–8pm; Oct–April school hols only 2–7pm; €7) is in Villevieille, a beautiful little hamlet of stone-built houses. Owned by the same family for some 750 years, it is one of the few noble castles to escape appropriation or destruction during the Revolution (due to the lord's friendship with Voltaire and Condorcet, who interceded on his behalf). Today it boasts a sumptuous interior; the furnishings, including sixteenth-century Flemish leather "wallpaper" and the first mirror in France are classed as national monuments, plus the beds in which three kings of France and Cardinal Richelieu slept are still in their respective rooms. One of the best things about the visit is that you're shown around by members of the family – an unassuming, friendly bunch who are disarmingly frank, and genuinely welcoming. Next door, the restaurant Les 4 Vents (℗04.66.77.79.66) has home-cooked *menus* (€18–29) and **chambres d'hôtes** (❸).

The best of the **local walks** (detailed in tourist office's brochure) is an excursion to the twelfth-century **church of St-Julien**, 5km north of Sommières along the right bank of the Vidourle (the turn-off is marked on the left after 3km). It makes a good stop for a picnic, though the church itself is usually closed: if you want to look inside, check first at Sommières tourist office. The villages of the *garrigues* stretching north from Sommières do not contain any sights of particular interest, but the relative tranquillity of the highways makes for very pleasant **cycling**.

Sauve

The first town of any interest on the road from Nîmes to Ganges is **SAUVE**, 40km to the west of the capital of Gard and 20km upriver from Sommières. It's a quiet little town, once fortified and still presided over by the castle which was centuries ago the summer retreat of the bishops of Maguelone, and although there are no specific monuments, it is a particularly good example of a typical medieval-era town of northern Gard. The **old town** is a maze of twisting alleys, some of which are covered, and the **view** from the other side of the bridge over the Vidourle is inspiring. In recent years it has been revived due to an influx of cosmopolitan urban refugees who have opened up some interesting, ethnic restaurants and cafés, and organize an annual African music festival in mid-July.

Sauve's only **bus** link is with Nîmes and Ganges: the stop is just off the main road, at the edge of the town. The small seasonal **tourist office** is in place René Isouard (July & Aug Mon–Fri 10am–noon & 2–6pm; ℗04.66.77.57.51). There's a very comfortable **hotel** ⚜ *La Magnanerie* (℗04.66.77.57.44, ⓦwww .lamagnanerie.fr; ❸) in town, and an agreeable **gîte**, *La Pausamanque*, 2km east of town on the Nîmes road (℗04.66.77.51.97, ⓦwww.lapousaranque .com; English spoken; ❷), with a restaurant (from €11). There are two good **restaurants** in town: *Le Micocoulier*, at 3 place Jean-Astruc, (mid-April to Sept Thurs–Sun dinner only; ℗04.66.77.57.61; *menu* €17) a cosy little *auberge* serving up intriguing un-French food and lavish desserts, and Anne Tourneux's *Villa Eugénie*, route de Villesèque (closed Dec–March; ℗04.66.77.05.22), which provides excellent dinners and lunches (about €30) in a garden setting. Finally, you can stock up on your own supplies at Sauve's country **market**, held on Thursdays and Saturdays in the town centre.

St-Hippolyte-du-Fort

ST-HIPPOLYTE-DU-FORT, eight kilometres west of Sauve, across undulating farmland, is the highest town on the Vidourle's course. Beyond lies Ganges, where the road dips into the Hérault valley, having crossed over into the *département* of the same name. St-Hippolyte, like so many old cloth towns of the Cévennes, switched over to silk production in the period before the Revolution, and prospered until a nineteenth-century epidemic wiped out the mulberry plants on which the silkworms depended. Today the town is trying to generate interest as a tourist stop, encouraging its inhabitants to attach **sundials** to the fronts of their houses in order to develop a rather contrived identity. Some of the solar clocks are quite attractive, but most are unremarkable; the tourist office distributes a route map which takes you past all of them. Rather more interesting is the **silk museum** (April–June & Sept–Nov Tues–Sun 10am–12.30pm & 2–6pm; July & Aug daily 10am–12.30pm & 2–6.30pm; €5) behind the old military school, a five-minute walk west of the main square, place de la Canourgue. Displaying reconstructed silk-weaving machinery and an exhibition of live silk worms doing their stuff, the museum makes for a good stop for both adults and children. Another good stop for children is the nearby **Musée du Sapeur Pompier** (June to mid-Sept Wed–Mon 10am–noon & 12.30–6.30pm; mid-Sept to May Sat & Sun same hours; €3), featuring a collection of historical fire trucks and fire-fighting equipment.

Buses roll through the town centre, stopping just before place de la Canourgue. The town's **tourist office** (July & Aug Mon–Wed & Fri 10am–4pm, Sat 10am–3pm & Sun 10am–1pm; Sept–June Mon–Fri 10am–4pm; ℡04.66.77.91.65, ⓦwww.multimania.com/sainthippolyte) is in the courtyard of the same building as the silk museum. **Accommodation** is limited to the *Auberge Cigalois* (℡04.66.77.64.59, ⓦwww.multimania.com/aubergecigaloise; closed Dec–Feb; ❸), off the D999 1km or so east of town, or the small and basic *Les Cévennes* at 3 boulevard le Temple (℡ & Ⓕ04.66.77.90.20; €32). The **campsite** *Figaret* (April–Sept; ℡04.66.77.26.34, ⓦwww.campingfigaret.com) is on route de Lassalle. There are several unexceptional **restaurants** and **cafés** clustered around place de la Canourgue.

Travel details

Trains

Trains run west from Nîmes along the coast to Sète and Béziers, and east to Provence via Beaucaire (hooking up with the north-south Rhône rail corridor), while a secondary line runs north via Alès to the Massif Central. SNCF buses may run in lieu of trains on these lines; services are reduced on Sundays and holidays.

Aigues-Mortes to: Le Grau-du-Roi (5 daily; 5min); Nîmes (2–5 daily; 50min).

Beaucaire/Tarascon to: Montpellier (10–11 daily; 1hr 5min); Nîmes (10–11 daily; 25min).

Nîmes to: Agde (18–23 daily; 1hr 10min); Aigues-Mortes (2–5 daily; 50min); Beaucaire/Tarascon (10–11 daily; 24min); Béziers (18–23 daily; 1hr 15min); Carcassonne (15–18 daily; 2hr 5min–3hr 10min); Le Grau-du-Roi (2–5 daily; 55min); Lunel (12–15 daily; 15–28min); Montpellier (18–23 daily; 30min); Narbonne (18–20 daily; 1hr 45min); Paris (frequent; 3hr); Perpignan (15–18 daily; 2hr 45min); Sète (18–23 daily; 48min); Toulouse (15–18 daily; 2hr 45min to 3hr); Vauvert (2–4 daily; 20–45min).

Buses

The principle bus routes run from Nîmes to Uzès via Remoulins and the Pont du Gard, and to Grau. Services to the upper Vidourle, Sommières and Beaucaire are less frequent, and routes are often reduced or cancelled on Sundays and holidays. In summer extra services run from Nîmes to Aigues-Mortes, Grau and La Grande-Motte. For full schedules, see ⓦwww.stdgard.com.

Aigues-Mortes to: Le Grau-du-Roi (2–9 daily; 10min); Montpellier (5 daily, increased service in summer; 1hr 20min); Stes-Maries-de-la-Mer (summer 1 daily; 30min).

Beaucaire to: Remoulins (1–2 daily; 45min); St-Gilles (1–2 daily; 30min).

Nîmes to: Aigues-Mortes (2–9 daily; 1hr 5min); Avignon (4 daily; 1hr 30min); Beaucaire (4–10 daily; 35min); Collias (1–2 daily; 1hr 5min); Ganges (3–6 daily; 1hr 15min); La Grand Motte (2–9 daily; 1hr 30min); Le Grau-du-Roi (2–9 daily; 1hr 15min); Lunel (1–6 daily; 40min–1hr 5min); Montpellier (1–2 daily; 1hr 30min); Pont du Gard (4–16 daily; 45min); Quissac (3–6 daily; 40min); St-Gilles (5 daily; 50min); St-Hippolyte (3–6 daily; 1hr); Sauve (3–6 daily; 50min); Sommières (2–8 daily; 45min); Uzès (2–12 daily; 30min–1hr); Vauvert (4 daily; 35min); Villevieille (8 daily; 40min).

Quissac to: Ganges (4–7 daily; 35min).

St-Hippolyte to: Ganges (4–7 daily; 15min); Montpellier (1 daily; 1hr 45min); Quissac (4–7 daily; 35min); Sauve (4–7 daily; 30min).

Sommières to: Montpellier (4 daily; 1hr 10min); Nîmes (2–8 daily; 45min); Villevieille (2–8 daily; 5min).

Uzès to: Nîmes (2–12 daily; 30min–1hr); Pont du Gard (3–7 daily; 25min); St-Hippolyte (1–2 daily; 25min).

5

Montpellier and around

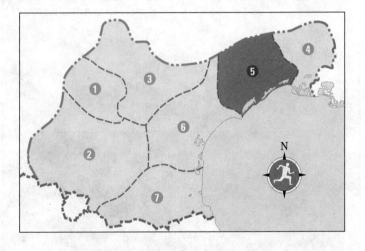

CHAPTER 5 # Highlights

✳ **Beaches** A long swathe of sand girds the Mediterranean coast: you can find both solitude and crowds here. See p.257

✳ **Café-littéraires** Take in Montpellier's lively student culture in these provocative salons. See p.270

✳ **Water-jousting** This curious Sètoise sport has grown in the last centuries into a regional tradition. See p.276

✳ **Seafood** Whether cultivated in the Bassin de Thau or fished from the sea, the coastal cuisine of this area is a gourmet's delight. See p.283

✳ **Pézenas** Walk the streets of Languedoc's old capital for a taste of life in the age of Molière. See p.283

✳ **Cirque de Navacelles** A spectacular ox-bow canyon, etched deep into the *causse* of upper Hérault. See p.292

△ La Grande Motte beach

Montpellier and around

Together **Montpellier** and the surrounding country comprise the most varied and exciting region in Languedoc. The city is a capital in every sense of the word – a zesty centre of government, education, culture and economy for the whole of Languedoc-Roussillon *région* and, best of all, it is minutes from the beach. While Languedoc's **coast** may not be able to hold a candle to the likes of Provence's Côte d'Azur, if you can put up with the often-strong wind, its some forty kilometres of nearly uninterrupted sand bar – as well as providing ample opportunities for sun-soaking and watersports – means you can escape the crowds if you wish. Moreover, the seaside towns, although unavoidably busy in high season, have not sunk into the irretrievable triteness of their Provençal counterparts; the continuing role of **Palavas**, **Mèze** and **Sète** as fishing ports balances their beach-town roles, endowing them with life and energy throughout the year. Just inland, **Pézenas** was the capital of Languedoc in the glory days of French Absolutism, and the many palaces which cram its old town preserve it as one of the most beautiful in the Southwest. The River Hérault gives its name to the *département* of which Montpellier is the administrative centre, and dominates its **interior**. Less travelled than the coast, its beautiful highlands are home to a wealth of natural wonders and historic sites. Dusty and provincial **Clermont-l'Hérault** acts as a gateway to the dramatically varied landscape at nearby **Lac du Salagou**, while **Lodève** – still lorded over by its hulking medieval cathedral, is the best place to set off for the breathtaking **Cirque de Navacelles**. East of the cirque, Ganges sits on the banks of the Hérault at the point where the river completes its descent from the high Cévennes mountains to the north; just downstream you can visit one of France's most celebrated caverns, the **Grotte des Demoiselles**, before following dramatic gorges southwest past the ancient monastic centre of **St-Guilhem-le-Désert**, or bearing due south towards the towering **Pic-St-Loup**.

Getting around by **public transport** in the region around Montpellier is easy. The city sits on the main coastal rail artery, uniting it with Sète to the west and Nîmes to the east, while the area of greater Montpellier, the *agglomération*, is served by the city's transport network (TAM), whose far-ranging buses reach Palavas and Maguelone on the coast. Inland, the lack of train lines is compensated by regular bus services connecting the bigger towns. Only the smaller

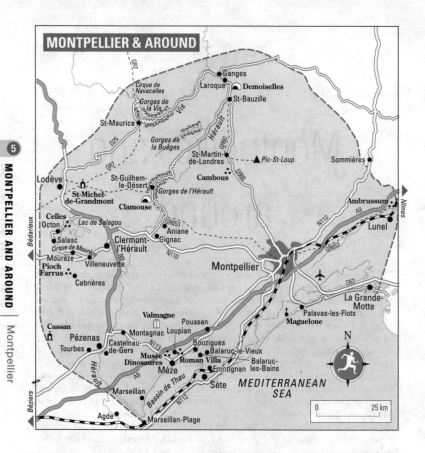

villages, such as the hamlets around Lac du Salagou and Navacelles, do not have useful bus services; to explore these you'll need a car or bike, or be prepared to hitch-hike.

Montpellier

Home to a youthful and dynamic university culture and a host of artistic festivals and events, **MONTPELLIER** is the most exciting city in Languedoc proper. In addition, it boasts a beautiful architectural fusion of the classical and the avant-garde, and is even close enough to the Mediterranean to have the beach within reach of public transport. With fine museums, a charming old centre and a bouncy rhythm of life, Montpellier offers an ideal place for either a longer, relaxing stay, or a whirlwind two-day tour of its highpoints, notably the many Renaissance **mansions** of the old town.

Montpellier is a medieval city, and can't claim the same venerable Roman past of rival Nîmes. Starting off as a market town for nearby **Maguelone** in the tenth century, in 1204 it was acquired by marriage by the count-kings of

Barcelona, who favoured it as a residence – both Jaume I "the Conqueror" and his son Jaume II of Mallorca were born here. By the late thirteenth century it had become second only to Paris in size, thanks partly to its famous **university**, and a major centre for medicine, law and the arts. With Jaume I's posthumous divison of his realms, the city was incorporated into the Kingdom of Mallorca until 1349, when Jaume II sold it – afflicted with plague, banditry and famine – to the French Crown. In the era that followed the city was sustained by its university, through whose doors passed the pioneering Renaissance poet Petrarch and, later, the satirist Rabelais, who received his doctorate here in 1537. Despite the transfer of the bishopric of Maguelone here in 1537, Montpellier became strongly **Protestant** in the sixteenth and seventeenth centuries, losing many of its old church buildings in factionalist struggles, and was only saved from destruction at the hands of Louis XIII, who had personally waged war on the Huguenot stronghold in 1622, by an eleventh-hour truce. In a good position for trade and with a varied economic base, Montpellier managed to escape the post-Religious Wars depression which afflicted most of Languedoc, and the wealthy burghers vied with each other to build decadently outfitted **manors** in the surrounding vineyards. The city's leftist tradition began with a bang in 1789, and the revolutionary anthem known as "La Marseillaise" was in fact first sung by a local medical student. Another wave of serious unrest came during the wine crisis of 1907, during which it was the strongest centre of popular agitation in reaction to plummeting grape prices (see p.404). The last shake-up was in 1962; with the dismantling of the Algerian colony, 13,000 French (*pieds-noirs*) and Maghrebi (*harki*) refugees arrived in the city, two groups whose integration into Montpellier society generated considerable friction, but whose presence brought a revitalizing dynamism to the city. Not long after this, Montpellier became the official capital of the administrative *région* of Languedoc-Roussillon.

Recently, solidly-socialist Montpellier has garnered kudos for its ecological initiatives, notably the development of its public transport system and most recently the effective banning of cars from the historic centre. Now you can stroll around the medieval city soaking up the atmosphere, free from exhaust fumes, tooting horns and traffic.

Arrival, information and city transport

The city's **airport** is 8km southeast of the centre, beside the Étang de Mauguio: from here a **navette** (timed for flights; 15min; €5) runs to a stop on rue de Crète beside the Antigone (by the Léon Blum tramstop), or a **taxi** costs €12–30. The **gare SNCF** (no left luggage) and **gare routière** are next to each other at the southern end of rue Maguelone – it's a five-minute walk along this street to the central place de la Comédie. If you're driving, the simplest option for **parking** is to head for the "Comédie" car park, under the famous *place* – if however you want to avoid paying, you will be banished to the metered zones on the periphery of the old town. Alternatively, outlying public car parks charge €4 for parking and a return tram fare for each passenger.

The main **tourist office** (July & Aug Mon–Fri 9am–7.30pm, Sat 10am–6pm, Sun 9.30am–1pm & 2.30–6pm; Sept–June Mon–Fri 9am–6.30pm, Sat 10am–6pm, Sun 10am–1pm & 2–5pm; ☎04.67.60.60.60, ⊕www.ot-montpellier.fr) is on the northern edge of place de la Comédie, with seasonal branches at the *gare SNCF* (July–Sept Mon–Fri 9am–1pm & 2–6.45pm, Sat 9.30am–1pm & 2–5.30pm) and in the Antigone, at 78 av de Pirée (April–Oct Mon–Fri 9am–1pm & 2–6pm). All these offices can reserve the official **guided tours** (Sat at

Festivals in and around Montpellier

Most of the action in Hérault *département* is centred on Montpellier, which is renowned for its cultural vitality, hosting a range of annual **festivals**. Also worth looking out for are the *fêtes* on the coast, which invariably feature the local tradition of water-jousting – throughout July and August in Palavas and Sète (see box, p.276) – as well as *tauromachie* (both Spanish and Camargue styles). The uplands of the Hérault valley also have a few small local festivals. Where no specific information number is given, contact the relevant tourist office for details.

Late Jan to early Feb Montpellier: Christian Cinema Festival ☎04.67.64.14.10, Ⓦwww.chretiensetcultures.free.fr. A diverse programme of inter-religious film, music and dance.

First or Second weekend Feb Montpellier: *Swing Danse Festival* Ⓦwww.montpellier swing.com. One of France's biggest swing festivals, featuring lindy-hoppers, boogie-woogiers and swingers from around the country.

Feb or March Pézenas: *Carnaval*. Lent kicks off with a three-day Mardi Gras (Shrove Tuesday) festival here, featuring folkloric displays and a parade led by the local totem-animal, *Le Poulain*.

Pentecost (5 weeks after Easter) Lunel: *Estivales*. Early summer celebration featuring three days of *courses camarguaises*, a massive street market and livestock fair.

May Pézenas: *Cavalcade*. A popular festival with a bustling handicrafts market, culminating in a medieval period-costume parade led by *Le Poulain*. Held over one weekend in May.

Early June Maguelone: Maguelone music festival. ☎04.67.60.69.92, Ⓔparnasse .lr@wanadoo.fr. Medieval and Baroque music concerts held several nights a week in the cathedral.

June Pézenas: *Pézenas sous regard de Molière*. A historical reconstruction of Pézenas in its greatest period of glory. Lots of costumed townsfolk, activities and a market. Held over one weekend in June.

Mid-June Palavas: Water-jousting tournaments. ☎04.67.07.73.34, Ⓦwww .palavaslesflots.com.

Mid-June to mid-July Montpellier: *Le Printemps des Comédiens* ☎04.67.63.66.67, Ⓦwww.printempsdescomediens.com. Theatre, dance and music festival held in the grounds of Château d'Ô, a mansion northwest of Montpellier (tram #1 to "Château d'Ô").

Mid-June to mid-Aug St-Guilhem: *Musique Sacrée* ☎04.67.63.14.99. Religious and Baroque music series, performed in the former abbey-church.

Late June to mid-July Montpellier: *Montpellier Danse* ☎04.67.60.83.60, Ⓦwww .montpellierdanse.com. A three-week festival of traditional music and dance from around the world, held in the old Ursuline convent, the Comédie, Le Corum and other venues around town.

First weekend July Sète: *Fête de la St-Pierre*. Traditional fishermen's festival with a religious procession, street party and jousting.

Second Sunday July Palavas: *Fête de la Mer* ☎04.67.07.73.34, Ⓦwww.palavas lesflots.com. Religious procession and blessing of fishing boats, followed by jousting, fireworks and *tauromachie*. Also night-time *joutes* on July 14.

Mid-July Mèze: *Festival du Thau* ☎04.67.18.92.80, Ⓦwww.festivaldethau.com. A week-long alternative, ska and World-Music festival on the banks of the Bassin du Thau, with three concerts per evening.

5.30pm; advance reservation obligatory; ☎04.67.60.19.27; €6.50), which allow you access to certain normally off-limits sights, like the medieval *mikvé* (Jewish

Mid-July Sète: Worldwide Festival ⓦ www.worldwide-festival.com. A new, small festival gathering together electronic music artists from around the world.

Mid- to end July Montpellier: *Electromind* ⓦ www.electromind.fr. The Languedocian version of Barcelona's Sónar, held outdoors at the beachside Espace Grammont, and featuring an impressive line-up of DJs and musicians from France, Europe and North America.

Mid- to end July Montpellier: *Le Festival de Radio-France et de Montpellier* ☎ 04.67.02.02.01, ⓦ www.festivalradiofrancemontpellier.com. Music festival representing styles from classical to jazz, held at Le Corum and other venues. Half the concerts are free.

Mid- to end July Sète: *Festival de Sète*. Mediterranean-music festival featuring folk and pop music from African and European shores.

July 21–23 St-Guilhem: *Fête*. Local town *fête*, featuring costumes, music and traditional market.

Throughout July St-Martin-de-Londres: *Les Musicales de St Martin* ☎ 04.67.55.09.59 Weekly concerts at the abbey, with styles ranging from Jazz to Celtic.

Late July Lodève: *Voix de la Méditerranée*. Poets, musicians, story-tellers and comedians from around the Mediterranean participate in a progamme of free outdoor performances.

Late July Bassin de Thau: *Festival de Thau* ☎ 04.67.18.70.83, ⓦ www .festivaldethau.com. Annual week-long World Music festival, held in Mèze, Marseillan, Loupain and Frontignan. Headliners in 2006 included Salif Keita and Willy DeVille.

Late July to early Aug Sète: *Fiest'a Sète* ☎ 04.67.74.48.44, ⓦ www.fiestasete.com. Two-week celebration, with nightly performances of music and dance at the Théâtre de la Mer (from €26), as well as street theatre and plenty of parties.

Throughout July & Aug Pézenas: *Mirondela des Arts* ☎ 04.67.98.36.40, ⓦ www .mirondela.com. International theatre festival with excellent quality performances held at the town's Théâtre de Verdure, in the old town's squares and other venues.

August 15 Palavas: Feast of the Assumption. Water-jousting.

End Aug Sète: *Fête de St-Louis*. One-day extravaganza of fireworks, street parties, jousting and medieval pageantry.

Sept 29 to Oct 1 Palavas: *Feria d'Automne* ☎ 06.61.46.68.85. Local Camarguaise-style festival of horsemanship and *tauromachie*.

Late Sept to early Oct Montpellier: *Quartiers-Libres* ☎ 04.67.34.88.44, ⓦ www .quartierslibres.montpellier.fr. A new festival, aimed at bringing the city's artists out into the streets.

Late Oct Montpellier: *Internationales de la Guitare* ☎ 04.67.66.36.55, ⓦ www .internatinalesdelaguitare.com. Europe's only festival dedicated to the history, culture and music of the guitar.

Late Oct to early Nov Montpellier: *Festival du Cinéma Méditerranéen* ☎ 04.99.13. 73.73, ⓦ www.cinemed.tm.fr. Festival of feature-length films and shorts, with symposiums and awards.

Third week Dec Pézenas: Occitan Christmas. Christmas festivities featuring the folk traditions and customs of the Languedocian plains.

ritual bath) or the interior of the Arc de Triomf. They also sell one-, two- and three-day **city passes** (covering buses and trams, admission to many city sites and other discounts), as well as handing out the free student guide *L'Indic*; the fortnightly *Sortir*, with entertainment listings; and *Montpellier Côté Coeur*, which also lists shops.

The star of the city's transport system (TAM; 27 rue Maguelone; ☎04.67.22.87.87, ⓦwww.tam-way.com) is its new fleet of **trams**, which has its hub at place de la Comédie. At present, one line is in service, running a twisting course northwest to southeast across town. Coupled with the **buses**, which run out to Palavas on the coast, they make an incredibly comprehensive transport network. Both buses and trams operate from 5am to 1am, and **maps** and **passes** (one-day pass €3.20; weekly pass €11.10) are available at

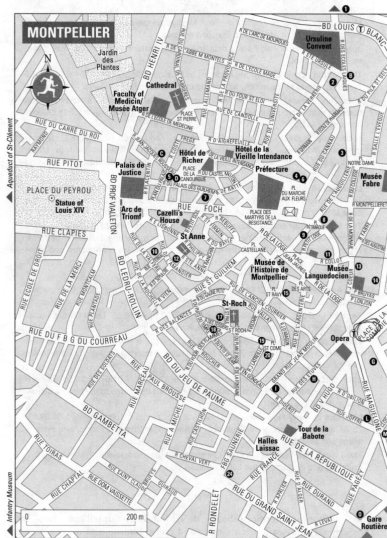

the TAM office, although you can also buy **tickets** (single €1.30 valid for one hour including transfers) from drivers, at tobacconists or at the vending kiosks at major stops (credit cards accepted). Other green transport initiatives include the city's comprehensive 120km **bike** path network: bikes can be rented at Vill'a Vélo at the *gare routière* (℡04.67.92.92.67), or direct from TAM (€7 per day).

Accommodation

With its roles as a student and administrative centre, Montpellier has abundant **hotel** facilities in all price ranges. Most accommodation is concentrated in the

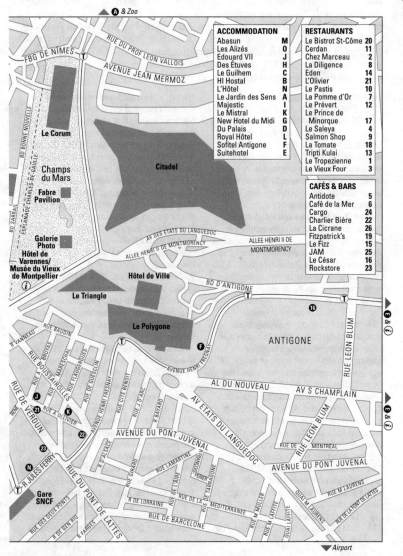

ACCOMMODATION

Abasun	M
Les Alizés	O
Edouard VII	J
Des Étuves	H
Le Guilhem	C
HI Hostal	B
L'Hôtel	N
Le Jardin des Sens	A
Majestic	I
Le Mistral	K
New Hotel du Midi	G
Du Palais	D
Royal Hôtel	L
Sofitel Antigone	F
Suitehotel	E

RESTAURANTS

Le Bistrot St-Côme	20
Cerdan	11
Chez Marceau	2
La Diligence	8
Eden	14
L'Olivier	21
Le Pastis	10
La Pomme d'Or	7
Le Prévert	12
Le Prince de Minorque	17
Le Saleya	4
Salmon Shop	9
La Tomate	18
Tripti Kulai	13
Le Tropezienne	1
Le Vieux Four	3

CAFÉS & BARS

Antidote	5
Café de la Mer	6
Cargo	24
Charlier Bière	22
La Cicrane	26
Fitzpatrick's	19
Le Fizz	15
JAM	25
Le César	16
Rockstore	23

compact grid of streets between the *gares* and the place de la Comédie. You may be tempted to stick to this area for convenience, but there are options in the old town which are worth searching out, particularly in the area west of the central place des Martyrs de la Résistance. The city's tourist office runs a "*Bonne Week-end*" programme giving a free second night at selected hotels (Nov–March).

A good low-budget option for medium to long stays and students is the network of over six hundred **rooms and apartments** in the greater Montpellier area, administered by L'Association des Résidences Internationales, at 2 rue Germain, just north of the Marché aux Fleurs (Mon–Fri 8am–noon & 1.30–5pm; ☎04.67.60.36.00, ℻04.67.60.36.58). Alternatively, there are a couple of organizations that can arrange short or long **stays with a French family**: the Association Accueil en France at 214 rue Louis Lépine (☎04.67.64.96.65, ⓦwww.aef-asso.fr), and the Association Accueil en Famille VBI, at 7 rue de Verdun (☎04.67.56.73.87, ⓦwww.frenchfamily.fr). The closest **campsite** to Montpellier is *L'Oasis Palavasienne* (April to mid-Oct; ☎04.67.15.11.61), just south of town on the D21 to Palavas (bus #28), though you'll have much more choice in Palavas itself (see p.274).

Abasun 13 rue Maguelone
☎04.67.58.36.80, ⓦwww.abasunhotel montpelliercentre.com. Centrally located and newly renovated. The best value for these amenities. ❷
Les Alizés 14 rue Jules-Ferry ☎04.67.12.85.35, ⓦwww.hotel-alizes.com. Perhaps over-priced, but with a convenient station-side location. Amenities include en-suite bath, satellite TV in every room and a restaurant serving from 5am–1am. ❹
Edouard VII 10 rue Aristide-Ollivier ☎04.67.58.42.13, ⓦwww.hoteledouard7.com. Friendly place in a great old nineteenth-century building with a striking facade and spacious interior. Every room has en-suite shower, toilet and TV. ❸
des Étuves 24 rue des Étuves ☎04.67.60.78.19, ⓦwww.hoteldesetuves.fr. Simple, spotless rooms in the south of the old city, all with en-suite bathrooms and TV. ❷
Le Guilhem 18 rue J-J-Rousseau ☎04.67.52.90.90, ⓦwww.leguilhem .com. Beautifully restored sixteenth-century town house whose cheerful rooms mostly overlook quiet gardens, and with a sunny breakfast terrace. ❺
HI hostel Impasse Petite Corraterie, off rue des Écoles Laïques ☎04.67.60.32.22, ⓔmontpellier @fuaj.org. Fifteen minutes' walk from place de la Comédie in a renovated old building at the northern boundary of the old town (bus #6 to "Ursulines"), this hostel has a bar, billiards room and a luggage check; the curfew is at 2am. Closed mid-Dec to mid-Jan. Dorm beds €12.50, doubles ❶
L'Hôtel 6 rue Jules-Ferry ☎04.99.13.33.44, ⓔlhotel@wanadoo.fr. Newest and best of the station-side hotels – modern, clean and soundproof, with good amenities. Some rooms with bath. ❸
Le Jardin des Sens 11 av St-Lazare ☎04.67.79.63.38, ⓦwww.jardindessens.com

The best of the upper-bracket hotels, and the epitome of restrained and tasteful luxury, Le Jardin boasts a swimming pool, elegant rooms and one of the region's most acclaimed restaurants. ❾
Majestic 4 rue du Cheval-Blanc ☎04.67.66.26.85, ℻04.67.66.11.42. Very basic but clean, quiet and central, with rooms with en-suite showers. ❷
Le Mistral 25 rue Boussairolles ☎04.67.58.45.25, ⓦwww.hotel-le-mistral.com. Comfortable and clean, a good mid-range option, offering satellite TV and garage parking (€5 extra). ❸
New Hôtel du Midi 22 bd Victor-Hugo ☎04.67.92.69.61, ⓦwww.new-hotel.com. A rather pricy, luxury option with a great view of the Comédie. ❾
du Palais 3 rue du Palais ☎04.67.60.47.38, ⓦwww.hoteldupalais-montpellier.fr. Tastefully renovated eighteenth-century mansion on the west side of the old town, blending modern and antique touches. Cosy rooms, most with en-suite facilities. ❻
Royal Hôtel 8 rue Maguelone ☎04.67.92.13.36, ⓦwww.hotel-royal-34.com. Good amenities (including Canal Plus) in this three-star hotel between the Comédie and the *gare*, with an old-world ambience. ❻
Sofitel Antigone 1 rue des Pertuisanes ☎04.67.99.72.72, ⓦwww.sofitel-montpellier .com. Suitably futuristic design, with a somewhat cold predominance of concrete over glass set in the city's flagship Antigone development. Four-star service and amenities including a pool. ❾
Suitehotel 45 av du Pirée ☎04.67.20.57.57, ⓦwww.suite-hotel.com. This new three-star hotel in the Antigone offers roomy suites with all mod-cons and excellent service. There are discounts for weekends and for stays of four nights or more. ❻

The Town

More or less everything you will want to see in Montpellier can be found in or on the edge of its compact and largely pedestrian **old town**, which spreads out north and west from the **place de la Comédie**, at the heart of the city. Bounded on the north by the boulevards Pasteur and Louis Blanc, on the east by the **Champ de Mars** park and on the west by the **Jardin des Plantes** and **place du Peyrou**, the terminus of the town's old aqueduct, the old centre is marked off into two unequal halves by the avenue made up of rues de la Loge and Foch. The north side was the most prosperous part, as the **mansions** which pepper it testify, and is also home to the city's old university buildings and **cathedral**. The crowded lanes of the south side were inhabited by the city's workers and artisans; its buildings are correspondingly less showy. East of the place de la Comédie you'll find the sprawling **Antigone** development, Montpellier's boldly designed but sterile modern quarter. Beyond the old town are mixed commercial and residential quarters, which provide interesting backdrops to stroll past, if lacking in significant sights, while further out still, various **châteaux** ring the town.

The place de la Comédie and the Champs de Mars park

The **place de la Comédie** is a broad plaza which was opened up in the mid-nineteenth century with the inauguration of the then new **opera hall** at its southern end. Although superseded by the new Corum hall, the gaily domed building still hosts music and theatre performances. Today the *place* to its northeast is a busy crossroads for both pedestrians and trams, and is lined on each side by a series of old cafés and fast-food joints, although it retains its traditional role as morning market-place (Mon–Sat 7.30am–1pm). At the northern end, the tourist office's pavilion marks the beginning of the **Champs de Mars**, a park with both a formal promenade and a network of paths and ponds which attract sunbathers and strollers in good weather.

The main attraction in the vicinity of the park is the huge **Musée Fabre** (currently closed for renovation), situated halfway up its west side. When the museum re-opens, it will display many of its immense collection of paintings – overwhelmingly French and post-eighteenth century in content and bridging a range of styles including the local "luminophile" movement of the early nineteenth century. Works by better-known names include David's *Portrait of the Doctor, Alphonse Leroy* and Delacroix's *Fantasia*, as well as pieces by Dufy, Maillol and the local Frédéric Bazille. In addition to these, there are works by well-known foreign artists such as Reynolds, Zurbarán and Rubens. The museum also owns a palace next door, the **Hôtel Cabrières**, which has luxuriously appointed rooms in eighteenth- and nineteenth-century styles (also closed for renovation). While the museum is closed, its **pavilion** (hours and prices vary) in the park opposite houses rotating exhibitions featuring a selection of the main collection. To the south of this you'll find the small **Galerie Photo** (Tues–Sat 1–7pm; free) which hosts temporary exhibitions of contemporary photographers from around Europe. Across a small bridge by the pavilion you'll see the city's massive star-shaped seventeenth-century **citadel**, built in 1622 to guard the suspiciously Protestant-leaning town and now converted into a school. Finally, at the northern end of the park looms the concrete and pink granite **Le Corum** (July & Aug Sat & Sun 2–7pm; Sept–June Sat 2–7pm), designed by Claude Vasconi to house the city's 2000-seat opera hall – the Opéra Berlioz – plus a convention centre and exhibition hall. During opening hours you can poke around the building and take in the sweeping **views** of the old city from its terrace.

Back at the place de la Comédie heading east brings you to the Triangle shopping centre, which marks the beginning of the Antigone development (see p.268); south down to the *gares* is a bustling neighbourhood of shops and restaurants; while northwest from here is the core of the old town.

From place de la Comédie to place de la Canourgue

Montpellier's greatest attraction is its old town, richly adorned by elaborate mansion facades and home to a series of small museums. Rue de la Loge, the city's main shopping street, leads northwest into the old centre from in front of the former opera. Just off this at 7 rue Jacques-Coeur is the impressive fifteenth-century facade of the Hôtel des Trésoriers de France, now home to the **Musée Languedocien** (Mon–Sat 2/2.30–5/5.30pm; €6), whose fine seventeenth-century courtyard can also be visited (€2). This museum is worth visiting not only for its collection of medieval artefacts, which include thirteenth-century ceramics and a curious lead baptismal font, but for the impressively vaulted Gothic interior of the main exhibition room. You'll also find luxurious Flemish tapestries, pre-Revolution furniture – including a seventeenth-century Italian celestial globe – and a collection of *faïence*, whose manufacture was an important industry here throughout the 1700s. Just northwest of here, the compact, triangular place Pétrarque is closed in by a clutch of palaces, the largest of which is the **Hôtel de Varennes**, at no. 2, whose ground floor is almost entirely Gothic in style, and includes the beautiful fourteenth-century **salle de Pétrarqueh**, a long hall vaulted with delicate stone ribs. On the first floor is the **Musée du Vieux Montpellier** (Tues–Sat 10.30am–12.30pm & 1.30–6pm; free) whose dull collection is dominated by portraits of city luminaries and assorted regalia of the town's public offices. On the next floor up, the **Musée Fougau** (Wed & Thurs 3–6pm; free) houses a similarly unexciting exhibition on traditional rural life, including nineteenth-century costumes, tools and household implements.

South of place Pétrarque, the lively café-lined place Jean Jaurès is home to the **Musée de l'Histoire de Montpellier** (Tues–Sat 10.30am–12.30pm & 1.30–6pm; €1.50), set in the ancient Romanesque crypt of the Notre Dame des Tables church. West of place Pétrarqueh, rue Foch leads into the wide *place* dominated by the city's *préfecture*, adjacent to which is a colourful market square, the place du Marché-aux-Fleurs. Around here you'll find a concentration of mansions, particularly on **rue du Cannau**, whose string of facades, decked out with ornately carved doorways and casement windows, attest to the wealth of this street – a prestigious neighbourhood three centuries ago. If you continue north along Cannau you'll eventually reach the hulking stone mass of the former **Ursuline convent**, built in the seventeenth century and later converted into a prison; today it is a centre for dance performance. Heading west from Marché aux Fleurs, will take you past the **Hôtel de la Vieille Intendance**, the former governor's mansion at no. 9 on the street of the same name, a stately palace which was later home of the philosopher Auguste Comte and writer Paul Valéry. South of here, quiet place du Chabanneau, whose modest old houses box in a gurgling eighteenth-century **fountain**, makes a good place to pause and enjoy a terrace-side drink before you continue to **place de la Canourgue**. This larger plaza served as the eighteenth-century administrative hub of the city. Its eastern side is dominated by the huge **Hôtel de Richer**, the former town hall, whose broad square courtyard is decorated in the finest Neoclassical pomp of the late 1700s. The square is ringed by further magnificent frontages; including the stone-carved faces which cap each window of the Hôtel de Cambacères across the square at no. 3.

The cathedral and around

From here it's just a short descent north to Montpellier's **cathedral** (Mon–Sat 9.30am–noon & 2.30–7pm, Sun 9am–1pm), with its strikingly bizarre entrance, a porch flanked by two straight towers capped with high conical roofs. The effect, which resembles two old-fashioned rockets, smacks of a Viollet-le-Duc initiative but is, in fact, original – dating back to the church's fourteenth-century foundation. It is also the most interesting feature of the cathedral, whose dark and bare interior is hardly worth poking your head inside. The cathedral has a covered cloister, which you can't enter, but can view from the back porch of the **Faculty of Médecine**, next door in rue de l'École de Médecine. The stately Neoclassical faculty building occupies the grounds of the now-vanished Benedictine monastery which the cathedral once served as chapel. Passing through the main doors, flanked by bronzes of local medical giants Barthez and Lapeyronie, you'll find the interior is decorated with marble columns and rich low-relief detailing around the windows and ceilings. The back porch is opposite the entrance, while up on the first floor, you'll find two noteworthy museums. The larger of these is the **Musée Atger** (Mon, Wed & Thurs 1.30–5.45pm; free), named after the local artist Xavier Atger, whose sketches make up the core of the collection, which also displays contemporary southern French art, as well as paintings by noteworthy Flemish artists such as Rubens and Van Dyck. Also on the first floor, the strong of stomach can also visit the **anatomy museum** (2.30–5pm; free) a library of specimens, models and manuscripts relating to vivisection.

At the end of rue de l'École de Médecine, which is lined with nineteenth-century university buildings, the **Jardin des Plantes** (July & Aug noon–8pm; Sept–June 2–5pm; free) marks the transition to the new town. Managed by the university's botany department, its well-maintained paths lead among an impressive variety of plant specimens, from tropical to temperate. The garden dates back to 1593, when it was founded by order of the former Huguenot king, Henry IV, in order to cultivate and study herbal remedies.

Place du Peyrou and south of rue Foch

Rising above the Jardin on the edge of the old *enceinte*, the flat paved expanse of the **place du Peyrou** stretches west, flanked on either side by wide beds of colourful flowers. The plaza itself is dominated by a Roman-style equestrian statue of the "Emperor" Louis XIV – an 1838 replacement of the original statue of 1692, which was destroyed during the Revolution. The great bronze king is frozen in motionless stride towards the **Arc de Triomf**, opposite the eastern end of the park, at the head of rue Foch. The arch, designed on the ancient Roman model, consists of a single, free-standing entryway, whose sides are covered with low-relief sculptures celebrating the military victories of the "Sun King" over the Dutch and the Huguenots, the revocation of the Edict of Nantes and the construction of the Canal du Midi. Behind Louis' statue, at the western end of the place du Peyrou, an octagonal, colonnaded pavilion marks the terminus of the 880metre-long aqueduct of St-Clément, built in the late eighteenth century to carry water to the city from a nearby spring. The Neoclassical pavilion was the work of Jean Giral, the same architect who designed the Faculty of Médecine. From the two levels of terraces over which the pavilion stands, you can enjoy views over the city and a hazy panorama of the flat Languedocian littoral fading off towards the distant Mont St-Loup.

From Peyrou, passing through the triumphal arch you'll come face to face with the striking Neoclassical **Palais de Justice**, which features a Doric-columned facade capped by an impressive tympanum in relief. From here, rue Foch sets out eastwards towards the *préfecture*, but before you reach it take a right into rue Petit

Scel; here, at no. 4, sits the former palace of Francese de Cazelli, a noblewoman named as governor of the coastal town of Leucate by the king in 1590 after she commanded its defence, refusing to surrender even in exchange for the life of her captured husband. The nearby plain stone nineteenth-century **church of St-Anne** is only really of interest for the occasional art exhibitions it houses; it's also the epicentre of the "L'Isle aux Créateurs", a collective of a dozen or so designers of decorative goods who have set up workshop-boutiques throughout the zone. South of the church on rue de l'Huile, you'll enter the city's old **artisanal quarter**, containing houses that survive from as early as the thirteenth century.

This neighbourhood is bounded on the east by rue St-Guilhem, a street of functional, quotidian shops, beyond which you'll find a succession of squares – good territory for restaurant-hunting. At the northernmost of these, place St-Ravy, are the scant remains of the **palace** of the kings of Mallorca and, crossing the colourful rue de l'Ancien Courrier, you'll pass the ruined church of St-Roch to arrive at a busy little bar-lined plaza at the end of rue Plan d'Agde. Just to the east, on the far side of the terrace-choked place St-Côme, squats the marvellous **hôtel** of the same name, girded by a double row of columns and capped by a low cupola. This edifice, built by Giral in the eighteenth century as an anatomical theatre, was donated to the city at the bequest of the Royal Surgeon François Gigot. Just to the south of it you'll come upon a final small *place*, set in the shadow of the **Tour de la Babote**, the only surviving portion of the town's twelfth-century defences. Crowned by an observatory in the 1700s it was also incorporated into the same semaphore system used at the Tour Chappe in Castelnaudary (see p.106).

The Antigone

Cut off from the main part of the old city by the hideous sprawl of the Le Polygone shopping complex and defended on the north and south by a whizzing expressway, the **Antigone**, twenty-first-century Montpellier, is a world apart from that of the eighteenth. Laid out on an esplanade stretching east from the city for almost 2km, this self-contained and car-free development of residences, shops, services and restaurants is endowed with an uncompromising unity of form and design. The Catalan architect Ricard Bofill has created a massive low-rise building complex, drawing largely on Classical motifs, including smooth columns, triangular window lintels and roof cornices reminiscent of ancient temples, but with a net effect that looks somehow futuristic–Georgian. The first section, the westernmost part of the complex, was inaugurated in 1984, and the latest, a library designed by Paris-born architect Paul Chemetov, opened in 2000. The whole thing, a striking if not entirely convincing Utopian landscape of broad cypress-lined courtyards, culminates in the monumental Esplanade de l'Europe on the bank of the River Lez, across which it gazes at the recently inaugurated Hôtel de Région, the governmental seat of Languedoc-Roussillon. It's an ambitious project, and you cannot deny it a certain graceful beauty, but it is somehow disappointing – perhaps it just needs some weathering to shake off the air of contrived novelty. For the time being, the grandeur of the buildings and the breadth of its plazas only serves to reinforce a feeling of emptiness. As a visitor to Montpellier, it would be a mistake not to see Antigone for yourself, but in the end it is nothing more than an elaborate suburb, and a quick walk through will likely exhaust your interest.

The suburbs

There are number of sights scattered around the outskirts of the city. Just to the southwest of the old town in the local military academy on avenue Lepic,

△ Montpellier's Antigone

the **infantry museum** (Mon & Wed–Sat 2–5.30pm; bus #7 from the *gare*; €3) holds a collection of uniforms and memorabilia from over the last five centuries. To the north, the city's eighty-hectare **Parc Zoologique de Lunaret** (daily: July & Aug 8am–7pm; Sept–June 8am–6pm; free) is a sprawling park with nearly 10km of paths leading through to spacious animal enclosures (bus #9 to "René Bouginol"). Also, north of the old town, at 951 av d'Agropolis, **Agropolis** (Mon & Wed–Fri 10am–12.30pm & 2–6pm; Sat & Sun 2–6pm; €7) is a multimedia museum exploring the history of agriculture and food, with the emphasis on Languedoc; its interactive displays make it an entertaining stop for children (shuttle bus from tram stop St-Eloi).

The main attraction of Montpellier's hinterland, however, is the series of **follies** raised by the town's wealthiest citizens as summerhouses in the 1700s. In a game of social one-upmanship, merchants and aristocrats vied to construct ever more luxurious estates, a few of which have been opened to the public, and are accessible by city transport. To the east of the centre at 2235 route de Vaugières (tram #1 "Odysseum"), the eighteenth-century **Château de la Mogère** (June–Sept daily 2.30–6pm; Oct–May Sat & Sun 2.30–6pm or by appointment Ⓦ www.lamoguere.com; €5) is one of the most sumptuous mansions, and contains a considerable collection of period furniture and artwork. The oldest and most elegant, however, is the **Château de Flaugergues** (June–Sept 2.30–7pm; Oct–May by appointment; €7.50; Ⓦ www.flaugergues .com), north of la Mogère at 1744 avenue Albert Einstein (bus #12 "Louis Lépine"). Still owned by the original family which built the palace in 1696, the luxurious apartments, decked out with contemporary tapestries and *objets d'art*, and accompanying formal French gardens, sit amidst the vineyards of its *domaine* (Mon–Sat 9am–12.30pm & 2.30–7pm; July & Aug also Sun 2.30–7pm; €5). The furthest out is former bishop's palace, the **Château de Lavérune**, which houses the **Hofer-Bufy museum** (Sat & Sun 3–6pm; €2), where you can see some temporary painting exhibitions (check with the tourist office for the current programme). It's a considerable walk from the bus stop "Les Bouisses" (lines #4, #7 & La Ronde).

Eating, drinking and nightlife

No other city in Languedoc and Roussillon, with the possible exception of much larger Toulouse, can compete with Montpellier in terms of either dining possibilities or cultural life. Cuisine in Montpellier is a combination of the bounty of the sea, the rich garden produce of the plain and the meats of the hills. Fish lovers should look out for the savoury, tomato-based seafood stew known as *tielle*, or crab-stuffed squid tails (*enocrnets farcis*) while *gâteau d'aubergine* (aubergine cake) makes a delicious meat-free option. Far from the *manades* of Gard, pork makes a triumphant reappearance here as sausage, cured ham and paté, with duck and goose in strong supporting roles. In addition to its *terroir* options, the city has a wide range of ethnic **restaurants**, rich *gastronomique* pickings and a lively **café** culture sustained by the university community.

The **nightlife** in Montpellier is also excellent, with an incredible number of **bars**, **clubs** and **live music** options. You'll be able to find everything you need in the old town and its environs, but die-hard clubbers will want to head for the string of nightclubs (*boîtes de nuit*) on the route de Palavas in Lattes. Fortunately, many of these are served by l'Amigo, TAM's night bus (till 5am), so you may not have to take a taxi home (TAM can provide a list of nightclubs served by the route). These clubs are supplemented by a profusion of **café-littéraires** on a variety of themes: *Le César*, 17 pl du Nombre d'Or (Ⓣ04.67.20.27.02), holds two regular *café-littéraires* – an astrology colloquium on the third Thursday of each month (8.30pm), and a feminist one once a month (days vary, 6pm). **Concerts**, ranging from chamber music to classical as well as opera, are held at L'Opéra de la Comédie (Ⓣ04.67.60.19.99, Ⓦwww.opera-montpellier.com), the L'Opéra Berlioz in Le Corum (☎04.67.61.66.16), which also serves as a major venue for pop music, and at other venues – the tourist office has a complete list. The **theatre** scene thrives here too, with nearly a dozen regular stages scattered throughout town. Major performances are held at the Opéra, while you'll also find informal *café-théâtres*, like *La Cicrane*, on 9 rue St-Ursule (☎04.67.60.74.11, Ⓦwww.lacicrane.free.fr). The Diagonal complex at place Pierre-Enaidel (☎04.67.58.44.74) is the best place to go for **cinema**.

Restaurants

Practically all the squares in Montpellier's old town have a **restaurant** or two, so if you don't feel like searching out something special, just wander around and pick from among the many terraces.

Le Bistrot St-Côme 2 pl St-Côme. The best of the open-air eateries dominating the south side of pl St-Côme. Service from noon till 11.30pm, and a range of *menus* with standard but dependable French fare (€12–22).

Cerdan, 8 rue Collot ☎04.67.60.86.96. High quality cuisine combining Norman and Algerian specialities, just off of the Comedie. Lunch from €10 and dinners from €14–27. Closed Sun & Mon lunch.

Chez Marceau 7 pl de la Chapelle Neuve ☎04.67.66.08.09. Excellent-value Languedocian cuisine (both inland and coastal varieties) with a wonderful shaded terrace. The *pâtés de canard* are particularly notable. *Menus* €12 at lunch and €18 at dinner. Closed off season Sun & Wed.

🏃 **La Diligence** 2 pl Pétrarque ☎04.67.66.12.21. Atmospheric vaulted medieval setting for innovative French dishes. Menus are €18–60, and offer a good-value dip into the finest French cuisine. Closed Sat lunch, Sun & Mon lunch.

Eden 12 bd Sarrail ☎04.67.66.18.04. An airy bistro, featuring Lyonnaise cuisine as well as the usual Gallic stand-bys. Expect to spend €12 and up. Also has a parkside patio. Open Mon–Sat 8am–midnight.

Le Jardin des Sens 11 av St-Lazare ☎04.67.79.63.38. One of the top restaurants in Languedoc and universally acclaimed as Montpellier's best, just north of Le Corum. Excellent *terroir*-based creations in elegant surroundings. *Menus* €50–190. Closed Sun, Mon & Tues & Wed lunch.

L'Olivier 12 rue Aristide-Olivier ☎04.67.92.86.28. Pretty little restaurant north of the station offering excellent-value traditional French cuisine. *Menus* €32–47. Closed Sun, Mon and Aug.

Le Pastis 3 rue Terral ☎04.67.02.78.59. Great southern French cooking in a fine old mansion. Lunch *menu* at €14, dinner from €26. Closed Sat.

La Pomme d'Or 23 rue du Palais des Guilhem ☎04.67.52.82.62. Arty restaurant-bar with a predominantly gay clientele. A very wide selection of inventive *menus* at €18.

Le Prévert 8 rue Ste- Anne. A funky little place in the shadow of St-Anne's church. The tiny dining room with its clutch of tables is supplemented by a terrace which spills out into the adjacent square. Imaginative *menus* in the €13–18 range. Open for lunch Tues–Fri.

Le Prince de Minorque, 1 rue des Tessiers ☎04.67.66.05.77. Great-value Mediterranean food, in a cheerful setting with a streetside patio. Solid *plats du jour* at only €8, *menus* from €16. Closed Mon.

Le Saleya Pl du Marché aux Fleurs ☎04.67.60.53.92. In fine weather, join the locals at the outdoor tables to feast on a daily selection of market-fresh fish and regional fare for €12. Closed Sun.

Salmon Shop 5 rue de la Petite-Loge. Novel "mountain cabin" interior offering oak-smoked salmon main courses in half a dozen guises from €14 to €30 (including wine). Just off place Jean-Jaurès. Closed Sun lunch.

La Tomate 8 rue Four de Flammes. Unmissable with its tomato-coloured facade, this restaurant serves solid, *terroir* standards from only €8 at lunch and €11–18 at dinner. Closed Sun and Mon.

🏃 **Tripti Kulai** 20 rue Jacques-Coeur. Quirky, friendly women-run vegetarian restaurant. Dishes with oriental flair, including a good choice of salads, from €9. Closed Sun.

La Tropézienne 55bis rue de la Cavalerie ☎04.99.58.18.91. Elegant but modern restaurant featuring a range of dishes, from fresh shellfish to specialities of Aveyron. Open for dinner till 11.30pm with *menus* from €15 to €25.50 and a lunch special for €10. Closed Sat & Sun lunch.

Le Vieux Four 59 rue de l'Aiguillerie ☎04.67.60.55.95. Carnivores will love this cosy, candlelit place specializing in *grillades au feu de bois* – meats roasted on an open spit. *Menus* €14–25. Eves only; closed Sun in summer.

Cafés, bars and clubs

Antidote Pl de la Canourgue. Snappy bar which attracts the arty set. Techno-music dominates, and there are occasional art exhibitions. Mon–Thurs till 1am, Fri & Sat 2am.

Café de la Mer 5 pl de Marché-aux-Fleurs. Popular gay-friendly establishment with a busy terrace. Mon–Sat 8am–1am, Sun 3pm–1am, open till 2am in July & Aug.

Cargo Pl St-Denis ☎04.67.92.56.05. Montpellier's best nightclub and live venue for blues, funk and soul. A ten-minute walk south of the old town. Tues–Sat 7pm–1am. Entry free, up to €4.50 at weekends, or for concerts or special events.

Charlier Bière 22 rue A. Olliver. Grungy beer bar for under-25s. The slogan "Helping ugly people have sex since 1862," says it all.

Fitzpatrick's 5 pl St-Côme. The place to go if you're craving Guinness. Often has live music. Daily 10am–1am.

Le Fizz 4 rue Cauzit ⊛www.lefizz.com. Downtown club featuring techno and house that attracts a decidedly younger crowd. Tues–Sat midnight to 4/6am.

JAM (Jazz Action Montpellier) 100 rue Ferdinand-Lesseps ☎04.67.58.30.30. Jazz bar, concert venue and home of the regular *café-littéraire* "Ethnologue" on the first Wed of month (8pm–midnight).

Rockstore 20 rue Verdun. Legendary Montpellier club and concert venue. You can't miss the half-Cadillac protruding from the front of this former Calvinist temple. Free except for concerts. Mon–Sat 6pm–4am.

Listings

Airlines Air France ☎04.67.22.65.05, ⊛www.airfrance.com; Air Liberté ☎08.03.80.58.05; British Airways ☎08.02.80.29.02, ⊛www.britishairways.com; Ryanair ☎04.68.71.96.65, ⊛www.ryanair.com.

Airport Aéroport de Montpellier Méditerranée ☎04.67.20.85.00, ⊛www.montpellier.aeroport.fr.

Banks All major French banks are represented, most with branches in rue de la Loge, place de la Comédie or rue de Maguelone.

Books English books at Book in Bar, 8 rue du Bras de Fer, and Book Shop, 4 rue de l'Université. Travel books at Les Cinq Continents, 20 rue Jacques-Coeur.

Bus information ☎04.67.92.01.43.

Car rental ADA, 58bis bd Clémenceau ☎04.67.58.34.35; Avis, 900 av Prés d'Arènes ☎04.67.92.51.92, ⊛www.avis.com; Europcar, 6 rue Jules-Ferry ☎04.67.06.89.00, ⊛www.europcar.com; Hertz, 18 rue J-Ferry ☎04.67.58.65.18, ⊛www.hertz.com; Rent-a-Car, 111 av de Palavas ☎04.67.22.42.52.

Consulates Britain, 64 rue Alcyone (by appointment only, ☎04.67.15.34.04).

Cultural associations Centre Culturel Juif, 5000 bd Antigone ☎04.67.15.08.76; Institut Franco-American, 55 rue du Mistral ☎04.67.20.05.09; Maison de Cambridge, 1 rue du Général-Riu ☎04.67.64.07.86.

Internet access There are lots of cybercafés around town, including Cybersurf, 22 pl du Millénaire in Antigone (Mon–Fri 8am–9pm, Sat & Sun 10am–6pm).

Language courses French courses are offered by several academies including: APRE - Institut Culturel Français, 25 av St-Lazare (☎04.67.72.22.77, ⊛www.institutfrancais montpellier.com); IMEF Montpellier, 34 rue Saint-Guilhem (☎04.67.91.70.00, ⊛www.imef.fr); and Langues Sans Frontières, 3 impasse Barnabé (☎04.67.91.31.60, ⊛www.lsf.fr).

Laundry 11 rue Sérane (daily 7.30am–10pm).

Markets There are two main covered markets: Castellane, rue de la Loge; and Laissac, pl A. Laissac (both Mon–Sat 7.30am–1pm). There are also outdoor markets (Mon–Sat 7.30am–1pm) in bd des Arceaux (organic food); av de Heidelberg (flea market, also Sun); cours Gambetta (food and clothes); and pl de la Comédie (food and clothes), as well as Antigone (Wed & Sun only).

Medical emergencies ☎04.67.22.81.67 or ☎15; Centre Hospitalier de Montpellier, 555 rte de Ganges (☎04.67.33.93.02) – take bus #16 from the *gare* to "Route de Ganges" or the tram to "Hôpital Lapeyronie".

Police Hôtel de Ville ☎04.67.34.71.00.

Regional Products Maison Régionale des Vins et des Produits du Terroir, 34 rue St-Guilhem (Mon–Sat 9am–8pm).

Swimming Piscine Olympique d'Antigone, av Jacques-Quartier (☎04.67.15.63.00; tram to "Léon Blum").

Taxis Allo Taxi d'Oc ☎04.67.47.26.80; Taxi 2000 ☎04.67.03.45.45; Taxi à Montpellier ☎04.67.20.35.20; Taxi Bleu or 5 ACTM ☎04.67.03.20.00.

Train information ☎04.99.74.15.10.

Travel agencies USIT Connect, 1 rue de
l'Université ☎08.25.08.25.25, ⓦwww
.usitconnect.fr; Nouvelles Frontières, 4 rue Jeanne
d'Arc ☎04.67.64.64.15, ⓦwww.nouvelles
-frontieres.fr.

Youth information CRIJ, 3 av Charles-Flahault
☎04.67.04.36.66. Youth information and a
ride-sharing service, Allostop ☎04.67.04.28.28,
ⓦwww.allostop.net. Also Espace Montpellier
Jeunesse, 6 rue Maguelone (Mon–Fri noon–6pm;
☎04.67.92.30.50, ⓔsej.dj@ville-montpellier.fr).

The coast: La Grande-Motte to Marseillan-Plage

From its narrowing point at Le Grau-du-Roi, south of Nîmes, the Petite Camargue trails off westwards in fits and starts – a string of salty *étangs* and scrubby flats populated by birds and bulls respectively, passing close by Montpellier and continuing as far as Agde (see p.328). The easternmost town along this stretch is **La Grande-Motte**, a bizarre 1960s planned resort handy for getting to the ruins of **Ambrussum** a few kilometres inland, where the great Via Domitia once carried goods from Cadiz, past Gibraltar, all the way to Rome. The other towns along this coast – **Palavas**, **Sète** and **Mèze** – have been fishing centres for generations, and their maritime heritage lives on in popular local traditions, such as the water-joust. Only **Maguelone**, once a bustling port, was unable to stand the test of the ages, and has been reduced to an ancient and romantically sited **cathedral**. Extremely popular and flooded with people in the summer months, all of these towns offer the makings of a good beach holiday, but they are far from being merely soulless seaside resorts.

La Grande-Motte

Separated by only a few kilometres of sandy beach from Le Grau-du-Roi to the east and less than 20km southeast of Montpellier's centre, **LA GRANDE-MOTTE** is undoubtedly the oddest resort town on the French Mediterranean. A Sixties-era beachside version of Montpellier's Antigone development, this "futuristic" planned community, executed by Jean Balladur has aged about as gracefully as the beanbag chair and eight-track tape. Begun in 1967, the town consists of an immense array of weirdly shaped sand-coloured condos and apartment complexes with evocative names like "Le Calypso" and "Temple du Soleil", set on a long boardwalk. Traffic is banished to the background; you park (if you can find space) in the back streets, and reach the beach on foot. The strange aspect of the seafront is compounded by the absence of trees – nothing breaks up the pale beige landscape sandwiched between sea and sky – and, to cap it off, the proliferation of restaurants and shops on the promenade makes the whole place feel like an enormous shopping mall that just happens to have a beach. Aside from its peculiar looks though, the town is a run-of-the-mill family-holiday seaside resort, where apartments and hotels are usually booked for two- to four-week blocks. It's as good a place as any to stop for a swim, and if you want to spend a couple of days on the beach, you'll find all the facilities and services you would expect.

Practicalities

La Grande-Motte's **tourist office** (daily: July & Aug 9am–9pm; Sept–June 10am–12.30pm & 2–6/6.30pm; ☎04.67.56.42.00, ⓦwww.ot-lagrandemotte .fr) is on allée des Parcs, at the entrance to the town. **Buses** arrive at the *gare* *routière*, just to the east of the tourist office on avenue de Melgueil. The most appealing among the town's dozen or so near-identical **hotels** is the *Azur Bord de Mer* (℡04.67.56.56.00, ⊛www.hotelazur.net; ❺), dramatically set on the extremity of the town's quay. A cluster of seven **campsites** sits just west of the tourist office, among them *Louis Pibols* (April–Oct; ℡04.67.56.50.08) and *Le Garden* (March–Oct; ℡04.67.56.50.09), both close to the beaches and with good facilities. The only **restaurant** which stands out above the uniform beachside fare is *Alexandre Amiraute* (closed Sun eve & Mon; ℡04.67.56.63.63) on esplanade de la Capitainerie, with good views of the port (*menus* from €25). **Bikes** and scooters can be rented at Bumpcycles, 172 rue des Artisans (℡04.67.29.87.73), Holiday Bikes, 476 avenue de Melgueil (℡04.67.29.14.30, ⓔgrandmotte@holiday-bikes.com), and at numerous other beachside outfits.

Lunel and Ambrussum

Marking the northwestern extent of the Petite Camargue, **LUNEL** is just 14km north of La Grande-Motte, on the western side of the Vidourle river. Aside from a few medieval buildings scattered about the decaying old town, the place is unforgivingly nondescript, and the only reason to stop here is to partake in the town's lively tradition of *tauromachie* – bullfights are held occasionally from spring to mid-autumn – or to visit the nearby ruins of Roman Ambrussum.

The Roman settlement of **AMBRUSSUM** (admission free; guided tours July & Aug Tues & Wed at 10am; reserve at Lunel tourist office; €2) once commanded the bridge which carried the Via Domitia over the Vidourle, but is now reduced to a couple of massive supports rising romantically out of the river. To get to the ruins, climb the stairs on the hillside, to the old Roman **road**. Where this forks, taking the left will lead you past a series of indecipherable foundations and on to the remnants of the town's once formidable five-metre-thick walls. There are good **views** from the top, and it's a popular spot for locals – the riverside is quite beautiful, its trail makes for a pleasant walk and the area is prime for picnicking. The ruins themselves, however, are disappointingly insubstantial, and there is a lack of informative plaques.

A stop on the Montpellier–Nîmes line, Lunel's **gare SNCF** is on rue Verdun; from here it's a fifteen-minute walk south to the **tourist office** (July & Aug Mon–Sat 9am–7pm, Sun 9.30am–12.30pm; Sept–June Mon–Sat 9am–noon & 2–6pm, Sun 9.30am–12.30pm; ℡04.67.71.01.37, ⊛www.ot-paysdelunel .fr) on cours Georges-Péri, beside the church in the old town. The summer-only (mid-June to mid-Sept) "Comet" **bus** service from La Grande-Motte stops at the main roundabout by the rue République, where you can also get the bus towards Ambrussum (Tues & Thurs at 12.20pm; dir. Villetelle), which drops you within a few kilometres of the ruins (follow the signposted gravel road). If you get stuck in Lunel for the night, *Les Mimosas*, on Avenue de Vidourle (℡04.67.71.25.40, ⓔhotellesmimosas@free.fr; ❷) provides cheap and adequate **accommodation**, and you can get a decent **meal** at *L'Auberge des Halles* beside the tourist office (closed Sun eve, Mon & Feb; *menus* from €18). There are several **campsites** in the neighbourhood, including *Bon Port* on route de Camargue, just south of town (April–Oct; ℡04.67.71.15.65, ⊛www.campingbonport.com).

Palavas and Maguelone

PALAVAS-LES-FLOTS is Montpellier's own beach town, now absorbed into the metropolitan *agglomération* and even served by regular city buses. The town has been a popular seaside destination for almost a century, a fact attested to by the satirical caricatures of its inhabitants and visitors drawn by Montpellier artist Albert Dubout (1905–76). It's not as dismal as it seems, either, for once you penetrate the surrounding developments you'll find that the oldest part, where the banks of the canalized River Lez reach the sea, still retains the air of a pretty old fishing town. That said, Palavas is a busy, modern resort complete with all that that implies: restaurants of dubious quality, stores selling colourful junk and crowds of people enjoying themselves swimming, sunbathing, sailing and cycling. Like so much of the coast, the town is built on a sand bar which encloses a series of *étangs*, the smallest of which, the Lac du Levant, on the north side of the old quarter, has a small eighteenth-century fort, La Redoubte, in the middle. Reached by a long causeway, the fort now houses the **Musée Albert Dubout** (Jan & Dec Sat & Sun 2–6pm; Feb–June Tues–Sun 2–7pm; July & Aug daily 4pm–11pm; Sept–Nov Tues–Sun 1–6pm; €5 including the Musée du Train), where you can see the artist's work. Back on the mainland, a **Musée du Train** (same hours and ticket as Musée Dubout) houses the steam locomotive which used to run between here and Montpellier and was a favourite subject of Dubout (you'll see it in several of the works on display in the museum). The *étangs* themselves are replete with birdlife, and are one of the few places on the French coast where you will see flamingoes in their habitat; the tourist office can arrange **bird-watching** trips (Mon–Fri 9am–noon; €5).

The most interesting section of **beach** and the best for swimming and sunbathing lies west of the main town, past the campsite. You can get there by TAM bus or, if you drive, you will be obliged (mid-June to mid-Sept) to use the free car park. From the parking area, a narrow sand spit stretches west, separated from the *étang* behind by a shrubby embankment; the beach here is a popular gay spot and given over generally to nude bathing. A road runs along the inland side of the embankment on which a free *petit train* runs every twenty minutes, ferrying people from their cars to the beach and on to the isthmus of **MAGUELONE** (TAM buses do the route out of season).

You wouldn't guess it, but the Romanesque **cathedral**, built in the 1100s and dominating the green promontory today, was for centuries one of the most important churches in the medieval South of France. Before accumulating silt linked it to the mainland, Maguelone was an island, most likely first settled by the Phoenicians. In the early eighth century, the town here was taken by Muslim forces, but Charles Martel, court chamberlain and de facto ruler of France, pushed back the Muslim advance and destroyed the settlement in 737 to prevent its recapture and use as a forward base for further attacks. Refounded in 1030, the strongly fortified church became an important religious centre and a place of refuge for bishops and popes in their quarrels with the nobility and kings of Europe. In 1096, Urban II proclaimed Maguelone as the second church after Rome – an indulgence which guaranteed the complete forgiveness of sins of whoever was buried there. Shortly thereafter, the church was rebuilt in its present form. With the papal blessing and in its recovered role as port, the town thrived from the Middle Ages until the Wars of Religion, when Louis XIII destroyed it for its unrepentant Protestantism. Nowadays, all that remains is the ancient church. The building is still a place of worship, so you can't enter it in beachwear, although you'll be able to see its marble **portal**, with excellent mid-twelfth-century low-relief carvings of apostles Peter and Paul. The **interior** (10am–6/6.30pm; free), which has suffered total looting through the ages, is dominated by a huge overhanging gallery. You'll find some ancient tombstones down by the altar, and from the gallery you can look down through the sluices over the entrance, which were intended to have hot oil poured through them onto the heads of attackers. The rest of the island is a verdant idyll, and on the north shore, some restored fishermen's huts evoke the Maguelone of the early twentieth century, when it was a poor fishing hamlet.

Practicalities

TAM **buses** (route #17; from tram stop "Port Marianne" in Montpellier) circulate throughout the town. Palavas' **tourist office** (July & Aug daily 10am–8pm; April–June & Sept daily 10am–noon & 2–6pm; Oct–March Mon–Sat 9am–noon & 2–6pm; ☎04.67.07.73.34, ⊚www.palavaslesflots.com) is in the unmistakable lighthouse building which towers above the port. For **accommodation**, try the central *Le France*, at 9 quai Clémenceau (☎ & ℉04.67.74.00.35; ❹), or the down-beat *du Midi*, 191 av Saint Maurice (☎04.67.68.00.53, ⊚www .hotel.du-midi.com; ❹), half of whose rooms look out over the beach; both are good value with excellent locations. There are several **campsites** around town, most along avenue Saint Maurice, but the best situated is the beachside *Palavas Camping* (mid-April to mid-Sept ☎04.67.68.01.28, ⓔpalavascamping@free.fr) at the westernmost end of town. You'll have no problem finding a **restaurant** here: the ones that stand out include the riverside *La Marine* 1 Quai Paul Cunq (☎04.67.68.00.05), for its original seafood creations (upwards of €28); *Les Flots Bleus*, at 21 quai Georges-Clémenceau (☎04.67.68.01.73; closed part Jan), for its grilled monkfish (*menu* from €19); and the elegant *Les Embruns*, 3 avenue Général-de-Gaulle (☎04.67.68.16.95), which specializes in lobster and turbot (*menu* €20–45) and has fine views over the canal.

Sète

Some 38km west along the marshy coast from Maguelone, and a twenty-minute ride by train or car from Montpellier, the cranes and winches of **SÈTE**'s busy port rise above the expanse of *étangs*. Entering town from this direction you find yourself surrounded by grey warehouses, fenced-in storage yards and stacks of freight containers. This initial vision is somewhat disconcerting, but once across the wide Canal Maritime, you'll arrive at the colourful old quarter, which straddles the westernmost of the two north–south canals, the Canal Royal. On the west bank of the canal, the land rises dramatically, hedging in the historical centre. This slope is the eastern side of the 175m-high rocky promontory, **Mont St-Clair**, whose presence has determined the growth of the town. As

Water-jousting

The origins of the curious Sètois sport of **water-jousting** are lost, but the practice seems to have originated in the late seventeenth century, when Sète was thriving as a port thanks to its link to the Canal du Midi and the Canal du Rhône. The sport consists of two sleek boats, each manned by eight oarsmen, charging at each other on a near head-on course. At the stern of each boat, a long, raised tail supports the platform on which a jouster stands, dressed in white. Six other jousters provide a counterweight to the platform, while the rest of the crew, a coxswain and two musicians, keep the boat on course and in time. As the boats approach each other, the jousters steady their small shields, aim their long lances and attempt to strike their adversary from his mount. The spectacle is repeated seven times in each tournament, or *joute*, and the winning team is the one that unseats its opponents the most times. There are about a dozen *sociétés des joutes* in Sète (other Languedocian ports also have their own teams). The season runs from late spring through early autumn, with more frequent tournaments taking place in the summer. The most important championships are held here on August 25, the *fête de St-Louis*.

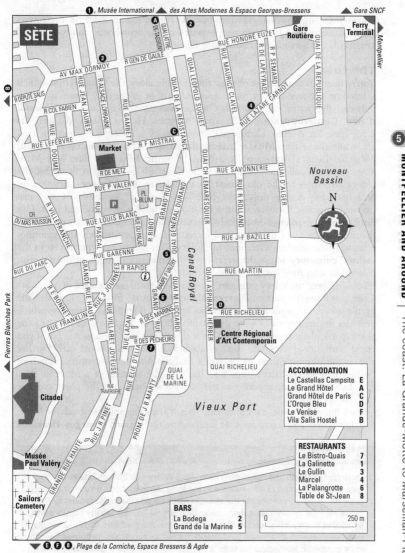

SÈTE

Gare
Routière

Ferry
Terminal

Montpellier

Nouveau
Bassin

Market

Canal Royal

Centre Régional
d'Art Contemporain

Pierres Blanches Park

Citadel

Vieux Port

Musée
Paul Valéry

Sailors'
Cemetery

ACCOMMODATION

Le Castellas Campsite	E
Le Grand Hôtel	A
Grand Hôtel de Paris	C
L'Orque Bleu	D
Le Venise	F
Vila Salis Hostel	B

RESTAURANTS

Le Bistro-Quais	7
La Galinette	1
Le Gullin	3
Marcel	4
La Palangrotte	6
Table de St-Jean	8

BARS

| La Bodega | 2 |
| Grand de la Marine | 5 |

0 ————— 250 m

▼ ⓔ,ⓕ,ⓖ, Plage de la Corniche, Espace Bressens & Agde

it expanded early in the last century, Sète grew as a long corniche completely circling the *mont*, but recently suburbs have begun to climb its steep slopes. The attractive town has a couple of small museums and a park, but primarily makes a good base for enjoying the twenty-kilometre long unbroken stretch of beach west towards Agde – it also has accommodation, excellent pleasure-port facilities and lively nightlife in summer. The best beach reachable by public transport (buses #6, 7 & 9) – with showers and other amenities – is the Plage de la Corniche, where you'll also find restaurants and accommodation (see p.279). It's also worth trying to time your visit to coincide with one of the many

water-jousting tournaments (see box, p.276) which are held on the town's canals; the quaysides jam with people watching the boat-borne combatants, and afterwards the bars fill with boisterous revelry.

The town

You're likely to spend most of your time in Sète along the Canal Royal, which is lined on the west side by restaurants and bars, or in the tight scrum of streets between the water and the hill. On the waterfront, the **Centre Régional d'Art Contemporain**, at 26 quai Aspirant Herber (Mon & Wed–Fri 2.30–7pm, Sat & Sun 12.30–7pm; free), houses a varied collection of local art, while the quirky **Musée International des Arts Modestes**, at 23 quai Maréchal-Lattre (10am–noon & 2–6pm: July–Aug daily; Sept–June Wed–Mon; €5) contains a collection of art made from cast-off goods. Apart from this, the closest attraction to the old quarter is the **Musée Paul Valéry** (10am–noon & 2–6pm: July & Aug daily; Sept–June Wed–Sun; €3), southwest of the canal on rue François-Desnoyer, about a ten-minute walk west of the old port. This doubles as a municipal historical museum, whose collection focuses on the nautical traditions of the town and includes documents, models and paintings relating to the sport of water jousting. Valéry's (see box below) remains lie in the **sailors' cemetery** across the street from the museum, along with many Sètois fishermen who have lost their lives at sea.

Looking over the Valéry museum, on a broad plateau on the west of Mont St-Clair, you'll see the park of **Pierres Blanches** (bus #5 from the Hôtel de Ville or the museum), a scrubby habitat for lavender, thyme and rosemary, which provides impressive views over the shellfish beds of the Bassin de Thau to the north, particularly towards sunset. This is also a great spot for a picnic, but if you come without supplies, you can get a snack at the small on-site café. Further east, at the summit of the mont, you'll find the nineteenth-century church of Notre-Dame-de-la-Salette (bus #5), built on the remains of a medieval fort; the church is nothing special but the views from here over the ports, old and new, are spectacular.

From the canal front, it's a long ride (bus #3) to the northwest side of Mont St-Clair, where you'll find another local shrine, the **Espace Georges-Brassens**

Paul Valéry

Though of Corsican and Italian parentage, **Paul Valéry** was born in Sète in 1871, and spent his childhood and adolescence in the town. An introspective youth, he whiled away his hours contemplating the sea. On reaching adulthood, he moved to Paris, where he took up work as a legal clerk; by this time he had already begun writing **Symbolist poetry** influenced by Poe and Mallarmé. His great and largely unrequited love, however, was for science, and despite his literary successes, he turned towards more pragmatic intellectual pursuits in the sciences. He was a great admirer of da Vinci, in whom he saw the "universal man" – a cerebral Renaissance figure whom he brought to life in his stylized novel *Monsieur Teste* (1895). Valéry did his best to live up to the da Vincian ideal which he professed. In his forties, at the urging of André Gide, he returned to poetry, while his scientific pursuits brought him into personal contact with contemporaries such as Albert Einstein. His acute observational powers and political insights made him a popular *salon* guest in inter-war Paris, and official accolades followed with his election in 1925 to the Académie Française and his appointment to the Collège de France as the first Professor of Poetry. Valéry remained in Paris through the Nazi occupation and, having lived to see the Liberation, died the following year and was buried as a national hero.

(July & Aug daily 10am–noon & 2–7pm; June & Sept daily 10am–noon & 2–6pm; Oct–May Tues–Sun 10am–noon & 2–6pm; €5). Brassens (1921–81) was perhaps France's most popular folk singer of the postwar era, a sort of Gallic Bob Dylan, whose simple guitar melodies served as platforms for irony-edged sentimental lyrics.

Practicalities

Sète's **gare SNCF** (☎04.67.46.51.00) is on quai Maréchal-Joffre, on the north bank of the Canal Latéral; from here it's a forty-minute walk into town so your best bet is to take bus #3 to the "Les Pénitents" stop, near the tourist office. The **gare routière** is a little bit closer in, on quai de la République; from here it's a ten-minute walk west along rue Honoré Euzet to the Canal Royal, and then another fifteen minutes south to the tourist office, or you can take bus #4 to the Hôtel de Ville, at the northern end of the old town. Across the Canal Maritime, to the east of the *gare routière*, you'll find the **ferry terminal**, Gare Maritime Orsetti (☎04.67.46.68.00; bus #4), which has regular departures for Mallorca and Morocco. The **tourist office**, at 60 Grand'rue Mario Roustan (July & Aug daily 9.30am–7.30pm; Sept–June Mon–Fri 9.30am–6pm & Sat & Sun 9.30am–12.30pm & 2–5.30pm; ☎04.67.74.71.71, ⓦwww.ot-sete.fr), has exchange facilities, and sells local bus tickets (€1 one-way). Buses #6, #7 or #9 will take you to the Plage de la Corniche, the town's best beach. You can rent **bikes** at Déferlantes, 6 quai Commandant Samary (☎04.67.74.82.30), and **scooters** at Cabello, 9 quai Vauban (☎04.67.74.50.29). There's **Internet** access at Le Cyber Snack, 10 av Victor-Hugo (Mon–Fri 9am–noon & 2–6pm). For **boat** rides, Sète Croisières on Quai Général Durand, runs a number of regular trips in the summer for €10–15.

Hotels, hostel and campsite

Le Castellas campsite 10km west of town on the RN112 ☎04.67.51.63.00, ⓦwww.le-castellas .com. This mammoth complex is the biggest and best around. Open May–Sept.

Le Grand Hôtel 17 quai de Lattre de Tassigny ☎04.67.74.71.77, ⓦwww.legrandhotelsete.com. Alongside the northern part of the Canal Royal, this elegant hotel has good views over the canal, and secure parking. ❺

Grand Hôtel de Paris 2 rue Frédéric-Mistral ☎04.67.74.98.10. Decaying but funky, this atmospheric hotel is a good option in high season when others fill up. Few amenities, but clean and central. Open May–Sept. ❸

'Orque Bleu 10 quai Aspirant-Herber ☎04.67.74.72.13, ⓦwww.hotel -orquebleue-sete.com. At the southern end of the Canal Royal, this converted nineteenth-century mansion is the best deal in town – try to get a quayside room, as the views over the canal to the old town are great. ❸

Villa Salis Hostel rue du Général-Revest ☎04.67.53.46.68, ⓦwww.fuaj.org. Unhospitably basic, and a stiff half-hour walk west of the *gare routière* on the eastern slopes of the *Mont*. Open mid-Jan to Nov. €20 per person for compulsory half-board.

Hôtel le Venise Plage de la Corniche ☎04.67.53.02.86. Steps from the sand, this hotel makes a good alternate to staying in the centre of town. Closed Dec & Jan. ❷

Restaurants, cafés and bars

There's a barrage of restaurants along quai Général-Durand, from the pont de la Savonnerie right down to the pleasure port, all offering seafood in the €15–30 bracket.

Le Bistro-Quais 50 Grand'rue ☎04.99.04.99.90. This traditional French bistro has a cosy dining room and an excellent wine selection. *Menus* from €16–25. Closed Sun & Mon.

La Bodega 21 quai Noël-Guignon. A cocktail bar playing jazz, Latin and rock music (nightly 10pm–4am).

La Galinette, 26 place des Mouettes ☎04.67.51.16.77. On the north side of town, this restaurant serves great-value seafood, with *menus* from €15. Closed Jan–June & Sun eve, Fri lunch & Sat lunch out of season.

Grand de la Marine 90 quai Durand. A good bar to start the night off.

Le Gullin 1 rue du 11 Novembre. The best deal for lunch with a four-course *prix fixe* for €12.

Marcel rue Lazare-Carnot ℡04.67.74.20.89. A great deal with grilled fish and local wines from €15.

La Palangrotte 1 rampe Paul Valéry ℡04.67.74.80.35. A local favourite, famous for its mussels and bouillabaisse (€23–36) and solid wine list. Closed Sun noon & Mon & Wed off-season.

Table de St-Jean Plage de la Corniche ℡04.67.53.02.57. A good bet next door to the *Le Venise*. Serves local specialities including *la tielle*, a spicy octopus pie, and biscuits, such as the sweet *zézette*, best washed down with muscat or champagne. Closed Mon.

Around the Bassin de Thau

North and west of Sète lies the shallow expanse of the **Bassin de Thau**, which, at 18km long and some 5km wide, is one of the biggest salt lakes in Languedoc. From its northeastern end above Sète it extends along the town's 14km stretch of beach southwest to Agde. The Bassin is a major centre of shellfish cultivation, particularly oysters and mussels, with approximately 13,000 tonnes of oysters raised here annually, ninety percent of which are the larger Pacific variety. At the eastern end of the lagoon, between Bouzigues and Sète, the wooden oyster racks protruding from the water make a curious aquascape. The oysters are harvested using a nineteenth-century technique of cementing them to ropes which hang from the racks: the strong winds which blow along the surface of the water compensate for the lack of tidal movement, which the shellfish depend on to move water through their gills. The water itself is a tepid, murky green – safe enough to swim in, although most prefer the clearer waters of the Mediterranean side. The closest you'll probably get to the oysters, however, is a steaming bowl of *coquillages*, enjoyed on a pier-side terrace.

There are two ways around the *étang* from Sète. The most direct route is to follow the windswept and narrow strip of dunes which separates the lagoon from the sea, a deserted stretch of highway punctuated only by the massive *Camping Castellas* (see p.279) and by windsurfers' camping vans. There are parking areas along the length of the road (with two-metre height barriers to prevent RVs from entering) and you can swim anywhere along its sandy length, though there are no showers, so you'll have to put up with a salty, post-swim crust until you reach accommodation. The inland route, while it has no major tourist sites, is a unique area well worth exploring, especially for its gastronomical delights. Either route can be managed by **bike** (the whole circuit is about 40km), but the usual warnings regarding the high speed traffic on the narrow secondary roads apply and strong winds add to the challenge.

Balaruc and Poussan

Coming from Sète, after 3km you'll arrive at Balaruc, which actually consists of two villages: **Balaruc-les-Bains**, an ancient fishing port turned spa town; and **Balaruc-le-Vieux**, a tiny *circulade* set dramatically on a low spur just inland. Here, you can see the remains of a third-century palaeo-Christian **basilica** (free). Don't let the built-up agglomeration of holiday flats around Balaruc-les-Bains put you off: its compact old town has managed to retain its charm, even

---

Museum discount pass

If you plan on visiting more than one of the museums around the Bassin, ask for a *"Passeport des 5 Sites"* at the first museum you visit; the free card will give you discounts at the remaining four. The Musée de l'Étang, Villa-Loupian, the Écosite, the dinosaur park, and the Abbey of Valmagne (see p.287) are all included.

in high season, and the views over the *étang* towards Sète and Mont Saint-Clair are striking. Five kilometres north is another ancient *circulade*, **Poussan**, dating from the tenth century. Its streets make for excellent strolling, with several fourteenth-century palaces, a still more ancient church, and a picturesque early-twentieth century metalwork **market** building.

Balaruc-les-Bains makes a good base for exploring the area, with a small **tourist office** in the old spa complex (Mon–Sat 9am–noon & 2–6/7pm, Sun 10am–12.30pm; June–Sept also Sun 4–7pm; ℡04.67.46.81.46, ⓦwww .balaruc-les-bains.com). It also has several good **hotels**, including the central *Neptune*, at 5 rue Montgolfier (℡04.67.48.53.17, ℱ04.67.43.56.44; ❸), with a pool, and the quieter *Arcadius* in the new town (℡04.67.80.90.00, ⓦwww .arcadius.com; ❸). The municipal **campsite**, *Du Pech d'Ay* (March–Dec; ℡04.67.48.50.34, Ⓔpechday@wanadoo.fr), is on avenue de la Gare just south of the central pedestrian area. There are a raft of **restaurants** along the water-front: two of the best, both with good seafood *menus* and views across the bay, are the *La Barge* (*menus* from €12–25), next to the campsite, and the more upmarket *Le Sainte Claire*, on Quai du Port (from €28–49), whose *bouillabaisse* is hard to beat. Weekly **markets** are held on Tuesday in Balaruc and Friday in Poussan.

Bouzigues and Loupian

A few kilometres from Balaruc on the north shore, **Bouzigues** seems like a fishing town which has slept through the last century, with its narrow, laundry-strung streets and strong salt-air. It is also *the* place to eat shellfish, and the long waterfront boulevard, avenue Louis Tudesq, is girded by a phalanx of colour-ful restaurants, offering generous, fresh *coquillages* (normally €36 for two): *Le Grand Bleu* is one of the best here, having been serving *coquillages* since 1926. After lunch, head to the **Musée de l'Étang de Thau** (daily: July & Aug 10am–12.30pm & 2.30–7pm; Sept–June 10am–noon & 2–6/7pm; €4), whose array of imaginative multimedia displays explains the art of shellfish raising (including tanks with live specimens) as well as traditional fishing techniques. If you want to stay, there's a surprisingly chic **hotel**, *À la Voile Blanche* on avenue Louis Tudesq (℡04.67.78.35.77, Ⓔalavoileblanche@wanadoo.fr; ❹).

Heading inland 5km to the west, the medieval hamlet of **Loupian** is the site of an excavated **Gallo-Roman villa** (late June to mid-Sept 11am–3.45pm; mid-Sept to late June Wed 3.30pm, Sat 2–5pm & Sun 11am–5pm; guided tours €4.60), dating from the tail end of the Roman period and containing some impressive figurative and geometric mosaics.

Mèze and around

The largest village on the Bassin de Thau's northern shore, **Mèze** is an ancient fishing hamlet whose old town is a dense maze of narrow streets flanked by low houses. As it isn't directly on the sea it gets relatively few visitors, and provides some respite from the crowded coastal towns. The village has a pleasant, laid-back feel, with two beaches, a beautiful old fishing port and a fine old **market** building, making it an excellent stop for families. It's also the main service centre for the Bassin de Thau: its **tourist office** (July & Aug Mon–Fri 9am–12.30pm & 2–7.30pm, Sat 9am–12.30pm & 2–7pm, Sun 9am–12.30pm; Sept–June Mon–Fri 9am–12.15pm & 1.30–6pm, Sat 9am–12.30pm; ℡04.67.43.93.08, ⓦwww.ville-meze.fr) is near the village centre on rue Massaloup. There's one **hotel**, the economical *de Thau*, on rue de la Parée (℡04.67.43.83.83, ℱ04.67.43.69.45; ❸), and a string of near-identical **restaurants** along the waterfront quai Descournut, all serving up shellfish fresh from the *bassin*: *Le Chabichou* and *Le Coquillou* are well regarded by locals, but any of them will do (*menus* from €15). The sprawling **campsite** *Beau Rivage* (April–Sept; ☎04.67.43.81.48) is located off the highway RN113. **Sailboats**, ideal for exploring the broad and calm *étang*, can be rented at Le Taurus in rue de la Méditerranée (☎04.67.43.59.51).

Three kilometres southwest of town along the shore, is the three-hectare **Écosite** (daily: April–June, Sept & Oct 2–6pm; July & Aug 10am–7pm; €4.60): set up to preserve the habitat of the salt lagoon, it has exhibitions on the flora and fauna of the *étang*, and on techniques of aquaculture. Also nearby, 5km north of Mèze, just off the main RN113 road towards Pézenas, is the **Musée-Parc La Plaine des Dinosaures** (daily 10am–5/7pm; €6), a museum and excavation area established on the site of a major palaeotological find: its highlights include a 12m-tall Brachiosaurus skeleton and one of the biggest caches of dinosaur eggs yet discovered.

Marseillan and Marseillan-Plage

Marseillan and Marseillan-Plage, which anchor the southern end of the Bassin, reflect how the economy of the region has shifted in the last generation. Once a flourishing fishing town, Marseillan now lies all but forgotten, ignored by the masses of weekenders who inundate the seashore at its namesake, Marseillan-Plage. This is good news for the few who do come to Marseillan, now the most picturesque and atmospheric town in the area, with a very evocative **old port** and a fine seventeenth-century **market**. There is little for the visitor to do aside from soak up the atmosphere, although a trip to the famed Noilly Prat **distillery** (daily 9.30am–noon & 3.30–7pm; €3.50) is a good excuse to soak up the local vermouth as well. Separated by nearly 10km of marshy reeds, Marseillan-Plage is, by contrast, the epitome of noisy Mediterranean hedonism. Its one sight, other than the hordes of near-naked bodies which crowd its beaches, is the **débouché**, the terminus of the great Canal du Midi, whose earthworks protrude strikingly into the Mediterranean here.

Marseillan-Plage's **tourist office** (July & Aug daily 9am–7pm; Sept–June Mon–Sat 9am–12.30pm & 3–6pm, Sun 9am–12.30pm; ☎04.67.21.82.43, ⓦwww.marseillan.com) is right after the main roundabout at the entrance to the resort. The best-value **hotel** here is *Le Richmont* on allée Filliol (☎04.67.21.97.79, ⓦwww.hotel-marseillan.com; ⑤), and there are over a dozen **campsites**, the largest of which, *Les Méditerranées* (April–Sept ☎04.67.21.94.49, ⓦwww.lesmediterranees.com) is on the appropriately named avenue des Campings. In

Marseillan, there's just one hotel, *Le Boulevard* in rue de Gaulle (T04.67.77.21.11, F04.67.26.50.95; ❷).

There's no shortage of **restaurants** to choose from in Marseillan-Plage, although few rise above the beach-town standard: one of the better ones is *Chez Philippe* at 20 rue de Suffren (T04.67.01.70.62; closed Sun–Tues Sept–June), an excellent traditional-style bistro where you'll spend €15–30. Marseillan's best restaurant is *La Table d'Émilie* by the covered market (T04.67.77.63.59; from €19), though you may prefer to drive 4km north of Marseillan to the splendid *L'Auberge du Domaine de la Mandoune* (T04.67.77.21.14; July & Aug Tues–Sun; Sept–June Fri–Sun; from €18) set in a nineteenth-century vineyard: it's signposted at the junction of the D18 and the D51.

Pézenas and around

Fifty-four kilometres southwest of Montpellier along the N113, and more or less halfway between Mèze and Béziers, **PÉZENAS** is the last large inland settlement on the Hérault river, as it meanders south to Agde through the vineyards of the Languedoc plain. One of the most singularly beautiful towns in the French Southwest, endowed with an almost overwhelming concentration of grand architecture, it is also a centre for **arts and crafts**, and thus very popular – packing out with tourists in July and August.

Although it had been an important market centre for centuries, Pézenas catapulted to glory when it became the seat of the Languedoc parliament and the residence of its governors in 1456, and reached its zenith in the late seventeenth century, when Armand de Bourbon, prince of Conti and governor of Languedoc, made it a "second Versailles", drawing artists and writers of the stature of Molière to his court with his wealthy patronage. On and off, the playwright spent a good four years here performing for the prince and garnering inspiration for the plays which would later make him famous. But with the prince's death in 1666, stagnation soon set in, and Pézenas reverted to the sleepy provincial town which – outside high season – it remains today. The rolling countryside around Pézenas is dotted with atmospheric old villages, such as **Tourbes**, as well as medieval castles, and the country's largest wine-producing monastery, the **abbey of Valmagne**.

Pézenas Town

Pézenas' compact **old town** is set on the west bank of the Peyne river, occupying the area between the hill on which the town's castle once stood, and the village church. It is best accessed from the broad café-lined place du 14 Juillet, a lively square which now hosts the town's market and is set on the riverside just to the west of the *gare*. Entering from here, the first of the fine *hôtels* which you'll encounter is the **Hôtel Lacoste** (10am–noon & 3–7pm; free) at 8 rue Oustrin, a fifteenth-century palace with a beautiful but compact vaulted courtyard framed by a monumental staircase; the mansion now houses temporary painting exhibitions. As you continue west, place Gambetta is home to the tourist office (see p.286), once the shop where Molière idled away his afternoons. Across the narrow, cobblestoned *place* stands the handsome sixteenth-century council house, whose broad and square vaulted interior once held sessions of the Estates of Languedoc, but now houses the **Maison des Métiers d' Arts** (10am–noon & 3–7pm; July & Aug also Wed & Fri 8.30–11pm; free), a showcase for local crafts, including painting, decorative sculpture, stained-glass items and the like.

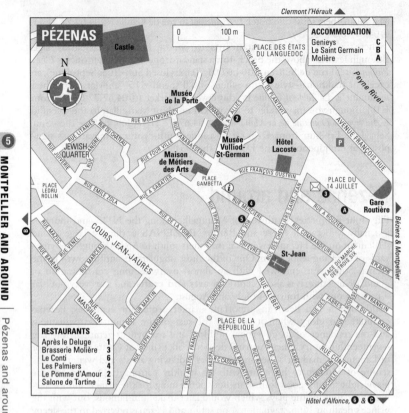

PÉZENAS

Castle

ACCOMMODATION

Genieys	C
Le Saint Germain	B
Molière	A

Peyne River

0   100 m

PLACE DES ÉTATS
DU LANGUEDOC

RUE MARÉCHAL DE PLANTAVIT

Clermont l'Hérault

Musée
de la Porte

RUE BÉRANGER

RUE ALLIÉS

RUE MONTMORENCY

Musée
Vulliod-
St-German

Hôtel
Lacoste

AVENUE FRANÇOIS HUE

RUE LITANIES

RUE DU CHÂTEAU

RUE CANABASSERIE

RUE FOUR VILLE

JEWISH
QUARTER

RUE ANDRÉ

RUE JUVERIE

Maison
de Métiers
des Arts

RUE FRANÇOIS OUSTRIN

PLACE
GAMBETTA

PLACE DU
14 JUILLET

PLACE
LEDRU
ROLLIN

RUE ÉMILE ZOLA

RUE SABATIER

RUE THIPRERIE LITTLE

RUE MERCIÈRE

RUE DES CHEVALIERS SAINT-JEAN

RUE A ROUZIÈRE

Gare
Routière

RUE DE LA FOIRE

RUE THIPRERIE LITTLE

RUE JUIFS

RUE ORFÈVRES

RUE COMMANDEURS

St-Jean

RUE DU MARCHÉ
DES TROIS SIX

COURS JEAN-JAURÈS

RUE MAZUC

RUE VENEL

RUE BARÊME

RUE MARCEAU

RUE BARÊME

RUE MASSILLON

RUE CONDORCET

RUE KLÉBER

RUE DES FABRES

RUE J. ROUSSEAU

R PLAUCHE

R FRANKLIN

R DU CAPT DAVID

RUE DOCTEUR MARTIN

RUE JOSEPH CAMBON

PLACE DE LA
RÉPUBLIQUE

RUE ANATOLE FRANCE

RUE RASPAIL

RUE H C CASSAN

RUE BARRATERIE

RUE DE JUVENEL

RUE RABELAIS

RUE BABRES

RUE CONTI

RUE DU VIEUX SALIN

R MICHELET

Béziers & Montpellier

RESTAURANTS

Après le Deluge	1
Brasserie Molière	3
Le Conti	6
Les Palmiers	4
Le Pomme d'Amour	2
Salone de Tartine	5

Hôtel d'Alfonce, **G** & **C**

From here, wandering off in any direction will lead you to the carved stone facades of the wealthy merchants and nobles of Renaissance Pézenas; a glance up as you stroll around will almost certainly reveal a playful human face, a stately lion or regal sun carved out of a window casement or doorframe. North of the square, down rue Alliés, is the mansion housing the **Musée Vulliod-St-German** (Mon–Sat 10am–noon & 2–5pm, Sun 2–5pm; €2) – purportedly dedicated to the life and times of Molière, but in fact containing all manner of sixteenth- and seventeenth-century artefacts, from classically themed Aubusson tapestries to displays dwelling on the daily life of the humbler classes. The famous playwright is recalled in a room containing some of his papers and personal effects. Beyond this museum, you'll see the watchtower that forms the sole remnant of the medieval fortifications, while on the hill at the end of rue Béranger lie the ruins of the **castle** (closed) destroyed by Richelieu and dating back to as early as 1500 BC. At the foot of the castle's rise, sits the small and rather dull **Musée de la Porte** (July & Aug Mon–Fri 10am–12.30pm & 3.30–7pm, Sat & Sun 3.30–7pm; Sept–June Sun 2–6pm; free), celebrating Pézenas' tradition of ironwork, most evident in the elaborate balustrades which can be seen around town.

On the far side of the castle's base through rue Litanies, is the town's old **Jewish quarter**, marked off by gates, as was the custom during the Middle Ages – there's not much of interest here but snaking east, between the gate

△ Pézenas' old town

of rue Juiverie and place Gambetta, are a warren of narrow streets jammed with magnificent *hôtels*; make sure you check out the doorway of the **Hôtel Grave** on rue du Château, the fifteenth-century **Hôtel de Jacques Coeur** at 7 rue Émile-Zola and the impressive ironwork railing in the courtyard at 12 rue Sabatier. From the old Jewish quarter, rue de la Foire eventually leads to the incongruously plain **church**, the Collegiate of St-Jean; south of this, at no. 32 rue Conti, the **Hôtel d'Alfonce** (July & Aug Mon–Fri 10am–noon & 2–6pm; €2) features a spacious courtyard girded by an ornately balustraded stone balcony; it was here that Molière's players put on performances during the winter of 1655–56.

If you like to **shop** while travelling, Pézenas will not disappoint, as two out of every three frontages seem to conceal a store or workshop, and in July and August many stay open till midnight on Wednesday & Friday. Quality varies incredibly, and if you persevere, you may turn up some interesting and original *objets* amongst the tack. Cheaper and considerably less durable souvenirs can be bought in the form of *petits pâtés*, bite-sized mince tarts based on the recipe of an Indian cook in Lord Clive's household – the British Governor of India holidayed here in 1768 and the recipe stuck. The best place to pick these up, piping hot, is at Maison Aleary, 9 rue des Chevaliers de St-Jean. Another speciality, the "*Berlingot*," is a hard candy which comes in a variety of flavours and continues to be made in the town. If you happen to be around for one of the local festivals (see box, p.260), keep an eye out for **Le Poulain** – the town's traditional totemic animal. A mock horse, constructed of a cloth-draped wooden frame and borne through the streets by a bunch of burly men, Le Poulain was adopted in honour of a foal which King Louis VIII's favourite mare gave birth to here in 1226.

Practicalities

Buses stop in Pézenas at the open-air *gare routière* on place Molière, from where it's a five-minute walk west to the main **tourist office**, on place Gambetta (July & Aug Mon–Tues, Thurs & Sat 9am–7pm, Wed & Fri 9am–10pm, Sun 10am–7pm; Sept–June Mon–Sat 9am–noon & 2–6pm, Sun 10am–noon & 2–5pm; ☎04.67.98.36.40, ⓦwww.ot-pezenas-valdherault.com). On Sundays, the town centre is taken over by a busy **market** from 10am to 6pm.

There are three **hotels** in Pézenas, all with good amenities: *Genieys*, at 9 rue Aristide-Briand, near the end of rue Conti (☎04.67.98.13.99, ⓦwww.logis-de-france.fr; ❸); the splendid old *Molière*, on place du 14 Juillet (☎04.67.98.14.00, ⓦwww.hotel-le-moliere.com; ❻); and the newer *Le Saint Germain*, at 6 av Paul Vidal (☎04.67.09.75.75, ⓦwww.hotel-saintgermain.com; ❹). If these are full, try *Les Rocailles* on the N113 in Montagnac (☎04.67.24.00.27, ⓕ04.67.24.06.70; ❸), or the luxurious **gîte** *Domaine l'Eskillou* in nearby Pouzolles (April–Nov; ☎ & ⓕ04.67.24.60.50, ⓦwww.perso.wanadoo.fr /domaine-eskillou; ❹, including breakfast), **Campsites** in the area include the municipal site *Castelsec* (April–Oct; ☎04.67.98.04.02, ⓔg.benezech @agglohm.net) and *St-Christol* (mid-April to mid-Sept; ☎04.67.98.09.00, ⓦwww.campingsaintchristol.com).

There are a couple of excellent **restaurants** in Pézenas: *Les Palmiers*, 50 rue de Mercière (June–Sept; ☎04.67.09.42.56), is a beautiful and welcoming establishment serving inventive Mediterranean-style cuisine from about €28, while *Après le Deluge*, 5 rue Maréchal de Plantavit (☎04.67.98.10.77; closed Mon eve & mid-Nov to mid-Dec), is in a fourteenth-century building with several separate dining-rooms (*menus* €17–45). For lunch, the comfortable *La Tartine* at 17 rue des Orfèvres, serves home-style meals in a funky, informal atmosphere (open lunch only; about €15). Aside from these, there's no shortage of unremarkable restaurants serving *menus* for under €18: *La Pomme d'Amour* on rue Albert-Paul-Alliés (March–Dec; closed Mon eve & Tues in winter) and *Brasserie Molière* on place du 14 Juillet (notable for its good whisky selection) both serve *terroir* food, while *Le Conti*, 27 rue Conti (closed Mon in winter & Sun), is a pizzeria. You can **rent bikes** at Cycles Garin in av Émile-Combes (☎04.67.98.34.04), and **cars** at *Citer* on rte de Béziers (☎04.67.98.82.08). For **Internet**, head to Aranhi at 30 rue Conti (daily 10am–10pm).

Around Pézenas

The immediate surroundings of Pézenas offer good possibilities for walking, cycling or exploring by car. The attractive old town of **Montagnac**, with a well-preserved fourteenth-century church, lies halfway between Pézenas and the twelfth-century Cistercian **abbey of Valmagne** (daily: mid-June to Sept 10am–noon & 2.30–6.30pm; Oct to mid-June 2–6pm; closed Tues in winter; guided tours in English available; €6). Set in a romantic wooded park, Valmagne was once one of the richest abbeys in the south of France and is now the largest wine-producing monastery in the country. It has a well-preserved cloister, a gothic church and chapterhouse, and hosts temporary art exhibitions and occasional concerts.

To the south of Pézenas, **Castelnau-de-Guers** was once a way-station on the Roman Via Domitia, while 3km southwest on the road to Béziers, the medieval village of **Tourbes** boasts a maze of narrow alleys with a porticoed square and a medieval church. More impressive, however, is the priory, **Château de Cassan** (mid-April to late June & early Sept to early Oct Mon–Fri 2–7pm & Sat & Sun 10am–7pm; late June to early Sept daily 10am–7pm; early Oct to mid-Dec Sat & Sun 11am–6pm; €7), 10km west of town, just beyond Roujan. Founded in 1080, its abbots ruled over extensive territories in the 1200s, answering only to the Pope. Following the Hundred Years' War and Wars of Religion, it fell into decline until the 1700s, when it was rebuilt as a huge Neoclassical palace. Aside from the Romanesque church, and the remains of a medieval hospital, the main attraction today is its immense cloister, which contains a fine iron-forged staircase. Also in the grounds is an elaborate Oriental garden founded by Armand de Bourbon.

Inland from Montpellier

The area **inland from Montpellier** is dominated by two rivers: the mighty Hérault, which cuts down southwest from the Cévennes mountains through the plains above the city, and the Vis, which runs along the northern rim of the *département* and into the Hérault at Ganges. Between them, their underpopulated and lesser-travelled valleys – a world apart from the fishing towns and beaches of the coast – offer some remarkable scenery and attractions, and, taken in conjunction with a couple of absorbing towns, also form a naturally circuitous tour of the region by car, with plenty of hiking opportunities along the way.

The circuit starts with quiet **Clermont-l'Hérault**, poised on the eastern edge of the Haut Languedoc uplands 40km west of Montpellier, which provides access to the nearby reservoir **Lac du Salagou** and an array of interesting sites: the old industrial centre of **Villeneuvette**; **Cabrières'** prehistoric copper mines; and the eerie landscape of **Cirque de Mourèze**. North of here is **Lodève**, an eminently explorable town which boxes in the Orb valley to the west and provides a good base for local excursions, as well as for the route eastwards across the high plateau des Garrigues to the beautiful **Cirque de Navacelles** in the Vis valley. From here, you pass down through the Vis gorge to link up eventually with the Hérault just north of **Ganges**. The area on the southern border of the Cévennes – with its gnarled olive trees and sturdy oaks – is a far cry from the Mediterranean scrub of the plains further south, a zone whose cloth industry was supported by the flocks of sheep which still roam its long valleys. Ganges provides easy access to the cavernous chambers of the **Grotte des Demoiselles**, which open up under the calcite plateau – you'll pass the *grotte* on either of two routes south to Montpellier. The first follows the **Hérault valley** itself, veering southwest to the deep Hérault gorge and the ancient hamlet and UNESCO

World Heritage site of **St-Guilhem-le-Désert**, while the second, more direct route heads straight south via the **Pic-St-Loup**, standing sentinel above the coastal plain, and the old town of **St-Martin-de-Londres**.

Clermont-l'Hérault and around

Some 40km west of Montpellier, a short distance from the banks of the River Hérault, lies quiet **CLERMONT-L'HÉRAULT**, a dull little cantonal capital whose only recommendation is as a jumping-off point for visiting the area around **Lac du Salagou**. The town itself merits little more than a brief walk, with a stop to look at the thirteenth-century **church**, fortified in the fourteenth century to defend it against the English, and the small Gothic chapel of **Notre-Dame-du-Peyrou**, at 8 rue Louis Blanc, once a way-station on the *chemin de St-Jacques*.

More interesting is nearby **Villeneuvette**, 4km west. A model factory town founded by Colbert in the seventeenth century to produce high-quality wool for sale in the Mediterranean, Villeneuvette stayed in business until 1954 and still has 85 inhabitants. The walled-in compound is entered through a monumental gate bearing the legend *Honneur au Travail* ("honour to work"), and inside, a square, flanked by the church and *mairie*, opens onto neat rows of low, flower-bedecked workers' houses and the decaying factory. In its wooded surroundings, the little settlement presents a curious but enchanting idyll. A further 5km south of Villeneuvette, at Cabrières, you can visit the site of the **copper mines** of **Pioch Farrus** (April–Nov daily 10am–7pm; €7), which were exploited by the region's Neolithic inhabitants over 5000 years ago – the engaging hour-long tour takes you through 200m of galleries. Wrap up warm; the temperature in the mine is 15°C.

Northwest of Villeneuvette is the village of Mourèze in the midst of an eerie zone of eroded dolomite known as the **Cirque de Mourèze**, featuring a landscape of ancient seabed eroded by rainfall into a forest of rocky pinnacles. You can stroll though the myriad of paths which crisscross the area, or enjoy an impressive panoramic view from the **Courtinales** (daily: July & Aug 10am–7pm; Sept–June 10am–6pm; €4), a private park whose footpaths lead through a garden of local fauna and reconstructions of the prehistoric dwellings of the region – good fun for adults and children. Mourèze was also the first town that the Resistance group, the Maquis Bir Hakeim, liberated from the Germans – a monument to 140 of their dead (including one English officer) sits a kilometre or two south of the entrance to town.

Continuing towards **Salasc**, a tiny crossroads hamlet 4km further west, the landscape looks Martian, as the ground gives way to red iron-rich dunes. From Salasc, the road marked for Laiusson leads to the south shore of **LAC DU SALAGOU**, a reservoir whose shallow waters teem with birdlife, as well as fish and tiny crabs. The north shore, east of the larger village of **Octon**, is more developed and the landscape less striking. As the road follows the cliffs above the shore, it passes the ghost town of **Celles**, which was expropriated in the 1970s when the reservoir was built. The waters, however, never reached the hamlet, which now sits abandoned. Today, it is the scene of a lively mix of families on outings and nude bathers. After another eight kilometres of winding road, you'll join up with the busy *route nationale* just north of Clermont.

Practicalities

Trains and **buses** arrive in Clermont-l'Hérault at the **gare SNCF** on place Frédéric-Mistral, five minutes' walk south of the town centre. The **tourist office**

In 1942, with the dissolution of the puppet **Vichy regime**, the formal **German occupation** of Languedoc began, and once again the natives of the region found themselves fighting an outside power against enormous odds. Although research has dispelled the romantic vision that every Frenchman was pro-Resistance (in fact, it seems, just as many were against it), in Languedoc the movement was particularly strong and determined. This was due to a number of factors, not the least of which was a sense of regional identity. The highlands of Languedoc were traditionally a home to nonconformists, originally Cathars and Huguenots, but in the 1940s to "white" royalists, "red" communists, supplemented by refugee leftists from Franco's fascist Spain (some of whom were wanted by the Gestapo), Wehrmacht deserters and Jews escaping from occupied northern France. Local people were additionally embittered by the fact that citizens had suffered involuntary transportation to Germany to substitute factory workers gone to the front, and others, who had volunteered, seeing this as the only escape from a devastated rural economy, had found themselves in concentration camps. Given these conditions, men and women of the highlands of Languedoc took up arms with determination. Soon they became known as "*maquisards*" or "**maquis**", a term which refers to the scrubby Mediterranean landscape – the isolated and difficult terrain which was their home and their refuge.

In the first two years of German occupation, the *maquis* groups were comprised of mere handfuls of individuals, who tended to be ideologically committed enough to die for the anti-Nazi cause, mostly **Communists**. The main resistance group, which operated primarily in the Cévennes and eastern Haut Languedoc, was known as the Maquis Bir Hakeim, named after the heroic defence of Bir Hakeim in Libya by Free French Forces in June 1942. They were extremely active in the region until surprised by German forces in the hills near La Parade in May 1944 and wiped out. In the Sidobre of western Haut Languedoc and Tarn, the **Resistance** was more durable, and the feared Maquis de Vabre carried out a campaign of raiding and sabotage despite the brutal retaliations which such acts provoked. In 1944, with the invasion of Normandy, Allied successes in Italy and Russian advances in the East, the writing was clearly on the wall for the Germans, and more and more French began to join the Resistance. Meanwhile, the Allies began to provide support for the Resistance, supplying them with air cover and sending in agents. In August of that year, fifteen commandos of the OSS (the fore-runner of the CIA) were parachuted into Vabre, one day before a British agent, Major Davies, arrived. Davies' notebook, which he called a report on "the war in Languedoc Rouge", recalls the fighters as "mainly youths who were not very experienced, but they made a profound impression on me. They were fine upstanding fellows with fresh keen faces, from all social classes. In England, of course, they would (still) have been at school." Davies was also impressed by the participation of people from all walks of life. "This was the sort of war that Mr. Smith, Jones and Robinson of France were engaged in, nothing very tremendous perhaps but brave work nonetheless..." Despite their lack of arms and equipment, in August 1944, *maquis* action turned the German withdrawal from Albi into a military debacle – many vehicles were lost and the 4500-strong garrison of Castres surrendered. In the wake of this retreat, the Resistance squads were organized into the Forces Françaises de l'Interieur and sent to Lyon to bolster the Allied presence.

(Mon–Fri 9am–12.30pm & 2–7pm, Sat 9am–noon & 2–5/6pm; July & Aug also Sun 10am–noon; ☎04.67.96.23.86, ⓦwww.ot-clermont-l-herault.com) for the town and surrounding area is at 9 rue Gosse, between the station and the church. **Bikes** can be rented at Ozone on rte du Lac du Salagou (☎04.67.96.27.17).

If you have to stay overnight in Clermont itself, the best bet is the basic **hotel** *Le Terminus*, at 11 allées Salegro, by the station (☎04.67.88.45.00,

Ⓔleterminus@wanadoo.fr; ❷). However, the Lac du Salagou area offers better possibilities, including Villeneuvette's friendly *La Source* (Ⓣ04.67.96.05.07, Ⓦwww.hoteldelasource.com; closed Jan to mid-Feb & late Nov; ❺), with great amenities and a good restaurant (*menu* €22–34), and *Les Hauts de Mourèze* in Mourèze (Ⓣ04.67.96.04.84, Ⓕ04.67.96.25.85; closed Nov–March; ❹), a comfortable inn in a rustic setting. There's a **gîte** in Salasc, the *Auberge Campagnarde* (Ⓣ04.67.96.15.62, Ⓦwww.aubergedusalagou.fr; ❸, including breakfast), while at Octon there's the comfortable old *La Calade* (Ⓣ04.67.96.19.21, Ⓦwww.hotel-lacalade.com; March to mid-Dec; ❷) in the village centre (*menu* €15; closed Tues & Wed out of season). Overlooking the lake, 4km from Octon in Hameau de Basse, the area's best hotel is the luxurious Swiss-run 🅰*La Palombe* (Ⓣ04.67.95.40.07, Ⓦwww.lapalombe.com; ❼). There's a **campsite**, *Les Rivières* (Ⓣ04.67.96.75.53; June to mid-Sept) just west of Clermont, and two on the lake: the year-round *Le Salagou* (Ⓣ04.67.96.06.18, Ⓦwww.le-salagou.fr) at the eastern end, and the nudist *Village du Bosc* (April–Sept; Ⓣ04.67.96.07.37, Ⓦwww.villagedubosc.net) near Octon. The best **restaurant** in Clermont, out of a poor selection, is *L'Arlequin* in place St-Paul, by the church (closed Sun & Mon; *menus* from €14), while Mourèze has a couple of pizzerias by the entrance to Les Courtinales.

Lodève and around

Located on the eastern spur of the massif that forms the bulk of the Parc de Haut Languedoc, and just 10km north of Lac du Salagou, **LODÈVE** is everything which Clermont-l'Hérault is not – a pleasantly situated and friendly little town with a couple of surprisingly good sights. Heading southwest from the *gare routière*, you'll arrive in a few minutes at the greatest of these, the **Cathédrale St-Fulcran**, built in the town's second great period of prosperity in the twelfth and thirteenth centuries (the first was under Nero in the first century BC, when it had been important enough to have an imperial Roman mint). The current cathedral was raised on the riches of the woollen cloth industry, which dominated this area in the Middle Ages, and named in honour of a tenth-century bishop. Although it's mostly late medieval, traces of an earlier cathedral's sixth-century foundations can be seen, while the **cloisters** preserve part of the cathedral building raised by the saint himself in the tenth century. The nave's dimensions are impressive – 58m in length and 25m high – and its biggest bell weighs in at 2000 kilograms; in a small interior chapel opposite the door, you'll find where the remains of the town's 84 bishops lie interred. Next door to the church, the later **bishop's palace** has been converted into the *mairie*, and during business hours you can peek in at the Italianate salons and staircases.

From the cathedral, the old town spreads out east, bounded on three sides by a dramatic bend in the Lergue river. Just southeast of the church, you'll find the beautiful medieval bridge, the **Pont de Montifort**, while in the centre of town, up nearby rue de la République, is the surprisingly good **Musée Fleury** (Tues–Sun 9.30am–noon & 2–6pm; €3.20, €6 for special exhibitions), a gallery which draws the best fine-arts exhibitions between Castres and Montpellier, as well as a good selection of archeological finds and historical items dating from the prehistoric to the post-Revolutionary. Just east of the museum, in the place du Marché, the nineteenth-century *halle* has been converted into the **Hôtel Dardé** (daily 9am–7pm; free), a showcase for local sculptor Paul Dardé (1888–1963). Unfortunately, little survives of medieval Lodève, as the town was nearly razed in retribution for its support of Montmorency's revolt.

You can, however, gain an insight into the local cloth-making industry (which only ceased in 1960) by visiting the **Atelier National de Tissage de Tapis** (Tues, Wed & Thurs 1.30–3.30pm; €3.20; call ahead ☏04.67.96.40.40) south of the old town, across the river: as well as looking round the exhibition of looms and other machinery, you can watch textiles being woven according to traditional methods.

Lodève makes a pleasant base for exploring the surrounding area, including the upper Orb valley to the west and Lac du Salagou to the south, but the nearest attraction is the **priory of St-Michel de Grandmont**, just 8km away, on a wooded rise to the east of town. The old monastery and its grounds can

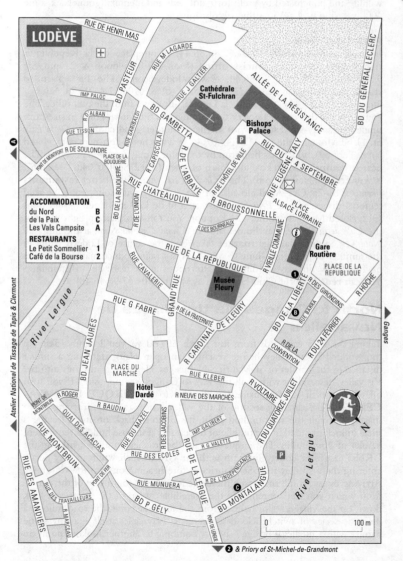

LODÈVE

RUE DE HENRI MAS

RUE M LAGARDE

RUE J GALTIER

BD DU GÉNÉRAL LECLERC

ALLÉE DE LA RÉSISTANCE

BD PASTEUR

IMP PALOC

R D'ALBAN

RUE TISSON

R DE SOULONDRE

PONT DE MONTFORT

PLACE DE LA BOUQUERIE

BD GARIBALDI

RUE CAPISCOLAT

BD GAMBETTA

RUE DE L'ABBAYE

RUE CHATEAUDUN

BD DE LA BOUQUERIE

R DE L'UNION

R DES BOURNEAUX

Cathédrale St-Fulchran

Bishops' Palace

RUE DE L'HÔTEL DE VILLE

R BROUSSONNELLE

RUE DU 4 SEPTEMBRE

RUE EUGÈNE TAILY

PLACE ALSACE LORRAINE

R VIEILLE COMMUNE

RUE DE LA RÉPUBLIQUE

RUE CAVALERIE

Gare Routière

PLACE DE LA RÉPUBLIQUE

R DES GIRONDINS

R HOCHE

ACCOMMODATION
du Nord   B
de la Paix   C
Les Vals Campsite A

RESTAURANTS
Le Petit Sommellier 1
Café de la Bourse   2

Atelier National de Tissage de Tapis & Clermont

River Lergue

RUE G FABRE

GRAND'RUE

R DE LA FRATERNITÉ

Musée Fleury

R CARDINAL DE FLEURY

BD JEAN JAURÈS

BD DE LA LIBERTÉ

R BARRA

R DE LA CONVENTION

R DU 24 FÉVRIER

Ganges

PLACE DU MARCHÉ

Hôtel Dardé

RUE KLEBER

R NEUVE DES MARCHÉS

R VOLTAIRE

R DU QUATORZE JUILLET

PONT DE MONTBRUN

R ROGER

QUAI DES ACACIAS

RUE DU MAZEL

R DES JACOBINS

IMP GALIBERT

R G VALETTE

RUE DE LA LERGUE

R DE L'INDÉPENDANCE

RUE MONTBRUN

RUE DES AMANDIERS

RUE DES TRAVAILLEURS

PONT DE FER

RUE DES ECOLES

RUE MUNUERA

BD P GÉLY

BD MONTALANGUE

PONT DE LERGUE

R MARCEAU

River Lergue

N

0   100 m

▼ ❷ & Priory of St-Michel-de-Grandmont

be visited as part of a **guided tour** (July & Aug daily at 10.30am, 3pm, 4pm & 5pm; June, Sept & Oct daily at 10.30am, 3.15pm & 4pm; Feb–May daily at 3pm; Nov to mid-Dec Sat & Sun 3.15 & 4pm; €5.40), but you can also poke around the buildings on your own (June–Oct daily 1–2.45pm; €4) Built in 1128, it was one of the first convents of the extremely strict Grandmontine Order of hermits, whose alarming popularity with the faithful prompted the power-jealous John XXII to clamp down on them in 1317. The buildings which remain today comprise one of their best-preserved houses, including a cloister, reception hall and an austere late thirteenth-century church. The spacious **grounds** are well worth a visit; their shaded woods are stocked with deer and other wildlife and punctuated by prehistoric dolmens and menhirs (going back some 4000 years) as well as Visigothic sarcophagi.

Practicalities

Lodève's **gare routière** (☏04.67.88.86.44) is on place de la République, right beside the town's **tourist office** (Mon–Fri 9am–noon & 2–6pm, Sat 9.30am–noon; ☏04.67.88.86.44, ⓦwww.lodeve.com). The best place to **stay** is the well-renovated ⚑ *Hôtel du Nord* (☏ & ⒻF04.67.44.92.78, ⓦwww .hotellodeve.com; ❷) at 18 bd de la Liberté, just down from the post office. The young couple that run it are very welcoming, and the rooms range in size from singles to family-sized suites with kitchen. Another good choice is *De la Paix* on 11 bd Montalangue (☏04.67.44.07.46, ⓦwww.hotel-dela-paix.com; closed Jan & Feb; ❸), which has been run by the same family for over a century. The nearest **campsite** is *Les Vals*, just south of town (April–Sept; ☏04.67.44.36.57, ⓦwww.campinglesvals.com). The *de la Paix* has one of the better **restaurants** (*menus* €18–25; Oct–April closed Sun eve & Mon), with solid, home-cooked regional dishes, and *Le Petit Sommelier*, at 3 pl de la République (*menus* from €12; closed Mon) is another good option. You can also pick up light meals at the *Café de la Bourse*, 1 av Fumel, and *Le Grand Café du Nord*, at the hotel *du Nord*. On Saturdays a large **market** takes over the centre of Lodève, while in the summer months (mid-June to mid-Sept) a *terroir*-produce market convenes on Tuesday, Wednesday and Thursday afternoons in the place de la République. You can **rent bikes** at Club House, in av Vallot (☏04.67.96.46.48).

North to Ganges via the Cirque de Navacelles

Taking the D25 eastwards from just north of Lodève, you'll climb 15km up the wooded Brèze valley before reaching an open plain stretching a similar distance to the hamlet of St-Maurice-Navacelles. Here the road drops into the Vis valley, descending with it all the way to Ganges (see opposite). If you turn off to the north at St-Maurice, you'll come to the **CIRQUE DE NAVACELLES**, a breathtaking section of the valley where the river, carving down sharply through the surrounding plain, has doubled back on itself, leaving a small hillock stranded in the middle of the cirque; at its base huddles the ancient hamlet of **Navacelles**. The cirque can also be reached in a day's **hiking**; the GR653 east from Lodève links up with the GR7, which winds its way north, entering the Vis valley near St-Maurice before heading on into the Cévennes. Arriving by car, you'll first reach the belvedere on the south side of the cirque, from which you can contemplate the incredible sweep of the gorge and look down on the village 600m below. From the lookout point, the road follows a dramatic series of switchbacks descending to Navacelles itself – a tiny stone hamlet with a medieval bridge – before climbing to another lookout point on the north side. The **information centre** (daily 10am–noon & 2–6pm) for the cirque is located at the southern belvedere; it has a small exhibition explaining the formation of the curious canyon and conducts two- and three-hour walking tours (€5; frequently in English). A good alternative walk which you can easily manage unguided is the spectacular six-kilometre hike to the underground *source de la four*, along a trail leading west along the canyon floor from Navacelles itself.

East of St-Maurice, the road snakes down into the Vis gorges for the remaining 26km to Ganges. Contrasting with the open scrub around Navacelles, this section of the valley is a steep and lush canyon, whose tree-clad banks at times close off the sky above with thick boughs. As you continue, it gradually widens, passing occasional signs of life – riverside *relais*, ancient bridges and abandoned factories – before opening up abruptly when it reaches the Hérault at Ganges.

As you'd expect, services are rather minimal in this neck of the woods: in Navacelles village, there's the **chambre d'hôtes** *Casa Lou Haîdouc* (T04.67.81.51.54; ❷), while a CAP **gîte** at La Vacquerie, halfway between Lodève and St-Maurice (T04.67.44.60.50; ❶), provides shelter if you're hiking along the GR7. There are other possibilities along the Vis gorge, the most luxurious of which is the splendid *Château de Madières* (closed Nov–March; T04.67.73.84.03, W www.chateau-madieres.fr; ❾), a renovated fourteenth-century castle. All of these establishments serve **meals**, as does the café *Baume Auriol* at the southern belvedere (*plat du jour* €11).

Ganges and around

GANGES, the largest town in the upper Hérault valley, is primarily of interest as a transport hub and service centre for the more interesting places just to the south (which you can also access travelling along either of the two routes down to Montpellier – see p.258), and for the busy recreation industry which has grown up on the banks of the river. The town, like many villages of the Cévennes region to the north, enjoyed prosperity first as a hub for the wool trade then subsequently as a silk centre, until the advent of synthetic fabrics and ravages of phylloxera disease in the late 1800s drove the industry under. It was also here, in August 1944, that the local *maquis* managed to repulse a column of three thousand German troops after a fierce ten-hour battle. Nowadays, there's little to see or do, although a walk through the old quarter will take you past a few remaining medieval houses, a pretty eighteenth-century market square and an imposingly dour Huguenot temple. All in all, though, these do not suffice to dispel a certain lingering air of stagnation.

The **gare routière** is on rue Jules-Ferry, just west of the central plan l'Ormeau, which is where you'll find the **tourist office** (Mon–Sat 10am–noon & 2–6pm; July & Aug also Sun 10am–noon; T04.67.73.00.56, W www.ot-cevennes.com), and the **hotel** *de la Poste* (closed Jan; T04.67.73.85.88, W www.hoteldelaposteganges .com; ❷), with surprisingly good amenities. The *Domaine de Blancardy*, 7km out of town towards Nîmes (T04.67.73.94.94, W www.blancardy.com; dorm beds €20, doubles ❸), operates a comfortable and well-equipped **gîte** with some private rooms, while the municipal **campsite** (mid-June to Aug; T04.67.57.92.97) is along the river at the southern end of Ganges, with the town's only laundry.

Of the local **restaurants**, the best is ⚘ *Le Mélodie* (closed Wed; T04.67.73.66.02), a homey little Lyonnais place at 4 place Fabre d'Olivet (*menus* €9 at lunch, €14 at dinner), while *La Rose de Saigon*, at 12 place des Halles (closed Tues), serves good Vietnamese cuisine (dinner *menus* at €11 & €14). For something lighter try the creperie *La Luciole* next door at no. 11.

There are various **banks** with exchange services along rue Frédéric-Mistral, and **Internet** access at Médi@gora, beside the *gare routière*. Intersport, on route de Vigun (☎04.67.73.75.75), rents **bikes**.

Laroque, the Grotte des Demoiselles and St-Bauzille

A couple of kilometres south of Ganges, the first place you come to is the hamlet of **LAROQUE**, attractively situated on a hillside along the Hérault river. It has a cheerful bank-side promenade, with narrow medieval streets zigzaging up to the remains of its castle. At the entrance to the town, there is a small twelfth-century church, while on the south side lie the ruins of a huge nineteenth-century textile plant. A few kilometres further south, you'll come upon the area's biggest draw, the **Grotte des Demoiselles** (March & Oct daily 10 & 11am & 2–4.30pm; April–June & Sept daily 10am–5.30pm; July & Aug daily 10am–6pm; Nov–Feb Mon–Fri 2–4pm, Sat & Sun 10 & 11am & 2–4pm; €8), a little more than 2km east off the road. This incredibly vast cavern, discovered in 1770, stretches out below the plateau de Thaurac, the highland southeast of Ganges, and is famous for its huge stalactite and stalagmite formations. The obligatory one-hour **guided tour** (expect a long wait in high season; last departure 1hr before closing) is made aboard an underground funicular (hourly; last departure 45min before closing), which lends the whole thing an amusement-park air, and though the cave is spectacular, it can be a bit of a let-down after all the crowds and fuss. Just south of the grotto, **ST-BAUZILLE** is of note only as a centre for river-oriented sports; it's a good place to shop for a canoe trip south down the Hérault.

Without doubt, the nicest place to stay in the area is **Laroque**, at the **hotel** *Le Parc aux Cèdres*, 120 avenue de l'Europe (☎04.67.73.82.63, ℱ04.67.73.69.85, ❹), in a park on the northern edge of town. There is also a **campsite**, the two-star *Le Tivoli* (June–Aug; ☎04.67.73.97.28), near the *Cèdres*. You can get excellent **food** at *Aux Trois Arches*, on the main promenade (April–Oct; ☎04.67.73.86.80), while the nearby *Bar des Ramparts* has decent Belgian beers and home-made desserts.

South to Montpellier

Heading south from Ganges to Montpellier, you can choose between two routes, whose paths diverge at **St-Bauzille** (see above). The longer, more spectacular of the two leads down the Hérault gorge to the medieval abbey-town of **St-Guilhem-le-Désert**, emerging from the canyon shortly before **Gignac**, from where you can either head 30km east to Montpellier or continue to Clermont-l'Hérault. Unfortunately, only the St-Guilhem–Gignac leg of this route is served by buses, and then only in summer, so if you don't have your own transport, doing the whole thing will involve some walking or hitching. The other option is to head due south, a forty-kilometre route which takes you to St-Martin-de-Londres, from where you can hike to the Pic-St-Loup and surrounding sights. St-Martin is, in fact, only 6km from the banks of the Hérault, but is separated from the river by a series of low peaks; if you have a car or are willing to hitchhike or walk, you could link up the two routes by heading first to St-Martin and then doubling back on the treacherously winding D122 to the village of **Causse-de-la-Selle**, north of St-Guilhem on the valley route (a distance of 14km). Stopping at Causse also gives you the opportunity of making the trip to St-Guilhem by river raft (see opposite) – the most thrilling way to take in the gorges.

Via St-Guilhem-le-Désert

The route from Ganges to St-Guilhem follows the course of the Hérault via the D4 on the river's right bank, which you access by crossing the bridge at

St-Bauzille. After 15km, the road cuts southwest across a plateau, passing the hamlet of Causse-de-la-Selle – the turn-off for St-Martin-de-Londres (see p.296) – before rejoining the river midway through the dramatic **Gorges de l'Hérault**. Hugging the western bank, the road follows the tortuous canyon to reach the stunningly situated hamlet of **ST-GUILHEM-LE-DÉSERT**. There is no mistaking the great antiquity of this village; nestled in a steep and wooded ravine rising from the gorge, the reddish roofs of its medieval houses contrast with the electric green of the surrounding trees. The town grew up around the abbey founded by Charlemagne's counsellor Guilhem, who returned from Rome in 800 with three pieces of wood said to be remnants of the Cross. Thanks to these relics, the monastery and the village around it thrived through the centuries that followed, both as a pilgrimage destination in its own right, as well as a stopping point on the way to Santiago de Compostela. Today, the immaculately preserved town, designated a UNESCO World Heritage site, is still presided over by the eleventh-century **abbey-church of Gellone** (daily 8am–12.10pm & 2.30–6.20pm; free), at the upper end of the village, by the obligatory car park (€5; the lower car park is €4). Crowned by a chunky, fifteenth-century bell tower, the church is the only surviving part of the once powerful monastic house. Its magnificent entryway, flanked by columns pillaged from Roman ruins, passes through a small vaulted narthex and opens into the cavernous but plain nave, ending in a curiously oversized transept and apse. Inside the church is the casket holding the remains of Guilhem (who was canonized after his death) and a reliquary holding one of the famous bits of wood. From the church you can climb down to the **crypt**, which dates from the eighth century, as well as the ruined **cloister**, whose north and west galleries are still in place. There is also a small **museum** here (July & Aug daily 11am–noon & 2/2.30–5/6pm; Sept–June Mon & Wed–Sat 2–5pm, Sun 2.30–5pm; €2) containing religious sculptures recovered from the destroyed abbey. The rest of the village consists of low, ancient houses which follow the narrow lanes leading down the ravine, interrupted by medieval pilgrims' fountains marked with the scallop-shell symbol of St James. Looking back as you descend past the church, you'll be treated to views of its impressive apsidal chapels.

St-Guilhem's **tourist office** (daily: July & Aug 9am–7pm; Sept–June 10.30am–12.30pm & 2–7pm; ⓣ04.67.57.44.32, ⓦwww.saint-guilhem-le-desert.com) is at the foot of the village, just above the main road; the office has an ATM, and they can give you a coupon offering you €2 off entry to the Grotte de Clamouse (see p.296). The most comfortable of St-Guilhem's **hotels** is *Le Guilhaume d'Orange* at 2 av Guillaume d'Orange (ⓣ04.667.57.24.53, ⓦwww.guilhaumedorange.com; ❺), while a more modest choice is *La Taverne de l'Escuelle* at 11 chemin Val Gellone (Feb–Nov; ⓣ04.67.57.72.05; ❸). The budget option is the English-speaking Gîte *de la Tour* (ⓣ & ⓕ04.67.57.34.00; ❶), located in a medieval tower in the village. The hamlet's best dining is at *L'Auberge sur le Chemin* (Tues–Sun; ⓣ04.67.57.75.05), where you can enjoy an excellent *terroir menu* (€25) in an atmospheric medieval room. A dramatic approach to the town can be made from the riverbank 3km east of Causse on the D122, from where Canoë La Vallée des Moulins (ⓣ04.67.73.12.45) runs **canoeing** excursions downriver to St-Guilhem. St-Guilhem's **rafting centre** is at the bottom of the hill, across the road (ⓣ04.67.55.75.75) from the entrance to the village.

A one-hour **hike** leads up from the car park in St-Guilhem to the ruins of a castle, from where you get the best **views** of the town. Just after this, the GR trail splits, with the GR74 climbing through a canyon towards Mont St-Baudille, and the GR653 looping south before merging again with the GR74 to proceed west to Lodève. The tourist office (see opposite) can give you information on the several AR trails which run through the hills hereabouts. Leaving St-Guilhem by road, the D4 continues 4km further along the dramatic canyon, passing the mouth of the **Grotte de Clamouse** (Feb–May & Oct daily 10am–5pm; June & Sept daily 10am–6pm; July & Aug daily 10am–7pm; Nov–Jan Sun–Fri noon–5pm; €8), famous for its immense and delicate crystal-line formations. Only 500m later, the gorge abruptly opens up at the beginning of the low Languedocian coastal plain; the transition is marked by a great medi-eval *pont du diable*, which crosses the river above a gravelly bank now serving as a popular river-beach.

Shortly beyond, you pass the unremarkable hamlets of **ANIANE** and **GIGNAC**, the former most visited because of its nudist beach and the latter serving as a bus interchange for Montpellier and Lodève. There's not much to see in either, although Aniane is presided over by its hulking **abbey**, founded in 782 and rebuilt in the seventeenth-century, and has various **medieval vestiges**, including tanners' tubs, a market and the remains of its town walls. Gignac has a **tourist office** in its central square (Mon–Fri 9.30am–12.30pm & 3–5/6/7pm, Sat 10am–12/30pm, in July & Aug also Sat 3–7pm & Sun 10am–noon; ☎04.67.57.58.83, ✉oti.gignac@wanadoo.fr), and both hamlets have good **accommodation** and dining. In Aniane, the *Hostellerie Saint Benoit* on rte de Saint-Guilhem (March–Nov; ☎04.67.57.71.63, ✉hostellerie .st-benoit@wanadoo.fr; ④) is an oasis of comfort (complete with pool), while just south of Gignac on the D131E, the *Domain du Pelican* (☎04.67.57.68.92, ⓦwww.domainedepelican.fr; ④) runs a homely **chambres d'hôtes**. In Gignac, you'll find one of the area's best **restaurants**, *Liaisons Gourmandes Capion*, at 3 boulevard de l'Esplanade (☎04.67.57.50.83; off-season Fri–Sun only), with superlative *menus* from €17–45. You can **camp** in Aniane at *Le Moulin de Siau* (June–Aug; ☎04.67.57.51.08, ⓦwww.camping-moulin-de-siau.com) or *La Meuse* (June–Sept; ☎04.67.57.92.97).

Via the Pic-St-Loup and St-Martin-de-Londres

Some 20km due south of St-Bauzille looms the great **Pic-St-Loup** (658m), which, dominating the plain of Hérault, can be seen from Béziers almost to Nîmes. **ST-MARTIN-DE-LONDRES**, 13km south from Ganges by road or hiking trail (the GR60, leaving St-Bauzille), makes the best base for hiking the remaining 10km to the *pic*'s wooded summit – a site from which you can enjoy impressive panoramas, but which cannot be reached except by foot (drivers can get as close as 4km away by taking the D113 to the hamlet of Cazevielle). St-Martin is another town of great antiquity and, contrary to appearances, its name has nothing to do with England's capital, London ("Londres" in French); it is named after the Plaine de Londres (from the Celtic word for "swamp") in which the town is located. Testament to the town's history is the beautiful knot of buildings focused around the eleventh-century Romanesque **church**, founded by monks from nearby St-Guilhem. Its interior is plain, but is more than made up for by the three-lobed Byzantine-style exterior, which blends in harmoniously with the surrounding buildings. Elsewhere in the town, you can see how the two concentric sets of walls and towers were swallowed up by houses over the centuries.

If you're **hiking** into town, or if you're not up to tackling the *pic*, about 2km north of St-Martin a leg of the GR60 leads off eastwards into the Ravin des Arcs, a high but narrow canyon which makes an excellent two-hour walking circuit; be sure to bring water along, as there is no drinkable source on the way – you can fill up at the public fountain in front of the tourist office. Another option is the ninety-minute walk south of St-Martin (but also on the Montpellier bus route) to Viols-en-Laval, where you'll find the excavated **prehistoric village** of **Cambous** (May, June & Sept–Nov Sat & Sun 2–6pm; July & Aug Tues–Sun 2–7pm; €2.50), once home to the "Fontbouisse" culture, which practised copper-smelting and ceramic production as well as agriculture and herding some 5000 years ago.

St-Martin's **tourist office** (May, June & late Aug to mid-Sept Mon & Tues 9.30am–12.30pm; July to late Aug daily 9am–1pm; ☎04.67.55.09.59, Ⓦwww .tourismed.com) is on the main road in the centre of town and there's an excellent **chambres d'hôtes**, 🏃 *De ci…De là!* (☎04.67.86.36.83, Ⓦwww .decidela.fr; ④) on the edge of town. The **campsite**, *Pic de Loup* (April–Sept; ☎04.67.55.00.53, ⓔcamping-pic@tourisme.com), is just east on the main road. 🏃 *Les Muscardins* **restaurant** at 19 rte des Cévennes (☎04.67.55.75.90; closed Feb, Mon & Tues) has superb Cevennoise *menus* from €29, while the cheaper but also very good *La Mas Cevenol* at 12 rte du Littoral (☎04.67.55.70.22), serves excellent *terroir* meals from €17.

Travel details

Trains

The main coastal rail line (with TGV) connects Montpellier to Béziers and Nîmes, while a secondary line runs north via Clermont-l'Hérault to the Massif Central. SNCF buses may run in lieu of trains on these lines; services are reduced on Sundays and holidays.

Montpellier to: Agde (12–18 daily; 35min); Beaucaire/Tarascon (10–11 daily; 1hr 5min); Béziers (18–23 daily; 30min–1hr); Carcassonne (15–18 daily; 1hr 30min–4hr); Lunel (12–15 daily; 15min); Narbonne (18–20 daily; 45min–1hr 15min); Nîmes (18–23 daily; 30min); Paris (frequent; 3hr 15min–6hr); Perpignan (15–18 daily; 2hr 15min); Sète (18–20 daily; 15–20min); Toulouse (15–18 daily; 2hr 15min–2hr 55min).

Buses

Hérault's bus hubs are in Montpellier and Béziers. Many lines have no Sunday service; service on Saturdays and holidays may be reduced. Summer lines, *lignes estivales*, serve St-Guilhem and other tourist sites. For a route map, full schedules and information on discount tickets, see Ⓦwww .herault.fr or ☎08.25.34.01.34.

Clermont-l'Hérault to: Lodève (4–6 daily; 25min); Pézenas (3–6 daily; 35min).

Ganges to: Montpellier (6–7 daily; 1hr 10min); Nîmes (3–7 daily; 1hr 15min); Quissac (3–7 daily; 55min); St-Hippolyte (3–7 daily; 15min);

St-Martin-de-Londres (3–7 daily; 25min); Sauve (3–7 daily; 25min).

Gignac (summer only) to: Pont du Diable (1–5 daily; 20min); St-Guilhem (1–5 daily; 35min).

La Grande-Motte to: Lunel (2 daily; 35min).

Lodève to: Béziers (3–6 daily; 1hr 50min); Clermont-l'Hérault (4–6 daily; 25min); Pézenas (3–6 daily; 1hr 20min).

Lunel to: Villetelle (for Ambrussum; 1–4 daily; 20min).

Montpellier to: Aigues-Mortes (8–12 daily; 1hr 5min); Béziers (4–7 daily; 1hr 55min); Bédarieux (3–6 daily; 1hr 45min); Clermont-l'Hérault (5–25 daily; 40min); Ganges (6–7 daily; 1hr 10min); Gignac (for St-Guilhem; 5–25 daily; 40min); La Grande-Motte (8–12 daily, in summer hourly; 30min); Lamalou (3–6 daily; 2hr 5min); Le Grau-du-Roi (8–12 daily; 45min); Lodève (2–12 daily; 1hr 15min); Lunel (1–5 daily; 35min–1hr 15min); Nîmes (1–2 daily; 50min); Pézenas (4–7 daily; 1hr 25min); St-Hippolyte (2 daily; 1hr 45min); St-Martin-de-Londres (3–6 daily; 45min); St-Bauzille (3–6 daily ; 55min); St-Pons (1–3 daily; 2hr 25min); Sète (3–11 daily; 45min); Sommières (4 daily; 1hr 10min).

Pézenas to: Béziers (6–10 daily; 32min).

Sète to: Balaruc-les-Bains (6–18 daily; 20min); Bouzigues (2–5 daily; 35min); Loupian (2–5 daily; 40min); Mèze (2–5 daily; 45min); Marseillan (1–3 daily; 40min); Marseillan-Plage (1–3 daily; 30min).

Narbonne, Béziers
and around

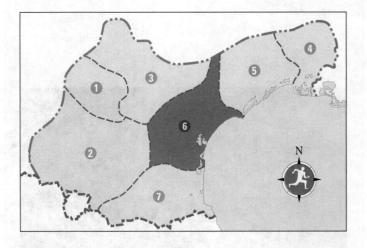

CHAPTER 6

Highlights

* **Lagrasse** A sleepy little village which grew up around a once-powerful monastery.
  See p.316

* **Canal du Midi** France's seventeenth-century engineering wonder is now a sublimely beautiful thoroughfare for cyclists, walkers and boaters.
  See p.317

* **Oppidum d Ensérune** A pre-Roman settlement, perched on a ridge above the vineyards of Béziers.
  See p.323

* **Old Béziers** Atmospheric streets and a splendid cathedral which provides views as far west as the Canigou.
  See p.326

* **The Orb valley** Rarely visited, this river course boasts unique micro-climate zones and near-forgotten hamlets.
  See p.331

△ Boating on the Canal du Midi

Narbonne, Béziers and around

The provincial towns of **Narbonne** and **Béziers** dominate the flat expanse of marshy alluvial plain formed by the outpourings of the Hérault, Orb and Aude rivers, whose mouths all reach the Mediterranean within a 15km strip. The former town is the smaller, but generally livelier centre, with a compact medieval core and vibrant nightlife, while the latter is a historically proud and defiant place which, though somewhat more sedate these days, springs to life in the summer with its renowned *feria*. Poised just north of the Étang de Bages' long expanse, Narbonne is best situated for excursions into the **Corbières**, an isolated range of hills stretching south to Roussillon; once forming the Cathar heartland, they harbour the idyllic village of **Termes**, with its *château*, and the strikingly beautiful hamlet of **Lagrasse**. Swinging sharp east at Carcassonne, the River Aude makes its way along the northern edge of the Corbières, shadowed by the **Canal du Midi**, the incredible waterway which has dominated the whole of this area since the seventeenth century. The canal route takes you past the various monuments of the **Minervois** – the region squeezed in between the Corbières and Haut Languedoc – and attractive Languedocian scenery before it splits, with the Canal de la Robine heading south towards Narbonne and the main waterway meandering on, via Béziers, to the Bassin de Thau. Skirting Béziers, the route up the **Orb valley** threads north along the border of the Parc Naturel de Haut Languedoc, passing a succession of villages which have survived the centuries thanks to the river's fertile banks. The coastal stretch curving between the two towns is, for the most part, an area of uninviting marsh, but at either end two chunks of terra firma, the Montagne St-Loup and de la Clape, provide anchors for a couple of old ports, **Agde** and **Gruissan**, each of which have modern beach-resort alter egos. Although those interested in sun and swimming will find prettier surroundings in the Côte Vermeille to the south, both of these old settlements are worth a visit for their gentle ambience – Agde from Béziers and Gruissan from Narbonne.

Public transport facilities in this region vary considerably. At Narbonne, the busy coastal rail line to Perpignan branches off from the main Toulouse–Marseille route, on which Béziers can be found. In the hinterland, you'll have to depend on bus services, which are fairly good for the major towns along the coast and the Orb valley. Out-of-the-way sites are more difficult: Minerve,

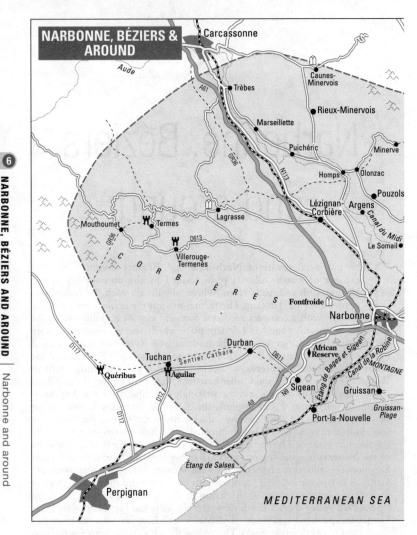

for example, isn't served at all by public transport (although the narrow-gauge ATM train does approach it). But in any case – if you have time – the best way to travel through the region is by canal, either by piloting a houseboat, or biking or hiking along the towpath.

Narbonne and around

There's no mistaking **NARBONNE** as you approach it, its towering cathedral rising up over the rooftops and dominating the coastal plain for miles

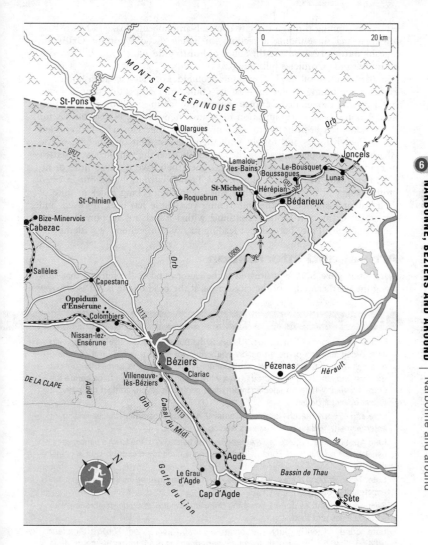

around. Once the capital of the Roman province of Gallia Narbonensis, it flourished as a port and communications centre from ancient times into the Middle Ages, and was home to an important Jewish university in the twelfth and thirteenth centuries. But in the mid-1300s things suddenly went awry: the Jews were expelled, the plague struck, the Black Prince burnt down the town, the dykes of the Aude burst and the port silted up, a series of disasters which brought ruin to Narbonne's economy. A tentative prosperity returned only in the late 1800s with the birth of the modern wine industry, which continues to support the town. Today, it's a pleasant provincial town with a small but well-preserved old core, centred on the great truncated choir of the **cathedral** and bisected by the **Canal de la Robine** (see p.322), whose banks provide a grassy esplanade running through the city centre. Narbonne also makes a handy base for exploring surrounding attractions, including the old port of **Gruissan**, Sigean's **nature reserve** and the abbey of **Fontfroide**, which you can also visit en route to the Corbières hills (see p.314).

In the summer of 1991 Narbonne acquired notoriety as a flashpoint in France's continuing problems with its ethnic minorities, this time a long-suffering and disregarded minority desperately forcing itself on public attention. Among its mixed population of relative newcomers, Narbonne has for thirty-odd years been home to a group of *harkis*, Algerians who had enlisted in the French forces and fought with them against their own people in the Algerian war of independence in the late 1950s. After the war they were settled in France for their own protection, and since then have received little or no help. Eventually the *harkis'* children, now French citizens, broke out in open protest, angry at finding themselves still last in the pecking order in spite of their parents' sacrifice. In the intervening years little has been resolved, and occasional sit-ins and protests continue, with *harki* claims supported by the French Socialist Party but still not leading to any comprehensive settlement.

Arrival and information

Narbonne's **gare SNCF** is situated at the eastern end of the railyard that runs along the northern edge of the city centre, at the head of the RN9 as it leaves

---

Festivals in and around Narbonne and Béziers

In this little corner of Languedoc, Béziers is the hot spot for popular festivals, with its five-day *feria* the prime attraction. Narbonne, for its part, is big on theatre and also has a good *Carnaval*. There are summer music cycles and parties throughout the area and, as can be expected from a wine region, local festivals to celebrate the grape harvest. Where no specific information number is given, contact the relevant tourist office for details.

Late Jan to early March Narbonne: *Carnaval*. A series of parades, dances and street entertainment held on the weekends leading up to Lent.

Late April Béziers: *Fête de la St-Aphrodise*. The feast day of the town's patron saint, usually held on the third Sunday, and featuring a curious procession with a camel float.

Late May Béziers: *Fêtes Médiévales*. A medieval market, with costumed re-enactments, food and fun.

Second weekend in June Capestang: *Fête du Canal*. Canalside celebration with music, games and food.

Late June to early July Narbonne: *Festival National de Théâtre Amateur* ✆04.66.32.40.50. Free nightly theatrical performances (9.15pm) on the cours de la Madeleine and at the Archbishop's Palace.

July 7–10 Agde: *Grande fête des pêcheurs*. Three-day fishermen's celebration in honour of St. Peter, patron of the sea.

Throughout July Narbonne: *Orgues d'Été*. Evening organ recitals every Sunday in the cathedral.

First two weeks of July Béziers: *Festival de Musique de Béziers*. Classical choral performances of international quality held in various venues.

July 12–15 Narbonne: Bastille Day. Huge four-day outdoor party in cours Mirabeau.

Mid-July Béziers: *Festa d'Oc* ✆04.67.31.76.76, ⊛www.ville-beziers.fr. A celebration of all things Occitan, in particular the region's music.

town (enquire at the information desk for **left luggage** facilities). From here it's about a fifteen-minute walk to the place de l'Hôtel de Ville in the centre, or a short hop on buses #1, #2 or the Petit Bus. Just to the southwest, on the far side of the freight terminal, you'll find the **gare routière**. If you're **driving** into town, you can park just about anywhere you find a spot – most plazas and streets have meter-parking. The town's main **tourist office** (mid-June to mid-Sept Mon–Sat 9am–7pm & Sun 9.30am–12.30pm; mid-Sept to mid-June Mon–Sat 8.30am–noon & 2–6pm & Sun 9.30am–12.30pm; ℡04.68.65.15.60, Ⓦwww.Mairie-Narbonne.fr) is on tiny place Roger-Salengro, just to the north of the cathedral, but there is also canalside **information kiosk** at the southern end of the centre on quai Victor-Hugo (June–Sept Mon–Sat 10am–7pm; Oct–May daily 8am–noon & 2–6pm). Information on festivals and events in Narbonne and the surrounding area can be found in the free fortnightly events magazine, *Olé!*, which is available from the tourist office and news-stands.

Narbonne has an efficient municipal **bus** system. You can buy single tickets (€1) from drivers and ten-trip TICTEN passes (€9) at tobacconists. For **bike** rental, try Cycles Cancel, 50 boulevard Frédéric-Mistral (℡04.68.65.12.26).

Accommodation

It's easy to find reasonable **accommodation** in Narbonne, which has a fair number of good value hotels, as well as a hostel and a couple of decent

Mid-July to mid-Aug Orb valley: *Festival de la Vallée de l'Orb* ℡04.67.89.65.32. Choral music and folk activities related to wine, held in town squares and churches throughout the region.

Late July Cap d'Agde: *Fête de la Mer*. After an open-air Mass for victims of the sea, the boats are blessed, and there's water-jousting and general celebration.

Late July Gruissan: *Fête des Pêcheurs*. Sea-faring rituals, including boat blessings and a procession with the statue of St Peter.

Late July to early Aug Sigean: Musical ℡04.68.40.40.95. Street festival featuring music, theatre and children's activities.

Throughout July & Aug Bédarieux: *Soirées Musicales*. Evening performances of comedy and music (from medieval to jazz to reggae) in the place Nouvel, which are usually free.

Throughout July & Aug Lamalou-les-Bains: *Festival National d'Opérettes* ℡04.67.95.70.91, Ⓔomt.lamalou@wanadoo.fr. Operetta troupes from around France perform in Lamalou's casino.

Throughout July & Aug Villerouge-Termènes: *Fête Médiévale* ℡04.68.70.06.24. Medieval market, fair and events held in even-numbered years.

Aug 5 & 6 Narbonne: *Fête du Commerce et du Vin*. Wine festival.

Second weekend Aug Narbonne: *La Via Mercaderia*. Medieval street market and fair.

Mid-Aug Béziers: *La Feria*. Four-day festival with street entertainment, fireworks, music and a daily Spanish-style *corrida* (tickets €24–83).

Aug 25–28 Narbonne: *Semaine Bavaroise*. Narbonne's summer version of the Munich Oktoberfest, with plenty of lager and lederhosen.

Mid-Oct Béziers: *Semaine du Goût - Festival de la Tartine*. A week-long celebration of one of the town's favourite dishes.

Late Oct Béziers: *Les Primeurs d'Oc*. The best of the local wine festivals, with wine competitions, music and traditional activities.

campsites. The two main concentrations of accommodation are in the immediate vicinity of the gare SNCF and along the Canal de la Robine, which flows through the centre.

Hotels

Alsace 2 av Carnot ☎04.68.32.01.86, @hotel-lalsace@wanadoo.fr. Just across from the station, this small, old-fashioned two-star is clean, but the rooms are on the small side. ③

De France 6 rue Rossini ☎04.68.32.09.75, @www.hotelnarbonne.com. A quiet nineteenth-century establishment south of the old town, and close to the covered market and the canal. It has TVs in the rooms and parking facilities, and is also wheelchair accessible. ③

De la Gare 7 av Pierre-Sémard ☎04.68.32.10.54. Cheap, basic accommodation in a rather run-down stationside hotel. ①

Grand Hôtel du Languedoc 22 bd Gambetta ☎04.68.65.14.74, @www.hoteldulanguedoc .com. Located on the ring road, a five-minute walk south of the cathedral in an attractive old building. This nineteenth-century house which has been converted into a well-appointed and comfortable hotel is one of the better deals in town. ④

Hôtel du Midi 4 av de Toulouse ☎04.68.41.04.62, @www.hoteldumidi.net. A comfortable but afford-able all-mod-cons option, with a garage and wheelchair access. ③

Le Régent 50 rue Mosaïque/15 rue Suffren ☎04.68.32.02.41, @www.leregentnarbonne.com. Reasonable accommodation in the quieter and newer part of the city centre, two minutes' south of boulevard Gambetta. Rooms have TV. ②

La Résidence 6 rue du 1er Mai ☎04.68.32.19.41, @www.hotelresidence.fr. An early nineteenth-century converted house, in a great location on a quiet street near the pont Voltaire. Comfortable rooms with AC, and there's a garage and lift. ⑥

Will's 23 av Pierre-Sémard ☎04.68.90.44.50, @willshotel-narbonne .com. Friendly place and a travellers' standby, which accepts pets and has amenities like TV and cable, but fills up quickly. Right by the train station. ③

Hostel and campsites

Camping Club Les Mimosas Chaussée de Mandirac ☎04.68.49.03.72, @www.lesmimosas .com. Big three-star site with all mod-cons, located 6km south of town on the Étang de Bages (no public transport). Open late March to Oct.

Les Floralys rte de Gruissan ☎04.68.32.65.65, @www.lesfloralys.com. The closest campsite to town, located 3km from the centre on the road heading south towards the coast, this is a small, thirty-pitch site with good services (including laun-dry and restaurant). Open all year round.

MJC Centre International de Séjour pl Roger-Salengro ☎04.68.32.01.00, wwww.cis-narbonne .com. Modern hostel right by the tourist office, with dorm beds for €12 as well as limited private rooms (①). Nice lounge with TV and a simple restaurant.

The Town

If Narbonne's name lends itself to a certain sense of grandeur, you'll be shocked by its diminutive size. The whole of the **old town** – which is where all the sights are – fits snugly into a 1km-by-750m rectangle, bisected north–south by the **Canal de la Robine**. Of the two halves it is the eastern side that holds the main draws, with the **archbishop's palace**, its **museums** and the **cathedral** dominating affairs, plus a number of medieval attractions on their periphery. The western side of the canal, though less salubrious than its eastern counter-part, also harbours a couple of interesting sights.

A single ticket, costing €5 and valid for three days, gives entry to all Narbonne's monuments and museums (unless otherwise noted): it can be purchased at participating sites.

The Archbishop's Palace

The broad square of the place de l'Hôtel de Ville, in whose centre you'll find a recently uncovered section of the Roman Via Domitia, is marked on its south-ern side by the grand old Aux Dames de France department store, while the entire north side is taken up by the great facade of the **Archbishop's Palace**,

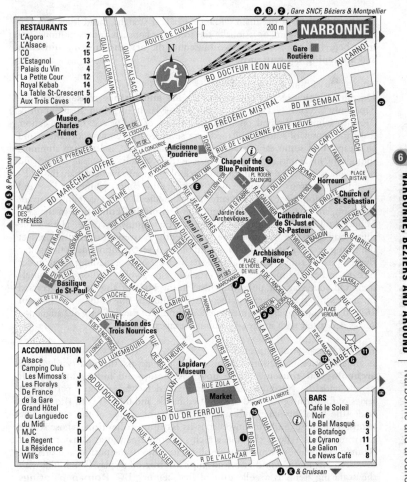

RESTAURANTS

L'Agora	7
L'Alsace	2
CO	15
L'Estagnol	13
Palais du Vin	4
La Petite Cour	12
Royal Kebab	14
La Table St-Crescent	5
Aux Trois Caves	10

NARBONNE

0   200 m

ACCOMMODATION

Alsace	A
Camping Club	
Les Mimosa's	J
Les Floralys	K
De France	I
de la Gare	B
Grand Hôtel	
du Languedoc	G
du Midi	F
MJC	D
Le Regent	H
La Résidence	E
Will's	C

BARS

Café le Soleil	
Noir	6
Le Bal Masqué	9
Le Botafogo	3
Le Cyrano	11
Le Galion	1
Le News Café	8

peppered by pointed ogival windows and decorated with Gothic-looking vegetal flourishes. But while you marvel at its medieval beauty, it is worth bearing in mind that what you are looking at is in fact one of Viollet-le-Duc's imaginative repair jobs (see box, p.124), an ersatz bit of medievalia. Now the town hall, the palace's rambling complex also incorporates the city's two major museums, plus the entrance to the cathedral (see p.308). Passing through the main doors of the palace, which are directly on the square, on the left you'll find the entrance to the towering **donjon** (Mon–Fri 9am–noon & 2–6pm) commissioned in the late thirteenth century by the town's lord and archbishop, Gilles Aycelin. This ponderous 42m defensive tower is a fine example of late thirteenth-century military architecture – its splayed-out base, which was constructed over the remains of the previous Roman wall, was designed to prevent battering and better withstand attempts to undermine the keep. There's not much to see inside, but from the top (after climbing a 162-step key-stone staircase) you can enjoy excellent **views** of the cathedral and the surrounding countryside. Back at the main entrance, heading straight ahead leads you out into a broad courtyard, occasionally the scene for concerts and exhibitions, and from here you can access the two museums: the **art and history museum** and **archeological museum**.

The art and history museum

On the left you'll see the entrance to the **art and history museum** (April–Sept daily 9.30am–12.15pm & 2–6pm; Oct–March Tues–Sun 10am–noon & 2–5pm), which is located on the upper floors of the palace. The collection, featuring scores of canvases of mediocre seventeenth-century portraiture and landscape, plus some early modern pottery and *faïence*, is less than stunning, though the luxurious interior of the palace itself, with its *artesonado* ceilings and other details, is more rewarding; rooms to look out for in particular are the audience hall, the king's chamber – with seventeenth-century painted walls – and the grand salon. That said, a smattering of medieval pieces certainly warrant attention, and the museum's highlight, the **Orientalist collection** in the salle Hippolyte Lazerges, alone almost justifies the admission price. Here some thirty-odd works, dating from the seventeenth to twentieth centuries, reflect the European fascination with the world of the desert: paintings depicting sultry Berber girls staring enigmatically at the viewer, or eyes flashing from under turbans, as bearded men pose with cruel-looking swords on horse- or camel-back. On your way out, poke your head in the **Hall of the Synods**, accessed from the same grand staircase as the museum. Built by one of the archbishops in 1628, it was used for clerical meetings and sittings of the *parlement* of Languedoc and is decorated with impressive Aubusson tapestries.

The archeological museum

A much better collection can be found just across the courtyard at the **archeological museum** (same hours as the art and history museum). It begins with the Neolithic period, represented by various skull parts and a series of footprints preserved in solidified muck, and follows with Bronze Age finds (the usual brooches and weapons) from the *oppida* of the region. The mainstay of the exhibition, however, is its **Roman collection**, whose strong maritime streak reflects the role which Narbonne played as a major port of Roman Gaul. Various stone carvings illustrate ships of the period, and there's a towering 3.5-metre wood-and-lead ship's **anchor** on display. Combined with the seafaring items is a collection of first-century BC **Roman paintings** – the best of its kind in France. Most of the pieces came from a villa in the northern part of the Roman town, and include elaborate borders, depictions of country scenes and "portraits" of gods. The collection winds up with an impressively large mosaic from the same period as the paintings, and a number of paleo-Christian sarcophagi.

The Cathédrale de St-Just et St-Pasteur

From the archeological museum a narrow alley, the passage de l'Ancre, leads further into the complex, towards the entrance to the **Cathédrale de St-Just et St-Pasteur** (April–Sept 9.30am–noon & 2–6pm; Oct–March 10am–noon & 2–5pm; free). Christianity in the city dates back at least to the time when Constantine the Great proclaimed it the empire's official religion in 328 AD; as a provincial capital Narbonne became seat of an archbishop, and a cathedral was raised. Its exterior is pure Gothic – the tall and narrow core of the building, dominated by expanses of stained-glass window, is braced by sturdy buttresses, from which delicate-looking flying buttresses launch up to support the highest points on the walls. The building which you see today is the fourth to sit on this site, and was begun in 1272. With the completion of the hulking 49-metre choir some fifty years later, construction of the nave, which was meant to extend westwards, was held up after the first couple of stages, because extending it would have involved knocking down the old Roman defensive wall – still very useful in those uncertain times. Thus, as with Toulouse's cathedral, the project was never completed, leaving the church with its strikingly odd form. As you climb the short flight of stairs from the street you'll arrive first at the compact **cloister**, from where there's a good view of the seemingly delicate array of buttresses which support the light Gothic-style walls. A door on the west side of the cloister leads to the formal-style **Jardin des Archevêques**, with even better views, and around to the so-called **Cour St-Eutrope**, which is in fact the sealed-off stub of the aborted nave. The entrance to the church itself can be found on the north side of the cloister.

On entering, the first thing that will strike you is the tremendous space inside the unfinished building – its soaring ceiling the third highest for a French cathedral. Along with the upward dynamic of the design, the predominance of stained glass over stone on the walls is a hallmark of high Gothic style – some of the windows date from the original construction. The centre of the church is taken up by elaborate eighteenth-century **choir stalls**, presided over by a massive **organ** of the same era. Facing it is the high altar, and behind this a series of chapels hung with fine Gobelin and Aubusson tapestries. Directly behind the altar, a badly damaged – but nevertheless beautiful – fourteenth-century stone **retable** illustrates themes of the Redemption with exceptionally carved and incredibly kinetic high-relief figures. From the southernmost of the chapels, a spiral stair leads up to the beehive-shaped chamber housing the cathedral's **treasury** (€2.20), the centrepiece of which is a sumptuous fifteenth-century tapestry depicting the Holy Trinity, personified as three kings. Other fine pieces include a ninth-century ivory panel and an eleventh-century pyx of Muslim origin. On your way out of the church complex, after descending the stairs from the cloister, take a peek in the cathedral's gift shop (same hours as the church), not so much for the stuff on sale, but because it's housed in the elegant **Salle au Pilier**, an airy fourteenth-century chamber whose Gothic vaulting is supported by a single delicate pillar, and in which you'll find rare carvings dating back to the Visigoths of the sixth century.

Around the palace and cathedral

It's worth taking time to explore the lesser sights in the vicinity of the palace and cathedral. First among these is the small **chapel of the Blue Penitents**, just steps from the tourist office on the west side of place Salengro, in the heart of the "quartier del' Europe", as this part of the old town is called. Originally founded in 1149 for the Hospitaller Knights, the chapel has suffered a bout of Baroque, and its interior (hours vary) is a bland white with pale blue detailing, but you can still recognize the fine Romanesque features of its doorway. South of the square two small streets lead directly away from the massive east wall of the cathedral and into a compact **medieval neighbourhood**, which was once the *quartier* of the choristers and other functionaries of the great church: rue du Lieutenant-Colonel-Deymes and the next street along, rue Rouget de l'Isle, both contain houses with distinctly medieval windows and doors. On the latter street, at no. 7, is the **Horreum** (April–Sept daily 9.30am–12.15pm & 2–6pm; Oct–March Tues–Sun 10am–noon & 2–5pm). Despite Narbonne's importance in Roman times, this is the only structure in the city which has survived from that era – in fact it disappeared until 1838, when the building covering it was demolished. Its name means "granary" in Latin, and that's precisely what it was: an underground grain store which was most likely attached to a market building or depot above the ground. Its 40m-by-50m area is divided into a series of small storage chambers leading off a rectangular passage. There's not much to see inside, apart from some ancient graffiti, but it does make for an atmospheric visit.

From the Horreum, head east to the bend in rue Maréchal, where an ancient Roman **stela** sits in the courtyard of the grandiose Hôtel de Poulhariez (now apartments). Following this street further will take you to place Bistan, where you'll see the meagre remains of the Roman forum and capitol, while the once graceful yet flamboyant Gothic **church of St-Sébastian** rises up in rue Michelet, just to the south of the square. From the *place*, atmospheric rue Droite traces the route of both the Roman and medieval main street west back to the place de l'Hôtel de Ville. Heading north from here along the canalside will bring you to Rue de l'Ancienne Porte-Neuve, where you'll find the **Ancienne Poudrière**, a squat and sobre seventeenth-century powder magazine now housing temporary exhibitions.

West of the Canal de la Robine

Narbonne's old town extends over the Canal de la Robine to the west, but in the Middle Ages, as today, this neighbourhood is a humbler section of town. The narrow lanes and crooked streets are home to the city's marginalized North African community, and the plethora of police who comb it are testament to the social problems which grip the area. Even so, it is eminently explorable; there are fewer shops and restaurants here, and the tiny windows of the ageing buildings hang with laundry but the main reason for visiting is to see the two parish churches which share this side of the river. The first is the **Basilique de St-Paul** on rue Dupleix, which you can reach by crossing the canal at pont Voltaire and proceeding south. It's a tall thirteenth-century construction, chipped and battered on the outside over the years, but inside possessing a pleasant mixture of Romanesque and Gothic. The main attraction is the **crypt** (Mon–Sat 9am–noon & 2–6pm & Sun 9am–noon; free): built over a paleo-Christian necropolis and dating back to the fourth century, it is where the town's first bishop was buried. Scattered about the low-ceilinged room are various amphora, sarcophagi and a small mosaic.

Leaving the crypt, around the far side of the church, pick up rue de l'Hôtel Dieu, where you'll find the magnificent sixteenth-century facade of the **Maison des Trois Nourrices**, at the corner of rue Quinet. Taking the next left will lead you to place and rue Belfort, and another crop of medieval dwellings, while at the end of the street, a car-filled *place* opens up in front of the former abbey-church of Notre-Dame-de-la-Mourguié. This is now home to the town's **lapidary museum** (daily: March–Sept 9.30am–12.15pm & 2–6pm; Oct–Feb 10am–noon & 2–5pm), housing a large, but rather monotonous, collection of over thousand statues, inscriptions, tombstones and sarcophagi, most dating back to Roman days. The town's beautifully restored nineteenth-century **covered market** (daily 7am–1pm) is beside the church on the banks of the canal, while along its south side runs the boulevard de Dr-Ferroul, whose stately facades braced by elaborate wrought-iron balustrades testify to the wealth which the wine industry brought in the late 1800s. Finally, the town has a quirky attraction in the home of native **Charles Trénet** (Wed–Mon: April–Sept 10am–noon & 2–6pm, Oct–March 2–6pm; €5.30), at 13 avenue Charles Trénet. A local legend (1913–2001) known as the "singing fool," he was half of the popular 1930s act "Charles and Johnny", and in post-war France became an international cabaret star. Jammed with personal effects, his house recalls in a campy spirit the nostalgic simplicity of still-colonial 1930s and 1950s France.

Eating, drinking and nightlife

Whilst Narbonne is definitely not the culinary capital of the Southwest, you won't starve. There are a couple of **restaurants** which stand out, as well as an array of unexceptional brasseries and bistros where you can eat for under €18. The best place to browse is along the cours de la République on the southern portion of the canal, where you'll also find lots of informal snack places, and the boulevard Gambetta which runs off it to the east.

Restaurants

L'Agora 9 pl de l'Hôtel de Ville ⊕04.68.90.10.70. Despite the Roman name, this is a *terroir* which specializes in foie gras and *magret en confit*, as well as doing a fine line in tapas. *Menus* €10.

L'Alsace 2 av Pierre-Sémard ⊕04.68.65.10.24. Just opposite the train station, this is undoubtedly Narbonne's best restaurant, featuring terroir and northeastern French dishes. Great decor, mammoth servings and menus from €10–29. Closed Tues & Wed.

CO 1 rue Rossini ⊕08.20.39.12.91. Narbonne's swishest eating establishment is surprisingly sophisticated, with arty decor, modern furniture and subtle lighting. The *gastronomique carte* is a welcome relief from *steak frites*. *Menus* from €19–25.

L'Estagnol cours Mirabeau ⊕04.68.65.09.27. On the market side of the canal, this no-frills *terroir* restaurant also has a good fish selection. Solid *menus* in the €10–28 range; less at lunch time. Closed Sun & Mon eve.

Palais du Vin Domaine de St-Crescent le Viel rte de Perpignan ⊕04.68.41.47.20. A *terroir* restaurant, that's part of the local vintners' complex – a showroom for over 2500 regional wine

growers. *Menus* start at around €17. To get there, walk 30min west of the town centre or take bus #3 to "St-Crescent".

La Petite Cour 22 bd Gambetta ⊕04.68.90.48.03. Fish and seafood are the order of the day in this high-ceilinged room decked with seascape murals. There's a good choice of *menus* from €16, or up to €45 in the evening; closed Sun & Mon.

Royal Kebab 14 bd Docteur-Lacroix. The town's Turkish *table*, with all the usual suspects: shish and doner kebabs, salads and sweets.

La Table St-Crescent Domaine St-Crescent-le-Vieil ⊕04.68.41.37.37. It's worth the effort of getting to this excellent gastronomique located in an ancient eighth-century oratory, amongst vineyards and olive groves, that is part of the same complex as the Palais du Vin. Expect to spend about €40 per person. Closed Sat noon, Sun eve & Mon.

Aux Trois Caves, 4 rue Benjamin-Crémieux ⊕ 04.68.65.28.60. Quirky place whose modern decorative touches clash incongruously with their surroundings. Inventive dishes based on local standbys are served in an excavated Roman cellar. Expect to spend €10–22.

Bars and clubs

Narbonne's **nightlife** is far more interesting than its restaurant scene, with a profusion of energetic bars and clubs – curious in a town so quiet and lacking a university. A good place for an early evening **drink** is *Café le Soleil Noir* in place de l'Hôtel de Ville (open till 2am in July & Aug, otherwise till 9pm), a small corner café with sleek décor, a mixed crowd and good sandwiches. Livelier late-night venues include *Le Cyrano*, 26 boulevard Gambetta, a bar with pool table, or *Le Galion* on avenue Anatole France (9pm–2am) which has different nightly themes and dancing. The coolest places are the cocktail bars *Le News Café* and *Le Bal Masqué*, at no. 4 and no. 6 rue Marcelin-Coural, respectively. The former (Mon–Sat until 2am) has live music and DJs with a predominantly 1960s play-list, while the latter (till 2am) has a better variety of music (including salsa on Fridays), with live bands occasionally playing on Thursday nights. Another **club** option is *Le Botafogo*, at 8 avenue des Pyrénées (Tues–Sun 6pm–2am).

Listings

Banks and exchange Narbonne has branches of several major French banks; all have ATMs and most will change money during normal banking hours. Try the Caisse d'Épargne in bd Docteur-Ferroul, beside the indoor market, or the Crédit Lyonnais opposite the *passerelle* in cours de la République.

Bike rental Cycles Cancel, 50 bd Frédéric Mistral (℡04.68.65.12.26, Ⓔ cycles.cancel@wanadoo .fr; and Narbonne Insertion, 12 av Charles Trénet and Quai Victor Hugo (℡04.68.42.45.27, Ⓦ www .narbonne-insertion.com) which also has electric bikes.

Boat tours and rental For canal trips, Berges de la Robine, cours de la République (℡06.11.75.36.98) rents electric boats by the hour (from €19), while Connoisseurs Cruisers, promenade des Barques (℡04.68.65.14.55), is the best place for houseboats.

Car rental ADA, 12 av des Pyrénées ℡04.68.42.44.81; Avis, 21 bd Marcel-Sembat ℡04.68.32.43.36; Europcar, 52 bd Frédéric-Mistral ℡04.68.32.34.54; Locabest, 2 rue Romain ℡04.68.65.35.50.

Hospital Centre Hospitalier de Narbonne, bd Docteur-Lacroix (℡04.68.41.00.00; bus #1, #2 or #3 to "Hôpital").

Internet access Versus, 73 & 82 rue Droite (Mon–Thurs 10am–8pm, Fri 10am–midnight, Sat 2pm–midnight, Sun 2–8pm).

Launderettes 24 av des Pyrénées; 25 bd Docteur-Ferroul; 3 av Karl-Marx.

Pharmacies Pharmacie de l'Hôtel de la Ville, pl de l'Hôtel de la Ville. For night-time and weekend, check the notice on the door.

Police Gendarmerie, rue Anatole-France ℡04.68.90.38.50.

Rugby Local team RCNM play at the Parc des Sports et de l'Amitié, southeast of the old town (bus #3 to "Parc des Sports"; ℡04.68.41.76.93).

Swimming Espace Liberté, rte de Perpignan ℡04.68.42.17.89; bus #3 to "Roches Grises" or "Hautes de Narbonne".

Taxi ℡04.68.32.03.00.

Theatre Théâtre-Scène Nationale de Narbonne, 2 avenue Domitius ℡04.68.90.90.20, Ⓦ www .narbonne.com/letheatre. Mon–Fri 12.30–6.30pm & Sat 3–6pm; bus #2 to "MI Juin".

Train departures All trains leave from the main gare SNCF (℡04.68.80.77.74), except the ATM (Autorail Touristique Minervois) service to Sallèles and Bize (see p.320), which leaves from a separate station on place de la Constituante, just off place des Pyrénées; the fare from Narbonne to Bize is €9.50 return.

Gruissan and Gruissan-Plage

Some 20km southeast of Narbonne, the quiet fishing town of **GRUISSAN** cuts a striking figure from the distance, with its circular streets huddled around an ancient tower, and filling a dramatic-looking promontory in the inland *étang* which bears its name. Arriving, you may be surprised to find little sign of life among the fading colours of Gruissan's houses, or even around the ruins of the **watchtower** (no set hours; free entry) – development has turned its back on the town, which basically consists of an array of low-roofed houses. The "action" is to be found on the long shore, partly in a smattering of bars and restaurants, but mainly in the daily business of the fishermen, tending to their boats or bringing in the catch. The salty Étang du Grazier separates Gruissan from the narrow spit of sand marking the Mediterranean's shore. Here, a concrete expanse of low-rise hotels has choked the banks of the inlet, and spreads north to the equally vacuous development of **GRUISSAN-PLAGE**. Apart from the traditional array of beachside activities and sights for which the towns are admirably equipped, there is virtually nothing to see or do on this stretch of the coast. When you tire of wandering Gruissan's near-deserted streets, you can head to the tourist office, which distributes a series of **biking** and **walking** itineraries in the low but rugged mountain of La Clape, separating Narbonne from the coast. The most popular is the one- to three-hour (depending on whether you start from town, or a car park up the hill) excursion to the local sailors' graveyard and hill-top chapel of Notre-Dame-des-Auzils. The landscape along the way is archetypically Mediterranean, with scrubby pines

Wines of Languedoc and Roussillon

With its perfect weather and excellent soil, Languedoc has been producing wine since Roman times, and is still today responsible for approximately one third of France's wine production. Traditionally a region that produced affordable, everyday wine, in recent years Languedoc has seen a blossoming of small vintners and co-ops producing excellent high-quality wines using blends of grapes similar to those over the Rhône in Provence. One of the joys of visiting Languedoc and Roussillon is to sample a variety of wines, with most co-operatives and domaines welcoming prospective buyers and providing free tastings.

History and tradition

It was the **Romans** who brought wine to Languedoc in the fourth-century BC and production has continued ever since; many of the coastal areas have been growing grapes without interruption for over two thousand years. With the establishment of **Christianity**, wine took on a new significance as a necessary component of the sacrament of Eucharist, and in the Middle Ages the Church became the major consumer and producer. Most of the oldest and most famous varieties of the region, including Gaillac and Blanquette de Limoux, were first made by **monks**.

▲ Monks have been making wine in Languedoc since the Middle Ages

The Rule of Saint Benedict allotted a daily ration of just under half-a-litre of wine per monk, and in a time when water could not always be trusted for drinking, wine became the beverage of choice for those who could afford it. Moreover, wine was considered to have important **medicinal and therapeutic qualities**, and was used to treat ailments and maintain a healthy constitution. Over the centuries as transport and distribution improved and the standard of living rose, wine became even more popular, with national output reaching an all-time high in 1875. By 1887, however, production had fallen to less than a third, as the vine-killing disease **phylloxera** ripped through France. Disaster was avoided only by pulling up the native stock and replacing them with vines from the United States (which themselves had been raised from cuttings taken earlier from France) – the basis of the region's wine production today.

Wine regions

Aside from the uplands of the Pyrenees and Haut Languedoc, vines are grown more or less throughout the region. The southernmost wines are those of the **Côtes du Roussillon**, which produce fruity and exciting reds. Some of the best **Muscat**, a sweet wine, obtained by adding alcohol during the fermentation process, also comes from Roussillon, of which the most famous is the **Byrrh of Thuir**. Just north of Perpignan lie the *domaines* of **Fitou**, a recent AOC (*Appellation d'Origine Contrôllée*), founded in 1948, which combines characteristics of the heavy,

▲ Grape harvest in the Fitou *domaines*

Top 10 tasting tips

- Find a *domaine* – look for the *"dégustation"* (tasting) sign.
- Hold the glass by the stem – don't warm the wine.
- Study the wine, swirling it gently in the glass.
- Look at the wine, holding it up to the light.
- "First nose" - several short snorts with your nose deep in the glass.
- "Second nose" - swirl the wine then gently sniff it.
- Loudly slurp it through your teeth, mixing it with air.
- Slosh it around your whole mouth.
- Spit it out in the bucket provided.
- Compliment the vintner and do it again.

▶ Hold the glass by the stem and swirl it gently

robust vintages yielded by the neighbouring Corbières regions hills and littoral; **Corbières** wines are one of the great AOCs of Languedoc, as varied as the terrain which stretches along the Aude and the hillsides on its southern bank.

Closer to the sea, but sheltered from strong coastal winds by the mountain which separates Narbonne and Gruissan, the **Clape** AOC produces robust and flavourful reds. The vineyards of the coastal plain stretching from Béziers to near Nîmes and inland along the Hérault valley are grouped together as the AOC **Côteaux de Languedoc**, which produces a solid if unexceptional range of reds, whites and rosés. On the other hand, the vintages of the **Costières de Nîmes**, which spread south and east of the city to the marshes of the Camargue, produce well-regarded reds, known for their strength and subtlety. Lastly, **Listel**, a rosé, is one of the best of the vins de sable, the "sand wines" of the Camarguaiseh coast, which originated around Aigues-Mortes and Le Grau-du-Roi.

▼ Château Valmagne in the Coteaux du Languedoc

But the coast does not exercise a monopoly on fine wines in Languedoc and Roussillon. The foothills of Haut Languedoc, stretching west from Narbonne as far as the Montagne Noire, are home to the full-bodied reds of the **Cabardès**, and the honey-tinted whites and fruity reds of the **Minervois**. South of Carcassonne, you'll find **Blanquette de Limoux**, Aude's most famous *appellation*: a sweetish sparkling white produced since

▲ Gaillac produces some of Languedoc's best vintages

the mid-sixteenth century. Curiously, one of Languedoc's most venerable and well-reputed vintages comes from far inland, in the district around **Gaillac**, the transitional zone between the Atlantic and Mediterranean climatic systems where cool ocean-borne winds take the edge off the harsh southern weather. First established as an AOC over a thousand years ago, it is best known for its whites, but also produces excellent reds and rosés. Virtually every tourist office in the region has a brochure on local vintages and a list of domaines which can be visited for tasting. For a general orientation on the wines of the region, consult ⓦwww.vins-du-roussillon.com.

A tradition in crisis

Despite the region's high quality vintages and deep-rooted traditions, Languedoc's wine industry is in **crisis**: vineyards are being torn up; growers are demonstrating; wine stock sits backed up in *caves*; and in 2005 alone more than half-a-million litres of wine were dumped at Sète in response to falling prices. A militant vintner group, **CRAV** (*Comité Régional d'Action Viticole*) has even attacked consignments of foreign wine arriving for sale. The main cause of this crisis is **foreign competition**, as once-marginal areas such as the US, Australia, South America and Eastern Europe now produce top-quality wines at a cheaper price. But **changing French habits** are also contributing to the problem: people are increasingly health-conscious and less likely to drink wine at lunch. Furthermore, with the rising price of wine and cost of living, fewer diners will order a bottle with lunch knowing they may leave much of it at the table. What the future holds is difficult to say, but wine-makers are being forced to become increasingly creative and selective and to reassess both production strategies and marketing: it is good news for consumers, but disquieting for a land proud of its *terroir* traditions.

▶ New production methods are being adopted

and slender cypress sprouting up between the red stones; from the top of the hill, there's a dramatically sweeping panoramic view: the slender band of yellow sand set against the turquoise sea to the east, and the vineyards and *châteaux* of the La Clape *appellation* to the west.

Arriving by **bus** in Gruissan, you'll stop by the **tourist office** (July & Aug daily 9am–1pm & 3–7pm; Sept–June Mon–Sat 9.30am–noon & 2–6pm; ☎04.68.49.09.00, ⓦwww.ville-gruissan.fr), on boulevard Pech-Maynaud between the old and new towns. Given the town's proximity to Narbonne, there's no real reason to spend the night here, but if you are intent on a bout of beach-side hedonism, you'll find a selection of modern, near-identical two- and three-star **hotels**. Right on the beachfront, *Le Floride* (☎04.68.49.04.06, ⓦwww.hotellefloride.com; ❸) is a reasonable choice with good amenities, while the *Port* (mid-April to mid-Oct; ☎04.68.49.07.33, ⓦwww.gruissan-hotel-du-port.com; ❸) is closer to the old town, on Boulevard de la Corderie. The best value of the several **campsites** in the area, is the municipal site (April–Nov; ☎04.68.49.07.22, ⓦwww.ville-gruissan.fr), on route de l'Ayrolle in the old town. If you're looking for a **meal** in town, well-priced seafood and fish can be enjoyed at *L'Estagnol*, on avenue de Narbonne (March–Sept; ☎04.68.49.01.27) whose patio dining area has good views (*menus* from €14), and *Le Phoebus* (☎04.68.49.03.05) in old Gruissan, at 4 rue Amiral-Courbet (*menus* €19–43). **Bikes** and scooters can be rented from Luc Mallien on rue de la Croix Blanche (April–Sept; ☎04.68.49.49.52).

Sigean and Tuchan

Heading south from Narbonne, the road hugs the base of the rising hills, separated from the sea by a wide buffer – a series of salty *étangs* – and accompanied by a landscape characterized by scrubby trees, red soil, and an impossibly blue sky in summer. Travelling by rail south from Narbonne provides a different perspective, as the line threads the marshy spits connecting the salt pans and lagoons; on board you'll feel no hint of the steady and unforgiving wind which lashes in from the east. There's little along the coast to detain you until you arrive at **SIGEAN**, just north of which is a large **African nature reserve** (daily 9am–4/6.30pm; €22). This immense drive-through park (no motorcycles) recreates several equatorial habitats, including brushland, savannah and plain, and lazing around you'll see lions, giraffes, rhinos and hippos, as well as graceful oryx and springboks. There's also a bear area and a bird reserve, while chimpanzees are exiled to their own island at the southern end of the park. For those without cars, a series of footpaths have been laid out among the habitats in a limited area. Sigean itself is nothing special, although it does have a small **archeological museum** by the tourist office (open on request during tourist office hours; €3), displaying artefacts recovered from the nearby *oppidum*: the remains of this hill-top settlement, just outside of town and dating back to the sixth century BC, can also be visited on the same ticket, though there's little to see there (check with the tourist office for directions and opening times).

Buses from Narbonne, Perpignan and Port-la-Nouvelle stop right in Sigean's centre, near the **tourist office** (July & Aug Mon–Sat 9–noon & 3–7pm; Sept–June 9.30–11.30am; ☎04.68.48.14.81, ⓔsisigean@wanadoo.fr) on place de la Libération. Accommodation hereabouts is limited to two **campsites**: the municipal site, at the Étang Boyé (☎04.68.48.43.68; July & Aug), a few minutes' walk from the town centre, and *La Grange Neuve* (☎04.68.48.58.70), near the reserve. To eat, head to the **restaurant** *Le Ste-Anne* on 3 avenue Michel-de-l'Hospital (*menu* €17). Or, if you are just passing town, you might pause for a drink in the wonderful old glassed-in *Café La Rotunda*, at the centre of town on the main street.

Tuchan

In the hills southwest of Sigean, along the Cathar trail, the hamlet of **Tuchan** is presided over by the **Château d'Aguilar** (daily: April to mid-June & mid-Sept to mid-Nov 11am–5pm, mid-June to mid-Sept 11am–7pm; €3.50), with a well-preserved thirteenth- and fourteenth-century curtain wall and keep. Tuchan is also home to the rather over-priced *Relais d'Aguilar* (℡04.68.45.47.84, Ⓦwww .relaisaguilar.com; ❺), which also has a campsite, a restaurant (from €14) and a pool. Alternatively, *l'Amandier* (℡04.68.45.89.48, Ⓔhotelamandier@aol.com) in Durban, half-way between Sigean and Tuchan, can provide decent **accommodation** (❷) and a meal (from €11).

The Corbières

To journey into the heart of the hilly **Corbières** region, which fans out southwest of Narbonne, bordered to the west by the upper Aude valley and to the south by the Fenouillèdes hills of northern Roussillon, is to enter a world very distinct from the coastal plain. As the land rises, the roads narrow, twisting and writhing up into the forests of the low mountains, tenaciously following the streambeds which cut into the slopes. Once the heart of Cathar territory, this district has suffered centuries of abandonment and neglect, and many hamlets lack even a café or a proper payphone, let alone a restaurant or hotel. For all of this, it is a splendid place to drive through, offering the ancient monasteries of **Fontfroide** and **Lagrasse**, and the Cathar sites of **Villerouge-Termenès** and **Termes**. Without your own transport, however, the Corbières is difficult to access, the only bus route following the D613 from Narbonne.

Fontfroide

Passing through the rocky *garrigues* west of Narbonne, the D613 leads you past the narrow turn-off to the **Monastery of Fontfroide**, 22km out of town. Following this road south for four kilometres, you'll come across the stout walls of the ancient Cistercian foundation, tucked inside a shallow valley hidden amongst cypress groves. Founded in the late eleventh century by a count of Narbonne, it saw its greatest prosperity in the two subsequent centuries, after which, like so many monastic centres, it began to decline. The monastery's best-known abbot was Jacques Fournier, who as Bishop of Foix commanded the Inquisition which investigated the Cathars of Montaillou (see p.141), and went on in 1337 to be elected pope as Benedict XII. In private hands for the last hundred years or so, the abbey can only be visited as part of a one-hour **guided tour** (on the hour daily 10am–noon & 2–4pm; €9). It's best to come early in the morning or late in the day in order to avoid crowds; but be warned, this is a popular stop on bus tours, and in high season is frequently too busy to be enjoyable.

The visit starts in the open courtyard, the *cour d'honneur*, built by the sixteenth-century abbots. From here, you're led to the refined beauty of the **cloister** – originally built in the 1200s, but added to as late as the seventeenth century. From the east side you enter the marvellously vaulted **chapterhouse**, and then the **church**, a simple twelfth-century Romanesque basilica, on the south side of which is an interesting ossuary, the salle des Morts, which contains a fifteenth-century Crucifixion scene. After a visit to the storage

cellars which, going back a thousand years, are the oldest surviving part of the monastery, the tour concludes with the monks' living quarters above. Afterwards, you can wander freely along the paths which lead through the surrounding groves and gardens.

There's no accommodation at Fontfroide, so if you're travelling by **bus** you'll want to make sure you are at the main road in time to catch the last one back to Narbonne or further on up into the hills. There is, however, an excellent **restaurant** at the monastery, *La Bergerie* (closed Dec–Feb), which is divided into two parts: the less expensive lunch-time dining room serves traditional but well-executed dishes (*menus* from €15); while the evening-only *gastronomique* will set you back €35 or more (closed Mon).

Villerouge-Termenès and Termes

If you continue west from Fontfroide along the D613, you'll arrive at St-Laurent-de-la-Cabrerisse, where the road forks right for Lagrasse (see p.316), and left towards the hills. Following this second route will lead you into some of the wildest back-country of the region, where forested uplands are capped by the tumbled remains of nameless castles. The road first climbs to the 404-metre-high Col de Villerouge, and as you round the top, you'll get a startling view of the castle and **VILLEROUGE-TERMENÈS** below. The village is dominated by the tall keep of its impressively restored **castle** (Feb, March & late Oct to Dec Sat, Sun & school hols 10am–5pm; April–June & Sept to mid-Oct daily 10am–6pm; July & Aug daily 9.30am–7.30pm; €6). The earlier Cathar fort here was destroyed in the wake of its conquest by Crusaders in 1210, and the present structure, dating from the 1300s, was designed not to protect but to dominate the inhabitants of the surrounding hills. A visit involves an engaging audiovisual show which recaps the history of the area and recounts the tale of Guilhem Bélibaste, the Cathar *parfait* who was burned at the stake here in 1321. Afterwards it's worth taking a walk through the village huddled around the castle; the town was almost certainly fortified in the twelfth century, but the walls which are visible today were built to fend off the English and their allies during the Hundred Years' War. South of the *enceinte* you'll find the **church** of St-Étienne, which houses an immense sixteenth-century retable.

Leaving Villerouge, another steep ascent takes you to the **Col de Bedos** (485m), where a narrow paved road veers off to the right. Carefully following this relentless succession of hairpin curves will take you over hill and into valley until you make a sharp descent to **TERMES**. Little more than a cluster of ancient houses set on cramped but orderly streets, this extraordinarily beautiful hamlet would be worth a visit even if it weren't for its famous castle. Trees crowd over the narrow stream, bridged by a centuries-old stone bridge, and the sharply rising slopes above are covered by a blanket of beech, ash and stunted oak. The only thing which ruins the effect is the modern reception centre across the river, which is the point at which you begin the arduous ascent to the ruins of the **castle** (March & mid-Oct to Dec Sat, Sun & school hols 10am–5pm; April–June & Sept to mid-Oct daily 10am–6pm; July & Aug daily 10am–7.30pm; €3.50). You wouldn't know it from either the ruins or the village, but this castle was dominated by one of the greatest feudal domains of Languedoc. Ruled by an unrepentant heretic lord, Raymond, it was a prime target for de Montfort, who besieged it for four months, until the disease-ravaged garrison could resist no more. After it was taken the castle continued to be used, and it was not destroyed until the seventeenth century, when Richelieu systematically cleared the land of possible points of resistance to central rule. Clambering among the remains of the two concentric sets of walls, you'll find the chapel and take in breathtaking **views** over the hills around. From Termes, you have two options: continue on for another twenty hair-raising kilometres to reach the main road heading north to Lagrasse, or double back the way you came, and descend the Col de Bedos to **MOUTHOUMET**. This sleepy village serves as the end for the bus line which runs up from Narbonne and, if nothing else, makes a welcome rest stop on the GR36 as it winds its way south from Termes to Peyrepertuse, or on the west towards Arques and Rennes-le-Château.

Practicalities

Services are extremely thin on the ground in this neck of the woods, with accommodation limited to an unofficial **campsite** on the riverside outside Termes, just before you enter town. **Eating** is a little better: in Villerouge you can enjoy a lively meal in the castle's *Rôtisserie Médiévale* (closed Sun eve & Mon except hols, open weekends by reservation only off-season; ☎04.68.70.06.06) for about €27, while in Mouthoumet's main square there's the *Auberge du Terroir* (lunch only; closed Sat), a homely little place serving excellent salads, and *menus* from €13.

Lagrasse

Just over halfway from Narbonne to Carcassonne and separated from the Aude valley by the low ridge of the Montagne d'Alaric, **LAGRASSE** is the largest and most beautiful village of the Corbières highlands. A compact walled hamlet set idyllically where the Orbieu opens up in a broad hollow, it hugs the right bank of the shallow river, while the magnificent abbey squats on the far side. Delightfully, but surprisingly, Lagrasse is not very touristy; the grid of streets in the old town is almost completely residential, and you'll hardly see a postcard stand or gift shop. It's a real pleasure to wander the cobbled lanes down to the arcaded *place* and its ancient **covered market**, with flowers cascading from the windows of the houses which hem the streets and crowd around the fort-like **church**. Much of the old *enceinte* is intact, and as you cross the eleventh-century bridge, try to crane over its protective walls to look at the

△ Lagrasse

town's riverside fortifications, now pierced by the scores of windows of the houses built against them – an especially evocative sight at dusk. It's only about a five-minute walk from the far side of the river to the **abbey of Ste-Marie d'Orbieu** (late Jan Sat & Sun 2–4.30pm; Feb, March & Nov to mid-Dec daily 2–4.30/5pm; April–June, Sept & Oct daily 10.30am–noon & 2–5pm; July & Aug daily 10.30am–6.15pm; €3.50). This is one of the region's oldest monastic houses, founded in an era when it was a dangerous, underpopulated frontier of the eighth-century Carolingian empire. Cultivating the extensive lands with which they had been endowed, the monks slowly increased the monastery's wealth until its golden age in the fourteenth century, which saw the building of the town's walls and market. The complex is now a pastiche of styles, with components dating from the tenth to eighteenth centuries. The abbot's Renaissance **palace** and cloister were built during the monastery's second great period of revival – just before the storm of Revolution swept it away – whereas the bulk of the **abbey-church** and the old Romanesque-style **cloister** date from the thirteenth century, although both have since been substantially remodelled. Look for the distinctive mark of the "Master of Cabestany" (see box, p.108) in the cloister and on one of the abbey's entrances. You'll also get a look at the monks' cavernous **dormitory**, and have the chance to climb the Gothic-tinged fifteenth-century **clock tower**, whose heights afford impressive vistas of the town and valley. Leaving the abbey, continue along the riverside to a low dam bridging the river – you can walk across here and re-enter the town.

Heading on from Lagrasse towards Carcassonne, the most scenic route takes you west through the Gorges d'Alsou.

Practicalities

Lagrasse's services and shops are mostly strung along the tree-lined boulevard de la Promenade, including the **tourist office** (July & Aug 10.30am–12.30pm & 2–7pm; Sept–June 10.30am–12.30pm & 2–5.30pm; ℡04.68.43.11.56, ⓦwww .lagrasse.com) at no. 6. Further along at no. 9, you'll find the friendly **hotel** 🍴 *Hostellerie des Corbières* (℡04.68.43.15.22, ⓦwww.hostelleriecorbieres.com; ❹; closed Nov to mid-March), which also has an excellent restaurant (*menu* from €20). Otherwise, there are **chambres d'hôtes** in the old town at *Les Trois Grâces*, 5 rue de Quai (closed Jan & Feb, and Wed & Thurs; ℡ & ⓕ04.68.43.18.17; ❹), which also has an excellent restaurant (€21), and with the Hughes (℡04.68.43.14.54, English spoken; ❸), who can also provide bicycles. There is a basic municipal **campsite** (March–Oct; for details, contact the tourist office) on the edge of town. The most interesting **restaurant** here is *Les Temps de Courges* at 3 rue des Mazels (closed Tues & Wed lunch; ℡04.68.43.10.18), where you can order vegetarian or meat dishes and dine on a cosy little terrace (*menus* at €17–28). Otherwise there are a string of family-run establishments on the boulevard de la Promenade, including *Le Petit Saint* and *L'Affenage*, both of which have basic *terroir menus* for under €20 and pavement terraces.

Along the Canal du Midi east from Carcassonne

Heading east from Carcassonne, the **Canal du Midi** (see p.110) follows the course of the lower Aude valley, past the shady port at **Trèbes**, and on into the wine country of the **Minervois**, bounded by Haut Languedoc to the north and the hills of the Corbières to the south. Here the small port of **Homps** provides a jumping-off point for the old Cathar stronghold of **Minerve** and the monastery at **Caunes**, while bustling **Lézignan** is a hub for non-fluvial transport. Just after the old way-station of Le Somail the canal splits; the offshoot **Canal de la Robine** glides past the ancient wine centre of **Sallèles**, and on through Narbonne to reach the sea near Gruissan, while the main channel edges on to pass the magnificent **Oppidum d'Ensérune**, before reaching Béziers and, eventually, Agde (see p.328). As with the western leg of the canal system, you needn't commit yourself to boating to enjoy this archetypal southern French landscape, since the two towpaths which run along the canal's length make for excellent **biking** and **walking**.

Trèbes and Puichéric

The first and prettiest port of call along the eastern stretch of the Canal du Midi is **TRÈBES**, just a few kilometres east of Carcassonne. The canal makes a broad curve here, following the wide meander of the Aude; arriving at Trèbes, two canal bridges, the second designed by the military architect Vauban in 1686, carry the watercourse over the Frequel and Orbiel rivers. Aside from being an attractive place with a canal port overlooked by the town walls at its western

The Black Prince: Languedoc's first English tourist

The end of the Cathar Wars ushered in an era of peace and prosperity for Languedoc, but it wasn't fated to last, as events far off at the courts of Westminster and Paris brought warfare once again to the already severely devastated region. This time the occasion was the **Hundred Years' War**, which flared up in 1330 when Edward III of England, who already controlled a significant part of north and western France, claimed that he, rather than Philip VI, was the rightful king. At that time, Edward III's eldest son and heir, also named Edward, was only two years of age, but by the time he was 16, he was experienced enough in war to be given partial command at the Battle of Crécy in 1346, which saw a resounding victory over the forces of the French king.

Young Edward, who was the first heir to the throne to carry the title "Prince of Wales", was also Duke of Aquitaine, and once he had proven his mettle, he was sent off to Bordeaux to take command of the province. Here the local Gascons were only too happy to join the English in looting and pillaging their neighbours; contemporary chronicler Jean de Froissart commented that the Gascons "love the English in preference to the French, for the war against France is the most profitable; and this is the cause of their preference". Edward, by then known as the **Black Prince** after the colour of his armour, would give them every opportunity.

Although most of the war was being fought in northern France, Edward mounted a massive *chevauchée* – a scorched-earth campaign designed to terrorize civilians and destroy infrastructure – into Languedoc in 1355. Striking out towards Toulouse, he and his men covered nearly 675 miles in 68 days of raiding. Castelnaudary, as well as the *bastide* of Carcassonne, Trèbes, Limoux and Narbonne, were just a few of the towns he and his troops sacked and put to the torch; in all his troop of five thousand men laid waste to nearly 18,000 square miles of territory. The following year Edward went on to further glory by capturing the French king, John II, in battle at Poitiers. It would be many years before the horror of the raid would be forgotten. For his part, Froissart ventured a rather restrained assessment of the foreign forces, saying that he had "witnessed the great haughtiness of the English, who are affable to no other nation than their own".

end, Trèbes is home to the remarkable **church of St-Étienne** (July & Aug Mon–Fri 10am–noon & 2–7pm; at other times, ask the parish priest; free), the wooden-beamed ceiling of which, dating back to the early fourteenth century, has over 350 individual faces painted on the ends of its roof supports, including caricatures of various professions and social classes, exotic foreigners and grotesques. For boaters the town is a well-equipped stage-post, just as it was in the seventeenth century, with mooring facilities and a range of services.

Trèbes' **tourist office** is by the former canal *auberge*, on rue Pierre-Loti (March–April & Oct daily 2–6/7pm; May Mon–Sat 10am–noon & 2–7pm; June–Sept Mon–Sat 10am–noon & 2–7.30/8pm & Sun 2–7.30/8pm; ℡04.68.78.89.50, ⓦwww.ot-trebes.fr.st). The nearby Sautès Le Bas commercial zone just west of the town centre is home to two decent **hotels**: *La Gentil-hommière* at 6 Zac de Sautès Le Bas (℡04.68.78.74.74, ⓦwww.lagentilhom .com; ❹) and the *Sarl L'Andalou*, at 12 rue de l'Industrie (℡04.68.78.88.48, ⓔandalou@wanadoo.fr; ❶). The town's **campsite** is on chemin de la Lande on the west side of Trèbes (April–Sept; ℡04.68.78.61.75). There are a number of inexpensive **restaurants** in Trèbes, including *Les 3 B*, on avenue Pasteur, and *Le Relais des Capucins*, at 34 rte de Narbonne – either of which can set you up with an €11 midday *menu*. For **boat rental**, head to the canalside boat basin, where the port office (℡04.68.78.83.08) and Connoisseur (℡04.68.78.73.75, ⓦwww.connoisseur.com) have a selection of house-boats, and you can also rent electric boats for shorter trips (two hours €35). For **boat trips**, contact Les Croisières Entre Deux Mers, also at the boat basin (℡04.68.94.42.02, ⓔcroisieresentre2mers@net-up.com). **Bike rental** is available at Loca Velos (℡04.69.78.68.81) in the village.

From Trèbes, the canal meanders east to **Puichéric**, a Cathar town that survived the Crusade, but was put to the torch by the Black Prince a century later. Today there's little to see, as its medieval castle is now private.

The Minervois

As the canal arcs northward it passes **HOMPS**, a town which suffered destruction in the Crusade and the Wars of Religion, but revived with the construction of the waterway. It's the main port of the **Minervois** region, a sun-bleached wine-producing territory stretching from the north bank of the Aude up to the hills of Haut Languedoc. The principal town of the Minervois, **OLONZAC**, lies just 2km north of the canal, linked to Homps by the D910. There are no sights here but it makes a convenient stop on the road to the former Cathar stronghold of **MINERVE**, a further 15km north. A tiny medieval hamlet, located at the cirque where the deep gorge of the River Cesse doubles back on itself, Minerve's main attraction is its stunningly dramatic location – only a single pile of stones remains of its **fortress**, which resisted Simon de Mont-fort for five months in 1210. When it was taken, 140 Cathars who refused to recant their beliefs voluntarily jumped into the fire which the Crusaders had prepared for them. Neither of the town's museums merit much attention: the **archeological museum** (March–Oct daily 10am–6.30pm; €1.70), with its shambolic collection set in dusty fly-specked display cases, is quite a specimen itself, while the **Musée Hurepel** (April–Sept daily 11am–12.30pm & 2–6pm; €2) is nothing more than a thinly disguised shop, where you can pay to see a series of cheesy miniature dioramas recounting the Cathar saga. A visit to the town is best spent hiking the path through the **canyon** which surrounds it, and where you can walk in natural tunnels bored through the cliffs. The trail can be picked up just over the bridge which enters town. It's best to avoid Minerve in high season and at weekends, when the volume of visitors threatens to obliterate its charms.

The Cesse river meanders eastwards for 10km from Minerve and can be followed by road, veering south and descending to the quiet, walled hamlet of **BIZE-MINERVOIS**. Set just off of the main Béziers-Carcassonne highway and 8km from the Canal du Midi, Bize is the final stop on the Narbonne–Sallèles ATM rail line (see p.322). Although there are no specific sights, it's a pleasant and atmospheric spot, and in summer, the canalized Cesse river here is a favourite local bathing spot.

CAUNES-MINERVOIS, the region's capital, lies 20km west of Olonzac on the far western edge of the Minervois. Its centre is dominated by a hulking **abbey** (daily: April–June, Sept & Oct 10am–noon & 2–6pm; July & Aug 10am–7pm; Nov–March 10am–noon & 2–5pm; €4.50). There's not much to see here, although the crypt holds the foundation of the original fourth-century church, and some eleventh-century pavement has been uncovered in the cloister. Otherwise, the town is fairly unremarkable, although a wander through its streets discloses a peppering of the abbots' luxurious mansions, which were constructed in the Middle Ages and through to the sixteenth century. Caunes is most famous for its marble quarries, which supplied stone for many of the churches throughout the region. Along the way you may want to stop in **Rieux-Minervois**, where the town's **Église de Notre Dame** contains a fine example of the handiwork of the "Master of Cabestany" (see box, p.108) in its chapel of the Assumption, as well as a fine fifteenth-century tomb.

Practicalities

There are **tourist offices** in the centre of Olonzac, at 9 boulevard Blazin (July & Aug 9am–noon & 2–6pm; ℡04.68.91.34.95, ℻04.68.91.21.08), and behind the church in Minerve, at 9 rue des Martyrs (July & Aug 10am–noon & 2–6pm; ℡04.68.91.81.43). Comfortable **hotels** and **chambres d'hôtes** in the region include the *Eloi Merle* on avenue de Homps in Olonzac (℡04.68.27.62.03; ❹), and the excellent ✤ *Maison des Rossignols* in Pouzols, just east of Olonzac (℡04.68.46.03.59; ⓦwww.maison-des-rossignols.com; ❸), with superb quality meals (€15). In Minerve, the only hotel is the *Relais Chantovent* (℡04.68.91.14.18, ℻04.68.91.81.99; ❹; closed mid-Dec to mid-March), which is also an excellent place for a local meal (*menus* from €8). In Bize-Minervois, you can stay at the rustic but well-appointed *chambres d'hôtes Du Menhir* (℡04.68.46.16.90, ⓦwww.domainedumenhir.com; ❸), with a private pool, or the nearby luxurious *domaine*, ✤ *La Bastide Cabezac* (℡04.68.46.23.05, ⓦwww.labastidecabezac.com; ❺), in Hameau de Cabezac, 3km south of Bize on the main road (a 20-min walk from the ATM station). In Caunes, the *d'Alibert* in place de la Mairie (℡04.68.78.00.54, ⓔfrederic .dalibert@wanadoo.fr; ❸; closed Sun & Mon in low season & late-Dec to Feb) has a good restaurant. Caunes also has a municipal **campsite** (mid-June to mid-Sept; ℡04.68.78.07.83). Along the canal route, there are also several accommodation options, including *Hôtel la Muscadelle*, on the route de Languedoc in Marseillette (℡04.68.79.20.90, ⓦwww.ferien-frankreich.fr; ❷), *L'Auberge de l'Arbousier* at 50 av de Carcassonne in Homps (℡04.68.91.11.24, ⓦwww.logis-de-france.fr; ❸; closed mid-March to mid-April), and the *Logis de Merinville* on avenue Général-Clémenceau in Rieux (℡04.68.78.12.49, ⓔcathy .morin@wanadoo.fr; ❸).

Olonzac is home to the highly-rated *Du Minervois Bel* **restaurant**, 2 rue des Écoles (℡04.68.91.20.73; from €20; closed Sun & Mon), though the *Auberge de* *l'Arbousier* in Homps (T04.68.91.11.24; closed Sun eve to Tues eve off season and Mon & Tues noon in summer), is a better option, with *terroir menus* from €15. Alternatively, the waterside *La Guinguette* in Argens (T04.68.27.55.73), 6km or so down the canal from Olonzac, is another excellent option, as are *Le Templier*, just inside the medieval gate in Bize-Minervois, with a pleasant dining room and hearty local food (around €18), and *L'Olivier*, a renown *gastronomique* at Hameau de Cabezac, (closed Mon & Tues noon & Sat noon & Sun off-season; *menus* from €23).

For **boat rental** and **cruises**, contact Les Camalous Sud in Olonzac (T04.68.91.25.99, Wwww.camarguesplaisance.com), or Connoisseur in Homps' port (T04.68.91.24.00, Wwww.connoisseur.com), which also rents out bikes.

Lézignan-Corbières and Le Somail

Veering south and east after Homps, the Canal du Midi enters a particularly beautiful stretch, passing a series of castles as the landscape settles into vine-covered plain. Some 5km south of the canal sits **LÉZIGNAN-CORBIÈRES**, the capital of the rugged region rising gradually to the south. Lézignan has been in the business of wine production since the time of the Romans and today remains a small but bustling centre of the viticulture industry. There's no overwhelming reason to visit, although if you're dependent on public transport you may have to change buses or trains here.

Buses will let you off as they pass through the town's centre, while **trains** stop at the **gare SNCF**, 3 rue Turgot. There's also a **tourist office** (July & Aug Mon–Sat 9am–7pm, Sun 10am–12.30pm; Sept–June Mon–Fri 10am–noon & 2–6pm; May, June & Sept also Sat 9am–12.30pm; T04.68.27.05.42, Wwww .lezignan-corbieres.fr/tourisme) at 9 Cours de la République, on the southern side of the ring road which skirts the old town. You'll find a good selection of shops, services and **hotels** in Lézignan, the best of which is the *Tassigny* on rond-point de Lattre-de-Tassigny (T04.68.27.11.51, Wwww.logis-de-france .fr; ❸), with clean rooms and good amenities. You can also get a bed at the local MJC **hostel**, 25 rue Marat (T04.68.27.03.34, Wwww.mjc-lezignan -corbieres.com; doubles ❷, dorm beds €18), and there's a **campsite**, *La Pinède* (March–Oct; T04.68.27.05.08, Wwww.campinglapinede.fr) on the main road on the eastern edge of town. **Bikes** can be rented from Plancade, at 33 avenue Président-Wilson (T04.68.27.29.13, Ecyclesplancade@yahoo.fr). Wednesday morning is **market** day.

From Lézignan, this leg of the canal continues over the canal bridge of Répudre – France's first, and an invention of Riquet himself – on to **LE SOMAIL**, the last port before the Canal de la Robine splits off to head south towards Narbonne. As a whole, the town, mired among modern housing devel-opments on a broad expanse of flat land, looks unpromising as you approach, but the area along the canal, which formed the seventeenth-century port, is a world apart. Here a single-arched stone **bridge** dating from the eighteenth century spans the canal, still attached to the old post-house *auberge* on the east bank and a small **chapel** on the west. There's little to do here aside from enjoy-ing a drink or meal and soaking up the canalside ambience before moving on, although if you're not in a hurry you might take a look at the private **hat museum** (June–Sept daily 9am–noon & 2–7pm; Oct–May Mon–Sat 2–6pm, Sun 2.30–7pm; €3.20), located at the south end of town, where you'll find more than six thousand hats on display from around the world. Bibliophiles will enjoy browsing around the famous **Librairie Ancienne** a huge used and antique book shop housed in an old wine *cave*.

There's a small canal **information office** (irregular hours; ☎06.84.81.96.20) by the old bridge, and decent *chambres d'hôtes* **accommodation** in an old canal *auberge* at *Chez Pierrette Bernabeu*, on the east side of the bridge (☎04.68.46.16.02, ✉pierrette.bernabeu@wanadoo.fr; ❸). The neighbouring *Auberge Lou Somaillou* (March–Nov; ☎04.68.46.19.41) serves satisfying meals in a comfortable dining room or on the canalside terrace (*menus* €16–36). Minervois Cruisers, at 38 chemin des Patiasses (☎04.68.46.28.52) rents out cruising **boats** for longer trips, while *Comptoir Nature*, at 1 chemin de Halage, hires electric boats by the hour.

Along the Canal de la Robine

From Le Somail, the **CANAL DE LA ROBINE**'s short trajectory carries it almost directly south, crossing the course of the wide and, here, tame Aude, and continuing through Narbonne before penetrating the marshy extent of the Étang de Bages et de Sigean. After Narbonne there are two legs; the longer tracks the same spit of land as the railway, skirting the bird-lovers' paradise of Île de Ste-Lucie, before arriving at Port-la-Nouvelle and the sea, while the shorter cuts east past the vineyards of La Clape, passing Gruissan (see p.312) and the salt pans of St-Martin before reaching the Mediterranean.

The only major port of call on the Canal de la Robine, a few kilometres before it merges with the Aude, is **SALLÈLES**. Like Lézignan, Sallèles is a wine town of great antiquity, whose vintages graced the tables of Rome more than two thousand years ago. Bearing testimony to this are the town's Roman pottery works, now incorporated into the **Amphoralis** museum on Sallèles' northern edge (July–Sept daily 10am–noon & 3–7pm; Oct–June Tues–Fri 2–6pm, Sat & Sun 10am–noon & 2–6pm; €4). Named after the distinctively tapered vessels (*amphorae*) once made here, it's a well-laid-out and entertaining museum, which includes the excavation site of the pottery itself. The walk out to the museum from the tourist office is interesting too, thanks to the six sets of **locks** which grace that part of the canal. While you're in town, you might also head to the rather less imaginative **Musée du Vieux Sallèles** (May–Sept Sat & Sun 2.30–6.30pm; €3) in the centre, a traditional small-town French museum with extensive but familiar collections of tools relating to traditional crafts, viticulture and nineteenth-century life. The old town itself, a tight knot of narrow lanes, is also as good a place as any to stretch your legs. Finally, at Sallèles' canalside station, you can hop on board the narrow-gauge **Autorail Touristique Minervois** (☎04.68.27.05.94, ⓦwww.trains-fr.org/unecto/atm), a 1950s-era tourist train which uses the old line connecting Narbonne in the east with the quiet, walled hamlet of Bize-Minervois to the west. The ATM runs on Saturdays (July & Aug 3 daily), Sundays (July & Aug 3 daily; Sept to early Oct 1 daily) and occasional weekdays. The fare for the Sallèles to Bize leg is €5.50, for Narbonne–Bize €9.50.

Sallèles' canalside **tourist office** (Mon–Fri 10.30am–12.30pm & 4–6.30pm; ☎04.68.46.81.46, ⓦwww.sallelesdaude.com) is in the centre of town at 3 Grand'Rue. The best **accommodation** is at the canalside B&B, ⚐ *Les Volets Bleus* (☎04.68.46.83.03, ⓦwww.salleles.net; English spoken; ❹; closed Dec to mid-Mar), set in an old canal master's house, with comfortable rooms and generous meals available (€22). The municipal **campsite** (mid-June to mid-Sept; ☎04.68.46.86.46) is a ten-minute walk from the centre on the east side of the canal. There are a couple of **cafés** along the main road where you can get a meal, and **bikes** can be rented Velo's, at 13 rue Victor-Hugo (☎04.68.46.18.59, ✉velos.salleles@free.fr).

The Canal du Midi: from Le Somail to the sea

East of Le Somail, the Canal du Midi enters its most picturesque stretch, snaking through a rugged landscape of low and rocky vine-clad hills whose only reminder of civilization is an occasional bell tower. Beyond Béziers, the Canal finally empties into the Bassin de Thau, from where you can reach the sea or connect with the other great inland waterway of Languedoc, the Rhône–Sète Canal (see box, p.240), which carries on past the Petite Camargue into Provence.

Capestang

Sixteen kilometres from Béziers, the Canal du Midi passes under the old hill-top town of **CAPESTANG**, whose small castle is capped by a distinctive tower. With a tree-lined square snuggled up against its medieval church, Capestang is an exceedingly pleasant little town, where you can climb the church's **bell tower** to enjoy sweeping views over the Aude valley, or simply enjoy a snack or drink and observe the unhurried life of the *place*. The nondescript-looking **castle** is currently private property, but there are plans to open it in the next few years, at which time its 161 fourteenth-century **ceiling paintings** will become a must-see for those following the canal route. These vivid caricatures depict monsters, musicians, court ladies and even a mischievous jester pulling a rather exaggerated "moon" at the viewer: for entry details enquire at the **tourist office**, on the main street, adjacent to the castle (Mon–Sat 10am–noon & 3–6pm: Nov–April closed Sat; ℡04.67.93.34.23, ⓦwww.ville-capestang.fr). Capestang has a couple of worthwhile **accommodation** options, both along cours Belfort, the main road through town: the two-star hotel *Le Relais Bleu*, at no. 39 (℡04.67.93.31.26; ❸), and the *chambres d'hôte*, *La Bellifontaine* at no. 44 (℡04.67.93.69.68, ⓦperso.orange.fr/la-bellifontaine; ❹). The *mairie* runs a **campsite** *Tounel* (May–Sept; ℡04.67.49.34.23), in av de la République. One of the best **restaurants** in town is the popular *La Grillade* on the main square, which serves excellent grilled meats from €9. Alternatively, there's the slightly fancier *Le Provence* (℡04.67.93.36.54) on the west side of the square, with *menus* from €16–25.

Colombiers, the Oppidum D'Ensérune and Nissan-lez-Ensérune

After cutting through the ancient hamlet of Poilhes, some 5km beyond Capestang, the Canal du Midi passes through a long tunnel, eventually arriving at the tiny village of **COLOMBIERS**, where you can visit the **Cave des Ducs de Castries** (daily 10am–12.30pm & 4–8pm; €2) in place du Millénaire, a sumptuous nineteenth-century *bodega* designed by wood carvers who studied under Eiffel, which hosts art and archeological exhibitions. Colombiers is also home to the area's best **restaurant**, the elegant *Château de Colombiers* (℡04.67.37.06.93; closed Wed noon, Thurs & Sun off-season) set in the town's *château*, which uses local produce for its fine fare (from €20). **Boats** can be rented here from the riverside Rive de France (℡04.67.37.14.23, ⓦwww.rivedefrance.com).

Two kilometres west of Colombiers and set on a long ridge towering over the surrounding plains, the site of the **OPPIDUM D'ENSÉRUNE** (*oppidum* being Latin for "town", referring generally to pre-Roman hill-top settlements) has attracted settlers for over 2500 years. Even before Hannibal and the Romans took it over in turn, it was an important centre for trade, maintaining commercial ties with Greece, while under the Romans it served as one of the postal way-stations on the busy Via Domitia. The site itself, a rocky spur crowned with cypress and brambles, is characteristically Mediterranean, and climbing to the top, looking north, you'll get a view of a strange array of fields resembling a spoked wheel. This was once the *étang* of Montady, one of the many salt lagoons of the lowlands here that were drained and cultivated in the thirteenth century. The **excavations** (April, May & Sept daily 9.30am–6.30pm; June–Aug 9.30am–7.30pm; Oct–March Wed–Mon 2–5pm; €5) of the ancient ruins, covering most of the hill-top, are impressive, with remains of defensive walls, villas and a large array of cisterns and sunken grain stores. The small **site museum** inside the grounds holds a collection of statuary found here, including small devotional pieces and larger civic portraits.

If you have the time, **NISSAN-LEZ-ENSÉRUNE**, the largest town near the ancient settlement – just 4km to the south on the main road – is worth a look. The thirteenth-century Gothic **church** contains inscriptions in Occitan and some fine medieval statuary, and it has a small **museum** (open by prior arrangement through the tourist office; free), housing Roman finds from the surrounding area. Nissan is also home to the main **tourist office** in the vicinity of the *oppidum*, on place René-Dez (Mon–Sat 9am–noon & 2–5.30pm; ⊺ & Ⓕ04.67.37.14.12), and the best **hotel** hereabouts, the *Résidence*, set in an old mansion at 35 avenue de la Cave (⊺04.67.35.00.63, Ⓦwww.hotel-residence .com; ❹; closed late Dec to early Jan). There's also a pretty and well-equipped **chambres d'hôtes**, *Domaine Salabert,* just outside the town (⊺04.67.37.00.27, Ⓔsalabert34@hotmail.com; ❸).

Villeneuve-Lès-Béziers and the neuf écluses

As it arrives at the foot of Béziers' ridge, the canal descends another set of multiple locks, the **neuf écluses**. Billed as a tourist attraction, and endowed with footpaths and snack bars, the lock complex draws families and tour groups who dutifully stand around watching the boats make their slow descent – altogether about as exciting as watching someone take the lift. Five kilometres futher on, tiny **VILLENEUVE-LÈS-BÉZIERS** is the last mooring point on the Canal du Midi before it follows a flat and featureless course to Agde (see p.328) and empties into the Bassin de Thau. Villeneuve's **tourist office** is on rue de la Fontaine (July & Aug 9am–7pm; Sept–June Mon–Fri 9am–noon & 2–6pm; ⊺ & Ⓕ04.67.39.48.83), while **accommodation** can be found at *Las Cigalas*, 28 boulevard Gambetta (⊺04.67.39.45.28, Ⓦwww.las-cigalas.com; ❸). The municipal **campsite**, *Les Berges du Canal* (mid-April to mid-Sept; ⊺04.67.39.36.09, Ⓦwww .lesbergesducanal.com) is on Promenade des Vernets. Villeneuve's country **market** is held on Tuesdays and Sundays.

Béziers and around

Just inland from the mouth of the Orb river and dominating the strip of plain between the coast and Haut Languedoc, **BÉZIERS** could be held up as a metaphor for Languedoc – it's a town with a long and proud past, and a history of independent spirit, which it has more than once paid for in blood. Like neighbouring Narbonne, Béziers was already a sizeable settlement when the Romans took it over in the second century BC; it thrived under *pax Romana*, and was the seat of a bishop and a prosperous market town through the Middle Ages. The last great event here was the attack it suffered in the Albigensian Crusade, and since then it has been something of a sleepy bywater – Paul Riquet, the genius behind the Canal du Midi, is the town's biggest claim to fame. Still, its former grandeur is evident from afar; as you approach, its great **cathedral** towers over the Orb river, high up on a dramatic ridge. Until only recently the city had fallen into decay, its dusty streets and deteriorating shop-fronts betraying the slump into which the town has settled in the last century or so. Determined civicism has turned the situation around, however, and Béziers has become a delight, its atmospheric **old quarter** now bustling with busy shops. Modern Béziers is the home to two great Languedocian adopted traditions: English **rugby**, and the Spanish **corrida**, both of which it follows with a passion. The best time to visit is during the mid-August **feria**, a raucous four-day party which you will enjoy even if you don't find bullfighting to your taste. Béziers is also a useful staging point for excursions up the **Orb valley** (see p.331) towards Haut Languedoc, or down to **Agde** and the coast.

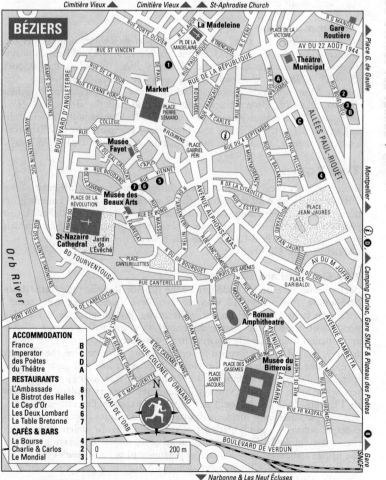

Narbonne & Les Neuf Écluses

Arrival, information and accommodation

If you arrive at the **gare SNCF** on boulevard de Verdun, about fifteen minutes' walk southeast of the old town, the best way into the centre is through the landscaped gardens of the Plateau des Poètes, opposite the *gare* entrance, and up allées Paul-Riquet to place de la Victoire. The **gare routière** is on place Général de Gaulle, just to the east of Victoire, while the **tourist office** is in the Palais des Congrès at 29 avenue Saint-Saëns (July & Aug Mon–Sat 9am–7pm, Sun 9.30am–12.30pm; Sept–June Mon–Sat 9am–noon/12.30pm & 1.30/2–6pm; ☏04.67.76.47.00, ⓦwww.ville-beziers.fr). There are also a couple of small seasonal offices: one in place Lavabre in the old town (May & June Mon–Fri 10am–noon & 2–6pm; July & Aug Mon–Fri 10am–1pm & 2–7pm); and one by the canal locks (May–Sept daily 10/11am–5/7pm). The tourist offices sell **a pass** (€3.30) which is valid for one visit to each of the town's museums. **Drivers** will find plenty of metered street **parking** in and around the town centre, and you can rent **bikes** at La Maison du Canal (☏04.67.62.18.18) beside the Port Neuf, south of the gare SNCF.

Accommodation

For a central place to **stay**, try the smart *Hôtel du Théâtre*, right beside the municipal theatre at 13 rue Coquille (☏04.67.49.13.43, Ⓔhoteldutheatre .beziers@9online.com; ②), or the *Hôtel des Poètes*, 80 allées Paul-Riquet (☏04.67.76.38.66, ⓦwww.hoteldespoetes.net; ③), overlooking the gardens. More upmarket options include the new *France* at 36 rue Boïédieu (☏04.67.28.44.72, ⓦwww.hotel2france.com; ④), and the de luxe ⚜ *Hôtel Imperator*, at 28 allées Paul-Riquet (☏04.67.49.02.25, ⓦwww.hotel-Imperator.fr; ④), which is a notch above the rest. The nearest **campsites** are at Villeneuve-lès-Béziers (see p.324) and 6km east at Clariac (April–Sept; ☏04.67.76.78.97).

The Town

Béziers' vaguely semicircular **old town** snuggles into a gentle meander of the Orb, which, along with the canal – the Ruisseau de Bagnols – bounds it on three sides. The eastern limit is marked by allées Paul-Riquet, which has a broad pedestrian concourse running down its centre. From place Jean-Jaurès, which opens up off allées Paul-Riquet, you can descend rue de la Citadelle to place Gabriel Péri, the old town's centre.

The Cathédrale St-Nazaire

Béziers' main attraction is undoubtedly the majestic Romanesque **Cathédrale St-Nazaire** (daily 10am–12.30pm & 2–6.30pm; free), about five minutes' walk west from place Péri on the western rim, just off place de la Révolution. Constructed in the thirteenth century, the cathedral's marriage of style and function is immediately apparent in its west face, which has a great rosette window flanked by two fortified towers. From the entrance here, the first part of the cathedral you enter is the cloister. Within its low and austere gallery, there's a collection of old funerary stones, including one with Hebrew characters, while on its east side a stairway descends into the airy gardens, the **Jardin de l'Évêché**, built off the south side of the great church. The cathedral's voluminous, predominantly unadorned **interior** is dominated by an outrageous Baroque retable – a gaudy starburst of saints and cherubs which clashes with the sobriety of the building. The high point of the visit is the dizzying climb to the **upper galleries** (free) – a rare opportunity to get a pigeon's eye view of a cathedral's interior. Climbing the well-worn, narrow keystone staircase, you traverse a small landing before continuing up to the top – the balconies which circle the pinnacles afford spectacular **views**. Almost directly below the cliffs on which the cathedral stands, you'll see the evocative twelfth-century *pont vieux* as it crosses the Orb below and, beyond to the west, the whole of the Biterrois plain stretching off into a haze – on a clear day you might make out the form of Le Canigou on the horizon. Take care when climbing the stairs and circulating up top, particularly if you're travelling with children – the only protective fencing here is the old stone balustrade.

The rest of the old town

North of the cathedral, at the far end of the pleasant place de la Révolution – where republican protesters were fired upon in 1851 – is the Hôtel Fabrégat, a mansion which houses the **Musée des Beaux Arts** (Tues–Sun July & Aug 10am–6pm; otherwise 9/10am–noon & 2–5/6pm; €2.45), a collection of works by local painters as well as better-known artists such as Delacroix and Dufy. The museum's sculpture annexe is lodged in another aristocratic residence, the nearby **Musée Fayet**, whose collection is dominated by nineteenth-century works, notably by local sculptor Injalbert (same hours and ticket). Continuing north from here, you'll pass the beautiful wrought-iron covered **market** (Tues–Sun 7.30am–12.30pm), set in the attractive place Pierre-Sémard and, further on up rue Paul-Riquet, the church of **La Madeleine** (irregular hours; free), scene of the murder of the Trencavel viscount in 1167 and the **massacre** of seven thousand Catholics by the Crusaders in 1209 (see *The Land of he Cathars* Colour section). Continuing north from La Madeleine, for some 250m, up to place St-Aphrodise – follow the pedestrian signs – you'll come across **St-Aphrodise church** (Mass only), an incredibly old structure with a tenth-century nave and Gallo-Roman crypt. A further five minutes' walk north along rue de la Faïence brings you to the **cimetière vieux** (daily 8am–5.45pm; free), founded in 1838. It contains a series of impressive mausoleums and monuments raised by the town's prospering bourgeoisie, featuring sculptures by Jean-Antoine Injalbert (a native, whose ponderous works grace Paris Hôtel de Ville and Palais de Justice) and other noteworthy artists.

Heading east from La Madeleine, rue Trencavel takes you towards the pretty Art Nouveau-style **Théâtre Municipal Molière** at the top end of allées Paul-Riquet, a broad, leafy esplanade lined with cafés, *crêpes* stalls and restaurants; on Friday mornings, the weekly flower market is held here. The boulevard ends at the gorgeous little park of the **Plateau des Poètes**, whose ponds, palms and lime trees were laid out in the so-called English manner by the brothers Denis et Eugène Bülher, who created Paris Bois de Boulogne. Finally, to the west of the park on rampe du 96ème, you'll find the impressive **Musée du Biterrois** (Tues–Sun: July & Aug 10am–6pm; Sept–June 9/10am–noon & 2–5/6pm; €2.45), housed in an old barracks and containing sections on natural history, ethnography and archeology. The first two, respectively illustrating the biological diversity of the marshy coast and the rural and craft traditions of the region, are passable, but it's the last section, most of which is given over to the Gallo-Roman period, which makes the museum well worth a stop. This important collection ranges from locally produced pottery and ceramics, to funerary monuments and milestones, and there are also various artefacts dredged from ancient shipwrecks off the coast, but the highlight is the "treasure of Béziers" – a rich cache of silver platters found in a nearby field. The medieval period is represented by locally sculpted medieval capitals and bas-reliefs.

The most dedicated Romanophiles can cap off their visit to Béziers by taking a look at the remains of a modest Roman **amphitheatre** (by appointment only), two streets north of the museum. The building was quarried for stone in the Middle Ages and filled with rubble. There's not much to see here, and you'll strain to make out the ghost of the structure beneath the grassy undulations.

Eating and drinking

There's a whole string of economical **restaurants** (with patios) along the west side of allées Paul-Riquet, serving the usual *steak-frites* type *menus* for about €12. Better fare can be found in the old quarter, where rue Viennet has a good choice of places. The best is ✦ *Le Cep d'Or*, at no. 7, serving mostly seafood (*menus* from €13–20; closed Sun eve & Mon out of season), with the nearby *Les Deux Lombards*, at no. 32, dishing up more upmarket fare (with *menus* from €30). Lighter meals can be found at *La Table Bretonne*, at no. 21, an airy crêperie with a large street-side patio where savoury or sweet pancakes start at €9 (closed Mon). *L'Ambassade,* at 22 boulevard de Verdun (℡04.67.76.06.24; closed Sun & Mon), is another good choice (*menus* from €28), while *Le Bistrot des Halles*, further north on place de la Madeleine behind the market square, is popular for its varied, well-priced *menus* (from €15; closed Sun & Mon). A good **café** is *La Bourse* at the corner of place Jean-Jaurès and allées Riquet, while a livelier time can be enjoyed at two tapas **bars** on opposite corners of rues Boïeldieu and Solferino, *Charlie & Carlos* and *Le Mondial*.

In addition to the town's covered **market** (Mon–Sat mornings), a regional produce market is held on Fridays in place du 14 Juillet.

Listings

Banks All the major French banks are represented here, most with offices in allées Paul-Riquet or place Jean-Jaurès. On the former you'll find BNP at no. 34, Banque Populaire du Midi at no. 39 and Crédit Lyonnais at no. 16.

Boat rental At Béziers' port: Ad'navis-Amica Tours (℡04.67.62.18.18) and Béziers Croisières (℡04.67.49.08.23), which also runs canal trips. Voies Navigables de France (℡04.68.11.81.30, ℡www.vnf.fr) has an office in av Duy Prado.

Book Store Le Bookshop, 18 rue des Anciens Combattants (Tues–Sat 10am–noon & 2–6pm) sells English books.

Bus information ℡04.67.28.23.85.

Car rental ADA, 23 bd Verdun (℡04.67.62.65.39); Avis, 18 bd Verdun (℡04.67.28.65.44,

℡www.avis.com); Budget, 35 bd Verdun (℡04.67.35.84.54, ℡www.budget.com), Europcar, 70 allées Paul-Riquet (℡04.67.62.09.89, ℡www.europcar.com); Hertz, 83 av Pt-Wilson (℡04.67.62.82.00, ℡www.hertz.com).

Internet access Cyberia, 7 rue St-Ferignon ℡04.67.72.99.91 (Mon–Fri 10am–12am, Sat 1pm–2am, Sun 2am–12am).

Police Pl Général-de-Gaulle.

Rugby Béziers has one of the star rugby clubs in France, A.S.B.H., based at the Stade de la Méditerranée in the eastern suburbs (℡04.67.11.03.76, ℡www.asbh.net).

Taxis ℡04.67.35.00.85.

Train information ℡08.36.35.35.35.

Agde and the coast

Thanks to the few kilometres which separate it from the sea, **AGDE**, just 12km east of Béziers, is one of the most unspoilt towns on the Languedocian coast. It boomed as a port 2500 years ago under the Phoenicians and on through the Middle Ages, until competition from neighbouring towns and the silting up of the Hérault pushed the seashore from its walls. Today, its compact old town has resisted intensive development and remains a quiet respite from the crowds – the best time to arrive is on one of Agde's market days: Thursday for produce and Wednesday and Saturday for the flea market. Set along the now canalized river, the town is dominated by a twelfth-century fortified **cathedral**, St-Étienne, on its south bank, whose appearance is more castle than church, its three-metre-thick walls and hot-oil sluices having formed the strongpoint of the town's defences: you can climb the **bell-tower** (Mon–Fri 10am, 11.45am & 4.30pm; €2) to get striking views of the village and coastal plain. A series of *places* follows the riverside from east to west: the lively Jean-Jaurès, with its sidewalk cafés; Picheire, where you'll find the small porticoed medieval **market**; and de la Marine, a grittily authentic fishermen's quarter. Heading south from place de la Marine, the residential rue Poissonerie is a step back in time – a neighbourhood of fishermen's families living in modest and ancient houses. Following rue Poissonerie to the end, you'll arrive at the old convent housing the **Musée Agathois** (daily 9am–noon & 2–6pm; €4). It's one of the better of the region's "local" museums, with exhibitions on life in the area from the prehistoric era to the present day; relics of the town's seafaring past range from ancient Greek *amphorae* to nineteenth-century navigational instruments. Continuing, you'll pass the new market building and the **church of St-André**, occupying a site on which there's been a church since as far back as 506 AD, when an episcopal council was held here. Just south is the wide tree-lined La Promenade, with its multitude of terraced bars, while close by, rue de l'Amour and rue Jean-Roger are lined with tacky souvenir shops. If you're looking to escape the crowds, head to the shady nineteenth-century gardens of **Château Laurens**, set on Belle-Isle, a twelve-hectare park bordered by the Hérault and the Canal du Midi, just across the bridge from the old town.

Cap d'Agde and Grau d'Agde

Agde's evil twin, **CAP D'AGDE** lies to the south of Mont St-Loup on the seashore, some 7km south. A sprawling and characterless modern resort, its only redemption is the abundance of colourful plants and flowers which line its broad streets, only partially concealing a uniform sea of cream-coloured holiday villas behind. But the Cap has everything you would want for a mindless, cultureless beach holiday – nightclubs, watersports and restaurants, although here you will pay dearly for them. If you're just passing through though, a worthwhile stop is the **Musée de l'Éphèbe** (daily 9am–noon & 2–6pm; €4), in the central Parc de la Clape, which holds a collection of Greek and Roman relics retrieved from the sea bed, including the beautiful little Hellenistic bronze statuette known as the Éphèbe d'Agde, formerly housed in the Louvre. There is also an **aquarium**, at 11 rue des Deux-Frères (daily: July & Aug 10am–11pm; Sept–June 2–6pm; €6.50), and a huge Aqualand **amusement park** (mid-June to mid-Sept 10am–7pm; €23), at the west end of town. The former prison of **Fort de Brescou**, built in 1680, lies just offshore and can be reached by ferries departing from the ports at either Cap d'Agde (Sarl Croisières: July & Aug Thurs–Mon 10.30am, 2.30 & 6.30pm; €6) or le Grau d'Agde (Île de Brescou: July & Aug daily 2.30 & 4.30pm; €7). The grim fortress, which evokes Marseille's famous Château d'If, can be visited on a **guided tour** (timed with boat arrivals from mid-June to early-Sept; €3), or you can simply explore the rocky seagull-infested island for free.

If you fancy a dip, the best **beaches** are on the west side of the cape stretching over towards La Guirandette; on the east side there's a huge, self-contained **nudist colony** (see box, p.330). Nearby **GRAU D'AGDE** is the beach-town antithesis of the Cap: a dispersed settlement of weathered houses and ageing bungalows, this dissipating suburb distils into an old fishing town as you reach the lighthouse-capped wavebreak.

There are two very distinct sides to Cap d'Agde. On the one hand there is the conventional and somewhat tacky tourist resort – the largest in France – with its overpriced restaurants, busy beaches and homogenous personality. Meanwhile, on the western edge of the town lies the world's largest nudist resort.

Cap d'Agde's **quartier naturiste**, which in the height of summer attracts as many as 60,000 visitors, owes its existence to a small group of lost German tourists and two enterprising winegrowers. Looking for a secluded spot away from prying eyes, a caravan-load of German naturists arrived more or less by accident at the modest beachside vineyard owned by René and Paul Oltra in 1958. Next year they returned, now in a small convoy of caravans, and the rest is history. The Oltra brothers were granted permission by the local council to establish a naturist campsite on their land, and by the early 1960s a small office had been set up at the entrance, while the campsite itself was full of bungalows, tents and caravans. The first brick construction went up in 1971 next to **Port Ambonne**, to be followed soon after by other apartment complexes and commercial centres such as **Héliopolis** and **Port Nature**.

Nowadays, the *quartier naturiste* is really a small town in its own right. There are supermarkets, restaurants, cafés, bars, discos, thousands of holiday apartments for rent, a hotel and a campsite with more than 2500 places, all catering to a naturist clientele. Nudity is permitted – although not absolutely required – at all times anywhere within the confines of the resort, and while not everyone chooses to do their shopping or go to the bank in the nude, the two-kilometre stretch of sandy beach around which the resort has developed remains almost entirely "textile free".

Just as the landscape of the *quartier naturiste* has changed dramatically over the years, so has the type of people who visit the resort. Until about the early 1990s, most of the people who came to Cap d'Agde did so simply because they enjoyed spending their time naked, with no other connotations attached. Gradually, however, another type of naturist, described by French commentators as "*à poilistes*", began to arrive. For these people nudity and sex were inextricably linked, and soon the beach became unofficially segregated into various sections: for families, for sexually liberated heterosexuals and for gays. The resort's infrastructure also evolved to cater to this new breed of visitor. For example, there are more boutiques selling X-rated clothing in the *quartier naturiste* than in most large cities, and some of the raunchiest and most famous **swingers clubs** in Europe are located here. Cap d'Agde is now perhaps the world's ultimate "sea, sex and sun" destination.

The nudist **season** in Cap d'Agde runs from mid-March to mid-October, although most of the shops, restaurants and bars in the resort are open from around mid-May to mid-September. One-day access is €9 with a car or €5 for pedestrians and cyclists. No tickets are sold after 8pm. For more information, contact the Bureau d'accueil (℡04.67.26.00.26, ⓦwww.agdenaturisme.com), or read Ross Velton's *The Naked Truth About Cap d'Agde* (ⓦwww.wordcrafting.com).

Practicalities

Trains and **buses** arrive in Agde just across the river from the old town. To continue south to the Cap you can take a municipal bus (€0.60) from the *gare*, or use the superb network of cycle paths – once there you'll realize it's no place to walk, and end up using one of the two *petits trains* which circulate around the town (€2), or the various **water taxis**. Agde's **tourist office**, on place Molière, near the main roundabout (daily 9am–noon & 2–6pm; ℡04.67.94.29.68, ⓦwww.ville-agde.fr), sells the **Agde Pass** (€12), which gives access to all the towns' museums: it's also the departure point for a two-hour **guided tour** of the town (in English Tues & Thurs 10am; €5). In Cap d'Agde, you'll find the **tourist office** (daily: June–Aug 9am–7/8pm; Sept–May 9am–noon &

2–6/7pm; ℡04.67.01.04.04, ⓦwww.capdagde.com) on the huge roundabout which marks the centre of the settlement. There's also an **information kiosk** in Grau (June–Sept daily 9am–noon & 1.30–7pm).

   Bike rental is available in Agde from La Cadotière, 1 place Jean-Jaurès (℡04.76.94.26.20), while Les Bateaux du Soleil (℡04.67.94.08.79) at the port runs **river trips.** Nautic, in Chemin de la Pagèze (℡04.67.94.78.93), and Locarama, in av Passeur Calliès (℡04.67.26.26.45), both rent out **boats.** You can get **Internet** access in Agde at Globe Trotter, 4 place de la Marine.

Accommodation

The best **hotel** in Agde is the Dutch-run 🎋 *La Galiote* (℡04.67.94.45.58, ⓦwww.lagaliote.fr; ❺), located in the old bishops' palace on place Jean-Jaurès, with *Le Donjon* on the same square (℡04.67.94.12.32, ⓦwww.hotelledonjon .com; ❺), a close second. Some of the cheapest but still decent digs can be had at the *Hôtel des Arcades* (℡04.67.94.21.64; ❸) in an old convent at 16 rue Louis-Bages. A good option at the Cap is *La Voile d'Or* on place du Globe (℡04.67.01.04.11, ⓦlavoiledor.com; ❻), while Grau has the sea-side *El Rancho* (Feb–Nov; ℡04.67.94.24.35, ⓦwww.logis-de-france.fr; ❸). In the nudist colony, try *Hôtel Eve* in Impasse Siassan (April–Oct; ℡04.67.26.71.70, ⓦwww .hoteleve.com; ❼), with its own campsite (℡04.67.01.06.36).

   There are no fewer than 24 **campsites** in the area – they are pretty indistinguishable, but you could try *Sud Loisirs* near Agde (℡04.67.21.09.10, ⓦwww.campingsudloisirs.com), or *La Clape* at the Cap (mid-March to Sept; ℡04.67.26.41.32, ⓦwww.camping-laclape.com).

Eating

One of the area's best **restaurants** is at *Le Jardin de Beaumont* (℡ 04.67.21.19.23) set in a wine domaine 3km north of Agde, where you can dine on *tapas* and excellent wines inside or out (about €30). A good choice at the Cap is the seafood specialist, *Le Brasero*, Port Richelieu II (℡04.67.26.24.75; *menus* from €13) or the *gastronomique, Le Caladoc* in the Île des Loisirs (℡04.67.26.87.18; *menu* €25). In Agde itself, there are a number of places right on the quayside or in rue Chassefière, which runs along it, or try *La Fine Fourchetté* at 2 rue du Mont-Saint-Loup (℡04.67.94.49.56), with an intriguing *carte* featuring unusual *gastronomique* variations on local *terroir* dishes (*menus* from €9.45).

The Orb valley

The **River Orb** winds a twisting path down from its source in the hills of Haut Languedoc north of Béziers, descending some 120km through the highlands and across the broad coastal plain to skirt the city before emptying into the Golfe du Lion. Heading up its valley from Béziers provides rapid access from the coast to the lesser-travelled uplands of Haut Languedoc. Just after **Roquebrun**, a centre both for viticulture and rafting, the valley delves into the rugged uplands, wheeling off to the east to pass **Hérépian** and the old spa town of **Lamalou-les-Bains** – both good bases for walks into the Parc Naturel de Haut Languedoc – and following the park's edge round until the land opens up into a compact but fertile plane around **Bédarieux** – another possible departure point for exploring the highlands. Heading further north into the **upper valley** you eventually reach a series of tiny hamlets high up at the river's origins.

Roquebrun and around

Journeying 21km upriver from Béziers, the D14 joins the course of the Orb at Cessenon, just before it ascends into the rugged uplands. The border of the Parc du Haut Languedoc (see p.194) has recently been pushed south to incorporate the area around **ROQUEBRUN**, less than 10km further along. This old town, clumped on a hillside beneath the ruins of its medieval tower, is located in an exceptionally mild microclimate, making the valley floor, which is still wide here, an ideal place for vine cultivation – indeed the town has produced several award-winning vintages (AOC Saint-Chinian), which you can sample and buy at the various *domaines* scattered around the valley. The good weather also provides a suitable climate for the town's **Jardin Méditerranéen** (July & Aug 9am–7pm; mid-Feb to June & Sept to mid-Nov 9am–noon & 1.30–5.30pm; €4.50), a collection of exotic, primarily arid-climate plants from around the world, while in winter the valley around the town bursts into colour with the blooming of mimosas. After Roquebrun the valley begins to meander drunkenly, reeling between the ever-higher peaks which gird it until, at last, you reach the mill at **Terassac** 14km on, where the Jaur and the Héric join the Orb; here the river course takes an abrupt swing to the east on towards Lamalou. The mill is also the place to rent **canoes** (℡04.67.97.74.64) for the exciting rafting journey downstream to Roquebrun, the terminus for this and trips from higher up in the hills.

Roquebrun has a small **tourist office** (July & Aug Mon–Sat 10am–1pm & 3–7pm; Sept–June Mon–Fri 9am–noon & 2–6pm; ℡ & ℻04.67.89.79.97) in av des Orangers. Accommodation consists of the English-run **chambres d'hôtes** *Les Mimosas* (℡04.67.89.61.36, ℮04.67.89.61.36; ❹) in a nineteenth-century house in avenue Orangers, which also does meals (€28), and the *Le Nice* **campsite** (mid-March to mid-Nov ℡04.67.89.61.99).

△ Roquebrun's Jardin Méditerranéen

Lamalou-les-Bains and Hérépian

Built on the hot springs which have brought it prosperity for the last thousand years, **LAMALOU-LES-BAINS** lies just a kilometre north of the river course. In the late nineteenth and early twentieth century it came into fashion, and notables such as the writers Alphonse Daudet and André Gide came to enjoy its curative waters. It's still a popular therapeutic spot today, and the more or less constant parade of ailing people moving among its faded *fin-de-siècle* mansions gives it the strange air of a large outdoor hospital. The town is most useful as a stopover for hikers making their way through the hills, but there is also a beautiful old parish church here, **St-Pierre-de-Rhèdes**, which dates back to the spa's earliest beginnings. The church's pastiche of stylistic touches, overlaying its basic Romanesque form, results from immigrants to the region, including Mozarabs from Spain, who left Christian inscriptions written in Arabic.

Lamalou's **tourist office**, on avenue Dr-Ménard (Sept–May Mon–Fri 9am–noon & 2–5/6pm & Sat 9.15am–noon; June & July Mon–Fri 9am–noon & 1.30–6.30pm, Sat 9.15am–noon & 2–5pm & Sun 10am–noon; ☎04.67.95.64.17, ℱ04.67.95.23.62, ⓦwww.ot-lamaloulesbains.fr), provides information on nearby towns and sells SNCF bus tickets. There is no shortage of **accommodation** here and the hotels *De la Paix l'Arbousier*, 18 rue A-Daudet (☎04.67.95.63.11, ⓦwww.lolgis-herault.com; ❹), and *Galimar*, 17 boulevard St-Michel (☎04.67.95.22.99, ⓔhotelgalimar@tiscali.fr; ❷), are both good value, with decent **restaurants**. There are at both towns, Lamalou has a **campsite**, *Le Verdale* at Le Bois de Lon (May–Sept; ☎04.67.95.86.89), and there's also one at nearby Hérépian, *Le Riviéral* (☎04.67.95.19.25). Lamalou has a good range of services, including several banks, a laundry and a car rental office.

A few kilometres upstream, **HÉRÉPIAN** is a pleasant workaday town with a more salubrious air than its neighbour, and only the most basic of services. It's home to one of the country's last functioning bell foundries, the **Bruneau-Garnier foundry** (daily: July & Aug 10am–noon & 2–7pm; April–June & Sept 10.30am–noon & 2–6pm; Oct–March 10am–noon & 2–7pm; €5), and also makes a good base for the hike up to the ruins of the **Castle of St-Michel**, 300m above the riverbed on the slopes of the **Pic de la Coquillade**. The trail head begins on the Orb's south bank, just west of the hamlet of Les Aires, and the gruelling 6km walk will take you first to the extensive ruins of the castle, which was founded in 990, and on to the summit, where you'll find a small chapel.

Bédarieux

Continuing from Hérépian, the valley broadens suddenly, forming a wide pocket of flat land dominated by **BÉDARIEUX**, the biggest place north of Béziers on the course of the Orb. The town is something of a transport hub and, as an administrative centre, it's also busy, but you're not likely to want to stay too long. Bédarieux's one tourist attraction is the mediocre **Maison des Arts** (Mon, Tues & Thurs 3–6pm; €3), on avenue Abbé Taroux, whose collection is dominated by local painter Pierre-Auguste Cot. Otherwise, the tourist office can set you up with detailed information on **walks** in the local countryside (€1 for their booklet). One of the better short ones is the trail, through vines and bulrushes, to the twelfth-century pre-Romanesque **chapel** of St-Raphaël, on the far bank of the river, while a more challenging option is the ascent of the Pic de Tanajo (518m) to the southwest.

Bédarieux's **gare SNCF** (☎04.67.95.02.92), which is also where **buses** stop, is a good twenty-minute hike north of the old centre, where you'll find the regional **tourist office** on place aux Herbes (Mon–Sat 9am–noon & 2–6pm & Sun 3–6pm; Oct–May closed Sat morning; ☎04.67.95.08.79, ⓦwww .bedarieux.fr),. The town's only **hotel**, *Hôtel de l'Orb* (☎04.67.23.35.90, ⓦwww.hotel-orb.com; ❸) is on route de St-Pins, near the station, with the **campsite** *Trois Vallées* (mid–June to Aug; ☎04.67.23.30.19) on the south bank of the Orb, just west of town. The best value **restaurant** is *Le Rapier*, by the Hôtel de Ville on rue de la République, where you can get a four-course meal including dessert, coffee and wine for around €17. **Car rental** is available from Wallgren, 4 rue de la République (☎04.67.23.18.23), while Cycles Horizon, at 13 av Abbé Tarroux (☎04.67.95.24.25), rents out **bikes**. There are **markets** in the town's *places* on Monday and Saturday mornings.

The upper Orb valley

Moving north, the valley continues to rise, with the river petering out to little more than a brook near its sources in the Monts d'Orb. Proceeding from Bédarieux, you should take the turn-off 6km north of town and ascend to the tiny medieval hamlet of **BOUSSAGUES**, an extremely well-preserved walled town, replete with church, fountain and *donjon*, which is surprisingly unvisited; the only service you'll find here is a (frequently closed) café. The ruins of its castles, on the hill above, are little more than foundations overgrown by vine and bramble, but the views they provide are great. **Hikers** on the GR7 will pass by Boussagues as they make their way between Lamalou and Lodève. **LE-BOUSQUET**, 10km further up the valley, has a strange air, as if everyone is waiting for something to happen – nothing ever does, however, and aside from taking a fleeting look at the old quarter gathered in a mound on the right bank, there is no reason to stay.

LUNAS, just a few kilometres further (and on the GR653) makes a much more pleasant option. Here the river glides past the walls of a pitched-roof *château*; you'll find an old bridge and a church which, it is claimed, dates back to the fifth century – nothing particularly stunning, but, with the low, forest-clad hills rising on either side of the river valley, an attractive and peaceful scene, and a good stop before braving the spectacular mountain road which leads east along the steep ridge to Lodève (see p.290). **Accommodation** in Lunas includes the *Auberge Gourmande* (☎04.67.23.81.41, ⓦwww.auberge-lunas.fr; ❷) whose restaurant (closed Fri–Sun in winter) has *menus* from €14–40, or the more attractive and better equipped *Manoir de Gravezon* on the route de Bédarieux (☎04.67.23.89.79, ⓦwww.hotel-manoir-de-gravezon.com; ❸). Alternatively, 5km from Lunas in the little hamlet of Briandes, there's the **chambres d'hôtes** *Gîte de Briandes* (☎04.67.23.73.91, ⓦwww.gitesdebriandes.fr; ❸), and there's a seasonal **campsite** in nearby Le-Bousquet (mid-June to Aug; ☎04.67.23.80.89).

Five kilometres north of Lunas is the evocative mountain hamlet of **JONCELS** (ⓦwww.joncels.com), which grew up around the seventh-century Benedictine monastery of St-Pierre, and became an important stop on the *Chemin de St-Jacques*. In the thirteenth century the town was fortified, with further amendments made in the eighteenth century, but the monks still live there today (forbidden by papal order from leaving the confines of the abbey) and still provide rest for passing pilgrims. There's an excellent **hotel** in the village, ⚜ *Villa Issiates* (☎04.67.23.20.93, ⓦvilla.issiates.free.fr; ❸), a **pilgrims' hostel** (☎04.67.23.80.89; dorm beds €15), and a **campsite** (mid-June to Sept; ☎04.67.23.89.89).

Travel details

Trains

Main-lines link Narbonne to Béziers/Montpellier and Peprignan, as well as to Carcassonne/Toulouse, while a secondary line climbs the Orb from Béziers towards the Massif Central. The infrequent Autorail Touristique Minervois (see p.322) also connects Narbonne to Sallèles and Bize. SNCF buses may run in lieu of trains on these lines; services are reduced on Sundays and holidays.

Béziers to: Agde (12–18 daily; 15–45min); Bédarieux (6–9 daily; 40min); Le Bousquet (3–6 daily; 50min); Lunas (1 Mon & 1 Fri; 55min); Lunel (12–18 daily; 1hr 15min); Montpellier (18–23 daily; 30min–1hr); Narbonne (18–20 daily; 14min); Nîmes (16–23 daily; 1hr 30min); Paris (30 daily; 4hr 30min–12hr); Sète (18–23 daily; 30min); Toulouse (14 daily; 1hr 35min).

Narbonne to: Agde (12–15 daily; 28min–1hr); Béziers (18–20 daily; 14min); Carcassonne (13–17 daily; 35min); Cerbère (7–10 daily; 1hr 30min); Lézignan (8–12 daily; 14min); Lunel (12–15 daily; 1hr 30min); Montpellier (18–20 daily; 45min–1hr 15min); Nîmes (16–20 daily; 1hr 45min); Paris (very frequent; 5–11hr); Perpignan (11–16 daily; 36–45min); Rivesaltes (13–16 daily; 40min); Salses (7–11 daily; 30min); Sète (18–20 daily; 45min); Toulouse (7–8 daily; 1hr 18min–1hr 50min).

Buses

Main bus lines in the Aude *département*, run up the valley to Quillan and down to Narbonne. Services

may be reduced on Saturdays and school holidays. No buses run on Sundays in the Aude, and on many lines in the Minervois (for Hérault bus schedules, ☎08.25.34.01.34 or ⓦwww.herault .fr). In summer extra services run from Béziers and Narbonne to the beach towns.

Agde to: Cap d'Agde (winter 4–6 daily; summer every 30min; 15min); Pézenas (1–3 daily; 40min).

Bédarieux to: Le Bousquet (1–2 daily; 15min); Lamalou-les-Bains (1–3 daily; 20min); Lunas (1–2 daily; 15min); Montpellier (3–6 daily; 1hr 45min); St-Pons (3 daily; 1hr 20min).

Béziers to: Agde (2–5 daily; 30min); Bédarieux (1–2 daily; 1hr–1hr 20min); Capestang (3–8 daily; 40min); Castres (2 daily; 2hr 50min); Colombiers (4–9 daily; 20min); Lamalou (1–2 daily; 1hr 10min); Marseillan (2–5 daily; 45min); Montpellier (4–7 daily; 1hr 55min); Nissan-lez-Ensérune (4–9 daily; 35min); Olonzac (2 daily on Fri; 55min); Pézenas (6–10 daily; 32min); Roquebrun (4 daily; 50min); St-Pons (4 daily; 1hr 20min).

Carcassonne to: Caunes-Minervois (1–4 daily; 30min); Lagrasse (1–2 daily; 1hr 40min).

Narbonne to: Bize (1–2 daily; 40min); Carcassonne (2 daily; 1hr 25min); Gruissan (3–5 daily; 30min); Lézignan (2–6 daily; 35min); Mouthoumet (1–2 daily; 2hr 5min); Perpignan (1 daily; 2hr 30min); Sallèles (1–3 daily; 30min); Salses (1 daily; 1hr 55min); Sigean (1 daily; 35min); Sigean Reserve (2–4 daily; 30min); St-Julien/Fontfroide (2–5 daily; 40min); Villerouge-Termenès (1–3 daily; 1hr 40min).

Roussillon

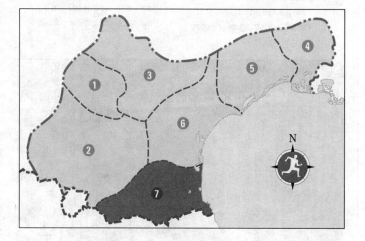

CHAPTER 7

Highlights

✱ **Christmas festivals** Roussillon celebrates Christmas in distinctive Catalan style featuring traditional folk art: *pessebres*, *caganers* and *cagatiós*. See p.349

✱ **Le Canigou** The Catalans' sacred mountain; join the mid-summer firelight pilgrimage. See p.363

✱ **Train Jaune** A revived narrow-gauge line takes you up through a string of villages

that make perfect hiking bases. See p.366

✱ **Romanesque churches** A series of rural churches painted and sculpted by local masters one thousand years ago. See p.381

✱ **Collioure** The region's most beautiful beach-town; swim in the shadow of the royal castle and soak up the atmosphere that inspired the town's Fauvist artists. See p.382

△ The Train Jaune

Roussillon

oussillon, bordered by the Mediterranean to the east, the hills of the Corbières along the north, and the upper Aude and Ariège valleys to the west, is France's southernmost region, sometimes known as French Catalonia; the peaks of the eastern section of the Pyrenees, which it shares with Spain, mark its southern limit. Although absorbed by France some three and a half centuries ago, and now known officially as the *département* of Pyrénées-Orientales, it hasn't entirely lost its Catalan flavour: in the mountains there are many people whose language of choice is Catalan, and even in the larger towns you'll find the survival of customs such as the *sardana* dance and unique Paschal rituals. You'll also notice the influence of traditional Catalan ingredients and recipes in the region's *terroir* cuisine. But despite these particularities, and recent efforts by Catalan speakers to broaden the currency of the language, Roussillon is fundamentally French in cultural orientation, and unlike other French regions, such as Corsica, it has no significant separatist movement or regionalist political party – most likely, your only encounter with the language will be overhearing the conversations of the many visitors to the region from Catalonia proper. Traditionally a poor and neglected area, Roussillon's people have historically lived off fishing on the coast; agriculture, herding and lumber in the hills; and, until recently, smuggling, which, with the region's frontier position and the inhospitality of its landscape, provided a meagre source of income. In the last decade or so though, the mild climate has provoked its resurgence as a retirement spot for northern French, viewed by some of the local inhabitants with a jaundiced eye as "foreign" encroachers.

It is a beautiful region, marked by the variety and contrasts of its landscape. North of the cosmopolitan main city, **Perpignan**, a marshy coastline hems in the **Fenouillèdes** hills stretching up to the northeast corner of the *département* – home to the easternmost Cathar castles and a number of prehistoric caves. Southwest from the capital you can follow the course of Roussillon's jugular, the River **Têt** (or **Conflent**), up the valley to **Canigou**, the peak which still symbolizes all of Catalonia, and the scene of a patriotic torchlight procession on midsummer's eve. Roussillon's mountains begin with the Canigou massif and include the zones of the **upper Têt** – shadowed by the spectacular route of the *Train Jaune* – the **Capcir** plateau, stretching up to the Aude, the **Cerdagne**, tucked away in the far southwest corner of the *département* and, north of that, the forbidding **Carlit massif**; all of these regions – recently incorporated into the **Parc Régional Naturel des Pyrénées Catalanes** (see p.367) – offer excellent **hiking** and **skiing** amidst superb scenery. There are also many architectural treasures worth seeking out here, in particular the sturdy Romanesque **monasteries** which cropped up along this length

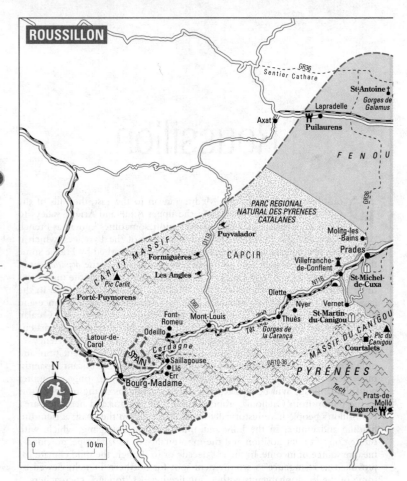

of the Pyrenees in the eleventh and twelfth centuries. The **Tech valley** runs a vaguely parallel course to the Têt, leading up from the plains south of Perpignan and along the Spanish border; a favourite zone with refugees from Franco's repression, its villages are some of the most traditionally Catalan in the whole region. Finally, the rugged **Côte Vermeille**, the seashore to the north of the frontier, is ideal for swimming and relaxing, its rocky harbours, cut out of wind-blown precipitous hills, forming a mirror image of Catalan Empordà on the far side of the Pyrenees.

Despite its relative lack of development, Roussillon is fairly easy to get around, as long you stick to the main **transport** routes, which run along the coast, and up the major valleys – the Têt, Tech and rivers of the Fenouillet. Travelling between the valleys is more problematic, and unless you have your own transport you'll have to resort to hiking or hitching. The main road and rail links to Spain head south from Perpignan, the latter passing through the towns of the Côte Vermeille.

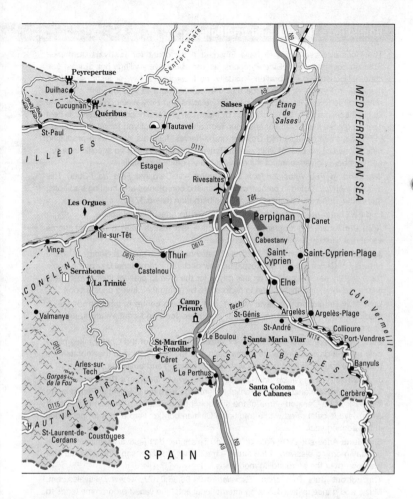

Perpignan and around

PERPIGNAN (or Perpinyà, in Catalan), the capital of Roussillon, is the most multinational city in the Southwest. A substantial part of its population is descended from Spanish Catalans who poured across the border in the final days of the Spanish Civil War, desperate to avoid reprisals at the hands of Franco's Castilian and Moroccan troops. There's also a sizeable Romany contingent, while some of the suburbs were settled by French colonists who fled the upheavals associated with the Maghrebi independence movements of the 1950s and 1960s. Finally, a run-down zone in the centre has become the quarter for recent arrivals from Morocco and Algeria, who moved here fleeing unstable and repressive political regimes or simply in search of a brighter economic future. The melting-pot atmosphere of the city makes it difficult for a distinctly Catalan ambience to coalesce, but the people are nonetheless happy to set themselves apart from the rest of their countrymen by promoting this identity – even if

Roussillon's festivals and traditions

The Roussillonaise seem to have inherited a penchant for **festivals** from their Spanish cousins south of the Pyrenees, as just about every village has at least one cheerfully energetic celebration – usually the local saint's day, or *festa major* (*fête majeure*, in French). It is in these that the region's Catalan and Spanish character come to the fore, with *sardanas*, *corridas de toros* and Holy Week processions. The last of these, a solemn barefoot march by taper-carrying and hooded penitents, is best seen in places like Collioure, Arles-sur-Tech and Céret. Lest you forget that you are in France, there are also mid-October grape-harvest festivals in the wine-producing regions, two of the best of which are at Banyuls and Elne. Where no specific information number is given, contact the relevant tourist office for details.

Weekend in Feb Arles-sur-Tech & St-Laurent-de-Cerdans: *Fête de l'Ours*. This ancient festival, rooted in prehistoric shamanistic ceremonies and hunting traditions, marks the time when bears come out of hibernation (see p.377).

End Feb Prats-de-Molló: *Fête de l'Ours*. Similar to Arles' festival above.

April Perpignan: *Confrontation*. Retrospective film festival with a different theme each year. Held in the Palais des Congrès.

April 22 Perpignan: *San Jordi*. Festival of Catalonia's patron saint, St George. Also the birthday of Cervantes and Shakespeare, now declared International Day of the Book; the – slightly sexist – custom on this day is for the men to present their sweethearts with a red rose, and the women to reciprocate by giving their loved ones a book.

Late May Perpignan: Medieval Market. The old town centre is transformed into a medieval open-air market replete with costumed food-and-craft vendors, jugglers and street entertainers.

Early June Céret: *Grande Fête de la Cerise*. The Festival of the Cherry takes place over several days: Céret is the cherry capital of the Pyrenees, and it celebrates the traditional source of its prosperity with music, dancing and bullfights.

June 23 Têt valley: *Nit de Sant-Jaume*. On the eve of St John's Day people come from all over Catalonia for the torchlight pilgrimage from the Castillet in Perpignan to the peak of Le Canigou – one of the symbols of the Catalan nation. In Banyuls, St John's eve is celebrated with a traditional Catalan bonfire: leap over it for good luck in the coming year.

End June Arles-sur-Tech: *Fête de St-Éloi*. This three-day festival culminates in the Sunday morning blessing of the mules – traditionally indispensable here, as the only transport over the surrounding mountains.

Throughout July Perpignan: *Estivales* ☎04.68.35.01.77, ⓦwww.estivales.com. Music and dance festival featuring international acts; the varied programme tends to have a heavy Spanish influence.

July & August Villelongue-dels-Monts: *Festival Lyrique* ☎04.68.89.68.35. On Saturday evenings at 9pm, the Romanesque chapel of Santa Maria Vilar hosts top-notch medieval music ranging from Gregorian chant to troubadour recitations.

Second weekend in July Céret: *Feria de Céret* ☎04.68.87.47.47. A month-long festival featuring regular bullfights, as well as bull-running. Also a Flamenco programme around the middle of the month.

July 14–21 Perpignan: *Día de Sant-Jaume*. The second biggest Catalan holiday kicks off a week of medieval pageantry in Perpignan, with a medieval-style market held in the place de la Loge and around the cathedral on July 14 itself.

Mid-July Céret: *Céret de Toros*. A three-day celebration featuring bullfights and bull running.

Mid-July Prades: *Ciné-Rencontres* ☏04.68.05.20.47, ⊛www.cine-rencontres.org. A week-long film festival with an international but retrospective programme.

Mid-July to late Aug Perpignan: *Les Jeudis de Perpignan*. Thursday evening festival, featuring street performers and live music in many bars and squares.

July 28–30 Arles-sur-Tech: *Festa Major*. Typically boisterous Catalan festival, featuring processions and loaded with medieval traditions.

Late July Thuïr: *Tuïr la Catlana*. Festival celebrating Catalan culture and the cuisine of Roussillon and La Cerdagne.

Late July Argelès-sur-Mer: *Festival International Flamenco* ☏08.71.34.91.03, ⊛www.flamenco-production.com. Three nights of international top-quality flamenco singing, dancing and music. All three nights for €81, or €30 per night (under-12s half-price).

Late July Saint-Génies-des-Fontaines: *Festival Lyrique*. Celebration of Catalan song and verse.

Late July Céret: International *Sardana* Festival ☏04.68.87.46.49. Three days of traditional dance performances and contests, held in the town's streets, as well as a market, and evening concerts and dancing.

End July to mid-Aug Prades: *Festival Pablo Casals* ☏04.68.96.33.07, ⊛www.prades -festival-casals.com. A world-famous classical music festival, featuring over 25 concerts with soloists and groups from around the world, and a programme which ranges from Bach to Ravel. The venues include the monastery at Cuxàc and other regional churches.

Aug 16 Collioure: *Festa Major*. The town's saint, Vincent, is feted in the finest Catalan and Spanish styles, with merrymaking, fireworks, dancing and a *corrida*. It's a very popular event, and you must book ahead with the town's tourist office if you want to see the *corrida*.

Mid-Aug Argelès-sur-Mer: *Festival Lyrique*. Celebration of Catalan song and verse.

First week Sept Elne: *Festival de Musique en Catalogne Romane*. A classical music festival featuring mostly French artists, held in the medieval cathedral.

First weekend Sept Arles-sur-Tech: *Fête Médiévale*. A rollicking medieval festival, complete with dancing bears and fire-eaters.

First two weeks Sept Perpignan: *Visa pour l'Image* ⊛www.visapourlimage.com. International festival of photojournalism held at the Palais des Congrès, with seminars, exhibitions and screenings of journalistic photos by leading photographers and rising stars.

Mid-Sept Céret: *Ronde Céretaine*. A Catalan music and culture festival with *correfocs* (fireworks parades) and *sardanas*.

Last two weekends Oct Perpignan: *Jazzebre* ☏04.68.51.13.14. Eclectic programme ranging from mainstream jazz to klezmer, performed by musicians and groups from around the world.

Penultimate weekend in Oct Banyuls-sur-Mer: *Vendîme*. Grape harvest and wine festival.

November Perpignan: *Foire de la Saint-Martin*. Perpignan's month-long autumn fair, complete with old-fashioned attractions, rides and games. Held at the Palais des Expositions, across the river from the Palais des Congrès (free *navette* service).

Last two weeks Dec Perpignan: Christmas activities that include a market, *pessebres* (Nativity scenes), a public *cagatió* and concerts.

their own spoken Catalan is frequently nonexistent or limited to a few phrases pronounced with a distinctly Gallic accent. Unfortunately, though, Perpignan is far from a model of tolerance – Le Pen's Front National party and its derivatives have done well here at the polls, peddling a racist vision of white French nationals "swamped" by outsiders.

Perpignan has had a quiet history. Too far from the sea to serve as a port itself, it was a sizeable if unremarkable town until the thirteenth century, when it began to boom as a cloth-making centre. Jaume II of Mallorca and Roussillon enhanced this prosperity in 1276, when he made the town his alternative mainland capital (Montpellier being the other, and Palma de Mallorca the king's principal residence). When that kingdom evaporated in 1349, however, the city was absorbed by the Catalan-Aragonese Crown, whose own main capital was nearby Barcelona, bringing an end to Perpignan's elevated status. In the centuries that followed it was the object of repeated campaigns of conquest by France, finally becoming French territory in 1659 with the Treaty of the Pyrenees.

Aside from taking in the pleasant Mediterranean ambience of the place, there are a number of interesting monuments and museums worth seeking out here, and the one sight that shouldn't be missed is the **Palais des Rois**, in the south of the old town. In addition, Perpignan is the principal transport hub of the region and serves as a handy base for exploring nearby **Salses**, as well as **Tautavel** on the way into the Fenouillèdes (see p.355), plus the beaches of the Côte Vermeille.

Arrival, information and city transport

Perpignan's small **airport**, Perpignan-Rivesaltes, 5km north of town, handles daily flights to and from Paris, Montpellier, Lyon and Strasbourg, as well as services from London in summer; its meagre facilities include shops, a bar and restaurant, and car rental offices. An airport **navette** (shuttle service) (€4.50) makes the twenty-minute trip into the centre up to six times daily (though it is rather tightly timed to meet the flights), stopping at the gare SNCF, place de Catalogne and the *gare routière*; a **taxi** into the centre will cost around €12.

Perpignan's **gare SNCF**, at the west end of avenue Général-de-Gaulle, was once dubbed "the centre of the world" by Salvador Dalí, and is now topped by a large statue of the artist, falling over backwards or reaching out to embrace the heavens. To get into the heart of the city from here, walk along the avenue, over place de Catalogne and cross the River Basse at **place Arago**, close by the *quartier piéton* (pedestrian zone) – a twenty-minute walk – or take one of the frequent #2 buses to "Castillet". If you arrive by local or long-distance bus or airport *navette*, you'll be dropped at the **gare routière** just off avenue Général-Leclerc, a short distance northwest of place de la Résistance. From the station the free *navette* does a circuit of the old town, but does not run during lunch hour. If you're arriving by **car**, follow signs for the "Centre" to get to the old town: the Palais des Rois' car park is a good option, and there's also free and metered street parking on most roads outside the pedestrian area, but avoid leaving your car in the seedier areas of the old town.

The **municipal tourist office** (mid-June to mid-Sept Mon–Sat 9am–7pm, Sun 10am–6pm; mid-Sept to mid-June Mon–Sat 9am–6pm, Sun 10am–1pm; ℡04.68.66.30.30, ⓦwww.perpignantourisme.com) is in the Palais des Congrès, the white building at the eastern end of the leafy promenade des Platanes which runs parallel to boulevard Wilson – they can supply you with the free *Perpig-*

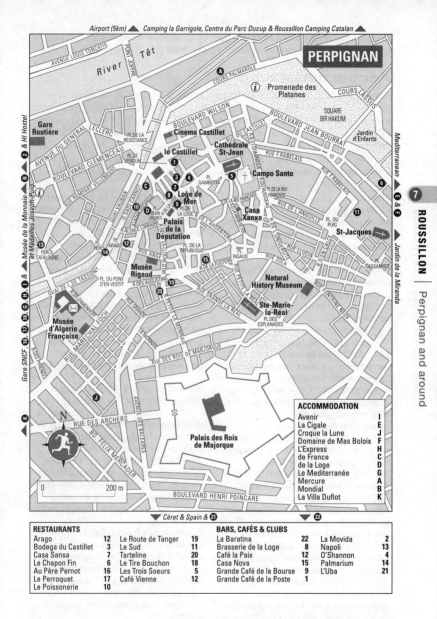

Airport (5km) ▲ Camping la Garrigole, Centre du Parc Ducup & Roussillon Camping Catalan ▲

PERPIGNAN

ACCOMMODATION

Avenir	I
La Cigale	E
Croque la Lune	J
Domaine de Mas Boloix	F
L'Express	H
de France	C
de la Loge	D
Le Mediterranée	G
Mercure	A
Mondial	B
La Villa Duflot	K

▼ Céret & Spain & ㉑ ▼ ㉒

RESTAURANTS					
Arago	12	Le Route de Tanger	19		
Bodega du Castillet	3	Le Sud	11		
Casa Sansa	7	Tarteline	20		
Le Chapon Fin	6	Le Tire Bouchon	18		
Au Père Pernot	16	Les Trois Soeurs	5		
Le Perroquet	17	Café Vienne	12		
Le Poissonerie	10				

BARS, CAFÉS & CLUBS					
La Baratina	22	La Movida	2
Brasserie de la Loge	8	Napoli	13
Café la Paix	12	O'Shannon	4
Casa Nova	15	Palmarium	14
Grande Café de la Bourse	9	L'Uba	21
Grande Café de la Poste	1		

nan Mag (monthly in summer, otherwise quarterly) for events listings. There's also a less useful **departmental tourist office** (Mon–Fri 9am–12.30pm & 1.30–6pm; ☏04.68.51.52.53, ⓦwww.cg66.fr) at 1 avenue des Palmiers, just off boulevard Georges-Clémenceau.

As far as transport goes, there are plenty of **city buses**; the CTP kiosk in place Péri, near the *Palmarium* café, supplies information and tickets (a single costs €1.10, and is also available from drivers); and there's also a free *navette* circulating the old town. However, the best way to see the city is **on foot** – you can walk across the compact old town in twenty minutes – or by **bike** (see "Listings," p.352).

Accommodation

Accommodation is plentiful in Perpignan, with a selection of establishments in all price ranges, although the most common are small and serviceable, few-frills hotels. There's a range of reasonable **hotels** strung along the lively avenue Général-de-Gaulle, beginning just as you leave the train station. This is a fair distance from the old town though, so for more central options, head around the place de la Loge or along the promenade des Platanes. Perpignan also caters well for the budget-conscious traveller, with a number of **hostels** and **campsites**.

Hotels

Avenir 11 rue de l'Avenir ☎04.68.34.20.30, ⓦwww.avenirhotel.com. Unprepossessing, simple but comfortable and near the train station, with a wide range of rooms from singles to a family room; also has secure parking. ❶

La Cigale 78 bd Jean-Bourrat ☎04.68.50.20.14, ⓦwww.hotel-cigale-perpignan.com. Renovated, comfortable hotel at the far end of the promenade des Platanes, near the church of St-Jacques. Good facilities and service. ❸

🏃 **Croque la Lune** 3 Rue François Boher ☎04.68.34.17.39. Quiet and comfortable old-town B&B not far from the royal palace; ask for the room with the private terrace. Close to parking. ❺

Domaine du Mas Boluix Chemin du Pou de les Colobres ☎04.68.08.17.70, ⓦwww.domaine-du-boluix.com. Well-appointed B&B with five rooms, sitting room and garden. ❺

L'Express 3 av Général-de-Gaulle ☎04.68.34.89.96. One of the small, old hotels near the station. The rooms don't rise much above functional but they do all have TV. ❷

de France 16 quai Sadi Carnot ☎04.68.34.92.81, ⓦmonsite.wanadoo.fr/hotel2france. Beautifully appointed nineteenth-century hotel in a perfect location on the edge of the old town, overlooking the canalized Basse river. ❸

de la Loge 1 Rue Fabriques D'en Nabot ☎04.68.34.41.02 ⓦwww.hoteldelaloge.fr. A well-priced option in the heart of the old town with spacious rooms and good facilities. ❷

🏃 **Le Mediterranée** 62bis av Général-de-Gaulle ☎04.68.34.87.48, ⓦwww.hotel-mediterranee.com. Hip hotel near the station, which is very popular with the backpacking crowd. The building isn't the most modern and the service is relaxed to say the least, but its bar, cybercafé (Wi-Fi for guests) and laid-back atmosphere more than compensate. ❷

Mercure 5bis cours Palmarole ☎04.68.35.67.66, ⓦwww.mercure.com. Ideal for families, this distinctive-looking hotel has five suites in addition to its well-equipped rooms. Just within the confines of the old town, north of the tourist office. ❻

Mondial Hôtel 40 Boulevard Clémenceau ☎04.68.34.23.45, ⓦwww.hotel-mondial-perpignan.com. Solid two-star hotel with good amenities, near the Musée Joseph-Puig, a short walk from the Castellet. ❺

La Villa Duflot Rondpoint Albert Donnezan (Serrat d'en Vaquer) ☎04.68.56.67.67, ⓦwww.villa-duflot.com. Halfway between the city centre and the airport, Perpignan's most luxurious hotel is set among a sixteen-acre spread of ancient olive gardens and has an excellent in-house *gastronomique* restaurant (*menu* from €30). ❻

Hostels and campsites

Camping la Garrigole 2 rue Maurice Lévy ☎04.68.54.66.10. Small and basic but shady campsite 5km to the northwest of the city. Bus #19 will drop you off nearby. Open all year.

Centre du Parc Ducup Rte de Prades ☎04.68.68.32.40. Large park-side hostel run by the local Catholic diocese, some 5km north of the city centre. Singles from €34, with a family-sized room and full-board available. No membership necessary, but no cheaper than a hotel. On the bus #19 route.

HI Hostel Av de la Grande-Bretagne ☎04.68.34.63.32, ⓕ04.68.51.16.02. Modern, well-run hostel beside a park, fifteen minutes' walk from the centre, between the *gare routière* and the gare SNCF, but with a noisy road running behind it. Curfews 11am–4pm & 11pm. Open March to mid-November. Dorm beds €12.40. Camping is permitted.

Roussillon Camping Catalan Rte de Bompas ☎04.68.62.16.92. Large two-star site, 8km northeast of the city, with shop, swimming pool and laundry service. Also rents caravans and is wheelchair accessible. No service by municipal bus. Open March–Oct.

The City

Perpignan's medieval walls, though spared by Richelieu, were demolished early last century to allow for expansion, and replaced by wide boulevards. This, in fact, maintained the separation of the city's older districts from the new, and it's still easy and enjoyable to get around the compact **old town** on foot. The overriding impression is favourable: the Mediterranean is visible to the east, the River Têt skirts the town to the north, while the narrow River Basse threads through the centre, dispensing welcome greenery along its banks. Most of the city's sights are concentrated in the dense clutch of pedestrian streets northeast of riverside **place Arago**, and stretching towards the geographical centre of the old town, while between **place de la Loge** and place Rigaud just to the southeast, you could be on the Left Bank in Paris, the old streets now a maze of chic boutiques. On the north side of the pedestrian area you'll find the **cathedral**, from where you can follow the course of the old walls, through the Romany and **Maghrebi quarter** to the church of St-Jacques, marking the eastern limit of old Perpignan. To the south of this the land rises towards the massive **Palais des Rois de Majorque**, crowning the hill which dominated the southern quarter of the medieval town. In the **new town**, to the west of the River La Basse, you won't find many sights, but the avenues leading west towards the train station make for excellent hotel- and restaurant-hunting.

Place Arago to Le Castillet

The heart of the city is café-lined **place Arago**, on the flower-decked bank of the canalized Basse river. From here, head south along rues Porte-d'Assaut and Maréchal Foch to reach a tiny thirteenth-century *faubourg*, whose quiet grid of streets contains well-restored houses and the odd café: at 52 rue Maréchal Foch is the small **Musée d'Algérie Française** (Tues & Wed 12.30–6pm; free), commemorating France's domination of North Africa with bitter nostalgia. But you'll most likely prefer to dive directly east into Perpignan's historical centre. Heading from the *place* along rue Ange, you'll find the **Musée Rigaud** on the right at no. 16 (Wed–Mon: May–Sept noon–6.30pm; Oct–April 11am–5.30pm; €4). This museum is housed in a seventeenth-century palace, originally the workshop of local artist Hyacinthe Rigaud, a favourite of Louis XIV, and it later served as studio and living space for Picasso, Dufy and Cocteau. Today it holds a good collection of modern art, including works by Maillol, Alechinsky and the aforementioned artists. Just beyond the museum, rue Ange crosses the evocatively named rue Cloche d'Or ("street of the Golden Bell"); turning right on this street will lead you uphill towards the hulking Palais des Rois (see p.350), while turning left will lead you further into the medieval quarter.

Museum discount passes

For €8 you can purchase a Passeport Musées, which gives you access to any four of Perpignan's museums, except the Palais des Rois. The latter, however, is covered by the Inter-site discount card, which gives reductions of fifteen to fifty percent on the entrance fees of up to eleven out of a total of 38 museums and monuments in Pyrénées-Orientals, including those on the coast and the most important fortresses and churches of the Tech and Conflent valleys. The Inter-site card is free and valid for one year after you have visited your first monument. Both passes are available at participating museums and monuments, and you can get the Inter-site at tourist offices throughout the *département*.

At the northern end of Cloche d'Or, is place Jean-Jaurès, centre of the pedestrian zone and the city's shopping district: bustling with life during the day, it's all but deserted at night. Next along is **place de la Loge**, the centre of activity in fourteenth-century Perpignan: on its eastern side, you'll find three of the city's most important administrative buildings. The first of these is the fifteenth-century Gothic-style **Palais de la Députation**, where the Catalan count-kings once convened the Roussillon parliament, while next door, the sixteenth-century **Hôtel de Ville** is worth a peek for the Aristide Maillol bronze, *La Méditerranée*, which sits in the courtyard. The last of the three great buildings is Roussillon's famous **Loge de Mer**; built in 1397, it served as the region's stock exchange – the meeting place and court for its merchants. High on the south wall is a blazon bearing three arms, which stand for the three classes of city folk who ran the town council: merchants and drapers; doctors and notaries; and artisans and gardeners. The building remains a marvel, with a gracefully vaulted interior and gargoyles adorning the upper parts of its facade – a fine and rare example of Gothic civic architecture – that is now home to a tastefully arty café-restaurant. The square, which spreads around the Loge, long served as the scene of grisly executions, notably of the rebels housed in Le Castillet (see below), while during World War II, the *place's* busy pavement cafés were the place to find *passeurs*, the men and women who guided refugees across the Pyrenees into Spain.

If you feel like exploring around place de la Loge, take a wander through the series of ancient lanes which run off towards the river, including tiny rue Fabriques d'En Nabot, where you'll come across a number of notable thirteenth- and fourteenth-century houses, with magnificent doorways and ogival windows. Following any of these streets, or taking the wider rue Louis-Blanc at the north end of place de la Loge, will lead you to Perpignan's distinctive red-brick **Le Castillet**, the lone surviving tower of the old town walls. Also known as the Casa Païral ("The House of the Ancestors"), it now houses a **museum** celebrating Roussillonaise rural culture (Wed–Mon: May–Sept noon–6.30pm; Oct–April 11am–5.30pm; €4) and in particular commemorating the anti-French rebellions of 1661–74, when the tower held captured Catalan insurgents. The place de Verdun, on the south side of Le Castillet, is the setting for summer evening performances of the *sardana*, the perplexingly insipid Catalan folk dance. Nearby, at 1 boulevard Wilson, is the battered but splendidly ornate **Cinema Castillet**, the oldest cinema in France, now converted into an eight-screen complex.

The cathedral and east
Two hundred metres east of Le Castillet, but most easily accessed from the north end of place de la Loge, is another ancient square, place Gambetta, scene of the town's open-air market since the Middle Ages. At its eastern end towers the **Cathédrale St-Jean** (daily 9am–noon & 3–6.30pm; free), commissioned in 1324 and elevated to cathedral status in 1602 when the diocese of Elne was transferred to Perpignan. Next door, its predecessor, the impressive Romanesque St-Jean le Vieux (currently closed for renovations), is linked to the cathedral by mammoth buttresses. The cathedral's striking exterior sports bands of rounded river stones sandwiched by brick, while inside there's a majestically columned nave, whose side chapels, though badly damaged, retain some elaborate sixteenth- and seventeenth-century retables. Leaving through the south transept, poke your head in the **chapel** on the left, which is presided over by an excellent fourteenth-century polychrome Crucifixion, known as the *Dévot Christ*, and most likely the work of a Rhineland sculptor. Past the

chapel, on the left, is the entrance to the **Campo Santo**, one of France's oldest cemeteries, going back some 600 years (April, May & Sept Tues–Sun noon–7pm; Oct–March Tues–Sun 11am–5pm; closed July & Aug) – it is now used for concerts in summer.

On the far side of Campo Santo, down the evocatively named rue de la Main de Fer is **Casa Xanxo** (Tues–Sun: April–Sept noon–7pm; Oct–March 11am–5.30pm; free), a luxurious residence constructed by the local merchant Bernat Xanxo and renovated in the seventeenth and eighteenth centuries: it now houses temporary exhibits. Close by, the lively rue de la Révolution Française, populated by arty cafés and hip bars, runs east to the *place* of the same name. From here you can turn right to ascend into the slums of old Perpignan, which spread south from here almost as far as the great palace, and east to place Cassanyes, at the former limits of the city walls. Inhabited almost exclusively by recent arrivals from North Africa, with a Romany enclave centred on **place du Puig** (pronounced "pooch"), this can seem an intimidating district, although it has improved in recent years; the cramped quarters are littered with refuse and hung with washing, a stereotype of immigrant poverty. But it's worth persevering – the various squares dotted around are rich with history, such as place Fontaine-Neuve, which dates back some 700 years to the time when the "new well" after which it is named was dug here. If its interminable renovations have finally been concluded, you might also look in at Perpignan's **natural history museum**, at 12 Fontaine Neuve (Mon–Fri: May–Sept noon–6pm; Oct–April 11am–5.30pm; €2), which holds the usual stuffed specimens of local fauna, as well as a prized Egyptian mummy.

Northeast of place Fontaine-Neuve and just east of place du Puig is the fourteenth-century **church of St-Jacques** (daily: July & Aug 3–7pm; Sept–June 2.30–5.30pm), the nucleus of Perpignan's oldest parish, originally founded by Jaume I in honour of his patron saint (Jacques being French for Jaume) a hundred years earlier. The king was also a donor to the confraternity of Sanch – a parish-based social organization typical of the Middle Ages, dedicated to the Holy Blood of Christ ("sanch" means "blood" in old Catalan). On Maundy Thursday each year, they hold a Spanish-style procession of penitents, who walk from the church through the town hooded (so as not to take pride in their

The Catalan Christmas Cagatió

Among the many Catalan folkloric customs which have survived centuries of French domination are two rather strange practices associated with **Christmas**. Like the Provençals, the Roussillonnaise are known for their elaborate Nativity scenes (*pessebres*), populated by hordes of figurines. However, if you look carefully at the Catalan version, among the various shepherds, angel choirs and wise men you'll note a small figure, usually dressed in peasant garb and sporting a traditional Catalan red cap. This is the **caganer**, a crouching man, poised with pants around his ankles, in some stage of the act of defecation. Similarly, although Catalan children customarily receive presents on the Epiphany (Jan 6), the **cagatió** (literally, the "shitting log") ensures that they don't go completely empty-handed at Christmas. It consists of a log with a painted-on face, draped with a red cloth at its posterior end. As children gather round the *cagatió*, beating it with sticks and singing a song invoking bowel movement, the blanket is withdrawn to the delight of all, revealing the sweets which it has apparently excreted. You can purchase your own *caganers* (which now come in various forms, including policemen, referees and political figures) and *cagatiós* at Perpignan's Christmas market, held in front of the cathedral during the four weeks of Advent.

piety) and barefooted, carrying heavy candles or crosses. Behind the church, the **Jardin de la Miranda** (daily 8am–noon & 2–5.30pm), built on a section of the city's old fortifications, provides an airy respite for the inhabitants of this quarter. If you want to avoid the seedy part of the old town, the church and garden can also be reached from place de la Révolution Française, by heading north and following rue Pierre Ronsard, in the shadow of the city's remaining **walls**, or, further north still, alongside square Bir Hakeim, and the adjacent Jardin d'Enfants, a grassy, tree-lined park crisscrossed by paths and complete with the usual assortment of children's rides, bandstands and *buvettes*.

The Palais des Rois de Majorque

Perpignan's most famous sight, and the kernel around which the city grew, is the massive **Palais des Rois de Majorque** (daily: June–Sept 10am–6pm; Oct–May 9am–5pm; €4) on the southern fringe of the old city; the entrance is on the west side of the complex in rue des Archers, around fifteen minutes' walk from place de la Loge, and slightly longer from the church of St-Jacques.

The history of Perpignan is more or less synonymous with that of the palace, originally built in the late thirteenth century as a residence for Jaume II of Mallorca, son of Jaume I ("The Conqueror"), Count of Barcelona and King of Aragón and Valencia, who captured Mallorca from the Muslims. At his death "The Conqueror" divided his kingdom between his two sons: to the elder, Pere II, went the titles of King of Aragón and Valencia and Count of Barcelona, but only a portion of the actual kingdom; the remainder, including Roussillon and Mallorca, went to the younger Jaume. The two branches of the family were immediately at each other's throats, and stayed that way until Roussillon was reunited with Aragón and Catalonia in the early fourteenth century by the powerful Pere III. Having passed to the French, then back to the Catalans, Perpignan changed hands for the last time in 1642, a couple of years after France had occupied Roussillon in the wake of the Catalans' revolt against the Hapsburg rulers of Madrid; in September, after a siege that was at times commanded personally by Louis XIII and Richelieu, Perpignan fell. Vauban, military engineer to Louis XIV, constructed the imposing outer walls in the fit of over-enthusiastic fortification that followed consolidation of French sovereignty accorded by the 1659 Treaty of the Pyrenees.

After ascending an impressive zigzagging ramp, large enough for several cavalry to ride abreast, you enter a grassy park, with the square thirteenth-century **castle** ahead of you, standing incongruously with its curious stone and mortar construction. Passing into the splendid two-storey **courtyard**, whose upper level opens into graceful Gothic galleries on the east and west sides, you ascend the stairs to the former kings' apartments, now a boutique for Roussillon vintages. Across from these you'll find the unsullied but sparsely furnished queens' apartments, which have delicately vaulted period ceilings and windows. Between the two sets of royal apartments are the so-called king's and queen's **chapels**, one on the upper floor and one on the lower, and both with interesting details in Gothic style, from carved corbels to fading frescoes. The palace frequently holds temporary exhibitions on local history and culture (included in admission).

The new town

Although the far bank of the Basse opposite place d'Arago fell within the boundaries of the medieval ramparts, its character resembles more that of the new town which grew up around it. There's little in the way of specific sights here, but a stroll through the series of attractive nineteenth-century *places* – Gabriel Péri, Bardou-Job and Jean-Payra – is pleasant. The last of these leads into the large place de Catalogne, dominated on its east side by the beautiful and derelict Aux Dames de France department store. From here, avenue du Général-de-Gaulle heads due west to the *gare*, the main artery of a surprisingly lively neighbourhood, with workaday shops, grungy bars and tattoo salons, as well as many good hotels and restaurants. Running north from the place de Catalogne, the busy cours Lazare-Escarguel leads to avenue de Grande Bretagne, where, at no. 42, you'll find the **Musée de la Monnaie et Médailles Joseph-Puig** (Tues–Sat 10am–6pm; €4), an impressive early twentieth-century mansion, with some 1500 coins on display, ranging from ancient small change to monies of medieval France, Aragón and the Catalan lands. Prize of the collection is the "treasure of Bompas", a Gallo-Roman coin hoard found by a local farmer.

Eating, drinking and nightlife

Don't dally when pondering dinner: most of Perpignan's **restaurant** shutters seem to roll down at 10pm sharp, though several **brasseries** stay open till midnight, including the popular *Arago* and *Café Vienne* in the palm-shaded place Arago – this and avenue Général-de-Gaulle have the greatest concentration of places to eat. For a fix of Asian or North African food, head for the eastern side of the old town, particularly rue Llucia, where several modest establishments serve up stir-fries and couscous/*tajine* dishes.

Restaurants

Bodega du Castillet 13 rue Fabriques Couvertes ☎04.68.34.88.98. An atmospheric little place which specializes in small portions of local Roussillonaise cuisine. Dine on tapas for around €16. Closed Mon.

Casa Sansa 2 rue Fabriques-Nadal ☎04.68.34.21.84. Catalan cuisine served up in this comfortable establishment, founded in 1846, in one of the old town's most beautiful streets. Wheelchair accessible. Closed Sun. Menus €24–38.

Le Chapon Fin 18, bd Jean Bourrat ☎04.68.35.14.14. Perignan's dining at its most sophisticated (and expensive), the *Park Hôtel* restaurant features a stunning Mediterranean *gastronomique carte*. *Menus* €55 at lunch, and €100 dinner. Closed Sun.

Au Père Pernot 16 av Général-de-Gaulle ☎04.68.51.33.25. Locally respected Catalan cooking featuring a variety of meat and fish dishes, as well as a tempting array of home-made soups. *Menus* €12–30. There is also an all-you-can-eat pancake brunch on Sat noon–4pm. Closed Sun.

Le Perroquet 1 av Général-de-Gaulle ☎04.68.34.34.36. Very close to the station on the north side of the street, with a good choice of Catalan specialities; *menus* from €20. Closed Wed Sept–April.

La Poissonerie 12 rue Lazare Escarguel ☎04.68.34.02.01. Cheery seafood place not far

from the Loge. Snack on a plate of a dozen oysters (€12.50) or splurge on the "Super Neptune" platter that feeds four or five people for €120.

La Route de Tanger 1 rue du Four St-Jean ☎04.68.51.07.57. Welcoming Moroccan restaurant serving traditional *tajines* and couscous, as well as more adventurous fusion recipes. *Menu* €12. Closed Sun & Mon lunch.

Le Sud 12 rue Basiul ☎04.68.34.55.71. Eclectic and delicious Mediterranean cuisine served up in the heart of Perpignan's Romany quarter. No *menu*, and *à la carte* for about €30. Closed Jan–March.

Tarteline 10 rue la Petite Monnaie. Good stop for delicious home-made quiches and tarts, to eat in or take away. Open lunchtime only Mon–Fri (except hols). *Menu* for €8 (also children's *menu*).

Le Tire Bouchon 20 av Général-de-Gaulle ☎04.68.34.31.91. A small family-run brasserie, the best of those around the station. *Menu* at €13, although an à la carte meal for two can easily run to more than €50. Closed all Sun, Mon & Wed eve.

Les Trois Soeurs 2 rue Fontfroide ☎04.68.51.22.33. Off pl Gambetta, this campy Spanish-flavoured restaurant features free jazz concerts (Oct–June Wed at 7.30pm) and a "women-only" male revue and dinner on Saturdays (Oct–June at 7.30pm). In addition to the carte, there are tapas and a lunch menu from €15. Closed Sun.

Cafés, bars and nightlight

Perpignan is not great for nightlife, but it has plenty of **cafés**. Start on place de la Loge – call in at *Brasserie de la Loge* or *Grand Café de la Bourse* – and place de Verdun, where the *Grand Café de la Poste*, shaded by huge plane trees, is the best. *Café la Paix* in place Arago is another popular choice, but best of all is the huge, airy *Palmarium*, on the opposite side overlooking the River Basse, a low-key, self-service place, where you can linger for hours over a coffee. All of these serve reasonably priced *menus* at mealtimes.

There are **bars** scattered throughout town, including *Casa Nova*, at 8 rue de la Fusterie, which features Afro-Cuban sounds, and the Spanish *bar musical*, *La Movida*, at 45 avenue Général-Leclerc, while *O'Shannon*, at 3 rue de l'Incendie, is the local headquarters for stout. Most of Perpignan's **clubs** are on the fringes of town, but in the centre you can dance at *Napoli*, 3bis place Catalogne (Wed–Sat 11pm–3am; €8), and *L'Uba*, 5 boulevard Mercader (Wed–Sat 11pm–3am; closed mid-July to mid-Aug; €10). *La Baratina* is a large disco at 5bis place de la Sardane (Thurs–Sun), which caters for crowds from 18–70 (Tues–Sun 11pm–3am; free–€10). In July and August the town comes alive on Thursday nights with a **street festival** featuring markets and music.

Listings

Airlines Ryanair ☎08.92.55.56.66, ⓦwww .ryanair.com; Flybe. ☎00.44.13.922.685.29, ⓦwww.flybe.com.

Airport Aéroport de Perpignan Rivesaltes ☎04.68.52.60.70, ⓔaeroport@perpignan.cci.fr.

Banks and exchange All major French and some Spanish banks have offices in the centre, many along bd Clémenceau, and quai Vauban – most have ATMs.

Bike rental Véloland, 95 av du Mal Juin ☎04.68.08.19.99; and Cycles Mercier, 20 av Gilbert Brutus ☎04.68.85.02.71.

Bus departures *gare routière* (☎04.68.35.29.02).

Car rental Avis, 13 bd du Conflent ☎04.68.34.26.71; Budget, 9 av Général-de-Gaulle ☎04.68.56.95.95; Europcar, 28 av Général-de-Gaulle ☎04.68.34.65.03; Leclerc, 27 av Général-de-Gaulle ☎04.68.34.77.74; Sixt, 48 av Général-de-Gaulle ☎04.68.35.62.84. Europcar, Budget and Avis also have offices at the airport.

Cinemas Rive Gauche, 29 quai Vauban ☎04.68.51.13.84 has four screens, with some VO.

Internet access La G@re, 62bis av Général-de-Gaulle; and at the hotel *Le Méditerranée*, 62bis av Général-de-Gaulle (daily 10am–2am).

Laundry Laverie Foch, 23 rue Maréchal Foch (daily 9am–7pm); and Laverie St-Jean, 3 rue Cité E. Bartisol, near Campo Santo (daily 7.30am–7pm).

Markets General market in pl de la République (Mon 7am–1pm, Tues–Sat 7am–12.30pm &

4.30–7.30pm), plus antiques in allées Maillol (Sat 8am–6pm) and organic food in pl Rigaud (Sat 8am–noon). The most colourful market takes place on Saturday and Sunday mornings in the tree-shaded place Cassanyes, with a mixture of French, Arab and African traders selling cheap clothes, crafts and all sorts of local produce.

Medical Centre Hospitalier, av du Languedoc ☎04.68.61.66.33, on the north side of the city, reached via av Maréchal-Joffre.

Police av de Grande Bretagne ☎04.68.35.70.00, and allée Marc Pierre ☎04.68.66.30.70.

Rugby Perpignan's Rugby à XV team, USAP, has long held a place in France's First Division, and has won the championship four times. It plays at Stade Aimé Giral on allées Aimé-Giral; for ticket information call ☎04.68.61.18.18, or go to ⓦwww.usap .fr. The rugby à XIII team, XIII Catalan, plays at stade Jean-Laffon, on av des Sports ☎04.68.55.13.13.

Swimming Champs de Mars, rue Paul Valéry (Mon & Sat 12.15–1.30pm, Tues, Thurs & Fri 6.30–8pm; €3).

Taxis ☎04.68.35.15.15 or 06.09.36.96.86. There are also taxi stands at pl de Verdun, at the gare SNCF and on pl Arago.

Train information ☎08.36.35.35.35, ⓦwww .voyages-sncf.com.

Travel agency Nouvelles Frontières, 40 bd Clémenceau ☎04.68.35.50.55.

Youth information Bureau d'Information Jeunesse, 35 quai Vauban ☎04.68.34.56.56.

Around Perpignan

The main attraction heading north from Perpignan towards Narbonne along the N9 is the enormous stronghold of **Salses-le-Château**, built to dominate the strategic strip of land between the Étang de Leucate and the uplands of the Corbières. East of Perpignan is its beach resort, **Canet-la-Plage**, with a good rather windswept beach, while the village of **Cabestany**, to the southeast, has a museum dedicated to the eponymous medieval master-sculptor.

Salses-le-Château

Fifteen kilometres from Perpignan is the fortress of **SALSES-LE-CHÂTEAU** (daily: June–Sept 9.30am–7pm; Oct–May 10am–12.15pm & 2–5pm; €6.50),

△ Salses-le-Château

constructed by the Spanish in the fifteenth century to guard the northern border of Roussillon from French attack. It's a curious structure – set low within a deep moat, like a cannon-age fortress, but with the basic design and overall squareness of a medieval castle, it represents an intermediary stage in the evolution from early to modern fort. Salses withstood four sieges before it was taken by the French in 1642; with the shift of the frontier south to the mountains, the fortress was first abandoned and then later used as a prison until being declared a monument in 1886. In the village, which lies to the east of the castle, the **Musée Catalan d'Histoire** (hours vary – check with the tourist office in Perpignan; free) has a small collection of arms as well as archaeological relics dating from the Roman period, when the Via Domitia passed through town.

The narrow strip of sand which hedges in the Étang de Leucate to the northeast of Salses is buried under a holiday conurbation but **wind-surfers** may be attracted to this part of the coast for the relentless winds which pelt the lagoon. The northern end of the *étang* has parking along the spit and is the best place to get in the water.

Salses is a fairly easy **bike** ride (wind permitting) from Perpignan, but it also has a **gare SNCF**, just west of the fortress. **Buses** stop at the place de la République, where you will find a small **tourist office** (July & Aug daily 9am–7pm; Sept–June Mon–Fri 9am–6pm, Sat 10am–5pm; ☏04.68.38.66.13). The only accommodation is the **chambres d'hôtes** *La Salsepareille* (☏04.68.38.61.70, ⓦwww.salsepareille.com; English spoken; ❸) in a century-old house in the village centre. Otherwise, there's the **campsite** *International* on RN9 (☏04.68.38.60.72, ⓦwww.camping-roussillon.com). The only good **restaurant** is the twelfth-century farm house and bakery *Auberge de Vespeille*, on route d'Opoule (☏04.68.64.19.51; Sat & Sun only in spring and autumn, Sun only in winter), with an open-hearthed fire in its rustic dining room. Alternatively, stock up on supplies at the Wednesday-morning **market**.

Canet-la-Plage

Perpignan's own beach resort, **CANET-LA-PLAGE**, is 12km to the east (bus #1 from Perpignan; departures every 20min), with everything that you would expect from a beach town: sun, fun, bars and music. The only sight here is the **aquarium** (daily: July & Aug 10am–8pm; Sept–June 10am–noon & 2–6pm; €5.70), home to over 3000 species including shark, piranha and coral. The town's **tourist office** (July & Aug daily 9am–7pm; Sept–May Mon–Sat 9am–12.30pm & 2–6pm, Sun 10am–noon & 2–5pm, ☏04.68.86.72.00, ⓦwww.ot-canet.fr), is in the central Espace Mediterranée, while the *Clair-Soleil*, at 26 avenue de Catalogne (☏04.68.80.32.06, ⓦwww.hotel-clair-soleil.com; ❸), is a good-value **accommodation** choice, just 150m from the beach. There are several **campsites**, including the year-round *Le Domino* (April–Sept; ☏04.68.80.27.25, ⓦwww.campingdomino-canet.com) in rue des Palmiers, which also rents out tents. Among the wide range of **restaurants**, a good option is *Le Don Quichotte* at 22 avenue de Catalogne (☏04.68.80.35.17; closed Sun & Mon out of season), with *gastronomique menus* from €25–43. The local **market** is held in the village (Wed) and at the beach (Tues & Sun).

Cabestany

Fans of medieval art and sculpture will want to make a pilgrimage to **CABESTANY**, 5km southeast of Perpignan, where the eleventh- to fourteenth-century church of Notre-Dame-des-Anges is home to a remarkably vividly carved tympanum, the discovery of which in 1930 led to the identification of the Master of Cabestany (see box, p.108). You can see further examples of his sculpture at the museum and resource centre, the **Musée Maître de Cabestany**, in the church of Ste-Marie in the village centre (Tues–Sun 9.30/10am–5/6pm; €3).

The Fenouillèdes

Stretching out to the northwest of Perpignan, the **Fenouillèdes** is the range of scrubby limestone hills that marked the inland border between France and Spain until the Treaty of the Pyrenees gave Roussillon to France in 1659. It is a rich area to discover, with highlights including the caves at **Tautavel**, where some of Europe's earliest hominids have been discovered, and several Cathar castles, the most famous being **Quéribus** and **Peyrepertuse**. Further west, you can explore the dramatic **Gorges de Galamus** and continue to another Cathar stronghold at **Puilaurens**. The main artery through the Fenouillèdes is the D117, running westward from Perpignan to Quillan (see p.134); all the sights can be accessed from various points along this road, whether you're driving or reliant on the bus. If you have time to take the hills in by foot, however, head out on the **Sentier Cathare**, which leads west into the Pays de Sault (see p.137), or the **Tour du Fenouillèdes**, a seven-day circuit that links the main sights of the region (for information on this see the tourist office in Perpignan, or visit their website – see p.344).

Tautavel

In 1971, archaeologists working at the Caune de l'Arago, a cave near the village of **TAUTAVEL**, 20km northwest of Perpignan on the edge of the Fenouillèdes, discovered the front part of a skull of *Homo erectus* – an evolutionary midpoint between the African *Homo habilis* and modern *Homo sapiens* – dating back to half a million years ago, a period from which scarcely any other human remains have been found in Europe. The reconstructed skull, with its enormous cranial ridge and low eye sockets, is displayed in Tautavel's **Centre Européen de la Préhistoire** (daily: April–June & Sept 10am–12.30pm & 2–6.30pm; July & Aug 10am–7pm; Oct–March 10am–12.30pm & 2–5.30pm; €7), the centrepiece of a small but extremely moving exhibition which includes stone tools, animal bones and casts from the floor of the cave. The **cave** itself (April–June visits by arrangement with the museum) is situated in a low hill on the opposite side of the Verdouble valley. All the finds – some 250,000 objects – have been removed, but it's exciting to stand where primordial hunters dwelt half a million years ago.

Local **information** can be obtained from the *mairie* in either Tautavel (☎04.68.29.44.29, ✉tautavel.mairie@wanadoo.fr) or Estagel, 7km south on the main road and bus route (☎04.68.29.10.42, ✉agly-verdouble@wanadoo .fr). Estagel's *Charmotel les Graves*, 9 boulevard Jean Jaurès (☎04.68.29.00.84, ℱ04.68.29.30.26; ④) is the best place to stay, with the closest **campsite** on the west side of town, on route d'Estagel (☎04.68.29.41.45, ⓦwww.le-priourat.fr). Local **markets** are held at Tautavel in front of the town hall (Tues & Thurs) and at Estagel's allée des Tilleuls (Mon & Fri mornings).

Quéribus and Peyrepertuse

The Cathar stronghold of **QUÉRIBUS**, the easternmost of "mother" Carcassonne's five "sons", is a short detour off the D117, from the turn-off at Maury, 10km beyond Estagel. If you don't have transport of your own, take the

Perpignan–Quillan bus to Maury, from where it's a steep two-hour uphill walk. Visible on its turret of bare rock long before you reach it, the **castle** is much bigger than it looks, since much of the **interior** (Jan Sat, Sun & school hols 10am–5pm; Feb daily 10am–5.30pm; March & Oct daily 10am–6pm; April–June & Sept daily 9am–7pm; July & Aug daily 9am–8.30pm; Nov & Dec daily 10am–5pm; €5) is below ground level. A single stairway links all the various structures, including the so-called **salle du palmier** in the polygonal keep, where the vaulted ceiling is supported by a graceful pillar sprouting a canopy of intersecting ribs.

Quéribus was constructed at the end of the tenth century, and belonged successively to the count-kings of Barcelona and Aragón and the counts of Fenouillèdes. After the fall of Montségur in 1244 it became the refuge of some of the last surviving Cathars (see *The land of Cathars* Colour Section), an affront that King Louis IX decided to erase. His opportunity came in 1255, when the local lord who sponsored the Cathars, Chabert de Barbaira, was captured by royal forces and forced to cede this and other castles as his ransom. But, unlike at Montségur, the Cathar garrison here had time to escape, probably south across the mountains.

The closest amenities to Quéribus are 3km west, in **Cucugnan**, which has crumbling vestiges of its own castle and vineyards all around. It also has a **tourist office** (July & Aug daily 9am–7pm; April–June, Sept & Oct Mon–Sat 10am–noon & 2–5pm; Nov–March Mon–Fri 9am–noon & 2–4pm; ℡04.68.45.69.40, ⊛www.ot-hautescorbieres.com), and a couple of places to **stay**, both in the centre of the village: the *Auberge du Vigneron* (℡04.68.45.03.00, ⊛www.auberge-vigneron.com; ❻), and the *Auberge de Cucugnan* (℡04.68.45.40.84, ℻04.68.45.01.52; ❸ ; closed Jan & Feb). Each has a **restaurant**, but the *Vigneron* (closed Sun eve & Mon; €20–30), is outshone by the *Cucugnan* (closed Wed), where you can enjoy abundant four-course *menus* ranging from €16 to €40 (including house wine) and *cargolades* (Catalan barbecues) in an interior garden.

Four kilometres northwest of Cucugnan, another of the five "sons" of Carcassonne, **PEYREPERTUSE** (daily: late Jan, Feb, March, Nov & Dec 10am–5pm; April–June & Sept 9am–7pm; July & Aug 9am–8.30pm; €5) is the largest and one of the best preserved of the **Cathar castles**. Its age and history are nearly identical to those of Quéribus, with Paris assuming definitive control here by treaty with Catalonia-Aragón in 1258. It's a ten-minute drive along the D14 from Cucagnan, or you can approach the *château* on

foot via the Sentier Cathare, or along the GR36 from Rouffiac (see below). The setting of the castle, draped the length of a jagged ridge with sheer drops at most points, is its most impressive feature. No single architectural feature amongst various cisterns, chapels and towers claims attention, but from the highest chamber, the **Chapelle San Jordi**, there are sweeping views east to the Mediterranean and Perpignan, with Quéribus perched on its rock stalk in between.

Near Peyrepertuse, the village of **Duilhac** coils picturesquely at the eastern foot of the castle ridge. Here you'll find a shop and bakery, plus the comfortable, stone-clad *Auberge la Source* (mid-Feb to mid-Dec; ℡04.68.45.02.17, ℻04.68.45.02.18; ❷), on the northerly through-road, with a restaurant (*menu* from €10.50; closed Tues off season). Better **accommodation**, however, can be found in **Rouffiac des Corbières**, 3km north, where the *Auberge de Peyrepertuse* on the main through-road (mid-Jan to mid-Dec; ℡ & ℻04.68.45.40.40; ❷) has excellent en-suite rooms and serves hearty food (€16; closed Wed). There's also a **campsite**.

The Gorges de Galamus and Puilaurens

From Rouffiac, the D14 winds westwards to the **GORGES DE GALAMUS**, a short but impressive limestone *défilé* worn through the ridge by the River La Boulzane, although most visitors enter the gorge at its downstream end, 3km out of St-Paul-de-Fenouillet. At this end there's a free car park and the start of a path to the exquisitely sited **Ermitage de St-Antoine**, about halfway down the gorge's east flank (10am–6pm) – a huge, sanctified grotto thrusting deep into the cliff, from where a steep path, culminating in a rock ladder, drops down to pools below. The river is deep enough for swimming, and the gorge is also a popular **rafting** venue: contact Sud Rafting, 16km west of St-Paul at the crossroads near Axat (℡04.68.20.53.73, ✉esudrafting@libertysurf.fr), which also offers canyoning through Galamus, as well as rafting and hydrospeed trips through the Aude gorges.

St-Paul-de-Fenouillet has little to offer aside from its role as staging point for **buses** west, and a jumping off point for exploring the Galamus Gorges: you can get detailed information at the **tourist office** (℡04.68.59.07.57, ◍www.st-paul66.com) on boulevard d'Agly. There are two **hotels**: *Le Châtelet*, on the main road (℡04.68.59.01.20, ◍www.chatelethotel.com; ❹), and the more upmarket *Relais des Corbières*, at 10 av Jean-Moulin (℡04.68.59.23.89, ✉relais.corbieres@france.fr; ❹), with a **restaurant**. The **campsite** is in av 16 Août, along the riverbank, south of the main road (open year-round; ℡04.68.59.09.09, ◍www.camping-agly.com). You may also want to stock up on local produce at the weekly **market** (Wed & Sat) in place du Foyer Rural.

Some 18km west of St-Paul along the D117, at Lapradelle, you'll find the turn-off for the **castle** at **PUILAURENS** (Feb, March & Oct to early-Nov Sat, Sun & hols 10am–4.30pm; April–June & Sept daily 10am–5.30pm; July & Aug daily 9am–7.30pm; €3.50), another of Carcassonne's "sons", perched majestically on a 700-metre-high ridge. Built originally by the Visigoths, Puilaurens was enlarged not long before its captured lord, the Cathar Chabert de Barbaira, turned it over to Crusader forces as a condition of his release. You enter from the west, via a stepped maze of *chicanes* or staggered low walls; much of the interior is dilapidated, but make sure you catch the view east over pined hills from outside the southeastern gate, and the point on the **western donjon** complex where you're allowed briefly on the curtain wall to take in the vista in the opposite direction.

The lower Têt valley

From Perpignan, the Têt valley (also known as the Conflent), provides a fast if initially not very scenic route southwest into the Pyrenees. The **lower Têt valley** is that stretch running up to the peak of Canigou, and its most interesting parts are found some 30km west of Perpignan, where **Ille-sur-Têt** provides a jumping-off point for the spectacular rock formations of **Les Orgues** to the north and, just west, the narrow Boulés gorge climbs south to the region of Les Aspres, within whose wooded isolation you'll find the magnificent Romanesque **priory of Serrabone**. Further west along the valley, you'll come to **Prades**, a good access point for the Canigou mountain and, skirting the north side of the famous massif, you reach **Villefranche-de-Conflent**, which marks the transition to the upper valley, covered on p.366. Both regular trains and buses run along this part of the valley.

Upstream towards Prades

Heading out of Perpignan along the N116, a detour from the river's course at St-Féliu will take you 6km south to **THUIR**, although if you are driving or cycling you can reach it more directly by taking the D612. The town is known chiefly as the main producer of the red aperitif wine called Byrrh (pronounced "beer"), and you can visit the **winery** at 6 boulevard Violet (daily: April–June, Sept & Oct 9–11.45am & 2.30–5.45pm; July & Aug 10–11.45am & 2–6.45pm; €1.60) and taste the sweet ferment, which is aged in a cathedral-like gallery designed by Gustave Eiffel.

From Thuir you can head directly to Ille-sur-Têt along the D615 or go via **CASTELNOU**, 4km west. Capping a hill-top, this lovely stone village is strong on medieval ambience, and has a well-preserved gate and walls, as well as a tenth-century **castle** (daily: late-June to late-Sept 10am–7pm; Oct to mid-June 11am–5/6pm; €4.50), with good views and a restaurant (noon–2pm & 7–10pm, closed Wed off-season; roughly €15). The best day to come is Tuesday, when a local **market** breathes extra life into the village (June–Sept).

Back on the river, 12km beyond Castelnou, **ILLE-SUR-TÊT** has an attractive medieval quarter of narrow alleys, within which a well-run **Centre d'Art Sacré** (April to mid-June Wed–Sun 2–6pm; mid-June to Sept Mon–Fri 10am–noon & 2–7pm, Sat & Sun 2–7pm; Oct–March Mon & Wed–Fri 2–6pm; €3.50) is housed in the seventeenth-century **Hospice d'Illà** – the local headquarters of the medieval Hospitaller Knights – and hosts temporary exhibitions of local religious art. More remarkable are the clay cliffs just across the River Têt, a kilometre or so on the road north towards Sournia, and which the elements have eroded into extraordinary figures known as **Les Orgues**, so called because of their resemblance to organ pipes. Rising dramatically up from a deep tributary of the Têt, they can be explored by a series of **footpaths** laid out within the gorge (April–June & Sept daily 10am–6.30pm; July & Aug daily 9.30am–8pm; Oct–March Mon–Fri 10am–12.30pm & 2–5pm, Sat & Sun 10am–5pm; €3.50).

The priory of Serrabone

The most compelling stop en route to Prades involves a detour south from Bouleternère, 5km after Ille-sur-Têt, up a perilous eight-kilometre track to Roussillon's celebrated **priory of Serrabone** (mid-Jan to Oct daily except public holidays 10am–6pm; €3). The location of the simple church, set as it is on a high hill-top, against a precipitous and wooded drop, is impressive; in the grounds around the priory, a botanical garden has been set up to showcase the region's diverse flora. The building's modest facade conceals a strange cloistered gallery, which looks out on the hills, and leads inside to the church's equally curious interior. Here, the almost windowless nave is dominated by an exquisitely decorated tribune of rose marble – an unusual "indoor" cloister, reminiscent of some Spanish Mozarabic churches and perhaps a faint echo of Córdoba's great mosque. Excavated columns found here suggest that much of the original priory – founded in the twelfth century – was as elaborate as the tribune. From the foot of the hill on which the priory sits, the road continues 5km south to the village of Boulès d'Amont. From here a harrowing nine-kilometre drive brings you to the chapel of **La Trinité**, just before the Col Xatard (752m). Superb ironwork adorns the outside of the door, and inside there's a *Christ en Majesté* – a Gothic sculpture in which a regally robed Christ reposes impassively on the Cross. If you're **hiking**, you can get to Serrabonne and La Trinité by taking a trail from Vinça, 6km beyond Bouletenère on the N116.

Practicalities

Ille's gare SNCF is a five-minute walk south of the town centre, which is where you will find the town's **tourist office** in square de la Poste (July & Aug Mon–Sat 9am–noon & 2–6.30pm, Sun 9am–noon; Sept–June Mon–Fri 9am–noon & 2–6pm, Sat 9am–noon; ☎04.68.84.02.62, ⊛www.ille-sur-tet .com). Accommodation in the area is limited to **chambres d'hôtes**, such as the palatial *Les Buis*, 37 rue Carnot in Ille (☎04.68.84.27.67, ⊛www.lesbuis .com; English spoken; ➎); the atmospheric and comfortable *Peu del Causse*, at 6 Carrer del Canigó in Thuir (☎04.68.53.42.47, ⊛www.peudelcausse.com; ➍); the deluxe *Casa del Arte*, set in a renovated eleventh-century farmhouse also in Thuir (☎04.68.53.44.78, ⊛www.casadelarte.fr.fm; English spoken; ➎); and *La Figuera* at 3 carrer de la Fond d'Avall in Castelnou (☎04.68.53.18.42; ➌). The municipal **campsite**, at the foot of the hill (☎04.68.84.72.40), is open year-round. The best **restaurant** hereabouts is *Le Patio* (closed part Oct & part Jan; ☎04.68.53.23.30), just up the street from Castelnou's old gate, which offers Catalan cuisine in a relaxed, intimate atmosphere from €15.

Prades and around

Midway along the Têt valley, **PRADES** is by far its biggest town. Distinctively pink with its marble masonry and pavements, it is the birthplace of Thomas Merton, the twentieth-century Catholic mystic who eventually settled in a Trappist monastery in Kentucky. But it is best known for hosting the annual summer music festival founded in 1950 by the Catalan cellist **Pablo Casals** (or Pau Casals in Catalan). In exile from Franco's Spain, Casals spent the second half of his life here, composing such works as the oratorio *The Crib* and the popular *Song of the Birds*. The one-roomed **Musée Pablo Casals** (July & Aug Mon–Fri 9am–noon & 2–6pm; Sept–June Mon–Fri 9am–noon & 2–5pm; free), in the same building as the tourist office (see p.360), commemorates the virtuoso, who died in 1973, two years before Franco. In the main place de la République, you'll find the **church of St-Pierre**, which contains a huge and sumptuous seventeenth-century retable, a masterpiece by the Catalan sculptor Joseph Sunyer. Prades is in fact conspicuously Catalan in feel, hosting a summertime Catalan university course (ten days in August; ⊛www.ucestiu.com) and having established the first Catalan-language primary school in France. On Tuesday and Saturday mornings there is an excellent produce **market** in the square and surrounding streets.

Much of the music festival takes place at the restored ninth-century Benedictine monastery of **St-Michel-de-Cuxà** (May–Sept Mon–Sat 9.30–11.50am & 2–6pm, Sun 2–6pm; Oct–April Mon–Sat 9.30–11.50am & 2–5pm, Sun 2–5pm; €3.80), whose single, ponderous square tower suddenly appears above a copse of poplars 3km south of the town, on the orchard-lined road to Taurinya. St-Michel reached its peak in the eleventh century and then went into slow decline: closed and abandoned in 1790, much of its stone was pillaged during the Revolution, some of it eventually finding its way – like many other Romanesque fragments from the region – to the Cloisters Museum in New York. Today the highlights of a visit include a subterranean crypt consisting of a circular chapel dating back to the monastery's foundation, and the remains of the broad cloister, whose columns are capped by fine twelfth-century detailings. The church, accessed from a tiny door off the cloister, contains a puzzling mishmash of features, superimposed on each other during the long series of renovations which followed the building's construction.

From the north side of Prades, the D14 winds 10km up into the hills to the beautifully sited thermal spa of **Molitg-les-Bains**, which has good spa facilities (see below) and a landscape well-suited for rambling.

Practicalities

The **gare SNCF** is at the southern edge of Prades, about ten minutes' walk from the centre; **buses** set you down on avenue Général de Gaulle (RN116), which is the main road through the centre of town. The **tourist office** (July & Aug Mon–Sat 9am–noon & 2.30–6pm, Sun 10am–noon; Sept–June Mon–Fri 9am–noon & 2–5pm, plus Sat 9.30am–noon in June & Sept; ℡04.68.05.41.02, Ⓦwww.prades-tourisme.com) is at 4 rue Victor-Hugo, with the **music festival office** next door (℡04.68.96.33.07, Ⓦwww.prades-festival-casals.com): it's a mine of information on walking trails, biking trails and climbing the Pic du Canigou, as is the office in Molitg, on rte des Bains (℡04.68.05.03.28, Ⓦwww .molitg.com). You can **rent bikes** at Cycles Flament, 8 rue Arago, and Cycles Cerda on chemin de las Bouchères (near the "Super U" supermarket).

For good value **accommodation**, you can't beat the faded elegance of the white-painted, simply-furnished *Hostalrich*, at 156 av Général de Gaulle (℡04.68.96.05.38, Ⓕ04.68.96.00.73; ❶), run by a family who were friends of Casals. Alternatively, *Les Glycines*, at no. 129 on the same street (℡04.68.96.51.65, Ⓦwww.glycines.com; ❷), is spotlessly clean and friendly. More luxurious accommodation is available in Molitg, including the excellent *Château de Riell* (April–Oct; ℡04.68.05.04.40, Ⓦwww.relaischateaux.com/riell; ❽), and the well-equipped spa *Grand Hôtel Thermal* (April–Nov; ℡04.68.05.00.50, Ⓦwww .chainethermale.fr; ❸). The beautifully sited municipal **campsite**, (April–Sept; ℡04.68.96.29.83, Ⓦwww.leconflent.net/seml) in the valley just east of the centre of Prades off chemin du Gaz, also has chalets for rent.

The *Hostalrich*'s spacious **restaurant** is the best value in town, with a €12 *menu*, or try *El Patio*, at 19 place de la République (closed Wed), which serves both traditional and Andalucian-style food for about €20 per person. Molitg's *Château de Riell* is the high end option (from €43). **Café** life is centred on the place de la République, where the *Café de France* has a reputation for the best *plats du jour*.

Villefranche-de-Conflent and around

Beyond Prades, the Têt valley narrows dramatically, becoming a gorge 6km further on, where the high walls of **VILLEFRANCHE-DE-CONFLENT**

△ Villefranche

almost block the way. As there's almost no construction outside the walls, externally at least the town looks much as it did three hundred years ago: an elongated, two-street place squeezed between the palisade just to the south and the river. Within the ramparts, the most evocative area is along the bank of the Têt, by the thirteenth-century church of **St-Pierre**; the best view is from the far side, from where the weathered red-tiled roofs and the tower of the twelfth-century church of **St-Jacques** peer over the ramparts. But more satisfying, perhaps, than any man-made constructions are the vast **cave** complexes (see below) which riddle the strata below and around the town.

Villefranche dates from 1092, when Guillaume Raymond, Count of Cerdagne, granted the charter for the town, meant as a strategic bulwark against the counts of Roussillon. Some remnants from that period still stand, notably the **Tour d'en Solenell** on the little square known as the **Placette**. In 1654 Villefranche – then controlled by Spain – was besieged by Louis XIV's troops, and fell after eight days' fighting. After the Treaty of the Pyrenees confirmed their annexation of Roussillon, the French rebuilt the Spanish fortifications according to plans drawn up by Vauban.

As you walk the immense and maze-like **ramparts** (daily: late Jan to May & Oct–Dec 10am–12.30pm & 2–5/6pm; July & Aug 10am–8pm; June & Sept 10am–7pm; €4.50), their vulnerability to attack from the surrounding heights is obvious – a defensive weakness that Vauban remedied by adding various bastions and building the upper fort now known as **Fort Libéria** (daily: June–Sept 9am–8pm; Oct–May 10am–6pm; €5.80), rising high above the main town on the steep northern bank of the Têt. The castle has seen more service as a prison than as a fortress; its interns have included a group of seventeenth-century noblewomen of the court of Versailles, locked up in isolation and silence for over thirty years, on allegations of witchcraft and poisoning. You can reach the fort by hiking up the winding dirt road which starts just outside the eastern gates, or by catching the complimentary minibus, either from outside the Porte de France or at the insipid new **museum** opposite the ticket office for the ramparts.

The caves

The most celebrated incident in Villefranche's history was the 1674 revolt against French rule, which culminated in the betrayal of the rebellion's leader, Charles de Llar, and his co-conspirators by Llar's own daughter, Inès. His hiding place was the Cova Bastéra, now known as the **Grottes de la Préhistoire** (daily 10am–6pm; €7), a cave which he could enter and exit from within the walls of the town – today the entrance is just west of the town walls on the N116. If you plan on visiting the cave, consider buying a combined ticket (€10), also good for the limestone formations of the **Grottes des Canalettes** (daily 10am–6pm; 45min guided tour; €7), 1km along the road south towards Vernet-les-Bains. The most spectacular caves, however, are the adjoining **Grottes des Grandes Canalettes**, which require a separate ticket (daily 10am–6pm; 1hr guided tour; €8, or €11 including *son et lumière*). Entry is via a 160-metre passageway, hollowed out by water over the past four hundred million years; the water dripping down the sides is now directed over moulds to create limestone images for sale at the shop. Beyond a door you then enter a succession of huge chambers crammed with stalactites, stalagmites, pillars and tiny, feathery formations.

Practicalities

Main-line trains from Perpignan terminate in Villefranche, at the **gare SNCF** (☎04.68.96.56.62), 400m north of the town; for onward *Train Jaune* services (see box, p.366), simply change platforms. **Jeep excursions** up the Canigou depart from outside the *gare* (to book, call M. Bouzan on ☎04.68.05.62.28). The **tourist office**, in a booth at the entrance to the ramparts (Feb–Dec Tues–Thurs, Sat & Sun 10am–noon & 2–5pm; ☎04.68.96.22.96, ⊜otsi -villefranchedeconflent@voila.fr), sells local hiking and biking guides (€5–10). The only **hotels** are south of the old town: the magnificent old ⚜ *Auberge du*

Cèdre (℡ & 🅵04.68.96.05.05; ❷) just east of the old walls, near the *gare*; and the lovely *Therminus* (℡04.68.05.27.03; ❸) in the old station itself. There is a welcoming **chambres d'hôtes** *Mireille Pena*, located off the same lane as the *Cèdre* (℡04.68.96.52.35, 🅴mpebafain@aol.com; ❹), with a swimming pool, and the *mairie* (℡04.68.96.10.78) can provide information about **gîtes** in the area. The **campsite**, *Mas de Lastourg* (April–Nov; ℡04.68.05.35.25, 🅦www .camping-lastourg.com), is just off the main highway. The most interesting **restaurant** is *Le Ménestrel*, in rue St-Pierre, the alley leading down to the Pont St-Pierre (and on to Fort Liberia), which serves some vegetarian dishes. **Market**-day is Saturday, with vendors gathered around the place de l'Église.

The Pic du Canigou and around

Rising to a height of 2785m between the Tech and Conflent valleys, **Pic du Canigou** (*Canigó* in Catalan) is the great landmark of Catalonia, dominating the whole of the Roussillon lowlands. Situated well inside French territory, the mountain became a symbol for Catalonia's lost independence in the course of the nineteenth-century literary renaissance, and came to signify Catalan cultural unity, endorsed today by the small flags and other patriotic parapher-nalia festooned from its summit cross. Before modern geographic surveys had covered the whole of the Pyrenees, the Canigou was thought erroneously to be the range's highest peak – it does, however, overshadow the rest of the **Canigou Massif**, wedged between the two rivers. The massif has been protected as a nature reserve and the peak (when not clouded) affords breathtaking views; if you're intent on reaching the summit, you must **hike**, and the most direct route is from the **Chalet des Cortalets** (2150m) on the peak's northeastern slopes – you can get to this by vehicle or on foot. There are, however, other, more challenging hikes up to the peak either from the Tech valley to the south or from the amenable village of **Vernet-les-Bains** on its northwestern slopes; if you choose to take on these trails or explore the massif further you should purchase either the 1:50,000 "Canigou/Vallespir/Fenouillèdes" *carte de randonnée* published by IGN, or the TOP 25 1:25,000 **map** (no. 2349ET "Massif du Canigou"), readily available at shops in the area. Vernet is also the place from which to get to the key sight around Canigou – the **monastery of St-Martin-du-Canigou**, easily accessible by car. For all route information, contact the regional tourist office in Perpignan (see p.344), or visit their website. Before setting out to the summit, either by car or foot, be sure to check the weather conditions. In general, the best time of year to hike up is the autumn, when there is no snow on the summit (as in late spring); summer is not the best of times to make the ascent, as the heat can be uncomfortable and humidity reduces visibility from the top.

To the summit via the Chalet des Cortalets

Most hikers tackle Canigou from the *Chalet des Cortalets*, a busy refuge a couple of hours from the summit. You can get to the chalet from either the east or the north. The easternmost route is the quiet and impressively steep (but not difficult) approach from **Valmanya**, which you can drive or **hike** to (along the GR36) from Vinça – some 20km to the north. From the village, a narrow road climbs a further 5km west, before petering out – you must then use the GR36 to complete the remaining 8km to the chalet. Approaching from the north, there is a jeep track from near **Prades**. A scenic but busy alternative, this route provides the gentlest ascent to the chalet and is the one used by **jeep-taxis** (roughly €30 per person) from Prades; booking offices in the town include Ria (T04.68.05.27.08) and Corbières Grand Riad (T04.68.05.24.24). If you're **driving**, take the D35 out of the south side of Prades to Villerach (8km; signposted as "Clara-Villerach"), from where an unpaved *route forestière* dirt track rises to the chalet − an hour's drive. This is a superb approach, often running close to the River Llech, each turn revealing a new arrangement of rock, water, sky and forest. An ordinary car can easily get as far as the ruined hut at Prat Cabrera (1650m), an hour's walk from the *Chalet des Cortalets*, and − with extra care and ideal conditions − all the way to Cortalets itself.

A maquisard hideout in the last war, and consequently heavily shelled by occupation forces, the restored **Chalet des Cortalets** (May–Oct; Nov–April emergency shelter only; T04.68.05.63.57) is run by the Club Alpin Français. There are double rooms (**2**) as well as dorm beds (€20), while **meals** in the bar-restaurant cost about €15. Be warned that the main lodge can get over-crowded, and the tracks bring up jeeps full of revellers (as opposed to walkers) at weekends to picnic at the tables around the little lake, ten minutes' walk west of the refuge. **Tents** are tolerated on the lakeshore, and next to another smaller pond closer to Cortalets.

The summit

The well-marked **hike to the summit** goes past the larger lake, with its fine view up into the summit cirque, then climbs south along the ridge connecting with the **Pic Joffre**, which often teems with lizards at sunset. It takes about ninety minutes and provides only a slight sense of exposure as you reach the wrought-iron summit cross and *table d'orientation*. Even though it's the process of getting to the top that makes Canigou so memorable − rather than the experience of standing on the peak − the views encompassing everything from Andorra to the sea are wonderful.

At midsummer (technically June 21 but in Catalonia observed on the eve of June 23–24, the *Festa de Sant Joan*), the refuge and the peak are a frenzy of activity as seemingly half the population of Catalonia congregates for merry-making and the kindling of the traditional bonfire, which is then relayed to light numerous others in Catalan villages on both sides of the frontier. Even at other times there is often a patriotic Catalan or two prepared to camp for the night beside the peak's highest cairn.

Vernet-les-Bains and St-Martin-du-Canigou

The biggest village on the Canigou's slopes and the major stop en route to the famous abbey of St-Martin is the pleasant if slightly stuffy spa town of **VERNET-LES-BAINS**, whose easiest approach is via the D116 for 10km south from Villefranche. English visitors such as Rudyard Kipling made the place fashionable during the last century and a waterfall, 3km out of town on a well-marked track, is even called the **Cascade des Anglaises**. Along with the thermal paraphernalia of plunge-pools and institutional adjoining therapy wings − first installed in 1377 − a range of more contemporary pastimes is now offered (mountain-biking, canyoning, hydrospeed and caving), though the baths are still the focus of activity. Often overlooked, the old quarter's warren of alleys is capped by the ninth-century but much-restored double church of

Notre Dame del Puig/St-Saturnin, which incorporates remaining bits of a castle. You can also visit the town's **geological museum** in Parc du Casino (April–Oct daily 10am–noon & 2–6pm; €3), which has a collection of local silex and other fossils.

From Vernet-les-Bains, a paved road and a footpath lead 2.5km south to **Casteil**, an appealing, quiet hamlet, close to the **monastery of St-Martin-du-Canigou**, a ubiquitous sight on local book covers, postcards and posters. Access to the monastery is only by a thirty-minute climb up the continuation of the footpath, or by jeep transport from Casteil along a steep, narrow road. Inaccessibility helps protect the place from becoming over-commercialized – as does its continuing use by an active religious community. Built from tan stone and roofed with grey slates, the monastery ranks as one of the most gorgeous monuments in the eastern Pyrenees, and the surrounding woods of sweet chestnut, beech and aspen form an unbeatable backdrop to the pinnacle of rock on which it stands. Founded in 1001 by Count Guifred de Cerdagne, it was severely damaged by an earthquake in the fifteenth century and thoroughly pillaged after abandonment in 1782. Restored through the twentieth century, the glory of the place resides in its **cloister capitals**, reassembled in unity by a bishop of Perpignan. The monastery is now occupied by an unusual mixed order of monks and nuns, called the "Beatitudes", with a sprinkling of lay workers. Ordinarily, visitors are allowed only on (French only) **guided tours** (hourly departures: Mon–Sat 10am–noon & 2–5pm, Sun at 10am, 12.30pm & 2–5pm; Oct–May last tour at 4pm; €4). Descending from the rear of the complex, you can take an alternative marked footpath back to Casteil (30min) via the entrance to the **Gorges du Cady**, where the river falls 500m over a distance of 3km, making this a popular spot for **canyoning**.

Practicalities

Vernet's **tourist office** is quite central, on place de la Mairie, near the corner of boulevard Lambert-Violet and rue du Canigou (July & Aug Mon–Fri 9am–noon & 2–6.30pm, Sat 9am–noon & 2–5pm & Sun 10am–noon; Sept–June Mon–Fri 9am–noon & 2–6pm; ℡04.68.05.55.35, ⓦwww.ot-vernet-les-bains .fr), close to where the buses stop. **Jeep-taxis** to the monastery and up Canigou (roughly €30 per person) can be arranged through Garage Villacèque (℡04.68.05.51.14).

Vernet has three good-value two-star **hotels**: *Eden*, 2 promenade du Cady (April–Oct; ℡04.68.05.54.09, ⓦwww.logis-de-france.fr; ❷); the *Moderne*, 7 avenue des Thermes (℡04.68.05.52.17; ❸); and the *Princess*, rue des Lavand-iers (mid-March to Nov; ℡04.68.05.56.22, ⓦwww.hotel-princess.com; ❸). A better option, however, is the cosy ⚘ *Le Molière*, a couple of kilometres out of Vernet in Casteil, (℡04.68.05.50.97, ⓦwww.lemoliere.com; ❸), whose restaurant serves fine country cooking. There's also a gîte d'étape in Vernit, in chemin St-Saturnin, on the left bank of the Cady next to the municipal pool (℡04.68.05.51.30; dorm beds €20), as well as plenty of **campsites**: the nearest are *Les Cerisiers*, on the same side of the river as the *gîte* (April–Nov; ℡04.68.05.66.38, ⓦwww.camping-les-cerisiers-vernetlesbains.com), and *del Bosc*, 1km north on the Villefranche road (April–Sept; ℡04.68.05.54.54, ⓦwww.camping-del-bosc.com). There's also a **campsite** in Casteil, *Camping St-Martin* (April–Sept; ℡04.68.05.52.09, ⓔcamping-stmartin@ifrance.com), with a swimming pool.

Aside from Casteil's delightful *Molière* **restaurant** in an apple orchard (€17–25), there's the elegant *Le Cortal* (closed Mon and in Oct & Nov), up in Vernet's old quarter behind the church at rue du Château, where you can easily spend

The best way to move into the uplands of the Parc Régional Naturel des Pyrénées Catalanes is on the **Train Jaune**, once an essential local service, but now more of a fun ride – in summer some carriages are open-air. Built in the early twentieth century, the railway climbs for 63km from Villefranche (427m) up to Latour-de-Carol (1231m), where it connects with the Transpyrenean railway (Toulouse–Barcelona). Tourism saved the scenic narrow-gauge line from closure early in the 1970s, but its future remains uncertain. As it is, return tickets are valid for only 24 hours, with **fares** double those of French main-line services; for example, Villefranche to Mont-Louis and back (the most popular stretch) costs €16.60.

From late May through to September there are six **departures** a day in each direction; between 5.25am and 4.20pm from Latour-de-Carol and between 9.05am and 6.25pm from Villefranche. The descent takes just over two hours and the ascent an extra 30 minutes; there are connections with the Villefranche-Perpignan line within 10–25min of each arrival and departure. Since most of the line is single track, there are often delays caused by long halts at Mont-Louis or Font-Romeu to allow the uphill train to pass. The train is scheduled to stop only at certain stations, and if you want to alight at one of the smaller, unstaffed stations (designated *arrêts facultatifs* on carriage placards) you have to notify the driver in advance. Similarly, to get on at such stations, you have to flag the train down. Beware when walking near the line, as the electrified "third rail" which provides power for the train is exposed and is a potential safety hazard.

For **information** on timetables and prices call ☏08.92.35.35.35 or check ⓦwww.trains_touristiques-ter.com.

around €40 a head. On Mondays, Thursdays and Saturdays Vernit's place de la République is home to a bustling morning **market**.

The upper Têt and the Capcir

The lower Têt valley finishes at Villefranche-de-Conflent, above which the shaggy flanks of the **upper Têt** (Conflent) close dramatically around the narrow-gauge *Train Jaune* rail line and N116, which forge their separate ways along the river up to **Mont-Louis**, at the top of the Têt. En route, interspersed with abandoned villages colonized by hippies and New Age travellers, are a number of small hamlets, on the valley floor or perched just above, which make serviceable bases for excursions into the hills. Of these, the hot springs and the splendour of **Carança gorge** near **Thuès** make it one of the most accessible and rewarding. North of Mont-Louis, a sedimentary plateau called the **Capcir** spreads towards the gorges of the upper Aude. Bare and extremely flat, dominated in the centre by the large artificial lakes of Matemale and Puyvalador, it is cradled by densely wooded slopes that sweep up to Pic Madrès and the Carlit Massif, with only the pistes of the **ski resorts** Les Angles, Formiguères and Puyvalador interrupting the trees. One of the harshest winter climates in southern France also makes this excellent **cross-country skiing** terrain. The Capcir woodlands, with their sprinkling of *gîtes* and hotels, provide ample opportunities for **hiking** during warmer months, well within the capabilities of a novice walker; for information on the area's more challenging trails or longer circuits like the four-day **Le Tour du Capcir**, which winds around the bleak Capcir plateau (see p.368), contact local tourist offices. In July and August, and during the ski season, all the main Capcir villages and resorts are served by a taxi-bus, which departs from the Mont-Louis/La Cabanasse train station.

In 2004, the three upland regions of the Haut Conflent, Capcir and Carilt were incorporated into the **Parc Régional Naturel des Pyrénées Catalanes**, covering almost 1400 square kilometres including 64 communes and villages and their 21,000 inhabitants. The aim of the park is to protect and preserve the fragile habitat and indigenous traditions of the region, and to provide services for visitors. The park's **administrative office** is at 1 Rue Dagobert, 66210 Mont-Louis (℡ 04.68.04.97.60, ⓦ www.pyrenees-catalanes.fr).

The Carança gorge area

At **NYER**, less than an hour from Villefranche on the *Train Jaune*, the road south from the station to the village climbs on into the impressive Gorges de Nyer, but you're probably better off staying on the train until **THUÈS-CARANÇA**, four minutes above the small spa of Thuès-les-Bains and the gateway for the even more spectacular **Gorges de Carança**. The gorge is clearly signposted from the train station and from Thuès village, and more notices at its mouth (over which the *Train Jaune* clatters across a bridge) advise you of entry at your own risk. After a short walk from the car park, the path divides: the left-hand path (signposted for Roc Madrieu) climbs steeply up the wooded side of the valley, while the right-hand path (over a small bridge) follows the more spectacular corniche route; the two paths converge at the *pont des singes* (suspension bridge). The first ninety minutes of corniche walkway are the most amazing, poised over sheer four hundred-metre drops – not for the vertigo-prone. Next is a series of nerve-wracking catwalks, ladders and wobbly, metal suspension bridges, these last not advisable for heavily laden walkers. If you want to **hike** further, beyond the narrows the route becomes a shady streamside trail on the west bank; soon the countryside opens out, and you should reach **Ras de Carança** (1830m), with its summer-staffed refuge, in about four to five hours – here you can join up with the GR10-36 (see p.368).

As you would expect, there is little by way of services in this rugged and underpopulated stretch, but you'll find enough accommodation to make even an overnight visit possible. At Nyer, there's a **campsite**, *La Catalane* (℡ 04.68.97.07.63), but more enticing is Thuès-entre-Valls' delightful **gîte-campsite** next to the church, *Mas de Bordes* (℡ 04.68.97.05.00, ⓕ 04.68.97.11.51), with self-catering suites (❸). This restored farm is part of a substantial property which includes its own outdoor hot springs, a remote log cabin and a meadow for pitching tents. The place is always packed in July and August, when you must book ahead, but it's worth trying to fit it into your plans for a night or two. Good *table d'hôte* suppers are provided for overnight guests for about €14, a blessing, since there's little in the village itself. Information on local excursions can be obtained from the local Maison de la Réserve in Nyer (℡ 04.68.97.05.56, ⓔ reserve.nyer @libertysurf.fr). The **nature reserve** itself (open year round; free) consists of over 22 square kilometres of mountain wilderness between 700 and 2663m in altitude, and is home to rare and varied Pyrenean flora and fauna, including the Pyrenees lily, bearded vulture and royal eagle, as well as wildcats.

Mont-Louis and around

Approaching Mont-Louis, the *Train Jaune* crosses the 150-metre-long **Pont Gisclard** suspension bridge, which carries the track 80m above the river; it was designed early last century by the mathematician and engineer Albert Gisclard, who was tragically killed by a runaway train on the very day of the official bridge trials in 1909. Soon afterwards you'll find the turn-off for **PLANÈS**, whose peculiar triangular church was once thought to be an adapted Muslim structure. To get to Mont-Louis from here you can get back on the train (stop at La Cabanasse) or **hike** the 4km down the GR10-36.

At 1600m, the garrison town of **MONT-LOUIS** is the highest on the Têt, only 14km southeast of the river's source, the Lac des Bouillouses. Known as the gateway to the Cerdagne, Mont-Louis is the quintessential work of Louis XIV's military engineer Vauban, and its massive moat-ringed **ramparts** (July & Aug daily 10am–noon & 2–6pm; Sept–June Mon–Sat 10am–noon & 2–5/6pm; €4.50), built between 1679 and 1682, represent a glorious but failed effort to close off the Spanish frontier. Though promoted as a resort, Mont-Louis is still essentially a military town (now a commando training centre), and apart from the walls, its only other attraction is the world's first **solar oven** (*four solaire*), built in 1949 and now open for one-hour **guided tours** (mid-June to mid-Sept daily 9.30am–12.30pm & 2–7pm; mid-Sept to mid-June Mon–Sat 9.30am–12.30pm & 2–6/7pm; €5.50); the huge mirror for the *four* stands in the moat, just to the left of the main gate (Porte de France).

In Mont-Louis there's a **tourist office** in rue du Marché (daily 10am–noon & 2–6pm; Sept–June closed Sun & Mon; ℡04.68.04.21.97, ⓦwww.mont-louis .net), while the best deal for **accommodation** is the attractively furnished *La Taverne*, in 10 rue Victor Hugo (℡04.68.04.23.67, ⓦwww.latavernebernagie .fr; ❸), which has excellent-value *menus* (€16–42) and delicious pizzas from a wood-fired oven. The closest **campsite**, *Pla de Barres* mid-June to mid-Sept; no reservations), lies 3km west along the road towards Lac des Bouillouses. Mont-Louis's **market** days are Tuesday and Thursday.

The Capcir ski resorts

All the **Capcir ski resorts** (ⓦwww.capcir-pyrenees.com) lie on, or just off, the D118 road served by the taxi-bus. Nearest to Mont-Louis, **LES ANGLES** (ⓦwww.lesangles.com) is the area's largest and a favourite with snowboarders: it has 50km of pistes – half of them red, with the top run at 2325m. Chalets predominate rather than high-rises, but the old village has still been almost completely swamped. Six kilometres further north, **FORMIGUÈRES** (ⓦwww.formigueres.com) is far more attractive with its shops (some selling outdoor gear), cafés and crêperies giving it the feel of a county town. Its church of **Ste-Marie** features an unusual triangular facade culminating in the belfry; inside is an excellent seventeenth-century *majestat*, or "Christ in Majesty," typical of the Catalan regions. The pistes here total just 20km, with no really tough runs, but a good-value seasonal pass is available at the local tourist office (see below). Moreover, standing at the heart of 100km of marked trails, Formiguères is the perfect place for **cross-country skiing**; this sort of skiing requires no lessons – experience teaches you how to avoid falling over – and equipment rental can cost less than half downhill piste rates. The ski station at **PUYVALADOR** (⊛www.puyvalador.com), at the north end of the Capcir plateau, is 5km west of its namesake reservoir and village (which has no amenities). There are only 25km of pistes, but with a top station at 2380m it has breathtaking views, and is known for its excellent off-piste skiing. In summer the Formiguères and Puyvalador **télésièges** provide access to the Lac Bouillouses nature reserve (early July to Aug; €5).

Practicalities

There are **tourist offices** (both daily: June & Sept 9am–12.30pm & 4–6.30pm; July & Aug 9am–1:30pm & 2.30–7pm; Oct–May 8.30am–1pm & 3.30–7pm) at Les Angles (℡04.68.04.32.76, ⊛www.les-angles.com) and at Formiguères (℡04.68.04.47.35, ⊛www.formigueres.net). The Bureau Montagne in Les Angles (℡04.68.04.34.30, ⊛www.guide-montagne-pyrenees.com) can provide **guides** and equipment for summertime activities, such as horse-riding, mountain-biking and canyoning.

Formiguères has two **hotels**: first choice is the *Auberge de la Tutte*, on the road out of town by the junction for Les Angles (℡04.68.04.40.21, ⊛www.latutte.waike9.com; ❸), or try the one-star *Picheyre* behind the church (℡04.68.04.40.07, ⊛www.picheyre.com; ❸; closed mid-April to early June & Nov to early Dec). In Angles you can choose between five hotels, including the good-value *Llaret Hôtel*, 12 av de Balcère (Jan–March, July & Aug; ℡04.68.30.90.90, ⊛www.logis-de-france.com; English spoken; ❺). The municipal **campsite** (℡04.68.04.66.73, ⊛www.campingladeveze.site.voila.fr) is in Formiguères, on route de la Devèze.

The best **restaurant** in the area is the excellent *Al Cortal* near Puyvalador (℡04.68.04.45.00; eve only during ski season; also lunch time in summer; otherwise weekends only), with slightly pricey four-course *menus* from €28. Alternatively, the *Picheyre*'s restaurant is old-fashioned and rather dull, but good value for about €18. **Market** days are Saturday in Formiguères and Tuesday in Les Angles.

The Cerdagne and the Carlit Massif

The French **Cerdagne** is half of the ancient Catalan county of La Cerdanya, chopped in two by the Treaty of the Pyrenees. It is the highest point of the Sègre watershed which descends south to Catalan Lleida, and the sunniest area in the French Pyrenees, the ripe colours of summer grain and hay on its treeless, rolling hills reinforcing this impression. Due to a technicality in the treaty, the Cerdagne consists of the hamlets and countryside surrounding the sizeable Spanish enclave of Llívia. To its northeast, the ski-centre of **Font-Romeu** is the biggest town in the region. To the south, **Saillagouse**, **Err** and **Bourg-Madame** ring the island of Spanish territory and can be traced west to **Latour-de-Carol**, which marks the terminus and frontier-crossing of the railway which ascends the Ariège valley from Toulouse; north of Latour is the excellent ski-station of **Porté-Puymorens**, with its renown 3km long red piste, "La Coulée". The granite ridges of the lake-spangled **Carlit Massif**, the last truly alpine region of the Pyrenees, occupy a compact area just north of the Cerdagne and offer one of the most challenging regions for serious **hiking**. As with the upper Conflent valley, the *Train Jaune* provides the best access to the entire area.

Font-Romeu and around

Sprawling at the foot of Roc de la Calme, in the southeast corner of the Carlit Massif, **FONT-ROMEU** (ⓦwww.font-romeu-station.com), together with the nearby **Pyrénées 2000** (ⓦwww.pyrenees2000.com), is one of the best known ski areas in the Pyrenees. Its reputation though, is somewhat unjustified, since the much-touted Cité Préolympique was little more than an altitude training camp for the 1968 Mexico summer games: its top station is a mere 2200m, with a maximum vertical descent of just 400m, and there are few pistes challenging to the good skier. It does, however, have a state-of-the-art *télésiège* and some good cross-country skiing – more than 110km of marked trails. In summer you can also get up to the **Lac Bouillouses nature reserve** by *télésiège* (early July to Aug; €5) or via *navette* (June to early Sept; €5), which departs every fifteen minutes from Pla du Barrès in Font-Romeu.

Aside from the nightlife, the town is known for its famous Virgin statue, a source of devotion and the origin of Font-Romeu's name, meaning "pilgrim's spring" in Catalan. The legend tells of a cowherd uncovering a buried figure of the Virgin – a recurring motif throughout upland Catalonia – having been led to the spot by a bull. The statue is now housed in the **Ermitage**, a short stroll from the main town, off avenue Emmanuel Brousse (early July to early Sept daily 10am–noon & 3–6pm; free), much altered since its fourteenth-century construction. The Catalan artist Joseph Sunyer sculpted the retable in 1707, and five years later created a flamboyantly Baroque "bedroom" for the Virgin, known as the *camaril*. On September 8 the Virgin is taken down the hill to **ODEILLO**, returning on Trinity Sunday the following year. Odeillo has the only other sight in the immediate area – the **Four Solaire**, or solar power station (daily: July & Aug 10am–7.30pm; Sept–June 10am–12.30pm & 2–6pm; €5). It no longer functions as a generator, but rather as a museum and PR exercise, with occasional full-moon-powered demonstrations on summer evenings.

Practicalities

The *Train Jaune* **station** is at Via, from where it's a fairly steep two-kilometre walk north to Font-Romeu, passing Odeillo about halfway. **Accommodation** in Font-Romeu tends to be expensive, but with eighteen thousand beds you should be able to find something. For a list of holiday apartments ask at the **tourist office** (daily 8.30am–7pm; ☎04.68.30.68.30, ⓦwww.font-romeu.fr) near the top of avenue Emmanuel Brousse. The best **hotel** deal is *L'Oustalet*, in rue des Violettes (☎04.68.30.11.32, ⓦwww.hotelloustalet.com; ④), with an outdoor swimming pool. Alternatively, there's the two-star *Le Regina*, on avenue Emmanuel Brousse (☎04.68.30.03.81, ⓦwww.le-regina-hotel.com; ④), or the *Hôtel Y Sem Bé* west of town (☎04.68.30.00.54, ⓦwww.hotel-ysembe.com; ⑥), with views over much of the Cerdagne. *La Chaumière*, at 96 avenue Emmanuel Brousse (☎04.68.30.04.40; closed Sun & Mon, part June & July), is one of the town's best **restaurants**, with *menus* from €18, while the nearby *L'Équirol* is an excellent option for regional food (*menus* from €15–30). **Market** day is Wednesday.

West to Porté-Puymorens

Beyond Odeillo, the *Train Jaune* winds its way across the wide open plain to the south side of the Cerdagne, to depopulated **SAILLAGOUSE** (1320m), also along the N116, and a base for the glorious twelve-kilometre round-trip **hike** through the **Gorges du Sègre**. The road snakes southeast from the village, passing through the extremely picturesque hamlet of **LLÓ**, before continuing up the gorge as a *route forestière*. The next *Train Jaune* stop is on the north edge of **ERR**, a tiny village at the foot of heavily wooded Puigmal – and another place with a "found Virgin" legend. The twelfth-century effigy is housed in the **Chapelle de la Vierge**, considerably enlarged in the eighteenth century. Separated from it by the cemetery is the church of **St-Genis**, on which an almost indecipherable inscription says is the burial place of Bishop Radulf of Urgell, a close relative of Guifré el Pelós of Ripoll (known in English as "Wilfred the Hairy" and hailed as the first of the line of the great Catalan count-kings). The cloister which was once attached to the church is now in the Philadephia Museum of Art. Skirting the Spanish enclave of Llívia, the *Train Jaune* reaches the frontier at **BOURG-MADAME**, which in 1815 changed its name from Les Guinguettes d'Hix in honour of the wife of the Duc d'Angoulême, bearer of the title "Madame Royale". In the eighteenth century, the town was a major bazaar, both as a smuggler's entrepôt and legitimate competitor to Puigcerdà across the Spanish border. Today, however, it's visibly depressed and fading, its vitality sapped by its more favoured neighbour. It is the best place, however, to buy souvenirs such as earthenware. From Bourg-Madame, the *Train Jaune* continues for fifteen minutes to the end of the line, the Gare Internationale of **LATOUR-DE-CAROL/ENVEITG**, the interchange for trains south towards Barcelona and north towards Toulouse. The *gare* lies between the two villages, though it's actually much closer (700m) to Enveitg, the larger place. Finally, north of Latour-de-Carol on the N20 or by train, on the western slopes of the Carlit Massif, the ski station above the village of **PORTÉ-PUYMORENS** (Ⓦ www.porte-puymorens.net) is probably the best the French Catalan Pyrenees has to offer. For although the nearby Col de Puymorens marks the shift from the arid Cerdagne to the damp Ariège, a lot of snow often falls on the Cerdan side and stays there, protected from the worst of the wind. The seventeen runs here are fairly evenly distributed amongst all difficulties, with the highest points at a respectable 2400m and 2500m. There are also 25km of trails for *ski de fond*, a snowboarders' "board park" and a whole gamut of non-ski leisure facilities (including horse-riding, bike trails and fitness). The village itself has a pleasant valley setting, off the main road.

Practicalities

Saillagouse's *Train Jaune* station is actually across the river, about a fifteen-minute walk from the town's *mairie*, where you'll find a small **tourist office** (July & Aug Mon–Sat 10am–1pm & 3–7pm: Ⓣ04.68.04.55.35, Ⓔmairie-saillagouse @wanadoo.fr). You can stay at the *Hôtel Planes*, place de Cerdagne (Ⓣ04.68.04.72.08, Ⓦwww.planotel.fr; ❸), whose atmospheric fire-side dining room serves up elaborate *gastronomique* fare (menu €22). Alternatively, there's the **chambres d'hôtes** *Mas Rondole*, an eighteenth-century farmhouse on the outskirts of town (Ⓣ04.68.04.00.51, Ⓔmas.rondole@wanadoo.fr; ❹), or one of two **campsites**, *Le Sègre* (Ⓣ04.68.04.74.72) and *Le Cerdan* (Ⓣ04.68.04.70.46). In Lló, the only choice is the three-star *Auberge Atalaya* (Ⓣ04.68.04.70.04, Ⓦwww.atalaya66.com; ❻), which provides expensive accommodation and more affordable high-quality meals. Local produce can be found at Saillagouse's **market** (Tues & Fri).

Bourg-Madame's best-value **hotel** is the two-star *Celisol* (☎04.68.04.53.70; ❷), though there's also two **campsites**, both open year round: *Le Sègre* on route de Toulouse (☎04.68.04.65.87), and the *Caravaneige Mas Piques* (☎04.68.04.62.11, ✉campiques@wanadoo.f). The **market** is held on Saturdays.

Because it's on the main road between Spain and the Ariège, **Latour-de-Carol/Enveitg** has some very tacky **hotels** which can get away with charging too much. One of the more reasonable options is *Auberge Catalan* (☎04.68.04.80.65, ✉carolee@club-internet.fr; ❷), which also has a decent **restaurant** (€15–28; closed Sun eve & Mon). A pleasant alternative is 🏌*Mas Franc* (☎04.68.04.88.21, ⓦwww.relaismasfranc.com; ❸) a rural chambres d'hôtes, 6km from Enveitg, with hiking and horseback riding (€70 a day). Otherwise, you can **camp** at the Latour-de-Carol's riverside *Municipal de l'Oratoire* (Jan to mid-Oct; ☎04.68.04.83.70, ⓦwww.cerdagne-capcir.com).

Porté-Puymorens (ⓦwww.porte-puymorens.net) has a small *gare* SNCF and accommodation at *Hôtel Restaurant du Col* (☎04.68.04.52.39, ⓦhotelducol .free.fr; ❸) down in the village. The valley-bottom **campsite** – *La Rivière* (☎04.68.04.82.20) – is open all year, but you'd have to be a polar bear to stay in winter.

The Carlit Massif

Being easy to access, the mountains of the **Carlit Massif** are popular, and the lakes – even where not dammed – are sometimes a little overly manicured, but still provide opportunities for several days of **trekking**. Three major walking routes which range in difficulty from moderate to extreme – the **HRP**, the north–south **GR7** and the trans-Pyrenean **GR10** – as well as marked secondary trails, cross the massif, while parts of the GR7 and GR10 comprise sections of the less demanding **Tour du Carlit**, aimed at hikers of medium experience. For all of these explorations you'll want the IGN 1:50,000 *Carte de Randonnées no. 7*, "Cerdagne-Capcir"; the IGN TOP 25 no. 2249 ET is also well worth having. The ascent of **Pic Carlit** (2921m) itself is within the capabilities of any reasonably fit person, especially from Lac des Bouillouses, accessible either by car or foot, on its eastern slopes.

Climbing Pic Carlit

A quick approach to the summit can be made from Mont-Louis on the **east** side, up the very narrow but paved D60 road. On a fine summer day, expect hundreds of cars at the **Lac des Bouillouses** parking area 13km along, with an even greater number of trippers milling about – definitely not virgin wilderness, and with family groups crammed four to a vehicle, you've little chance of hitching a lift. For purist hikers who don't mind a long slog, the **GR10** out of Bolquère, two stops west of Mont-Louis on the *Train Jaune*, climbs gently through woods to the **Col del Pam** (2005m), where it links with the HRP from Font-Romeu, both continuing past ski lifts and pistes to Lac des Bouillouses (5hr from either town).

There's plenty of **accommodation** and **food** at the Bouillouses lake, actually a huge reservoir constructed in the early 1900s. The CAF-run *Refuge des Bouillouses* (☎04.68.04.93.88; obligatory half-board ❹), the cheapest option, stands east of the dam wall at just under 2000m. Tucked inconspicuously behind this is the smallish, privately managed *Auberge du Carlit* (☎04.68.04.22.23, ⓦaubergeducarlit.free.fr) which has rooms (❷) as well as half-board (❺), and a **gîte** (dorm beds €11.50). Just above the west end of the dam at 2050m looms the gigantic *Refuge Le Bones Hores* (Easter–Oct; ☎04.68.04.24.22, ✉boneshores@wanadoo.fr; obligatory half-board ❸), popular with families.

From next to *Le Bones Hores,* where a placard informs fishermen which lakes are legally open, you get on the **HRP**, whose course is scantily marked with faded paint splodges but deeply grooved into the terrain. You arc up gently through the woods, between **Étang Noir** and **Étang Vive**, reached after twenty minutes; the next natural lake, **Dougues**, is a mere 45 minutes above the dam, and thus a hugely popular outing. However, the crowds do thin somewhat as you press on past the necklace of smaller lakes – Casteilla, Trébens and Soubirans – under the shadow of **Touzal Colomé** (2804m), and finally up the ridge that leads to the summit from the east. This is a superb climb, with the tarns glinting in the sun, the grass green in June but usually a faded ochre by August, and the scree-strewn pyramid of Carlit overhead. There and back from Lac des Bouillouses is at most six-and-a-half hours, a day's walk in good conditions – though rather ominously there are green sheds by most of the lakes, for sheltering from the foul weather which is often not long in appearing. If – as so many do – you just want to take in the lakes, it's only a three-hour round trip from the dam to the highest one, Soubirans, at 2320m.

The Tech valley and the Albères

Running more or less parallel to the Têt valley, but roughly 30km further south, the **Tech valley** (or Vallespir) is the southernmost in France, endowed with exceptional sunshine (300 days a year) and relatively low rainfall which nurtures a flora that includes oranges, cacti and bougainvillea – as well as dense forest on the higher, wetter slopes. Heading up the valley will take you through the Spanish ex-pat art centre, **Céret**, and on to **Arles-sur-Tech**, the gateway to the exciting **Gorges de la Fou**. Further upstream, the upper Tech is dominated by **Prats-de-Molló**, where the main road departs from the river to reach the Spanish frontier. The northern face of the Pyrenees, rising out of the sea at the rugged Côte Vermeille and bordered by the Tech to the north, is known as the **Albères**. Here, a myriad of paths – a traditional route of shepherds, refugees and smugglers – cross the frontier into Spain, which is officially marked by the village of **Le Perthus**. Access into both regions from Perpignan by car or bus is via **Le Boulou**, where the N9 splits to head straight south for Le Perthus, and west to shadow the Tech valley as the D115.

South to Le Perthus

The cork capital of France, **LE BOULOU**, 20km south of Perpignan, is a fairly nondescript little spa town, although it is worth stopping at the **Église Ste-Marie,** the doorway of which features a fine frieze by the "Master of Cabestany" (see box, p.108). There is also a small **history museum**, the *Espace des Arts* (Tues–Sun 9am–noon & 2–6pm; free), with more works by the master. Die-hard fans should drive or cycle 14km north to the outskirts of Passa, where the cloister, **Monastir del Camp Prieuré** (Fri–Wed tours at 10 & 11am & 3, 4, 5 & 6pm €4), features more of the anonymous sculptor's work. To further tempt, the monastery is now a wine *domaine*, where you can taste local vintages. Le Boulou's **tourist office** (July & Aug Mon–Sat 9am–12.30pm & 2–6.30pm; Sept–June Mon–Fri 9am–12.30pm & 2–6pm & Sat 9am–12.30pm; ☎04.68.87.50.95., ⓦwww.ot-leboulou.fr) is in the central place de la Mairie. The best **accommodation** options are the *Le Grillon d'Or*, 40 rue de la République (☎04.68.83.03.60, ⓦwww.grillon-dor.com ❸; *menus* from €18– 35), and the more luxurious, but elegantly rustic ⚑ *Le Relais des Chartreuses* (Feb to mid-Nov; ☎04.68.83.15.88, ⓦwww.perso.orange.fr/relais.des.chartreuses; ❹), set in an old Catalan *masia*, at 106 avenu d'En Carbouner in Le Boulou.

Heading east from Le Boulou will take you past a number of other Romanesque monuments (see box, p.381), or head a few minutes south, where the Tech cuts by on its way to the sea, to visit the remarkable **chapel of St-Martin-de-Fenollar** (mid-June to mid-Sept daily 10.30am–noon & 3.30–7pm; mid-Sept to mid-June Mon & Wed–Sun 2–5pm; €3) in Maureillas-las-Illas. Its twelfth-century frescoes are the best Romanesque wall-paintings in Roussillon, and their clarity and simplicity of line may well have influenced Picasso, who sometimes stayed in nearby Céret.

Nine kilometres further south, **LE PERTHUS** was marked in history on the night of February 5, 1939, when a column of twenty thousand Spanish Republicans arrived at the border post to seek sanctuary in France. Nowadays consumer armies descend here every day, disgorging from coaches to spend their money on foodstuffs, booze and perfume, or to cross the border to fill up their tanks in Spain. The main landmark hereabouts is **Fort de Bellegarde** (July–Sept 10.30am–6.30pm; €3), which looms on a peak above the town. Built in the sixteenth century and later reinforced by Vauban, it comprises two rows of dilapidated buildings and the deepest well in Europe (63m) within an enclosure of mighty walls, and gives superb views south into Spain and north across Roussillon. In Roman times the Via Domitia crossed the Albères 2km to the west at the **Col de Panissars**, accessible by the narrow road which continues past Fort de Bellegarde, and is probably the way that Hannibal came in 218 BC. When Pompey returned to Rome fresh from putting down a rebellion in Spain a century and a half later, he ordered a triumphal monument to be built at the col, and the excavated base of this edifice is now visible through a cordon of barbed wire.

For **accommodation**, there's *Chez Grand-Mère*, at the summit of the main road (☎04.68.83.60.96. ℱ04.68.8363.72; ❷), or the municipal **campsite** *Les Oliviers* (mid-Jan to mid-Dec; ☎ 04.68.83.12.86), east of the town centre. The best option for a meal hereabouts, is to hop across the border to Spain, where any of La Jonquera's many bustling **roadside eateries** will lay out an all-you-can-eat buffet or a hefty four-course meal in the €8–12 range. If you do nip into Spain, taking the toll *autoroute* (less than €3) will avoid the excruciatingly long delays through bottle-necked Le Perthus.

Céret

Just 10km or so upstream along the Tech from Le Boulou lies the cherry capital of southern France, **CÉRET**, a friendly and bustling place with a shady old town of narrow and winding streets, still dominated by its much built-into medieval fortifications. The best time to visit is during any of the town's famous **festivals** (see box, pp.342–343), which have a markedly Catalan and Spanish flavour, including *sardanas* and *corridas* held in the arena to the north of town – but you'll have to plan ahead, as accommodation sells out well in advance. At the entrance to the town, the single-arched **Pont du Diable** was said to have been built by the Devil in 1321 in return for the soul of the first Cérétan to cross. The engineer who made the bargain duly sent a cat over first, but the trick backfired as none of the locals would then risk the Devil's vengeance by using the bridge themselves. Like Prades on the Têt, Céret was a place of refuge for escapees from Franco's fascist regime, with many artists passing through or staying here. At that point, the town was already a creative colony, having been a temporary home to luminaries such as Pablo Picasso, Marc Chagall and a clutch of Catalan and French artists, including Pierre Brune, who in 1950 opened the **Musée d'Art Moderne** at 8 bd Maréchal Joffre (daily 10am–7/8pm; €8). This museum's small but varied collection includes works by the Fauvists, Cubists and Surrealists, as well as pieces by recent artists such as Tàpies, but the highlight is a series of painted bowls with bull motifs by Picasso. Other sights in the town include the small **archeological museum** (July & Aug daily 10.30am–noon & 2–6pm; Sept–Dec & Feb–June Mon–Fri 10am–noon & 2–5pm; €2.50) tucked behind one of the old gates, the **war memorial** by Aristide Maillol in the old town and the **monument** to the composer Déodat de Séverac by the Catalan sculptor Manolo in avenue Clémenceau. If you head north 100m from the town centre on avenue d'Espagne, you'll come upon **Le Capelleta** (Sat 10.30am–12.30pm & 3.30–7pm; free), a tiny church with a well-executed Romanesque lintel over the entrance, which houses temporary art exhibits.

Practicalities

The **tourist office** (July & Aug Mon–Sat 9am–12.30pm & 2–7pm; Sept–May Mon–Fri 10am–noon & 2–5pm, Sat 10am–noon; ☎04.68.87.00.53, ⓦwww.ot-ceret.fr) is at the top of avenue Clémenceau, on the corner of boulevard Maréchal Joffre. Céret Les Sentiers de Pyrène, in 11 rue Maillol (☎04.68.87.06.93, ⓔleyaouanq@aol.com; English spoken), can organize guided **hikes**, while VTT 66 at 27 rue des Mimosas (☎04.68.87.44.16) runs **biking** trips. The most central **accommodation** is at the atmospheric one-star ⚜*Vidal*, housed in the old bishop's palace, off place Soutine (☎04.68.87.00.85, ⓦwww.hotelvidalceret.com; ❸). Alternatively, there's the two-star *Arcades*, opposite (☎04.68.87.12.30, ⓦwww.hotel-arcades-ceret.com; ❸), or the *Pyrénées* on rue de la République (☎04.68.87.11.02, ⓔericlegentil@wanadoo .fr; ❸). For more luxury, there's the well-equipped, four-star *La Terrasse au Soleil* on route de Fontfrède (Jan–Oct; ☎04.68.87.01.94, ⓦwww.terrasse-au-soleil .com; ❾), though it's only really good value in low season when prices are halved. The best option, however, is ⚜*Le Mas Trilles* at Le Pont de Reynes, 2km outside Céret (☎04.68.87.38.37, ⓦwww.le-mas-trilles.com; ❼), set in a seventeenth-century *mas* overlooking the Tech. There are several local **campsites**, two of them on route de Maureillas: *Les Cerisiers* (Feb–Dec; ☎04.68.87.00.08) and *Saint-Georges* (☎04.68.87.03.73).

The best place to **eat** is the bistro-crêperie, *Le Pied dans le Plat* (closed Sun; from €14), and adjacent pizzeria, both on place des Neuf-Jets, with outdoor seating. For finer dining, there's *Les Feuillants* (☎04.68.87.37.88), set in a grand old house at 1 boulevard La Fayette (*menus* €30 and €46). Social life at the *Grand Café* in boulevard Maréchal Joffre is not what it was when the "bande Picasso" hung out there, but it's still a good place to sit outside with a glass of wine and a plate of *frites*; there are more **cafés** around the corner by the Porte de France. Saturdays see a morning farmers' **market** along the old walls, the street stalls groaning with local produce.

Arles-sur-Tech and around

Continuing upstream from Céret, the next town which merits a visit is **ARLES-SUR-TECH**, renown for having preserved the curious folk traditions of the eastern Pyrenees – try to make it for one of the several festivals that are celebrated throughout the year (see box, pp.342–343). The heart of the town is formed by its compact medieval quarter, centred on the eleventh-century **abbey-church of Ste-Marie** (daily: July & Aug 9am–7pm; Sept–June 9am–noon & 2–6pm; Nov–March closed Sun; €3.50). Before passing through the main door built into its impressive facade, check out the grilled-off marble block just to the left. This is the *sainte tombe*, a fourth-century sarcophagus, revered for the pure water which it miraculously issues, and which plays a key part in the town's ancient religious rituals. The interior of the church has a number of good **chapels**, as well as an elegant thirteenth-century **cloister**. The cloister itself leads to the **Musée du Fer**, which recreates the town's medieval iron-smelting and mining industries (same hours; €2).

From Arles, you can **hike** up the northbound GR10 towards the Canigou, but a less ambitious and more spectacular option is the nearby **Gorges de la Fou** (☏04.68.39.16.21; April–Nov daily 10am–6pm weather permitting; €5), one of the great – if touristy – spectacles of the eastern Pyrenees. Follow the signposted turning off the main highway west of Arles or ascend the trail leading off the D115, 3km west of town. You need at least an hour to cover the 1500m of metal walkway to the end and back, squeezing between 200-metre-high walls, so close together that they have trapped falling rocks. In places, water erosion has made the walls as smooth as plaster, and the force of the torrent during storms in 1988 swept part of the walk away – when storms threaten, the route is closed. If you have your own transport, you should consider leaving

△ Gorge de la Fou

the main road at Arles, and continuing past the top end of the Gorges de Fou trail to Corsavy and on to **MONTFERRER**, which, with its ruined castle and Romanesque church, is one of the most attractive settlements in the upper Tech. Set amongst dense forest and crags, with sweeping views east to the opposite side of the valley, it enjoys its status as the truffle capital of Roussillon.

South of the main road a tortuous side road ascends through forests of sweet chestnut to the village of **ST-LAURENT-DE-CERDANS**, an important junction on the World War II refugee route to Spain. Here the local history museum, **Musée des Arts et Traditions Populaires** (June–Sept daily 9/10am–noon & 2/3–6pm; July & Aug daily 10am–noon & 2–7pm; Oct–May Mon–Fri 9am–noon & 2–6pm; €2), preserves rural arts such as the manufacture of espadrilles, the traditional esparto woven shoes favoured by refugee guides (*passeurs*). If at all possible, visit the town in early February, for the colourful *Fête de l'ours* (see box below). The **market** is held on Saturday. Further on at tiny **COUSTOUGES**, the spine of the Albères rises northeastwards to the highest point of the chain at **Roc de France** (1450m).

Practicalities

Buses stop in Arles a short walk from the **tourist office** (Mon–Sat 9am–noon & 2–6pm; ☏ & 🖷 04.68.39.11.99, 🌐 www.ville-arles-sur-tech.fr), in rue Barjou

---

The Pyrenees: Bear facts

Although Languedocian *tauromachie* and the Mediterranean obsession with bulls may date from pre-Classical times, local peoples' fascination with **bears** goes back to the very dawn of our species. Cave paintings depict them, while excavations at Chauvet cave (near Nîmes) suggest that bears and hominids shared living space 32,000 years ago. For early societies around the world bears were feared and respected as embodiments of the power of nature and of virility – a force to be reckoned with and a rival to be hunted down. Until modern times, when they were hunted almost to extinction, bears continued to roam the wooded slopes of the Pyrenees, preying on wild game and herds, inspiring awe among village-dwellers and resentment among farmers.

Since the 1980s **conservationists** have been struggling to save the species, whose habitat had been encroached on not only by herders and hunters but by the massive development of ski resorts. Sadly, these efforts have come to nothing, and the remaining three indigenous bears have now been shot by poachers: the last – "Canelle" – was found dead in August 2004 in Béarn's Valle del Aspe. Even before then, the French and Spanish governments had initiated a programme to reintroduce the species, importing Slovenian and Croatian bears and releasing them in the high valleys along the frontier between the two countries. But this is no easy task. There are few protected habitats on the French side of the *cordillera*, and shepherds oppose the programme claiming that it puts their herds in danger, despite generous (and often-abused) compensation payments. A further force to contend with is the Hunting and Fishing Party, which runs in local elections on a platform advocating the right to kill the animals. For more information on the conservation programme, contact Pays de l'Ours - ADET, Maison des Association, 31160 Arbas (☏ 05.61.97.48.44, 🌐 www.paysdelours.com).

Today, ursuline totems and costumes are standard features of folk festivals in the mountains, and the closest you're likely to come to seeing a bear is at the **fêtes de l'ours**, celebrated in villages such as St-Laurent-de-Cerdan. The ancient festivals mark the date when hungry bears emerged from hibernation. Traditionally village youths would go out to capture a live animal to prove their masculinity, but gradually this was transformed into a symbolic hunt, in which gangs of youths pursued a villager dressed in a bear costume – an occasion for good-natured revelry and youthful mayhem (a vivid recreation can be seen in the 1983 film *The Return of Martin Guerre*).

at the top of the town, which has suggestions for walks and trails around Arles, and also stocks a list of *chambres d'hôtes*. The place to **stay** is the comfortable two-star *Les Glycines*, 7 rue du Jeu-de-Paume (☎04.68.39.10.09, ✉hotelglycines @wanadoo.fr; ❸), which also has the town's best **restaurant**, with a shaded terrace and Catalan specialities (*menus* from €18). There are several **campsites**, including the scenic *Riuferrer* (☎04.68.39.11.06), on the west side of town, near the mouth of the Freixe stream; *Le Vallespir* (April–Nov; ☎04.68.39.90.00, ⓦwww.campingvallespir.com) on the road to Amélie-les-Bains; and the naturist camp *Le Ventous* (May to mid-Nov; ☎04.68.87.83.38, ⓦwww.leventousnaturiste .com) on the road to Prats-de-Mollo. Arles' best eating options include the **restaurant** at *Les Glycines*; *La Treille* at the beginning of boulevard Riuferrer (☎04.68.39.89.59; closed Mon Sept–May), with a pleasant vine-shaded terrace (€14 *menu*); and the grill-bar at the Musée Jean Cordomi (March–Dec 10am– 10pm), opposite the *mairie*.

Prats-de-Molló

From Arles, the road climbs 19km to the medieval city of **PRATS-DE-MOLLÓ**, and its sister town of **La Preste**, famous as a spa since 1302. The present road follows the path of a former railway (the station houses can be seen along the way), since the old road, along with houses and bridges, was washed away in the disastrous floods of October 1940. In the seventeenth century, when the Treaty of the Pyrenees subjected this area to the outrageous tax policies of Louis XIV, Prats-de-Molló and a number of other towns and villages revolted against the French Crown. Living at the far end of what was then a densely wooded valley, the rebels probably felt themselves invulnerable when they murdered the king's tax collectors. And indeed, they held off two battalions before the forces of Maréchal de Noailles made a surprise attack over the western flanks of Canigou to put down the insurrection.

Fort Lagarde (April–June & Sept–Nov Tues–Sun 2–5.30pm; July & Aug daily 11am–1pm & 5–7pm; €3.50), which dominates the town from above, was built in 1680 under the direction of Vauban, as much to subdue the local population as to keep the Spanish at bay; the town walls, raised on fourteenth-century foundations, are another Vauban relic from this period. To make the 25-minute climb up to the fort, head for Porte de la Fabrique on the north side of town, then either follow the footpath which winds up the hill from behind the church or take the covered walk which starts in a ruined building to the right of the cemetery entrance. The fort itself has been beautifully restored, and there are superb views all around from the ramparts. An extra attraction here is the **Visite-Spectacle** on summer afternoons, when horsemen dressed as cavaliers recreate eighteenth-century cavalry training, with trick riding, sword fights and the firing of muskets and cannons.

With Canigou at its back and the River Tech in front, picturesque Prats-de-Molló has now become a tourist attraction but is still surprisingly unspoilt – particularly the old *ville haute* within the city wall, with its steep, cobbled streets and ancient fortified church. In summer, the pedestrianized streets buzz with activity; the rest of the year the hotels are locked up, and the locals pass the time playing *boules* under the plane trees of El Firal, the huge square outside the walls, where markets and fairs have been held since 1308.

Practicalities

The **tourist office** in place du Foiral (July & Aug daily 9am–12.30pm & 1.30– 6.30pm; April–June, Sept & Oct Mon–Sat 9am–noon & 2–6pm; Jan–March,

Nov & Dec closed Sat; ☎04.68.39.70.83, ⓦwww.pratsdemollolapreste.com) has a wealth of information, including maps and advice for walking in the Haut-Vallespir. Nearby, the Maison de la Réserve in La Preste (☎04.68.39.74.49, ⓔresnatprats@wanadoo.fr) can arrange **guides** for 1–5 day hikes into the upper Tech. There is a good selection of **hotels** here. The best value is the *Hôtel des Touristes* at 3 avenue Haut-Vallespir (April–Oct; ☎04.68.39.72.12, ⓔrestauranthotel touriste@wanadoo.fr; ❶), decorated with original antique furniture. Otherwise the family-oriented *Le Relais*, no. 3 on place Joseph Trinxeria (☎04.68.39.71.30, ⓦwww.hostellerie-le-relais.com; ❷) and the friendly *Bellevue* overlooking place du Foiral (mid-Feb to Nov; ☎04.68.39.72.48, ⓦwww.lebellevue.fr.st; ❸) are both good and also serve reasonable meals. A better choice of **restaurant**, however, is *Costabonne* at 6 place du Foiral (☎04.68.39.70.24), renown for its home-made *foie gras* (*menus* from €12.50–18). There are plenty of local **campsites**, too, including *St Martin* in av de Vallespir (Feb–Dec; ☎04.68.39.77.40, ⓔcamping .st.martin@wanadoo.fr) and *Can Nadal* (April to mid-Nov; ☎04.68.39.70.89) about 1km along the road towards La Preste. Stock up on supplies at the local **market**, held Wednesday and Friday mornings.

The Côte Vermeille

When the nineteenth-century Fauvists discovered the **Côte Vermeille**, which extends southeast from Argelès-sur-Mer to the Spanish border, they found natural inspiration for their revolutionary use of colour: the sunsets (from which the coast earned its name) are a gentle red, the sea is turquoise and, as Matisse wrote, "no sky is more blue than that at Collioure". **Elne**, inland, and once Roussillon's main town, is the gateway to the coast, and proceeding south you'll pass the broad beaches of **Argelès**, before reaching the characteristically rocky coves of **Collioure**, **Banyuls** and **Cerbère**. The beauty of this stretch of coastline has inevitably been exploited, but cut up along the trails into the hills at the back of the resorts and you'll often be on your own. Public transport along the coast is good, with a regular train and bus service connecting all the major points of call.

Elne

Standing on a hill just 6km from the sea, the first stop on the coastal transport line is **ELNE**, an ancient fortified town which was once the capital of Roussillon. Despite the heavy beach-bound traffic whizzing past on the main road, the old town, inside the sixteenth-century ramparts, is eerily quiet after dark. Its one great attraction is the former **cathedral of Ste-Eulalie** (daily: April & May 9.30am–6pm; June–Sept 9.30am–6.45pm; Oct 9.30am–12.15pm & 2–5.45pm; Nov–March 9.30am–11.45pm & 2–4.45pm; €5), the seat of Roussillon's bishops until their transfer to Perpignan in 1602. The **cloister**, built from Céret marble, is the highlight: one intact side of twelfth-century Romanesque pillars and capitals, immaculately carved with motifs such as foliage, lions, goats and biblical figures, is complemented on the other sides by fourteenth-century Gothic work. A small museum in the twelfth-century St-Laurent chapel, which you access from the cloister, is mainly given over to exhibits found in the excavations of Roman villas around Elne. Opposite the cathedral, at 3 rue Balaguer, is the **Musée Terrus** (same times and ticket as the cathedral), dedicated to the landscape painter Etienne Terrus (1857–1922), a contemporary of the Fauvists and friend of sculptor Aristide Maillol (whose bust of Terrus stands on the Plateau des Garaffes, nearby); the *salon de thé*, on the first floor, has a panoramic view.

Practicalities

The **gare SNCF** (℡04.68.22.06.15), on the main line from Perpignan to the Côte Vermeille, lies about ten minutes' walk west of the old town; **buses** stop at the parking area in the centre, near the cathedral. The **tourist office** is at 2 rue du Docteur Bolte (June & Sept Mon–Fri 9.30am–noon & 2–5pm, Sat 9.30am–noon; July & Aug Mon–Fri 9.30am–noon & 2–6pm, Sat 9.30am–noon; Oct–May Mon–Fri 9.30am–noon & 2–5pm; ℡04.68.22.05.07, ⓦwww.ot-elne.fr), between the post office and Hôtel de Ville. Of the **hotels**, the rather pricey *Cara Sol*, in boulevard Illibéris on the edge of the old town (℡04.68.22.10.42, ⓦwww.hotelcarasol.com; ➎), has great views from the front rooms over the Tech valley, the Albères and Canigou, though the two-star *Le Weekend*, 31 avenue Paul Reig (℡04.68.22.06.68, ⓦwww.hotel.weekend.chez-alice.fr; ➌), is better value, with a celebrated garden **restaurant** (*menus* from €16). There are two municipal **campsites** (June– Sept): *Les Pédraguets* (℡04.68.22.21.59) on the Argelès road; and *El Molí* (℡04.68.22.08.46) on boulevard d'Archimède, in the direction of St-Cyprien. The local **market** is held on the place de la République (Mon, Wed & Fri).

Saint-Cyprien

Five kilometres northeast of Elne lies the sleepy, old village of **SAINT-CYPRIEN**, clumped around a tiny square, the place de la République, where you'll find **Les Collections de Saint-Cyprien** (10am–noon & 2–6/7pm: July & Aug daily; Sept–June Wed–Sun; €3.50). Its tiny permanent collection contains a few pieces of interest, notably Dalí's sculpture *Venus de Milo with Drawers*, but it also hosts excellent and often provocative temporary exhibits of contemporary and modern art. Five kilometres east of the village is the beach town of **Saint-Cyprien-Plage** and the Dantesque holiday development of Saint-Cyprien-Sud. Beyond the densely built-up developments which surround Saint-Cyprien-Plage, there's a beach with abundant amenities and which is quieter and more suitable for families than nearby Argelès.

Saint-Cyprien-Plage's **tourist office** is on quai Rimbaud (July & Aug daily 9am–8pm; Sept–June Mon–Sat 9am–noon & 2–6pm, Sun 10.30am–noon & 3–7pm; ℡04.68.21.01.33, ⓔtourisme@saiknt-cyprien.com). There's no shortage of **accommodation** at the beach, including the functional *Mar i Sol*, 8 rue Auguste-Rodin (℡04.68.37.31.00, ⓦwww.hotelmarisol.com; ➍), and the four-star *Île de la Lagune* on boulevard de l'Almadine (℡04.68.21.01.02, ⓦwww.hotel-ile-lagune.com; ➒), with a highly recommended **restaurant**, *L'Almadine* (from €46).

Argelès-sur-Mer and around

Poised on the northern edge of the Côte Vermeille, **ARGELÈS-SUR-MER** has the last wide, sandy beach on the coast. At the end of the Spanish Civil War thousands of refugees lived in camps here, their numbers including the Republican poet Antonio Machado, who failed to survive the first harsh winter of his arrival. Not surprisingly, given camp conditions, nearly ten thousand of the inmates volunteered to serve in the French army upon the 1939 outbreak of hostilities. Nowadays, more than any other resort on this section of coast, this is a mass-tourist town, wooing its visitors with holiday essentials like mini-golf, gambling tables and beauty contests.

The town itself is divided in two: the old **Argelès-Ville**, a little inland, and the new **Argelès-Plage**, which receives an annual inundation of up to 300,000 French, Belgian, Dutch and English visitors. Plage Nord and Plage des Pins are **beaches** of the smooth, sandy and potentially windblown variety, whereas **Le Racou** – the first bay of the Côte Vermeille – is more intimate and offers a taste of mountain coastline. Either way, Argelès-Plage is a centre for noisy,

Romanesque in the Albères

The northern slopes of the Pyrenees and the plains which spill out below them were heavily populated in the Middle Ages, a fact attested to by the numerous churches and monasteries which were built here a millennium ago. This was not the wealthiest area, and these humble foundations cannot compete with the grandeur of Toulouse or the North of France, but the very fact that they were relatively isolated and poor means that many of their original features, which would have been remodelled and effaced elsewhere, have been left intact. **Romanesque churches** here are typically compact and squat, with few windows and single-naved chapels capped by primitive barrel-vaulting. The surviving artwork from this period is chiefly in sculpture and painting. Sculptors, the most famous of whom is the "Master of Cabestany" (see box, p.108), devoted their attention to capitals and corbels, which they shaped into complex vegetal and geometric patterns or carved into biblical scenes peopled by bulbous-featured human figures; their best work is often found on the lintel above a church's main door. Rarer, and more striking, are the magnificent frescos which once fully covered the interiors of many of these buildings. Fresco painting lends itself well to the bold and colourful (and surprisingly modern-looking) designs favoured by these artists. These frescoes served to dramatically illustrate biblical scenes for the illiterate parishioners; Old Testament patriarchs, apostles, God and the angels were brought to life in vivid, kinetic scenes.

In addition to the better-known sites, such as Elne, St-Génis and St-Martin-de-Fenollar, several other churches can be taken in on a circuit of the area. Touring by bicycle, scooter or car will take a day, or you can walk, if you don't mind taking longer – either way, it's a stimulating break from the easy beach-side hedonism of Argelès and Collioure. Heading west out of Argelès, you'll pass the N114, after which a minor road leads 3km to **St-André** (non-suicidal cyclists should avoid the busy D618). Here an old abbey-church in allée de la Liberté houses the **Musée Transfrontalier d'Art Roman** (mid-June to mid-Sept Tues–Sun 9am–noon & 2.30–7pm; mid-Sept to mid-June Tues–Sat 10am–noon & 2–6pm; €2), which is visited on an hour-long guided tour. A further 5km takes you to **St-Génis**, once home to an ancient Benedictine abbey: although most of it has disappeared, the remaining two-metre lintel over the doorway of the church, dating from 1020, is one of the earliest examples of Romanesque sculpture in France – a disarmingly archaic array of apostles and angels. When the **church** is open (daily: June–Sept 10am–noon & 2/3–6/7pm; Oct–May 9.30am–noon & 2–5pm; €2) you can visit its fine thirteenth-century Romanesque cloister, whose single row of short columns supports semicircular arches of multicoloured marble (white from Céret, pink from Villefranche, black from Baixas), and has capitals carved with engaging primitive figures: half-human and half-beasts, fantastic creatures, and Christ crucified. From here the D11 leads 3.5km south to Laroque, then west to Villelongue-dels-Monts, where a steep and winding road, intermittently sign-posted to the "*Église*" leads up to the former Augustine convent and pilgrims' hostel of **Santa Maria Vilar** (daily 2.30 & 6pm; 1hr guided tour €4). Originally founded in 1089, the present church dates from 1149, although sections, like the impressive Carolingian hall, are older. The main attractions here are the beautiful eleventh- and twelfth-century fresco murals, featuring both geometric and human motifs. Santa Maria is also home to a well-reputed *Festival Lyrique*, featuring Gregorian Chant and troubadours (☎04.68.89.64.61; July & Aug Sat 9pm; €16). A further 2km along the road brings you to the ancient chapel of **Santa Coloma de Cabanes** (irregular hours). From here you can follow the D2 back east to Argelès, or continue on the D11 to Montesquieu-des-Albères (3km) before descending to Le Boulou.

ebullient, youthful hedonism, a landscape of neon, fast-food with a background of loud music and the rattle of scooters. The only cultural attraction is the old town's **Casa de les Albères**, in place des Castellans, a small museum of local art and traditions, mostly agricultural tools and implements (June–Sept Mon–Fri 9am–noon & 3–6pm, Sat 9am–noon; €2). Otherwise, a great attraction for children and adults alike is **Les Aigles du Château de Valmy** (April–June & Oct Tues–Sun 1.30–6.30pm; July & Aug daily 1.30–6.30pm; €8.50), which puts on displays of birds of prey and sheep dogs at the nineteenth-century folly, Valmy castle, just over the RN112 from Argelès (exit 12).

Practicalities

The **gare SNCF** is a few minutes' walk west of the centre of the Argelès-Ville, while **buses** stop opposite the Hôtel de Ville. An hourly bus service (€2) runs in summer between the station, the old town and Plage-Nord. There is a summer-only **tourist office** in the old town by the Hôtel de Ville on allée Ferdinand-Buisson (July & Aug Mon–Sat 9.45am–12.15pm & 3–6.15pm; ℡04.68.95.81.55); Argelès-Plage has its own office in place de l'Europe (July & Aug daily 8.30am–8pm; Sept–June Mon–Fri 9am–noon & 2–6pm, Sat 9am–noon; ℡04.68.81.15.85, ⓦwww.argeles-sur-mer.com), on the corner of avenue des Platanes and avenue des Mimosas. Several places, including Velocation on the beachside av du Tech (℡04.68.81.61.61, ⓦwww.aregelesvelolcation.com), rent out **bikes** and **motorbikes**.

Accommodation can be difficult to find in midsummer, especially for a short stay. The best choice in the old town is ⚜ *Auberge du Roua* (℡04.68.95.85.85, ⓦwww.aubergeduroua.com; ⑥) a renovated *masia* on Chemin du Roua, or for those on a budget, the two-star *Clair Logis*, 78 route de Collioure (℡04.68.81.03.27, ⓕ04.68.95.93.01; ❷). Of the dozens of hotels in Argelès-Plage, the two-star *Les Mimosas*, 51 avenue des Mimosas (℡04.68.81.14.77, ⓦwww.hotel-mimosas.com; ❹), and *Al Pescadou*, rue des Aloès (℡04.68.81.31.12, ⓦwww.argeles-sur-mer.com; ❸), are reasonably priced and well situated. There are more than fifty **campsites** in the neighbourhood: two with good beach access are the three-star *Beauséjour* near Centre Plage (April to mid-Oct; ℡04.68.81.10.63, ⓦwww.camping-lebeausejour .com), and *Les Pins* on Avenue du Tech (mid-May to late-Sept ℡04.68.81.10.46, ⓦwww.les-pins.com). The **restaurants** in Argelès rarely rise above mediocre beach-town fare: one of the few that stands out is *Amadeüs* on avenue des Platanes, by Argelès-Plage's tourist office (℡04.68.81.12.38 closed Mon April–Nov & all Jan), which serves reasonable Catalan dishes, with *menus* from €20.

Collioure

Eleven kilometres down the coast from Argelès-sur-Mer, **COLLIOURE**, a true Côte Vermeille town, which to a certain extent still banks on its maritime and artistic past, sits nestled in a picturesque cove. Established as a trading port by the Phoenicians and ancient Greeks, Collioure was later occupied by Romans, Visigoths and Arabs. Altogether, the place has been the focus of nearly a dozen territorial squabbles, including four invasions by the French and two by the Spanish. The sixteenth-century **Fort St Elme** overlooking the town from the south (now privately owned), and the seventeenth-century **Fort Miradou** to the north (still used by the military), are reminders of this turbulent past. In the early 1900s, invaders of a different sort came; the group of painters – including Matisse and Derain – known as the **Fauvists** (*les Fauvistes*) made Collioure their summer base. Some of their original work adorns the bar at *Les Templiers* (see p.384); you can also follow the "Chemin du Fauvisme" around the town, a trail of twenty reproductions of paintings by Matisse and Derain placed on the sites where they were painted (a map is available from the tourist office; regular guided tours €6). Housed in the beautiful Villa Pams on the edge of the town on route de Port-Vendres, Collioure's **Musée d'Art Moderne** (June–Sept daily 9.20am–12.30pm & 3–7pm; Oct–May Mon–Fri 10am–noon & 3–6pm, Sat & Sun 3–6pm; €6), has a small permanent collection, which includes Picasso's poster *Hommage à Antonio Machado*, commemorating the Spanish Republican poet and martyr, who is buried in the town. It also hosts temporary exhibitions by artists associated with the region.

The artistic tradition of Collioure survives today, albeit with less distinction; the forest of easels that occupies the promenade in summer produces mainly tourist souvenirs, but there are also a few serious commercial galleries. Many of these are in the old quarter of the town, the **Mouré**, whose steep, narrow streets are lined by pastel-tinted houses and assorted shops and cafés. Lateen-rigged fishing boats might be moored in the **harbour** itself, or drawn up on the palm-lined beach; those no longer used by fishermen are now beautifully restored and sailed as pleasure vessels by their new owners. The **château-royal** (daily: June–Sept 10am–6/7pm; Oct–May 9am–5pm; €4), the imposing fortress which dominates the harbour, was founded by the Templars in the twelfth century, rebuilt and used as a sometime residence by the kings of Mallorca and Aragón two hundred years later, and modernized by Vauban after the Treaty of the Pyrenees. Impressive as it is from the inside, the fortress is hardly worth going into unless you are going to attend one of the concerts held in the ramshackle courtyard; the bare rooms hold a few mediocre exhibitions that lack explanatory information (a French-only pamphlet is available for €2). On the other hand, the two **beaches** which bookend the castle are worth the time, although they become hopelessly crowded in summer months. One is sandy and the other stony, so you can take your pick, or head up to the **nude beach** just around the cape at the town's north end.

At the opposite end of the harbour, the **church of Notre-Dame-des-Anges** was erected in the seventeenth century, replacing the ancient Ste-Marie, razed on the orders of Vauban. The distinctive round bell tower – once doubling as the light-house – onto which it was grafted, has been damaged many times by storm and war: the base dates from the thirteenth century, the middle from the fourteenth to seventeenth centuries, and the bell chamber from the nineteenth. It's worth taking a look inside (8am–noon & 2–5.30pm) to see the magnificent gilt retable, carved and painted in three tiers, another work by Joseph Sunyer. Beyond the church, the tiny **Chapelle-St-Vincent** stands above the sea on a rocky peninsula, with the south-facing St Vincent beach on one side and the Plage Nord on the other.

Practicalities

Collioure's **gare SNCF** is less than ten minutes' walk west of the centre, along avenue Aristide Maillol; **buses** stop at the central car park, off avenue Général de Gaulle. **Parking** on the street is almost impossible: head, instead, for the large and reasonably priced car park on the hill which rises over the sea behind the castle. The very helpful **tourist office** is just behind the harbour on place du 18 Juin (July & Aug Mon–Sat 9am–8pm & Sun 10am–6pm; Sept–June Mon–Sat 9am–noon & 2–6/7pm; ☎04.68.82.15.47, ⊛www.collioure.com) and there is also a seasonal information kiosk (July–Sept Mon–Sat 9am–5pm) in the small tower by the beach on the other side of the castle.

The quieter Plage Boutigue, southeast of the harbour, has some desirable sea-view **hotels**, the best of which is ♣ *Triton*, 1 rue Jean-Bart (☎04.68.98.39.39,

@www.aswfrance.com/hotel-triton; ❺). The most unusual accommodation is *Hostellerie des Templiers*, 12 quai de l'Amirauté (☎04.68.98.31.10, @www .hotel-templiers.com; ❺; reservations essential), in which the individually deco-rated rooms, staircases and dining rooms are filled with original artworks; try and get a room in the main building, rather than in the less attractive annexes. For something quieter, but pricier, there's the very attractive *La Casa Païral*, in impasse des Palmiers (mid-Feb to Dec; ☎04.68.82.05.81, @www.hotel-casa -pairal.com; ❾). There are two seasonal (April–Sept) **campsites** to the north of the town, near the coast: *Les Amandiers* (☎04.68.81.14.69, @www.camping-les -amandiers.com) is in the sheltered bay known as L'Ouille, though *La Girelle* on plage d'Ouille (☎04.68.81.25.56), is better located and more attractive.

For **eating**, there's a great choice of very reasonable crêperies, sandwich bars and pizza-pasta places around the old Mouré quarter, but it's worth paying extra to sit at a table on the fashionable rue Camille Pelletan, by the harbour, to watch the world go by – the most atmospheric is *Les Templiers*, a café-bar well known to the Fauvists, and now filled with drawings and paintings donated by Matisse, Maillol, Picasso and Dufy, among many other artists. While in town, try to sample the famous salted anchovies, a local standby and an important component in Roussillonaise cookery. **Markets** (Wed & Sun morning) are held in place du Maréchal Leclerc. *Collioure Location* (☎04.68.82.24.59) at 7 av Général du Gaulle rents **bikes** and **scooters** by the day or week.

Port-Vendres

The next settlement southeast, **PORT-VENDRES**, a five-minute ride from Collioure, is marred by the busy main road, but for a genuine, unsophisticated fishing port, this is your best (indeed only) choice on the Côte Vermeille – though you probably won't want to stay longer than it takes to have a look around the port and tuck into a fish lunch. A huge fish-processing factory dominates one side of the harbour, while sardine- and tuna-fishing boats are moored under the Maillol-designed war memorial opposite, with nets and other paraphernalia piled along the harbour wall. Salt has taken its toll on Maillol's work, and the uncharac-teristically draped figures have lost limbs, noses and various other features.

To the Romans, the town was Portus Veneris (Port of Venus), a place of strate-gic trading importance. By the Middle Ages its significance was diminishing in direct relation to the rising star of neighbouring Collioure, but by the eighteenth century it had recovered somewhat through the business of shipping Roussillon wines. In 1830 it became the primary port for dispatching soldiers and supplies to the French colony in Algeria, a link that lasted for more than a century. There is a regular Saturday **market** in town, as well as a Thursday-morning "Peasants' market" (mid-June to mid-Sept), but it's worth stopping in for lunch or dinner at the numerous quay-side fish **restaurants** on any day of the week.

Banyuls-sur-Mer to the Spanish border

As the road crosses the Col du Père Carnère and drops down towards the Plage des Elmes, the once-elegant wine town of **BANYULS-SUR-MER**, 6km south of Port-Vendres, comes into view, with dry-stone walls and orderly rows of vines stretching into the hills behind it. Banyuls is famous for its dessert wine, which the French tend to drink as an aperitif; if you fancy a tipple, take a 45-minute **guided tour** of one of the larger cellars, such as the Cellier des Templiers in route du Mas-Reig (April to early Nov daily 10am–7.30pm; early Nov to March Mon–Sat 10am–1pm & 2.30–6.30pm; €2). Less fashionable than Collioure, Banyuls is still a lively and popular seaside resort. The busy road which runs along the seafront spoils it, and the wide, stony main beach is less attractive than some of the smaller bays to the north and south, but the whole town comes alive in the evenings when everyone gets together to promenade along the seafront, play *boules* or eat out at one of the many beach cafés and seafood restaurants.

You shouldn't leave Banyuls without visiting the **Laboratoire Arago**, a large white building overlooking the port. Run by the marine biology and land ecology department of the Sorbonne, its **aquarium** (daily: July & Aug 9am–1pm & 2–9pm; Sept–June 9am–noon & 2–6.30pm; €4.20) comprises over forty tanks of fascinating local specimens, including seahorses, bright red starfish and wicked-looking eels, and is supplemented by a comprehensive display of local birds. The coastal waters of this area, rich in marine life due to the Pyrenees' steep underwater descent, were the first *réserve marine* to be declared in France, indeed throughout the Mediterranean. If you have the necessary qualifications you can **dive** within the reserve area by contacting Plongez Rederis Club, at the port (℡04.68.88.31.66, 🌐www.rederis.com).

Practicalities

The **gare SNCF** is at the very western edge of town, while **buses** stop on the coastal boulevard. The **tourist office** is on the seafront, opposite the *mairie* (July & Aug daily 8.30am–8pm; Sept–June Mon–Sat 9am–noon & 2–5/6pm; ℡04.68.88.31.58, 🌐www.banyuls-sur-mer.com). Recommended one-star **hotels**, open all year, include the quaint and unpretentious *Hôtel Canal*, 9 rue Dugommier (℡04.68.88.00.75, 📧hotelcanal@aol.com; ❶), and the slightly smarter *Le Manoir*, 20 rue de Maréchal-Joffre (mid-March to Nov; ℡04.68.88.32.98; ❷), both in the quieter back streets. ✦ *El Llagut*, 18 avenue du Fontaulé (℡04.68.88.00.81, 🌐www.al-fanal.com; ❹; closed Nov & Dec), is a reasonably priced hotel on the seafront near the port, where many of the rooms have a balcony and sea-view. Another good option is the comfortable and well-equipped *Les Elmes* (℡04.68.88.03.12, 🌐www.hotel-des-elmes.com; ❼) perched on the cliffs at the north end of town, with a private beach. **Camping** is at *Les Bambous*, rue Jean Bouin (April to mid-Nov; ℡04.68.88.35.66, 🌐www.campinglesbambous .com), or the cheaper *Camping Municipal La Pinède* nearby, on route du Mas-Reig (April–Nov; ℡04.68.88.32.13, 🌐www.banyuls-sur-mer.com).

Banyuls has a good choice of **restaurants** specializing in fresh seafood. The most expensive, with starched tablecloths and live lobster tanks, are lined up opposite the seafront, but there are also several less pricey choices: the best is *Les Canadells*, just off the main boulevard at 4 avenue du Général de Gaulle, with delicious *menus* (from €12 at lunch, €16 at dinner; closed Sun eve & Mon Oct–March) and specializing in *zarzuela* and other fishy dishes. Nearby rue St-Pierre is home to a number of restaurants, including *Casa Miguel*, at no. 3, which has Spanish and Catalan specialities, and the livelier *La Paillotte*, at no.14. The best choice, however is *La Littorine* in *Les Elmes* hotel, where you can savour roast lobster, fire-grilled bass, or squid in its own ink (expect to spend around €35). The local morning **market** is held year-round on Sundays and Thursdays.

Maillol's tomb

The four-kilometre **hike** from Banyuls to **Maillol's tomb** and house makes a pleasant excursion up into the vine-clad Albères. Sculptor **Aristide Maillol** (1861–1944) was a Banyuls native famous for his fleshy nude sculptures. He is buried at his farm, La Baillaurie, now restored as the **Musée Maillol** (daily: May–Sept 10am–noon & 4–7pm; Oct–April 10am–noon & 2–5pm; €3.50), which contains his personal art collection, featuring works by Duchamp, Bonnard and Picasso. The artist's tomb is topped by his *La Pensée*. To get here, walk the length of avenue Général de Gaulle, until you pass under a bridge. Shortly afterwards, where the road curves around to the right, take the left-hand road, following the line of a river: signs from here point to the "Musée et Tombeau de Maillol". The round trip takes about two-and-a-half hours.

Cerbère

The Côte Vermeille comes to an end at **CERBÈRE**. The harbour is quite pretty and the mountain backdrop impressive, but the beach is negligible. Depending on the service, train passengers have to change either here or on the Spanish side of the border, at the much nicer **Port Bou**, where the rail line changes track size. In Cerbère, you can **stay** and **eat** at *La Dorade* on the harbour (☎04.68.88.41.93, ⓦwww.hotel-ladorade.com; ❸) or **camp** at the municipal *Camping Cap Peyrefite,* on the beach of the same name (☎04.68.88.41.17).

Travel details

Trains

The main rail-line runs along the coast via Perpignan. SNCF buses may run in lieu of trains on these lines; services are reduced on Sundays and holidays. The *Train Jaune* (see p.366) also runs a service up the Tech valley to Latour-de-Carole (linking with the Ariège valley rail line to Toulouse), and the *Train du Pays Cathare et du Fenouillèdes* (p.356) serves the Fenouillèdes to Axat.

Perpignan to: Argelès (10–14 daily; 20min); Banyuls-sur-Mer (10–14 daily; 30min); Carcassonne (15–18 daily; 1hr 15min–2hr); Cerbère (10–14 daily; 40min); Collioure (10–14 daily; 25min); Elne (10–14 daily; 10min); Ille-sur-Têt (6–8 daily; 22–35min); Montpellier (12 daily; 2hr 15min); Narbonne (11–16 daily; 36–45min); Nîmes (12 daily; 2hr 45min); Port-Vendres (10–14 daily; 25min); Prades (6–9 daily; 45min); Rivesaltes (13–16 daily; 10min); Salses (7–11 daily; 15min); Toulouse (15–18 daily; 2hr 30min–3hr 45min); Villefranche-de-Conflent (6–8 daily; 50min).
Villefranche-de-Conflent to: Font-Romeu (6–8 daily; 1hr 15min); Ille-sur-Têt (6–8 daily; 30min); Latour-de-Carol (6 daily; 2hr 45min); Mont-Louis (6–8 daily; 1hr); Perpignan (6–8 daily; 50min); Prades/Molitg (6–8 daily; 10min).

Buses

Many lines have no or reduced service on Saturdays, Sundays and holidays, and in summer months. Main bus lines follow the coast or run up the Fenouillèdes, Tech and Conflent valleys. The Roussillon Interplages shuttle runs frequently from Port-Bacarès to Collioure and back (July & Aug only), connecting the beach towns inbetween. See ⓦwww.cg66.fr for a route map and full schedules.

Argelès to: Céret (1–2 daily; 1hr 15min); Le Boulou (1–2 daily; 1hr); St-Génis (Tues & Thurs 1 daily; 50min).
Arles-sur-Tech to: Coustouges (1–3 daily; 35min); St-Laurent-de-Cerdans (1–3 daily; 30min).
Latour-de-Carol (Sat, Sun & hols 1 daily) to: Bourg-Madame (10min); Font-Romeu (25min); Formiguères (1hr 30min); Mont-Louis (55min); Puyvalador (1hr 35min).
Mont-Louis to: Font-Romeu (3 daily; 15min); Latour-de-Carol (3 daily; 1hr).
Perpignan to: Argelès (2–6 daily; 35min); Arles-sur-Tech (2–8 daily; 1hr); Banyuls-sur-Mer (6 daily; 1hr 15min); Cabestany (10 daily; 10min); Cerbère (2 daily; 1hr 35min); Céret (2–4 daily; 45min); Collioure (6 daily; 45min); Elne (10 daily; 20–45min); Font-Romeu (2–3 daily; 2hr 30min); Ille-sur-Tet (12 daily; 15–35min); Latour-de-Carol (2–3 daily; 3hr); Le Boulou (2–9 daily; 25–30min); Le Perthus (3 daily; 50min); Narbonne (1 daily; 2hr 30min); Passa (4 daily; 45min); Prades (8 daily; 1hr); Prats-de-Molló (2–4 daily; 1hr 55min); Rivesaltes (12 daily; 20min); Quillan (2 daily; 1hr 30min); St-Cyprien (4 daily; 15min); St-Génis (4 daily; 35min–1hr); St-Paul-le-Fenouillet (5 daily; 50min); Salses (8 daily; 15min–1hr 5min); Thuir (3–5 daily; 25min); Vernet (4 daily; 1hr 25min); Villefranche-de-Conflent (8 daily; 1hr 20min); Vinca (8 daily; 55min).
Prades to: Bourg-Madame (2 daily; 1h 55min); Casteil (3 daily; 20min); Mont-Louis (4 daily; 55min); Thuès (1 daily; 40min); Vernet-les-Bains (4 daily; 25min); Villefranche (1–12 daily; 15min); Vinca (1 Mon; 15min).
Rivesaltes to: Tautavel (3 daily; 30min).
St-Paul-le-Fenouillet to: Axat (2 daily; 30min); Quillan (2 daily; 45min).
Villefranche-de-Conflent to: Casteil (1 daily; 15min).

Contexts

Contexts

History

The two areas of Occitan Languedoc and Catalan Roussillon, in addition to their own cultural particularities, have strong historical differences. Languedoc was traditionally ruled by a native aristocracy, while Roussillon fell into the ambit of Catalonia, fated to become part of modern Spain. Even before they were integrated into the nation-state of France, though, their geographical proximity meant there were parallels and connections; each enjoyed its "golden age" in the Middle Ages, which may account for the nostalgia with which the inhabitants regard the period, and their shared borders saw considerable movement and contact.

Prehistory

The earliest traces of the human occupation of Languedoc and Roussillon date from the early **Palaeolithic era** (Stone Age): the cranial remains of the slight but upright *Homo erectus*, discovered in the 1970s at Tautavel, near Perpignan, date back nearly half a million years. These early ancestors, who do not appear to have harnessed fire, hunted with the aid of simple stone weapons and tools and lived off the abundant (and dangerous) fauna of the region, which included wolves, hippos, rhinos, wild sheep and goats and the ferocious cave bear, whose claw marks are still visible on cave walls in the region (for example at Limousis, in the Montagne Noire). As the evolutionary tree branched off, taller and smarter **Neanderthal** humans appeared, dominating the local scene during the mid-Palaeolithic era (approximately 150,000–35,000 BC). With a better tool-making capability than *Homo erectus*, the Neanderthals were able to pursue the mammoths and elephants of the Languedocian plain, and the remains of burial places scattered about the Pyrenean foothills dating from this time point to the beginnings of culture and religion.

It was not until the late Palaeolithic era that **modern humans** (*Homo sapiens*) came to monopolize the area, thriving especially in the Magdalenian period, some 14,000 years ago, which followed the last retreat of the glaciers. The earliest **cave paintings** of the Ariège valley (at Niaux and Mas d'Azil) date from this period and show the preoccupation of this early people with the hunt. In addition to cave art, they fashioned the small corpulent "Venus" statuettes, which are generally considered to relate to fertility rites.

With the invention of the harpoon, the development of fishing began to draw people towards the coasts of modern Roussillon. Nevertheless, the mid-altitude caves remained the favoured habitat into the Mesolothic and Neolithic (middle and new Stone Age) periods, which lasted here until about 1500 BC. Several important innovations occurred in the Neolithic era: **agriculture** and **animal husbandry** came into being in the fifth millennium BC, as did the use of grain-storage facilities. **Mining** and smelting were developed for the crude utilization of metals, such as copper, and better management of fire also permitted the manufacture of ceramics. Technical improvements encouraged specialization and this, in turn, trade, which seems to have first arisen among the lowland settlements of the Narbonnais plain. It was also in the last millennium of the Stone Age that the **dolmens** (megalithic henges) and **tumuli** (burial mounds) which dot the mid-level Pyrenees and Haut Languedoc appeared.

The Bronze Age

The Bronze Age in Languedoc and Roussillon was an era of great move-ment and change. Around 800 BC, the **Celts** arrived and began displacing the indigenous peoples, and an area roughly analogous with modern Languedoc – stretching from Nîmes in the east past Toulouse in the west – came under the hegemony of the Volcae, one of several large Celtic tribal groups who dominated the South of France. Meanwhile, **Phoenicians** and **Greeks** began to arrive on the region's shores. They set up outposts (such as Maguelone and Port-Vendres) and began to trade with natives, who lived for the most part in fortified hill-top towns now known as **oppida** (plural of the Latin *oppidum*, or "town"), like the settlement of Ensérune. As archeological finds have confirmed, the native tribes were not uncivilized "barbarians" as Romans were later wont to claim, but participants in complex, technologically capable societies linked to extensive trade networks. Their rich culture is evinced by the objects which have survived them: skilfully worked bronze weapons and jewellery. Although perhaps not comparable with contemporary civilizations of the eastern Mediterranean, they had their own diversified agricultural and craft-based economies and stratified social structures. Their one weakness was that they were not oriented towards the sea and so needed intermediaries like the Phoenicians to reach foreign markets.

The Romans

In the fourth century BC, the **Romans** embarked on a series of campaigns of conquest which brought the whole Iberian peninsula and the bulk of Greek possessions under its power and set it against the **Carthaginians**, heirs of Phoenicia in the western Mediterranean. The Romans were the ultimate victors, and the futile rumble of **Hannibal**'s elephants across the length of Languedoc in 218 BC presaged the beginning of a long colonial period in southern France. A few decades later the **Via Domitia**, the Rome–Cadiz superhighway, was built along the Languedoc coast, facilitating Roman military and economic expansion, and the Roman city of Narbo was founded. By about 70 BC all of what is now France south of Lyon and Toulouse constituted Narbonensian Gaul. With the completion of the conquest by **Julius Caesar** and his successor, the Emperor **Augustus**, the zone was elevated to the rank of an imperial province, and subdivided (in 27 BC), so that Narbonne became the capital of the lands from the Rhône to the Pyrenees.

Enjoying the benefits of *pax Romana*, the region enjoyed an easy prosperity under the first emperors. Trade flourished (wine was a big export item) and there were major settlements at Baeterra (Béziers) and Nemausus (Nîmes). Nîmes became the region's most important city in the mid-second-century under Antoninus Pius – an emperor who lavished favours on his home town. During this period, Roman organizational infrastructure and slave labour permitted the elaboration of architectural projects of a scale and complexity which were not to be duplicated for fifteen hundred years. This is particularly true in the case of public civic architecture, such as Nîmes' huge amphitheatre, **Les Arènes**, the nearby aqueduct, the **Pont du Gard**, and the **bridges** at Sommières and Ambrussum. Religious buildings, the finest surviving example of which is Nîmes' **Maison Carrée**, were based on Greek styles – temples usually consisting of a *cella* or inner sanctum (the abode of the god), ringed by a colonnade of columns which were topped by decorative capitals. Less grandiose remains of civic and residential structures can be found at Loupian and Ensérune, along the length of the Via Domitia. The cities and settlements of Roman Languedoc-Roussillon have yielded a wealth of intricate mosaics and Roman-style civic and religious statuary.

But there were rocky times ahead for the empire, as the expansion on which its prosperity had depended slowed. Domestic economic crises were compounded by the growing threat of neighbouring powers: Persia in the east, and "barbarians" in North Africa and northwest Europe. While the frontiers under attack by **Franks** and **Goths** were far from Languedoc, the disruption of the empire's stability had economic repercussions which reached Gallia-Narbonensis. The growing dissatisfaction and malaise in the empire encouraged a certain trend towards new religions such as the Mithras cult and **Christianity**, which spread rapidly through urban Languedoc. The latter was seen as a threat to the imperial order and a series of emperors set about trying to quash it. The fiercest persecutions, which saw Christians submitted to all manner of brutal public tortures and executions, were carried out under Valerian and Diocletian between 257 and 311 – many of the area's martyred saints date from this era.

When **Constantine the Great** became sole emperor in 324, he proclaimed Christianity a tolerated religion and it quickly took hold in the towns and cities of Languedoc. With the capital of the empire now in far-off Constantinople, the bishops, who were appointed in each Roman town after 391, helped hold together the decaying fabric of administration. In the new, contracting Christianized empire, Nîmes and Narbonne waned, as Roman cities in Provence, like Arles, came to the forefront. But great changes were afoot, and as central power declined, people left the cities, taking refuge in smaller fortified towns and villas, and frequently trading off their liberty for the protection of a powerful patron. Imperial policy in the east was to deflect the waves of semi-nomadic steppe peoples westward, a tactic which saved the core of the empire, but brought about its disappearance in the west.

After the Romans

In the fifth century wave after wave of these small but aggressive invading bands passed through Languedoc and Roussillon: first the Suevi, then the Vandals and finally the **Visigoths**. It was the last of these who set up a durable kingdom, which in its greatest extent covered the southwest of France and most of Iberia. Their first capital was **Tolosa** – modern Toulouse – and they initially ruled, in name, as Roman imperial governors. At this time, however, a rival group, the **Franks**, had coalesced in the Low Countries and, led by King Clovis (482–511), drove southwards, incorporating Toulouse into their Kingdom of Aquitaine. Most of Languedoc and Roussillon, however, known then as **Septimania** (either after its seven great cities: Narbonne, Agde, Béziers, Maguelone, Lodève, Nîmes and Uzès, or after the Roman Seventh Legion which was garrisoned in the area), remained under the Visigoths.

The weak and conflictive Visigothic kingdom was dealt a deathblow by **Muslim armies**, which arrived in Iberia around 711. Wiping out the Spanish Visigothic nobility in a single battle, they quickly conquered most of modern

Spain and Portugal, and small raiding parties crossed the Pyrenees, taking Toulouse and Septimania in the 720s. The most northern of these groups was turned back near Poitiers by Charles Martel in 732. Numerically too few to hang onto such an extensive area, the Muslims occupied the towns, exacting tribute and using them as raiding bases. In the years that followed the battle of Poitiers, the Muslims were turned out of Toulouse, Carcassonne and eventually their coastal enclaves as one by one these fell to the Franks; it was to prevent their return that Martel destroyed the town of Maguelone (see p.275). This long campaign was carried out under the leadership of **Pepin the Short**, the first Carolingian king (751–68), and it was his successor, **Charlemagne** (Charles the Great), who pushed the Muslims back over the Pyrenees. Languedoc was absorbed into the **Frankish Empire** and Roussillon became part of the semi-autonomous frontier region known as the **Spanish Marches**. After the decline of Roman power in the west, the empire continued in the east, but despite the fact that Constantinople was now its capital, its rulers continued to bear the title "Emperor of Rome". During Charlemagne's era, it so happened that it was a woman, Irene, who was in power in Constantinople; seeing an opportunity to enhance his prestige – given that no one actually held the title of "Emperor" – Charlemagne journeyed to Rome and had the pope crown him as "Holy Roman Emperor" in 800. Thus, his dominions, which covered almost all of western Europe, came to be known as the **Holy Roman Empire**, and the papacy, which up till then had been little more than an ordinary bishopric, gained justification for its later claims to be the power which could (or not) crown emperors.

The counts and feudalism

Despite his centralizing policies, Charlemagne followed Germanic custom, separating his kingdom among his heirs, and Languedoc fell into the **Kingdom of the Western Franks**, more or less contiguous with modern France. When its second king, Louis the Stammerer, died heirless in 879, the kingdom rapidly disintegrated, leaving power in the hands of local **counts**, although nominally Charlemagne's other descendants held the highest authority. Among the local nobility, one family, the "**Raymonds**" or "dynasty of St-Gilles", eventually came to dominate. They had ruled Toulouse since 840, thanks to a grant by Pepin II, and by the late 900s, they were to all intents and purposes independent rulers. As such, they began to expand, absorbing neighbouring territories, such as Albi, or co-opting other, lesser noble lines, such as the **Trencavels** of Carcassonne, as vassals. **Raymond IV** ruled a realm which stretched from Toulouse to the banks of the Rhône; it was he who adopted the surname of "St-Gilles", in honour of his favourite possession. Meanwhile, the most powerful lord of the Spanish March, **Guifré el Pelós** ("Wilfred the Hairy"), Count of the Cerdagne, Girona and Barcelona, was granted independence from the empire. Roussillon, then dominated by Elne, came under his power; it is at this point that Languedoc and Roussillon's histories as separate regions begin, and over the course of the centuries that followed their paths would be linked, but not united again until Louis XIV's formal annexation of Roussillon in the 1600s.

In these early medieval centuries, what little industry and urban life existed under the Romans all but disappeared. Western Europe became overwhelmingly agrarian, developing an economy of near subsistence in which the noble class siphoned off the meagre surplus and provided military protection to the masses. Local magnates depended on military strength to maintain their power and protect their subjects, obtaining warriors by granting lands in exchange for loyalty, and **feudal** structures developed. Religion too was a largely private and local affair: noble lords built churches and monasteries and put them under the charge of their friends and relatives, who lived comfortably off the income from these posts. The common folk continued to depend as much on traditional pre-Christian beliefs and magic – just as well, since most local priests knew no more than a smattering of Church Latin and were not particularly exemplary in their moral life. Learned culture too all but vanished with the disappearance of towns, and was maintained only by the monks who lived in isolated and introspective communities – fortresses of faith, hidden in isolated valleys and on remote mountainsides.

Twelfth-century revival

In the twelfth century the picture began to change rapidly. A shift away from subsistence, possibly as the result of climatic change and aided by improvements in agricultural technology, allowed the population to grow, while under the counts the region began to enjoy a stability which stimulated **trade** and **industry**. People started to move around Europe looking for better opportunities; towns expanded, shaking Toulouse and the cities of Septimania back to life. The agrarian social structures which had developed in the previous period were not suitable to town life, and the counts, anxious to promote economic growth, recognized that by extending liberties and privileges to the townsfolk, their own position could be improved. Oligarchic **town councils**, such as the **Capitolo** in Toulouse, were formed, sharing in or taking over urban administration and further stimulating growth.

Changes were afoot in the Church as well: the papacy was in the process of becoming a geopolitical power, initiating a level of bureaucracy and organization which would give it control of the resources and policies of local churches – traditionally the turf of the nobles. Some efforts were made to improve the priesthood too, to ensure that priests were educated and lived, at least in appearance, morally upright lives. On the popular level, **pilgrimage** played an important role, carrying ordinary believers across Europe, to Rome or Santiago de Compostela; along the way they visited local churches such as that at St-Gilles and came into contact with a wider Christian world. A wave of reformation also swept over the **monasteries**, where the degenerate and locally independent Benedictines were replaced by new, pious and strict orders, most importantly the Cistercians, who were controlled by a strong central organization.

With all of this new wealth, secular and religious culture began to revive. Great churches were raised in the towns, and old cathedrals were replaced by new, more grandiose and elaborate structures. The courts of the counts' palaces became the focus of a new culture as well, one which sought refinement in the **courtly traditions** of elaborate manners, rich clothes and imported luxuries. The most visible manifestation of this new culture was the tradition of courtly love and the **troubadours**. These singing poets – the first of whom is said to have been Guilhem de Peitieu, count of Poitiers and father of Eleanor of Aquitaine, Queen of France and, later, England – composed odes of yearning, unrequited love to anonymous "dark ladies", and satirical barbs aimed at local nobles. Their language of choice was not Latin, which had previously been the only voice of culture, but the local vernaculars, Occitan and Catalan. It was also in this era that the rites and rituals associated with feudalism, such as heraldry and the tournament, began to be formalized – precisely when the feudal world began to decline.

However, with this period of revival came a greater demand for fulfilment, directed at the Church from just about every corner. The newly wealthy and increasingly literate craftsmen, the **burghers**, who had no role to play in the warrior-aristocratic culture of the court, wanted a level of political power and social prestige which reflected their economic standing and, better educated than before, began to look for more satisfying theological answers than the still feudal-oriented Church could provide. Town life generated new social problems, particularly among the urban poor, which the Church – effectively a social welfare organization in the countryside – was not equipped to address. The peasants too were dissatisfied; although increasingly interested in Christianity, a shortage of priests meant they were frustrated by a lack of pastoral care. In short, the Church was seen as **corrupt** by everyone but the nobility, a situation aggravated by the taxes which people were forced to pay to support it. In addition, Latin, once widely spoken, was the only accepted sacred language – preserving the mystery of the Church, but now acting to cut off the faith and Scripture from the common folk.

Although their religious consciousness was high – local nobles, such as the Crusader Raymond of St-Gilles, distinguished themselves by reclaiming the Holy Land from the Muslim "infidels" – the upper classes in Languedoc began to find themselves turning against the Church too, but for a different reason. The nobility considered it their natural privilege to control local institutions, including bishoprics, parishes and monasteries and, unconcerned by the theological preferences of their subjects as long as they continued to pay their taxes, resented papal expansionism as a threat to their own power.

In the meantime, neighbouring Roussillon, though it went through most of the same social and economic processes as Languedoc, followed a distinctive political and religious course. In the centuries following Guifré el Pelós, his descendants, the **counts of Barcelona**, had been struggling to gain supremacy over their various rival counts in Catalonia, who did not want to recognize them as overlords. They were aided in this campaign in 1142 when Ramon Berenguer IV married the princess of Aragón, obtaining the title of King of Aragón for his heirs. Thus Barcelona became the capital of a multinational monarchy and its rulers, the count-kings, were to govern one of the great powers of the medieval Mediterranean. Linked by ties of marriage to noble houses in Languedoc and further east in Provence, they angled for political expansion, and for a time their holdings included Montpellier and various parts east of the Rhône. Indeed, the counts of Toulouse became their vassals – although this was merely a formality, amounting more to a pact of mutual assistance than a recognition of the count-kings' authority.

Catharism and the Albigensian Crusades

In the climate of dissatisfaction with the Church, popular **heresies** began to spring up, led by men who preached to the people in their own language and led lives of austerity and poverty, in emulation of the Apostles and in contrast to the wealthy and aloof Catholic clergy. The Church tried at first to quash the problem with force, but then, co-opting the impulses which drove the heretics, licensed two new groups, the Dominican and Franciscan preaching friars who – in contrast to the isolated monks – were to minister and preach among the common people. But the damage had already been done, and the most successful of the new heresies, **Catharism** (see *The Land of the Cathars* colour section), had become firmly entrenched. This doctrine was a variant on ancient Middle Eastern beliefs combined with Christianity, a dualistic creed which portrayed the material world as evil and the spiritual world as good. It resonated among the common folk (who appreciated its populism) and nobles (who wanted to set themselves apart from the influence of Rome and its northern French political allies), and a shadow counter-Church began to organize itself, holding its first Council at St-Félix-de-Lauragais in 1167. In most of the major towns of Languedoc, and the countryside around Toulouse and south of the Aude, this new Church gained a strong presence. Here, the nobility, including the counts of Toulouse, the Trencavels of Carcassonne and a whole array of minor barons, remained Catholic themselves, but gave free reign to Cathar preachers to spread their religious message. As Roussillon did not develop an urban society as quickly as Languedoc and the count-kings had a more favourable political attitude to the papacy, Catharism was discouraged from gaining a strong hold here. Preachers and refugees did arrive in Catalan lands, but they could not live openly in their faith, for fear of persecution.

By the end of the 1100s the Catholic Church had become a powerful corporation, and it was not about to brook the loss of Languedoc to the heretic Cathars – or **Albigensians**, as they are commonly known. When persuasion failed to convert the heretics or influence the Cathar-protecting lords of Languedoc, and excommunication had little effect, the papacy turned to military force. Although it hardly had a formal army, the papacy could count on the support of powerful multinational monastic organizations such as the Cistercian Order, whose headquarters, Cîteaux, was in northern France, and which was dominated by noble families from the north. These same families, which had been united under the Capetian kings of France, began to look hungrily at the extensive but fragmented lands of the counts to the south. Papal efforts to bring the Cathars back into the fold began as early as 1150, and in 1204 **Raymond VI** of Toulouse was excommunicated for refusing to persecute his Cathar subjects. However, the Albigensians and their lords would not cave in – the papal legate Pierre de Castelnau was murdered at a parley in 1208 – and **Pope Innocent III** called a Crusade, providing the northern nobles with the ideological justification to wage war on Languedoc. They were joined by knights from across Christendom, drawn by the allure of religious redemption and loot.

The campaign was led initially by **Arnaud Amaury**, abbot of Cîteaux, whose campaigns carried him rapidly across the littoral from Nîmes, which gave up without a fight, to Béziers. Here, faced by the refusal of the town's Catholics to give up their Cathar neighbours, he ordered the wholesale slaughter of the town's occupants; some 20,000 are said to have perished.

At about this time, the ageing Crusader **Simon de Montfort** set his sights on the Cathar lands and, taking up leadership of military operation, embarked on a campaign marked by its terror and efficiency. Carcassonne was taken, and with it **Count Raymond VI**; thereafter Cathar towns and fortresses were besieged one by one, including Lastours, Minerve, Hautpoul, Lavaur, Termes and Puivert. Almost without exception they fell or surrendered, and the unfortunate defenders were executed or mutilated and sent on as blunt warning to the next victims;

the only survivors were those on the inaccessible southern border: Quérigut, Peyrepertuse and Montségur.

After a brief exile in England, **Raymond VII** returned to lead a counter-attack, calling on the aid of various allies, including his liege-lord **Pere the Catholic**, Count-King of Catalonia-Aragón. Fresh from a decisive victory against Spanish Muslims at Las Navas de Tolosa, Pere went into the field at Muret (14km south of Toulouse) in 1213, but was singled out and killed by de Montfort's men, dealing a grievous blow to Raymond's forces.

It took five more years of fighting to turn the tide against the northern forces, who were deprived of their leader de Montfort (who had assumed the title of Count of Toulouse), when his head was smashed in by a missile outside the walls of Toulouse. His son Arnaud attempted to carry on the campaign, but could not sustain his position and returned to his lands in the north, carrying with him his father's dead body and broken dreams. After this long drawn-out battle, Raymond had no choice but to make **peace** with the papacy in order to recover his lands, reaffirming his Catholicism and recovering his scarred and battered territories. These he began immediately to fortify, founding strategic strongholds such as Cordes-sur-Ciel.

However, despite Raymond's concessions and preparations, **Occitan independence** was not to last. By the mid-1220s the French king, **Louis VIII**, swelled by victories over the English Crown, turned his own sights south, proclaiming a fresh Crusade against the Occitan Cathars, who continued to live discreetly in Raymond's lands, or openly under the defiant and unconquered barons of the south. This time the exhausted forces of the counts and local nobility could not respond, and after a brief campaign much of Languedoc came under the direct power of the king of France. Louis VIII's aggressive policy was followed up by his heir, Louis IX (later St Louis), who came to the throne in 1226 and finished off the job. With the counts out of the way, the papacy sent in the **Inquisition**, led by the Dominican Order. Their job was to investigate and root out heretics, employing torture if necessary, and urging them to recant before turning them over to the king's forces to execute. Needless to say, they were not popular among the local citizenry, and there was some relief when a band of renegade Cathars sallied out of their stronghold at Montségur in 1242 to **massacre** a band of Inquisitors at Avignonet-Lauragais. The royal reaction was immediate: an army of six thousand was assembled and laid siege to the fortress in 1243. Eight months later, when it fell, the garrison of two hundred was burnt alive. Subsequent mopping-up operations finished with the surrenders of Puilaurens and Quéribus in 1256. Catharism had disappeared as a political force and, confined to secrecy and isolation, was hunted into extinction over the next century.

But royal policy was not wholly destructive in Languedoc, as its aim was not to lay waste to the region but to extinguish possible sources of rebellion and resistance. From the time of de Montfort's death, the kings had worked to re-habilitate the area, particularly through the founding of royal **bastides**, such as Revel and Réalmont. These planned and usually fortified towns were set up by royal charter. Ruled by a council, they answered directly to the king rather than to an intermediary noble, and were given privileges such as the right to hold a market. Thus, they strengthened the royal position and, with their liberties and self-determination, helped to boost the economy.

On the fringes of Languedoc, mountainous **Foix**, like Toulouse, had been an independent county since about the time of the Carolingian disintegration. Over the following centuries, it remained isolated, even more than Roussillon, from the modernizing trends which were shaping Languedoc. That said, the counts of Foix were sworn enemies of the French Crown and allied themselves with the Raymonds during the Albigensian Crusade; in the campaigns that followed, the county managed to escape more or less unscathed, and when the French Crown threatened in the 1270s, the ruling house eluded their control by forging a marriage alliance with the neighbouring kingdom of Béarn.

Except for the loss in battle of Count-King Pere, **Roussillon**, too, all but escaped the effects of the Albigensian Crusades. The death of Pere, and the period of uncertainty that followed, when his 5-year-old son, Jaume, was made king, entailed the end of any Catalan-Aragonese pretensions in Provence, so the French Crown had a long breathing period in which to consolidate its power there. Roussillon, however, remained for the moment firmly in the Catalan-Aragonese ambit, and its nobility was drawn towards the campaigns of conquest which the count-kings carried out against their Muslim neighbours (Valencia, Mallorca and Menorca), and Sardinia and Sicily. When **Jaume the Conqueror** died after a 63-year reign, he divided his kingdom between his elder son Pere (who received the mainland holdings south of the Pyrenees) and Jaume, who became **king of Mallorca** and count of Roussillon and Montpellier. Perpignan served as his mainland capital. The kings of Mallorca allied with the French against their Barcelona-based rivals, and in the 1280s Roussillon served as the springboard for the French invasion of Catalonia, launched in retribution for Catalan seizure of French-ruled Sicily.

The Hundred Years' War

Under **Philip le Bel** (1285–1314), France became a superpower. The astute king managed his treasury well, disbanded and appropriated the funds of the wealthy Knights Templar and brought the papacy under his ominous protection in Avignon.

But royal domination of Languedoc brought only short-lived peace and prosperity to the region. Philip died without a male heir, and Edward III of England, who had married Philip's daughter, claimed the throne. Edward's family, the Plantagenets, were French in origin, and the language and culture of their court were northern French, but the prospect of Edward taking the throne was highly undesirable to a large section of the French nobility, who stood to see themselves marginalized by such a turn of events. So they invoked the ancient French Salic Law, which forbade succession to the throne through the female line, and resisted the English claim. These were the circumstances which provoked the series of conflicts which came to be known as the **Hundred Years' War** – essentially a struggle between two French royal houses.

England took the early advantage, defeating the French at Crécy in 1346 and capturing the French king shortly afterwards. Meanwhile, the king's son, Edward, Prince of Wales (known as the **Black Prince**), was unleashed on Aquitaine and ravaged the Aude valley. These military campaigns coincided with a series of disasters, including **crop failures**, the arrival of the **Black Death** and the Jacquerie peasant uprising. In 1360, a **truce** was called and part of western Languedoc remained under English control until nine years later, when **Charles V** began a campaign which all but expelled the English from France.

Unfortunately, Charles' successor, **Charles VI**, was considered mentally unfit to rule, and a struggle ensued between the dukes of Burgundy and Orléans, who had been entrusted with the care of the realm. The English intervened on the side of the Burgundians, against the Duke of Orléans and his Armagnac allies, and began to reconquer the country. After a series of defeats, including Agincourt in 1415, all seemed lost for the French Crown. It was then that the peasant girl **Joan of Arc** appeared on the scene, and helped to turn the tide against the invaders, claiming divine guidance and rallying the French forces in a campaign to push the English off the mainland. Five years later, **Charles VII** entered Toulouse in triumph; a French king was once again master of Languedoc, and although the reconquest of the former royal territories dragged out over the length of the fifteenth century, France emerged from the struggle as a unified, powerful national kingdom.

In this protracted period of **crisis**, the people of Languedoc coped as best they could. Population decreased, agriculture suffered and traditional industries, such as leather-working, which accounted for the prosperity of the Tarn region, were almost extinguished. However, in the mid-fifteenth century it was discovered that a local plant, **woad**, could be made to yield a fine blue dye, *pastel*, a high-priced luxury commodity much in demand by the fabric industry of the day, thus provoking an economic renaissance which lasted for over a century. Toulouse, still ruled over by a council of burghers, took the lead in this industry. Fortunes were made, fine palaces were raised, and the city's famous university was founded, turning Toulouse into a centre of culture. On the Occitan coast, Montpellier (which had been bought by the French Crown in 1349) was also driven by the growing textile industry and set up its own prestigious university.

As had happened with the Albigensian Crusade, Catalonia was not involved directly in the Hundred Years' War, but it did have to contend with France's relentless efforts to chip away at its holdings north of the Pyrenees, Cerdanya and Rosilló (the **Cerdagne** and **Roussillon**), and through the fourteenth and fifteenth centuries, they were shifted back and forth between the two powers. In 1462, when **Louis XI** mounted a military campaign against Roussillon – seizing it in response to the Catalan-Aragonese capture of French-dominated Naples – Catalonia was on the verge of a major realignment. The marriage of Ferran (Ferdinand) of Aragón and Isabel of Castile in 1469 laid the foundations for the creation of the Kingdom of Spain, and the ultimate submission of Catalonia and its dependencies to Madrid; it thus became a secondary concern, and Roussillon was set further on the periphery.

The rise of Protestantism and the Wars of Religion

Despite the peace which came with re-establishment of a strong monarchy in France under **François I** (1515–47), there was much dissatisfaction in Languedoc and Roussillon. This resentment took two forms: that towards the Church on the part of the people, and that towards the Crown and the northern nobility on the part of local lords and magnates. As had happened in the Cathar period, the interests of these two groups coincided, and even more so after 1483, when the Crown gained direct control over the Church in France. So social and political discontent was once again voiced on religious terms – this time the revolutionary movement was **Protestantism**.

The new faith first arrived in Haut Languedoc close on the heels of **Martin Luther**'s defiance of Church authority in 1519. However, French Protestantism, or the **Huguenot** movement (named after an obscure Swiss political event), tended to follow the teachings of **John Calvin** (Jean Cauvin), which had a clearer political message. Calvin had studied theology at the conservative University of Paris and had been swept up in the wave of reforming theology which very quickly provoked a clampdown by the religious and royal authorities. He fled into exile in Geneva, which became a hotbed for the Protestant creed that he formulated. His beliefs focused on the omnipotence of God and predestination, denying hierarchies and earthly elites and concentrating on hard work and pastoralism – a recipe for success among the artisanal classes – and it spread like wildfire in Paris and through Occitania.

By 1559, **Calvinism** was established as a religion and organization in France, and had the support of some of the kingdom's greatest noble houses, despite the persecution which had been carried out by François I's son Henri II. When Henri died (in an accident allegedly presaged by Nostradamus), the succession of two weak child-kings gave the rival **noble factions** led by the Protestant Bourbons and the Catholic Guises the opportunity to battle for control of the realm. Forty years of bloody and relentless civil war followed, of which the most notorious episode is the **St Bartholemew's Day massacre** of 1572, in which the Protestant elite, who had come to Paris for a royal wedding, were ambushed. A nationwide campaign against Protestants ensued, during which some 20,000 were killed. The violence was not all one-sided, however: the Calvinists committed atrocities as well, among them the murder of Nîmes' Catholic clergy in the **Michelade massacre** (1567).

The wars were finally concluded by the victory of Henri, King of Béarn (or Navarre, and a successor of Gaston Fébus of Foix), the leader of the Protestant faction. It was, however, politically impossible for him to become king as a Huguenot, so having decided that "Paris is worth a Mass", he converted and was crowned as **Henri IV** of France in 1593. Thanks to his accession, Foix was incorporated into the French realm. Six years later, he proclaimed the **Edict of Nantes**, which granted political and religious freedom to the Hugenots and the right to maintain certain fortified strongholds.

Although most of Languedoc had been ruled by the Catholic Guises, its population was strongly Protestant. Castres became a "protected zone" for Huguenots, and home to one of the four **courts** empowered to mediate legal disputes between Catholics and Protestants. In Nîmes, some three quarters of the population converted to Calvinism, while Montpellier was home to the Protestant Theological Institute. In the east, most of the towns – mainly herding and textile centres – were firmly Huguenot but, despite regional imbalances, the new pluralistic French society seemed to function well.

The Age of Absolutism

The liberal vision of Henri IV was not to last, however. When he was assassinated by a Catholic reactionary, his year-old son **Louis XIII** came to the throne under the strict control of his staunchly Catholic mother, Marie de Medici. In 1624, that supreme Machiavellian **Cardinal Richelieu** managed to wrest control from the queen. Richelieu made it his mission to establish France as an absolutist Catholic state, and for almost two decades he was the sole power behind the Crown. He immediately set about stripping the towns and cities of their defensive walls (to prevent revolt) and then began reducing Protestant strongholds. He also adopted an aggressive foreign policy, attacking France's neighbours and taking Roussillon. But his heavy-handedness provoked reaction at home. In 1622, the Protestant Duke of Rohan raised a **revolt** in the Cévennes (just north of Hérault) and although after seven years of fighting he was forced to make a settlement with Richelieu which stripped the Huguenots of political power, he maintained their freedom to worship.

Heavily Protestant Languedoc was not pacified, however, and shortly thereafter its royal governor, **Henri de Montmorency**, raised a revolt against Richelieu which spanned the region from Nîmes to Toulouse. He was no match for the cardinal, who defeated him in battle at Castelnaudary in 1632 and led him off to be beheaded on the place du Capitoule in Toulouse. The vindictive Richelieu then exacted revenge on Henri's heirs by transferring the title of First Duchy of France from the house of Montmorency to the loyally Catholic dukes of Uzès.

In 1643, the "Sun King" and supreme absolutist **Louis XIV** came to the throne. Continuing the centralizing policies initiated by Richelieu, he hamstrung the French nobility by obliging them to take up residence at his palace in Versailles and to participate in its expensive and regimented court life. His megalomaniac tendencies ("I am the state") led him to embark on a series of costly and ultimately disastrous military adventures, the successful episodes of which are recorded on the Roman-style monuments, such as the equestrian statue and triumphal arch of Montpellier, which he erected to commemorate his grandeur. He waged **war** in Flanders, Germany and Spain, managing to secure the permanent annexation of the Cerdagne and Roussillon with the **Treaty of the Pyrenees** in 1659.

The able management of his successive prime ministers, Mazarin and Colbert, managed to preserve the kingdom from financial ruin, and it was Colbert who gave the green light to Riquet's visionary project of linking the Atlantic and Mediterranean by canal. The main channel of the **Canal du Midi**, which stretched from Toulouse to Agde, was opened in 1666, sparking an economic recovery in the region, which had languished in depression since the wane in demand for the local pastel dye (thanks to the discovery of cheaper alternatives in the Indies); the canal allowed locally grown grain to be shipped to distant markets. But on the whole, Louis' reign was not a happy one for Languedoc and Roussillon. In 1674, the **Catalans** rose up against French rule, which they found even more oppressive than that of the Spanish Hapsburgs,

Signing of the Treaty of the Pyrenees, 1659

against whom they had risen a generation earlier. The **uprising** was brutally crushed, and its leaders imprisoned and executed in Perpignan.

A decade later, Louis moved against the Protestants by issuing a **Revocation of the Edict of Nantes** (1685), which deprived the Huguenots of their rights and outlawed their religion. Half a million Protestants chose to flee the country, including many merchants and textile workers, dealing a grievous blow to the industry on which the prosperity of eastern Languedoc depended. Those who remained were subjected to **oppression**; they were spied on and hounded, forced to carry on their services in secret and brook the humiliation of having soldiers billeted in their homes. Intransigent Protestants were imprisoned, among them Marie Durand, locked up for over thirty years in a tower in Aigues-Mortes. Some feigned conversion, some were deported to the colonies, and others fled to the "desert" – the wild and isolated hills of the Cévennes. It was here that they rose again in protest, in what is known as the **Camisard revolt**. The spark came in July 1702 when the parish priest of Chayla arrested and detained a small group of fugitive Protestants. A group of villagers stormed the castle to free them and in the course of the struggle the priest was killed. Knowing that retribution would be swift and cruel, Protestants across the Cévennes (mostly refugees from Languedoc proper) began a guerrilla war which pitted their forces, numbering between three and five thousand, against some 30,000 royal troops. The shirts they wore as a sign of recognition earned them the popular name of Camisards (from *chemise*, French for "shirt"). Battles raged across the region, with one of the greatest confrontations taking place at **St-Hippolyte**. The guerrillas and civilian population took refuge where they could, hiding in the remote hills or in caverns, like the Grotte des Demoiselles, south of Ganges.

In the course of the struggle two leaders emerged: the aristocratic **Jean Cavalier**, and the commoner **Roland**. Unable to conclude the struggle militarily, the French commander Villars began to negotiate with Cavalier at Nîmes, offering him the rank of colonel, command of a Protestant legion which would fight for the French abroad, and a hefty annual salary in exchange for submission. Cavalier accepted, greatly undermining the uprising. The former leader left France and served the English, eventually being named governor of Jersey. Roland continued the struggle, but later the same year was killed in battle, bringing an end to the revolt.

In the century or so before the Camisards episode, Languedoc had been tamed into discontented submission by France, ruled by the princes of Conti, members of the ruling Bourbon family, since the defeat of Montmorency. Pézenas, which had been the region's capital since the 1450s, became a paler southern Versailles, especially in the 1650s when **Armand de Bourbon** lavished his patronage on the town, playing host for a time to the playwright Molière and his company.

The absorption of Roussillon, while it aggrandized France, struck a blow against the towns of the Aude valley, which up until then had enjoyed a trade-based prosperity thanks to their position on the Spanish frontier. As part of Madrid's empire, in which Church institutions like the Inquisition kept a very tight lid on any potential sources of dissent or heterodoxy, Protestantism was basically unknown in Roussillon during its efflorescence, and by the time of the region's annexation, it was virtually a spent force.

The Revolution

Languedoc and Roussillon were not the only areas which chafed against the Sun King's absolutism. As the **economic crisis** deepened, taxes were driven up, forcing the masses of the kingdom, the *sans-culottes* ("trouserless"), into an ever more desperate state of poverty. A series of bad harvests compounded the problem, and indebted smallholders had their lands repossessed and were reduced to penury and near servitude. In order to gather the revenue which was necessary to maintain the court, fund expensive military adventures and service the spiralling national debt, the ruling class resorted to **tax-farming**. Speculators paid the Crown a set sum upfront and were then free to extract as much as they could from the area under their control. This excluded most of the nobility, many of whom enjoyed hereditary exemptions, and the largest single land-holder, the Church, which paid no royal taxes and continued to collect its own. At the same time, the Crown's growing obsession with control bred a fear of rebellion, which became self-fulfilling. Law was completely subverted to royal authority, and suspected troublemakers were imprisoned indefinitely without charges, by writ of the feared letters of cachet, or orders of detention.

These **dictatorial** tendencies worsened over the course of the eighteenth century, as Louis XIV's successors continued his absolutist style of ruling and his disastrous policy of foreign intervention. **Louis XV** (1715–74) carried France into the Polish and Austrian Wars of Succession and the Seven Years' War, as a result of which the kingdom lost all of its colonies. Ironically, the king also encouraged the extraordinary literary and philosophical blossoming, in which Voltaire and Rousseau figured, among others, and which laid the ideological foundations for the Revolution which was shortly to follow.

Poor grain harvests continued after Louis XV's death in 1774, provoking riots and unrest. Royal finance ministers attempted to institute reforms, but to little avail. In Languedoc, the new king Louis XVI's conciliatory policies were chiefly noted in the form of the **Edict of Toleration** (1787), which was aimed at diffusing the rebelliousness of the Protestants by restoring their rights and liberties. The situation was such that the king was forced in 1789 to summon the Estates General (the equivalent of parliament) for the first time in nearly two centuries. The newly constituted Third Estate, made up of commoners, who for the first time joined the nobility and clergy in government, called for the formation of a National Assembly.

When in the months that followed the country rose in **revolution**, Languedoc and Roussillon were solidly Jacobin (revolutionary). Even Montpellier, at that time a wealthy bastion of Catholicism and cotton lords, could not resist. In 1791, the French Republic was declared and as southern troop levies marched towards the capital, a young medical student from Montpellier composed the "War Song of the Army of the Rhine", better known as **La Marseillaise**, which was adopted eventually as the national anthem. The Revolution was a focus for the discontentment of diverse groups in the south: the Protestants, the poor, the Occitans and the local magnates, all of whom had a bone to pick with Paris or the monarchy. But although the monarchy fell, Paris persevered, emerging as the capital of a sharply centralized and thoroughly French state.

The short and bloody revolutionary experiment was centred in Paris, and Languedoc felt its influence chiefly in the administrative novelties which were introduced, the most durable of which was the division of the region (as with the rest of the country) into administrative **départements**. The rationalist (and centralist) policies of the new government ensured a break with historical traditions in defining these areas. They were based on geography, for the most part on the major river valleys. Roussillon became the culturally neutral Pyrénées-Orientales.

The Napoleonic era and the nineteenth-century republics

The rise of revolutionary France did not, however, bring about a change in foreign policy, which remained aggressive. The **armies** of the Republic, among whose leaders figured a young **Napoleon Bonaparte**, lashed out against their neighbours on all sides. Back at home, power had devolved to a five-member **Directory**, whose heavy-handed governance was met with growing resentment by the populace. When Bonaparte returned from his defeat by the British in Egypt, he set a coup d'état in motion, which saw him elevated initially, in 1799, to First Consul, and subsequently, to **Emperor**. His campaign of European domination brought him up against practically every other power in Europe and, after initial successes in Germany and Spain, his campaign in Russia brought about the decimation of his Grand Army and his ultimate ruin.

Although most of the Napoleonic Wars took place on foreign soil, Languedoc was to feel the sting of the emperor's defeat. **Wellington**'s British expeditionary force, which had been sent to aid Spain and Portugal, pushed its way across the peninsula and dealt the French a severe defeat at Toulouse in 1814.

For the next forty years France and Languedoc returned to monarchy, with the reigns first of the Bourbon **Louis XVIII** (1814–24) and **Charles X** (1824–30), and then **Louis-Philippe** (1830–48) of the house of Orléans. The Bourbons, who had obviously learnt nothing from previous experience, immediately embarked on a heavy-handed Catholic-oriented policy, and were brought down by popular revolution in 1830. The throne was then taken by Louis-Philippe, the candidate of the middle-class elite, a commercial nobility no less despised than their aristocratic forebears. He was unseated in the **revolution of 1848**, European socialism's *annus mirabilis*, which saw uprisings in capitals across the continent. But the Second Republic quickly gave way to the **Second Empire**, when Bonaparte's crafty nephew gained the throne as **Napoleon III** in 1852. Protests followed his seizure of power, such as the one in Béziers, where troops opened fire on a crowd of republican demonstrators led by the town mayor. As a tactician, Napoleon III proved as unsuccessful as his namesake, first embroiling the country in the bitter Crimean War, and then in 1870 provoking the ignominious **Franco–Prussian War**, which saw his own capture and the subsequent German siege of Paris.

Although Roussillon continued to drift in agrarian poverty, Languedoc weathered all these events with some measure of good fortune. While the bulk of the population suffered in poverty, the **textile industry**, based on wool and cotton and later on silk, boomed. The herds of the uplands of the Cévennes and Haut Languedoc were the chief source of raw material, and the fast-flowing rivers provided the energy to run the newly mechanized factories. All along the fringe of the mountains, towns which had up to then been insignificant villages – Castres, Mazamet, Ganges, St-Hippolyte – enjoyed unprecedented good fortune. As coal was discovered, new industries, such as **mining** and **glassmaking** (at Albi and Carmaux), sprang up, and when the railways arrived in the middle of the century, the towns along their route benefited additionally from better access to distribution networks. Of course, this good fortune tended to remain in the hands of a relative few – the factory owners and merchants – and this fact contributed to the popularity of egalitarian and **socialist ideologies** among the masses of the region.

The era of the **Third Republic**, which followed France's defeat at the hands of the Prussians, was one of introspection, not least because of the massive war indemnities which the state was forced to pay. Socialists were scapegoated, and there were mass executions at the hands of the new reactionary regime: in excess of 20,000 were killed in Paris alone. Nor was all well in Languedoc and Roussillon, as outside the industrial areas the people of the countryside still eked out only the most meagre of livings. Many left, frequently for Paris, compounding the capital's social and economic problems. The new, modern **wine industry** which had developed along the littoral provided a seasonal source of income for many, and stimulated related industries, such as bottle-, cork- and barrel-making, but in 1875 the vineyards were decimated by phylloxera. This was followed by a second epidemic which attacked mulberry trees, the silkworm's staple food, precipitating a crisis in the silk industry.

A marked tendency towards the Left continued to colour local politics, partially fuelled by resentment towards remote and indifferent Paris. These political trends were personified in **Jean Jaurès**. Born in Castres, he was drawn to Paris as a brilliant student but later returned to his home region of Tarn. Here he entered politics and embarked on a series of labour-oriented campaigns, helping to organize miners' unions, and setting up co-operative, worker-run factories. He joined other liberals in defending **Alfred Dreyfus**, a Jewish army officer wrongly convicted of espionage in 1898, and founded the communist newspaper *L'Humanité* in 1904 and a new socialist party in 1905. Speaking out against the anti-German nationalist hysteria which gripped the country in the years leading up to World War I, he paid with his life, assassinated by a nationalist in 1914.

However, popular politics in Languedoc and Roussillon were not divided strictly across ideological lines, as the cross-class solidarity of the **wine revolts** would show. As the wine industry recovered in the last years of the nineteenth century from the blow dealt by disease, it received further setbacks. A series of abundant harvests drove down the price of grapes, and the combination of competition from cheap Algerian vintages and a law permitting sugar to be added during fermentation (reducing the amount of grape pulp required) decreased demand. Wages plummeted and unemployment rose. Led by the innkeeper, Marcellin Albert, half a million protesters turned out in Montpellier in 1907, and similar numbers rose up in other wine towns, like Béziers and Narbonne. People across the class spectrum depended on the wine industry, so the uprising had the character of a regional revolt. The interior minister, Georges Clémenceau, responded by sending in the troops, but the locally levied 17th Infantry Regiment sympathized with their countrymen and mutinied. They were packed off to Tunisia in short order, and troops from the north were sent in to quell the "Midi madness". In the confrontations between army and civilians, shots were fired and there were some casualties, but the episode served to instigate the creation of a regional wine board to manage prices and quality and to bring stability to the industry.

The two world wars

In 1914, the diplomatic strain between Europe's uniformly conservative powers finally snapped, and the **assassination** of the Austrian Archduke Ferdinand at the hands of a Serbian nationalist in Sarajevo led to a diplomatic chain reaction which brought about **World War I**. The French were particularly anxious for revenge for their recent defeat at the hands of Prussia, which had deprived them of the Rhenish provinces of Alsace and Lorraine. After an initial German advance, both sides settled in for a long-drawn-out campaign of near-static trench warfare, along a 400km front stretching roughly from the Swiss border to Ostend, which was to last four years.

On the "Western Front" France (with allies Britain and eventually the US) and Germany ground away at each other in the first modern mechanized war; over its course the front shifted almost imperceptibly, but an exhausted Germany surrendered in 1918. France paid a high price for its eventual victory – almost one and half million dead. Although none of the fighting took place in Languedoc and Roussillon, the **cenotaphs** which mark the centre of every hamlet and village bear dramatic testimony to the price which they paid in the struggle.

Languedoc and Roussillon limped through the 1920s and 1930s, suffering along with the rest of Europe in the postwar **flu epidemic** (which claimed more lives than the war) and the **Great Depression**. Weak postwar democracies arose in Italy and Germany and were quickly replaced by dictatorial fascist regimes, and a prelude of the struggle to come took place in Spain, where General Franco's attempted coup set in motion a civil war in 1936. The bitter struggle, from which France – along with the rest of the Allies – remained aloof and uncommitted, lasted until 1939. As fascist troops took over Catalonia and the Basque country, tens of thousands of **refugees** poured over the border, the Catalans arriving initially in Roussillon.

A few months later, German soldiers poured over the Polish border, initiating **World War II**. The following year they circumvented France's defensive white elephant, the Maginot line, and arrived in Paris in June. For the first time in seven hundred years Languedoc and Roussillon found themselves independent of Paris as they were incorporated into the puppet **Vichy Republic**, which enjoyed a fictitious independence under the World War I hero turned traitor, **Henri Pétain**. He collaborated with the **Nazis**, facilitating the repression of their opponents, the deportation of "undesirable elements" and the wholesale transportation of southern French citizens to labour camps and factories in Germany.

In 1942, the Germans decided to dispense with even the illusion of autonomy in the South and brought the whole region under their direct control. Repression was intensified, but the local guerrilla **resistance**, the **Maquis**, benefited from a stiffened resolve on the part of the populace. Across France as a whole there were about as many active collaborators with Nazi rule as resisters, but Resistance activity in Languedoc and Roussillon was considerable, the efforts of local companies like the famed Maquis Bir Hakeim of Haut Languedoc, or of individuals like Jean Mance of Béziers, who founded the National Committee for Resistance, proving a significant element in the war. In their mountain redoubts in the Pyrenees and Cévennes and in the hills of Haut Languedoc, they withstood German air attacks and pacification missions, while the civilian population suffered direct reprisals for their collusion with the rebels. In the Cerdagne and Roussillon, clandestine *passeurs*, motivated by either ideals or profit (or a combination of the two), helped to slip people and contraband back and forth over the frontier with neutral Spain.

From 1943 on, the disasters of the Russian campaign focused German manpower in the east, and with the **allied invasions** of Italy in 1943 and Normandy in 1944, the undergunned maquis finally had a chance, and began to mount an open military campaign. The first towns which they managed to recover were mere mountain hamlets, like Mourèze, near Clermont-l'Hérault, but when the Germans sent a column of three thousand troops to retake the upper Hérault, they were fended off after a fierce day-long battle with the local Resistance. Memorial plaques which pepper the streets of Toulouse and other major towns recall the maquis who fell in the widespread **street-fighting** of 1944. By the end of that year, France had been liberated.

Recent history

In the postwar **Fourth Republic** France endeavoured to recover from the damage wrought by four years of occupation and two invasions. Europe's colonial age was coming to an end and for France this signalled nationalist revolts in Indochina and Algeria. In Languedoc and Roussillon, the wine industry recovered and mining continued, but with the advent of cheaper synthetic fibres, the textile industry all but disappeared. **Poverty** and **depopulation** continued and served to channel political consciousness ever more to the Left.

Former general and self-proclaimed liberator of France **Charles de Gaulle**'s conservative **Fifth Republic**, which came in 1958 on the heels of France's entry into the new European Common Market, gradually became something of a dictatorship. In the South, certain progressive economic policies were embarked upon, including the construction of **reservoirs** and **hydroelectric facilities** and the articulation of a region-wide irrigation plan.

Meanwhile in **Algeria**, native unrest led to open rebellion, and when de Gaulle reacted by announcing the abandonment of the **colony**, the *pieds-noirs* (so-called by the natives for their custom of wearing shoes) – the French population who had ruled it since 1830 – felt betrayed and carried out a brief armed resistance. With the **Accord of Évian** (1962), they agreed to be settled, along with the **harkis**, their native Algerian allies, in Languedoc. The influx of this population – a largely educated and skilled workforce – gave new life to the cities of the coast (notably Montpellier, Narbonne and Perpignan), although the welcome which the *harkis* received was hardly warm. Forty years later, they continue to protest the official neglect to which they have been subject.

The **Student Revolution** of 1968 presaged the departure of de Gaulle, who resigned in 1969 after a failed attempt to widen his already broad powers by popular referendum. The unrest of that summer also heralded an era of openly **left-wing politics** in Languedoc and Roussillon. In the elections of the years that followed, Languedoc voted massively in favour of the socialists and communists, encouraged by the areas' traditional economic marginalism and an antipathy to the conservative north.

The nation, however, remained under **conservative rule** through the presidencies of Georges Pompidou (1969–74) and Valéry Giscard d'Estaing (1974–81). In this era of baby boom and general prosperity, the infrastructure of Languedoc and Roussillon was improved by the construction of *autoroutes* and the improvement of roads. The **tourist industry** also received stimulus through the revitalization of the abandoned Canal du Midi and the creation of regional parks, such as that of Haut Languedoc. The area still retains a shadow of its former textile industry, but manufacturing has been dominated in the west by the high-profile **aviation industry**, based in Toulouse. The city had been a pioneer of flight since before the days of St-Exupéry, and served as a hub for Africa and South America between the wars. It was here that the Concorde was first tested, and the European joint-venture Airbus Industries was founded.

Despite these recent successes, the region remains underpopulated and relatively poor, and *départements* like Aude, Ariège and significant parts of Hérault are now actively stimulating tourism as a way of bringing investment and employment. Whether as a result of these efforts, or as a consequence of overcrowding and rising prices in traditional Anglo destinations like the Dordogne, British travellers and property-investors have moved into Languedoc and Roussillon, both as a holiday destination and as somewhere to set up home.

As the French population ages, waves of northern retirees are heading south to the affordable property and agreeable climes of Languedoc and Roussillon – a trend which is seen with a jaundiced eye by many natives, who perceive in it a modern reprise of the invasions of the past. Some also see the massive influx of North African immigrants from France's former colonies and protectorates as an invasion, and this has served to divert part of the traditional extreme Left vote, paradoxically, to the **extreme Right**. The 1995 municipal elections gave a surprisingly high return to the parties of the far Right, dominated then by Jean-Morie Le Pen's racist **Front National**. It is not without irony that Roussillon's "Perpignan la Catalane" should be ruled by an extremist French mayor. At the *région* level, the Right scored well in the 1998 elections; the UDF–FDR coalition's (President Chirac's power base) 22 seats added to the FN's thirteen made for a narrow majority over the 31 seats won by the socialists and resurgent communists.

As parties geared up for the 2002 elections, it appeared that the region would return to its traditional socialist orientation, with the FN splintered and the **Chirac government** discredited by an influence-peddling **scandal** involving government contracts which seemed to point at the president's office. Few were prepared for what was to come. The first electoral round was met with record voter apathy and abstention, particularly among socialist voters. This knocked out Jospin's party from the race and catapulted Le Pen into second position. In a typical irony of politics, leftist voters came out for the second round and voted in Chirac, seen as the lesser of two evils.

The social negligence born out of the elitism of Chirac's right and of the French political class in general was dramatically demonstrated in November 2005, when the death of two youths of North African descent while being pursued by police in a Paris ghetto ignited nationwide riots. Government arrogance fuelled the indignant desperation of France's marginalized Maghrebian youth – assimilated but unaccepted by the national mainstream. Presidential hopeful, Interior Minister and Chirac henchman **Dominique de Villepin**'s disdainful dismissal of the rioters as "scum," only added fuel to the fire. The *banliees* of Paris erupted, and as the evening news broadcast images of burning cars and clashes with police, unrest spread across the country and to Languedoc, most notably to Toulouse. By early 2006 tensions had calmed and attention focussed increasingly on the upcoming Presidential elections. In autumn 2006, the socialists elected a new leader, **Ségolène Royal**, who looks set to square off against the conservative **Sarkozy**, although the spectre of **Le Pen** and his racist Right is once again making its sinister presence felt.

Unlike some of France's other regions, such as Corsica, Alsace, the Pays Basque and Brittany, the issues of a distinctive language and identity do not seem to have made their way into the political dialogue of either Languedoc or Roussillon. For all the resentment which these regions may feel towards Paris, and despite the survival or revival of their native tongues, there is no doubt among the people of the region that their future lies within France.

Books

M ost of the books listed below are in print and in paperback – those that are out of print (o/p) should be easy to track down either in secondhand bookshops or through Amazon's used and secondhand book service (Ⓦ www.amazon.com). Note that while we recommend all the books listed below, we do have our favourites and these have been marked with a 🐾 symbol.

History

General

🐾 **Alfred Cobban** *A History of Modern France* (3 volumes: 1715–99, 1799–1871 and 1871–1962). Complete and very readable account of the main political, social and economic strands in French history, from the death of Louis XIV to mid-de Gaulle.

Colin Jones *The Cambridge Illustrated History of France* (o/p). A political and social history of France from prehistoric times to the mid-1990s, concentrating on issues of regionalism, gender, race and class. Good illustrations and a friendly, non-academic writing style.

The Middle Ages

Richard Barber *Edward, Prince of Wales and Aquitaine.* A weighty academic read, but perhaps the best of the biographies on the Black Prince, including much on his campaigns in Languedoc.

🐾 **Natalie Zemon Davis** *The Return of Martin Guerre.* A vivid account of peasant life in the sixteenth century Pyrenean village of Artigat. The return of a long-lost villager sparks a sensational and gripping courtroom drama.

🐾 **Emmanuel Le Roy Ladurie** *Montaillou.* Village gossip of who's sleeping with whom, tales of trips to Spain and details of work, all extracted by the Inquisition from Cathar peasants of the eastern Pyrenees in the fourteenth century.

J.R. Maddicott *Simon de Montfort.* An academic but readable treatment of this complex and

problematic figure – carefully reflecting de Montfort's combination of piety and ambition.

Stephen O'Shea *The Perfect Heresy.* Lively but partisan non-academic account of the history of the Cathar Church and faith and the Catholic campaign mounted to wipe it out.

Linda M. Paterson *The World of the Troubadours: Medieval Occitan Society, c.1100–1300.* Scholarly but clear survey of medieval Occitan culture and society.

Mark Pegg *The Corruption of Angels: The Great Inquisition of 1245–1246.* An intimate look at the lives of peasants, townsmen and nobles of the Lauragais seen through the eyes of the Cathar-hunting Inquisition.

Jonathan Sumption *The Albigensian Crusade.* Concise but eloquent portrayal of the Albigensian Crusades from the beginnings of the Cathar movement through to the fall of Montségur.

René Weiss *The Yellow Cross: The Story of the Last Cathars, 1290–1329.* Lively historical detective work built on the same sources as Montaillou. An energetic, engaging read, not overly academic in tone.

The Wars of Religion

Joseph and Francis Bergin *The Rise of Richelieu.* An interesting look at Richelieu's rise to power, presenting the cardinal as a complex Machiavellian figure, who was not without his convictions.

Willert Paul Ferdinand *Henry of Navarre and the Huguenots in France* (o/p). Ageing but interesting study of the French Protestant movement, focusing on the figure of Henri IV.

Mack Holt *The French Wars of Religion, 1562–1629.* A recent survey of the whole period of the Wars of Religion.

🏃 **Felix Platter** *Beloved Son Felix* (o/p). Fascinating diary of a young Swiss man who sets out to study medicine in sixteenth-century Montpellier.

James Valone *Huguenot Politics, 1601–1622.* Recently published, exacting study of the Huguenot situation during the reign of the former Protestant Henri IV.

Eighteenth and nineteenth centuries

Anthony Crubaugh *Balancing the Scales of Justice: Local Courts and Rural Society in Southwest France, 1750–1800.* Engaging new academic study of local court documents, revealing the subtleties of peasant life in Languedoc in the era of the Revolution.

🏃 **Norman Hampson** *A Social History of the French Revolution.* An analysis that concentrates on the personalities involved, with particular emphasis on the sans-culottes.

Christopher Hibbert *The Days of the French Revolution.* Well-paced and entertaining narrative treatment by a master historian.

🏃 **Peter McPhee** *A Social History of France, 1780–1880.* A scholarly work underscoring fundamental differences between how people lived and thought in 1880 compared to 1789, with particular reference to gender, education, economy, culture and physical environment.

J.M. Thompson *The French Revolution.* A detailed and passionate account, first published in 1943, but still the classic depiction in English.

Twentieth century

H.R. Kedward *In Search of the Maquis: Rural Resistance in South France 1942–1944.* Dry, but full of fascinating details about the brave struggles of the countless ordinary people across France who fought to drive the Germans from their country.

Barbara Tuchman *The Proud Tower.* A portrait of England, France, the US, Germany and Russia in the years 1890–1914. It includes a superb chapter on the extraordinary passions and enmities aroused by the Dreyfus Affair, and on the socialist movement in the run-up to World War I, centring on the life of Jean Jaurès.

🏃 **Paul Webster** *Pétain's Crime: The Full Story of French Collaboration in the Holocaust.* The alarming story of the Vichy regime's collaboration with the Holocaust, and the bravery of those, especially the

Alexander Worth *France 1940–1955* (o/p). Emotionally engaged portrayal of the taboo Occupation period in French history, followed by the Cold War and colonial struggle years in which the same political tensions and heart-searching were at play.

Society and politics

Jose Bové *The World is Not for Sale: Farmers Against Junkfood.* A manifesto by the US-raised self-proclaimed saviour of French ecology and cuisine.

Bernard Henri-Lévy *Adventures on the Freedom Road: The French Intellectuals in the 20th Century.* Clever and complex essays by the contemporary philosopher-celebrity, mercilessly analysing the response of great French thinkers to the key events of the century. Easy to dip into, surprisingly readable and very provocative.

Ian Ousby *Occupation: The Ordeal of France 1940–1945.* Non-academic book which reflects the recent trend

to deflate the myth of massive resistance to the Nazis. Examines the development of the Resistance and the counterweight of collaboration.

David Thomson *Democracy in France Since 1870.* An inquiry into why a country with such a strong socialist tradition should have had so many reactionary governments.

Harold R. Weinstein *Jean Jaurès: A Study of Patriotism in the French Socialist Movement* (o/p). First published in the 1930s, this ageing but eloquent study looks not only at the figure of Jaurès, but locates him in the wider context of late nineteenth-century French socialism.

Art and architecture

John Berger *The Success and Failure of Picasso.* Although most strongly associated with Provence, Picasso also was influenced by and influenced Roussillonaise artists. Perhaps the best one-volume study of Picasso in English.

Kenneth J. Conant *Carolingian and Romanesque Architecture, 800–1200.* Good European study with a focus on Cluny and the St-Jacques pilgrim route, which includes strong coverage of the sections through Languedoc.

Julia Bloch Frey *Toulouse-Lautrec: A Life.* An intimate look at the life of

the painter, with emphasis on his friends, family, and artistic contemporaries.

Walter F. Friedlaender *David to Delacroix* (o/p). Respected survey of French art from the late seventeenth to late nineteenth centuries, from Neoclassicism through to Romanticism, and including figures who were influential in Languedoc and Roussillon.

John Golding *Cubism: A History and an Analysis 1907–1914* (o/p). Excellent work on the formative stages of Cubism, particularly relevant for a journey to Céret.

Sarah Whitfield *Fauvism.* A survey of the movement, accompanied by colour plates, emphasizing the major figure of Matisse, but with good material on Maillol and lesser-known artists.

Regional literature

Anonymous *Aucassin et Nicolette.* Dating from the fourteenth century, perhaps the first European musical play. Recounts the impossible love between a prince of Beaucaire and a former Muslim slave-girl in Tarascon.

Michael Baigent, et al. *Holy Blood, Holy Grail.* Learn what happened to the Holy Grail, how Jesus didn't die on the cross, how the Knights Templars are a force to be reckoned with and how Rennes-le-Château is the key.

Alessandro Barrico *Silk.* Sensual love story set in the aftermath of the silk crisis of nineteenth-century Languedoc.

Sophie Burnham *The Treasure of Montségur: A Novel of Cathars.* A thirteenth-century bodice-ripper in which Cathar Jeanne recounts her sex-tinged heretical past to a Catholic lover.

Julius Caesar *The Gallic War.* A highly subjective but majestically written account of the Roman experience in France.

Charmaine Craig *The Good Men: A Novel of Heresy.* Another bodice-ripping tale of heretical lust and unrequited love set in fourteenth-century Montaillou.

Alphonse Daudet *In the Land of Pain.* Memoirs and notes which chart the nineteenth-century Beaucaire author's descent into the latter, fatal stages of syphilis.

Lawrence Durrell *Spirit of Place: Letters and Essays on Travel.* A collection of letters to friends and contemporaries, including T.S. Eliot, written during Durrell's retirement in Sommières.

André Gide *If It Die…An Autobiography.* Gide's spiritual autobiography, sensual and introspective, including his time spent in Uzès.

Arthur Guirdham *Cathars & Reincarnation.* In this non-fiction study an English schoolgirl is allegedly hypnotically induced to recall her past life as a Cathar.

Christopher Hope *Signs of the Heart: Love and Death in Languedoc.* Award-winning South African-born novelist writes about his life in Languedoc.

Zoé Oldenbourg *Destiny of Fire.* Historical novel set in the age of the Albigensian Crusade, written by a respected French historian.

Gaston Phébus *The Hunting Book of Gaston Phébus.* Beautifully illuminated facsimile edition of a 1405 manuscript of the count of Foix's hunting manual.

Antoine de Saint-Exupéry *Night Flight.* The Toulousain aviator and author of *The Little Prince* recounts in novel format the dangers and exhilaration of flying the southern Atlantic route in the 1920s and 30s.

Janet Shirley *Song of the Cathar Wars.* Translation of two contemporary accounts of the Cathar wars of 1204–1218, written by a Crusade-supporter and an Occitan sympathizer.

Gustaf Sobin *Luminous Debris: Reflecting on Vestige in Provence and Languedoc.* Sixteen essays stroll poetically through the distant past of Southern France.

Robert Louis Stevenson *Travels With a Donkey in the Cévennes.*

Traveller, spy and author, Robert Louis Stevenson tours Camisard country in the mid-nineteenth century, reflecting on the land and people of upland Languedoc.

Paul Valéry *Selected Writings*. A good introduction for English-speakers to the thoughts and writing of the Sètois Symbolist.

Travel books and guides

Jenny Baker *Simple French Cuisine: From Provence and Languedoc*. Comprehensive guide to southern French cooking with easy-to-follow recipes arranged thematically.

Sabine Baring-Gould *In Troubadour-Land: A Ramble in Provence and Languedoc*. A very British, late nineteenth-century aristocratic ramble through the French south, offering an interesting perspective of the region under the Third Republic.

James Bromwich *The Roman Remains of Southern France*. The only comprehensive guide on the subject – detailed, well illustrated and approachable. In addition to accounts of the famous sites, it will lead you off the map to little-known discoveries.

Glynn Christian *Edible France*. A guide to food rather than restaurants, concentrating on regional produce, local specialities, markets and the best shops for buying goodies to bring back home.

Cicerone Walking Guides. Neat, durable guides, with detailed route descriptions. Titles include *Walking in the Languedoc; The Way of St James; The GR10; Coast to Coast Through the French Pyrenees*; and *Walks and Climbs in the Pyrénées*.

Henry Cleere *Southern France*. Written by a true expert, this gives detailed information and background on 34 archeological sites, famous and obscure.

Nina Epton *The Valley of Pyrene* (o/p). Lively 1950s-era memoir of a

tour through Ariège, peppered with entertaining anecdotes.

David Everett *Buying and Restoring Old Property in France*. Recently updated, this is the classic reference book for *émigrés* and home-buyers.

Footpaths of Europe *Walking the Pyrénées* (o/p). Route guide covering the system of GR footpaths, illustrated with 1:50,000 colour survey maps. It is an English version of the Pyrenees *Topoguide des Sentiers de Grande Randonnée* (see opposite).

Peter Gorley *The Wines of Languedoc-Roussillon*. Lively, fact-packed guide to wines and *domaines*, with complete information on visiting times, recommended vintages and tips for the aspiring *oenologue*.

David Hampshire *Living and Working in France*. Now in its seventh edition, this comprehensive book offers everything for the long-term traveller or resident, from house purchasing to signing on.

Rion Klawinski *Chasing the Heretics: A Modern Journey through Languedoc*. A traveller's account of the Cathar heresy and the Albigensian Crusade, arranged in a guidebook format. A good handbook for those who want to make a Cathar-themed trip.

Polly Platt *French or Foe? Getting the Most Out of Living and Working in France*. Good-humoured guide to surviving life with the French.

Kev Reynolds *Walks and Climbs in the Pyrénées*. The classic English guide for walking in the Pyrenees.

Paul Stranq *Languedoc-Roussillon: The Wines and the Winemakers.* Richly detailed and well-illustrated survey of the *domaines*, vintners and vintages of southwest France.

John Sturrock *The French Pyrénées* (o/p). Well-written travelogue emphasizing the history of the French side of the range. Covers the mountains from coast to coast, with significant sections on Ariège and Roussillon.

Topoguide Series. Books featuring detailed maps and hiking instructions (in French, but not hard to follow for anyone with a working knowledge of the language). A volume is published for each *région* (50 routes) and *département* (30 routes) covered in this Guide. Widely available in French bookshops and tourist offices.

Henri de Toulouse-Lautrec *The Art of Cuisine*. Culinary masterpieces from the diminutive artistic genius.

Language

Language

Occitan and Catalan

B y the time the Roman Empire in the west disintegrated, Latin had become the language of daily speech in nearly all of what is now France. Over the course of the following centuries, spoken Latin began to evolve into local variants and eventually into new Romance languages, from Spanish to Romanian. In the south of France (and in part of modern Italy) Occitan (pronounced ok-si-tán) or the Langue d'Oc developed – so called for its word for "yes", which set it apart from the northern French Langue d'Oïl ("oui"). Occitan itself had discrete regional variants, chief among them Provençal in the east (including Nîmes), Limousin in the north, Gascon in the west (including Ariège and the Vall d'Aran in Spain) and Languedocien, from the Corbières to the Camargue. In northeast Spain and across the present-day border into southern France emerged the Catalan language, which bears similarities to both Occitan and Castilian Spanish. Ironically, the name Catalan derives from the same root as the name of its chief rival language, Castilian, both terms referring to the castles which covered the landscapes of each region.

Occitan language and culture

Around the turn of the first millennium, a distinct Occitan literary language emerged, thanks to the wealth of the southern counts and their patronage of **troubadours**. These poets composed and performed works which were sung accompanied by music, for which they were also known as *trovadors* or *jongleurs* ("players" [of instruments]). The themes of their works varied from popular or religiously toned epics, like the *Chanson de Roland*, to portrayals of courtly love, considered to be the most elegant of subjects. Across these could be found recurring motifs, including righteous battle (for example, against the infidel), unrequited love and, above all, the glorification of good manners, sophistication and virtues, such as knightly loyalty or pious chastity. The poetry of courtly love was not erotic in nature; the idea was that the poet should be recognized as honourable by the noble woman (or man) who was the object of the work. The genre was so idealized that the great troubadour Jaufré Rudel claimed to have fallen in love with the countess of Tripoli without having ever laid eyes on her. Troubadours were not merely court entertainers, as many were noble-men themselves, and the first is said to have been the powerful duke, William IX of Aquitaine, father of Eleanor of Aquitaine, later Queen of England. But the bulk of them were not wealthy, and they practised their art as a way of ingratiating themselves with a noble house, and entering its service, much as a knight would.

The Albigensian Crusades of the thirteenth century brought about the end of many of the native ruling families in Languedoc and led to an influx of northern nobles. Naturally, these were French in cultural orientation rather than Occitan, and the literature of the language declined as sources of patronage dried up and it waned as an administrative language. Occitan literature persevered in prose, which emphasized secular and narrative themes. The decline of the language was met with some alarm, and in 1323 a group of poets from Toulouse determined to save the poetic tradition of the troubadours by instituting the **jocs florals** ("floral games") – a sort of poetic Olympics in which winners were awarded gilded flowers. The tradition has continued since that time, held annually on May 3, although in 1694, Louis XIV Frenchified it and established in Toulouse a society called the Académie des Jeux Floraux, which administers the games to this day. With the establishment of the Jocs Florals, Occitan survived as a literary language for a time, but with the increasing centralization of the realm, devolved once again into an unwritten language of common speech. In 1539, on the eve of the Wars of Religion, François I declared at Villers-Cotterêts that French – the dialect of the **Langue d'Oïl** which was spoken in the area around Paris – was to be the only language of administration in his realms.

As the language of education and administration, French thus displaced Occitan, which was – and sometimes still is – referred to insultingly by Francophones as *patois* ("the dialect"). It was not until the mid-nineteenth century that it was revived in literature, in an intellectual environment which saw subject peoples across Europe establish or re-establish literatures for their own languages. The major figure in the new Occitan literature was **Frédéric Mistral**, the venerated Provençal poet and cultural messiah. Born in 1830, Mistral spent a lifetime working to revive and modernize Provençal Occitan as a written and spoken language, producing countless works of literature and grammar, and campaigning in favour of Occitan folk practices, such as *tauromachie*. His efforts were recognized on an international level when he received a Nobel Prize in 1904. Meanwhile, philologists strove to standardize the language, which had degenerated into countless local variants as a result of its subjugation to French.

Nevertheless, reform was slow. Although it may have been the common language of the villages and fields through the middle of the twentieth century, the relentlessly centralist policies of the state and the greater diffusion of French-language education and literacy conspired against Occitan's revival. In Toulouse, the **Escola Occitana** (1919) and the **Institut d'Études Occitanes** (1945) were founded to promote and modernize the language, but it was not until 1951 that it was permitted to teach Occitan in schools, and only in 1969 that educational authorities officially ranked it as a language.

Ironically, the only area which has Occitan as an official and dominant language is Spain's **Vall d'Aran**, a tiny valley high in the Pyrenees to the southwest of Toulouse. **Aranese**, as the seven thousand or so inhabitants call the language, is in fact the Gascon dialect of the Langue d'Oc. In Languedoc, proper efforts continue to revive the language, but since the 1920s the number of speakers has decreased from ten million to two million – an optimistic estimate which sets the proportion of Occitan speakers as fourteen percent of the whole of Languedoc. (By contrast, in Corsica some fifty percent of the populace speak native Corse.) Nevertheless, the language is experiencing something of a revival both across southern France and in northwest Italy, where there was a major Occitan festival in 2006. In addition, there are Occitan-language newspapers (such as the weekly *La Setmana*), radio stations (*Ràdio País*) and television broadcasts, and bilingual public schools have been established in Albi, Toulouse, Monestiès and St-Sulpice. Most importantly, in 2006, Occitan (and Catalan in Roussillon) became mandatory subjects in the region's schools, in a programme undertaken by the Montpellier Academy. As a visitor, you're unlikely to encounter Occitan either spoken or written, apart from the Occitan street signs which are frequently set alongside their French counterparts.

Although readership is limited, authors such as **Max Roqueta**, **Bernat Maciet** and **Marcèla Delpastre** have begun to publish novels in Occitan, theatre companies tour performing original and traditional works, and musical groups of the 1970s and 80s, like Massilia and the Fabulous Troubadours, created the modern Occitan musical style called **nòva cançon**, which blends traditional melodies and instruments with modern styles, and still has a hardcore following today. For the most part, however, Occitan musicians have adopted other genres, from jazz, blues and folk, to rap and punk fusions (here known as *ragga-aïoli*), and of course regional and linguistic identity do not necessarily coincide – Toulouse's **Zebda**, a strongly regional-minded group whose mix of politics and music is reminiscent of America's Rage Against the Machine, sings exclusively in French.

Although Languedoc is rich with customs and traditions which set it apart from the rest of France, such as water-jousting and *tauromachie*, it is thoroughly subsumed in the French identity. There is no independence movement here such as exists in Corsica, the Basque Country or Brittany, and regional identity is vague, focusing with romantic nostalgia on episodes of northern French oppression such as the Albigensian Crusades and the Wars of Religion. Bernat Lubat, a renowned Occitan jazz musician, expresses an opinion on the subject of regional independence which is representative of the overwhelming majority of the area's inhabitants: "The desire for independence seems to me neither interesting, nor realistic, nor even poetic."

Catalan language and culture

Most of the world's six to ten million Catalan speakers live in Spain, in a band of territory stretching south from the Pyrenees to Valencia, and in the Balearic Islands (though proponents of Valencian, Mallorquin and Menorquin hold these to be distinct languages). The 120,000 Catalan speakers of France live in the *département* of Pyrénées-Orientales, which incorporates the Catalan cultural regions of **La Cerdanya** and **Rosselló**, and has its capital at Perpignan (Perpinyà in Catalan). Here, they represent 34 percent of the population, although only half of that figure claim a high proficiency level.

The **Cerdagne** and **Roussillon**, traditionally part of the realms of the Counts of Barcelona, were long disputed in border wars waged with the French. The French Crown took permanent control of the territory in the 1620s under Richelieu, but the land was not formally ceded by Spain until the Treaty of the Pyrenees (1649), negotiated by Louis XIV. Curiously, a fine reading of the text of the treaty allowed Spain to maintain control of the town of Llívia, which has remained a Spanish enclave, a few kilometres inside the French border, to this day.

Catalan, like Occitan, was a language of troubadours of the Middle Ages, and had a healthy tradition of narrative literature before Spanish or English. One of the most famous early Catalan works is the autobiographical *Llibre de fets* (Book of Deeds), written in the thirteenth century by the great count-king,

Jaume I the Conqueror, son of Pere the Catholic, who was killed by Simon de Montfort at Muret. Throughout the Middle Ages, Catalan culture flourished thanks to the powerful maritime dominion of Barcelona. The count-king Joan I the Hunter (1387–96) instituted a Catalan version of the **Jocs Florals**, in imitation of the Occitan contest. Winners were given a real, rather than a golden flower though, an early reflection perhaps of the famous Catalan frugality. But as happened to Occitan, the domination of powerful "foreign" administration – in this case, the Hapsburgs of Madrid – contributed to the marginalization of the language, and literary usage declined after the fifteenth century. This process was exacerbated in Roussillon by the French takeover in the seventeenth century. Like Occitan, Catalan was proscribed from official use, and denigrated to the status of a peasant *patois*.

The wave of regional and national consciousness which swept through Europe in the mid-nineteenth century washed over Catalonia as well, where the linguistic renaissance was spearheaded by the philologist **Pompeu Fabra i Poch**, who set about standardizing the Catalan grammar, and writers, such as the poet **Manuel Milà i Fontanals**. In 1859, the Catalan Jocs Florals were revived. With the victory of strongly Castile-centric Franco in the Spanish Civil War, a stream of Catalan refugees spilled over the border into France, giving the native language and culture an additional boost in Roussillon and the Cerdagne. Catalan was proscribed under the fascist dictatorship in Spain, but the postwar period in France signalled a liberalization of language laws and the admission of Catalan to the state school curriculum, with mandatory instruction beginning in autumn 2006.

Today, however, while there is a lively literary, television and cinema culture in Catalonia proper, in Roussillon it is almost nonexistent. Some Catalan folkloric customs have survived the centuries of French domination though, and still contribute to the defined flavour of Roussillon. Among these are the distinctive **Christmas customs** (see box, p.349), and the penitents' processions of **Setmana Santa** (Holy Week). A recent addition is the **sardana**, brought to Roussillon by the refugees of 1939, and a symbol of Catalan nationalism. It is a popular dance, in which participants, frequently wearing the traditional woven *espardinya* shoes, form a circle linking hands and do a slow hopping dance to the minor strains of an eleven-piece *colbla* (orchestra). Each dancer places some object (frequently a handbag) in the centre, which is said to symbolize sharing; and the dance is undemanding enough that young and old alike can participate.

The sizeable independence movement in Spanish Catalonia advocates the unification of all of the *Països Catalans*, including Roussillon and the Cerdagne, as a separate state. Indeed, the most potent symbol of Catalan identity, towering **Mont Canigou** (*El Canigó* in Catalan), sits in French territory, between Prades and the border. An imposing mountain casting its shadow over all of Roussillon, it had long been venerated by the region's inhabitants when a monastery was founded on its slopes by the grandson of Guifré the Hairy in 1001. Over the centuries its symbolism intensified, and for Catalans it became their sacred mountain, celebrated in literature through to Jacint Verdaguer's epic *Canigó* of the late nineteenth century. To this day it is the site of a yearly midsummer torchlight pilgrimage to celebrate the *día de Sant Joan* (St John's Day) on the eve of June 24. The traditional pagan solstice holiday, celebrated here, as in many societies, by raising a great fire, stands as a Catalan "national" holiday, celebrated in both Spanish and French Catalonia. But aside from annoying graffiti on buildings and road signs, there is little evidence of nationalist fervour on the French side of the border. Although Catalan speakers of Roussillon, and even

Naturally, the best place to **study Catalan** is in Catalonia proper, but if you are determined to do so in Roussillon, your best option is to take a course at **Prades'** Catalan summer university (℡04.68.96.10.84 and ℡(34)933.172.411, ⊛www.ucestiu.com).

many non-speakers, delight in the distinctiveness which the region's diluted Catalan identity gives them, they tend to recall the revolts against the French merely for their sense of rose-tinted nostalgia. The region is culturally very much closer to Paris than Barcelona – convincing confirmation of its predominantly French sensibility can be found in the election in 1995 of the extreme right-wing mayor of Perpignan, Jean-Paul Alduy of the Nouvelle UDF, who has not only remains in power today, but was also made senator in 2001.

French

A lthough Occitan is still spoken among some older rural folk and by recent students of the language, it serves little purpose for the visitor. Catalan, while more current, is nevertheless a second language throughout Roussillon and the Cerdagne. As a foreigner speaking French, you will be understood by all and you will not offend anyone's regional sensibilities.

French can be a deceptively familiar language because of the number of words and structures it shares with English. Despite this, it's far from easy, though the bare essentials are not difficult to learn and can make all the difference. Even just saying "Bonjour Madame/Monsieur" and then gesticulating will usually get you a smile and helpful service. People working in tourist offices, hotels and so on, almost always speak English and tend to use it when you're struggling to speak French – be grateful, not insulted.

Of the **phrasebooks** and **dictionaries** available, the *Rough Guide French Dictionary Phrasebook* is a handy and comprehensive companion, with both English–French and French–English sections, along with cultural tips for tricky situations and a menu reader. There's also the *French and English Slang Dictionary* (Harrap/Prentice Hall) and *Dictionary of Modern Colloquial French* (Routledge) – both volumes are a bit large to carry, but they are the key to all you'll ever want to know about the French vernacular.

French pronunciation

One easy rule to remember is that **consonants** at the ends of words are usually silent. *Pas plus tard* (not later) is thus pronounced "pa-plu-tarr". But when the following word begins with a vowel, you run the two together: *pas après* (not after) becomes "pazaprey".

Vowels are the hardest sounds to get right. Roughly:

a	as in hat		i	as in machine
e	as in get		o	as in hot
é	between get and gate		o, au	as in over
è	between get and gut		ou	as in food
eu	like the u in hurt		u	as in a pursed-lip version of use

More awkward are the **combinations** *in/im, en/em, an/am, on/om, un/um* at the ends of words, or followed by consonants other than *n* or *m*. Again, roughly:

in/im	like the an in anxious		on/om	like the don in Doncaster
an/am, en/em	like the don in Doncaster when said with a nasal accent			said by someone with a heavy cold
			un/um	like the u in understand

Consonants are much as in English, except that: *ch* is always "sh", *c* is "s", *h* is silent, *th* is the same as "t", *ll* is like the "y" in yes, *w* is "v", and *r* is growled (or rolled).

French words and phrases

Basic vocabulary

French nouns are divided into masculine and feminine. This causes difficulties with adjectives, whose endings have to change to suit the gender of the nouns they qualify. If you know some grammar, you will know what to do. If not, stick to the masculine form, which is the simplest – it's what we have done in this glossary.

aujourd'hui	today		celà	that one
hier	yesterday		ouvert	open
demain	tomorrow		fermé	closed
le matin	in the morning		grand	big
l'après-midi	in the afternoon		petit	small
le soir	in the evening		plus	more
maintenant	now		moins	less
plus tard	later		un peu	a little
à une heure	at one o'clock		beaucoup	a lot
à trois heures	at three o'clock		bon marché	cheap
à dix heures et demie	at ten-thirty		cher	expensive
à midi	at midday		bon	good
un homme	man		mauvais	bad
une femme	woman		chaud	hot
ici	here		froid	cold
là	there		avec	with
ceci	this one			

Numbers

un	1		dix-huit	18
deux	2		dix-neuf	19
trois	3		vingt	20
quatre	4		vingt-et-un	21
cinq	5		vingt-deux	22
six	6		trente	30
sept	7		quarante	40
huit	8		cinquante	50
neuf	9		soixante	60
dix	10		soixante-dix	70
onze	11		soixante-quinze	75
douze	12		quatre-vingts	80
treize	13		quatre-vingt-dix	90
quatorze	14		quatre-vingt-quinze	95
quinze	15		cent	100
seize	16		cent un	101
dix-sept	17		deux cents	200

trois cents	300	deux mille	2,000
cinq cents	500	cinq mille	5,000
mille	1000	un million	1,000,000

Days and dates

janvier	January	dimanche	Sunday
février	February	lundi	Monday
mars	March	mardi	Tuesday
avril	April	mercredi	Wednesday
mai	May	jeudi	Thursday
juin	June	vendredi	Friday
juillet	July	samedi	Saturday
août	August	le premier août	August 1
septembre	September	le deux mars	March 2
octobre	October	le quatorze juillet	July 14
novembre	November	le vingt-trois	November 23 2002
décembre	December	novembre deux mille deux	

Talking to people

When addressing people, you should always use *Monsieur* for a man, *Madame* for a woman, *Mademoiselle* for a young woman or girl. Plain *bonjour* by itself is not enough. This isn't as formal as it seems, and it has its uses when you've forgotten someone's name or want to attract someone's attention.

Pardon	excuse me	s'il vous plaît	please
Parlez-vous anglais?	do you speak English?	merci	thank you
Comment ça se dit en français?	how do you say it in French?	bonjour	hello
Comment vous appelez-vous?	what's your name?	au revoir	goodbye
		bonjour	good morning/ afternoon
Je m'appelle ...	my name is...	bonsoir	good evening
Je suis anglais[e]	I'm English	bonne nuit	good night
irlandaise[e]	Irish	Comment allez-vous?/Ça va?	how are you?
écossais[e]	Scottish		
gallois[e]	Welsh	Très bien, merci	fine, thanks
américain[e]	American	Je ne sais pas	I don't know
australien[ne]	Australian	Allons-y	let's go
canadien[ne]	Canadian	À demain	see you tomorrow
néo-zélandais[e]	a New Zealander	À bientôt	see you soon
oui	yes	Pardon, Madame/ Je m'excuse	sorry
non	no		
Je comprends	I understand	Fichez-moi la paix!	leave me alone (aggressive)
Je ne comprends pas	I don't understand		
S'il vous plaît, parlez moins vite	can you speak slower?	Aidez-moi, s'il vous plait	please help me
d'accord	OK/agreed		

Finding the way

autobus/bus/car	bus	autostop	hitchhiking
gare routière	bus station	à pied	on foot
arrêt	bus stop	Vous allez où?	where are you going?
voiture	car	Je vais à ...	I'm going to ...
train/taxi/ferry	train/taxi/ferry	Je voudrais	I want to get off
bâteau	boat	descendre à ...	at ...
avion	plane	la route pour ...	the road to ...
gare (SNCF)	train station	près/pas loin	near
quai	platform	loin	far
Il part à quelle	what time does it	à gauche	left
heure?	leave?	à droite	right
Il arrive à quelle	what time does it	tout droit	straight on
heure?	arrive?	ale l'autre côté de	on the other side of
un billet pour ...	a ticket to ...	à l'angle de	on the corner of
aller simple	single ticket	à côté de	next to
aller-retour	return ticket	derrière	behind
compostez votre billet	validate your ticket	devant	in front of
valable pour	valid for	avant	before
vente de billets	ticket office	après	after
combien de	how many	sous	under
kilomètres?	kilometres?	traverser	to cross
combien d'heures?	how many hours?	pont	bridge

Questions and requests

The simplest way of asking a question is to start with *s'il vous plaît* (please), then name the thing you want in an interrogative tone of voice. For example:

S'il vous plaît, la boulangerie?	where is there a bakery?	**Question words:**	
		où?	where?
S'il vous plaît, la route pour la Maison Carrée?	which way is it to the Maison Carrée?	comment?	how?
		combien?	how many/ how much?
similarly with requests:		quand?	when?
S'il vous plaît, une chambre pour deux?	can we have a room for two?	pourquoi?	why?
		à quelle heure?	at what time?
S'il vous plaît, un kilo d'oranges?	can I have a kilo of oranges?	quel est?	what is/which is?

Accommodation

une chambre pour une/deux personnes	a room for one/two people	pour une/deux/ trois nuits	for one/two/ three nights
un lit double	a double bed	Je peux la voir?	can I see it?
une chambre avec douche	a room with a shower	une chambre sur la cour	a room on the courtyard
une chambre avec salle de bain	a room with a bath	une chambre sur la rue	a room over the street

premier étage	first floor
deuxième étage	second floor
avec vue	with a view
clef	key
repasser	to iron
faire la lessive	do laundry
draps	sheets
couvertures	blankets
calme	quiet
bruyant	noisy
eau chaude	hot water
eau froide	cold water

Est-ce que le petit déjeuner est compris?	Is breakfast included?
Je voudrais prendre le petit déjeuner	I would like breakfast
Je ne veux pas de petit déjeuner	I don't want breakfast
On peut camper ici?	can we camp here?
un camping/terrain de camping	campsite
tente	tent
emplacement	tent space
auberge de jeunesse	youth hostel

Cars

garage	service station
service	service
garer la voiture	to park the car
un parking	car park
défense de stationner/ stationnement interdit	no parking
poste d'essence	gas station
essence	fuel
faire le plein	(to) fill it up
huile	oil
ligne à air	air line

gonfler les pneus	put air in the tyres
batterie	battery
la batterie est morte	the battery is dead
bougies	plugs
tomber en panne	to break down
bidon	gas can
assurance	insurance
carte verte	green card
feux	traffic lights
feu rouge	red light
feu vert	green light

Cycling

régler	to adjust
l'axe	axle
le roulement à billes	ball-bearing
la pile	battery
tordu	bent
le vélo	bicycle
le logement du pédalier	bottom bracket
le cable	brake cable
les freins	brakes
cassé	broken
l'ampoule	bulb
la chaîne	chain
la clavette	cotter pin
dégonfler	to deflate
le dérailleur	derailleur
le cadre	frame
les vitesses	gears

la graisse	grease
le guidon	handlebars
gonfler	to inflate
la chambre à air	inner tube
déserré	loose
baisser	to lower
le garde-boue	mudguard
le pannier	pannier
la pédale	pedal
la pompe	pump
la crevaison	puncture
le porte-bagages	rack
remonter	to raise
réparer	to repair
la selle	saddle
visser/serrer	to screw
la clef	spanner
le rayon	spoke

redresser	to straighten	les cale-pieds	toe clips
coincé	stuck	le pneu	tyre
serré	tight	la roue	wheel

Health matters

médecin	doctor	mal à l'estomac	stomach ache
Je ne me sens pas bien	I don't feel well	règles	period
médicaments	medicines	douleur	pain
ordonnance	prescription	ça fait mal	it hurts
Je suis malade	I feel sick	pharmacie	chemist
J'ai mal à la tête	I have a headache	hôpital	hospital

Other needs

boulangerie	bakery	banque	bank
alimentation	food shop	argent	money
supermarché	supermarket	toilettes	toilets
manger	to eat	police	police
boire	to drink	téléphone	telephone
camping gaz	camping gas	cinéma	cinema
tabac	tobacconist	théâtre	theatre
timbres	stamps	réserver	to reserve/book

Menu reader

Basic food terms

l'addition	bill/check	lait	milk
beurre	butter	moutarde	mustard
bouteille	bottle	œuf	egg
chauffé	heated	offert	free
couteau	knife	pain	bread
cru	raw	poivre	pepper
cuillère	spoon	salé	salted/spicy
cuit	cooked	sel	salt
emballé	wrapped	sucre	sugar
à emporter	takeaway	sucré	sweet
fourchette	fork	table	table
fumé	smoked	verre	glass
huile	oil	vinaigre	vinegar

Snacks

Un sandwich/une baguette	a sandwich	au fromage	with cheese
		au saucisson	with sausage
au jambon	with ham	à l'ail	with garlic

au poivre	with pepper	pain bagnat	bread roll with egg, olives, salad, tuna, anchovies and olive oil
au pâté (de campagne)	with pâté (country-style)		
croque-monsieur	grilled cheese and ham sandwich	panini	toasted Italian sandwich
croque-madame	grilled cheese and bacon, sausage, chicken or egg sandwich	tartine	buttered bread or open sandwich

eggs (œufs)

au plat	fried	durs	hard-boiled
à la coque	boiled	brouillés	scrambled

omelette (omelette)

nature	plain	au fromage	with cheese
aux fines herbes	with herbs		

Pasta (pâtes), pancakes (crêpes) and flans (tartes)

nouilles	noodles	panisse	thick chickpea flour pancake
pâtes fraîches	fresh pasta		
pâte	pasta or pastry	pissaladière	tart of fried onions with anchovies and black olives
raviolis	pasta parcels of meat or chard – a Provençal, not Italian invention		
		tarte flambée	thin pizza-like pastry topped with onion, cream and bacon or other combinations
crêpe au sucre/ aux œufs	pancake with sugar/eggs		
galette	buckwheat pancake		
socca	thin chickpea flour pancake		

Soups (soupes)

baudroie	fish soup with vegetables, garlic and herbs	pistou	parmesan, basil and garlic paste added to soup
bisque	shellfish soup	potée auvergnate	cabbage and meat soup
bouillabaisse	soup/stew with chunks of assorted fish	potage	thick vegetable soup
bouillon	broth or stock	rouille	red pepper, garlic and saffron mayonnaise served with fish soup
bourride	thick fish soup		
consommé	clear soup		
garbure	potato, cabbage and meat soup		

| soupe à l'oignon | onion soup with rich cheese topping | velouté | thick soup, usually fish or poultry |

Starters (hors d'œuvres)

assiette anglaise	plate of cold meats	hors d'œuvres	plus smoked or
crudités	raw vegetables with dressings	variés	marinated fish
hors d'œuvres	combination of the above		

Fish (poisson), seafood (fruits de mer) and shellfish (crustacés or coquillages)

aiglefin	small haddock or fresh cod		(scampi)
anchois	anchovies	limande	lemon sole
anguilles	eels	lotte de mer	monkfish
barbue	brill	loup de mer	sea bass
baudroie	monkfish or anglerfish	maquereau	mackerel
bigorneau	periwinkle	merlan	whiting
brème	bream	moules (marinières)	mussels (with shallots in white wine sauce)
bulot	whelk	oursin	sea urchin
cabillaud	cod	palourdes	clams
calmar	squid	poissons de roche	fish from shore-line rocks
carrelet	plaice	praires	small clams
claire	type of oyster	raie	skate
colin	hake	rouget	red mullet
congre	conger eel	saumon	salmon
coques	cockles	sole	sole
coquilles	scallops	thon	tuna
St-Jacques crabe	crab	truite	trout
crevettes grises	shrimp	turbot	turbot
crevettes roses	prawns	violet	sea squirt
daurade	sea bream		

Fish dishes and terms

éperlan	smelt or whitebait		
escargots	snails	aïoli	garlic mayonnaise served with salt cod and other fish
favou(ille)	tiny crab		
flétan	halibut		
friture	assorted fried fish	anchoïade	anchovy paste or sauce
gambas	king prawns		
hareng	herring	arête	fish bone
homard	lobster	assiette du pêcheur	assorted fish
huîtres	oysters	beignet	fritter
langouste	spiny lobster	darne	fillet or steak
langoustines	saltwater crayfish	la douzaine	a dozen

frit	fried
friture	deep-fried small fish
fumé	smoked
fumet	fish stock
gigot de mer	large fish baked whole
grillé	grilled
hollandaise	butter and vinegar sauce
à la meunière	in a butter, lemon and parsley sauce

mousse/ mousseline	mousse
pané	breaded
poutargue	mullet roe paste
raïto	red wine, olive, caper, garlic and shallot sauce
quenelles	light dumplings
thermidor	lobster grilled in its shell with cream sauce

Meat (*viande*) and poultry (*volaille*)

agneau (de pré-salé)	lamb (grazed on salt marshes)
andouille, andouillette	tripe sausage
bifteck	steak
bœuf	beef
boudin blanc	sausage of white meats
boudin noir	black pudding
caille	quail
canard	duck
caneton	duckling
contrefilet	sirloin roast
coquelet	cockerel
dinde, dindon	turkey
entrecôte	rib steak
faux filet	sirloin steak
foie	liver
foie gras	(duck/goose) liver
gigot (d'agneau)	leg (of lamb)
grenouilles (cuisses de)	frogs (legs)
langue	tongue
lapin, lapereau	rabbit, young rabbit
lard, lardons	bacon, diced bacon
lièvre	hare
merguez	spicy, red sausage
mouton	mutton
museau de veau	calf's muzzle
oie	goose
onglet	cut of beef
os	bone
poitrine	breast
porc	pork
poulet	chicken

poussin	baby chicken
ris	sweetbreads
rognons	kidneys
rognons blancs	testicles
sanglier	wild boar
steak	steak
tête de veau	calf's head (in jelly)
tournedos	thick slices of fillet
tripes	tripe
tripoux	mutton tripe
veau	veal
venaison	venison

Meat and poultry dishes and terms

aïado	roast shoulder of lamb stuffed with garlic and other ingredients
aile	wing
au feu de bois	cooked over wood fire
au four	baked
baeckoffe	Alsatian hotpot of pork, mutton and beef baked with potato layers
blanquette, daube, estouffade, hochepôt, navarin, agoût	types of stew
blanquette de veau	veal in cream and mushroom sauce
bœuf bourguignon	beef stew with Burgundy, onions and mushrooms
canard à l'orange	roast duck with an orange and wine sauce

canard pâté de périgourdin	roast duck with prunes, foie gras and truffles
carré	best end of neck, chop or cutlet
cassoulet	casserole of beans and meat
choucroute	pickled cabbage with peppercorns, sausages, bacon and salami
civet	game stew
confit	meat preserve
côte	chop, cutlet or rib
cou	neck
coq au vin	chicken cooked until it falls off the bone, with wine, onions and mushrooms
cuisse	thigh or leg
épaule	shoulder
en croûte	in pastry
farci	stuffed
gigot (d'agneau)	leg (of lamb)
grillade	grilled meat
garni	with vegetables
gésier	gizzard

grillé	grilled
hâchis	chopped meat or mince hamburger
magret de canard	duck breast
marmite	casserole
médaillon	round piece
mijoté	stewed
pavé	thick slice
pieds et paques	mutton or pork tripe and trotters
poêlé	pan-fried
poulet de Bresse	chicken from Bresse – the best
râble	saddle
rôti	roast
sauté	lightly cooked in butter
steak au poivre (vert/rouge)	steak in a black (green/red) peppercorn sauce
steak tartare	raw chopped beef, topped with a raw egg yolk
tagine	North African casserole
tournedos rossini	beef fillet with foie gras and truffles
viennoise	fried in egg and breadcrumbs

Terms for steaks

bleu	almost raw
saignant	rare
à point	medium
bien cuit	well done
très bien cuit	very well done
brochette	kebab

Garnishes and sauces

américaine	white wine, cognac and tomato
arlésienne	with tomatoes, onions, aubergines, potatoes and rice
au porto	in port
auvergnat	with cabbage, sausage and bacon
béarnaise	sauce of egg yolks, white wine, shallots and vinegar

beurre blanc	sauce of white wine and shallots, with butter
bonne femme	with mushrooms, bacon, potatoes and onions
bordelaise	in a red wine, shallot and bone-marrow sauce
boulangère	baked with potatoes and onions
bourgeoise	with carrots, onions, bacon, celery and braised lettuce
chasseur	white wine, mushrooms and shallots
châtelaine	with artichoke hearts and chestnut purée
diable	strong mustard seasoning

forestière	with bacon and mushrooms	piquante	gherkins or capers, vinegar and shallots
fricassée	rich, creamy sauce	provençale	tomatoes, garlic, olive oil and herbs
mornay	cheese sauce		
pays d'auge	cream and cider	savoyarde	with gruyère cheese
périgourdine	with foie gras and possibly truffles	véronique	grapes, wine and cream

Vegetables (*légumes*), herbs (*herbes*) and spices (*épices*)

ail	garlic	oignon	onion
anis	aniseed	panais	parsnip
artichaut	artichoke	pélandron	type of string bean
asperge	asparagus	persil	parsley
avocat	avocado	petits pois	peas
basilic	basil	piment	pimento
betterave	beetroot	pois chiche	chick peas
blette/bette	Swiss chard	pois mange-tout	mangetout
cannelle	cinnamon	pignons	pine nuts
câpre	caper	poireau	leek
cardon	cardoon, closely related to artichoke	poivron (vert, rouge)	sweet pepper(green, red)
carotte	carrot	pommes de terre	potatoes
céleri	celery	primeurs	spring vegetables
champignon, cèpe, chanterelle	types of mushrooms	radis	radish
		riz	rice
chou (rouge)	(red) cabbage	safran	saffron
choufleur	cauliflower	salade verte	green salad
concombre	cucumber	sarrasin	buckwheat
cornichon	gherkin	tomate	tomato
échalotes	shallots	truffes	truffles
endive	chicory		

Vegetable dishes and terms

épinard	spinach	alicot	puréed potato with cheese
estragon	tarragon		
fenouil	fennel	allumettes	very thin chips
férigoule	thyme (in Provençal)	à l'anglaise	boiled
fèves	broad beans	beignet	fritter
flageolets	white beans	biologique	organic
gingembre	ginger	duxelles	fried mushrooms and shallots with cream
haricots (verts, rouges, beurres)	beans (French/string, kidney, butter)		
		farci	stuffed
laurier	bay leaf	feuille	leaf
lentilles	lentils	fines herbes	mixture of tarragon, parsley and chives
maïs	corn		
menthe	mint	gratiné	browned with cheese or butter
moutarde	mustard		

à la grecque	cooked in oil and lemon			courgettes and peppers
jardinière	with mixed diced vegetables		pimenté	peppery hot
			piquant	spicy
mousseline	mashed potato with cream and eggs		pistou	ground basil, olive oil, garlic and parmesan
à la parisienne	sautéed in butter (potatoes); with white wine sauce and shallots		râpée	grated or shredded
			sauté	lightly fried in butter
			à la vapeur	steamed
parmentier	with potatoes		en verdure	garnished with green vegetables
petits farcis	stuffed tomatoes, aubergines,			

Fruit (*fruit*) and nuts (*noix*)

abricot	apricot		noix	nuts
noix de acajou	cashew nut		orange	orange
amande	almond		pamplemousse	grapefruit
ananas	pineapple		pastèque	watermelon
banane	banana		pêche	peach
brugnon, nectarine	nectarine		pistache	pistachio
cacahouète	peanut		poire	pear
cassis	blackcurrant		pomme	apple
cerise	cherry		prune	plum
citron	lemon		pruneau	prune
citron vert	lime		raisin	grape
datte	date		reine-claude	greengage
figue	fig			

Fruit dishes and terms

fraise (des bois)	strawberry (wild)			
framboise	raspberry		agrumes	citrus fruits
fruit de la passion	passion fruit		beignet	fritter
grenade	pomegranate		compôte	stewed fruit
groseille	redcurrant		coulis	sauce of puréed fruit
mangue	mango		crème de marrons	chestnut purée
marron	chestnut		flambé	set aflame in alcohol
melon	melon		fougasse	bread flavoured with orange-flower water or almonds (can be savoury)
mirabelle	small yellow plum			
myrtille	bilberry			
noisette	hazelnut		frappé	iced

Desserts (*desserts* or *entremets*) and pastries (*pâtisserie*)

bombe	moulded ice-cream dessert		calisson	almond sweet
			charlotte	custard and fruit in lining of almond fingers
brioche	sweet, high-yeast breakfast roll			

chichi	doughnut shaped in a stick
clafoutis	heavy custard and fruit tart
crème Chantilly	vanilla-flavoured and sweetened whipped cream
crème fraîche	sour cream
crème pâtissière	thick, eggy pastry-filling
crêpe suzette	thin pancake with orange juice and liqueur
fromage blanc	cream cheese
gaufre	waffle
glace	ice cream
Île flottante/ œufs à la neige	soft meringues floating on custard
macaron	macaroon
madeleine	small sponge cake
marrons Mont Banc	chestnut purée and cream on a rum-soaked sponge cake
mousse au chocolat	chocolate mousse
omelette norvégienne	baked alaska
palmier	caramelized puff pastry
parfait	frozen mousse, some times ice cream

petit-suisse	a smooth mixture of cream and curds
petits fours	bite-sized cakes/ pastries
poires belle hélène	pears and ice cream in chocolate sauce
tarte tatin	upside-down apple tart
tarte tropézienne	sponge cake filled with custard cream topped with nuts
tiramisu	mascarpone cheese, chocolate and cream
yaourt, yogourt	yoghurt

Dessert dishes and terms

barquette	small boat-shaped flan
bavarois	refers to the mould, could be a mousse or custard
coupe	a serving of ice cream
crêpe	pancake
gênoise	rich sponge cake
pâte	pastry or dough
sablé	shortbread biscuit
savarin	a filled, ring-shaped cake
tarte	tart
tartelette	small tart

Glossary

French terms

ABBAYE Abbey

AUBERGE DE JEUNESSE Youth hostel

BASILIQUE Basilica

BASSIN Reservoir

BASTIDE Planned, usually fortified town of the thirteenth century, typically laid out on a grid in a square or octagonal area

BOÎTE Nightclub/discotheque

CABANE Shepherd's hut

CANTON District

CAUSSE A limestone plateau typically with deep crevices and near-vertical stratification

CHAMBRES D'HÔTES Bed and breakfast

CHÂTEAU Fort, castle, mansion or country house

CIRCULADE Ancient hamlet, laid out in concentric circles

CIRQUE Deep, steep-walled basin on a mountain usually comprising the upper end of a river valley

CITÉ Citadel: the fortified section (usually the oldest and highest part) of a town

CLOCHÉ Bell tower

COL Pass

COLOMBIER Dovecote

DÉCOUVERTE Open-pit mine

DÉFILÉ Narrow gorge, canyon

DÉPARTEMENT Administrative area, similar to an English county, within a *région*

DOMAINE Estate

DONJON Castle keep

ÉCLUSE Canal lock

ÉGLISE Church

ENCEINTE Area falling within the walls of a castle or town, or the defensive enclosure itself

ÉTANG Coastal lagoon, normally salt-water and connected to the sea

ÉVÊCHÉ Palace or property pertaining to a bishop, or archbishop (archevêché)

FAUBOURG Extramural suburb, usually referring to late medieval town extensions built outside the walls of the original enceinte

FÊTE Festival

GARDIAN Cowboy of the Camargue

GARE Station

GARE ROUTIÈRE Bus station

GASTRONOMIQUE Elaborate and imaginative gourmet cuisine

GROTTE Cave

HALLES Market building

HORLOGE Clock

HÔTEL DE VILLE Town or city hall

HÔTEL PARTICULIER Private mansion or palace

JOUTE Joust; water-jousting

MAIRIE Office of the mayor: town hall

MANADE Camarguaise cattle or horse ranch

MAQUIS World War II Resistance fighter

MASIA Traditional Catalan farmhouse

MONASTÈRE Monastery

MUSÉE Museum

NAVETTE Shuttle service

PAYS Country, land

PIC Peak

PLACE Square

PONT Bridge

PONT DU DIABLE Arched medieval bridge

PONT VIEUX Old bridge

PORTE Gateway

PRÉFECTURE Main office, headquarters

PRISE DE L'EAU Dam

RÉGION Administrative region

SON ET LUMIÉRE Sound and light show

SOURCE Spring

TERROIR Literally meaning "soil", refers to traditional peasant cooking, using local ingredients

TGV Train Grande Vitesse, high-speed train

THERMES Hot-springs or spa

TOUR Tower

USINE Factory, workshop

VILLE BASSE Lower town

Artistic, architectural and archaeological terms

AMBULATORY Passage round the outer edge of a church's choir.

APSE Semicircular termination at the east end of a church.

ART DECO Geometrical style of art and architecture popular in the 1930s.

ART NOUVEAU Ornamental style of art and architecture which developed in the late nineteenth century, emphasizing decorative detail and avoiding straight clean lines.

ARTESONADO Spanish-style cabinet-work ceiling.

BAROQUE High Renaissance period of art and architecture, distinguished by extreme ornateness, exuberance and complex spatial arrangement of interiors.

BAS-RELIEF A stone carving with a shallow three-dimensional aspect ("high relief" sculpture has very pronounced depth).

CAROLINGIAN Dynasty founded by Pepin the Short; mid-eighth to early tenth centuries, named after its finest king, Charles the Great (Charlemagne). Also refers to art, sculpture, etc of the time.

CARYATID Sculpted female figure used as a column.

CHAPTERHOUSE Room in a monastery or church where the clergy met daily to discuss business and administrative affairs.

CHEVET East end of a church.

CLASSICAL Architectural style incorporating Greek and Roman elements: pillars, domes, colonnades, etc. At its height in France in the seventeenth century and revived in the nineteenth century as Neoclassicism.

CLERESTORY Upper storey of a church, incorporating windows.

CRENELLATION Battlements along the top edge of a wall or tower.

CUBISM Early twentieth-century art movement which used overlapping planes and geometric shapes in defiance of pictorial perception.

CURTAIN WALL Straight upright medieval defensive wall.

DOLMEN Neolithic stone formation, frequently consisting of a henge.

FAIENCE Porcelain and glazed earthenware decoration.

FAUVISM Artistic school of early twentieth-century France, characterized by vivid colour.

FIN-DE-SIECLE Referring to the turn of the twentieth century.

FOLLY Overly ostentatious rural dwellings of seventeenth- to nineteenth-century aristocracy.

FRESCO Wall painting – durable through application to wet plaster.

FRIEZE Sculpted decorative band, typically along the upper or lower limit of a wall, and usually in low relief.

GOTHIC Architectural style of the thirteenth to sixteenth centuries, characterized by pointed arches, rib vaulting, flying buttresses, broad windowed surfaces and a general emphasis on verticality.

IMPRESSIONISM Late nineteenth-century French style of painting which emphasized the perception of objects through the effect of light, rather than shape.

MAJESTÉ Romanesque and early Gothic sculptures of Christ on the Cross (majestat in Catalan).

MEROVINGIAN Dynasty ruling France and parts of Germany from the sixth to mid-eighth centuries. Also refers to art, etc of the period.

MOULIN A mill.

MOZARABIC Arab- and North African-influenced art and architectural style from Spain, brought to France around 900–1100 by Christians.

NARTHEX Entrance hall of a church.

NAVE Main body of a church.

NYMPHAEUM Roman or Greek shrine to a nymph, typically located at a fountainhead or spring.

OPPIDUM Pre-Roman hill-top settlement.

OPUS MIXTUM Roman building technique consisting of interspersed layers of stone and brick.

ORIENTALISM Study of Eastern and, particularly, Middle Eastern peoples from a Western and usually imperialistic and heavily romanticized perspective, from the late seventeenth to nineteenth centuries.

PANTOCRATOR Depiction of Jesus as "Lord of all Creation".

POLYCHROME Painted in colour.

REFECTORY Dining room of a monastery.

RELIEF The three-dimensional quality of a sculpture; its depth.

RENAISSANCE Artistic/architectural movement developed in fifteenth-century Italy and imported to France in the sixteenth century.

RETABLE Altarpiece.

ROMANESQUE Early medieval architectural style distinguished by squat, rounded forms and naive sculpture.

ROOD SCREEN Barrier set in some churches between the area of the altar and choir and the rest of the nave (where the main congregation gathers).

SARCOPHAGUS Latin for "coffin," referring to carved stone tombs.

STUCCO Plaster used to embellish ceilings, etc.

SURREALISM Early twentieth-century art movement whose apparently irrational juxtaposition of contrasting images expressed subconscious thoughts.

TRANSEPT Transverse arms of a church.

TRIBUNE Apse containing a bishop's throne; a gallery or raised area in a church.

TROMPE L'OEIL Decorative technique popular in the Baroque period, wherein a two-dimensional painting gives the impression of being a three-dimensional object.

TUMULUS Neolithic burial mound, frequently concealing a dolmen.

TYMPANUM A sculpted panel above a church door.

VAULT An arched ceiling or roof.

VOUSSOIR Sculpted wedge-shaped stones in the arch over a church door.

Travel store

ROUGH GUIDES Complete Listing

For more information go to www.roughguides.com

ROUGH GUIDES

Small print and
Index

A Rough Guide to Rough Guides

Published in 1982, the first Rough Guide – to Greece – was a student scheme that became a publishing phenomenon. Mark Ellingham, a recent graduate in English from Bristol University, had been travelling in Greece the previous summer and couldn't find the right guidebook. With a small group of friends he wrote his own guide, combining a highly contemporary, journalistic style with a thoroughly practical approach to travellers' needs.

The immediate success of the book spawned a series that rapidly covered dozens of destinations. And, in addition to impecunious backpackers, Rough Guides soon acquired a much broader and older readership that relished the guides' wit and inquisitiveness as much as their enthusiastic, critical approach and value-for-money ethos.

These days, Rough Guides include recommendations from shoestring to luxury and cover more than 200 destinations around the globe, including almost every country in the Americas and Europe, more than half of Africa and most of Asia and Australasia. Our ever-growing team of authors and photographers is spread all over the world, particularly in Europe, the USA and Australia.

In the early 1990s, Rough Guides branched out of travel, with the publication of Rough Guides to World Music, Classical Music and the Internet. All three have become benchmark titles in their fields, spearheading the publication of a wide range of books under the Rough Guide name.

Including the travel series, Rough Guides now number more than 350 titles, covering: phrasebooks, waterproof maps, music guides from Opera to Heavy Metal, reference works as diverse as Conspiracy Theories and Shakespeare, and popular culture books from iPods to Poker. Rough Guides also produce a series of more than 120 World Music CDs in partnership with World Music Network.

Visit www.roughguides.com to see our latest publications.

Rough Guide travel images are available for commercial licensing at www.roughguidespictures.com

Rough Guide credits

Text editor: Amanda Tomlin
Layout: Jessica Subramanian
Cartography: Rajesh Mishra
Picture editor: Harriet Mills
Production: Aimee Hampson
Proofreader: Anne Burgot
Cover design: Chloë Roberts
Photographer: Jean-Christophe Godet
Editorial: London Kate Berens, Claire Saunders, Ruth Blackmore, Polly Thomas, Richard Lim, Alison Murchie, Karoline Densley, Andy Turner, Keith Drew, Edward Aves, Nikki Birrell, Alice Park, Sarah Eno, Lucy White, Jo Kirby, Samantha Cook, James Smart, Natasha Foges, Roisin Cameron, Joe Staines, Duncan Clark, Peter Buckley, Matthew Milton, Tracy Hopkins, Ruth Tidball; **New York** Andrew Rosenberg, Steven Horak, AnneLise Sorensen, Amy Hegarty, April Isaacs, Ella Steim, Anna Owens, Joseph Petta, Sean Mahoney
Design & Pictures: London Scott Stickland, Dan May, Diana Jarvis, Mark Thomas, Jj Luck, Chloë Roberts, Nicole Newman; **Delhi** Umesh Aggarwal, Ajay Verma, Ankur Guha, Pradeep Thapliyal, Sachin Tanwar, Anita Singh, Madhavi Singh, Karen D'Souza

Production: Katherine Owers
Cartography: London Maxine Repath, Ed Wright, Katie Lloyd-Jones; **Delhi** Jai Prakash Mishra, Rajesh Chhibber, Ashutosh Bharti, Animesh Pathak, Jasbir Sandhu, Karobi Gogoi, Amod Singh, Alakananda Bhattacharya, Athokpam Jotinkumar
Online: New York Jennifer Gold, Kristin Mingrone; **Delhi** Manik Chauhan, Narender Kumar, Rakesh Kumar, Amit Kumar, Amit Verma, Rahul Kumar, Ganesh Sharma, Debojit Borah
Marketing & Publicity: London Liz Statham, Niki Hanmer, Louise Maher, Jess Carter, Vanessa Godden, Anna Paynton, Vivienne Watton, Rachel Sprackett; **New York** Geoff Colquitt, Megan Kennedy, Katy Ball; **Delhi** Reem Khokhar
Special Projects Editor: Philippa Hopkins
Manager India: Punita Singh
Series Editor: Mark Ellingham
Reference Director: Andrew Lockett
Publishing Coordinator: Megan McIntyre
Publishing Director: Martin Dunford
Commercial Manager: Gino Magnotta
Managing Director: John Duhigg

Publishing information

This third edition published May 2007 by
Rough Guides Ltd,
80 Strand, London WC2R 0RL
345 Hudson St, 4th Floor,
New York, NY 10014, USA
14 Local Shopping Centre, Panchsheel Park,
New Delhi 110017, India
Distributed by the Penguin Group
Penguin Books Ltd,
80 Strand, London WC2R 0RL
Penguin Group (USA)
375 Hudson Street, NY 10014, USA
Penguin Group (Australia)
250 Camberwell Road, Camberwell,
Victoria 3124, Australia
Penguin Books Canada Ltd,
10 Alcorn Avenue, Toronto, Ontario,
Canada M4V 1E4
Penguin Group (NZ)
67 Apollo Drive, Mairangi Bay, Auckland 1310,
New Zealand
Cover concept by Peter Dyer.

Typeset in Bembo and Helvetica to an original design by Henry Iles.

Printed in Italy by Legoprint S.p.A.

© Brian Catlos 2007

No part of this book may be reproduced in any form without permission from the publisher except for the quotation of brief passages in reviews.

456pp includes index

A catalogue record for this book is available from the British Library

ISBN: 978-1-84353-790-8

Help us update

We've gone to a lot of effort to ensure that the third edition of **The Rough Guide to Languedoc & Roussillon** is accurate and up to date. However, things change – places get "discovered", opening hours are notoriously fickle, restaurants and rooms raise prices or lower standards. If you feel we've got it wrong or left something out, we'd like to know, and if you can remember the address, the price, the time, the phone number, so much the better.
We'll credit all contributions, and send a copy of the next edition (or any other Rough Guide if you

prefer) for the best letters. Everyone who writes to us and isn't already a subscriber will receive a copy of our full-colour thrice-yearly newsletter. Please mark letters: "**Rough Guide Languedoc & Roussillon Update**" and send to: Rough Guides, 80 Strand, London WC2R 0RL, or Rough Guides, 345 Hudson St, 4th Floor, New York, NY 10014. Or send an email to **mail@roughguides.com** Have your questions answered and tell others about your trip at
www.roughguides.atinfopop.com

SMALL PRINT

Acknowledgements

The author would like to thank: Helene Aznar; Caroline Berland, OT Montpellier; Lysiane Boissydanglas, CDT Gard; Laurence Boxall, Languedoc Sun; Mélissa Buttelli, OT Toulouse; Valérie Crouineau, CDT Ariège; John Dagenais, UCLA; Vincent Enaud, Domaine Monastrel; Michel Foussard, CDT Aude; Myriam Journet-Fillaquier, CDT Aude; Patricia de Pouzilhac, CRT Languedoc-Roussillon; Christian Rivière, CDT Tarn; and Núria Silleras-Fernández.

Readers' letters

Thanks to all the readers who have taken the time and trouble to write in with comments and suggestions:

Laura Bell; Tony Bellworthy; Gail Bishko; Olivier Couraud; Joe Dowdeck; Kevin Fitzgerald; Malcolm James; Panu Kalmi; Elizabeth, Malcolm and Rosina Lanyon; John & Carole LeBrun; Marcus Loxton; Lynn Merritt; Barbara Oakley; Gail Orton; Dave & Sally Pabst; Mark Radnan; Vivienne Scott; Richard Smith; Susy Taylor; Catherine Van de Wiele; Evelyne Waldvogel; and Tricia Wass.

Photo credits

All photographs by Jean-Christophe Godet © Rough Guides, except the following:

Introduction
p.1 Montpellier, Place de la Comedie © John Miller/Robert Harding
p.8 Chateau de Foix © Tony Gervis/Robert Harding
p.10 *Feria* in Nîmes © Getty Images

Things not to miss
03 Water jousting, Sète © Agence Images /Alamy
04 Rabastens church © Brian Catlos
07 Collioure © Michael Busselle/Robert Harding
08 Cordes-sur-ciel © David Noton Photography/Alamy
10 Camargue horses © J.P. De Manne/Robert Harding
11 Caganer © Catherine Karnow/Corbis
13 Eldorado: Aristide Bruant, 1892 (litho) by Toulouse-Lautrec, Henri de (1864-1901) © San Diego Museum of Art, USA/Gift of the Baldwin M. Baldwin Foundation/Bridgeman Art Library
14 Le Canigou © Agence Images/Alamy
17 Niaux, cave art © Jean-Marc Charles/Corbis
18 Orb Valley, Castle in Lunas © WoodyStock/Alamy
20 Tauromachie, Mauguio Arenas, Camargue © Agence Images/Alamy
22 Pézenas market © Agence Images/Alamy
24 Aigues-Mortes © Bruno Barbier/Robert Harding

Colour Insert: The Land of the Cathars
Queribus castle © Agence Images/Alamy
The expulsion of the Albigensians from Carcassonne, from 'The Chronicles of France, from Priam King of Troy until the crowning of Charles VI', by Boucicaut Master, (fl.1390-1430) (and workshop) © British Library, London, UK/British Library Board/Bridgeman Art Library
Minerve © Mark Zylber /Alamy
Villerouge © Andy Arthur/Alamy
Montségur castle © Agence Images/Alamy

Colour Insert: Wines of Languedoc and Roussillon
Vineyard near Carcassonne © David Noton Photography/Alamy
Wine Production in the Middle Ages, from the 'Redevancier de Saint-Germain-des Prés', c.1530 by French School © Centre Historique des Archives Nationales, Paris/Archives Charmet/Bridgeman Art Library
Grape harvest in Fitou domains © Hemis/Alamy
Swirling wine © FoodPix/Jupiter Images
Wine barrels stored in church, Château Valmagne © Joerg Lehmann/StockFood UK
Gaillac vineyard grape harvest © Hemis/Alamy
Pumping the fermented must into a tank © Joerg Lehmann/StockFood UK

Black and whites
p.114 Carnival at Limoux © Mark Zylber/Alamy
p.144 Mirepoix © Michael Busselle/Robert Harding
p.210 Flamingoes in the Camargue © DK Images
p.245 Aigues Mortes, cafe at Place St Louis © Duncan Andrews/Images of France
p.338 Le train jaune © Agence Images/Alamy
p.361 Villefranche © Images of France
p.376 Gorge de la Fou © Mervyn Leah/Images of France
p.400 Meeting between Louis XIV (1638-1715) and Philippe IV (1605-65) at Isle des Faisans, 7th November 1659 (oil on canvas), Artist Laumosnier (fl.1690-1725) © Musée de Tesse, Le Mans/Bridgeman Art Library

SMALL PRINT

Index

Map entries are in colour.

INDEX

451

Map symbols

maps are listed in the full index using coloured text

---	Chapter boundary	Tower
---	International boundary	Fortress
-- --	Regional boundary	Museum
IIIIIII	Steps	Abbey
═══	Motorway	Monastery
──	Road	Church (regional maps)
──	Pedestrianized street	Grave
──●──	Railway	Château
──×──	ATM Railway	Tram stop
-----	Footpath	Metro station
— —	Ferry route	Airport
....	River	Bus stop
◆	Point of interest	Accommodation
⚊	Campsite	Gate
▲	Mountain peak	Internet café
⬢	Mountain refuge	Parking
⌒⌒	Mountain range	Hospital
)(	Mountain pass	Tourist office
🀫	Gorge/cliff face	Post office
☼	Swamp	Skiing
☼	Viewpoint	Building
⌂	Cave	Church
🍷	Waterfall	Park
⋀	Spring	Cemetery
∴	Ruins	Saltpan
⍭	Lighthouse	Beach
⊙	Statue	Forest
♨	Castle